KURT EISNER: A MODERN LIFE

German History in Context

ALBERT EARLE GURGANUS

KURT EISNER

A MODERN LIFE

 CAMDEN HOUSE
Rochester, New York

First published 2018
by Camden House

Camden House is an imprint of Boydell & Brewer Inc.
668 Mt. Hope Avenue, Rochester, NY 14620, USA
www.camden-house.com
and of Boydell & Brewer Limited
PO Box 9, Woodbridge, Suffolk IP12 3DF, UK
www.boydellandbrewer.com

ISBN-13: 978-1-64014-015-8
ISBN-10: 1-64014-015-8

Library of Congress Cataloging-in-Publication Data

Names: Gurganus, Albert E., author.
Title: Kurt Eisner : a modern life / Albert Earle Gurganus.
Description: Rochester, New York : Camden House, 2018. | Series: German history in
   context | Includes bibliographical references and index.
Identifiers: LCCN 2017055940| ISBN 9781640140158 (hardcover : alk. paper) |
   ISBN 1640140158 (hardcover : alk. paper)
Subjects: LCSH: Eisner, Kurt, 1867–1919. | Socialists—Germany—Biography. |
   Bavaria (Germany) —History—Revolution, 1918–1919. | Germany—History—
   Revolution, 1918.
Classification: LCC HX276.E418 G87 2018 | DDC 943/.3085092 [B] —dc23 LC
   record available at https://lccn.loc.gov/2017055940

This publication is printed on acid-free paper.
Printed in the United States of America.

To Susan,
both Solveig and Iselin

CONTENTS

Photographs follow page 288.

ACKNOWLEDGMENTS

I F ALL BEGINNING IS DIFFICULT, as we read in Goethe's first novel, then so too must be all ending. For just as ambitious design undertaken is invariably fraught with obligation, some debt of gratitude incurred in the endeavor goes unpaid at end, as we are parted from benefactors by fate and mortality. Still, the tallying in and of itself affords perhaps a measure of discharge and solace.

This book had its genesis in the midst of the Cold War when, drafting a master's thesis in the University of Chicago's Social Sciences Division, I read an agitational one-act play by Kurt Eisner from June 1914. Like him, I was put off by perfunctory economic and theoretically driven analyses of the Wilhelmine German workers' movement, which in their formulaic constructs discount essential, disparate cultural influences on component parties of the Second International. How, after all, might one adequately quantify the effect of, say, a Käthe Kollwitz print on the psyche of the semiliterate urban proletariat? Drawn thus to precepts of the Frankfurt School and pondering long what a Venn diagram of philosophical, political, and aesthetic values might meld, I determined to continue my graduate studies in a philology department where critical interpretive methodology plumbs abstractions of causality, code, and character. In Germanic Languages and Literatures at the University of North Carolina then, three men in particular—Richard H. Lawson, Siegfried Mews, and Petrus Tax—encouraged an interdisciplinary approach to the examination of revolutionary ferment.

Funded by a *Sonderstipendium* of the German Academic Exchange Service (DAAD), I decamped in fall 1981 for a year at Munich's Ludwig-Maximilians-Universität. My adviser there was Wolfgang Frühwald, who introduced me to Freya Eisner, granddaughter of my subject and an astute historian of the German labor movement. She was so kind as to make available Eisner's university journal, which revealed the coalescence of his social consciousness and engagement. The internal documents from Eisner's three months as head of the Bavarian Republic, housed at the Geheimes Staatsarchiv in Munich, illuminated the heroic attempt to convert theory to practice. James G. Hardin and Frank Trommler, editors of the Camden House Studies in German Literature, Linguistics, and Culture, brought to print my dissertation on Eisner's political aesthetic and agitational fiction under the title *The Art of Revolution* (1986).

With the fall of the Berlin Wall, the archives of the Institut für Marxismus-Leninismus (IML) were soon opened to all comers, and the trove of Eisner's papers and manuscripts could be scanned firsthand. During summers and two sabbatical years I traveled repeatedly to the transforming capital to sort through the files, first at the IML, then at the Bundesarchiv-Lichterfelde. Additional sallies to the Internationaal Instituut voor Sociale Geschiedenis in Amsterdam, the Bundesarchiv-Koblenz, the Nürnberger Stadtbibliothek, the Stiftung Neue Synagoge Berlin-Centrum Judaicum Archiv, and the Leo Baeck Institute in New York filled in critical gaps. At every turn the research and writing were supported by generous grants from the Citadel Foundation and the DAAD.

To my colleagues at The Citadel, the Military College of South Carolina, who critiqued work in progress, I am deeply indebted: Michael B. Barrett, Robert Brown, Mark Del Mastro, Cathy Jellenik, Jack Rhodes, Katya Skow-Obenaus, David Smith, and Ann Voit. The extraordinary dedication of Betsey Carter, Debbe Causey, Elizabeth Connor, and David Heisser of the Citadel's Daniel Library brought light to the dark time and again. I thank here too members of the Charleston History Colloquium, the South Atlantic Modern Languages Association, and the Philological Association of the Carolinas who provided invaluable commentary to many a presentation, especially Otto Johnston and Hal Rennert of the University of Florida, Nancy Nenno and Tom Baginski of the College of Charleston, and George Harding of Francis Marion University. Sabina Grossmann of the Nürnberger Stadtbibliothek and Elizabeth Chenault of Davis Library at the University of North Carolina are due special mention, as are the reference staffs of Perkins-Bostock Library at Duke, Widener Library at Harvard, the Bayerische Staatsbibliothek, and Münchener Stadtbibliothek. Max Gnigler of the Bundesrealgymnasium Reithmannstraße in Innsbruck and Finnish historian Veli-Matti Rautio made me aware of sources without which the final product would be diminished.

Above all I am grateful to my wife, Susan, who in the course of this project saw me at my best and worst and remained pillar and beacon.

INTRODUCTION

In November 1918 in the Catholic stronghold of Munich a transplanted Jewish Berliner, just released from prison, led a nonviolent revolution that deposed the ancient Wittelsbach dynasty and established the Bavarian Republic, effectively ending both the Second German Empire and the First World War. The local head of the breakaway Independent Socialists, Kurt Eisner, had been jailed for treason in February after organizing a munitions workers' strike to force an armistice. Before his incarceration he served as arts critic for the *Münchener Post*, organ of the Social Democratic Party, having been demoted from political editor for opposing the war. For a hundred days as Germany spiraled down into civil war and the victorious Entente powers deliberated their vengeance, Eisner fought as head of state to preserve calm in the South while implementing a peaceful transition to democracy and reforging international relations. On 21 February 1919, on the way to submit his government's resignation to the newly elected constitutional assembly, he was shot by a protofascist aristocrat. The senseless murder shattered a tenuous equilibrium, plunging Bavaria into the political chaos from which Adolf Hitler would emerge to herald a new epoch— one that culminated in 1945 with the citizenry of Dachau, their faces clouded by complicit ignorance and worse, burying the concentration camp dead on orders from its American liberators.

For many mired in the tradition of Catholic, monarchist Bavarian politics, including the resident Majority Social Democratic leadership, it was unthinkable that a diminutive Prussian intellectual of *mosaisch* heritage could mount an uprising that toppled one of Europe's most fixed ruling houses literally in an afternoon. But during the war an influx of North German labor had been channeled to Munich to drive the armaments industry, significantly radicalizing the urban proletariat. At the height of the British blockade the Wittelsbachs stood accused of war-profiteering by selling goods from the royal Leutstetten dairy at inflated prices.[1] The western front was breached, the German Army in retreat, and still the very parties that championed the kaiser's preserve called for a *levée en masse* for national defense. People were war-weary, hungry, disillusioned, malcontent. For the length of his twenty-year career as a socialist publicist and theorist, Kurt Eisner had been acutely conscious of the watershed nature of the historical moment as conditioned by scientific and technological advances, social and political developments, frenetic colonial expansion of the European powers, and the concomitant military buildup. As early as 1905, in the wake of the first Moroccan crisis, he had warned in a cogent albeit unheeded jeremiad, *Der Sultan des Weltkrieges* (The Sultan of World War), that imperialism was leading inexorably to catastrophic conflict, the outcome of which would have the direst consequences for its losers. For that he was mocked by precisely those German comrades who in 1914 would abandon the Socialist International in their headlong rush to the colors. Now his time had come and he proved up to the challenge.

As a Jew, however secular, as a neo-Kantian ethicist schooled by Hermann Cohen himself, and as an aesthete, Eisner was ever an outsider within the Social Democratic Party, a party of outsiders, even after he had been handpicked by its cofounder, Wilhelm Liebknecht, to take his place as editor of *Vorwärts* (Forward), Europe's preeminent socialist newspaper. Eisner's credentials were impeccable. He was university trained and had learned his craft at Berlin's renowned Herold News Agency. He had authored a groundbreaking critique of Nietzsche, archantagonist to Marx. Moreover, Eisner was a charter member of the avant-garde People's Free Stage movement. He had an impressive track record of cultural and political activism. A conspicuous distinction was nine months behind bars for impugning His Majesty. Here was a man with a sharp eye and keen nose for privilege, excess, and malfeasance. Yet his greatest virtues came to be reckoned as flaws when he discerned within the Social Democratic leadership some of the worst traits of the ruling state. Confident in his talents and perspective, he declined to be guided by lesser lights—a grave transgression against party discipline. He proved ideologically suspect to some as well. No rigid historical materialist, Eisner envisioned social justice born of heightened consciousness, collective spirit, superior organization, and concerted moral action rather than of ineluctable economic determinism and a bloody reckoning. In his last decade he often spoke of "the religion of socialism." Determined to maintain a centrist stance between warring factions at *Vorwärts*, he fell victim to a purge adumbrating greater violence to be visited upon Marxists by Marxists. The paper's reputation never recovered.[2]

In April 1919 Wilhelm Hausenstein eulogized Eisner as a slight, frail man who was at once a towering intellect, humanist colossus, one of Social Democracy's two great journalists (together with Franz Mehring), seminal social historian, and irrepressible political idealist whose vision and will forged the Bavarian Republic. Readily recognizing Eisner's failings as lyricist and dramatist, his quixotic attraction to Napoleon as a cult figure, and the limitations of boundless faith in human reason, Hausenstein, himself a distinguished art critic, proposed that his friend's brilliant theater reviews for the *Münchener Post* be collected and published as exemplary for the genre.[3] In his lifetime and afterward, whenever Eisner's adversaries sought to besmirch his achievement, they typically characterized him as a misplaced literatus meddling in politics, a highbrow operating beyond his ken in the real world. That their villain was indisputably a singularly incisive commentator, critic, and public intellectual ironically lent some twisted credibility to the charge.

But other comrades of diverse stamp—Ignaz Auer, Jean Jaurès, Julius Kaliski, Georges Weill, Hermann Wallfisch, Albert Südekum, Lily Braun, Gustav Landauer, and Ernst Toller—put a premium on Eisner's perspicacity and resolve. And in the end the most prominent of his chief adversaries in the party were reconciled with him: Karl Kautsky, Franz Mehring, Hugo Haase, and Clara Zetkin. In both camps there was the recognition that he identified and combatted the germ of self-destruction in Social Democracy's rise to power. Even when the party split over the war, few socialists regardless of stripe could conceive of the internecine struggle to come. Once the tottering Ebert government employed the army against rival Spartacists, whose leaders Rosa Luxemburg and Karl Liebknecht were then murdered by *Freikorps* (Volunteer Corps) units, terminal malignancy set in. "The rift between the Social Democrats and the revolutionary workers was never healed," observes Louis Snyder. "To the proletarian radicals, the Social Democrats were 'Cossacks' and agents of the bourgeoisie. . . . Had the Social Democrats and Communists worked together in the critical days of early 1933, they might have eliminated the Nazi threat. But both sides refused, each preferring to take its chances with Hitler. It was a fatal mistake."[4]

To avoid like fratricide in Munich, Eisner elected to share power with the Majority Socialists, according to them greater representation in his government than to his own Independents and giving the freest possible rein to meetings and demonstrations of the Far Left. Again and again he publicly and privately repudiated all bloodshed. And yet Michael Doeberl's jaundiced history of the Bavarian Republic, written while Hitler began to consolidate his power base in Munich, skews Eisner's regime as Bolshevist, whereas the East German Marxist-Leninist Hans Beyer brands his overthrow of the monarchy and establishment of a provisional government of workers', soldiers', and peasants' councils as a half-baked revolution.[5] Where lies truth?

Eisner had foreseen that the Wilhelmine Prussian-Junker militarist regime, spurred on by industrialists, businessmen, and speculators who stood to gain from the colonial venture in China and Africa, would readily foment war to secure what the kaiser enticingly dubbed "Germany's place in the sun." Bismarck, after all, had never shrunk from starting a fight in order to further his ends. As Bavarian premier, Eisner rejected another central German government dominated by Prussia in favor of a confederation of autonomous equals, a "United States of Germany." And just as Ludwig II, fifty-two years earlier, had allied Munich with Vienna against Berlin, the Francophile Eisner sought ties with Paris in hope of permanently containing Sparta on the Spree.

This book then represents a biography against the backdrop of a great historical divide: the demise of hereditary feudal monarchy in Central Europe, the birth of the communist Soviet Union, and the emergence of "the classless society," the United States of America, as a world power. The war begun in 1914 was renewed in 1939, as both Marshal Foch and John Maynard Keynes predicted—from diametrically opposed rationales—just months after Eisner's assassination. In that sense the ill-fated Weimar Republic was merely a long ceasefire, as ample historians have alleged, and Kurt Eisner's attempt to launch "a golden age of humanity" but a glimmer through the murk. Although Hitler interrupted Germany's progression to republic, the cataclysmic Third Reich functioned to dispel the entrenched Wilhelmine notion of democracy as a fool's paradise—espoused by no less a cultural icon than Thomas Mann. Thus thirty-one years of political turmoil and untold human misery drew to a close, and shortly thereafter a forty-year incubation period commenced in the two states risen from the ruins. Although Germany is now a full-fledged Western democracy and an indispensable linchpin of the European Union, elsewhere the tensions of a bygone era seethe unabated a century on. With Vladimir Putin's expansionist incursions, with the architects of the 1995 Bosnian genocide yet on trial in The Hague, with Turkey perpetually rent by choice of word for the liquidation of its Armenian populace, the First World War is still being fought on multiple fronts.

In many respects Kurt Eisner was the personification of German modernity, a man who preferred scientific socialism to confessional faith, cosmopolitan community to nationalism; a consilient thinker who recognized the nascent twentieth century as a new dispensation, who marshaled the empiricism of Marx and Darwin against Nietzsche's romantic individualism. He showed himself to be a staunch feminist in his first book. At the shaky inception of aviation he grasped its potential to transcend borders. Eminently at home in the grimy metropolis, he was among the first political activists to strike out into the hinterlands via automobile. The continuum of Eisner's enlightened ideation, secular ethicism, and globalist vision is all too often lost in studies overwhelmingly focused on the last three months of his life as a politician at the expense of his quarter century as social pundit and cultural theorist.

Eisner embodied everything the Nazis' *Blut-und-Boden* (blood and soil) populist, racist nationalism opposed. Their campaign of defamation, coupled with that of Doeberl's ilk, so distorted his image that West German scholars readily accepted that Kurt Eisner was the alias of Salomon Kosmanowski, a Galician Jewish Bolshevik. Even after Franz Schade's *Kurt Eisner und die bayerische Sozialdemokratie* (Kurt Eisner and Bavarian Social Democracy, 1961) demythologized the ultramontane, monarchist, and fascist cant, the old lies still held sway in some quarters.[6]

Two subsequent book-length biographies in German provided further clarity. *Kurt Eisner: Die Politik des libertären Sozialismus* (Kurt Eisner: The Politics of Libertarian Socialism, 1979), by Eisner's granddaughter Freya, child of his eldest son, firmly fixes Eisner as a lifelong centrist in the fragmenting Social Democratic Party and stresses his philosophically grounded antiauthoritarian stance. In her discretion she is reluctant to detail his libertine lifestyle, the scandal of a socialist party mired in bourgeois morality. The first work to draw extensively on former East German archives, Bernhard Grau's Munich dissertation, *Kurt Eisner 1867–1919: Eine Biographie* (2001), offers a more balanced perspective of Eisner's prewar career, affording greater insight into his formative education, early literary ambitions, and the influence of Marburg's neo-Kantians. Yet Eisner's literary works as a journalist for Social Democracy—the reviews, essays, short stories, vignettes, one-acts, and *Sozialmärchen* (social fairy tales) that he regarded as integral to his mission of molding the mind of the masses—receive short shrift. Vital personal and professional relationships are omitted as well; no mention is made of Lily Braun, Georges Weill, Max Beer, Gustav Landauer, or Otto Falckenberg.

In terms of readership *Kurt Eisner: A Modern Life* has been cast for the broad band of English speakers with an interest in Wilhelmine politics and culture, the Jew in German society, turn-of-the-century journalism as practice and profession, European socialism and the labor movement, imperialism at its zenith, the First World War, the rise of fascism, and conceptions of modernity. Everything has been translated into English, most of it for the first time. Compared with past treatments, this study is more a chronological narrative—with equal emphasis on the personal and public realms—than a thematic overview of a prominent political trajectory.

As to outlook and underlying principle, the operable premises are, in the words of Marx, that "the world is recognizable and changeable" and, as Eisner demonstrated, that history is shaped to that end by individual commitment to collective action.

CHAPTER ONE

A NOVEL'S SUFFERING HERO: A YOUTH IN BERLIN (1867–1889)

IN 1867 ALFRED NOBEL PATENTED DYNAMITE, Joseph Lister introduced his phenol antiseptic, Johann Strauß composed the *Blue Danube* Waltz, Ibsen published *Peer Gynt*, Henri Fantin-Latour painted Manet's portrait. Livingstone explored the Congo, Tsar Alexander II sold Alaska to the United States, Garibaldi launched his second campaign to wrest Rome from the French. Emperor Maximilian died before a republican firing squad in Mexico City. The Austrian ruler, Franz Josef I, ascended the throne of Hungary to establish the Dual Monarchy. The Southern rebellion quelled, the government of the United States turned its attention to subjugating the Plains Indians. In English exile Marx completed the first part of *Capital.* Having made war on Denmark for Schlweswig-Holstein and on Austria to consolidate Prussia's autonomy, Bismarck assumed the office of chancellor of the North German Confederation's twenty-two states, and his liege, King Wilhelm I, became their royal president. Under Bismarck's leadership Berlin stood at the ready to reclaim the prestige it enjoyed a century earlier when Friedrich II confounded the Continental powers to become "the Great." The invasion of France was in the offing.

An unlikely beneficiary of resurgent Prussia was a Jewish émigré who dealt by royal appointment in military regalia. Emanuel Eisner had been born forty years earlier in the Bohemian town Husinec, son of Hermann and Therese, née Gans. The family soon moved to Studenec in southern Moravia, where Hermann Eisner kept a tavern. Therese died in 1832, and upon his father's death young Emanuel learned the tanning trade before he and his brother Ignaz were taken in by relatives in Berlin and apprenticed in business. Together they opened shops in the early 1860s on Berlin's regal avenue Unter den Linden and in Danzig's bustling Kohlenmarkt, from which they supplied the Russian Imperial court with the insignia, buttons, braid, epaulets, ribbons, and medals that festooned the officers' splendid uniforms.[1] On 5 October 1863 thirty-six-year-old Emanuel, widowed with two sons, wed Hedwig Levenstein, daughter of the deceased Jewish merchant Levin Jontoff Levenstein.[2] Two years later the brothers went their separate ways in business. Emanuel relocated his shop and residence to Friedrichstraße and added to his clientele the Prussian emperor and king, the duke of Braunschweig, and the prince of Schwarzburg-Rudolstadt. He was thus employed when his wife bore him a son, Kurt, on 14 May 1867—a son destined to topple one of Europe's most prominent ruling houses.

Wilhelm Hausenstein, the Bavarian Marxist who embraced Catholicism and served as Bonn's ambassador to Paris in the 1950s, described Emanuel Eisner as a "respected merchant," his wife as "a charming old *Berlinerin* at heart disinterested in the world capital of Wilhelm II," the type painted by Daniel Chodowiecki in the last half of the previous century.[3] She gave birth to four children: Paul in June 1864, Kurt three years later, Jenny-Paula in April 1870, and Martha in February 1872. Only Kurt and Martha saw their fifth birthdays.[4] Emanuel and Hedwig's children were imbued with the values of Berlin's bourgeoisie. A portrait made of Kurt on 20 April 1870 by the Imperial court photographers Pflaum and Co. shows an attentive, long-haired child in a lace collar and dark woolen suit with bright piping.[5] Two years later Carl Günther photographed the five-year-old boy with sister Jenny-Paula. In jaunty leather boots, knee-breeches with bows, matching velvet jacket, and a bow tie cinching his high white collar, Kurt strikes a cavalier pose, standing with his arm resting on the back of her fringed chair. The girl, in white and showing a fashionable coiffure, looks primly into the lens, a perfect salon hostess in miniature.[6]

Eisner's pampered early childhood "in the center of the asphalt culture" played against the backdrop of the North German Confederation's stunning victory over France in 1870, orchestrated by Bismarck to achieve German unification.[7] Those Germans who had opposed the war, the Eisenacher Socialists, were ruthlessly suppressed, their leaders August Bebel and Wilhelm Liebknecht charged with treason and jailed. Bismarck's new state was born of an uneasy marriage of convenience between the unabashedly reactionary Prussian Junker caste—the landed gentry and military elite—and the laissez-faire National Liberal Party, the constituency of which was the ambitious middle class. The proletariat's place in the new Reich, historian Peter Gay notes, "was to work hard and be obedient."[8]

The economy fueled by war sputtered in 1873. The two workers' parties, the General German Workingmen's Association (Allgemeiner Deutscher

Arbeiterverein) of Ferdinand Lassalle, which had backed war with France, and the Social Democratic Labor Party (Sozialdemokratische Arbeiterpartei) of Bebel and Liebknecht, first vied to organize labor, then merged in 1875 as the Socialist Labor Party of Germany (Sozialistische Arbeiterpartei Deutschlands). In the wake of German victory over France and the subsequent economic downturn, Emanuel Eisner's business declined to the point that in 1877 he affiliated with Jewish commercial magnate Eduard Sachs, for whom he would work the rest of his life.[9] In 1874 Emanuel had placed his son in the lower school of Berlin's nascent Askanisches Gymnasium to begin the classical education that would prepare him for university and a professional career, a goal to which but few sons of his class and creed could aspire.[10] The boy seems to have been well suited to his parents' plans. In retrospect he readily admitted to believing what he read in "the wretched liberal press." Referring to the two attempts in 1878 on Kaiser Wilhelm's life by gunmen whom Bismarck demonized as revolutionaries, Eisner recalled how the progressive bourgeoisie regarded the Left: "At that time I myself considered them a horde of wild criminals." Despite an "instinctive aversion to all patriotic humbug," he lit candles in the window to celebrate Wilhelm's survival.[11] By the fiction that the second assailant had Socialist accomplices, Bismarck convinced the Reichstag to outlaw the party altogether.

A formal, three-quarter portrait shot in August 1883 when Eisner was sixteen shows an earnest youth with a high forehead and hair combed back, thin lips, a full chin, protruding ears, and a melancholy gaze directed past the camera.[12] The young man performed creditably at school. After eight and a half years at the gymnasium he qualified for university on 13 March 1886. His final report records good marks in German and choral music; satisfactory in Latin, Greek, French, English, mathematics, physics, and athletics; and mostly satisfactory in history and geography. His behavior was deemed commendable, his diligence good.[13] The prior report, from Easter to St. Michael's Day 1885, indicates that his Latin essays and Greek recitations showed promise and that he was an attentive pupil.[14] An essay from February 1884 on the theme "How a Noble Man Thinks and Acts (according to Sophocles's *Aias*)" affords insight into the sixteen-year-old's sensibilities: "The precept of loving one's neighbor certainly achieved its most noble expression in Christianity. But who actually lives by this rule? In this regard we are just as pagan as the ancient Greeks, only we speak our mind with less candor and spontaneity. . . . With regard to honor we are less ideally minded in our practical century than the ancients."[15] Felix Fechenbach, Eisner's personal secretary during the Bavarian Republic, writes in his biography that Eisner's unconventional views brought him into conflict with his teachers, who sought to suppress in particular "his opinion on matters of religion." He remarks as well Eisner's sensitivity to social injustice, focused by walks through the workers' quarter on Berlin's northside, where he saw the need of the proletariat and "as the son of well-off parents felt partly responsible for the misery of the have-nots."[16] By his own word Eisner roamed the forest of the Tiergarten on rainy fall days to exult or to dispel his gloom and threw himself into piles of leaves in ditches along the Charlottenburger Chausee "to cool all the raging passion."[17]

His literary bent was manifest early. He was enthralled as a child by the puppet theater, the germ of a pursuit he would cherish throughout his life.[18] In a notebook given to him by his aunt Eveline Levenstein, he copied odes by Horace, a scene from the first part of Shakespeare's *Henry IV*, aphorisms from Keats in French translation, the choruses of Swinburne's *Atalanta in Calydon*, entries from Friedrich Hebbel's diaries, and his own translation of Longfellow's "Excelsior." He evidently circulated the notebook among friends, for on 2 April 1880 his cousin Ella Crohn inscribed in it a poem she had written.[19] He began to compose aphorisms and poems himself, then graduated to stories and plays. In 1885 he reviewed for a Berlin literary journal the work of three forgettable contemporary poets: Hugo Frederking's *Der Born der Liebe* (The Font of Love), Adolf Brieger's *König Humbert in Neapel* (King Humbert in Naples), and Heinrich Seidel's *Idyllen und Scherze* (Idylls and Jests).[20] In a notebook that he titled "Musings of an Unworldy One," dated spring 1886, Eisner included a poem that evinces his waning Jewish faith:

> Religion is a gentle hack,
> plies steady its pious trot;
> ride it, who's in thinking slack,
> it unseats him not.
>
> Philosophy though is a spirited steed,
> storms beyond rein and rail;
> whoever can't control its speed
> will soon be on his tail.[21]

A few weeks before his nineteenth birthday he penned a dramatic sketch, "Railway and Resort," a tragic story of two young lovers desperately alienated from their milieu, reflecting a growing conflict with his father, who was troubled by his son's libertine thought and increasingly bohemian inclination.[22]

On 28 April 1886 Kurt Eisner enrolled as a student of philosophy at Berlin's Friedrich Wilhelm University. In his first semester, from April to October 1886, he read logic and the history of philosophy but also attended classes on nineteenth-century German literature and the dramatist Lessing, the latter taught by Richard Meyer, a young docent who would distinguish himself as one of the nation's foremost literary historians.[23] On break at the Baltic resort Prerow, Eisner wrote in his journal entry for 13 August of a sleepless night and an exhausting journey—six hours in the train, five on a steamer—following "a frightful scene" with his father. Overwrought, he confesses that the notion of a "divine benefactor" strained all credibility: "I no longer care to believe in a dear God."[24] After two days' rest and relaxation he celebrates in panegyric style the poet's calling. "O could I but commit all my feeling to words, were I able to cast the silent singing of the soul, the shadowy, ethereal song of the spirit in earthly rhythms!"[25]

Second semester, October 1886 to March 1887, Eisner's focus shifted from philosophy to German philology, with courses in grammar, medieval literature, lyric, and Berlin's literary culture in the eighteenth century. He delved into psychology and heard the nationalist, anti-Semitic historian Heinrich von Treitschke lecture on political theory from Plato to the present. From April to October 1887 he read German romanticism with Goethe scholar Erich Schmidt and philosophy with Friedrich Paulsen, an adherent of Kant and the English utilitarians. The economics of Adam Smith and courses in experimental psychology and aesthetics rounded out his schedule. He began to compile sources and take notes for a dissertation, to be written under Schmidt's direction, on the romantic Achim von Arnim, poet and collector of folksongs.[26] On holiday before classes were to resume in October, Eisner returned on 16 September to Prerow. On this visit he set down impressions of a journalist for the German Conservative Party's daily paper, *Die Kreuzzeitung* (The Cross Newspaper): "Meyer constantly addresses by title: Gracious Lady! He knows too as a gallant cavalier how to lay forth lives and fates in most skilled reporter fashion for the gracious lady of the Patzenhofer beer family."[27]

In his fourth and most ambitious semester, Eisner registered for nineteenth-century drama and German classicism with Schmidt, Meyer's courses on comparative literature and the Old Saxon religious epic, Treitschke's history of parliamentary government, Hegelian Georg Simmel's recent philosophy and the natural sciences, physical anthropology with Emil du Bois-Reymond—who was wont to open his lectures with facetious psychoanalyses of peoples and cultures—and Paulsen's lectures on Spinoza. Although Treitschke, Du Bois-Reymond, and Simmel enjoyed considerable standing in the intellectual community and exerted significant influence on their disciplines, none left his mark on Eisner. On the first two he passed judgment: "Today one speaks exclusively of laws—historical laws and laws of nature, whereas one ought to speak of Herr von Treitschke's and Herr du Bois-Reymond's legal delusions. In every little *studiosus* today there glimmers a great solon. And in the war of science the lover of doubleclad truths intuits even historical laws of nature."[28] Later Eisner would belittle Treitschke as "the great trumpet of the Hohenzollerns."[29] Eisner's attraction to Kant through Paulsen set him at odds ideologically with Simmel, whose student Georg Lukács would become the codifier of Marxist-Leninist aesthetics, yet another lawgiver of sorts. Paulsen's course on Spinoza influenced Eisner so deeply that on 7 November he began to write a novel on the Jewish philosopher's life, a project that would engage his interest for the better part of two years.[30]

His fifth, sixth, and seventh semesters, from April 1888 to October 1889, were devoted entirely to philology and European cultural history. He studied Gothic, Old High German grammar and verse, Renaissance and baroque literature, and continued his doctoral research. On 30 August 1888 he borrowed Arnim's *Die Gleichen* (The Equals) and the fifth volume of Musäus's *Volksmärchen der Deutschen* (Folktales of the Germans) from the Royal Library.[31] At the family's third-floor apartment at Blücherstraße 62 in southwest Berlin, he filed hundreds of pages of notes for his thesis, "Achim von Arnim as Publisher, Adapter, and Imitator of Older German Poetry."[32] He was supported by a quarterly allowance of 40 marks from the Jewish Students' Auxiliary. Its board approved the grant in mid-December for the first half of the new year.[33] His extracurricular belletristic interests, however, detracted considerably from his work, and he would later regret spending so much time "between chestnut grove and Opera Square."[34]

In early October 1888, for example, he took an afternoon off to rough out a comedy of ten scenes set in contemporary Berlin. The characters include thirty-year-old Professor Ernst Wellner; his twenty-five-year-old nephew, Dr. Leberecht Wellner, who bears a striking resemblance to the author; Hedwig Schackow, the daughter of another professor; the cultivated Isolde Schulze; her friend Marietta Syruppi; and Privy Councilor Weisbier.[35] Eisner's abiding interest had become theater, yet his experiences at the capital's playhouses frequently left him cold. On his first visit to Berlin's elegant Lessing Theater, just before Easter 1889, he saw Ludwig Anzengruber's *Meineidbauer* (The Perjury Tiller) and fulminated afterward against the lavish gimmickry of the sets and the frivolity of the audience, who joked and flirted between acts, laughed at the intense dramatic moments, and failed to applaud good acting. Earlier he had attended what he deemed a good performance of Anzengruber's comedy *Die Kreuzelschreiber* (The Cross Signers) in an almost empty theater. Some officers seated beside him dismissed the piece as inordinately dull and rued a wasted evening. After his experience at the Lessing Theater he vowed not to return and declined a friend's invitation to see there a staging of *L'Affaire Clémenceau* by Alexandre Dumas *fils*, featuring the actress Lili Petri, whose hair was so long, the friend declared enticingly, that one would have stepped on it when she loosed it for bed.[36]

In spring and summer 1889 when Eisner's political consciousness began to jell, the catalysts were literature, culture, and theater. He read Ibsen's *Ghosts* and Zola's *Germinal*, naturalist manifestos that depicted the rotten core of bourgeois society.[37] He scanned the socialist press and noted that its papers and journals demanded more from their readers than did the average paper "for the cultured circles." Mulling this anomaly, he was one of a handful present in the Music College's concert hall the evening of 1 May, International Workers' Day, for a talk by Hermann von Maltzan titled "The Establishment of German People's Theaters: A National Mission." The speaker urged that stages be erected for the masses and patriotic works played that might bolster national pride and unity as well as combat the pernicious influence of Social Democracy. To Eisner's glee, Maltzan envisioned a clientele resembling spectators at a racetrack: diverse social classes sharing a common interest. Another aristocrat in attendance, Ernst von Wolzogen, whose comic novel *Die tolle Komteß* (The Mad Countess) was published that year, questioned whether the masses were sufficiently schooled to comprehend drama. A discussion ensued and then, prompted by remarks from the playwright Ernst von Wildenbruch, whose nationalist drama *Die Quitzows* (The Quitzows) had premiered in Berlin in November, the audience founded an association to realize Maltzan's ideal. "And thus," Eisner observed, "Berlin, which I think has twice as many associations as inhabitants, has yet another."

Afterward, the student of literature and philosophy wrote an account of the meeting, critiqued the positions he had heard stated, and offered a counterproposal. His article, "The Establishment of a People's Theater: Berlin's Social Debt of Honor," was published that summer in *Die Gesellschaft* (The Society), Michael Georg Conrad's arts journal.[38] Eisner began by contesting the desirability of turning the stage into a "nursery school for patriots." National consciousness, he asserted, is rooted in "love of family, the land and those who dwell on it, language, art, history, satisfaction with the existing social structure, and last and least allegiance to the current form of government and the administration." Unfortunately, national pride was too often bound up with the deprecation of foreign cultures. To his mind, the matter of conveying art to the masses was a social rather than national issue: "Art should not mold the German, but the man, who may then happen to be a German." As to Wolzogen's estimation of the common man's capacity for art, Eisner countered that having witnessed at Easter the enthusiasm of working-class children, despite streaming rain, for a sidewalk puppet show starring Kasperl, he believed them to understand at least as much of what they saw as the bourgeois patrons of the Lessing Theater. He reasoned that "what a child can do, so too can the uneducated man of sound mind."

Moreover, if the common man is expected to fathom the often absurd mysteries of religion, why should he be oblivious to the universal truths revealed by great art? The church was outmoded in any case and could no longer satisfy modern man's needs and desires, for "we want paradise on earth, not in heaven." There is a good deal of metaphorical talk about "spiritual sustenance," Eisner observed, but few realize that the phrase has literal significance. Citing ascetics such as Spinoza, he argued that when the mind and soul are sated, the flesh requires less. Intellectual stimulation would assuage the need of the materially poor. Knowledge had swelled beyond the confines of scripture, political and social ideals were fundamentally at odds with the old patriarchy. Science and art had superseded faith. Since science yet overwhelmed the mind of the masses, direction would derive from art. Proclaiming that "of all spiritual sustenance living drama is the most strengthening," Eisner advocated the people's theater as successor to the church.

To the end of raising the popular temple, he suggested that Berlin be divided into parishes that would jointly build or rent a theater. Tickets could be allotted at minimal cost to the parishes on a rotating basis, with some reserved for vocational students, teachers at the elementary schools, and factory workers. Berlin's theater for the masses might economize by eschewing luxurious appointments, ornate sets, and elaborate costumes. He called on idealistic actors, actresses, and artists to aid the cause and accept as their recompense a decent wage and the honor of serving the people. As to repertory, the audience should be challenged with works classical and modern, tragic and comic, German and foreign. He named Anzengruber and Raimund as exemplary playwrights for such an undertaking. Germany's capital, for all its modern amenities, had yet to give the world a cultural ideal, Eisner declared, "but an institution that elevates, fortifies, and consoles the poor—that would be our city's eternal claim to fame."

The essay proved prophetic. At the time it went to press, the Free Stage Society (Verein Freie Bühne), a bourgeois initiative headed by director Otto Brahm and actor Maximilian Harden, planned private productions of banned avant-garde drama in rented theaters for subscribers. The play selected to inaugurate the first of its three seasons was *Ghosts*, performed on 29 September 1889. It was followed by Gerhart Hauptmann's *Vor Sonnenaufgang* (Before Sunrise) on 20 October. In its brief life the Free Stage became the champion of naturalism, staging works by Arno Holz, Anzengruber, Tolstoy, Bjørnson, and Strindberg. Eisner's membership card for the 1889–1890 season entitled him to seat thirty-six in the right wing of the second balcony at the rented Lessing Theater.[39]

Lee Baxandall writes that "the founding of the Freie Bühne stirred great interest among the more culturally conscious workers and middle-class intellectuals who ranged themselves politically with the workers." The Berlin trade unions did indeed purchase joint subscriptions for their members, but by and large the Free Stage "remained a theater belonging to an elite."[40] In an article for the 23 March issue of the Social Democratic paper *Berliner Volksblatt* (Berlin People's Paper), which became *Vorwärts*, Dr. Bruno Wille proposed a People's Free Stage after Eisner's concept, an institution for "the education of the people through art, in which the word 'education' is not meant in the sense of a patronizing offering 'from above' but rather as self-education through participation of those who invigorate themselves by sharing with others." Wille envisioned the People's Free Stage sponsoring Sunday afternoon performances, concerts, recitations, and lectures in rented theaters at an entrance fee of 50 pfennige.[41] In response to his call over a thousand people assembled on 8 August to found Berlin's Freie Volksbühne. Kurt Eisner emerged as one of the enterprise's leaders.

Eisner's journal entries of the time reflect growing dissatisfaction with Prussian autocracy. Of the king who rejected out of hand constitutional infringements on his power and in 1849 spurned the imperial crown offered by the National Assembly, he wrote: "Friedrich Wilhelm IV's statement that the king rules easily and justly because he 'overlooks' everything contains an apt double entendre. Which prince would not tiredly allow the scepter to sink if he did not overlook the horrible, ominous, and insoluble in his task—a blind man on a mountaintop regarding the world below."[42] The twenty-two-year-old recognized early the arrogance of the new Prussian king and German emperor who ascended the throne in June 1888 and would soon pit Germany against Britain in a fateful contest for colonies and supremacy of the seas. On 21 September 1889 Eisner noted: "According to Wilhelm II the sole purpose of history seems to be to glorify the current ruler."[43] A month later Eisner equated Paris's Eiffel Tower with the future and humanity, Berlin's Victory Column with the present and barbarism.[44] The entry for 29 October reveals the extent of utilitarian influence: "Culture's mission is to banish chance by law. The word 'happiness' must be struck from the dictionary of human thought and replaced by 'one's due.'"[45]

In later life Eisner proved the sort of charismatic intellect who attracts a coterie of admirers and disciples. His circle of intimates during his years at university was small but gifted. His closest friend was fellow student Richard Baerwald, who became a leading scholar in the field of parapsychology, authoring studies on clairvoyance, spiritualism, and autosuggestion. For eleven years, beginning in 1887, he corresponded with Eisner on topics ranging from Mozart to politics to "fine young ladies."[46] A letter written from England on 4 December 1889, in which he derides "our German brute-force economy with its police system," attests that at that time he shared Eisner's sympathy with the fourth estate and antipathy to the government.[47]

Among the women to whom Eisner felt drawn was his cousin Margarete, daughter of Ignaz and Fanny Eisner. "I repeat for you now," she wrote on 13 January 1888, "what I told you recently: you are free, no chains bind you to me. . . . I know too that some brighter day a memory of the moments we shared in happiness will steal upon you." They remained on friendly terms. Grete eventually married a Jew of Russian descent. Their son Ernst Boris Chain, born 19 June 1906, would teach at Oxford and share the Nobel Prize for physiology and medicine in 1945 for the discovery of penicillin.[48] In 1889 Eisner became acquainted with three sisters, Doris, Lisbeth, and Toni, children of landscape painter August Hendrich, who had moved from Freienwalde an der Oder to Eberswalde, a scenic village northeast of Berlin.[49] The eldest daughter, Doris, fell in love with the student, but he preferred Auguste Ludowika Elisabeth, six months his junior, blonde, and "childlike" in her emotions.[50]

She was an anxious young woman whose refined tastes were well beyond her means. She had already tried to attach herself to an elderly scholar in order to escape the poverty of her home, where importunate creditors left empty-handed and threatening. She unsuccessfully sought work in Berlin's shops and factories, then settled into menial cottage industry, finishing goods in her room for a pittance. "Never," Eisner recalled, "have I met a person so disheartened and stunted, who cried out so passionately from the depths of a tormented soul for peace and—goodness." On the first evening they met, she confided to him that she could no longer endure her lot, that she would prefer life in a bordello to the drudgery of her existence.[51] In a black suit, starched white shirt, and formal tie, he sat by her at dinner on her twenty-second birthday in early November 1889, amid a swirl of gaily dressed young people, and guessed that she would surely have a beau. While the party drank a toast to "What we love!" Eisner determined it was she whom he would love.[52] On 13 November he recorded in his journal that his life had been uprooted, his old existence doomed, and fancied himself "a novel's suffering hero."[53]

Twelve years later he reminisced: "Love is easily found in the mists of autumn evenings. . . . I can only recommend to every innocent and yearning soul between seventeen and twenty-two to fix on this time of fall when secret love that must remain concealed longs to grow into iron-forging fate. Be advised by one with experience."[54] Elisabeth Hendrich was unlike anyone he had ever known and thoroughly receptive to his ideas—a veritable lab school for his social theories. That fall and early winter he prepared for her a "Christmas book for my love," to which he gave the telling title "Loving and Teaching." The dedication reads:

> I inscribe this book to you that all my thought
> inhabits your soul as its own address,
> that, shaping, it may there dwell, in love well caught,
> and, thus content, give rise to happiness.[55]

In it he copied musings, aphorisms, poems, and stories from earlier journals, meant to affirm his love, reveal his personality, and mold her thinking. He recommended texts she should read, confessed his feelings of alienation, and unwittingly foretold his own fate in the poem "Martyrdom," in which the wise man sinks down in the dust, bearing the ignorance and insensitivity of millions like a "crown of thorns."[56]

Lisbeth answered in verse of her own—decidedly romantic in mood, imagery, and form—printed in the 15 December 1889 edition of the *Berliner Salonblatt*, a society magazine:

> If you perchance as a bright star,
> in the evening sky did blaze,
> then would I be a little bloom,
> untouched, alone in forest gloom
> and up to the heavens gaze. . . .[57]

Eisner was by then midway through his eighth semester, enrolled in courses on Old Saxon grammar, *Parzival*, and Goethe's first draft of *Faust*, living in his own rooms at Friedrichstraße 10, and financially strapped.[58] His mother wanted him to enter and rejuvenate the family business in military accoutrements, a prospect thoroughly odious to him. Old Emanuel took a dim view of his interest in the painter's daughter; only a marriage into money would allow him to pursue comfortably an academic career.[59] Kurt Eisner made his choice. At the turn of the year he withdrew from university, abandoned his thesis, and took up work as a correspondent and editor for the recently established Herold News Agency directed by Ludwig Klausner.[60]

CHAPTER TWO

ARISTOCRATIZE THE MASSES: FROM BERLIN TO FRANKFURT TO MARBURG (1890–1893)

E ISNER STARTED WORK AT THE HEROLD in January 1890. His duties were to gather news, file reports for dissemination to newspapers throughout Europe, and write lead stories. He covered sessions of the Reichstag, the powerless popular national assembly commonly characterized as a debating club, and the equally farcical Prussian Landtag. The issue of the day was Kaiser Wilhelm's new course, the defining component of which was *Weltpolitik*, described by Walther Rathenau as a "dilettante foreign policy."[1] Bismarck had never seen the need for Germany to look overseas for colonies when Poland lay so near, but Wilhelm, obsessed with national prestige and supported by wealthy interest groups such as the Pan-German League (Alldeutscher Verband), the Navy League (Flottenverein), and the Colonial League (Kolonialverein), was determined to secure Germany's place in the sun. Years earlier in 1881 Bismarck had unwittingly drafted his own pink slip when he remarked that he had no interest in colonial expansion.[2] Although he softened his stance in the mid-1880s to accommodate public opinion, his commitment was never more than halfhearted. Consequently, Wilhelm dismissed the septuagenarian icon, demanding, receiving, and accepting Bismarck's resignation between 17 and 20 March 1890.

Eisner was assigned to cover the chancellor's departure from the capital on the twenty-ninth, one of a select group of journalists to ride with the old man as far as the Spandau station on his return to Friedrichsruh. The Herold's new retainer recalled the crowd that serenaded Bismarck at Berlin's main station, his banter with reporters who stood on the desolate platform at Spandau, the stern face of "the great misanthrope," and the indifference of workers boarding the train to Berlin. Eisner was surprised to see two days later how his account had been sentimentalized in a major foreign paper: "Gone was the rigidity of injured pride, and the melancholy exile's two great tears streamed like silvery pearls."[3]

Eisner and Lisbeth Hendrich became engaged in mid-autumn 1890. Much of his leisure time was spent in Berlin's libraries researching his articles and reading the yet obscure Friedrich Nietzsche. Struggling against the allure of Nietzsche's "anarchy of the elect," Eisner began to cast a critique. In the spring he had three vignettes and a long poem published in *Die Gesellschaft*. The vignettes, "Pictures in the Style of Max Klinger," depict dark, sexually charged street scenes of proletarian women.[4] "May Night: A Leaf of Life," a love poem in blank verse—a departure from the ponderous contrivance of earlier attempts—weaves a lyrical spell in the first verses but deteriorates into metaphysical cogitations. The opening of the second strophe celebrates the universality of intimacy:

Pressed body to body, we listen to the night.
On a secluded balcony entwined with wild grape
we look out into the dark,
and into the breath of sacred quiet flows
from our souls love's own ardent breath.[5]

Personnel changes at the Herold made Eisner's job difficult, prompting him to consider his options. He resigned in late spring 1891, together with his immediate chief, Alexander Buchholtz, over growing differences with the Herold's management. In a letter of recommendation Buchholtz attested that Eisner "rendered outstanding service to the bureau through his great diligence and enthusiasm as well as extraordinary circumspection and skill."[6] Eisner wrote on 26 June from the Hendrich home at Pfeilstraße 4 in Eberswalde, asking Eugen Sierke, editor of the *Braunschweiger Tageblatt* (Braunschweig Daily Paper), for help finding another job in journalism.[7] In a subsequent letter he outlined his education and experience, mentioned his recent engagement, and declared: "Politically, I have no dogmatic party convictions and respect the honest observer's critical judgment. As to economics, I believe in the future of socialism." His stated ambition was to devote whatever free time he might have to literary pursuits.[8] He supported himself by freelance work but worried how long it might be, having "given up a good, comfortable, and lucrative position out of ideal considerations and moral scruples," before he would be financially secure enough to marry his "little blonde joy."

On Sundays they made excursions into the countryside, strolling over the plains north of the city. On such an outing he and Lisbeth rested on a hillock and watched three young storks circling above. One of the birds swooped low, causing Lisbeth to wince. Eisner joked that she had nothing to fear; the storks were too young to bear her off. Within a week he himself was shaken by a frightful experience of his own. A young emigrant couple and their infant son returned destitute to Berlin from the United States. The relatives from whom they expected help shunned them. After a week, with funds exhausted, they turned to Eisner, whom they had known earlier as one who sympathized with the poor. At twenty-four, their benefactor was slight, his reddish hair thinning, and, as he freely admitted, "subject to moods, of fragile health and fragile nerves." No sooner had they settled into his second room than the overwrought woman fell ill. Their miserable straits confronted the idealist with an unwelcome, deromanticized insight into the responsibilities of marriage and impressed on him the absolute necessity of a regular income.[9] The opposition of Eisner's parents to his liaison with a gentile girl from a poor, bohemian family, if anything, strengthened his resolve.[10]

In early fall he left Berlin to begin work as a copy editor for the *Frankfurter Zeitung*, the premier Left Liberal newspaper, the German daily most widely read abroad and recognized at home for its expertise in foreign affairs. Its founder was Leopold Sonnemann, a leader of the preunification People's Party (Volkspartei) who sought to forge consensus between bourgeois democrats and workers but who opposed exclusively working-class political initiatives and organizations.[11] Eisner's new position, which entailed proofing everything from news articles and editorials to advertisements and lottery results, certainly broadened his journalistic experience, but soon became onerous.[12] A man whose interests lay in philosophy and the arts must have chafed at checking the accuracy of the monthly report for investors in May's Consolidated Gold Mining Company Ltd. of Johannesburg, prices of Havanas at Carl Ladendorff's smoke shop in Pforzheim, or J. Wehl's stock options in North American railroads.

On 11 October 1891 Eisner wrote to his parents from his new lodgings, a third-floor flat at Goetheplatz 3. He began the lengthy letter with a call for reconciliation, voicing his desire for "the clear, cheerful relationship that should exist between parents and children." He assured them that he had not written sooner only because of the demands of his grueling schedule. Every other week he worked the night desk. His hours on this shift were from two to four in the afternoon, five to seven in the evening, and then from ten at night to quarter of four the next morning. During the "recovery week" he worked only four hours each afternoon. The work itself was dull, and the paycheck of 166.66 marks per month was barely adequate given Frankfurt's high prices. He hoped to supplement his income by contributing articles and reviews to the paper's arts section. Here each acceptance fetched 50 to 100 marks. Perhaps his superiors would recognize his talents and further him accordingly. It was doubtful though, for professional jealousy had poisoned the spirit of collegiality: "No friendly tone exists here at all. Each slanders the other, each intrigues against the other." Little wonder that he complained of suffering from chronic gastritis. Discouraged as he was at work, Eisner relished excursions into Frankfurt's surrounding countryside. He related that on the previous Sunday he had taken a cruise on the Rhine from Mainz to Biebrich and then stayed the night just outside Wiesbaden at the villa of family friends, Herr and Frau Reinglass. He closed with an offer to send money, were Emanuel and Hedwig in need.[13] Later in the month Eisner confided to his fiancée the suspicion that his advancement was being hindered by political considerations and judged his superiors "frightful fellows."[14] He found an outlet for his creative energy in publishing on the side in literary journals and began filing reports for *Die kleine Presse* (The Little Press), a Frankfurt paper with a regional readership.[15]

In November and December his anti-Nietzsche, *Psychopathia spiritualis: Friedrich Nietzsche und die Apostel der Zukunft* (Psychopathia spiritualis: Friedrich Nietzsche and the Apostles of the Future), was serialized in *Die Gesellschaft*.[16] He called his first book "a scene from the drama of my intellectual self-liberation and self-realization" (99) and readily admitted that it was no exhaustive, systematic analysis but rather a compilation of "rambling aphoristic remarks" (iv) on the maladies of the age. In addition to Nietzsche, he treats the nationalist racism of Julius Langbehn, social Darwinism, and rampant laissez-faire capitalism. The first comprehensive critique of Nietzsche published in Germany, *Psychopathia spiritualis* chronicles the coalescence of Eisner's thinking.

The former student of literature and philosophy readily confesses the draw of Nietzsche's "brooding profundity, dazzling spirit, audacious wit, and . . . joyful, almost boyish roguishness" (6), but he also discerns the chaos of a mind seething with contradictions. He likens *Zarathustra* to *Faust* in both its poetic grandeur and unsuitablity as a practical guide to life (8). Eisner recognizes that Nietzsche, regardless of his denials, is a direct intellectual descendent of the Schlegel brothers and Tieck, romantics who "created an aesthetic world of self-indulgence in opposition to a prosaic, altruistic moral philosophy" (9). From Friedrich Schlegel in particular came the selectively idealized Hellenism. In true romantic fashion Nietzsche glories in the mystical, the orgiastic abandon of the cult of Dionysus, the oracular office of the poet speaking to and for the initiates.

In Nietzsche's first book, *Die Geburt der Tragödie* (*The Birth of Tragedy*), "one perceived the classically educated, imbued philologist in the recognition of the Apollonian, but only with the maenadization of Hellenism, with the Dionysus fanaticism, did he arrive at his true self" (14). Absent here is the 'classical equanimity' (14) upheld by Winckelmann and Goethe.

As singular as Nietzsche's Hellenism is, Eisner deems his notion of "oriental Aryanism" (14), personified by Zarathustra, even more suspect. Had Nietzsche any understanding of Indian culture, he would know the artificiality of his distinction between a Semitic slave ethic and Aryan master ethic. Indeed, India's defining, central value is human *development*. But the desire for truth is, after all, one of the values Nietzsche questions. "For Nietzsche truth is a woman, and he loves it the way a modern misogynist loves women" (26). This point arouses Eisner's fervor. How could one realize the will to power, how could one lead, if one did not know "what is, what to fear, and what to despise" (27)? Conversely, Eisner has no delusions about truth as an absolute. "Truths are born, they live, grow, and die when their time has come" (29). Nietzsche, he charges, demonstrates his truths through syllogism: the great truths cannot be proven, what I tell you cannot be proven, hence it is true.

Here Eisner pauses to reflect on what Nietzsche divulges of himself in his writings. By nature supercilious, unfeeling, and severe, Nietzsche therefore seeks to depict his vices as the superman's virtues. What he wholly lacks personally, joie de vivre, he lays claim to in his philosophy.[17] In like manner he espouses the "emancipation of the flesh," a corollary to the primacy of the 'will' over Schopenhauer's 'idea' and a fundamental component of the master ethic (47). The glaring contradiction of the quintessential intellectual yearning for the physical, the syphilitic misogynist commending licentiousness, would best "be explained medically" (52).

In love with the painter's daughter and secure in his sexuality, Eisner finds Nietzsche's misogyny repugnant and objects to the witticisms that ridicule all women, without regard for individual qualities or character, as commonplace. In this wise the Social Democratic leader August Bebel shows himself in his writings on women to be as genteel and aristocratic as Nietzsche is vulgar and plebeian. Moreover, the effect of Nietzsche's conceits on his young admirers is grotesque: "They behave wantonly in celebration of unadulterated manliness and deserve at best the attribute manlike" (52). As an example, Eisner cites Nietzsche's disciple Ola Hansson, who candidly acknowledged using Krafft-Ebing's *Psychopathia sexualis*, a study of perversion and violence, as inspiration for his *Alltagsfrauen* (Everyday Women), a collection of graphic novellas. That none misapprehend, Eisner disclaims prudishness in his judgment of

Nietzsche. The only moral law that should obtain as regards sexuality is that we should consider immoral any act harmful to the family, society, a gender, or a race.

At the heart of Nietzsche's misogyny and Judeo-Christian slave ethic Eisner discerns the superman's dictum "Harden yourself." In his discussion of anti-Semitism in Nietzsche's camp, Eisner reveals something of his own bearing toward his heritage. He alludes to section 195 of *Jenseits von Gut und Böse* (*Beyond Good and Evil*), where Nietzsche sees in the negative connotation of the Hebrew word for "world" the germ of the slave ethic. He shows how Nietzsche ascribes the ills of the modern era— compassion, conscience, altruism, and Christianity itself—to this curious linguistic phenomenon. Just as Nietzsche indiscriminately attributes all traits he deems negative to women as a sex, so too he defames the Jews as a race. When racial generalizations are tested by science, Eisner argues, they invariably break down. The statistics yielded by cranial measurement, for example, demonstrate that variations within a racial grouping are as great as those alleged to set it off from others. Moreover, biblical scholars document substantial vestiges of the pagan past in Mosaic texts, rendering Nietzsche's sample somewhat less than racially pure. And recent research suggested that the Greeks borrowed culturally from the Phoenicians, a Semitic people. Such revelations might serve as a purgative for those who "suffer from an unbelievable race constipation" (39–40).

Before racial fatalism, Eisner exhorts, we must "save ourselves with the Kantian leap of necessity into the world of practical reason" (40) if we wish to live productively. In fact, what constitutes race on the cusp of the twentieth century is radically different from what it once was. "Communities sharing a milieu of life and interest form races; contemporaries, colleagues, and members of the same class represent nations. Today's Parisian stands closer to today's Berliner than the Berliner to his German brother in Kuhschnappel: metropolitan milieu. The 1891 Frenchman is more like the contemporary German than the latter is to his compatriot of the year 1500: temporal milieu. The Gallic professor is more closely related to his German colleague than to a Gallic swineherd: occupational milieu" (44). With an equally straightforward argument Eisner dispatches the social Darwinists and their application of natural selection to human society, "individualism as the right of the stronger" (77). If people are capable of acting in concert to mitigate the havoc of natural disasters by establishing insurance agencies, surely they can act against man-made evils as well. Here too he employs statistics to expose fallacy: the richer a society, the lower its mortality and birthrate; hence poverty is not, as social Darwinism holds, a natural mechanism to limit population.

At this point in his critique, Eisner turns to Julius Langbehn, one of the apostles of his subtitle, whose book *Rembrandt als Erzieher* (Rembrandt as Educator) advanced "Germanness" as a *unio mystica* between the land and its inhabitants. He lampoons Langbehn's fixing the Elbe River as the physical and spiritual border between the 'warm' and 'cool' (40) peoples, politicians, poets, and painters, as well as his notion of racial degeneration, exemplified by Jews who have their side curls trimmed and refuse to keep kosher. This kind of "conceptual nonsense" (41), fomented by Nietzsche and furthered by his disciples, Eisner writes, is criminally unconscionable.

The true path to the future, the way to the superman, according to the young journalist, lies in a political philosophy that turns Nietzsche on his head. Nietzsche, he explains, is the culmination of one of the two seminal intellectual currents of the nineteenth century—romanticism; the other, rationalism, gave rise to Marx. "In socialism I see a clear, realizable goal; in Nietzscheism I sleepwalk in search of a blue flower" (86), Eisner declares, referring to the poet Novalis's enduring romantic symbol. For all his brilliance, for all his damning criticism of Western values, Nietzsche lends no direction. In his scorn for the hoi polloi, democracy, and altruism he fails to grasp that socialism aims at the unfettered development of the individual by abolishing artificial restrictions on productivity. The way forward is to "aristocratize the masses" (79) rather than subjugate them. As a political organization of the workers' movement, Social Democracy "should strive at least for this goal" (81).

To come to a clear understanding of Social Democracy, Eisner ventures, one must set aside political and philosophical biases and consider the basic social issue. Ultimately the consequence of the workers' movement is less the enfranchisement of the fourth estate than "the realization of the ideal of collectivism, of practical regulation of production and consumption" to supersede the capitalist system "eternally tottering between boom and bust, between gluttonous plenty and starving want" (84). Socialism represents a world order engineered to preclude the right of might and the rule of chance. He believes that although socialism is inherently rational and scientific, it also has ideal, even religious components that wed exultant secularism with social justice and Christian charity. The Kantian, ethical component of Eisner's political conception would color his thinking throughout his life and lead to fateful clashes with party ideologues, most of whom made their way to Marx via Hegel.

As greatly as Eisner supported socialism's ideal, he was hardly blind to the faults of the Social Democratic Party. The radicalism of the Berlin membership, the bumbling parliamentary faction, and the personal animosity in debate—particularly that of Franz Mehring, coeditor of the party journal *Die Neue Zeit* (The New Age), who "acted as if he wanted to win the title of North German Champion of the Insult"—damaged the party's credibility even among those sympathetic to its cause. In the last pages of his critique Eisner warns that romanticism exerts a powerful pull on ambitious, rebellious youth. Only recently a number of young party members had bolted to form their own League of Independent Socialists (Verein unabhängiger Sozialisten). He notes that the language of their leader, Bruno Wille, rife with allusions to Nietzsche, betrays their inspiration. The prophet of "an anarchy of the elect" remained "the most dangerous and seductive opponent of Social Democracy" (88).

When the second installment of Eisner's critique appeared in December, he was making ready for a visit to Berlin. On the eighteenth his adoring sister Martha wrote that the family, obviously proud of his literary success despite his political leanings, had taken great pleasure in his last letter, "especially at the news that you will spend Christmas with us."[18] After the holiday his mother fretted that he was not saving enough of his salary, and his father fervently hoped that he would complete his degree. At dinner three weeks after New Year's, they urged Lisbeth to work her influence on him. "Wouldn't it work, darling," she wrote the same night, "can't you submit a dissertation to a small university, as you once planned? . . . Do it, love, but don't overtax yourself—little by little, in time it will be done." Emanuel sweetened the pot with an offer of 500 marks if his son would heed the good advice.[19]

Back in Frankfurt Eisner was enjoying the success of his avocation. Wilhelm Friedrich, the Leipzig publisher of *Die Gesellschaft*, reprinted *Psychopathia spiritualis* as a book. An advertisement inserted in the journal's March issue announced its availability in octavo at a price of 2 marks. "Here for the first time Friedrich Nietzsche's philosophical Weltanschauung, which today stirs the entire cultured world, is subjected to a rigorous but just critique by a congenial mind. . . . This profound text highlights current social conditions, the race question, prevalent social Darwinism and its perverse application."[20] The work generated predictably partisan reviews. In *Die Neue Zeit* Franz Mehring disputed the threat Nietzsche posed to socialism, as his appeal was limited mainly to gifted bourgeois youths with literary aspirations. Mehring was unimpressed by Eisner's command of historical materialism and economics yet recommended *Psychopathia spiritualis* as a useful introduction and insightful guide: "In the penetrating critique of Nietzsche, the text affords a most graphic and instructive picture." Mehring reckoned its author just over halfway down the road to socialism and concluded that "one can wish nothing better for Herr Eisner than that he soon arrive at the goal of the way he has taken with insight and courage."[21] The anthroposophist and pedagogue Rudolf Steiner acclaimed the study and then wrote personally to Eisner that his own goal was "to establish ethical individualism scientifically and, of course, completely independent of Nietzsche."[22]

Encouraged by the book's reception, Eisner posted it to Danish critic Georg Brandes, Nietzsche's early champion, whose lectures in Copenhagen in April 1888, reported by Denmark's leading paper, brought Nietzsche to the public. Nietzsche himself had sent Brandes a copy of *Jenseits von Gut und Böse*, only to be ignored until *Zur Genealogie der Moral* (*On the Genealogy of Morals*) arrived and struck the Dane's fancy. In the latter Brandes found, as he wrote to Nietzsche on 26 November 1887, "much that harmonizes with my own ideas and sympathies, the depreciation of the ascetic ideals and the profound disgust with democratic mediocrity, your aristocratic idealism." Within half a year Brandes was signing himself "your faithful reader and admirer."[23]

Receiving no acknowledgment, Eisner wrote again to Brandes, who responded on 7 June 1892 that each day he received a number of such books whose authors were all desirous of his judgment. "Since you demand so zealously to hear my opinion, I will permit myself to send you a couple of hurried remarks. For more I have no time." Had Eisner bothered to read his articles, Brandes chided, this annoyance would be unnecessary. Equating *Zarathustra* with *Faust* was "tastelessness." Eisner had oversimplified Nietzsche from imperfect understanding. In her article for *Die freie Bühne* (The Free Stage), Lou Andreas-Salomé explicated more clearly than Eisner the progression of Nietzsche's ideas. "Your psychology appears to me to be lacking when you ascribe Nietzsche's struggle to the moods of the day." Brandes condescended to agree with Eisner on one main point in his "limp (and a bit boring) work"—the wrong-headedness of Nietzsche's bearing toward socialism. But Brandes protested associating Nietzsche with the likes of Langbehn: "Why in the world do you lump the great man together with the pitiful numskulls who parrot him?"[24]

In a critique of *Psychopathia spiritualis* for the May issue of *Die Gesellschaft*, C. Vedente of Leipzig praised Eisner's style, psychological insight, and criticism of social institutions but faulted him for treating Nietzsche's disparate thought as a unified whole and for advancing his arguments through sentimental analogies rather than thorough proofs.[25] Eisner, evidently stung, remonstrated against being maligned as an "intellectual cripple" who failed to see the obvious contradictions in Nietzsche's oeuvre, but the adjective "sentimental" provoked genuine personal offense, for he interpreted it as a charge of effeminacy: "I am obdurately against what one calls female character traits. I have always endeavored to cultivate in myself the human. . . . I am so misfortunate as to have no secret nerves and no antithetical sexual impulses, and if my head were not assaulted once and awhile by a migraine, I would doubt seriously whether this body part deserves to be called modern at all."[26]

In a review printed in the *Frankfurter Zeitung* on 18 May and rerun in the Sunday supplement on the twenty-second, Eisner critiqued the fourth and final part of *Also sprach Zarathustra* (*Thus Spake Zarathustra*), published in 1891.[27] The review bears the haunting title "From the Literary Remains of One Still Living" and imparts the moral of the proud superman laid low, a dazzling mind gone dark. What he can teach us above all, Eisner writes, is tolerance. Only by examining Nietzsche's work with the tolerance that he himself disdained could one appreciate the brilliance of his prose, the depth of his thought, and "the ecstatic yearning for joy and life's fullness" without succumbing to Nietzsche's monstrous prejudices, enervating cultural despair, and "absolute nihilism." Still, Nietzsche struck a chord of discontent with the spiritual poverty of materialism. "The hypertrophic development of three human activities—politics, trade and industry, technology—has led to a neglect of those human activities that we customarily summarize by the name 'soul.'" The want accounts for Zarathustra's appeal.

At the end of the month Eisner wrote to his publisher, cited favorable reviews of *Psychopathia spiritualis*, and requested an increase in his honorarium for both the book and future essays for the journal. Wilhelm Friedrich answered on 10 June that although he was well aware of the critical success, sales did not yet justify a second edition. He considered the terms binding until demand merited another run, and future articles would be accorded the highest rate of 3 marks per printed page.[28] The book's following certainly whetted Eisner's literary ambitions. Using the pseudonym Reinhard Fern, he authored a vignette, "Feverish Night: An Impression," describing the mental anguish of a young man who must pawn a silver watch given to him by his father.[29] Under his own name Eisner presented in the *Frankfurter Zeitung* a two-part survey of recent German literature, in which he pays tribute to Theodor Fontane, whose novel *Unwiederbringlich* (Irretrievable) had appeared the previous year, as "the honorary member of the moderns," and passes over Maria von

Ebner-Eschenbach to pronounce Maria Janitschek "the strongest poetic power among the literary women."[30]

During the spring Eisner's circle in Berlin was diminished by the death, after long illness, of Lisbeth's sister Doris. Grete Eisner commiserated in a letter of 29 April that although she had prepared for it, Doris's death had affected her deeply.[31] Eisner and Lisbeth determined to marry in the summer. She wrote to him the evening of 3 June about the decor of their Frankfurt apartment.[32] On the nineteenth Eisner announced in a letter to his mother that he would return home in July "to go through the necessary formalities in Eberswalde that will make it possible for Lisbeth to return together with me to Frankfurt." He was determined to marry as soon as possible, he advised, and no objection on his parents' part would deter him. Doris's death clearly played a role in his decision. Lisbeth's life at home was oppressive and pernicious, he confided to Hedwig. "I have the duty of liberating her from it." And marriage would stabilize his own existence: "I desperately need the peace attendant to a chosen fate. . . . Above all I require a comrade so that I can continue my literary activity. With my first attempt I scored a success beyond any expectation. . . . This winter I will try to find the time and frame of mind for a drama." He foresaw that within a year or two he would seek a better position that would permit him to contribute more substantially to his parents' support. Until then Lisbeth would help him endure his lot.[33] On 19 July 1892 they wed in a civil ceremony at the Eberswalde town hall.[34] In Frankfurt they took two furnished rooms on the fourth floor of a boarding house at Große Gallusgasse 5.[35]

Settling into married life, Eisner continued to earn his bread through the fall and winter at the *Frankfurter Zeitung* while enhancing his reputation in the serial press. In a note to a colleague whom he sensed to be a kindred spirit, he confessed that he had suffered the while in Frankfurt from lack of personal intellectual stimulation and voiced concern that his "socialist political sensibility" had isolated him from the paper's management.[36] So successful was he at his extramural pursuits that his employers suspected that he was slighting his duties and feared that he could compromise their confidential sources. Even while he was drafting one of his reports for *Die kleine Presse* in his office at the *Frankfurter Zeitung*, Eisner was informed by management that he had no further prospects at the paper.[37] He resigned effective 10 April 1893 and began the search for another job.[38] On his first day out of work he wrote to Franz Mehring to ask his assistance. "Having sampled the noble mind in its most sublime form, as it exists only among people purported to be Democrats, I am finally free of my service to the house of the *Frankfurter Zeitung*. . . . Can you, dear Sir, advise me how one can indulge one's willingness and ability to work without subjecting oneself to derision and ridicule?"[39] On the twenty-first he wrote to a potential employer at another paper that he had resigned his position in Frankfurt for personal reasons and spelled out his terms, "a monthly salary of 175 marks (besides a share of the profits)."[40] In a letter of 12 May, Maximilian Harden, now editor of the prestigious journal *Zukunft* (The Future), offered to meet with Eisner in Berlin on the coming Wednesday afternoon.[41] But no job materialized.

While searching for a new niche, Eisner made do with freelance work. Under a pseudonym, assumed that he might write freely without jeopardizing opportunities for employment, he became a regular contributor to *Das Magazin für Litteratur*, a venerable Berlin weekly edited by Fritz Mauthner and Otto Neumann-Hofer. He chose the pen name Sperans, or "Hoping," in all likelihood in affirmation of the Kantian axiom that the logic of hope is synonymous with the logic of social action. Eisner must have felt at home in the journal's pages; other collaborators included his professors Erich Schmidt and Richard Meyer, student chum Alfred Kerr, and former foil Ernst von Wolzogen. Joining Eisner as a political observer and social critic for the journal was Gustav Landauer, a fellow Jewish, leftist intellectual who would become his closest political ally, speak his eulogy, and ultimately share his grave.

Eisner's inaugural effort, an article titled "Militarism," was accorded front-page top billing on 20 May.[42] Here he examined the military appropriations impasse that prompted Chancellor Caprivi to dissolve the Reichstag and call for new elections. The German military, Eisner wrote, the ranks of which were filled by men whose former station in life was generally worse than their potential fate on the battlefield, was a feudal anachronism that served as bodyguard to the privileged classes rather than as national defense force. Accordingly, "the representatives of the propertied and educated classes, the Right and the National Liberals," supported the measure. That the other great European armies were similarly constituted augured nothing good: "The great world war of the future is in its cave crisping its claws." Only the Social Democrats had voted en bloc against the bill, for their party enjoyed the luxury of being able to wait; its day was coming rather than passing. Eisner put himself squarely behind the Social Democratic demand for a citizens' militia, "the free people in arms with no purpose other than defending national independence," for such a military would be a democratizing force in German society and a boon to its cultural ascent.

The niche Eisner sought opened in late May when Paul Bader, founder and editor in chief of the *General-Anzeiger für Marburg und*

Umgebung (General Gazette for Marburg and Vicinity), called him to Marburg an der Lahn, a university town in the central state of Hesse. Bader too had worked early in his career at the *Frankfurter Zeitung* and moved toward the Social Democratic camp.[43] When Eisner arrived to take up a temporary position as political editor, Bader was engaged in a personal campaign against the incumbent Reichstag deputy representing Marburg-Kirchhain-Frankenberg since 1887, Dr. Otto Böckel, whose popularity in the villages of the district had earned him the nickname "the peasants' king." Head of the Antisemitic People's Party (Antisemitische Volkspartei) and owner of the rival *Reichsherold* (Imperial Herald) in Marburg, Böckel had galvanized a constituency by championing legislation to secure credit for peasants and protect small business and trades. Bader pitted his paper against the Antisemites and declared a protest candidacy to gauge opposition to Böckel.[44] Together with Johann Becker, a local printer who wrote occasionally for the *General-Anzeiger*, Eisner stumped for Bader in Böckel's strongholds. During a strategy session at Becker's home, the printer informed Eisner of Böckel's weakness for "village beauties." Becker's son Matthäus later recalled their conversation and his mother's amusement. "He's become a papa again in a neighboring village," Becker remarked. "And why not?" Eisner responded, "He's channeled all his physical energies into expanding his electoral base!" On a foray into a village the two found themselves before a particularly hostile audience. Böckel's men had put out the word that a Jew was coming to calumniate him. Becker was a shepherd's son and spoke the dialect, but it was Eisner who quieted the catcalls with his wit: "I have heard the rumor that has been spread about my companion Johann Becker, and therefore I now solemnly assure you that he is not Jewish."[45]

Sperans presented in early June a commentary on the inherent weaknesses of each of the parties.[46] The Conservatives, who were losing their appeal to agrarian workers, attempted to obfuscate the issues by fanning up anti-Semitism wherever it smoldered. "For every Jew approximately," Eisner observed, "there is an anti-Semitic faction . . . , ranging from those . . . who cannot forgive the Jews for *crucifying* Christ to those who regard Israel as a world-historical calamity for *producing* Christ." The Center Party was badly fragmented between its democratic and ultramontane elements. The National Liberals, the party that had gloried in German unification and the struggle against Rome for Germany's cultural identity, now pandered to special interests. The old Progressive Party, renamed the Radical Party in 1884 after realignment, was Bismarck's perennial adversary, lost its raison d'être with his departure, and could not determine "whether its archenemy stands to the left or right." The party with the least to lose and the most to gain in the voting on 15 June was the SPD (Sozialdemokratische Partei Deutschlands). Three years after its return from outlawry and exile, Social Democracy boasted a loyal, disciplined base of support among workers and a complement of bourgeois auxiliaries, but Bruno Wille's youthful faction was certainly capable of disruption. Having posited socialism as the political extension of his utilitarian philosophy and, indeed, having written in its support, Eisner nonetheless balked at joining the party, opting instead for irregular status. "We who take pleasure in needing to represent no interest follow this development too with serene curiosity."

In the elections the Social Democrats polled almost 360,000 votes more nationally than in 1890 and gained nine seats. The National Liberals lost 180,000 votes but gained eleven seats by apportionment. The Conservatives, Center, and Radicals all lost representation. The Antisemites received 3.4 percent of the total vote.[47] In his district Böckel was returned to the Reichstag, easily besting all opponents.

Following the fourth Evangelical Social Congress, held in Berlin in early June, Eisner analyzed the phenomenon he termed "frock socialism," the clergy-led, patriotic workers' movement launched by Prussian court pastor Adolf Stöcker. The article appeared in *Das Magazin für Litteratur* two days after the elections.[48] A prominent anti-Semite, Stöcker had founded the Christian Social Labor Party (Christlich-Soziale Arbeiterpartei) in 1878 to combat godless socialism and its causes. He believed that capitalism and industrialization, bankrolled by the Jewish lending houses, had wrought intolerable suffering among the poor, whose cry of anguish in turn had called down upon Europe the scourge of Jewish-inspired socialism.[49] Although Stöcker's party was thoroughly reactionary, it was assailed by the Right as well as the Left, and eventually most of its constituency turned to Social Democracy: "The eternal prospect of heaven as the supreme insurance agency against old age and infirmity became too monotonous for people—they were, after all, Berliners—and thus Herr Stöcker, in the end, had recruited and drilled soldiers for the enemy."

The Evangelical Social Congress was a forum for Stöcker's ideological spawn, whose plans for social reform from above Eisner likened to "soup-kitchen beneficence and Christmas gifts for poor children." Pastor Friedrich Naumann of Frankfurt, whom Eisner praised as "one of the few clergy who understand their time," used statistical data to dispute the assertion of Court Pastor Braun of Stuttgart that the gap between rich and poor had narrowed in the areas of education and standard of living, and condemned his patriarchal outlook as conducive to the suppression of the individual. To those like Stöcker who regarded Naumann as a dreamer ahead of his time, Eisner answered: "No one can understand his own time who does not have a presentiment of the future, who is not already at home there intellectually. Only from the distance of the future does one get a clear view of the present." Conversely, Eisner warned that Social Democracy, devoted as it was to Enlightenment ideals, must not discount the power of the spirit, as the politicized clerics did the skeptical mind, for "we also have a soul, an irrationally roving soul" that requires free range.

Later that summer Eisner had more advice from Sperans's print pulpit for the party leadership after its electoral gains. Those radicals shunning parliamentary participation as capitulation to the system were reactionaries clinging to retrograde tactics. "In parliamentarism everyone has at present a way to win political power. Whoever fails to use it is a fool. Alley revolutions are a means of earlier times, at best still suited to Russia."[50] It was a remarkable observation, made two years in advance of Engels's own adjuration in his preface to Marx's *Class Struggles in France, 1848–1850.*[51]

Eisner reported to his mother on 20 June that his four-week trial at the *General-Anzeiger* was done and that he had been invited to stay on. "The position here is ideal, actually: relatively little work, good pay, complete freedom of action, nice people, and moreover the opportunity and time to work at the university." He was encouraged too by the reception of his weekly articles for *Das Magazin für Litteratur.*[52] The next week he wrote that he had signed a two-year contract stipulating an annual salary of 3,300 marks and four weeks' vacation. It was nearly double his starting pay in Frankfurt, and Marburg was far less expensive. He added a postscript: "I will now be able to complete my doctorate here."[53] Appearances were important. In a letter of 25 July he instructed Lisbeth to buy for their new abode a full complement of furniture in the style she had already ordered from Dittmar in Berlin. "I simply cannot disgrace myself now when all Marburg awaits my things (everything I do interests all Marburg) by owning up that I have none."[54] For the new furnishings the rising leftist luminary saddled himself with debt.

CHAPTER THREE

REFUGE OF ALL IDEALISTS: THROUGH COHEN TO KANT TOWARD MARX (1893–1896)

THE LEFT LIBERAL JOURNALIST Hellmut von Gerlach remarked that Eisner, in his four-year tenure as political editor of the *General-Anzeiger*, won for the publication "a significance extending far beyond the range of a provincial paper."[1] Hesse had been annexed by Prussia after siding with Austria in Bismarck's war for Schleswig-Holstein; in its intellectual capital Eisner gloried in deprecating the Prussian arrogance and ambition personified by the German emperor. In lead articles for the paper, Berlin weeklies, and the liberal daily *Vossische Zeitung* ([Christian Friedrich] Voß Newspaper) he achieved his earmark style "somewhere between Heinrich Heine and Kurt Tucholsky."[2] In light of Eisner's coruscating wit and irony historian Allan Mitchell surmised: "Had he not been the editor of a provincial newspaper, he might well have earned his living by writing for one of Berlin's political cabarets."[3] Eisner's years in Marburg were in many respects the happiest of his life, a period of both respite and preparation, alive with the promise of family, friendship, intellectual growth, and meaningful work. A regular income freed him from the anxiety of the past, Lisbeth gave birth to three of their children there, and Eisner was drawn into the circle of intellectuals around philosophy professor Hermann Cohen, master of the neo-Kantian Marburg School whose thinking shaped a generation of "reform" socialists. The association with Cohen, his colleagues, and students channeled Eisner's already strong philosophical and political inclinations; "he began to define his socialism as a Kantian ethical socialism."[4] And through his political involvement with Bader he learned the practical application of his ideas.

Hermann Cohen had succeeded his patron Friedrich Albert Lange, enunciator of ethical socialism, as philosophy chair at Marburg in 1876. Once Eisner was settled, he determined to take advantage of his proximity to the great Jewish scholar who, continuing Lange's work, was in the process of explicating systematically that socialism has both its moral justification and philosophical fundament in Kantian ethics rather than in Hegel's ideal metaphysics or Marx's historical materialism. Cohen believed that philosophy, not science, is the vehicle for studying ethics, and that man—specifically, the individual and his associations—is the focus of the discipline. The principles that govern the conduct of individuals in their dealings with others are ethics, and moral values determine politics and economics rather than vice versa.

From these premises Cohen developed a practical philosophy. He held that each individual belongs to a number of groups, or pluralities. The pluralities together compose the totality that is the state. The highest good is achieved when the wills and actions of the disparate pluralities are unified to further the interests of the whole. The individual or group guided exclusively by self-interest is immoral. The power state (Machtstaat) emerges when selfish will subverts the highest good to the benefit of a particular group or groups. Consistent with Kant's categorical imperative that one's actions should be governed by principles that might serve as the basis for a universal code of law, the legal state (Rechtstaat) conversely represents the interests of the whole by safeguarding the interests of each individual. Consequently, the legal state is democratic and cooperative, based on universal suffrage and equal access to public education; in it "private property is limited to personal property" and "the production of economic goods becomes a truly collective task and responsibility."[5] The best chance for Germany's transformation from power state to legal state, Cohen reasoned, lay in the Social Democratic Party. Whereas Marx judged morality to be irrelevant to historical development and viewed Kantian ethics as socially conciliatory and detrimental to the revolutionary character of the proletariat, Cohen deemed Marx's "eruptive revolution" unnecessary in a society with rudimentary democratic mechanisms and immoral in that violence and terror were fundamentally inconducive to the highest good.[6]

Having studied Kant with Paulsen in Berlin and having espoused in *Psychopathia spiritualis* many of Cohen's precepts, Eisner now began auditing Cohen's popular lectures. Adolf Koester, another of Cohen's students while Eisner was in Marburg, later recalled the familiar scene of the diminutive professor in a large hat, strolling with cane in hand beneath the chestnuts along Gisselberger Chaussee, a train of collegians in tow with whom he discussed the unity of all knowledge.[7] Eisner came to know Cohen well. They often walked home together through Marburg's winding streets, speaking of Judaism, philosophy, politics, art, and events of the day.[8] Eisner also made the acquaintance of Cohen's confederates, most notably philosophers Paul Natorp and Rudolf Stammler, social scientist Franz Staudinger, and historian Karl Vorländer. With Natorp he shared an abiding affinity for Condorcet's belief in man's inherent goodness.[9] On the occasion of Cohen's seventieth birthday in July 1912, Eisner wrote in tribute that the sage's thinking had molded the very "essence of my being."[10] In the end, though, they disagreed on one critical question: the inevitability of revolution in the progress toward a just society.

In Marburg, as elsewhere in Germany, a sharp contrast existed between town and gown. While the university had become the international center of neo-Kantian socialism, Marburg proper remained "a Conservative, National Liberal, Antisemitic idyll." Bader's campaign against Böckel had distinguished him and his new staffer as "dangerous rabble-rousers."[11] In addition to his work for the *General-Anzeiger*, Eisner continued to contribute to the serial press. In an article titled "A Corruption Trial," appearing in *Das Magazin für Litteratur* on 11 November 1893, he took aim as Sperans at the manifestations of anti-Semitism brought to light by the sensational trial in Hanover of a Jewish gambler named Abter, who with an accomplice had cheated a young officer, Lieutenant von Plessen, out of 30,000 marks. The case was being tried as surely in the press as in court.[12] A characteristic portrayal emerged of "Jews and Junker" in which the former were demonized, the latter sanctified.

Citing sensational examples of anti-Semitic opinion on the trial— among them the call for "forcible expulsion from our country" of the entire race—Eisner ridiculed the logical inconsistency of rejecting criticism from those who regarded the officer corps as profligate on account of the habits of a few, only to indict then a sizable national minority on similar grounds. The need for scapegoats he considered symptomatic of spiritual malaise in the bourgeois soul. "Literary dross of the sort I noted above does not occur in proletarian publications: perhaps the matter-of-fact insipidity, the overbearingly prosaic enlightenment are boring, but the striving for knowledge, reason, and clarity always compensates for it. . . . Whereas one in the fourth estate seeks, perhaps wrongly but always by clear laws, to construe, differentiate, and structure the things of the world, whereas one possesses here in historical materialism a worldview of genuine substance, there one reels dog-drunk between chance symptoms and wild generalizations, in desperate, senseless fear of intellectual infections, to entice the other over to his side."

Abter was found guilty of usury. Eisner had no quarrel with the verdict, but in an observation that amply evinces Cohen's influence, he pointed out that German law recognized only the financial damages that derive from games of chance, that violations were punished as crimes against property; in Austrian, English, and Italian law, however, these offenses were judged as crimes against public morality. To those who called for legislation to protect youthful officers from victimization at the gaming table, he impishly proposed a "national credit bank for paying gambling debts incurred in accordance with one's class and rank" and then asked what law would protect the honest poor from exploitation at the hands of the bourgeois nobility-of-property.

In an article for the 18 November issue, "Boycotted Elections," Eisner contemplated the meaning of the Radical Party's demise in the lower house of the Prussian Landtag, members of which were elected by the three-class suffrage system devised in 1851 to preserve the privilege of the Junker squirearchy.[13] The three electoral classes were determined by tax rate; the effect was that the rich had one hundred times the representation of the poor. In 1890, for example, when the national Reichstag, elected by universal and equal male suffrage, had thirty-five Social Democratic deputies, the Prussian Landtag had none.[14]

Over thirty years the number of Left Liberal deputies had dwindled to a fraction of their former total. The decline had nothing to do, Eisner observed, with people becoming more conservative, for the Reichstag elections proved the contrary. Rather it merely reflected changing circumstance. Bismarck's volatility and willingness to use repression against his adversaries necessitated a bourgeois party that would defend middle-class freedoms—a disgruntled party of loyal opposition, as it were. Without Bismarck bourgeois radicalism served no purpose; with no strong man to play them off against each other and then run roughshod over them individually, the other parties of property—the Conservatives, National Liberals, and Antisemites—sufficed as advocates of special interests. The Radical Party was simply passé. Bismarck's successor, Count Caprivi, allowed for a realignment of political energies. "The historical merit of Capriviism is its programmatically implemented tedium. It afforded the repose to dwell on the essential in modern culture: one could finally learn to think and perceive socially." Consequently, the Prussian Conservatives, uneasy with foreboding, were celebrating a hollow victory, for "the majority of the people . . . expressed their opinion clearly and unmistakably by *boycotting* the elections."

The masses had become too conscious of their potential power to be "content with the scraps of political rights." They were stirring to rise to a new day. The electoral system that deprived them of a voice in affairs of state was "immoral" and would prove the undoing of those

who profited by it. Cohen's influence shines through Eisner's criticism
of Prussia's ills and through his optimistic view of the ineluctability of
social justice through increased democracy: "Constitutionalism rests on
the principle that the people's voice should be heard. Parliaments do
not exist to provide a definitive explanation of Kant's *Critique of Pure
Reason* by majority decision; then one would be able to justify suffrage
based on education. Their purpose is even less to grant to the propertied, in addition to their other advantages, that of legislative influence;
only an age warped by proprietary mania can justify that. Parliaments
should be a virtual replica of the people's frame of mind. Whatever they
desire and crave, whatever foolish and wise, beautiful and ugly seethes
and surges within them, the people's duly reconstituted representation
should express. And reason will prevail, necessity will emerge victorious!" In a very few years the optimism would be tempered by bitter
experience, and Eisner would realize that progress toward social justice
could not be linear across time, rather that social justice would derive
only from a new dispensation.

A cordial letter from Alfred Kerr evinces the effect Eisner's pseud-
onymous writings were having in the capital.[15] Kerr, who in the 1920s
became counterpoint to Herbert Ihering, Brecht's chief proponent, had
studied together with Eisner under Meyer and Schmidt. Through tren-
chant reviews for the arts serials and press, Kerr was rapidly establishing
himself as one of Germany's eminent theater critics. On 25 November
1893 he wrote to his former classmate to exchange news and ask a favor.
He reported that he had attained his doctorate; he knew that Eisner had
left Germanics, wondered if political economy was now Eisner's field of
study at Marburg, and inquired as to future plans. His request was at
once simple and unusual: "A lady in my acquaintance (I do not dissemble
when I say she is a 'sensitive' woman) has fallen in love with one of your
Sperans articles (which I find understandable) and asks that I deliver the
head of the author, not like Herod in uncultivated times, rather with all
the comfort of the modern age, in a photograph." Kerr's letter must have
found Eisner preoccupied, for on the twenty-second Lisbeth had borne a
son, called Reinhard.[16]

In the same week a remark addressed to August Bebel, leader of the
Social Democratic delegation in the Reichstag, by Prussian finance minister Johannes Miquel drew a fanciful response from Eisner in his review of
a nonexistent book.[17] As a twenty-year-old student during the Revolution
of 1848, Miquel sympathized with the Left and corresponded with Marx.
He changed his colors to become a leader of the National Liberals and
served the party as a deputy in three national parliaments—Prussian,

Confederation, and Reich—before Wilhelm II named him to a ministry. In equal parts idealist, realist, and intriguer, Miquel achieved a longevity that his adversaries could but envy. He outlasted Bismarck by urging Wilhelm to eschew confrontation with hostile elements in the bourgeois parties and espouse instead a "policy of inclusion" (Sammelpolitik). "The great task at present," he wrote in 1890, "is, without prejudice or embarrassment because of past battles, to gather together all the elements that support the state and thereby to prepare for the perhaps unavoidable battle against the Social Democratic movement, which is often misunderstood and still almost always underestimated."[18]

On 27 November 1893 Miquel promised Bebel before the Reichstag that he would write a book someday containing a criticism, drawn from his own experience, of socialism's basic premise. Seizing upon this announcement, Eisner declared that having seen the manuscript, he offered an assessment. "Herr Dr. Miquel has written a kind of biographical novel in this book. It is an imposing pamphlet against his youth, indeed against youth in general, it is a polemic against fantastic yearning and rapturous hope. Never before has an author intoned with such fearless audacity: youth is a vice that must be surmounted." Proceeding from Miquel's belief that man's longing tends not to commonality but rather to individual wealth as a validation of self-worth, Eisner pronounced Miquel's novel similar in theme to Keller's *Der grüne Heinrich* (Green Henry), a rambling account of a young man's struggle to find himself—he never does, but he gets rich in the process.

Eisner praises the work's style, comparing it to the national finance code in brilliance. He assigns it the title *Green Johnny*, in recognition of its biographical elements, and prints an excerpted chapter, "Change of Fortune," in which the young protagonist realizes the true purpose of life. He acquires an account book and turns in self-recrimination from the study of the great revolts of history and his correspondence with rabble-rousers. The transformation is complete when a copy of Radical Party leader Eugen Richter's *Sozialdemokratische Zukunftsbilder* (Social Democratic Visions of the Future) falls into his hands; from it he learns that poverty and misery are merely manifestations of one's own pessimism. Johnny has beheld God, His name is Rothschild, and the gospel is "free competition." He turns his back on his old friends to dedicate himself to the unfettered pursuit of self-worth.

On 31 December Eisner's retrospective on the closing year appeared in the *General-Anzeiger*. He concluded that "the world yearns for new forms, new ideas, new systems" and that the point had been reached where it was time to take bearings "in order to blaze new trails."[19]

"The Second," published 6 January 1894 in *Das Magazin für Litteratur*, dealt with another leading politician, Chancellor Caprivi, but in a more favorable light than Miquel had been presented.[20] The essay's title refers to Caprivi's unenviable position as the empire's second chancellor. Comparison with his predecessor was inescapable, yet Caprivi's harshest critics were those of his own Junker caste who believed his trade policies afforded them too little protection. The detractors took greatest exception to the chancellor's view of the state as guarantor of the common good—a view Eisner regarded as enlightened beyond any expectation. In a speech that won him the undying malice of his brethren, Caprivi remarked: "Economic interests are always based more or less on egoism . . . whereas the state places demands on the willingness of its citizens to make sacrifices, on their idealism. The more the parties become entwined in economic life and its interests, the more it must be government's duty to represent the more ideal interests."

Perspicacious and circumspect, frank and forthright, colored with a tinge of "ideological liberalism," Caprivi had a distinct flaw in the eyes of his cavilers: he was not Bismarck, he lacked Bismarck's resourcefulness. "It is delightful indeed," Eisner quipped, "to look on, for example, as a Bavarian baron who, by hanging a sign at the gate to his palace grounds, bars entrance to 'dogs and Jews' brusquely demands . . . the Reichskanzler to be resourceful." A personality cult had emerged after Bismarck's retirement that ascribed to him the grand design to a host of triumphs that were in fact merely the workings of history. Thus it was that a man who was more honorable, thoughtful, and devoted to serving the whole people than was his predecessor was doomed to stand in his shadow, a fate Caprivi himself recognized.[21]

Upon the appearance of a new weekly, the *Mittwochsblatt für unsere vaterländische Gemeinsamkeit* (Wednesday Paper for Our National Community), put out by Moritz von Egidy as "complement to the dailies of all present-day parties," Eisner commended the editor's idealism and desire to effect a reconciliation between society's dissonant factions.[22] The effort to create social harmony and prosperity through reason and beneficence was reminiscent of New Lanark, the industrial commune established by British utilitarian socialist Robert Owen. How starkly Owen's view of man clashed with that of his Prussian contemporary Friedrich von Gentz, who wondered how the masses were to be ruled if they became comfortable and independent! The Junker invariably saw his own dominion threatened by others' success. Demonstrating that his Kant was tempered now by Marx, Eisner rejected Egidy's premise and urged the former Prussian officer swayed by religious conviction to choose a side, for "truly there is no recon-ciliation between them and us."

In early March Eisner appended a personal note to an article on political guile: his infant son, whose eyes were larger than his mouth, looked "as if he believed in a world of great deeds and great reason, in a human existence full of purity and truth, happiness and goodness."[23] A few months later a horrible crime of despair at a Berlin residence that shocked the most inured reporters caused the new father to reflect on the human toll of class conflict.[24] A master housepainter named Seeger, ruined by a swindle in the building trade, killed his wife, four children, and himself. In the tragedy of the housepainter, Eisner read also the dilemma of an entire subclass. As an independent artisan, Seeger was "a lesser entrepreneur ground under by the ups and downs of the capitalis-tic mechanism." His meager livelihood depended on work subcontracted by a greater entrepreneur, who in turn prospered or suffered according to the caprice of the market. Having witnessed his own father's business woes, Eisner knew firsthand the specter of insolvency and displacement, "the unspeakably sad, lifeless misery of the sinking petite bourgeoisie." For the independent tradesman the thing he feared most, displacement into the proletariat, actually would be a step up. The working class was imbued with an optimism foreign to the lower middle class. The belief in the inevitablity of labor's triumph represented a "joyful ideal and a hope born of faith, or even, if one prefers this expression, a new religion."

In June 1894 Paul Bader and his associates changed the name of the *General-Anzeiger* to the *Hessische Landeszeitung* (The Hessian Regional Paper), a banner recalling the title of the socialist tract *Der hessische Landbote* (The Hessian Herald), published by dramatist Georg Büchner in nearby Gießen exactly sixty years earlier. Philipp Scheidemann, who over the course of a quarter century would rise from printer to Social Democratic prime minister in the first government of the Weimar Republic, was then a compositor in Marburg, served as district chairman of the German Printers' Union, and contributed occasional articles to the *Hessische Landeszeitung*. In his memoirs Scheidemann writes of his association with Eisner and Bader, neither of whom were party members at the time: "These two men are due my great gratitude, for they led me to places that up to then had been virtually closed off: they opened the doors to literature and kindled my appreciation for diverse fine arts." With Eisner he discussed Gerhart Hauptmann's naturalist play *Die Weber* (*The Weavers*) and began to attend Cohen's lectures. Scheidemann felt at home in Marburg and refers to the six years there as his brightest.[25] The Eisners' roots in Marburg deepened with the death of Lisbeth's father, the painter August Hendrich, at age fifty-four on Christmas Eve in Eberswalde.[26] The next month Eisner joined the Marburg Civic Association, an affiliation followed by membership in the local Comenius Society, an organization dedicated to cultivating the pansophist principles of the Moravian theologian and educator.[27]

In late winter and early spring 1895 Eisner became increasingly concerned about encroachments on intellectual freedom. For journalists in Wilhelmine Germany the threat of jail was ever a grim reality, and now the Reichstag contrived anew to muzzle particularly the Social Democratic press. The Center Party had introduced a measure to expand the purview of the sedition bill of the previous December to include atheism as a form of subversion punishable by imprisonment, "whereby, apparently," Eisner quipped in an article for *Das Magazin für Litteratur*, "the soul should be given opportunity to convince itself somewhat earlier of its immortality." He invoked Spinoza's call for total freedom of thought and speech, issued in 1670, against this current assault on intellectual life and warned against entrusting the national conscience to a judiciary composed of "old boys from the dueling fraternities" who, by virtue of passing an exam or two, now ruled absolutely over the fate of others. Noting that the courts had interpreted the lèse-majesté law broadly, to the discomfort of even the solidly bourgeois press, he demanded "complete freedom of every artistic, scholarly, and journalistic expression of opinion that is brought to heel by *none*."[28] In a spoof edition of the *Hessische Landeszeitung* dated 26 February, the editors announced that rather than continue to publish an independent newspaper, they would convert it forthwith into an organ of whichever party was most closely aligned with the government and eschew henceforth "any opposition, any criticism, any expression of dissatisfaction" in order to concentrate on reporting market prices and temperature readings. On 7 April the *Hessische Landeszeitung* ran anonymously an article in which Eisner traced the history of laws aimed at stifling criticism of the government and preserving status quo.[29]

The political editor took time for belletristic and personal pursuits. As "E." he wrote a minute description of the landscape and inhabitants of the Schwalm, a region of Hesse bisected by its namesake river.[30] Its residents differed markedly in physical appearance, manner, dress, and custom from their Hessian neighbors, prompting the author to venture that they were of Magyar rather than Germanic descent. The 29 September issue of the *Hessische Landeszeitung* printed Reinhard Fern's musings on the attribution of Shakespeare's works to his contemporary Bacon.[31] A month later the Eisners announced by engraved card "the joyful birth of a healthy girl" on 23 October.[32] As Ilse Hedwig and her brother Reinhard grew, their father savored the pedagogue's pleasure in parenting and insisted that the children be allowed to enjoy their natural freedom. He recorded tenderly how his young son wept over a dead crow and attempted to revive it by pressing crumbs of cake to its beak.[33]

The collegiality of Bader's staff, so different from what Eisner had experienced in Frankfurt, contributed to his sense of well-being in Marburg. Johann Becker, typesetter for the *Hessische Landeszeitung*, had written for the paper some peasant tales in the local dialect. Favorably impressed, Eisner urged Becker to submit his work to one of the national literary journals, but the humble typesetter declined. Acting in concert with Frau Becker, Eisner obtained the manuscript of Becker's "Next in Line" and entered it in a contest announced in the 28 June 1896 issue of *Die Hilfe* (Help), Friedrich Naumann's Berlin weekly. A prize of 120 marks was to be awarded for a story realistically depicting "the life of the little people in the city or country." Some fifty years later Becker's son remembered vividly Eisner's joy as he burst into the household to announce that the story had taken first prize.[34]

The prevalent mood at the paper, despite a flurry of libel suits, was one of indomitable mirth, for Eisner brought to his editorial duties the same wit that animated the Sperans articles. When a semiliterate vegetable handler named Paul Zörb confided to Eisner a desire to see his name printed in the paper, the editor offered to accommodate him everyday. By agreement Zörb allowed his name to be listed on the masthead as the responsible party, while Eisner promised that the paper would pay any damages awarded by the court and smart money for time spent in jail. Whenever Zörb drew his brief confinements, the *Hessische Landeszeitung* hired three carriages—two for the Seven Ravens, a popular band, the garlanded third for Zörb alone—to convey the feted vegetable dealer from the editorial offices through the streets of Marburg to jail. When his time was up, the same show was made to fetch him back. The townsfolk reveled in the spectacle.[35]

In July 1896 Dr. Richard Wrede, a journalist trained in law, succeeded Karl Schneidt as editor of *Die Kritik* (The Critique), a weekly devoted to "public life." Wrede had contracted Eisner to provide a regular commentary to lead off each issue. Because of the author's remove from the metropolis, his thoughts took the general title *Provinzialbriefe* (Provincial Letters). For the new forum Eisner adopted a new pseudonym, Tat-Twam, from the Sanskrit *tat twam asi*: you are thus.[36] Like the Sperans pieces, the *Briefe* addressed in the main "political events of the day." For almost two years Tat-Twam goaded the worthies until his identity became known and he was made to suffer the consequences. He addressed his first letter to Wrede, speculating on why the editor had chosen a "poor provincial" to instruct the Berliner on affairs in Berlin.[37] "Perhaps you are even inclined to the view that one can distinguish the superficial and essential more easily from a distance." In any case there was much to be said for "the influence the lowing of oxen and the cackling of geese exerts on the self-purification of one's reason." In the body of this first letter Tat-Twam surveyed the chicanery of the Reichstag in skirting the issue of women's rights, preferring instead to extend protection to overhunted rabbit populations.[38]

An article that registers Eisner's divergence from Cohen's evolutionary camp, "Out!" was the second piece for *Die Kritik*.[39] Its title derived from an incident at the adjournment of the Reichstag for summer recess. When one of the forty-eight Social Democratic deputies remained seated during the customary salute to the kaiser, supporters of the monarchy shouted their abuse in the monosyllable "raus," a command used to banish beggars from the gate or dogs from the kitchen. Beyond being within his rights as a citizen, Eisner argued, Deputy Schmidt had demonstrated good taste in not making a sarcastic obeisance to an institution that Social Democrary vowed to abolish. To hail perfunctorily the man who constantly denigrated the party as "the enemy within" could be judged the most egregious lèse majesté, smacking of mockery. Eisner wondered as to the future protocol, for given the ineluctable growth of the party, it was only a matter of time before Social Democrats would control the Reichstag. Of immense significance is his statement: "It is not our concern whether in the meantime repressive measures interrupt this development. Our constitution, flawed in its most fundamental principle, has no cushion to soften and render harmless the clash of forces. Their final resolution is brutal conflict. Before that conflict, though, a state of affairs is conceivable in which the president of the Reichstag closes the sessions with a salute to revolutionary Social Democracy, liberator of peoples." In Germany, he observed, the adversarial forces marshaled themselves less into the opposing camps generally associated with class conflict—"capitalism and collectivism, bourgeois society and social state, property and communism, liberal individualism and socialism"—than beneath banners of monarchy and democracy. The state prosecutors whose job it was to redress offense to the crown doubtless scrutinized the second of the *Provinzialbriefe* and clamored to know its author's identity.

It could well be argued that the day on which Eisner definitively cast his lot with the party was 8 August 1896. On that date *Die Kritik* printed his thoughts on the meeting of the Socialist International in London.[40] At a peace rally in Hyde Park one of the SPD representatives, Paul Singer, said that whereas the bourgeois states had formed the Triple Alliance of Germany, Austria, and Italy and the Dual Alliance of France and Russia, the workers of the world formed a single united front, a league of one, to defeat the bourgeois state. Singer's declaration, Eisner wrote, had the ring of prophecy, for eventually "by the law of economic development we will effect humanity's mightiest ethical achievement with the host of recruits turned out by class conflict, the League of Culture." The triumph would come in the twentieth century after thorough, systematic preparation. Social Democrary, Eisner explained, was grounded in three premises: the ethics of community, the economics of collectivism, and the tactics of class conflict. Of the three, the party had come to grips with only the last, winning for itself an estimable measure of political power. In its prerevolutionary stage the party would have to use every tool at hand to educate the worker for his historical moment. But inevitably, Eisner warned, "the future will not be born of rational argument but in wild battles with victory and destruction." Only then could a collective community of equality emerge that would redefine human relations. He urged the intellectually and ethically whole who wanted to have a hand in shaping the future to make a commitment. "We must flee to Social Democracy even if we do not share its economic and tactical premises. It is the only refuge of all idealists. . . . And even if they themselves had no further merit, these Social Democrats, than that they are organizing the masses, training them in clear thinking and thus creating from dark chaos, with its unpredictable explosions, an ordered world coursing in a regular orbit . . . , this would suffice to sympathize with them. . . . One will never have the need to combat them, at most to reform them." He counseled the party to repudiate anarchism, a romantic holdover at odds with scientific socialism, and took for signs of maturity its work to further women's emancipation and public education and its recognition of the benefits of parliamentary participation to win gains in these areas.

Yet no sooner had Eisner commended the party on its efforts to improve education than he was embarrassed by its representatives in London and felt compelled, earlier than he had expected, to reform its policy.[41] On the fifth day of the International congress the Germans voted against a resolution, modeled on their own Erfurt Program of 1891, calling for universal, free, public education from kindergarten to university for every capable student, when Labourite Keir Hardie, himself an autodidact, proposed that "capable" be struck from the wording. Appropriating the term denoting the liberal economic philosophy of laissez-faire, Hardie denounced the restriction as intellectual "Manchesterism." No one who desired education, he argued, should be excluded on the basis of ability.

To do so would be elitist and contrary to the essence of socialism. The Germans considered Hardie's reasoning a misguided "exaggeration of the principle of equality." Eisner agreed, though, with the British delegation: "Even if one eliminates the capitalistic restraints and arrives at the so-called natural selection of capacity, then a new and hardly preferable source of injustice and repression is created in the process. The concept of ability does not end in an intelligence test. In the colossal multiplicity of talents it is by no means the most admirable qualities that win out in the intellectual competition tied to scholastic organizations. . . . The free play of forces must never be the principle for social organizations and institutions; it is justifiable solely as individual motivation." Despite the opposition of the German delegation, the resolution was adopted by a vote of fourteen to six.

Earlier in the spring Eisner had strolled with Cohen through Marburg and listened as the professor told of his recent visit to Berlin. There a friend, a Social Democratic Reichstag deputy, had taken him to a performance at the German Theater of Hauptmann's *Weber*, a play he detested. Why, Cohen asked, did people consider Hauptmann's drama great art? He expected an argument; Eisner admired Hauptmann and, indeed, had corresponded with him. To Cohen's astonishment, Eisner was pensive and then answered: "If you expected great art embodying the socialist worldview, then you had to be disappointed by Gerhart Hauptmann." Naturalism had served its purpose by dashing convention and freeing letters from the stultifying propriety and prudishness of the bourgeois salon, and Hauptmann was unsurpassed in his ability to translate contemporary attitudes into credible characters whose speech seamlessly matched their station, but there was no one at present with the depth and vision to convey to mankind in sublime measure and style the universality of their ideal, no one to shape "the mighty, affirming art that forges the new cosmos from the twilight of the gods."

In his capacity as political editor, Eisner followed closely the Social Democratic Party congress in early fall at Gotha in the neighboring state of Saxony. A topic of protracted debate was the party's bearing toward modern literature, an issue raised by criticism charging Edgar Steiger, editor of *Die Neue Welt* (New World), the party's cultural and literary weekly, with indecency for printing unexpurgated naturalist texts. His chief critics were Reichstag deputy and occasional poet Karl Frohme and the *Hamburger Echo*, a major party daily. A number of influential delegates questioned from an ideological perspective the inclusion of naturalist works in Social Democratic journals. Hermann Molkenbuhr remarked that with their graphic depictions of the misery of the poor their effect was depressing rather than liberating, inspiring thoughts of suicide, and Wilhelm Liebknecht, the aging editor of *Vorwärts*, pointed out that Hauptmann made no pretense of being socialist. Steiger argued effectively that whatever the naturalists' faults might be, theirs was the only writing of current relevance to the workers' movement. Party chairman Bebel and congress president Paul Singer effected a compromise whereby *Neue Welt* would continue to print the work of the avant-garde, but language that could be considered offensive to women readers would be carefully edited. The irony was weaker then in that virtually no bourgeois journal would print what Steiger had run.

The conversation with Cohen and the proceedings at Gotha were impetus to a seminal essay in which Eisner revised and consolidated his thinking on art and society and enunciated a political aesthetic. It was published in late October 1896 in *Das Magazin für Litteratur*.[42] The Gotha debate was more significant than most of its participants realized, he wrote, because "it concerns not just the education of Social Democracy, hence the proletariat, the masses, as to art; it concerns equally the shaping of art to the masses." The day-long debate encapsulated a decade of controversy in bourgeois circles over naturalism, and the issue was resolved quickly in a "victory for reason" over philistinism. But the question remained as to whether the naturalists, whose relentlessly realistic and graphic depictions of human misery now had official party sanction, furthered the ultimate goals of the movement. "An icy shudder ripples through the delicate bones of our literary mavens at the mere thought that one, even in jest, could dare require writing by party line." But an ascendant class striving nobly for the realization of its life-affirming ideal could not be content with the "tired resignation and arid pessimism" at the heart of naturalism.

Germany's most modern literature was for the masses no more than a bridge to an ultimately committed, class-conscious art heralding the "golden age of humanity," the Social Democratic vision. "Where a great culture movement crystallizes in a party—and the modern form of every culture movement is the party—there too art must be party art. Here the party is no refundable ticket but rather the essence of every progressive intellect. The poet who stands within the culture movement cannot be anything other than a party man. . . . The party of the future must also engender the poet of the future." The classical poet of the future would be he who could dramatize Marx. In the absence of that titan, Eisner determined to shape his own creative writing to the end he envisioned.[43] On 3 November *Vorwärts* took note of Sperans's comments and printed excerpts from the "worthy essay."

Eisner was deeply impressed with the openness and ingenuousness of the proceedings at Gotha. The way the Social Democrats conducted their business he likened to the new architecture that left superstructure visible. Although debate was at times heated and division sharp, the delegates behaved like members of a greater family, addressing each other with the familiar *du*. Their head was Paul Singer, who presided like one of the "Jewish patriarchs, almost extinct now, who with iron will, loving heart, and wise discretion brought together all members in their guardianship each Sabbath, however hostile some individuals cared to be." Perhaps recalling Bruno Wille's break with the party, Eisner identified as a breed of recalcitrant the students in their "political puberty," convinced of their own superior intellect and reason, who, when their point of view was rejected by their sturdy comrades, broke ranks and bolted, unwilling to undertake the tedious task of winning their opponents over time: "One simply has to have the democratic belief in the reason of the masses, and it solidifies only in later years when one has learned to abstract and knows how to separate appearance from reality." The young, bourgeois intellectuals' impatience was stoked, Eisner surmised, by the assurance of a privileged position in the existing state.

Of particular interest to Eisner, journalist and editor, was the party's changing view of the role of its own press. The venerable Wilhelm Liebknecht, editor in chief of *Vorwärts* and, at seventy, one of the last socialist leaders of Marx's generation, was criticized during debate as incompetent—a charge with which Eisner ruefully concurred. "The same party that in theory champions large-scale production founded nothing but puny, small-scale operations," local papers so poor in quality that their intended readers preferred the superior products of the enemy camp. Recently, though, the *Leipziger Volkszeitung* (Leipzig People's Newspaper) and the *Sächsische Arbeiter-Zeitung* (Saxon Workers' Newspaper) had shown how good a party paper could be and strengthened the demand for a national daily befitting Europe's premier socialist party. Eisner reckoned that the delegates at Gotha had set for themselves a herculean labor in overhauling their press, but the effort would benefit both the party in particular and German journalism in general.[44]

Having proclaimed his admiration for Social Democracy, Eisner now took aim at a rival movement, Friedrich Naumann's National Social Union (Verein der Nationalsozialen), which had grown out of Stöcker's Christian Social Labor Party.[45] At their recently concluded meeting in Erfurt, where "the Freiburg professor Max Weber cheerfully preached the gospel of a radical individualism," the National Social adherents stopped short of forming themselves into a party, opting instead for the title "union," and showing thereby, Eisner gibed, their "slight tendency toward coffee club." Its chief constituents were theologians ashamed of a church with no social conscience, social reformers put off by the rigid constraints of Marxist thought, bourgeois malcontents too sensitive for party discipline, the "lost sons" of National Liberal chief Rudolf von Bennigsen, refugees from a host of failed causes—an assembly of Hamlets incapable of forming their critical resolve.

However highly one regarded Friedrich Naumann personally, however greatly one supported a domestic policy centered on bettering the workers' lot, one nonetheless had to reject the National Social movement as neither fish nor fowl: the two descriptors were mutually exclusive. To seek to improve living conditions in Germany and elevate the national standard of living by advocating colonial expansion with its attendant militarism was akin to refurbishing one's rooms and then setting the house on fire. "In reality, no radical, domestic social reform is possible without concerted international efforts in the political and economic realm." Moreover, Eisner prophesied, imperial adventurism would lead inevitably to conflict in Europe and fatal competition with Asia and America. "If these National Socials are really serious about social salvation, why do they seek to intrude on the preserve of the party that through tireless work has finally become a power with which the ruling powers must reckon?" By supporting Social Democracy, Eisner concluded, Naumann and his followers could accomplish far more than they ever would on their own.

The contagion of colonialism had spread even into the Social Democratic Party, infecting particularly the trade-union ranks. Party theorist and functionary Eduard Bernstein, who argued for a revision of Marx's hypotheses on the development and decline of capitalist society, emerged as a leading spokesman for "social imperialism." The controversy, which over the course of a decade would split the party, had its roots in the economic boom of the mid- and late-1890s. After the depression that followed Bismarck's dismissal, the second half of the decade was a period of prosperity in which the German worker's standard of living began to rival that of his English comrade. Interest groups such as the Colonial League and the Pan-German League sought to convince the worker of his stake in Weltpolitik: if Germany could overtake Britain in the race for colonies, German industry would profit from the acquisition of raw materials and new markets, and the German worker would share the rewards.[46] As the trade unions' membership doubled between 1896 and 1900, exceeding 600,000, so too did their influence in the party.[47]

From the outset Kurt Eisner opposed imperialism. In a series of articles he lashed out at both the theory and practice of colonial aggrandizement.

In "The Bleeding Heart," the eighth of the *Provinzialbriefe*, he assumes the persona and blustering, jingoist style of an imperial enthusiast railing against the overly cultivated sensitivity, the "ethical diabetes," of those who decried the maltreatment of natives at the hands of German colonists and troops.[48] He characterizes the vanguard of imperialism as "the best men of German stock, who risked their lives for crown and country by dutifully impressing Africa's Negro brutes for the good of the fatherland." The detractors of Germany's colonial mission, led by August Bebel, with their lies alleging brutality, corruption, and abuse of women were, of course, in the pay of the English. The jingoist journalist presents an indigenous folktale, purportedly collected by a colonial governor, to illustrate the African natives' need for the civilizing influence of German culture. The tale's principal character is Bwana Bill, a wealthy and powerful prince served by a host of ministers and purveyors whom he pays by taking from the general populace half of everything produced. Since Bill's entourage hails him as a god of sorts and the law condemns his critics to death, the people languish in subjection. The analogy could be lost on no one.

A month later Eisner questioned the motives behind a propaganda campaign urging the nation to make war on Turkey over atrocities against Armenian Christians, thereby abetting the tsar's cause when Russian persecution of Jews matched the Turkish atrocities.[49] Citing a pamphlet that demanded "Germany must lay its strong and mighty hand on Asia Minor" to save Christendom from the Turkish barbarians, Eisner reminded his readers that Islam's august achievements in scholarship, the arts, and science had schooled Christian Europe of the Middle Ages. The atrocities committed in Russia and the German colonies voided any moral right to rebuke the Turks. "The humanitarian ideal is long since foreign to the Christian states. How can they civilize Turks in the name of Christianity?"

Eisner believed that as a result of the imperial rivalries developing between Germany and the democracies of Western Europe, the monarchy was moving toward closer relations with the Russian crown—a development he regarded as potentially catastrophic. He became convinced that the monarchy itself was the root of the nation's evils and began to write more vituperatively against Wilhelm and the emperor's total lack of accountability to his subjects. It proved a fateful course.

CHAPTER FOUR

DICTATORIAL MEGALOMANIA: LÈSE MAJESTÉ AND PLÖTZENSEE PRISON (1896–1898)

In 1894 Ludwig Quidde, editor of the Imperial *Reichstagsakten* (Reichstag Record) in Munich and former head of the Royal Prussian Historical Institute in Rome, published in *Die Gesellschaft* an article titled "Caligula: A Study of Roman Dictatorial Megalomania." It was reprinted the same year by Wilhelm Friedrich of Leipzig, Eisner's publisher, as a twenty-page pamphlet. Although the article purported to portray the notorious Roman despot in his madness, the reader readily recognized it as a deftly veiled tract against the "personal regime" of Wilhelm II. Convicted of *Majestätsbeleidigung*, or lèse majesté, Quidde lost his position as editor and was jailed for three months in 1896.[1] Typically, however, the law was brought to bear on less prominent critics of princes. In the 1 February 1896 issue of *Die Kritik*, a review of news items of the past week compiled by Mephisto deplored that a twenty-year-old worker had been sentenced to two years' imprisonment for shouting "Hurrah for anarchy!" while Wilhelm made an inspection tour of a warship under construction at the Hamburg shipyard of Blohm and Voß.[2]

The attorney Max Falkenfeld of Fürstenwalde wrote in the 13 September issue that the concept of lèse majesté was a product of the late Roman Empire, which had also endowed the word "Byzantine" with its modern, negative connotation.[3] He looked back to when the great Friedrich II ordered that handbills against him posted at riders' eye level be lowered that the populace might better read them. Friedrich's Berlin was a capital of the Enlightenment; in the present, Falkenfeld lamented, a "mystical twilight rules the minds." Every German citizen except the sovereign, he observed, could choose whether or not to seek legal redress for defamation. The sovereign alone had no say in the matter; the law and the state prosecutor relieved him of that right. Even more ironically, in cases of lèse majesté the accused was forbidden from arguing the merit of his assertion before a judge, on the premise that 'every deprecating assault on the inviolability of the sovereign is necessarily illegal.' Since the well-educated critic—by far the most dangerous—usually masked his criticism well enough to avoid prosecution, whereas the poor fool venting his spleen went to jail, Falkenfeld concluded that justice would be best served by striking lèse majesté from the code.

That year Eisner, in the guise of Tat-Twam, assailed both the institution of the monarchy and Wilhelm personally in a series of *Provinzialbriefe*. On 29 August *Die Kritik* printed "Morituri," a commentary on news of the loss of the naval vessel *Iltis*, with all hands, in a storm.[4] The title derives from the Roman gladiators' greeting to the emperor before their combat: "Morituri, Caesar, te salutant!" (Those about to die salute you, Caesar!). The editor of the dispatch embellished the story by reporting that just before their end the gallant crew sang patriotic songs and thrice cheered Kaiser Wilhelm. With the exception of a few Catholic papers, the bourgeois press printed the account unquestioningly. "Who heard the final cheer? Who was witness?" queried Eisner, for whom the dispatch editor's "hyperfeudal" mode of thinking was inconceivable a century after the French Revolution.

The attempt to create a German "Imperial legend" on the eve of the twentieth century Eisner reckoned as no less deviant than the black mass of the waning Dark Ages, particularly when fifty years earlier the nation had united in the failed quest for a constitution that delineated the rights of the people and their ruler. It was precisely the delusion of omnipotence that undid any ruler: "An unpretentious constitutional monarchy, even today, still has its privilege and power; romantic Caesarism has fallen into ruin." Germany might well recover from the blight of "court parasites" if the lèse-majesté law were repealed and the emperor could gain the "benefit of honest criticism." This notion Eisner knew to be wishful thinking at best, for the fatal flaw in the structure of the German state was that neither the monarch nor his cabinet was accountable to the people's representatives, that the public will could be flouted with impunity. Eventually, he foretold, the spurned would assert their rights by sweeping away the monarchy altogether. In light of the times, emperor worship, real or imagined, seemed perversely theatrical to the ascendant class: "We would prefer to renounce gods than to misuse them as florid, farcical operetta; we overturn altars, but we do not defile them."

A week later the upcoming visit of Tsar Nicholas II impelled Eisner to ridicule official sojourns by foreign princes as wanton and profligate exercises in futility.[5] "It is truly a silly superstition that history is made by palace conversations, after-dinner speeches, and toasts." Compared to the logistics and expense of the tsar's jaunt of a few weeks through Europe with his entourage, Nansen's recently concluded five-year expedition to the North Pole was trivial, although the latter dwarfed the former in terms of world-historical significance. At a time when peoples strove mightily to realize humanitarian ideals and democratic self-determination in both national and international affairs, the machinations and intrigues of a handful of royal houses bent on self-preservation were as out of place as their ornate, ceremonial coaches on streets teeming with bicycles and electric trams. The royal tête-à-tête to determine relations between states was antediluvian. "Modern administrative technique . . . requires a supreme council of nations, elected by the national representative bodies of the people, to consolidate international law and to supervise its scrupulous application in complete openness and unfettered discussion. At the least, international congresses should already be convened at regular intervals by our official governments, at which the pending issues of the day can be brought, if not to resolution, then in any case to beneficial discussion." Eisner's vision is all the more striking in that it predates the first Hague Convention by nearly three years.

During his German visit Tsar Nicholas led his father's elite regiment at parade in Breslau—a sight that inspired his host to wax eloquent in praise of the young Romanov as a mighty commander "in the service of culture and in defense of peace."[6] In his remarks Wilhelm assured his subjects that he and his royal cousin would act in concert to protect Europe's "holiest possessions." It was, Eisner noted, a telling choice of words. "The holy possessions, upon closer inspection, are always the unholy interests of particular classes. Life's fullness and value require no protection, they are indestructible." The last time the Russian tsar served as guardian of Europe's cultural heritage was under terms of the Holy Alliance during the period of reaction from Napoleon's defeat to 1848, when the "holiest possessions," the class interests of the aristocracy, were defended against revolution in the form of bourgeois nationalism, with its demands for constitutional government and freedom of the press. The bourgeois freedom fighters were as vigorous in pursuit of their goals as their aristocratic adversaries were in defense of privilege and particularism; in the struggle for self-determination, "the philosophy of the deed, which unites theory and practice, was proclaimed, and the national war of liberation was for them as valid as revolution as a legitimate means of attaining their desires." Wilhelm II's newly proclaimed Holy Possession Alliance between Germany and Russia was based by necessity on the maintenance of international peace—just as the earlier Holy Alliance had been—for there were seeds of revolution in every war: "Could not the Commune sprout up in the end from the ruins?" Alluding from time to time to the threat of war was a tactic the crowned heads of Europe employed to consolidate the reaction. "Our army is solely—it is simply no longer to be denied—a means of defense against the internal enemy."

In mid-November Eisner wrote in a piece provocatively titled "The End of the Monarchy" that the institution found its last, crumbling base of support among peasants and the petite bourgeoisie.[7] The aristocracy certainly wanted no more in a king than a malleable advocate of its interests, and the middle class by nature harbored pronounced republican sentiments. Eclipsed by Bismarck's forceful leadership, the monarchy had become "merely an illusion of power supported by hypocrites and speculators." Yet rather than try to win the masses through social reform, Wilhelm preferred to curry the favor of the parasites who privately ridiculed him. "It is not our affair," Tat-Twam concludes, "to be adviser to the monarchy, perhaps to counsel it to take the decisive step toward a radical popular monarchy championing social, cultural work. Our task is merely to show things as they are." A month later in an article on political scandal, police corruption, and the decline of the judicial system, he characterized the German state as "theocaesarian" and derided lawmakers who regarded criticism of the kaiser as a form of blasphemy punishable by imprisonment, "for both the humanized god and the deified man are the identical product of national consciousness lost in a dream."[8]

As 1896 drew to a close, Eisner, as was his custom, presented a review of the year.[9] This retrospective, "One Hundred Years Ago," had the twist of being cast as a look back from the year 1996 to the Berlin of a century earlier. The author of the chronicle marvels at the mix of the modern and archaic: burgeoning electrification, communications technology, and medical advances amid nationalism, militarism, and remnants of feudal classes. A worldview was in its death agony. "People no longer believed the old beliefs, they were not yet prepared to accept the new ideas, and so they established a nonsensical shaman cult in which persons highly placed in affairs of state were deified and their willful utterances, whims, and affects elevated to the status of law. Today we can no longer imagine how it is possible. . . . And yet at that time the absurd was reality."

In the first days of the new year Eisner continued in the same vein with another fictionalized retrospective. On 2 January 1897 *Die Kritik* printed "An Undiplomatic New Year's Reception," the twenty-fifth in the series of *Provinzialbriefe*.[10] In his opening paragraph Tat-Twam explains that he has come into possession of the transcript of a speech and that he must not reveal his source. Having written at length on the risk journalists took when treating such subjects, Eisner must have realized the gravity of his undertaking. As the fanciful remarks presented verbatim were addressed to the speaker's "noble and wise" advisers on a range of national issues, the reader had to surmise that it was none other than the kaiser himself reflecting on the past and future before his ministers and diplomats at the traditional New Year's Day reception. But the sentiments expressed were hardly those of the emperor, or if they were, the scales had fallen suddenly from his eyes.

The speaker begins by hinting that the content of his remarks would differ markedly from that on similar occasions in the past, for "were I not lord, my vassals would not elect me chairman of a smoking club if I knew nothing more novel and clever to say." Borrowing Quidde's term, Eisner put here these fateful words in his fictitious ruler's mouth: "It is said that megalomaniacal delusion clouds the head of the exceedingly privileged. . . . Only when we recognize and acknowledge the endlessly petty in our existence do we begin to find our greatness, and with a nation of free, severe, and demanding judges will we perhaps even be able to become kings."

Reviewing past efforts and results, the emperor bitterly regrets having squandered the opportunity to accomplish something profound and lasting. He cites events of the past year in Germany's foreign and domestic affairs—conflict with Britain in South Africa, the enlargement of the fleet, the tsar's visit—and despairs at the motivations and aspirations of the ruling elite. "I, at least, have no more joy in the pompous embalmment of the decaying and am ashamed that the solemnly consecrated, new-dawning century will take fright at our ghastly mummy." The sovereign commits himself to social reform and reconciliation and calls on those present either to help him frame his grand design or to expect to be sacked.

On Saturday evening, 16 January, the Berlin police raided the residence of Richard Wrede, editor of *Die Kritik*, at Hedemannstraße 9. Dr. Wrede was away at a private party. For four hours police scanned his files for information that might reveal the identity of Tat-Twam. When Wrede returned home, he noticed that his usually cluttered desk had been straightened but thought nothing of it before retiring. The next morning he discovered a notice from Inspector Schöne apprising him that the public prosecutor had ordered a search for the manuscript of "An Undiplomatic New Year's Reception" and that "a packet, manuscripts and miscellaneous papers, and 875 copies of issue 118 of the journal *Die Kritik* from 2 January 1897" had been confiscated. The police returned on Sunday to continue their search and divulged that the author of the article in question was to be charged with lèse majesté. On Monday Wrede announced the search to the journal's readers and protested in print the seizure of his personal financial records and the opening of sealed let-ters.[11] The business offices were searched repeatedly. Records of deliver-ies and payments were seized and depositions were taken from the staff, yet, as one newspaper reported, "Tat-Twain's [*sic*] pseudonymity still has not been breached."[12]

After informing Wrede that he would readily confess to having authored the article once the police named him a suspect, Eisner made use of his regular column to defend himself as Tat-Twam against the accu-sation.[13] Letter 28 took the title "Criminal Glorification of Majesty."[14] Here he described how upon receiving the Berlin papers on Tuesday, 19 January, he believed he was reading his own obituary. He insisted that he was wholly ignorant of committing the crime of which he stood accused. "We wanted to achieve two things in our essay: simply to present a com-pressed review of the year, and then to have the ideal clash in sharp con-trast with reality. To this end we created a dream figure modeled on that mythological ruler, whom we endowed with magical power to effect that rapid fulfillment of our impatient desires." Despite his admitted disdain for the doomed institution of monarchy, Eisner claimed that he had not intended to disparage Wilhelm personally; moreover, he failed to compre-hend how his idealized portrait of an enlightened and progressive mon-arch could be construed as an insult to the German emperor. His only crime was "to weave dreams and make up fairy tales in this splendidly unified German Empire." With a wife five months pregnant and two tod-dlers to support, he "shuddered, shuddered, shuddered" at his situation. Convinced that his home too would be searched eventually, he nonethe-less made a conscious decision to conceal no potential evidence, in the belief that he had done nothing illegal.[15]

In a fortnight the ring closed around him. On Sunday, 14 February, Eisner was subjected to the same indignity that had befallen his editor. While he listened to a Beethoven quartet at a concert in nearby Gießen, the police appeared at his residence. Acting on her husband's instruc-tions, Lisbeth accommodated the local inspector, to whom this duty was clearly unwelcome, by providing him with a copy of Eisner's handwriting. Upon his return Eisner himself produced upon request correspondence from Wrede and announced that he would cooperate fully in order to spare his associates further harassment.[16] Newspaper accounts incorrectly identified the suspect as "the former adjunct lecturer Dr. Kurt Eisner," conferring a title and office that Hermann Cohen had hoped to see his friend realize.[17]

Eisner immersed himself in work while awaiting first arrest and then trial. In February his review of Ibsen's penultimate drama appeared in

Sozialistische Monatshefte (Socialist Monthly).[18] Far from being diminished by his advance in years, Ibsen was, in Eisner's judgment, at the height of his powers with *John Gabriel Borkman*, whose ambitious protagonist betrays love for wealth and power, spends eight years behind bars for embezzlement, and fathoms the bitter tragedy of his life only at his death. A Nietzschean superman of sorts, he personifies the rank anarchism of free-market finance. "Borkman's guilt lies not in the theft. That was the compelling causality of his being, which embodies capitalism. The material demise of many is not the greatest of his debits. He fell because he laid waste to a *soul*." Ibsen's moral renders him an ally; "he complements socialism, he does not combat it."

Die Kritik continued to publish Tat-Twam's *Provinzialbriefe*, although the world now knew who the author was. In response to a lecture held by Friedrich Naumann in Marburg, he formulated his most comprehensive critique to date of the National Social movement.[19] Naumann's support of Germany's bid for world power was not only incongruent with his domestic agenda for social reform but also counter to the trend of history at the fin de siècle. "The modern era is moving toward individual nations existing freely side by side, which come together as cultural communities (Kulturgemeinschaften) in order to protect themselves from less advanced nations. The elimination of national slavery is as equally the will of the modern era as the abolition of personal slavery. Whoever has grasped the sense of our time is working to achieve a cultural community that joins at least the European states (except Russia) and America. Precisely because the modern attempts at colonization contradict the spirit of the time, they fail so miserably and suck the blood of their progenitors."

Eisner returned in late March to the theme of Germany's bid for world power, Wilhelm II's vaunted Weltpolitik.[20] In the age of humanism, Eisner remarked, the term "world policy" denoted the ideal of forging the brotherhood of man—the same ideal Schiller hailed in his ode "To Joy," immortalized by Beethoven's Ninth Symphony. This world policy required no warships or soldiers. Germany's current rendition was in reality a bellicose, international trade policy driven by the domestic interests of the ruling classes. It worked its "barbarizing effects" on colonizer and colonized alike. The attempt to legitimize the exploitation of primitive peoples by applying Darwin's precepts to economic development was as crass as it was callous. "World policy, which ought to be humanity policy, the education of mankind to the highest ethical and economic autonomy of the individual and the national state alike, becomes in the final analysis a monstrous chemical-mechanical experiment with powder and lead, conducted on the side while the masses' tolerance for burden and ability to resist is tested to the limit. World policy becomes world-power policy in which a single state—on the strength of its economic-military superiority, hardly its higher cultural standard—attempts to make other states, peoples, and races serviceable as objects of material exploitation." It was ironic indeed, Eisner quipped, that through its maintenance of intolerable social conditions, the German state compelled droves of its citizens to seek a better life in the wilds of Africa, and then clamored for warships and troops to defend the outcasts.

On 13 April the prosecutor sent out the summons requiring Eisner to appear before the Prussian criminal court at Old Moabit, Berlin's judicial and penal complex, on the morning of 27 April.[21] Both Eisner and Wrede, as responsible editor, were charged with lèse majesté. For his defense Wrede selected the Berlin attorney Dr. Henke; Eisner was represented by Dr. Albert Löwenthal of Frankfurt am Main, whose acquaintance he had made while working there.[22] If Eisner truly believed that he would be vindicated at trial, he was soon divested of the notion when the chairman of the panel of judges hearing the case closed the courtroom to the public even though the prosecutor had declined to request it. As one judge read the offending piece aloud to his colleagues in an "almost scornfully ironic tone," emphasizing and repeating passages he deemed incriminating, Eisner became increasingly embittered at the farce being played out before him. At the phrase "megalomaniacal delusion," the reader looked knowingly to his fellows and said softly "Caligula!" Eisner was then questioned as to his interpretation of Quidde's pamphlet.

The defendant argued that the idealized prince bore no resemblance to Wilhelm II. No mention was made in the text of any proclivity to hunting, parades, ceremonial pomp, building projects, or rash pronouncements. Nor did the speaker's style manifest "the train of thought, fanciful images, and passionate animation of the Imperial toasts and formal speeches." Indeed, if the speaker was intended to portray the kaiser, it was, to be sure, an unlikely glorification. The prosecution countered that Eisner's fictitious prince referred to both the Transvaal and sending telegrams. It was therefore reasonable to conclude that Eisner meant the celebrated Kruger telegram, which Wilhelm had sent to congratulate German colonists who repulsed the English raid led by Jameson—a bellicose show of support immensely popular at home and unsettling to the rest of Europe.

Disheartened and incredulous, Eisner noted that the chief judge had lost interest and stared at the clock. After protracted argument as to whether the royal speaker was meant to depict Wilhelm and whether the depiction was negative, the judges' decision hinged on an argument that the prosecutor had never presented: that the intent Eisner had already admitted, to create an ideal monarch, was in and of itself an affront to the actual monarch. Ruling in favor of the state, the judges conceded that they were never in doubt as to the defendant's guilt. Wrede received a six-month sentence for printing the article, Eisner was accorded nine months' imprisonment for writing it—one more month than the prosecutor had demanded. In a letter to the Berlin papers Eisner chronicled the peculiarities of the proceedings and declared that he would have been prepared to accept the verdict and bear his fate "with fatalistic dignity" had the state proven its case against him. As it had not, however, he vowed defiantly to defend himself "as directly and unambiguously as the court wishes."[23]

On 2 May, the week after the trial, Lisbeth gave birth in Marburg to a second daughter, Doris Hildegard.[24] The next week Eisner made good his promise to present his defense to the public, when *Die Kritik* printed "Dolus eventualissimus."[25] On the same day the newspapers reported his conviction, he wrote, they also reported that His Majesty had privately branded the Reichstag majority that rejected appropriations for two warships as an "unpatriotic pack." Those offended by being called thus by their liege ran the risk, if they responded in kind, of having paragraph 95 of the legal code invoked against them by the state prosecutor. Eisner vituperated against the press's tacit complicity in the enforcement of lèse majesté by passively accepting the state of affairs rather than universally demanding the same right of free expression the kaiser enjoyed. It was a dilemma for which the press itself bore the brunt of blame, Eisner charged, for its members had timidly acquiesced in their own muzzling to the detriment now of the whole society. He noted bitterly that only the independent, Left Liberal *Volkszeitung* had seen fit to print his letter to the Berlin papers, the official organs of the bourgeois "pack" believing evidently that Tat-Twam's protest of his treatment was nothing more than a play for publicity. In order for the press to exert any moral influence on its readers, journalists had to assert their right to answer candor with candor: "We too, for our part, must demand complete freedom of criticism and self-defense. Both morality and healthy reason inevitably require no less."

Turning to the court itself, Eisner gratefully acknowledged the objectivity of the prosecutor, then passed judgment on his judges: "Whoever has never before been in a courtroom readily presumes that the officers of justice—with a certain high-priestly dignity, solemnly and deeply moved—wield the law against the offender, without hatred or bias, with a strong feeling of human compassion for the sinners laid low by the rigor of unbending law. . . . In reality there are no such judges." The ideal of justice had fallen victim to class interest, personal prejudice, and the perfunctory civil servant's perception of duty to his employer. On 12 May the Social Democratic Party chairman August Bebel denounced the verdict before the Reichstag and called for the repeal of the lèse-majesté code. Referring to his own trial and imprisonment for treason, Bebel spoke: "I can say that I too experienced something quite similar to what Herr Eisner has . . . when I too was convicted on the basis of arguments that had never played a role in the trial itself."[26]

Waiting for the appeal to be heard, Eisner continued to write the *Provinzialbriefe*. He eulogized Heinrich von Stephan, the German postmaster general whose efforts in consolidating the national postal service and establishing that international letters need only the stamp of the country of origin were magnificent examples of socialist organizational centralization and a worthwhile Weltpolitik.[27] In an article on university reform, Eisner attacked Prussian minister of education Robert Bosse, who resolutely opposed broadening the science curriculum, evidently because "scientific" was associated with the subversive thought of Marx and Darwin.[28] And he castigated the bourgeois parties for their deference to the ruling house and its ministers: "When we have no free public life, when we suffocate in cowardice and untruthfulness and patiently endure the desecration and mockery of our human rights and humane ideals, when German politics spin continuously in a circle like a mad dog, and we suffer quietly the unbearable precisely because it disgusts us that we are supposed to demonstrate ever anew the necessity of social demands that have long been the inalienable right of other nations, when, in short, our entire political existence is polluted by the filth of reaction, then the blame falls heaviest on the ruling parties' weakness and worthlessness, as they have neglected to employ the means to power granted them by the constitution."[29] The government's frustration at denial of funds for warships was lost on neither Bebel nor Eugen Richter, and Eisner believed that Social Democrats might join with Radicals in the Reichstag to thwart the National Liberal and Conservative alliance. Electoral reform and greater civil liberty would then become feasible objectives.

"The Cogovernment," Eisner's forty-second letter for *Die Kritik*, identified the police as a government unto itself, auxiliary to Germany's ruling elite, "the bulwark on which the tide of revolution breaks."[30] Eisner wrote of the police now from firsthand experience, for as Wrede divulged in the 26 June issue, Tat-Twam's identity had been betrayed by a trusted young man who was in fact a police "stoolie."[31] Their appeal was heard on 24 September by the Supreme Court in Leipzig. Unable to secure Dr. August Munckel of Berlin as his counsel, Eisner engaged Dr. J. Stranz. Wrede elected to represent himself. Stranz argued that Eisner's fictional prince could be interpreted as representative of any monarch, not exclusively the kaiser. In any case there was nothing illegal in a citizen's voicing the sentiment that the ruler was not great; history did as much in appending unbecoming sobriquets to kings' given names. Wrede contended that no crime had ever been proven, the conviction being based on a premise never advanced by the prosecution.[32]

As Bebel had foreseen, the appeal was denied. Eisner was to serve his sentence at Wehlheiden Penitentiary in his home state of Hesse. On 16 October, a week before he was to report, he wrote to the state attorney's office at Marburg to request that he be permitted to serve out the sentence at Plötzensee in Berlin.[33] Citing illness, he also asked that the beginning date be postponed by a week, that he could regain the strength necessary to endure his internment. Both requests were granted. He settled his affairs and made ready for the departure to Berlin. Lisbeth and the children were to remain in Marburg in their apartment at Haspelstraße 37.[34] A sizable personal loan from the Frankfurt banker and Jewish philanthropist Charles Hallgarten maintained the family during Eisner's confinement.[35]

Upon his arrival at Plötzensee on 1 November 1897, Eisner deposited his gold watch and wedding band, received his uniform, and was assigned to cell 186 in the eighth solitary-confinement ward.[36] On a handwritten calendar he began ticking off the 274 days of his sentence.[37] He was alone in his cell but allowed to exercise and required to attend religious services with his fellow inmates, who included thieves, defrauders, assailants, pimps, counterfeiters, and the occasional murderer. It was no easy adjustment for a man accustomed to imposing order rather than having it imposed on him. He resolved to make the best of his time by treating imprisonment as an enforced sabbatical. Temporarily relieved of family and professional responsibilities, Eisner spent his time in isolation reading and writing. "I wanted to work," he reminisced, "and not lose this year of my life." He sought to avoid alienating himself from his "colleagues," as he called the other inmates, by showering the warden with endless petitions, which in any case would have hampered his own work, as each quarrel with the prison bureaucracy inevitably exacted its toll in time and annoyance.[38]

Typically he rose each day at six to wash before a breakfast of bread and weak coffee was passed through the window in the door. While the ordinary felons were assigned work detail, Eisner, as a political prisoner, remained in his quarters. Lunch at noon in his cell was followed by an

hour of exercise on the yard, during which the prisoners walked a circuit in pairs. After the afternoon work period, supper was served at six.
The fare at both lunch and supper generally featured some combination
of vegetables and cereal—peas, beans, lentils, turnips, potatoes, kraut,
rice, and oatmeal—and occasionally a herring, some giblets, or cheese.
Particularly odious was a bread soup dubbed "chocolate" by the prisoners.[39] Twice each day the inmates were brought a pitcher of water.
The two-liter allowance was to suffice for drinking, bathing, and wash-
ing one's bowl after meals. After going thirsty for a week, Eisner sought
advice from fellow prisoners as to how they managed. His complaint left
them incredulous: "But you have running water in the cell; you can get as
much as you want." Only then did he realize that the residents drew their
water from the toilet.[40]

Prisoners were known by cell block and cell number. During the week
most convicts worked twelve hours a day for a daily wage of 80 pfennige,
with the constant drone of machinery ringing in their ears. On Sundays
and holidays Eisner found the stark silence eerie and unsettling. Christmas
Eve he was summoned to the mailroom and confronted by supervisors
annoyed that a crated, live Christmas tree, replete with candles, tinsel,
and candies, had come addressed to him from Marburg. Once they had
determined to their satisfaction that he was without advance knowledge
of the delivery, they allowed him a glimpse of the tree, then confiscated it
and had him returned to his cell.[41]

Eisner chafed at the inaccessibility of reference works, the poor light
in his cell—the open flame of a fantail burner—and the policy of lights-
out at 20:30 on weeknights, 19:30 on weekends. He studied Ira Remsen's
thousand-page *Anorganische Chemie* (Inorganic Chemistry), having
missed the subject at gymnasium when a curriculum change shifted chemistry and mineralogy from the upper to lower fifth form.[42] He read more
deeply in philosophy and economy and filled notebooks with thoughts
on such topics as phenomenology, Kant's teleology, Hume's causality, the
chapter "Value and Price" in part one of Marx's *Capital*, and "patriarchal socialism" in Goethe's novel *Wilhelm Meisters Wanderjahre* (Wilhelm
Meister's Journeyman Years). Looking back on what he had accomplished
in ten years as a journalist, Eisner projected a collection of his best essays,
settling on the title *Taggeist* (Spirit of the Day).[43] In preparation for a
major study, he assembled casualty lists of victorious armies in battles of
the past 130 years.[44]

To amuse himself Eisner chronicled his prison experience in the
"Plötzensee Picturebook," a droll poem with illustrations. Attributed to
"a bad boy," it was published in four parts after his release by the Social

Democratic journal *Der wahre Jacob* (Just the Man). In gay iambs he describes the residents, their accommodations, diet, and daily routine. The worst lot was that of the political prisoners housed in strictest isolation in the "mask wing," so called because its residents were required to wear a mask hung from their caps whenever they left their cells:

> Here too they keep "politicos,"
> whose very countenance offends,
> anarchists and the Reds,
> that they not, through agitating,
> do harm to innocent souls.[45]

In the course of a few days he wrote a racy novella, the heroine of which, Elly, is a tramp involved in a destructive relationship with a former corporal named Gustav.[46]

Eisner began a more serious work in the spring, a farce with the working title "The Prince's Trial."[47] Having been convicted of lèse majesté, he apparently no longer felt compelled to circumvent the crime. The play, which he would not complete until twenty years later while imprisoned at Stadelheim in Munich for treason, is a merciless satire of Wilhelm II. It traces the development of a mediocre youth into a philistine, chauvinist monarch who commits the nation to a devastating war in order to secure his place in history. The names of members of the court are thinly disguised. Dr. Hinzpeter, for example, the tutor charged with young Wilhelm's education, appears as Hirnmeister, or Brainmaster. A tinted drawing Eisner made of his new lodging shows a narrow room with a barred window high in the wall opposite the door. A rack with a mattress is clapped upright against one long wall. Between bed and window a rack of shelves filled with books hangs on the wall. Across from the bed a wooden table stands beneath a single shelf for a pitcher, wash basin, and bowl. The artist himself sits reading on a stool with his back to the table. Pen, ink, and paper are spread on the tabletop before a photograph, a nosegay in a glass to the side. A birdcage is fixed to the wall next to the window. Looking through the door upon the scene, the viewer sees to his left the wooden lid of the toilet box. Inscribed in the lower margin is the caption "In Quiet Solitude."[48]

Once a month inmates were permitted to write letters or receive a visitor for a few minutes. Martha Eisner came to see her brother in December. At just over two arms' remove, they stood opposite each other behind waist-high barriers and exchanged a few words. A guard sat observing in the corridor between them to ensure that prisoner and visitor neither touched nor passed any object.[49] Although he was better suited than most by virtue of intellect, constitution, vocation, and habit to endure the long hours alone in a cell with his thoughts, Eisner nonetheless suffered pangs of separation from family, friends, and colleagues in Marburg. In midwinter he wrote of the problem to Hermann Cohen: "One of the characteristics of prison life is the virtually hermetic isolation from the outside world. Correspondence is therefore limited to a degree little commensurate with the dictates of familial longing and friendly interest. . . . This is my first opportunity to thank you for your letter. It brought to my cell something akin to Renaissance spirit."[50]

One of Eisner's in-house acquaintances was a procurer named Louis, a sensitive and elegant youth from a bourgeois family. Louis's kleptomania eventually landed him in jail. "His specialty had been pleasure trips for three," Eisner wrote in retrospect, "he, his darling, and the lover— some aging baron of substantial means." On an excursion to the Danish capital, Louis and his girl stole their client's wallet and fled. Both were jailed for theft. Louis confided to Eisner that upon release he wanted to wed a proper seamstress who had borne him a child already. His one fear was that his former partner would turn on him and accuse him, out of spite, of pimping. He despaired that he would return then and die in prison. Eisner suggested that if Louis would but wait awhile to marry the seamstress and avoid his former partner, the statute of limitations would preclude prosecution. Suddenly Louis became aloof. "You do not know people," he said sadly. Looking back on the incident years later, Eisner confessed that the experience had altered fundamentally his "intellectual and moral self-consciousness" and served as a constant reminder "whenever I feel tempted to play society's game of moral indignation." For the pimp already knew that he would lapse into his old vices no matter how desperately he wanted to change.[51]

In mid-June Lisbeth enclosed in a letter a glowing review of an exhibition of her father's paintings at Eberswalde's German House, "some twenty pictures, mostly landscapes with motifs derived mainly from the environs." One still life, a game bag with birds, by the painter's late daughter was included in the show.[52] Eisner pondered what he and Lisbeth were to do upon his release. New management at the *Hessische Landeszeitung* voided return to Marburg. "So now, too, my upright, joyous, passionate, and not inconsequential work of more than four years is gone with the wind. I come out of prison without knowing where to set foot. . . . After such a time one is not exactly psychically fit to resume the struggle for existence." He genuinely wondered whether he were suited to "so-called practical life in the age of Bismarck's epigoni."[53] He proposed that Lisbeth move with the children to Eberswalde while he lived with his parents in Berlin and sought to reestablish himself: "I shall do as the thousands of workers do who are with their families only from Saturday evening until Monday morning. Our marriage will be then one great holiday. . . . That sounds somewhat unusual, but we have done so much unusual, and the children's health and freedom is the *one* obligation that takes precedence over all others." Once he had found work, they would settle in one of Berlin's suburbs.[54]

In a letter to Bader he wrote that he was leaving Plötzensee with "various completed works and rough drafts." He expressed confidence in his talents; prison had taught him that he could bear anything but grinding anxiety over finances that smothers the creative spark. "Otherwise I know no bounds to my desire and energy to work."[55] He toyed with the idea of making his way as a freelancer, forgoing affiliation with any particular paper or journal. The impediment here was the debt he already owed, having been unable to publish from his cell. Without a reserve to fall back on, he knew he could not survive on piecework. A more realistic plan involved collaborating with Bader to produce political and literary columns "of a distinct slant" for syndication to papers across Germany. "What is put out here of that stamp is to be sure very clever but altogether amateurish, intellectually and morally characterless. I would write, for example, 'parliamentary impressions.' One could make a living doing that alone."[56]

Eisner wrote to Richard Wrede to request a meeting on the morning of 2 August, the day after his scheduled release, at Eisner's parents' home in Lichterfelde. He disclosed in his letter that he wanted to be named to the editorial staff of *Die Kritik* and that he had plans that would make the publication "a journal of *grand style*," the likes of which Germany had nothing. The reform hinged on shoring up the journal's financial footing to allow for five years' run regardless of subscription numbers. In that time the subscribers requisite for long-term success would be attracted. "For it is not a question of capturing subscribers who are completely virginal but rather of seducing subscribers away from other ventures. The subscriber, however, is conservative; he sticks with his usual journal and is mistrustful of parvenus. It is necessary then to ingratiate oneself with people gradually until they are finally won over to the new. Generally ventures begin to run dry at exactly the moment when the public begins to get accustomed to the upstart. For real, lasting success will not be achieved through dazzling advertisement and fleeting sensation. In the end the inner strengths make the difference—as well as confidence in the constant level of quality and sure, steady growth." The second measure that would ensure the journal's success was a thorough revision of content, the details of which Eisner promised to reveal as soon as they could settle on the terms of Eisner's elevation to coeditor.[57]

Excited by what he had heard from a recently interned forger, Eisner wrote to Lisbeth on his last day of confinement about Schlachtensee, a new suburb on the train line, where single-family houses with plumbing, a balcony, and surrounding yard could be rented for 400 to 800 marks. He pictured their life outside Berlin, "between forest and lake," where Lisbeth would paint landscapes, the children run free, and a dog watch over their domain. His aging parents might live on the second floor and share the rent. All of them would be spending less than they currently paid for lodging and live more comfortably. He planned to use the first opportunity to ride out to Schlachtensee and have a look for himself. His next priority was to hurry to Marburg to see Lisbeth and the children. Only then would he be sufficiently at peace to go out in search of work.[58]

CHAPTER FIVE

MAKING THE LEAP:
BACK TO BERLIN AS A
SOCIAL DEMOCRAT (1898–1900)

Back in Marburg Eisner renewed contact with the Cohen circle and
cast about to reestablish himself in journalism. On 20 August 1898
at Haspelstraße 37 he drafted a general letter of application in which he
cited years of experience as an editor, offered to make available reviews of
his work as Tat-Twam and Sperans, and listed as references—in addition
to Professors Cohen, Natorp, and Rathke—Dr. Fedor Mamroth, theater
critic and feuilleton editor for the *Frankfurter Zeitung*, and the dramatist
and critic Dr. Ludwig Fulda of Berlin. In return for his services Eisner
stated that he expected an annual salary in the range of 5,000 marks.[1]
Adrift, he sought to reaffirm his viewpoint in a two-part article that would
not be published until the following year in *Neue deutsche Rundschau*
(New German Review), journal of the People's Free Stage.[2] The setting
for both parts is a wineroom where three friends sit late in the evening
debating the import of the fin de siècle and speculating on the shape of
things to come. Eisner presents his own views in the third person, literally,
for the participants are a teacher, a doctor, and "the third one, who was
nothing." Although he hardly could have anticipated it then, he framed a
debate that came to rule his life for the better part of the next decade, for
in their discussion the three intimates consider issues of "reforming and
revolutionizing."

The teacher at the gymnasium, a pedantic grammarian in an unhappy
marriage, decries modern culture with its celebrated advances in science
and technology as a dehumanizing abomination that has made mankind
the subject of a perverse experiment in acceleration, extirpating all sense
of tradition and community. "When we return after two years' absence
to a city where we lived, we cannot recognize it anymore: . . . instead
of the earlier pedestrians we see bicyclists, automobiles, electric streetcars
shielded from the indecent nakedness of the cloudless sky by a sieve of

telephone wires. . . . Our memory no longer even has the power of the motion-picture projector to unite the countless still images into smoothly articulated animation."

The epicurean doctor could have been modeled on Arthur Schnitzler, the Viennese physician, author, and bon vivant whom Eisner knew as a collaborator on *Die Gesellschaft*. The doctor mocks the teacher's idealized view of tradition and constancy by calling into question the genuine permanence and, indeed, desirability of holy matrimony. Joie de vivre, he insists, derives from appreciating the irony inherent in the myriad contrasts and contradictions. "What misfortune if salvation befell us, if your utopias came to fruition, be they romantic-reactionary or rationalist-revolutionary." Nothing could be more boring than a world where no imperfections existed to give meaning and value to their opposites. He entreats his friends to abandon the yearning for an irretrievable past or an unattainable future and devote themselves to the pursuit of present worldly pleasures.

The third friend dismisses the teacher's sentimental fancy as harmless hypocrisy and suggests that he establish a stagecoach line to compete with the Orient Express, eschew postal service and telephone in favor of private courier, and have his garden blessed instead of fertilized. He finds far more inscrutable the doctor's complacent pessimism that denies man's ability to effect change for the better, even when within memory "the sinister demons have been transformed into generally intelligible, clanking, reeking, smoking constructions of steel, electricity, steam, and grease." Moreover, the third companion asserts that his hedonist friend errs in thinking the future a product waiting to be finished and not an eternal absolute synonymous with hope itself. Fear of the future and its possibilities stems from a grotesque grammatical misconception: the future perfect tense. In Hegelian fashion, the seer denies the perfectibility of the future: "Let us create forthwith paradise on earth as we envision it, confident in the knowledge that the striving, struggling, and ascendant among us will only be enticed onward to new, unimagined shores."

At their next meeting, the report of which constitutes the second part of Eisner's reaffirmation of principles, the teacher and doctor amuse themselves by drafting the nineteenth century's last will and testament. Their dispossessed fellow, however, vexed by feelings of superfluousness, grouses that the fading century has nothing of value to bequeath. In the nineteenth century man became myopic and lost the ability to view the world and its workings as a systematic whole. The specialists trumpet observation and induction as bases of the scientific method because they are incapable of abstract thinking. Once scholars delved into areas of expertise only after grounding in "a comprehensive philo-sophical worldview." In obvious reference to Marx, he declaims: "Only when the great clearer and consolidator arrives, when the universities are unified again by one animating spirit, when the philosophical system permeates all disparate disciplines that stake out boundaries and segre-gate domains, when methods of teaching permit the possibility of gain-ing an overview of the whole, of collaborating in independent research without remaining forever in a mole's tunnel, then our striving youth, to the extent that they may permit themselves the leisure for learning, will no longer succumb to neurasthenia, and maybe even the current great majority of our academically uneducated whom we are wont to call educated will be transformed into a small, disdained minority whose members cannot even make reserve lieutenant." The twentieth century, he concludes, would enrich itself immeasurably by laying claim to the great legacy the nineteenth had spurned, the treasure of the eighteenth: reason. Taking the tenets of the Enlightenment as its sustenance, the coming age would flourish and prosper.

With no immediate prospect of regular employment, Eisner deter-mined to maintain residence in Marburg until he had a firm offer. He shuttled continually to Berlin, where he stayed at his parents' home at Mittenwalderstraße 28 while interviewing with editors of various pub-lications. The most promising opportunity foundered, "after lengthy negotiations," on the scope of duties; he had no desire to function as both associate editor and business manager of a journal.[3] The eventual acceptable offer came from an unexpected quarter. Philipp Scheidemann records in his autobiography that he accompanied Wilhelm Liebknecht, editor in chief of *Vorwärts*, from Gießen to Marburg in hope of wooing Eisner to come to work for the Social Democratic Party's central organ.[4] Liebknecht too had served a prison term in 1897–1898 for lèse majesté and was considering now a replacement for Dr. Adolf Braun, his chief edi-torial collaborator and presumed successor, who, as an Austrian national, was to be expelled from Prussia as an "undesirable foreigner."[5] When Scheidemann approached Eisner to gauge his interest, Eisner was decid-edly noncommittal. But on 11 October Eisner wrote from his Berlin base to Liebknecht, thanking him for the invitation to meet and asking when it might be convenient.[6] Scheidemann later confessed surprise when he received word directly from Liebknecht that Eisner had joined his edi-torial staff. The professoriate in Marburg reveled in Eisner's good for-tune and the concomitant rise of their own stock. Natorp wrote on 27 November to Albert Görland, who had just been granted his doctorate: "*Vorwärts* has named as managing political editor to replace the expelled

A. Braun our K. Eisner, a most thoroughly schooled Kantian who studied Cohen and Stammler exhaustively in Plötzensee! It appears that philosophers do not exactly become kings these days, but something nonetheless, in the context of our time, remotely analogous."[7]

On 1 December 1898, the day he assumed his new post, Kurt Eisner formally joined the party to which he had lent allegiance for a decade. His membership card, issued in the suburb Greater Lichterfelde, listed his profession as editor.[8] The same day he wrote to Lisbeth, three months pregnant, that he was "making the leap to *Vorwärts*" and sent greetings to his friends in Marburg.[9] At Boninstraße 3 in South Lichterfelde, a quiet street lined with towering chestnut trees, he rented the house for which he yearned: a two-storey, red-brick structure with ample windows to the southeast, a palatial balcony, and a spacious yard for the children. The station at which he boarded the evening train to downtown Berlin was a scant ten-minute stroll away.[10]

At the time Eisner assumed his new duties, *Vorwärts* was hardly the prestigious publication it became under his direction. Liebknecht, who knew better than any the vicissitudes of the party press and the tenuousness of life as a socialist journalist, was seeking in Eisner an anchor. Historically, Berlin's Social Democratic paper had its genesis in the 1860s. Several years before the General German Workingmen's Association (ADAV) was constituted in May 1863, its first president, Ferdinand Lassalle, planned to found "a great Berlin newspaper" for the workingman. In early April 1861 Lassalle offered coeditorship to his houseguest Karl Marx, who declined but recommended Friedrich Engels in his stead. Only after Lassalle's untimely death in August 1864 was his plan realized. The first issue of *Sozialdemokrat*, the ADAV official organ, appeared on 4 January 1865. Its editor, publisher, and owner was the authoritarian Johann Baptist von Schweitzer, elected president of the association in May 1867. Marx himself joined Engels, the poet Georg Herwegh, and Liebknecht as early collaborators on the paper until Schweitzer's Prussian nationalism effected a rupture. Liebknecht was dismissed from the editorial board in July 1865. He moved to Leipzig, aligned himself a year later with Bebel's Left Liberal Saxon People's Party (Sächsische Volkspartei), and was named editor of its paper, *Demokratisches Wochenblatt* (Democratic Weekly Newspaper). The two men were instrumental in founding the Social Democratic Labor Party (SDAP) in August 1869 at Eisenach, which drew dissidents from the rival ADAV. *Demokratisches Wochenblatt*, renamed by Liebknecht *Volksstaat* (People's State), became the official organ of the SDAP.[11]

When Schweitzer left the ADAV altogether upon losing his Reichstag seat in 1871, his newspaper ceased publication on 30 April 1871. The ADAV funded a new organ, *Neuer Sozialdemokrat* (New Social Democrat), edited by Wilhelm Hasselmann and Wilhelm Hasenclever, which rapidly attained a circulation of 14,000. The SDAP, on the other hand, not only maintained a central organ but supported local publications in a dozen cities. Accordingly, *Volksstaat* had just over 6,500 subscribers in 1873, half the number of the Lassallean paper. *Neuer Sozialdemokrat* and *Volksstaat* took different tacks.[12] Whereas the former was a strident voice of agitation, the latter under Liebknecht aimed to "build the spirit and character, and educate the workers for their political and social mission, while offering them an understanding of present conditions."[13] Bismarck's persecution of socialists impelled the two workers' parties to close ranks. Among the victims of the persecution was Liebknecht, who together with Bebel was jailed on the charge of treason—one of fourteen times Liebknecht was made a prisoner of conscience. In May 1875 the ADAV and the SDAP met at Gotha and merged to form the Socialist Labor Party of Germany (SAPD). The next year *Neuer Sozialdemokrat* and *Volksstaat* amalgamated as *Vorwärts*, published in Leipzig and edited jointly by Liebknecht and Hasenclever. The new party's central organ immediately attracted 12,000 subscribers.[14]

When Bismarck's antisocialist law went into effect on 21 October 1878, the SAPD was proscribed, its leaders interned, its press shut down, and its members placed under police surveillance. Because of an oversight in the code, socialist deputies in the Reichstag and state legislatures and candidates for seats in those bodies were immune from prosecution. For the twelve years the law was in effect, the SAPD continued to function underground and in exile, becoming far more radical and growing, remarkably, into Germany's strongest single party. Less than a year after the law was passed, the first issue of *Sozialdemokrat*, the organ in exile, was printed in Zurich on 28 September 1879. Liebknecht, Bebel, and Friedrich Wilhelm Fritzsche composed the initial editorial board. The young Bavarian Georg von Vollmar was selected as editor in chief. Under Vollmar and his successor, Eduard Bernstein, *Sozialdemokrat* adopted a revolutionary Marxist stance; the old Lassalleans faded from the scene. *Sozialdemokrat* was smuggled into Germany via the Red Field Post, a collaborative of over a hundred agents directed by Julius Motteler.[15] For the duration of the twelve years of outlawry, Liebknecht and Bebel worked tirelessly to maintain and strengthen both the party organization and their own increasingly Marxist ideological hegemony.

After the antisocialist law lapsed on 30 September 1890, *Vorwärts* was reconstituted as the official organ of the renamed Social Democratic Party of Germany (Sozialdemokratische Partei Deutschlands, or SPD) and relocated from Leipzig to the capital, where it absorbed the *Berliner Volksblatt*, the local party paper as radical as its metropolitan constituency. Founded and largely financed by Paul Singer, the *Volksblatt* had appeared daily from 1 April 1884 as an independent "workers' paper" and, under the capable editorship of the economist Max Schippel, reached a circulation of 25,000 after the Social Democratic gains in the Reichstag elections of 1890. By the new arrangement, a single paper was to serve as both the party's central organ and the local Social Democratic daily. The first issue of the reincarnated *Vorwärts*, subtitled *Berliner Volksblatt*, was printed on 1 January 1891.[16] Confirmed as chief editor only after intricate negotiations between the national and local organizations, Liebknecht presided over "a bevy of coeditors, assistants, regular contributors, and correspondents" representing the gamut of opinion within the party itself—a situation he readily recognized as inconducive to a clarion for socialist unity.[17] Yet despite the ideological diversity of his own staff and pressure from the militant local membership, the "Old Man," one of the last survivors of Marx's generation, succeeded for the most part in maintaining collegial relations among his board and with the party proper.

At the time he interviewed Eisner, Liebknecht faced his greatest challenge to date at *Vorwärts*. Since 1896, when Eduard Bernstein began a series of articles expounding on Georg von Vollmar's 1891 call for a rethinking of the party's purpose, the party itself was divided by the controversy over revisionism. In brief, Bernstein observed developments in Germany in particular and industrial, capitalist societies in general that contradicted Marx and Engels's predictions. The skilled German worker, the backbone of the party, enjoyed a higher, not lower standard of living, as real wages in fact had risen during the last quarter of the nineteenth century. The middle class had grown rather than shrunk, and smaller industry, far from being absorbed by larger concerns, proliferated. The crisis point that Marx, Engels, and Lassalle had deemed imminent seemed ever more remote. With the growing class consciousness of the working class, the strength of the trade unions, and the party's impressive electoral increases in the national elections of 1890, 1894, and 1898, outpolling every other party, Bernstein reasoned that the goal of revolution avowed at the SAPD congress in exile in Copenhagen in 1883 had been superseded by parliamentary participation. Increased democratization had provided Social Democracy the means to political power, and even greater popular support would derive from the disavowal of bloody upheaval to achieve social justice.[18]

Support for reformism came primarily from Carl Legien and the trade unions, but Bernstein, who served as correspondent for *Vorwärts* in London, where he had lived in exile since 1888, had advocates on the editorial board as well.[19] On 29 September Clara Zetkin complained in a letter to Karl Kautsky that far from clarifying the party's ideological stance, *Vorwärts* functioned as "an organ for systematic contamination of principles" through seeking to smooth over the differences between the two camps.[20] By naming an external candidate as Adolf Braun's successor—one who would need to take his cue from Liebknecht himself—Liebknecht hoped to right his board. A month after Eisner's arrival, Liebknecht congratulated himself on his new charge in a note to Victor Adler, Austrian Social Democratic leader and Braun's brother-in-law: "In Eisner I doubtless hit upon a good choice. The main thing, though, is that the cause of *frictions* gradually be eliminated and some love and passion rekindled for the paper."[21]

Liebknecht's secondary consideration in appointing Eisner, who had won a devoted public following wherever he worked, must have been the desire to improve the organ's style and format. It was a daunting challenge, for as Stefan Großmann reminisced, the local press commission worked the traditional unholy influence of such bodies by naming as editors reliable trade unionists and aging functionaries "who could not write."[22] Großmann's verdict is confirmed by Walther Oschilewski in his study of the Berlin press. "Until about the turn of the century the Social Democratic newspapers scarcely got beyond the status of a 'club circular.' Even in the nineties they were in most cases dry compilations of material and agitational texts. Time and again the complaint arose that the party papers were too uniform, too one-sided, too little informative and topical, all too crammed with theoretical discussions and internal wrangling."[23] At the time Eisner came aboard, *Vorwärts* had 53,000 subscribers, all but a few thousand of whom were Berliners.[24] If the party voice were not to be obscured by well-managed, local party papers such as the *Leipziger Volkszeitung*, which under editor Bruno Schoenlank and his chief collaborator, Franz Mehring, boasted a national readership, it would have to better itself.

As managing political editor, Eisner was soon functioning in effect as editor in chief, since Liebknecht at seventy-two no longer concerned himself with the demands of the daily deadline.[25] Stepping into his new role, Eisner faced immense challenges that would prove insurmountable eventually, even for one with his talent and skill. The newcomer's rise surely engendered professional jealousy among his fellow editors, but Eisner quickly proved his worth, drawing on his experience as correspondent for the Herold, seasoned journalist and editor, and victim of the Prussian judiciary. Just as Liebknecht had done in 1863–1864, he observed and reported on sessions of the Prussian House of Deputies and, in what must have been a delicious irony, covered court cases against journalists.[26] His return to the press box of the Prussian diet resulted in a thirty-page agitational pamphlet chronicling the machinations of the East Elbian squirearchy during the summer to stymie a government proposal for a canal linking the Rhine and the Elbe. Published in-house by Vorwärts Press, *Eine Junkerrevolte: Drei Wochen preußischer Politik* (A Junker Revolt: Three Weeks of Prussian Politics) amply demonstrates that the reputed Junker fealty to the crown existed only so long as the state served exclusively as guarantor of their interests.[27]

Eisner began his booklet by reciting how the Junker Bismarck, "who exhausted every brutal means of force to gain and keep power," had been supplanted by Miquel, "the enterprising, bourgeois businessman who . . . endeavored to meet the needs of all esteemed customers and win them by gentle persuasion." Miquel's policy to unite the Middle and the Right against Social Democracy was threatened by economic conflict between the industrial and agrarian sectors. Industrialists in the Ruhr, their financiers, suppliers, and shippers demanded low tariffs to bolster exports; conversely, the Junkerdom required high tariffs to limit the import of foodstuffs and keep prices for their produce high at home. The conflict grew to dispute over the government's Central Canal project, which the industrialists backed unanimously and the Junker opposed as much for strategic political as for economic reasons. The Central Canal's most vocal advocate was Wilhelm himself. Having been entreated by Friedrich Alfred Krupp to appear, the emperor journeyed to Dortmund to dedicate on 11 August the Dortmund-Ems Canal, a link in the proposed network, and declared his "firm and unshakable" support for the greater project.

Emboldened by rampant growth and the monarch's favor, the industrialists, represented by the National Liberals and Radicals, challenged Junker political supremacy in the Prussian House of Deputies. In a bizarre switching of roles, the National Liberal and Radical parties and press extolled the kaiser's will as unassailable, whereas the Conservatives were left to defend their patriotism. Despite overwhelming popular support for the canal and a frenetic campaign in the press, the Junker, the Agrarian League (Bund der Landwirte), and the Conservative Party rallied to defeat the bill in mid-August and deal a stinging blow to Wilhelm's prestige. The liberals were confronted anew with the unhappy realization that "Prussia is ruled by a number of families who derive their absolute sovereign authority from having immigrated to Brandenburg earlier than the Hohenzollerns" and that the East Elbian aristocracy's power and influence was far disproportionate to its number: "It intrigues at court, drills the army, and resides in every administrative office." Incredulous at their loss, the Liberal and Left Liberal press fulminated against the forces of reaction and called for the dissolution of the Prussian diet and for new elections.

Vorwärts—that is, Eisner himself—suggested another solution. Were the government to strike the three-class electoral system and institute universal, direct suffrage, Junker tyranny would be ended. Social Democracy had supported the canal but, having boycotted elections to the Prussian House of Deputies, had no say in the voting. The worker, Eisner lamented, suffered by the proposal's defeat. Perhaps the time had come for the party to abandon the boycott and exert its will. "It is not inconceivable that sooner or later in the course of the canal affair, the Landtag indeed might be dissolved. How would we act then? . . . Social Democracy is strong enough to allow itself the luxury of strengthening even opponents temporarily if there is an advantage to it." Realizing that on this issue he was breaking ranks with party leadership and ranging himself with the reformists, Eisner was careful to disclaim any desire to reignite a debate in which taunts of "opportunism and compromise play a greater role than all the objective grounds of political reason together." In retrospect he believed *Junkerrevolte* to be one of his best writings.[28] He had to be chagrined to see juxtaposed to his plea on the final page an advertisement on the inside cover for Liebknecht's brochure *Kein Kompromiß! Kein Wahlbündnis!* (No Compromise! No Electoral Alliance!). Already his political leanings were being questioned, even as his contributions at *Vorwärts* were winning approval. But clearly the revisionists did not count him among their number. On 17 August Ignaz Auer, secretary of the party's executive committee, wrote to Bernstein that Eisner and Georg Gradnauer, his fellow editor at *Vorwärts*, were "nothing less than Marxist fanatics."[29]

Even as acting editor of the party voice, Eisner found time for his belletristic writing. He introduced a regular column, *Sonntagsplauderei* (Sunday Chat), in the entertainment supplement, which printed serialized novels such as Zola's *Work* and Gorky's *Foma Gordeev*, a calendar of cultural events, notes on medical advances and scientific discoveries, reports on archaeological expeditions, and an ever-popular sampling of the latest jokes. The chats were essays, stories, brief one-acts, musings on a variety of topics; like the *Provinzialbriefe* for *Die Kritik*, the new column was the forum for anything Eisner cared to address. Whimsical, pert, or caustic as the subject dictated, the column became Eisner's signature on the publication, driving interest and subscriptions and sticking in the memory of his admirers as the stuff of the paper's classical heyday and in the craw of his detractors as the blight of aesthetic sentimentality on scientific socialism. Inaugurating the column under the pen name Alpha, he later signed his work as Joc for Jocusus, "the jocular one." The column of 25 June is reminiscent of the biting satire that had won him a prison term.[30] It takes the form of an imagined conference in the Interior Ministry between Prince zu Hohenlohe, Miquel, Count Posadowsky, and Podbielski upon defeat of the prison bill, a measure proposed by Wilhelm himself as part of his campaign against Social Democracy, threatening with imprisonment anyone encouraging workers to strike. The bill's defeat in the Reichstag would not occur in fact until two months later.[31] In late summer Eisner began submitting commentaries on events of the day, from Weltpolitik to agricultural tariffs, to the Viennese weekly *Die Wage* (The Scales), edited by Rudolf Lothar.[32]

Eisner's first great opportunity to trip the tightrope before a full house came in October. The annual party congress of 1899, convened at the old Ballroom in Hanover, was dominated by the revisionist debate. In March Bernstein had published a systematic summary of his thought under the cumbersome title *Die Voraussetzungen des Sozialismus und die Aufgaben der Sozialdemokratie* (The Hypotheses of Socialism and the Tasks of Social Democracy). Its stated purpose was to "strengthen the realistic as well as the idealistic element in the socialist movement by combatting the remnants of utopian thinking in socialist theory." He concluded by attacking Eisner, without actually naming him, as a corrupting influence on the worker: "Precisely because I expect much from the working class, I judge everything that tends to corrupt its moral judgment much more harshly than what occurs in this respect in the ruling class, and I see with greatest regret how here and there a tone of literary decadence is spreading in the workers' press that can have only a confusing and ultimately corrupting effect."[33] Before the book's appearance Bebel had determined to expel Bernstein from the party; a month after its release Bernstein's growing popularity precluded the option.[34]

In daily reports from Hanover Eisner summarized and commented on the proceedings, putting the best face on the schism—just as Zetkin had accused—by emphasizing the party's unity while extolling its diversity.[35] "However greatly our thinking seems to diverge," he wrote in the opening paragraph, "it is only the lively play in the tips of widespreading branches emanating from the same mighty tree." The congress opened Sunday afternoon, 8 October, with the customary ceremonies welcoming delegates from across Germany and guests from Europe and the United States: brass bands, male choruses, and gymnastics clubs performed their specialties. That evening the spokesman for the host local, Karl Frohme, addressed the delegates, urging a free exchange of views. The next morning, Eisner reported, the radical Rosa Luxemburg and reformist Max Schippel were seated across from each other at their long table, as if to refute symbolically "the hostile rumor of irreconcilable differences in our party." The great debate on revisionism began on Tuesday morning. "Today the free parliament of the proletariat began the earnest, fervent contest for truth and justification, for the mature development and clear formulation of its worldview and party principles."

In a marathon speech party chairman Bebel refuted the premises of revisionism through theoretical argument and statistical data—citing even bourgeois economists whose estimation of capitalist development were not as optimistic as Bernstein's. In his reportage of Bebel's main arguments, Eisner employed the indicative mood for heightened immediacy and dramatic effect, eschewing the subjunctive of indirect discourse that formal writing dictated. Bebel insisted that the class struggle was ever the fundamental fact of life in Wilhelmine Germany and that only the destruction of the ruling order could ensure social justice and peace. Nonetheless, he conceded that limited cooperation with the bourgeois parties was indeed expedient and desirable if it were a matter of "strengthening the party in elections, or expanding the political rights and freedoms of the people, or substantially improving the social condition of the working class and advancing its cultural mission, or combatting efforts hostile to the worker and people." The chairman deplored the inroads reformism had made in the party, subjecting its program to ridicule by the bourgeois public. The ruling order would not be overturned by collective bargaining. And far from being too immature to manage affairs of state, the proletariat already had surpassed the bourgeoisie in political education and ability.[36] The revolution Bebel envisioned was no bloody upheaval but rather an "expropriation"—the same tool utilized by the nobility and bourgeoisie in their rise to power—that would result from the proletariat's political will, ironclad organization, steadfast discipline, and overwhelming economic might.

Since Bernstein, who was still wanted by the police for sedition, had lived in exile in London since 1888, Dr. Eduard David, a distinguished economist, spoke in his defense. David scoffed at Luxemburg's "empty radicalism" and insisted that Bernstein remained a loyal Social Democrat committed to the class struggle but believed the strength of the unions and cooperatives should be brought to bear politically as well as economically. David was echoed or rebutted by a dozen speakers, including Luxemburg, each of whom was allotted half an hour to weigh in on reformism. For his readership Eisner remarked that Frau Luxemburg "sometimes has the slight, unfortunate tendency to diminish the effect of her insightful, pointed comments through distracting crudities."[37] On Thursday afternoon debate became rancorous. Bitter protests were lodged against the personal attacks to which Bernstein and his advocates had been subjected. Vollmar likened the congress to an inquisition. Eisner, who admitted that his own "sympathies and aversions" made impartial reporting difficult, observed that the incivility bred distrust and division: "When the artificially driven sense of conflict is greater than the conflict itself, then the objectively unfounded impression of the conflict affects detrimentally our feeling of solidarity and ultimately exacerbates the conflict itself." He editorialized that the major difference between Bebel and Bernstein was much more one of temperament than substance, "of the decisive energy of the enthusiastic true believer and of the somewhat resigned doubt of a scrupulous, honest but irresolute skeptic."

On Friday morning Bebel's resolution affirming the party's Marxist fundament in theory and practice—with the concession that occasional cooperation with the bourgeois parties might be considered—was approved by a ten-to-one margin. The question of tactic in Landtag elections, which Eisner's recent pamphlet had addressed, remained a sticking point for some, and although the majority asserted that Social Democratic backing for Left Liberal candidates had been rejected, except in extraordinary situations, Liebknecht pushed through a resolution placing the issue on the agenda of the 1900 congress at Mainz. In reporting a matter that touched him more closely, Eisner recounted that the Berliners' motion to accord equal rights to the party executive and local press commission in governance of *Vorwärts* had been approved but a related motion to prescribe a uniform editorial perspective was rejected.

Writing in summary after the congress concluded, Eisner emphasized Bebel's resolution as "the common ground on which we all stand" and downplayed discord in the ranks. Proven wrong, he wrote, were both the reformists who regarded the radicals as visionary fanatics disdaining practical politics in favor of the "great day" of revolution and radicals who considered the reformists crass opportunists who, having lost sight of the goal, were willing to settle for "bourgeois sham-democracy."

Even after Eisner's effusive praise of his vision and leadership, Bebel harbored reservations about the man who by his position was now de facto chief spokesman for Social Democracy. A week after the congress Bebel wrote to Victor Adler, the Austrian socialists' official representative at Hanover: "I wanted to inquire whether you have a man thoroughly schooled in journalism, who stands on *Marxist* footing, *possesses the necessary character* not to let himself be pushed from this standpoint, and who at the same time understands the German circumstances, that he might eventually accept an editorial position at *Vorw.* . . . But if the man does *not* have the above qualities, he should *not* apply. We have opportunists enough at *Vorw.*, and the editorial staff's intellectual leader, Eisner, lacks the critical knowledge of party history and theory, otherwise he would be a top man."[38] Adler replied on 6 November that Otto Pohl showed promise, although his predominantly literary education rendered him suspect. "He does well for us because he can be driven on a tight rein. In Berlin he will be without direction. Like all our young people, he also has the tendency to Bernsteinism. . . . As a helper he would be quite good, but he's absolutely not battle-ready, and Eisner would have in him at once a blind follower."[39] Wilhelm Liebknecht himself favored Rosa Luxemburg's appointment, but Bebel, fearing even greater division, preferred Heinrich Ströbel.[40]

Whereas Bebel and Adler had doubts about Eisner, J. H. W. Dietz, the Stuttgart publisher of *Die Neue Zeit* (The New Age), the party's theoretical journal edited by Karl Kautsky, coveted Liebknecht's lieutenant. On 8 November he telegraphed Ignaz Auer: "Should Eisner become available, I would like to try to win him. Terms good. Mutual discretion." The next day Auer dutifully passed along the message. Upon learning from Georg Gradnauer, Eisner's closest associate editor, that Eisner was content in Berlin, Auer counseled Eisner not to reveal Dietz's interest to any other than the most trusted of his circle: "That you are not thinking of leaving pleases no one more than me. But there can be those who do not share my pleasure."[41]

Personal as well as professional considerations must have swayed Eisner's decision to stay put. In late May Lisbeth had given birth to a third daughter, Jenny Eva. Conversely, old Emanuel Eisner's health was deteriorating daily. He died at home on Friday afternoon, 10 November, and was interred three days later in the Jewish cemetery at Weißensee in northeast Berlin.[42] The same week the Berlin journal *Deutsche Dichtung* (German Letters), edited by Karl Emil Franzos, published "Death on Approval," a wry, Faustian tale Eisner had written on the mystery of the beyond.[43]

In the wake of his father's death and as the year, decade, and century drew to a close, Eisner had cause to reflect on his life's improbable course. In a little over a year he had gone from prison inmate to managing editor of *Vorwärts*. He returned home a hero to the vibrant capital that so recently had housed him as a pariah. And the return coincided with the moment of Social Democratic ascendancy on the eve of the century he himself had prophesied belonged to Marx. Being born Jewish had posed little detriment to either Eisner's career or personal life. He had studied at university, married the woman of his choice, and achieved notable success in his chosen field rather than as the merchant his parents had wished him to be. Perhaps Friedrich the Great and Lessing's North German Enlightenment and industrialism's need of capital had tempered animosity to Jewry. Hermann Cohen, after all, was philosophy chair at Marburg, and the leadership of Germany's largest party was disproportionately Semitic. The possibilities must have seemed then, if not infinite, at least expansive.

In the new year Eisner resumed his assault on the vestigial feudalism that still animated German politics. The impetus was discussion in the Prussian upper house of a proposal to establish reformatories. Joc observed in the *Sonntagsplauderei* of 14 January that the Prussian House of Lords spurned Rousseau's ideal of education to humanity, preferring instead "the omnipotence of constraint, which they consider useful in training humans as befits the interests of their masters." Eisner traced how the pedagogy of the rod, disdained by the eighteenth century, had reasserted itself in the nineteenth, applauded by the church and champions of reaction. By nurturing the pupil's individuality, personal interests, and abilities, the enlightened educator had resounding success in molding productive members of society and exemplary citizens—an ideal that found its resonance in Lessing, Goethe, and Schiller: "Our classical period of German letters was in essence and by the artists' design an aesthetic education of humankind." At the advent of the twentieth century, however, German pedagogy was designed to turn out docile slave labor. How could it be otherwise, he asked, "at a time when the ruling class is obsessed with the most violent brutishness and sees life's sole purpose in the barbarity of militarism, in the rape of other classes and peoples?" The unsuitability of Germany's education system was a theme he would treat again and again.[44]

Ibsen's final play, *When We Dead Awaken*, premiered in Stuttgart on 26 January and was performed in Berlin a few weeks later.[45] Before the local production Eisner reviewed the work, in Christian Morgenstern's translation for S. Fischer of Berlin, the German publisher.[46] Eisner surveyed for his readers Ibsen's half-century career spanning from the revolutions of 1848 to the fin de siècle, with this "dramatic epilogue," as the subtitle stated, serving as a profound, personal malediction on lost opportunity. At the master's touch the literary commonplace of a late-life marital mismatch becomes "a miracle cathedral with the entirety of moaning, yearning human existence fluttering high in the vaults with vengeful echo." The characters accurately depicted contemporaries, minutely and mercilessly observed: "These people are clothed in the style of 1900. We have spoken already with all of them; they just have not revealed their secrets to us yet because we are not poets." He praised Ibsen's natural language and sober tone free of pathos, and he read correctly that the play was a brutal self-indictment. "The greatest poet of our time" spoke here his confession. Professor Rubek's awakening, his resurrection, comes when he reconciles with the woman whose selfless love he spurned in his youth. Contrition and the desire to atone suffice, for absolution is but rarely man's lot. "That is the life's germ to Ibsen's art as to all great art: the thought of resurrection, man's rebirth in the elevation of the individual, the prophet's image of the future who sees a new heaven and a new earth."

In late January 1900 Eisner dedicated to his friend Professor Rathke in Marburg a long poem of iambic couplets affectionately commemorating the quaint architectural jumble of hilly streets where a gabled roof afforded on one side a ground-level view of the neighbor's garden: "In Marburg old, a crooked town, / A wondrous sight is often found."[47] Yet however fondly he recalled the provincial charm, Berlin offered access to theater. On 4 February Eisner used his column to inveigh against a novelty made possible by technology with which the theatergoer could well dispense: the same-night, "in flagranti" review that permitted its author's aesthetic impressions no time to settle before going to press. "For Gerhart Hauptmann's new comedy, which opens to the public this Saturday, the mechanical perfection of art criticism will make it possible for us to obtain from the hands of the newspaper salesmen—already upon exiting the German Theater—the considered judgment of two acts." And soon, he guessed, one would know what to think of the final act as well even before reaching the Viennese Café, where the morning papers were already available. Vernon Lidtke and others have documented the rich cultural life of the German proletariat at the turn of the century, yet the average working-class reader must have marveled at the glimpse Eisner afforded here into the the world of the Berlin theater habitué, "this nightlife of the moneyed," in all its sordid glamor. "However little the essence changes—the odious artifice, the depravity in too much makeup, the tired feebleness, the look of desire exhaustively rehearsed before the mirror, all the misery and the boredom that relishes with pride how terribly expensive this boredom is to buy—as unchanging as this masculine playworld is, . . . the fashion of vice changes constantly and the manners of its victims exhaust all the possibilities of idiocy."[48]

In February and March Eisner was alone at the helm while Liebknecht enjoyed his first trip to Italy, the gift of a generous friend.[49] With a decade of experience in the trade, Eisner conducted the paper's business adroitly, expanding its network of collaborators and strengthening its base of support. In many respects, Eisner's comrade-rival was the erudite and crusty Franz Mehring, a man Bebel described as a "psychological riddle."[50] Like St. Paul, he had been a vociferous critic of the cause he eventually championed, quitting the Left Liberal camp in 1891 for Social Democracy. In 1900 he resided in Steglitz, a suburb a few miles from Eisner's home in Lichterfelde, yet Mehring and his ally Rosa Luxemburg, whose home base was also the environs of Berlin, were chief contributors to the *Leipziger Volkszeitung*, voice of Bernstein's radical opponents and challenger to *Vorwärts* as the party's national daily. In bourgeois background, education, and literary interests he and Eisner had much in common; philosophically and tactically their politics were at odds more often than not, although they later moved closer. They met occasionally over beer at Berlin's Hofbräuhaus after *Vorwärts* had gone to press to discuss their divergent perspectives. On 11 February Mehring wrote to Eisner in response to his request for a meeting and proposed that they meet, as usual, at 22:00 at the beer hall: "Since the differences of which you write probably refer to today's article, I shall hold off on the continuation until then."[51]

On 25 February, as the snow melted and a cluster of sunny days presaged spring, Joc made light of the flu that afflicted the capital and rued that the North had no popular seasonal celebration corresponding to the Catholic pre-Lenten carnival.[52] The next column's butt was General von Stülpnagel, commander of the Fifth Army Corps in Posnania, whose noncomissioned officers could not marry without his permission.[53] On April Fool's Joc smirked at the prospects of the Goethe Society, recently founded to combat the Center and Conservative parties' effort at censorship. If the new organization followed the typical course of the well-meaning bourgeois association of its kind, its members' initial sincerity and enthusiasm would succumb quickly to their political ignorance, inexperience, and impatience. The most that could be expected was a few rousing after-dinner speeches at their annual banquets. A more fitting name for an organization mobilized "against intellectual barbarism," he suggested, would derive from someone other than Weimar's favored courtier. Indeed, the best namesake was no German at all but the French novelist Zola, "that most powerful tendentious author after Jean-Jacques Rousseau" and "the single great poet of socialism, albeit not in the strict sense of scientific theory."[54]

Dr. Karl Vorländer, another of Cohen's students with whom Eisner corresponded regularly, wrote on 6 April 1900 from Solingen regarding Kant and socialism.[55] Prompted perhaps by Vorländer's letter, Eisner responded now to Bernstein—who also claimed Kant as an influence—and the recent charge of literary decadence. In his Easter column Eisner clarified his bearing toward Bernstein's reformist tactic. For a 1906 anthology of his essays at *Vorwärts* Eisner titled the piece "At the Home of the Sage." The medium he chose is telling, for the column takes the form of a *Märchen*, a fairy tale. Toward the end of winter an insect-sized figure holds court beneath an upturned watering can amid a heap of refuse. The tiny guru's wisdom is that of infinite patience: "Only through the passage of immeasurable time can we hope for our wishes to be fulfilled." Anyone who disagrees is branded a "utopian." Yet within weeks the sage has disappeared, put to flight by the "revolutionary awakening" of spring.[56]

The sensational trial in early April of an unfailingly polite shoe salesman named Gönezi, accused of murdering two elderly women for the fortune he suspected they had tucked away, moved Joc to draw a comparison to European, especially German imperialism in Africa where the lofty language of patriotism, duty, and honor masked the most wanton "cultural crimes."[57] A scathing essay on mystical neoromanticism, "The Old Idol," was published in the May issue of *Sozialistische Monatshefte*, followed by a Sunday column on an equally quirky but less pretentious flight of fancy.[58] In mid-May Eisner visited Barnum and Bailey's "Greatest Show on Earth" near the Savigny Square station. He declined to see the Siamese twins and bearded lady, observed that American taste finds appeal in immense size and number, and remarked that it would require the combined efforts and facilities of the Busch and Schumann circuses, the Berlin Opera, the Winter Garden cabaret, the Residence and Apollo theaters, and the Prussian House of Lords to rival the Barnum and Bailey extravaganza of animals, acts, and clowns.[59] A week later he shared with his readers the trials of teaching son Reinhard, now six, to sound out and read monosyllables in his primer. The boy would spell the word correctly then blurt out another altogether, claiming it to be the word he had spelled. With a show of exaggerated anger the frustrated father would bellow: "Lex is coming!" Only the threat of draconian law, which every Prussian had reason to fear, produced any effect, for his son merely laughed at the bogeyman, and appeals to God were to just as little avail, as the child associated deity with the baker from whom they received their daily bread.[60]

In early June Eisner noted that with the Boers near defeat in the Transvaal, the European newspapers had fixed on the Boxer Rebellion in China. He imagined how publishing magnates August Scherl and the Ullstein brothers conspired at their barbershop as to which slant their various papers would take on the issue in order not to undercut each other's sales. The generally apolitical *Lokal-Anzeiger* (Local Gazette) would call for a "mailed-fist" policy, the jingoist *Feldpost* (Field Post) support the German Navy as standardbearer of the nation's honor, the Democratic *Morgenpost* (Morning Post) find solace in European unity against the yellow peril, the Left Liberal *Berliner Zeitung* attack imperial adventurism and compare the rebellion to Germany's own wars of liberation against Napoleon, and *Die Woche* (The Week), "the great filter for all the sewage of the other organs," provide a professorial commentary asserting the primacy of European culture vis-à-vis oriental particularism.[61] In the same vein Eisner fabricated arms dealer Friedrich Alfred Krupp's musings on the rosy state of international affairs. Contemplating the enormity of profits that a full-blown war in China would drive, Herr Krupp hails the Boxers' resistance to foreign incursions and pledges to equip their cause. "If you want to be rid of the Europeans, you mustn't stint. Call your entire race to arms—the women, old men, and children too! You'll receive my current price list in the next post. Arms for 400 million people: what a prospect, what hope for the future!" The only thing that could be better than Wilhelm's Weltpolitik, Krupp reflects gleefully, is its consequence: Weltkrieg.[62]

Through his column Eisner strove to stem growing enthusiasm among workers for imperialism, which especially unionized workers believed would raise their standard of living to that of the English worker.[63] Remarkably, a core of support for the government's colonial policy developed within the SPD. Social Democrats who advocated Weltpolitik became known as the "social imperialists." Their credo derived directly from Bernstein, who in *Die Voraussetzungen des Sozialismus und die Aufgaben der Sozialdemokratie* unabashedly embraced social Darwinism. German industry, he argued, would suffer by having to compete against foreign industries helped by their governments in securing raw materials and ample markets for finished products. And if German industry suffered so too would the German worker. Consequently, he supported not only the government's acquisition of concessions in Kiaochow to "open" China to free trade but also the establishment of German colonies abroad.[64] The moral question of exploitation of indigenous peoples was all relative. "It is neither necessary nor has it even generally been the case to date that European occupation of tropical lands harms the natives' quality of life. Moreover, the savages' right to the lands they inhabit is conditional at best. In the most extreme cases, the more advanced culture has the more legitimate claim. Cultivation rather than conquest grants historical title to its use."[65]

Amid the Boxers' xenophobic campaign of violence that claimed the life of Germany's minister to Peking, news of the joint European-American expedition to capture the capital, and a "witches' sabbath of jingoism," Eisner opened his 8 July column by quoting Confucius's moral law: "Do not require of your subordinates what is odious to you when required by superiors; likewise, do not serve your superiors in the manner you find displeasing in your subordinates."[66] He compared the maxim from the sixth century BCE to Kant's categorical imperative, enunciated in 1787, and declared that "however morals and customs change, however views of good and evil may flow and fluctuate under the decisive influence of economic relations, the quivering, floating, circling compass needle of moral conceptions constantly strives for the fast pole of a fundamental principle: the rule and measure of all morality is its universal validity, its exceptionlessness, its uniformity for all individuals, peoples, and races." To disregard this essential truth and presume to civilize a venerable civilization by force and material exploitation was the sheerest occidental hypocrisy, glorification of egoism, and negation of all cultural values. Little wonder, he reasoned, that the Chinese considered the Westerner a barbarian and met his brutality with brutality.

On 31 July Joseph Bloch, editor of *Sozialistische Monatshefte*, requested from his Berlin office that Eisner forward final copy of an essay on Dostoevsky for publication in the September issue. He included the table of contents for the August issue and asked that Eisner run it in *Vorwärts* the next morning.[67] The final draft on Dostoevsky was delayed by unforeseen circumstances. Wilhelm Liebknecht left the editorial offices in the wee hours on Tuesday, 7 August. Later that morning he died in his sleep at his Charlottenburg home after suffering a stroke. Only a week earlier he had spoken in Dresden on international affairs. Sunday, the twelfth, the day of the funeral and a five-and-a-half-hour cortège through Berlin, Eisner reminisced in print about the fallen leader and shrewdly made his eulogy serve double duty. Realizing that critics of *Vorwärts* on the press commission would see in Liebknecht's death an opportunity to turn back the clock and reassert their control over the organ, Eisner detailed how radically the newspaper trade had changed in recent years while at the same time he lauded Liebknecht's personal qualities and contributions to the workers' movement. While conceding that none of Liebknecht's younger comrades would be able to replace him as the party's stentorian voice, he intimated that the technical demands of modern journalism outstripped the experience of those who cut their teeth on penny broadsheets.

> Perhaps the last great journalist of the old stamp died with Wilhelm Liebknecht—from that era when the newspaper was nothing more than an expanded, regularly appearing flier; when the issues of the day only provided the pretext to a recruitment appeal; when the writer for a daily was agitator, missionary, a knight of the intellect. . . . The pedantic work that today's editor of a news daily must do was always foreign to Wilhelm Liebknecht's inspired impetuosity. He was no artisan but rather an artist who followed the dictates of his temperament, valued good style far more than a sensational report, and never understood that it was a question of whether the public got its news a day late or early. . . . Liebknecht had remained unfamiliar with the industrialization of the newspaper too, so that in spite of having been the guiding light of great papers for decades, he had never delved into the technical details of the operation. In this respect he remained as harmless as a novice. I believe the twin rotary press was always something sinister to him, and his heart hung on the little hand press of an underground printer, where the way from the brain to the finished page is not all that far.[68]

The next day Eisner composed a brief appreciation of Liebknecht's life and work for *Sozialistische Monatshefte*.[69] It too had a secondary function. Here he hailed Liebknecht's lifelong opposition to militarism, his commitment to the International, his distaste for expediency, and his aversion to violence. "Today we know that of all the means to revolutionize the world none is less effective than that of brute force and destruction passed on by our oppressors. Only the desperation of most extreme self-defense that leaves no other recourse legitimizes this mean. Social Democracy strives to win its revolution through the peaceful conquest of power; it will not be our fault if developments lead to harsher clashes." But Liebknecht's greatest legacy was the realization that however democratically and peacefully the proletariat might come to power, capitalism and its class structure would have to be eradicated. It was not enough simply to commandeer the state apparatus; the state had to be reconstituted so as to serve the needs of the masses. The message was a recapitulation of Bebel's resolution at Hanover, directed against the party extremists left and right.

The party commissioned Eisner to write a brochure biography of Liebknecht for immediate dissemination. His initial inclination was that the office of biographer rightfully belonged to one of Liebknecht's old comrades of the exile. It was he though whose vacation coincided with the funeral. Repairing to the seaside village Wenningstedt on the Frisian island Sylt with sheaves of papers placed at his disposal by the Liebknecht family, Eisner churned out a sixty-page sketch by September. On 2 September, with the work substantially complete, he reported to Richard Fischer, business manager of Vorwärts Press and member of the Reichstag for Berlin's second district, that he had settled on the title *Wilhelm Liebknecht: Sein Leben und Wirken* (Wilhelm Liebknecht: His Life and Work).[70] The constraints of time and place, he observed in the preface, were altogether fitting. "In the end the same fate befalls the necrologist in his work that his hero had to suffer in his career as a writer: Liebknecht too was constantly compelled to write on the march and in flight, on vacation or in custody."[71]

Any account of Liebknecht's life would need to record the rise of the German workers' movement as well. Eisner delineates in his introduction the irreconcilable worlds of modern humanity—that of the idle masters and that of their striving slaves—which, although concurrent in 1900, manifested different stages of historical development. He names Bismarck and Liebknecht respective personifications of the two. Whereas the imperious champion of the crumbling feudal-dynastic order employed guile, obfuscation, and brute force, the mendicant crusader for the ascendant proletariat worked as an ingenuous edifier, instilling purity of principle, righteousness of cause, and certainty of victory. Glowing tribute is coupled here with searing denunciation.

Eisner presents Liebknecht as one born to revolution. His uncle, Pastor F. L. Weidig of Butzbach, led an illegal republican party in Hesse and was jailed in 1834 for his collaboration with Georg Büchner on *Der hessische Landbote*. Weidig's suicide in his cell, when Liebknecht was but a boy, inspired the nephew's early attempts at verse and tragedy. Liebknecht's studies at Berlin University ended in 1846 with his first expulsion from Prussia for subversive political activity. An interlude in Zurich as a schoolmaster—which Liebknecht always considered his true calling—was followed by an abrupt move to Paris in March 1848 to join poet Georg Herwegh's German Legion. The attempt to export republicanism to Germany came to grief. Liebknecht narrowly avoided imprisonment, resettled in Geneva, and turned from romantic revolution to a sober study of Marx. Expelled from Switzerland, he lived for thirteen years in London. There he studied with Marx in the reading room of the British Museum and earned a meager living by reporting on British affairs for the Augsburg *Allgemeine Zeitung* (General Newspaper).

Employing the slogan "Vorwärts!" as leitmotif, Eisner traces Liebknecht's return to Berlin in 1862, the break with Lassalle and Schweitzer over Prussian nationalism, his winning Bebel to Marxism, the founding of the SDAP, the unification of the rival workers' parties, and the genesis of the party press. A portrait emerges of Liebknecht as a singular man of vision and purpose undaunted by imprisonment, exile, privation, and personal tragedy. Given the division in the party at the time he was writing, Eisner took care to show Liebknecht as both revolutionary and pragmatist who overcame his ideological aversion to electoral politics to serve the proletariat in the Saxon Landtag and finally the Reichstag, even while deriding that august assembly as "the fig leaf of absolutism." Parliamentary participation on the party's terms was necessary, indeed vital, but only a temporary tactic. Eisner situated his monument squarely on the middle ground, preempting radical and reformist claims to Liebknecht's patrimony: "It is one of the most valuable of Liebknecht's lessons, never to be forgotten, that theory and practice are inextricably linked."[72] Seventeen thousand copies of the biography were printed in the first run and sold at 30 pfennige apiece.[73]

As editor in chief of *Vorwärts*, Liebknecht had been granted privileges befitting his long service to the cause, including the right to sit in advisory capacity at all meetings of the party executive committee. Now the executive moved to curb the independence and influence of the faction-riven central organ by declining to bestow Liebknecht's title on his successor. The editorial collective was to be directed by a "principal editor." It was to this position that Eisner returned from his working holiday at Wenningstedt.[74]

CHAPTER SIX

NO IDLE DREAMER: AT THE HELM OF *VORWÄRTS* (1900–1902)

THE MONTH OF SEPTEMBER 1900 saw Eisner transported from the sleepy seaside village back to Berlin and then on to Mainz for the annual party congress and the renewal of debate, as Liebknecht had brokered a year earlier, on participation in Landtag elections. The second pressing topic was Germany's colonial policy. "After the nerve-racking discussions in Hanover," Eisner readied readers of *Vorwärts* on 16 September, "the congress in Mainz will be of no less significance."[1] By its end the reformists would hold sway on one debate and suffer short-term defeat on the other, and the cracks in Social Democracy's ideological pedestal would widen. Providing a brief history and overview of the coming electoral debate, Eisner recounted that the party's traditional tactic against Prussian three-class suffrage had been the boycott. As party ranks swelled, though, some members determined that the Conservatives could be trumped in the House of Deputies despite the stacked deck if Social Democracy backed Left Liberal candidates or even put forward candidates of its own.

Bebel supported the boycott, as had Liebknecht. The party radicals generally had no use for either the Reichstag or the Landtag, both of which they regarded as trappings of the ruling-class state and as such fundamentally incompatible with the interests of the worker: collaboration and eventually power sharing would inevitably vitiate the party's raison d'être. The radicals' weapon of choice for advancing the revolutionary cause was the general, or political, strike. Historian Peter Gay writes: "To them proletarian mass-action was an end in itself and was to serve as a substitute for parliamentarism."[2] The general strike to achieve political concessions rather than economic benefits or improved working conditions was opposed particularly by the trade unionists as counterproductive, playing havoc with the lives of the rank and file. The theorists who advocated the strike as a political tool were too removed, they charged, from the workers' real needs. The trade unionists were skilled labor, and it was they who drove reformism. Their representatives considered participation in Landtag elections an effective means of expanding the party's influence and broadening its base of support.[3] Once again Eisner took it upon himself to plaster the cracks: "Today many of our best fighters still consider this beginning extremely questionable. . . . If, though, the congress decides for general electoral participation, the minority is prepared to enter the fray as well. . . . Our democratic principles demand it of us."

On the subject of Weltpolitik, also placed on the agenda at Liebknecht's request, congress president Paul Singer attacked Germany's incursion into China and the militarist, nationalist, and capitalist interests that fueled it. Bruno Schoenlank saw the emperor's personal ambition as the driving force and urged that the Reichstag deputation join forces with other opposition parties to rein in Wilhelm's colonial adventurism. Challenging Rosa Luxemburg's assessment of imperialism as international reaction, Anton Fendrich and Georg Ledebour characterized it as capitalism's final stage of development.[4] In his report Eisner emphasized the contradictory nature of the government's policy. On the domestic front it accommodated the Junker demand for high tariffs on foreign grain, which drew reciprocal foreign tariffs on German finished goods, restricting production and doing injury to the industrial worker. In foreign affairs, however, the government championed expansion purportedly to increase trade. Consequently, "the protest against this Weltpolitik is linked to the demand for a rational free-trade policy that protects the working class."

Following the at times heated debate during the sessions, delegates relaxed over meals and sampled the local libation at day's end. At lunch on Friday, 21 September, Eisner congratulated Rosa Luxemburg, a native Pole, on her masterful command of the German language and added that her delivery was the best of the congress. Writing that evening to her lover, Leo Jogiches, Luxemburg reported with obvious pride Eisner's compliment, "which from his mouth constitutes enormous praise."[5] In a cozy wine nook one evening Eisner imbibed more than was his custom, delighted in the antics of the house wit, and offered roses to a young barmaid to affix to her blouse. He justified his unusual thirst as duty, for the stores of old wine had to be drunk to make room for the new vintage, which promised to the the best in memory.[6] Despite the divergence of opinion on critical issues, Eisner must have considered the wine harvest a good omen for the first congress of the new century. Reflecting on its accomplishments, he hailed the decision to take part in Landtag elections and took heart at Bebel's appeal for solidarity in the new tactic: "The feud among us is at end. . . . Now there is but the one fight: against oppressive Prussian-Junker rule!"[7]

More problematic was the stance on colonialism, which the party was prepared to condemn in its particulars but not necessarily in concept. Although he sided with the reformists on the issue of electoral participation, Eisner vigorously contradicted Bernstein's arguments for an enlightened colonial policy as beneficial to both the German worker and the native of a preindustrial land. In the week before Liebknecht's death Eisner had begun for Joseph Bloch's *Sozialistische Monathefte* an exposé of German imperialism in theory and practice.[8] He took the title, "The Golden Mount Magnet," from the perilous cliff in a medieval tale, a "mountain of horror" that drew passing ships to their doom on the rocks. What set Social Democracy apart from the bourgeois parties, he wrote, was indeed, as Kautsky had asserted, its constant opposition to militarism. And Weltpolitik was the fatal fusion of militarism, chauvinism, racism, and regenerate laissez-faire capitalism. Stymied at home by the workers' movement, growing social consciousness among the populace as a whole, and protective tariffs from the agrarian right, unbridled capitalism found its outlet in colonial expansion. Europe's imperialist encroachments in Africa and China amply demonstrated that colonialism was nothing more than the conquest of raw materials and slave labor in the guise of Christianizing the heathen and exporting a "higher" culture, or as Marx described it, a reversion of the state "to its blatantly simple form of saber and cowl." Opposition to it stemmed from a moral, humane worldview once espoused by Germany's liberal bourgeoisie, who had since been co-opted by the state.

Before delving into the particular evils of Weltpolitik, Eisner grounded his argument in Kantian ethics and countered criticism anticipated from Marxist theorists, who would likely condemn a foreign policy guided by ethical rather than economic dictates as hopelessly idealistic and naive. "The humane worldview is in truth the genuine Realpolitik because it makes cultural necessity possible—the task of all human endeavor is not to make the necessary possible but to make necessary the possible. . . . Because, however, human morality, purposeful reason, and necessary development are identical concepts, the moral condemnation of this policy signifies at the same time a judgment of its possibility in general. The moral philosopher is no idle dreamer discounting real conditions; on the contrary he is the man with scientific knowledge of realities, he is the prophetic admonisher who knows that the path of the short-sighted 'realist' leads into the abyss. To measure all political events by the principle of a moral worldview is not playing and dreaming but rather molding the future that *must* be." Decidedly unrealistic, misguided, and amoral was the industrial nations' desperate race for colonies and more warships:

"a reeling toward catastrophe." Since 1870, Eisner cited, the European states had spent lavishly on "the cult of armed peace." The rationale now for German government requests to the Reichstag for funding new gunboats was always the necessity to protect German citizens plying trade abroad. Yet the ragtag Boxers had proven that the combined European powers, despite huge expenditures, had been unable to safeguard their citizens a mere 150 kilometers inland from the Chinese coast, less than half a day's remove by rail.

Foreign Minister Bülow's pipedream of Germany's place in the sun had become a nightmare. Far from securing trade, the armed forces sent to police the desired trading partners had wrecked it. The Christian missionaries, stalwart "pioneers of European culture" whose teachings the Chinese for the most part had indulged as yet another curious manifestation of intellectual speculation, were now surely regarded as insidious propagandists and spies, for their talk of loving one's neighbor heralded only brutal oppression. The photograph in a German journal of the execution of six Chinese by a German Army firing squad certainly attested to the cultural advance the Chinese enjoyed under European tutelage, Eisner commented sardonically, "for previously it was not customary there to photograph such scenes of higher civilization!" Remarkably, though, when the Boxers responded in kind to violence, Germany's bourgeois parties and press, whipped into a frenzy by Wilhelm himself, clamored for bloody revenge on the yellow devils.

During the "Khaki Summer of 1900" Wilhelm had been at his melodramatic worst, proclaiming a "mailed-fist" diplomacy and invoking first the terrible prowess of the Huns, then the sanctity of the Christian crusader in order to cow the Chinese insurgents. "We know that the kaiser views himself in all matters as the romantic lead in a heroic drama, who through his superior strength overcomes all resistance of the petty and paltry," yet in this particular episode the German Michel had assumed the role of Kasperl in a garish puppet farce. Wilhelm's fulminations had excited the "byzantine, speculative cretinism" of the bourgeois press, inducing, among other absurd proposals, the call for an army of criminals to be assembled from German prisons and dispatched to China to combat the Boxers. The real danger Eisner saw in the kaiser's posturing was that to his foreign policy there was not the same orchestrated opposition that checked the excesses at home. Moreover, as commander in chief, Wilhelm was free to issue any imperious order, as he indeed had done when he instructed the army to take no prisoners in their campaign against the resisters.[9] In stark contrast to Germany's behavior, the Russians and Americans, who stood to gain in China a vast market for their agricultural produce, had acted circumspectly, realizing that "one does not embitter people with whom one wants to do business."

Back at his desk at *Vorwärts* the last week of September 1900, Eisner reflected on events of the last fifty days. The tranquilizing monotony of the North Sea surf and the congenial ambience of Mainz's wine cellars faded into memory as the metropolis's manifold sights, sounds, and smells reasserted their claim on the senses. Through the window of the building's inner court at Beuthstraße 2 drifted the odors of machine oil and sweating horses, the screech of a parrot and strains of a piano waltz. As the setting sun cast an autumnal, Alpine glow on the gray walls of the court, the principal editor paused from composing a lead article on China to note for his Sunday column the opening of Berlin's newest department store, Tietz, which outshone Wertheim in scale, opulence, and architectural flourish. "I, however," he mused, "am thinking, far from Tietz and Wertheim and Jandorf and those yet to come, of the Frisian thatched cottage on Sylt's heath, storm windows shut tight, and dream of a beauty that scoffs at the passing fancies of the millennia."[10]

The staff and regular contributors over whom Eisner now presided included political editors Georg Gradnauer and Heinrich Ströbel, city editor Julius Kaliski, trade-union officials Robert Schmidt and Hugo Poetzsch, legal specialists Arthur Stadthagen and Paul Büttner, theater critic Conrad Schmidt, economist Heinrich Cunow, and Paul John, who like Philipp Scheidemann had begun as a compositor. As was the case with most Social Democratic offices, the central organ's personnel served the party in various capacities, for example, as members of the Reichstag, labor organizers, or indeed as editors of other journals. University educated, Gradnauer was credited with improving the standard of the *Sächsische Arbeiter-Zeitung* in Dresden before joining *Vorwärts* in 1897 and had been elected to the Reichstag the following year.[11] Ströbel had been recruited from Kiel's *Schleswig-Holsteinische Volks-Zeitung* (Schleswig-Holstein People's Newspaper) by the party executive to act as foil to Eisner. Kaliski was a longtime local functionary. Poetzsch headed the union of hotel, restaurant, and café workers. From 1893 to 1898 Robert Schmidt represented Berlin's fifth district in the Reichstag. The attorney Arthur Stadthagen served simultaneously as a Berlin city councilman and member of the Reichstag. Büttner had studied law at Heidelberg, Berlin, and Greifswald, passing the *Examen rigorosum* in May 1899. Brother of the artist Käthe Kollwitz, Dr. Conrad Schmidt was cofounder and chairman of the People's Free Stage. An editor for the *Vossische Zeitung* and the *Züricher Post*, he had also lectured at Zurich University. Cunow worked as an accountant but wrote extensively on ethnology, publishing in 1894 a study of the Australian aborigine. Since 1898 he had been on Kautsky's staff at *Neue Zeit*.[12]

When Caprivi's successor, Prince Chlodwig zu Hohenlohe-Schillingsfürst, stepped down in October 1900, he was succeeded as German chancellor and Prussian prime minister by Count Bernhard von Bülow, who had served as foreign secretary under Hohenlohe since June 1897. On 21 October Eisner predicted that Hohenlohe, the ineffectual "prophet of doom" who provided cartoonist Thomas Theodor Heine of the Munich journal *Simplicissimus* with ample material for his caricatures, would overshadow Bülow, whom history would recall only for his weak jokes that drove the Reichstag to distraction. In a series of vignettes deftly written in the prince's style of speech, which Eisner had learned to mimic from countless hours in the press gallery of the Reichstag and the Prussian House of Deputies, he imagined Hohenlohe's rambling conversations with himself in the days leading up to his resignation.[13] The octogenarian is depicted as a tenacious but enfeebled old gentleman who, although he had tired of the machinations of his would-be successors, struggled to keep his office and who was incredulous in the end upon reading in the newspaper of his own resignation.

A week later Joc addressed an open letter of feigned admiration to "Posa," Count Arthur von Posadowsky-Wehner, vice chancellor and interior secretary since summer 1897.[14] The *Leipziger Volkszeitung* had come into possession of a letter circulated by Henry Axel Bueck, general secretary of the Central Association of German Industrialists (Zentralverband deutscher Industrieller) and former member of the Prussian House of Deputies, to fellow industrialists when the prison bill was still being debated.[15] In his letter Bueck explained that Posadowsky had appealed to the association for help in financing the campaign for antistrike legislation. Specifically, the government had asked for 12,000 marks, which Bueck was attempting to raise. Following the letter's publication, the SPD's Reichstag delegation used the incident to embarrass the government. Chancellor Bülow was compelled to admit that it had been a serious mistake and should not happen again. An undersecretary was dismissed, but Posadowsky was hard put to reestablish credibility.

In Joc's opinion Posadowsky's request was simply refreshing Realpolitik. The secretary's only fault had been his complete candor, since everyone knew the government had never been impartial in its "public" service. Joc applauded this frank admission: "You have acknowledged in all honesty the government's relations with interested clients and have thrust upon them—with beautiful economy—the business expenses for legislation to order." Rather than apologize for his actions, Posadowsky would do well to formalize the policy by declaring three principles: that government is a business for producing bills, that bills guaranteed to be enacted into law are substantially more expensive, and that the costs of advertising and selling the product to the legislators must be borne by the client. Moreover, Joc advised, the government should require in advance 10 percent of the anticipated profits and another 10 percent once the bill becomes law. The Agrarian League (Bund der Landwirte), for example, was pushing for a grain tariff worth 2 million marks annually for the twelve-year life of the law—a tidy sum in proposed legislative fees.

On a Sunday afternoon in mid-fall Eisner hiked the paths of the Grunewald, the sprawling park between Berlin and Postdam, savoring the bright foliage of maple and beech and reminiscing of his youth, when one went out hiking no earlier than mid-May, no later than early September. How different it was now, twenty years later; in fall and winter alike pedestrians shared the ways with bicycles, carriages, and even the "racket-dragons that strive to conceal their monstrous nature behind the Romance word 'automobile.'" Despite the damp chill in the air, people sat outside over coffee at a popular forest tavern. Professional photographers had set up their cameras for anyone wishing to preserve the moment on film. Toward twilight Eisner walked past the old Fisher's Hut and paused, umbrella in hand, as night fell on the bank of the Schlachtensee to watch the fog rise from the water, then caught the train home to warm himself before the gas stove, content that there was no deadline to meet, as *Vorwärts* printed no Monday paper.[16]

Perturbed in early November by published, firsthand accounts of atrocities committed by German troops in China, Eisner compared their brutality to that recounted by the author Grimmelshausen from his experience as a soldier in the Thirty Years' War. He wondered if the German government and ruling class understood the ramifications of schooling the populace at home in respect for property, reverence for the crown and cloth, the right of national self-determination, and the inviolability of another's life only to sanction, indeed encourage abroad the pillage of palace and temple, the slaughter of defeated enemies. German soldiers had reportedly ripped silk from the emperor's throne in Peking and rifled the empress's dressing chamber, "signs of an anarchistic dissolution of all moral convention and all belief in authority, which would have to fill with dread those guardians of throne and altar, the preachers of subordination, the defenders of property, were they capable of thinking."[17] How prophetic his words seem in retrospect.

On Wednesday evening, 21 November 1900, Eisner attended at the Royal Opera a concert arranged by Count Hochberg, director of the

Court Theater, to celebrate the Lutheran Day of Repentance. The program was to comprise Brahms's *Requiem*, an aria from Handel's *Messiah*, and a scene from Wagner's *Parsifal*, but Berlin's chief of police unaccountably forbade the performance of Handel and Wagner. Could the text of the Handel aria—"every valley shall be exalted, and every mountain and hill made low"—Eisner wondered, be construed as an exhortation to revolution? Upon learning that the *Messiah* and *Parsifal* had been struck from the program, many patrons turned in their tickets and demanded a refund. Eisner had looked forward to hearing the *German Requiem*, "this most splendid modern work of sacred music." But under the circumstances he confessed that its mystical quality was lost on him, anxious as he was that the police might suddenly appear in the half-empty house to disperse the remaining audience.[18]

In the first Sunday column of December Eisner focused on the Prussian census that began on the first of the month.[19] Although the government intentionally limited itself to gathering only information of interest to the tax office and police, the potential impact of the statistics was immense. When, for example, Prussian government revenue figures first revealed that only 4 percent of the population earned what was deemed a minimal middle-class income, Lassalle had used the statistic to good advantage in his agitation. By knowing their number, the masses became aware of their strength. Christ, Eisner pointed out, had been born during a Roman census, a symbolism that transferred to the current circumstance: "In the dry statistic glows the spark of salvation. The people gain perspective through the tally and thereby summon courage to become savior to themselves." In addition to the usual queries as to the respondent's age, place of birth, occupation, confession, number of children and fruit trees, Eisner proposed a series of questions that would gauge the cultural and educational milieu of the general populace. Did one own the Bible, dime novels, a copy of Grimms' *Tales*? Books by Goethe, Shakespeare, Kant, Marx, Darwin, Ibsen, Zola? To which newspaper did one subscribe? Did one frequent the theater, music hall, public library? Was one a member of a political association? Then he continued in a lighter vein with sample questions that would provide a more complete picture of the general social and psychological disposition. Here Eisner invited the reader to complete the questionnaire and return it to the editors of *Vorwärts*, where, he hinted, the results might be published. "Do you have debts? Do you pay them? . . . Do you regret being married? . . . Do you beat your children? . . . Do you play the lottery? . . . Do you drink schnapps? How often, on average, are you sober? . . . Do you buy at Wertheim or Tietz?"

The article on Dostoevsky for *Sozialistische Monatshefte*, originally slated for publication in September but delayed by Liebknecht's death, appeared in January.[20] Its theme is the tormented psyche of Raskolnikov, protagonist of *Crime and Punishment*, but Eisner's intent was to show that Dostoevsky's successor, Tolstoy, in his novel *Resurrection* (1899) engaged in the same flight from reality as his precursor, turning to neo-Pietism as a refuge from Russia's woes. Raskolnikov is the impoverished student who, anticipating Nietzsche's superman, rationalizes the murder of a horrid crone for her money—an act calculated to propel him to an imagined great destiny. Instead Raskolnikov is consumed with guilt, confesses his crime, and does penance in Siberian detention. Eisner recalled from his university years how Raskolnikov's desperate deed struck a chord in German bourgeois writers of his own generation, dispossessed by, and disenchanted with Bismarck's state: "Revolutionary ideas, vague and amorphous, ruled them; they cultivated the great passions, which are in reality just petty diversions, they yearned for violent lawlessness that smashes all values, awaited, rapt, the dawn of a thousand-year Reich, which, however, they did not *work* for, felt in the deepest depths that they were only rattling their chains, that they were purposeless and superfluous, apart from the sober, active world."

Raskolnikov's tale was indeed "a dangerous book" for romantic youth fascinated by the irrational and intuitive. The mature mind in due course typically rejects melancholy brooding in favor of "pure, productive, creative thought and deed," yet Dostoevsky's development had been stunted by the seeming hopelessness of Russian autocracy. The revolutionary ideals of his youth, for which he himself was made to atone in Siberia, withered, and by the time he wrote *Crime and Punishment*, communism was for him merely an intellectual abstraction, its chief advocate in the novel preoccupied with free love. And now Tolstoy too in his old age had embraced "Nazarenity," preferring asylum from the world to meaningful, concerted action that would change it.

In late January Eisner attended a masked ball at the Metropol Theater in order "to see how wealthy Berlin is entertained in carnival fashion." The 1-mark fee to check overcoat and hat, he confessed, imbued him with delusions of grandeur, as if he were accustomed to high-stakes gaming tables, the racetrack, and the patrons' boxes at the ballet. Eschewing Heidsieck champagne for the least expensive but still outrageously dear Rüdesheimer, he settled into a corner to observe the revelers. Wigged and rouged attendants lined the dance floor, where daring women in risqué costumes swirled to waltzes while paper streamers rained down from the loges. Girls vending white carnations, pralines, and cigarettes circulated among gentlemen in top hats and tails. As the evening progressed the air became charged with sensuality. Amid the opulence Eisner considered his own evening dress, a fifty-year-old tailcoat worn by three generations of Eisners. He had sat exams in it, was wed in it, and sentenced to prison in it. Toward dawn he determined that it had seen enough service for this particular outing. Outside on the street he encountered a living symbol of the disparity of life in the city. A shivering woman stopped him in his finery, looked him in the eye, and begged for a cup of coffee.[21]

In February Franz Mehring submitted to *Vorwärts* an article critical of his former ally Maximilian Harden, the influential and incendiary editor of *Die Zukunft*. One of Wilhelm's most persistent gadflies, Harden had been jailed in 1899 for lèse majesté and had just been convicted once again. Mehring believed that the court accorded Harden preferential treatment because he had highly placed friends and was no socialist. Although Eisner found Harden as little to his personal liking as did Mehring, he sympathized with anyone facing a six-month sentence and rejected Mehring's piece. When Mehring complained that his dealings with *Vorwärts* had become unbearably aggravating, Eisner wrote on 14 February a conciliatory letter explaining his editorial rationale and assuring Mehring of the staff's and his own highest regard: "With no one do we wish even the slightest difference so little as with you, to whom a sincere and lasting admiration has ever bound us and for whose collaboration we are grateful not just for practical reasons but for very personal ones as well."[22] On 7 March Mehring replied via postcard from his Steglitz residence. He apologized for not having responded sooner to the letter, "the friendly intention of which I most greatly appreciate" and appended a request that accentuated their philosophical differences: "Since you are a Kantian, could you tell me perhaps . . . where Kant calls Epicurus's theory of the declination of atoms 'outrageous?' I cannot locate the passage in the three *Critiques*."[23]

The death on 9 March 1901 of Saar industrialist Karl Ferdinand Freiherr von Stumm-Halberg marked in some respects the passing of an era. Perhaps Germany's most virulent opponent of organized labor, the iron and steel magnate was known as the "King of the Saar." Workers in his factories were regimented to the point that he personally dictated whether they might marry and which newspapers they were and were not to read.[24] The next day Eisner ran an editorial obituary as lead article in the Sunday edition of *Vorwärts* in which the deceased was hailed as "one of Social Democracy's most effective agitators," whose reactionary fanaticism and "pathological temperament" served to strengthen the party immeasurably. The disturbed millionaire, who personally lobbied

Wilhelm II tirelessly for a new antisocialist law, was at once a symbol and caricature of capitalism, "a possessed man of property," who in the Catholic South transferred the concept of papal infallibility to industrial management. As Baron von Stumm left no male heir, there was speculation that his conglomerate empire would be merged with that of Krupp, his counterpart in the Ruhr.

The ruling class's appropriation and perversion of Christianity was the theme of lead articles on Easter and Pentecost.[25] In the first, titled "Resurrection," Eisner wrote of the rains that had ushered spring into field and forest at Berlin's edge. The rebirth of nature, celebrated by the pagan Germanic tribes as deliverance from dark winter, had been coopted by early Christians celebrating Christ's resurrection. Over nineteen centuries Christianity itself had mutated beyond recognition. The early, pure tenets of renunciation of power and wealth were now cynically exploited by church and state to perpetuate their own power and wealth. And now "faith in man himself," socialism with its attendant precepts science and reason, drew the oppressed: "The need in our day is not the need in the declining Roman Empire, when hopelessness engendered belief in miracles and hope of salvation. The peoples of the present make difficult demands on themselves for deliverance from the base and wicked." Continuing with the messianic typology seven Sundays later, Eisner proclaimed that just as Christ's disciples were filled by the Holy Spirit with zeal to preach their new message of salvation, so too were the apostles of the new secular faith. "Our celebration is not for the blind workings of passionate forces and not for the celestial immaterialism of an imagined hereafter. . . . We exult in the force of the spirit, that immortal force that leads mankind through pain and suffering up from barbarism to civilization, from bondage to freedom." As a priest of the new creed, Eisner clearly believed that its animus was more than the recognition of historical materialism; the Kantian ethical component figured as an equally important article of faith: "Misery and suffering are not eternal institutions ordained by a god; they are the product of brutal state and social conditions that man effects, that man can eliminate, that it is man's duty to eliminate." Consideration of the demands of that duty would soon propel him toward confrontation with the party's left wing.

On the last Sunday in June appeared one of Joc's most celebrated and syndicated columns, a piece that would be rerun each June in the party press across Germany for years to come.[26] Cast in skillfully rendered Berlin dialect, "The Bench" is both paean and malediction, lauding the humble park bench and decrying its removal by overzealous guardians of public decency. In German culture two trees above all are endowed with meaning: the oak in its strength and steadfastness and the lime, or linden, symbol of love. In the last days of spring while the limes were in full bloom, Eisner reflected on young love in the city, for to urban youth the park bench beneath moonlit lime branches was as were hedgerow, hayrick, glade, and dune to their provincial peers. Here lovers inhabited a world of their own surrounded by tumult and chaos. "Trolley wires snap constantly, people are run over, loud drunks attract crowds of onlookers, policemen rush about, hackney horses collapse, the loveless and dull trundle past endlessly. There on the bench in the shade of dense foliage light cotton nestles against dark, manly raiment, there's chatting and teasing and giggling and kissing and yearning, lost in itself, as if miles away from mankind's mundane pursuits."

On a recent Sunday outing to Schildow, a suburb to the north of Berlin where he liked to stroll through peaceful, "utopian" neighborhoods of neat cottages amid well-tended gardens, Eisner noted that the splendid municipal parks seemed almost superfluous. In the past he had always relaxed on one of the many benches occupied by mothers with their children, by workers at their leisure, and in the evenings by soldiers and their girls. This Sunday, though, there was no bench to be found. A low iron railing bordering the grassy lawns afforded the only seating. Chancing upon the nightwatchman at the railway station pub, Eisner learned that upon complaints from two local worthies about unseemly public displays of affection, the town council had ordered all park benches hauled away to Berlin. It was simply a question, explained the nightwatchman, of preserving "communal morality." Back in Berlin late the same evening, Eisner rested on a bench at Dönhoff Square and speculated that soon the magnificent lime trees of Schildow would surely be felled.

The conundrum of to what extent a revolutionary party fundamentally opposed to the "monarchical-absolutist" German state could engage in electoral politics to promote short-term benefits for its constituency became even stickier in 1899 when Alexandre Millerand, parliamentary leader of the French Left, accepted the post of commerce secretary in the bourgeois government of Pierre Waldeck-Rousseau. Although Secretary Millerand brought about sweeping reforms, he was castigated as a traitor by many of his former comrades, and the controversy over his ministry split the French socialists. In an article for the mid-July 1901 issue of *Neue Zeit* Eisner questioned the logical consistency of affirming the work of the SPD's Reichstag delegation while opposing in theory the acceptance of a cabinet appointment that could advance the party's immediate and future goals.[27]

Over the years Social Democratic deputies in legislative bodies had moved from the "political Malthusianism" of abstaining even from debate on proposed legislation to putting forward motions of their own. The decision to field candidates for the Prussian Landtag effectively ended the last boycott of a diet. Given the party's steady growth and increasing representation at state and national levels, a parliamentary presidency loomed as a distinct possibility. Filling it would signify nothing more than laying claim to the proletariat's due, hardly an endorsement of the state so long as party deputies continued to reject budget proposals, an act that maintained the "sharp line of demarcation between socialism and the capitalist world."

> All the tactical discussions about participation of Social Democrats in bourgeois politics and administration, all the bitter strife, the bad division and rifts that have led to a lamentable fragmentation of socialist power, arise in the final analysis from insufficiently clear insight into the *dualistic* character of the Social Democratic program and the consequent dualistic tactic. . . . Our principal future program, which contains the actual requisites of socialism, can be realized only through the complete eradication of capitalist society—of that we are convinced—and this eradication can result only from the conquest of total political power by the party of the organized proletariat. . . . On the other hand there are a great number of demands for reform that we accept the bourgeois class state is quite capable of satisfying. . . . Therefore we ourselves, as disagreeable as it may be to us, must descend into the workings of the bourgeois parties. We must take part in all elections, we must politic, follow the maxim of choosing the lesser evil and the greater good, even support bourgeois opponents in runoff elections.

In order to act consistently and ethically, a Social Democrat in a cabinet post would have to continue to speak for socialism's ultimate goal but confine his actual work to the immediate needs of the worker. To critics who charged that a Social Democratic cabinet secretary would share responsibility for all policies of the government in which he served, Eisner answered that his responsibility would be indirect and formal rather than material; the party member, however, who declined a portfolio and allowed a bourgeois secretary to continue in office shouldered both formal and actual responsibility by default. As a case in point Eisner cited the Italian socialists, who having condemned Millerand now actively supported a liberal bourgeois government committed to social reform—a course of action less scrupulous than Millerand's.

Eisner reminded his audience that "only a fraction of the 96 percent of the population" that formed the proletariat were adherents of Social Democracy. Of those who had not embraced socialism many had succumbed to the constant campaign of libel by officials of church and state. If, however, a Social Democrat were to serve in a government, propaganda labeling the party a purely negative force would lose credibility. To be sure, a socialist minister in a bourgeois government was no end itself, merely a means, a precondition to, and preparation for the final appropriation of the machinery of state. Ladislaus Gumplowicz, writing for *Sozialistische Monatshefte*, hailed the "consequent decisiveness" of Eisner's "supremely significant article," which displayed "the customary traits of Eisnerian style: perspicuity, broad-mindedness, and vibrancy."[28] Victor Adler, on the other hand, cautioned readers of *Neue Zeit* not to be beguiled by Eisner's "equally brilliant and, in my humble opinion, errant article."[29]

On 14 July 1901 Eisner signed a contract with publisher John Edelheim for *Taggeist: Culturglossen* (Spirit of the Day: Culture Commentaries), an anthology of essays from 1889 to 1900, most of which had appeared in *Die Kritik* during his stint in Marburg.[30] In his introduction to the volume Eisner described its contents as "impressions from the first decade of the New Course," in reference to Wilhelm II's reign. None of the questions dealt with in the essays was yet resolved, he claimed, and none was of less interest than it had been then. He chose Goethe for the epigraph:

> Who in world history resides
> should by the moment himself define?
> Who into ages peers and strides
> is uniquely worthy to give voice and sign.

The terms of the contract specified an honorarium of 600 marks for the work, half to be paid upon delivery of the manuscript, half upon publication. Dr. Edelheim's press printed cheap, paperbound editions of works by party leaders, theorists, and publicists. Ernst Gystrow reviewed Eisner's book in the September issue of *Sozialistische Monatshefte*. Viewed chronologically, he wrote, the essays documented the author's transformation from a "social-reformist Democrat, ultraliberal socially, . . . skeptical of Marxism and its consequences" to Social Democrat. Gystrow praised Eisner's unique style but faulted him for an early tendency to imitate the abstruseness of Maximilian Harden and for abandoning historicism for dogma in the later writings. Despite these flaws, Gystrow numbered

Taggeist among the good books that elicit reflection and recommended it to "thinking readers."[31]

In the weeks leading up to the 1901 party congress at Lübeck, Eisner anticipated a less contentious gathering than at Hanover or Mainz. On Sunday, 22 September, the day the delegates convened, he dedicated a lengthy lead article to the agenda, which included discussion of the role, organization, and administration of the party press and book distributorship, factiousness within the trade unions, and the current housing shortage and rent gouging.[32] The housing crisis, in particular, afforded the party an arena for significant "practical work and immediate reforms." He called special attention to the tenth anniversary of the Erfurt Program, which had established Social Democracy's Marxist fundament and the dual tactic of working for democratic and economic reform in preparation for the eventual transformation of the means of production into social ownership. The wrangling of the last two congresses had been "necessary" to reiterate those principles. The deliberations at Lübeck, he assured, would yield nothing unexpected but rather confirm the tried and true: "Even if peripheral opinions may diverge, in its heart and soul the party is clear about itself and with crystal-clear vision of mission and goal, ways and means is working constantly to expand its sphere of influence." Hindsight reveals that the pep talk was giddily optimistic.

As usual, *Vorwärts* printed verbatim each day's proceedings. When the congress adjourned on Saturday afternoon, 28 September, Eisner summarized for the Sunday edition its accomplishments.[33] The Bernstein debate had recurred, igniting "overly great passion" and ending with another resolution, similar to that at Hanover, condemning accommodation of the ruling state and bourgeois parties. Also noteworthy were Dr. Albert Südekum's detailed report on the housing crisis and Bebel's protest against the new agricultural tariffs. The party executive's various annual reports lasted until Friday, leaving little time for "other important questions." What took Eisner completely by surprise was a charge leveled by Bebel in the context of both the Bernstein debate and the obligations of the party press that *Vorwärts* had been remiss in its duty by sending no reporter to a lecture by Bernstein in Berlin. The talk in question was titled "How Is Scientific Socialism Possible?" and had been given in May, shortly after Bernstein's return from exile, for the Social Sciences Society (Sozialwissenschaftlicher Verein), a student club. In addition to some of Bernstein's key supporters in the party, several leading figures of the bourgeois Left were present, including Theodor Barth, Friedrich Naumann, and Hellmut von Gerlach. Neither Eisner nor Gradnauer believed that Bernstein would break any new ground in a talk for students, but when they learned that Heinrich Ströbel planned to attend asked him to file a report. In addition, the editor in charge of public meetings assigned a reporter to cover the event.[34]

By all accounts Bernstein's two-and-a-half hour address was a disappointment. Lily Braun, an ardent reformist, observed that he lacked presence on the podium, spoke in disjointed snatches of sentences, and lost his audience on a sally into the abstruse: "At times it seemed as though the talk were nothing more than the verbalized brooding of a man over problems that still tormented him."[35] The distinguished economist Adolph Wagner readily admitted that he could not follow it.[36] Ströbel made detailed notes but determined that what he had heard had been "not just purely academic but in many respects purely pedantic." Asked to proof what the reporter had written, he deemed it sketchy and misleading. Consequently, *Vorwärts* ran no story. In response to Bebel's accusation Ströbel presented his account of events, and *Vorwärts* printed a statement signed by Eisner and Ströbel in its 22 September edition, while the party congress was still in session: "How Comrade Bebel could come to think, contrary to our declaration, that we informed him during his chance presence in the editorial offices that no reporter had been present at the gathering is completely inexplicable to us. We could not possibly have told him anything of the kind then, a few days after Bernstein's address, when all details remained fresh in memory." The spat with Bebel was but a prelude to graver differences.

In the last days of mild autumn weather when chrysanthemum, aster, and dahlia filled Berlin with a final spray of color, Eisner ventured out to wander the palace grounds of Sanssouci in Potsdam. "The one good thing about the monarchy—I ask that no one demand my expulsion from the party—is that it once created these parks. . . . If I were not at *Vorwärts*, I might well like to be a court gardener."[37] But Bebel's tiff with the paper had subsided for the moment. In preparation for the Austrian Social Democratic Party congress in Vienna the first week of November, he wrote on 23 October to Victor Adler that he, Kautsky, and fellow German delegate Franz Ehrhart would likely be joined by Eisner, if Eisner were not arrested for his refusal to testify in the trial of *Vorwärts* editors Robert Schmidt and Paul John for impugning Germany's war in China. If Eisner were to be able to travel to Vienna, Bebel wanted the German representatives booked into the same hotel.[38]

Just before the conference in Vienna was to convene, Eisner received from editor Joseph Bloch a circular mailed to party officials. Attached was a copy of an angry letter by Bloch to Bebel, charging the party chairman with favoritism. Referring to an article on the Lübeck congress that Bebel had authored for *Neue Zeit*, Bloch protested Bebel's "rebuking a number of party comrades for preferring to write for *Sozialistische Monatshefte* rather than *Neue Zeit.*" Bloch further questioned why his journal was not included on the list of "official" party organs when it regularly brought the party's leading voices to print.[39] Bloch's charge sheds light on Bebel's nervousness about the lack of a report on Bernstein's rambling at the university, word of which had surely filtered to the chairman. The row over revisionism would not subside, and Bebel clearly felt threatened. He had always been able to count on Wilhelm Liebknecht's support; since Liebknecht's death Bebel was struggling for control of the press. Anything that served to discredit the reformists was welcome news; the absence of it he perceived as both affront and challenge.

In the midst of the squabble came news from Leipzig that another stalwart of the party press was dead. On Wednesday, 30 October, Dr. Bruno Schoenlank, chief editor of the *Leipziger Volkszeitung* and Reichstag deputy, succumbed at forty-two to a degenerative nervous disorder. His obituary in *Vorwärts* the next day lamented the loss of "one of the most gifted and skillful from our ranks." In terms of education, scholarly ambition, and career, he and Eisner had similar experiences. Schoenlank had pursued a doctorate at Halle, worked on the staffs of the *Fränkische Tagespost* (Franconian Daily Post) and *Vorwärts*, spent nine months in jail, and written an acclaimed history of class conflict in medieval Nuremberg. His early demise, coming a little over a year after Liebknecht's, and the approaching Memorial Day celebrated by German Lutherans gave Eisner pause to consider different perspectives of death throughout history and pen a secular Sunday sermon.[40] Surveying the Greek, Hebrew, and Christian traditions, he concluded that no prospect was more terrible than endless life, for all human happiness is conditioned by fatality. "Because and *only* because death is our destiny does life attain its power and greatness, its glory and splendor. It is death that urges us to joy, to productive work, to a rational social order, to art, and to every cultural achievement. . . . If there were no dying, there would be nothing immortal in man." As we cannot choose when we die, he reasoned, we must make the most of the time allotted to us.

Eisner was not detained by the police in their investigation of the case against editors Schmidt and John. He left Berlin early enough to stop over in Prague. "Whenever I travel alone, wander quietly for myself," he wrote of this excursion, "the world begins to live anew for me." Late in the evening he boarded the train at Anhalter Station. He shared a compartment with an Austrian officer in mufti whose tender farewell from a beautiful young woman piqued Eisner's interest, but no opportunity for conversation arose. A nightowl who later in life graduated to chronic insomnia, Eisner rarely slept on trains. While the locomotive coursed through the night and the officer dozed furled in his blanket, Eisner peered into the dark and listened intently to the rhythmic din of the rails and the howl of passing trains. Arriving in Prague at dreary daybreak, he settled into a dim café and watched shopgirls outside on their way to work primp in the mirror of his window. A loquacious waiter ruefully apprised him which of them were whores.

Never having learned Czech in school, Eisner plied the streets with guidebook in hand. "In the last two decades," he observed, "the city has become completely Czech. A striving and ascendant nation exercises here its seigneurial right. . . . There are fewer German shop signs now in Prague than there are Russian ones in Berlin." Despite the city's wonderfully unique architecture, he found Prague's residents by and large indistinguishable from those of other industrial cities. For several hours he meandered through the old town's twisting streets, remarking that here too the web of power lines for the municipal trolley signaled ineluctable modernity. A foray into the old Ghetto still afforded a view of a way of life that was vanishing across Europe. "Just as they did centuries ago, the poor sons and daughters of Israel are sitting and standing before the black, ill-smelling vaults of secondhand shops, reminiscent of the age of boundless misery. Faces there have nothing of the charm and beauty of youth. The spirit of the sad wares they deal has penetrated their faces. They are musty old clothes in dark dungeons, 'worn items' that become human by chance. Yet I kneel shuddering before your ugliness, martyrs of the centuries!" In the Jewish cemetery Eisner walked among the tangle of gravestones and elder bushes, accompanied by an unwanted guide-for-hire reciting the names and histories of worthies from the Ghetto and passing silently by the nameless poor.[41]

In addition to filing reports for the German party press on the Austrian congress, Eisner made new acquaintances, explored Vienna's fabled cafés, and recorded his impressions of the city and its inhabitants for his Sunday column. Kautsky, who was Austrian by birth and had studied in Vienna, took some offense at the *Plauderei* of 10 November. Himself the author of voluminous petrifying theoretical tracts, he enclosed the column in a letter to his wife the next day and pronounced it "very weak, superficial, and unimaginative." Eisner's perceptions, he judged, were all too colored by life in Berlin. "I had to laugh at his indignation that the coffee houses are 'already' closing at two. What business does a sensible man have in the coffee house after two in the morning? For the rest he says much that is true, but very dully. Now Heine wrote travel impressions of a different sort! Dear Eisner gets solemn and trite when he should be amusing. The article shows me that Eisner is no independent thinker and observer; all his wit lies in his style."[42]

As 1901 drew to a close, Robert Schmidt and Paul John were convicted of undermining Germany's war effort in China. Schmidt was sentenced to six months' imprisonment—twice what the prosecutor sought—for his report on the execution, ordered by Major General von Kettler, of twenty-two Boxers implicated in the murder of Chinese Christians. The only inaccuracy in Schmidt's account with which the prosecution found fault was that the executed had been accused by two Christian Chinese witnesses rather than only one. As the editor responsible for publication of the *Hunnenbriefe* (Hun Letters) series—actual soldiers' accounts of the campaign, including graphic reports of rape and pillage—Paul John received a seven-month sentence, three more than the prosecutor called for. At no time in the trial did the prosecution dispute either the authenticity or accuracy of the letters. Ironically, the German War Ministry charged that the letters' publication, not the events they related, constituted the crime.

In the lead article of 3 December, titled "The Impossibility of Truth," Eisner termed the sentences drawn by Schmidt and John sheer "draconianism" that had to cause the public to wonder at the vagaries of German justice. A host of newspapers across Germany, he argued, had printed similar correspondence, yet Social Democratic editors had been singled out by the War Ministry for criminal prosecution. In Stuttgart and Frankfurt am Main bourgeois journalists charged with writing critically of the war against the Boxers had received fines or at worst a few weeks' jail time, although in the case of the Stuttgart Left Liberal paper the criticism had been far more virulent than anything in the party press. "The more severe the punishment that befalls our comrades, the more shameful the verdict on the politics of the Chinese campaign and the greater our moral victory."[43]

At Christmas Eisner revisited the trial of his editors in a bitter homily, "Unholy Night."[44] Returning to his fateful analogy of 1898, he branded Germany the new Rome, an "empire of violence and human oppression" bent on the conquest and exploitation of weaker peoples. The state's pretense to Christianity was merely a veneer of propaganda meant to disguise the design of domination "that steals other peoples' land and compels them by Hunnish force to endure injustice, that consigns to prison those who refuse to call the Antichrist Christ." In the quiet of hearth and home faithful readers were admonished to gather strength of resolve. On the twenty-sixth, the second Christmas holiday in Germany, traditionally spent with friends, the Eisners hosted Karl and Luise Kautsky, Rosa Luxemburg, art critic Eduard Fuchs and his wife, recently moved from Munich to Berlin. Luxemburg wrote on the twenty-ninth to Leo Jogiches that on this, her first visit to the Eisner household she was received "exceptionally cordially" and had enjoyed a pleasant stay.[45] Also on the twenty-ninth Paul Natorp wrote from Marburg to Eisner, thanking him for a family photo Eisner had sent and giving news of Cohen, Tönnies, and Karl Vorländer.[46]

Vorwärts began the new year with a review of 1901. The lead article on 1 January examined domestic events of note, followed on the third by reflections on foreign affairs.[47] At home legislation had been dominated by the intrigues of the Agrarian League to secure a state-subsidized price for their grain and increased tariffs on imported produce while at the same time thwarting canal construction. Despite impressive gains in national and, particularly, municipal elections, the party learned the hard lesson that in runoff elections the Left Liberals could not be counted on to support Social Democrats over candidates from the bourgeois Right when the race hinged on agricultural issues. In the past year former chancellors Bismarck and Hohenlohe had been laid to rest, yet scandals in the officer corps served as a reminder that the spirit of Prussian militarism and reaction was alive and well. The costs of expanding the German fleet, which Baron von Thielmann, minister of finance, had assured the public would be covered by the projected growth of the economy, had sent him begging to New York for credit.

On the world stage Russia alone of the foreign adventurers in China derived significant benefit: "Its power is immensely enhanced, its territory secured all the way to the Yellow Sea, Manchuria almost fully in its sphere of interests." England's prestige had suffered from the protracted war against the Boers—a war that ground down the crown's crack troops and tarnished the luster of their vaunted commanders. Stymied in South Africa, the English had been compelled to watch nervously as St. Petersburg prepared to intervene in the succession to the Afghan throne. And in the New World, where Washington's protectorate stretched now from Baffin Island to Patagonia, London reluctantly agreed to concessions levied by the Americans for the construction of the Panama Canal. If 1901 augured the shape of things to come, then Russia soon would be the dominant power in Asia, the United States in the entire Western Hemisphere, and both would enjoy greater influence in Europe. Indeed, the Americans' "colossal economic might" was already evident in the huge exports of grain, meat, tobacco, coal, iron, and finished goods that flowed across the Atlantic.

Eisner concluded his first lead article of 1902 with a grim assessment of what the economic downturn of 1901 would mean for his readership: "Hard fights lie ahead." A fight Eisner personally relished was that against child labor, an issue that afforded *Vorwärts* an opportunity to attack the Junker landowners and industrial management simultaneously. By the most recent census, 544,283 children younger than fourteen were employed outside factories, in which government regulations prohibited them from working. The number was actually far greater, since there was no means of accurately counting those employed in cottage industry and in the fields. Cottage industry was the way by which manufacturers were able to cut costs and skirt compliance with protection laws. Whole industries relied almost exclusively on the piecework of children assembling toys, brushes, even cigars at home for a fraction of what adult workers would be paid in the factories, thus driving working-class families further into poverty. A teachers' organization in the Ruhr noted that as a result of the lagging economy and the surge in unemployment, "we see in our classrooms in greater number than before sickly, insufficiently nourished, or inadequately clothed children of poor parents." Similarly, teachers in the rural East reported that after the turnip harvest, when school was canceled altogether that children might assist, pupils suffered from chronic back pain and other work-related ailments. Interior Minister Posadowsky had proposed a bill that would allow children twelve or older to work a four-hour day in the factories and exempted cottage industry and agriculture from any regulation whatsoever. The bourgeois parties, by nature of their constituencies, Eisner wrote, were incapable of demanding the only remedy to the abuse: a complete ban on child labor, coupled with the improvement of conditions for all workers.[48]

On Sunday, 19 January, Rosa Luxemburg served a sumptuous dinner at her flat in Berlin-Friedenau for the Eisners, Kautskys, and Arthur Stadthagen. After courses of caviar, salmon and eggs, borscht with dumplings, pickled fish, roast sirloin and vegetables, compote, pudding, cheese and radishes, black coffee and cognac, the guests called in jest for champagne and were amazed when the hostess returned from the kitchen with a bottle she had held in reserve. Lingering long past midnight, they wrote a card to Paul Singer, who had been invited but had a speaking engagement. The next day Luxemburg wrote to Jogiches that Lisbeth Eisner had presented her a "charming" tinted family photo in a golden frame, displayed now on her end table.[49]

Monday evening, 27 January, Eisner and Lisbeth attended with other members of the *Vorwärts* staff and their spouses a feminist meeting in the Reichshalle on Leipzigerstraße at which the poet Clara Müller recited from her works. The next Sunday Luxemburg planned to bring Clara Zetkin on an afternoon visit to the Eisners, hoping to "draw Eisner thus a little into our circle." Luise Kautsky proposed that she and her husband might join them. Luxemburg was then hard put, she confided to Jogiches, to dissuade them tactfully, as "Eisner, who can abide her even less than him, would look vexed" and the visit's purpose would be defeated.[50] Luxemburg's hope was thwarted in any case, to her incredulity, when Zetkin, still in a snit over something Eisner had written about her at the Hanover party congress a year and a half earlier, declined to accompany her.[51]

"You promised me in October to write in due time an essay on *Ibsen*," Joseph Bloch wrote plaintively to Eisner on 3 February. "Ibsen has his seventy-fourth birthday on 20 March. I would very much like to publish the essay in the *March edition*. The editorial deadline for it falls on *10 Febr*. Can you write the essay by that time? I really need not add that you would make me most happy by doing so."[52] The piece on Ibsen would have to wait, as Eisner was absorbed at the time in other literary projects. Published as the work of Hans Wandrer, his review of a judge's revealing book on the practice and punishment of beggary in Russia appeared 9 February in the literary supplement of *Vorwärts*.[53] Drawing on his experience as a justice in Charkoff, August Löwenstimm classed beggars in seven categories, ranging from the run-of-the-mill hunchbacks and cripples to the sophisticated con artists. His concern was less for the causes of vagrancy than for adequate legislation to combat it by sending the old and truly infirm to asylums, the layabouts and sots to the workhouse, for poverty in Russia was so universal that begging had become a standard vocation. What His Honor failed to apprehend, Eisner emphasized, was that beggary in Russia was rooted in the appalling economic and social conditions.

In a series of articles in mid-March Eisner commemorated the Revolution of 1848, when the liberal bourgeoisie of the Continental capitals pressed for increased democratization and free trade. For the edition of Tuesday, 18 March, anniversary of the day two hundred workers died on the barricades in Berlin after General von Prittwitz's troops scattered a crowd, Eisner recounted the causes and course of the rising and the role of the proletariat.[54] Urban workers, who across Europe suffered from food shortages, poor housing, intolerable working conditions, and low wages, rushed to close ranks with the liberals against the tottering absolute monarchies, only to be rebuffed and reviled by their intended comrades in arms. When a meeting attended by workers in Berlin resolved that the Prussian king should create a labor ministry and that the people be protected from capitalist avarice, the leading liberal newspaper demanded that the military prevent such assemblies of rabble. Within a year the government and army had reestablished their firm control and reaction once again held sway. "Through its scandalous ineptitude and narrow-minded fear of the proletariat, the German bourgeoisie had forfeited the victory. Upon liberation from the feudal burden that had caused them to take an active interest in the revolution in its beginnings, the peasants sank back into their apathy." Without a coherent ideology, specific demands, or effective organization, the workers were doomed to fail, yet March 1848 was a station on their way to class consciousness.

The morning of the eighteenth, Eisner took part in a wreath-laying ceremony at Friedrichshain Cemetery, where the martyrs of 1848 were interred. Representatives of diverse organizations of the Left—the Social Democratic Women of Berlin, party precinct workers, metalworkers' and masons' locals, the People's Free Stage, a bevy of anarchist and Left Liberal associations—moved in a cordon in driving rain toward the entrance. Disgruntled policemen in spiked helmets lined the route. A lieutenant inspected the wreaths and their ribbons, exercising his duty as censor by tearing off any inscriptions expressing inflammatory sentiments. The wreath from *Vorwärts*, among the desecrated, bore a red ribbon with lines from a poem by Adolf Strodtmann celebrating revolution's immortality. Once the ribbons had been mutilated, the bearers were allowed to lay their wreaths and then ordered to disperse.

Outraged by the indignity, Eisner reported the incident in the Wednesday edition and then returned to the theme on Sunday.[55] "The entire development of the second half of the previous century," Joc declared in his *Plauderei* of 23 March, "is reflected in this police guard over the March dead." The hypervigilant lieutenant embodied the absurd imperiousness of desperate absolutism. The confiscation of ribbons was a sacrilege against human spirit that strives for an ideal. Joc wondered what fate would befall one who ripped ribbons from wreaths laid at the mausoleum of Friedrich Wilhelm IV, a mere king, who in no way merited the veneration accorded martyrs.

In late March Eisner asked Rosa Luxemburg to review the second volume in Franz Mehring's edition of Marx and Engels's literary remains. She responded on the twenty-seventh, having just returned to Berlin from a week in Leipzig, that her commitments to the *Leipziger Volkszeitung* would prevent her from reading the book over Easter but she would gladly furnish the review if he could but be patient. After the holiday she hoped to pay a call in Lichterfelde, and closed with regards "in the meantime to you and your joviality."[56]

The Berlin Choral Academy's annual performance on Good Friday of Bach's *St. Matthew Passion* induced Eisner once again to muse on theological typology.[57] How superficial was the faith of the bourgeoisie who ignored the sublime expression of Protestantism's towering artist in order to peer through their opera glasses up to the court loge. "Interest in the living grandeur of secular majesty far outweighs devotion to the tragic suffering of the Jewish proletariat's martyr, so profoundly unworldly to this society." And why would it be otherwise for the genteel? Christ, after all, had been judged by his betters as a traitor and rabble-rouser. The workers, on the other hand, who subscribed to the new faith were possessed of a "finer sensibility for the content of the 'Christian' holidays," for it was they who were bearing their own cross toward rebirth and salvation. One who had gone on before was to be honored Easter morning, Eisner summoned the faithful, when the monument to Wilhelm Liebknecht would be unveiled at Friedrichshain.

On the calendar of German socialism's high holy days, May Day came to be preeminent by the 1890s. Workers and their families celebrated the international Labor Day with gala processions to all-day, outdoor festivals where they ate and drank, cheered speeches of local activists, and were entertained by skits, chorales, athletic contests, and fireworks while police and informers circulated to intimidate participants.[58] On 20 April Eisner reported that Berlin's Union of Employers' Associations (Bund der Arbeitgeber-Verbände) had announced that its members would dismiss employees who did not report to work on 1 May and that no other member would rehire them for two weeks.[59] In light of this threat, the past winter's unemployment, and Germany's foray into China, *Vorwärts* proclaimed in its lead article on May Day that this year's observances should serve to demonstrate proletarian solidarity, reassert the demand for an eight-hour day, and protest imperialism.[60] In addition to relieving unemployment, the shortened workday would render the worker's time at work more productive and meaningful, and allow time in the evenings for intellectual and cultural pursuits that mold the "whole man." Imperialism had to be recognized rightly as the spread of exploitative capitalism to preindustrial societies. Competition for raw materials, cheap labor, and markets would inevitably lead the imperial powers into a cataclysmic international war. It was the duty of international socialism to oppose both imperialism and attendant militarism. "The economic principle of capitalism, competition, the struggle of all against all, dominates the relations of nations to each other just as it determines the relations of individuals united into so-called nations." Sadly, the international movement had been weakened by the willingness of workers in France and England to accommodate imperialism in return for short-term gains.

Articles in *Vorwärts* were generally unsigned, yet references here to the English worker's lack of concern for "ethical, philosophical, and aesthetic problems," to the brotherhood of man as the "humanitarian ideal of the most brilliant and noblest minds," to the "farce of the bourgeois peace propagandist," as well as the strident agitational tone deftly ratcheted up to the occasion and the mystical significance with which the holiday is endowed all argue for Eisner's authorship of this lead article. As such it represents a signal change in his bearing toward the French party, effected by its concessions to the government's colonial policy. However greatly one admired Millerand's social reforms, he wrote, the price paid for them was "a hundred times too dear." English workers had been seduced by promises of prosperity via colonial expansion, revealing unmistakably "that they are completely divorced from the socialist worldview," their cultural aspirations supplanted by a festering petit-bourgeois mentality, which unfortunately was also perceptible in elements of the German proletariat. It was therefore imperative that the German worker reconsecrate himself to his noble ideal on May Day: "One cannot serve both capitalism and socialism. Here there is only an either-or."

In April 1902 Friedrich Stampfer, acting editor of the *Leipziger Volkszeitung*, resigned when the local press commission acquiesced in Franz Mehring's demand that Rosa Luxemburg be named joint editor. Stampfer moved to Berlin to try his hand at freelancing and became a regular contributor to *Vorwärts*. He took up residence initially in Friedenau in the neighborhood of Kautsky and Luxemburg. He noted then that Eisner was suspect to the "radikalinskis," who envied his influence. Soon Stampfer relocated, at the Eisners' urging, to a cottage next door to the Eisner household in South Lichterfelde, "where one could live splendidly." Over half a century later Stampfer detailed in his memoirs the pleasure he took in the Eisner brood, who romped in the garden outside his study and beckoned until he joined their games. The parents, he wrote, "had a wonderful way of being friends to their children." Stampfer came to know the family well. In the evening he frequently accompanied Eisner to the *Vorwärts* offices. When they returned late at night, they walked together from the East Lichterfelde station, last stop on the train line at that hour, and "talked of philosophy and history, of literature, art, and mostly of course of politics and party."[61]

Eisner used his time on the train to reflect, relax, and observe minutely the behavior and mannerisms of people in transit. He recorded impressions of fellow commuters in a *Sonntagsplauderei* from June

1902.[62] On the morning train to Berlin vibrant shopgirls sat with a carefully wrapped, midmorning snack on their laps, reading novels or love letters. At noon they returned home for lunch, then boarded the train again to go back to work. As they dozed, the insatiable student of humanity lost himself in reading faces for clues as to circumstance, disposition, and dreams. In late afternoon elegant, suburban housewives taking the train into town to shop gossiped and skimmed their favorite tabloids. Eisner savored one day the consummate irony of a scene created by an inebriated artisan down on his luck and an immaculate bourgeois. When the gentleman threatened to have the grumbling drunk put off the train, the latter retorted that he would report the incident to the *Lokal-Anzeiger*. Once he had stumbled from the car at the next station, an indignant blonde matron scoffed at the very notion, as his stripe surely read *Vorwärts*.

CHAPTER SEVEN

MY LIFE'S PURPOSE: MOLDING THE READERSHIP (1902–1903)

THE RUTHLESSNESS OF MEHRING and Luxemburg in consolidating control at the *Leipziger Volkszeitung* and converting it into the organ of the extreme Left angered many besides the purged staff, and soon the contentious coeditors turned on each other. By early summer they were scarcely on speaking terms, yet in an attempt to discredit Eisner's moderate leadership of the central organ, they printed a series of attacks on *Vorwärts* by Parvus, pen name of Alexander Helphand, an unstable Russian émigré who served as Bebel and Kautsky's cudgel against anyone they suspected of harboring revisionist sympathies or even of willingness to hear the reformist viewpoint.[1] Eisner protested directly to Mehring in a letter dated 14 July. "Whenever the *L.V.* prints now Comrade Parvus's hallucinations that we—infinitely insidious and base conduct on our part—schemed hypocritically to compromise and undermine the *L.V.* or indeed the view it represents, I fail to understand how a serious paper can repeat obsessive accusations of that kind. At the least I would move simultaneously that the fellows pushing such a filthy agenda at *Vorwärts* be expelled from the party at once. I have enough sense of party camaraderie to want every party paper, including the *L.V.*, to be so superior as to serve as a model for us colorfast *Vorwärts* editors."[2] Eisner was particularly concerned about public perceptions of discord among the leadership with the annual congress set to convene in September in Munich. He considered this meeting of crucial importance in preparation for the elections of 1903. "This time," he wrote in the lead of 31 July, "we have no time to appear divided."[3]

In the same article Eisner proposed for discussion at Munich two measures he deemed prerequisite for success in the coming elections. The first was the development of a strategy to overturn state suffrage statutes depriving the proletariat of its rightful voice, as Prussia and Saxony could no longer simply be forfeited to the "unchecked forces of reaction." The second was a concerted campaign to break the Center Party's stranglehold in Catholic states on wards with sizable constituencies of industrial workers, miners, and farm laborers. Defeating the Center was the key to national progress, for with the largest Reichstag deputation, it figured in shaping all government policy, facilitating Weltpolitik, militarism, protectionism, and social inequity: "Clericalism is the sanctuary of stagnation here too and the impediment to any freer and purer development. Our public life is suffocating in the Center's monastic dank."

Hermann Cohen, who celebrated his sixtieth birthday in July, wrote on 14 August from the Hotel Sonne in Silvaplana, on vacation with his wife, to express appreciation for a special gift and to congratulate Eisner on the campaign against the Catholic party. The gift was Lisbeth's scenic rendering of Coswig on the north bank of the Elbe. "Although I raved to you about Judaism much more than you liked, you still discerned the love for my German homeland, for my little hometown as a living root of my being . . . of my Jewish German identity." Cohen then turned to politics. "It is a real satisfaction and source of hope for me that there exists no more difference between us in the assessment of the Center. I told Singer years ago that the party could perform no greater service than the destruction of the Center. It is my deepest conviction that there is no greater impediment to a free moral code than the papal church, and it is an ill even to express respect for its organization."[4]

On the issue of Landtag elections in Prussia Eduard Bernstein wrote to *Vorwärts* to restate his position.[5] Although it countered his own stance, Eisner chose to run Bernstein's statement as the lead on 9 September. Bernstein fully recognized that it was only through three-class suffrage that the Junker continued to wield their ponderous influence on national politics, thwarting democratic reform and social progress demanded by most Germans. Yet as pressing as the abolition of three-class suffrage was, he argued, the party would be ill served by either fielding its own candidates or supporting Left Liberals, for "whatever our electoral participation can contribute toward bringing fresh blood and life into the Landtag will be negated by Eugen Richter's influence." Bernstein therefore advocated extraparliamentary means—the boycott and fierce agitation—as the best course for undermining three-class suffrage.

On the eve of the Munich congress Eisner gave the delegates a rousing front-page charge on Sunday, 14 September.[6] As they would be holding a virtual "council of war," he entreated them to forgo intramural feuds and to close ranks. Hanover, Mainz, and Lübeck had served to clarify the party's objective and tactic. Now was the time to take the fight to the foe rather than to one's comrade. Within the party, he reasoned, there was certainly room for individual differences of opinion on the particulars, but the fundamental issues had been resolved. In keeping with Social Democracy's democratic principles, the individual now had to give way to the will of the majority.

Historians give the Munich congress of 1902 short shrift. The revisionist debate flared up once again but was confined for the most part to discussion of the status and role of Joseph Bloch's *Sozialistische Monatshefte*. In his summary for the readership Eisner regarded it as a manifestation of the disagreement on particulars to which he had referred. Kautsky, as editor of *Neue Zeit*, asserted in his own defense that Bloch's journal owed its popularity less to the "personal style of its editors" than to ongoing theoretical debate in the party, an assessment with which Eisner officially concurred. He wondered why, though, the two camps continued to favor one venue over the other when the majority of the party clearly believed that their differences were essentially quarrels over form rather than substance. He then allowed himself a dig at Helphand and his masters. "There is no more gratifying confirmation of the view we have held consistently in these matters than that in Munich the comrades of the so-called radical faction complained chiefly that the alleged 'opportunists' submitted their articles to the *Monatshefte* of a private publisher instead of to the zealous scourge of 'opportunists,' the official party journal *Neue Zeit*. . . . We might be permitted to mention in passing . . . that in the columns of *Vorwärts* the two sides have steadily worked in harmony beside and with each other."[7] As if to underscore his paper's impartiality, Eisner asked Rosa Luxemburg before the congress adjourned to review the third volume of Marx and Engels's collected works.[8]

However great his disappointment that no crusade against the Center was born in the capital of Catholic Bavaria, Eisner was mollified by Bebel's ringing indictment of government policy and the bourgeois parties' particularist platforms. The chairman of Germany's only truly national party had sounded the call to arms. The mobilization for the election campaign was underway.

In the last week of September 1902 Eisner eulogized Emile Zola, dead at sixty-two, as naturalism's great pioneer, an icon of modernity who preferred truth to beauty, the "epic portraitist of the capitalist age" whose novels of seamy city life in the shadows of the factory influenced politics as well as art.[9] He then wrote for *Neue Zeit* a more formally academic and critical appreciation in which praise was tempered by sober assessment of Zola's limitations.[10] Eisner readily conceded that Zola's creative imagination and descriptive powers placed him among the greats, but he was neither psychologist nor teacher, and his philosophy was too linear, too simplistic to yield a clear vision of human development. "It was not the slant in itself that weakened Zola's art, but the wavering vagueness of his slant." Despite his avowed goal of wedding science and literature, Zola never fully connected with the political philosophy that embodied his aesthetic ideal. With *Germinal* he seemed to be on the verge of embracing scientific socialism, but in his final works Zola rejected "the mature forms of the modern workers' movement" in favor of Fourier's utopianism. Signing himself only "E__r," Eisner recapitulated his critique, without partisan references, for the readership of the highbrow *Neue Deutsche Rundschau*.[11] Here too he emphasized that what was lacking in Zola's life and art was the sense of personal growth: "For that reason we meet him but once on our road of life. We can settle accounts with him by paying the due tribute he deserves, but he does not belong to the poets who are fathers and friends to us, whom we meet with again and again because we ourselves change."

On 1 October 1902 *Vorwärts* formally moved its base from the cramped halls at Beuthstraße 2 to new quarters several blocks away at Lindenstraße 69. The modern facility, with electric lighting and elevators, was designed and constructed by the firm of Kurt Berndt to house the party's own printshop, bindery, and bookstore in addition to all aspects of the central organ's operation. Its construction capped years of planning by the party executive, the press commission of Berlin, and the paper's business manager. The *Vorwärts* building and its state-of-the-art equipment were financed in large part by donations and loans from the trade unions. The larger of the two König and Bauer electric rotary presses, purchased at a cost of 60,000 marks, could print, sort, and fold 24,000 copies of a twenty-four-page newspaper each hour—the first of its kind to go into use in Germany. Eisner used the opportunity to counter critics of *Vorwärts* by tracing its eighteen years' progress from humble beginnings to "now when . . . it boasts the most readers of all the political daily papers in Berlin."

He underscored the credentials of its staff as frontline combatants in the class struggle. In the proud tradition of Liebknecht, Schoenlank, and August Jacobey, their collective jail time as enemies of the regime totaled more than eight years to date, with editors Robert Schmidt and Paul John still behind bars. Having linked his colleagues with the heroes of the past, Eisner then appealed to the local readership for continued support: "From now on every organization led by workers, every association affiliated with the party, must bear in mind that it promotes its own good by promoting the party enterprise, that the success of our new house is tied to the success of Social Democracy in Berlin."[12]

Wounded personally by the continuing campaign of the *Leipziger Volkszeitung* against *Vorwärts*, Eisner wrote candidly on 28 October from his editorial office to Franz Mehring, from whom he now distanced himself formally. That Mehring made public sensitive information Eisner had shared in confidence was "a question of personal code of conduct" that Eisner did not hold against him, for he himself had made an error of judgment by divulging it to Mehring. To Mehring's repeated charge that *Vorwärts* was ruled by a literary clique—the radicals' code for reformist intellectuals—Eisner replied cooly. "I hope never to be placed in the position of having to attest publicly that I am a good party comrade, that I place the party's interest above personal and professional interests, that I do not sacrifice party solidarity with class-conscious workers to the affected conceit of this or that literary clique. Those who do not already believe it of me would not begin to believe it were I to declaim so pathetically the patently obvious."

In any case he would ignore whatever further invective Mehring cared to write or print, as he had no intention of debasing his professional dignity by engaging in a "competition for the sympathy of the working class" by pandering to popular prejudices. Eisner closed with an accusation and a reproof. "Whoever spawns misconceptions in the masses about the 'literati' as you do continually, whoever incites the callused fist against party comrades of the press, does wrong not to his colleagues but to the party."[13]

The next month it was Eisner himself who through a strategic gaffe embroiled *Vorwärts* in a crisis that would threaten its existence. In November 1902 Germany was shaken by a sex scandal that tainted the highest echelons of the ruling elite. Their desperate attempts first to deny the well-documented truth, then to discredit and destroy its publishers reveal as no other single episode the ethos of corruption that animated the Wilhelmine state. For his part in the drama Kurt Eisner was both censured and celebrated, with some of the worst rebukes coming from his own comrades.

On 8 November the staunchly Catholic *Augsburger Postzeitung* broke a story in Germany that had appeared in September and October in the socialist paper of Naples. The *Postzeitung* declined to identify the principal other than as "a great industrialist of the highest reputation who is intimately connected with the Imperial court."[14] Friedrich Alfred Krupp, arms magnate, former Conservative deputy in the Reichstag, and privy councilor to the kaiser, had been invited by Italian officials to leave the country the previous spring following an investigation of sexual misconduct. Police evidence included photographs of frolics at Krupp's retreat at the Hotel Quisisana on Capri, where the forty-eight-year-old maintained a harem of local youths. The Berlin police had already investigated Krupp's aberrant appetites after the manager of the Bristol Hotel complained of orgies in Krupp's suites there. Paragraph 175 of the German penal code declared homosexuality a felony, but prosecution was selective, as the kaiser's cabinet and court, the Imperial general staff, and the Gardes du Corps Regiment were conspicuously suspect. When Margarethe von Ende Krupp learned of her husband's indiscretions in Italy, she appealed directly to Wilhelm for assistance. The kaiser sounded his closest advisers on the feasibility of relieving his friend of the management of his own company. One of them, Admiral von Hollmann, managed to get word to Krupp in Essen, who responded by having his wife forcibly removed to an asylum in Jena.[15]

In the wake of the *Postzeitung* article, Eisner believed that Krupp's troubles could be exploited. By revealing the identity of the eminent offender, he could compel the government either to prosecute a favorite or to strike paragraph 175 altogether. The party had long opposed prosecution of homosexuality, holding that practitioners "acted under the irresistible impulse of an unfortunate predisposition."[16] Friedrich Stampfer recounts in his memoirs it was rumored that the Berlin police files contained the names of many powerful and influential men whose reputations hung in the balance. "In this way the lists became a dangerous weapon in the hands of the police. On the other hand, there were male prostitutes who supplemented their income by blackmailing well-heeled clients. Paragraph 175, its application or nonapplication, formed in fact a dark chapter in the history of public morality."[17]

Eisner polled his staff and, despite warnings not to proceed, gambled that the government would choose the second option. On Saturday, 15 November, in an article titled "Krupp on Capri," *Vorwärts* exposed Croesus's private life to the nation, tactfully detailing what the foreign papers had already reported of the "Blue Grotto," incriminating photos, the investigation ordered by the Italian interior minister, and the Cannon King's banishment. As justification for the exposé *Vorwärts* cited the mercenary aspects of Krupp's penchant and the capriciousness of the German authorities in enforcing the law in question: "The case must be discussed publicly with the necessary earnest discretion, since it affords both a picture of capitalist culture in the most garish hues and perhaps the incentive finally to remove paragraph 175 from the German penal code, which does not just affect vice but damns to eternal fear morally sensitive persons with an unfortunate predisposition and holds them firmly in constant threat between incarceration and extortion." The article concluded with a challenge to the government to prosecute Krupp or decriminalize homosexuality.

What Eisner failed to gauge was the fear of the highly placed who stood to be compromised if the investigation of Krupp expanded. Krupp had never been formally charged in Italy. He agreed to leave and never return in order to avoid prosecution. His friends in Berlin were prepared to take any step necessary to whitewash him. Italy had a certain deserved reputation. Affidavits and photos in Rome could be made to disappear, as could plaintiffs if need be. The German government and Wilhelm himself were ready to intervene. Indeed, if Krupp were but willing to deny under oath the allegations printed by *Vorwärts*, the paper's credibility could be dealt a crushing blow. Instead of pursuing Krupp or scuttling the suspect law, Chancellor Bülow determined to charge *Vorwärts* with libel.[18] On Tuesday, the eighteenth, the Social Democratic central organ reported that police had raided its offices on Monday, confiscated Saturday's issue from cafés and taverns, and illegally searched the desks of members of the Reichstag. "Mr. Krupp," it announced, "evidently intends to file suit against *Vorwärts* for libel."

For whatever reasons, Krupp elected not to proceed against the paper. On Saturday, 22 November, he took his own life at his home in Essen. He had revised his will when the *Postzeitung* ran its article. His secretary and physicians concocted the story that Krupp died of a stroke, but glaring discrepancies in their subsequent statements aroused suspicion.[19] No autopsy was ordered and the coffin sealed to prevent examination of the corpse, giving rise to the speculation voiced by the Catholic *Kölnische Zeitung* that a guilty conscience had led Krupp to kill himself.[20] Eisner summoned the staff when the report of Krupp's death reached Berlin. He sat sullenly at the head of the table as they waited for him to speak. "It was," Stampfer recalls, "as if we could see the blood flowing over the table." Paul Singer arrived with the first reproach: "One just does not do such a thing!" His judgment was the mild prelude to a firestorm of criticism.[21]

Dr. Magnus Hirschfeld, distinguished physician and pioneering researcher on sexuality, wrote to Eisner on Saturday from Berlin-Charlottenburg upon receiving news of the death that Krupp was but *"one of the very numerous victims"* of paragraph 175, as research indicated that "nearly *one-third of all suicides* stem from conflicts arising from homosexuality." He divulged that some years earlier Krupp had sought out a Berlin doctor to cure his condition through hypnosis. The treatment had failed, of course, as homosexuality is no disease but rather "an *innate, singular nature.*" Dr. Hirschfeld advised Eisner to emphasize in his report that Krupp was subject to blackmail and "that *the sword of Damocles hung* over his entire life."[22] On Sunday *Vorwärts* printed the the death-by-stroke announcement exactly as it had come off the wire and issued a terse statement that it was suspending further discussion of the Capri affair. Within the party, concern that *Vorwärts* had sunk to the level of tawdry tabloid in airing Krupp's dirty laundry brought "hard times" for its editor.[23] The Conservative press howled that *Vorwärts* had hounded an innocent man to his grave.[24] Recriminations were exchanged on the floor of the Reichstag.

Depending on Margarethe Krupp's willingness to prefer charges, Eisner faced—beyond eroding support from his comrades—the prospect of another lengthy jail term that surely would have meant forfeiture of the directing editor's position. His salvation came from the unlikeliest source of all. After Krupp's funeral on the twenty-sixth, Kaiser Wilhelm addressed the Krupp firm's board of directors and a delegation of workers at the Essen train station. In his anger he accused Eisner, without naming him, of murder, "for there is no difference between one who mixes and serves another the poison draught and one who from the secure covert of his editorial office destroys with the poisoned arrows of his calumny the good name of a fellow man and kills him by the mental anguish arising from it." Then warming to his topic, Wilhelm implicated the Social Democratic Party as a whole. "Men who claim to be the leaders of the German workers," he told his audience, "have robbed you of your dear master."[25]

Eisner responded immediately to the slur and, with well-reasoned argument, reconfigured the issue as a debate on the monarchy itself. "The kaiser," he wrote in *Vorwärts* on 28 November, "spoke of the secure covert of a Social Democratic editor's office. Well, an editorial staff is accountable, legally and morally, for what it does. . . . The German monarchy, however, is constitutionally unaccountable. The monarch can attack, but a single spirited word in reply is prohibited by the lèse-majesté article." Were *Vorwärts* prosecuted, he questioned, how could a fair trial be possible if the emperor had already publicly asserted the guilt of the defendant? And heeding Dr. Hirschfeld's counsel, Eisner laid the blame for Krupp's demise squarely on paragraph 175. It was the fear of prosecution, not the revelation of the truth, that brought about his death. Having lectured the emperor in print on the misadministration of justice, Eisner concluded his rebuttal defiantly by declaring that whether *Vorwärts* had been right or wrong to publish its exposé, socialism's triumph would be unhindered by whatever fate befell a newspaper editor.[26]

Now even Eisner's harshest critics leapt to his defense. Franz Mehring wrote in *Neue Zeit* that although opinion was divided within the party as to the "tactical expediency" of the *Vorwärts* exposé, even if the intent were to repeal a repugnant law, "we would be cowards if we did not join battle as it is being offered to us." He then launched his own offensive against the Prussian crown by reiterating that Friedrich the Great's Capri was Sanssouci. Mehring surmised that the anticipated libel suit against *Vorwärts* could spell real hardship for a few, but their sacrifice would yield rich dividends for the party's propaganda campaign.[27] The reformist Paul Göhre, a Protestant theologian who had joined the party two years earlier, faulted *Vorwärts* on moral grounds for revealing Krupp's secret but praised the paper for its composure in the face of Wilhelm's attacks. In an article for *Sozialistische Monatshefte* he hailed Eisner's rebuttal as a dispassionate, "truly Christian and sublime" response to Wilhelm's invective. "Who can deny," he queried, "that this polemic against the monarchy, born of coolest calm, supreme confidence, and the certainty of victory of our own world-winning cause has a publicity value for us even in circles that acknowledge us only with great reluctance?"[28]

Knowing the truth of the matter and having been betrayed and humiliated when she turned to the kaiser in her need, Frau Krupp had no desire to abet his campaign against Social Democracy. At her insistence the chief public prosecutor, Dr. Isenbiel, announced on 15 December that the libel charge against the editor of *Vorwärts* was withdrawn.[29] By then though the Krupp affair had so inflamed passions on both sides that it took on a life of its own. Well into the new year skirmishes erupted on the Reichstag floor, where Bebel finally laid the issue to rest on 22 January by taking Eisner's tack of assailing the institution of monarchy. Nevertheless, Eisner's miscalculation in running the exposé had alienated significant figures in the party leadership, especially Bebel, who now regarded Eisner's effusive praise as a liability.[30]

In the first weeks of the new year two pieces by Eisner appeared in national publications. The first, a two-part article for *Die Neue Welt* (New World), the party's weekly *Illustrated Supplement for Science, Instruction, and Entertainment*, dealt with the history, culture, and lore of the hamlet Rantum on Sylt.[31] The second was the long-past-due appreciation of Ibsen that Joseph Bloch had solicited more than a year earlier for *Sozialistische Monatshefte*.[32] Rantum lies almost midway on the finger of island between the towns of Westerland and Hörnum. With thirty-two permanent residents, the tiny community practiced a unique form of proprietary communism, which economist Gottlieb Schnapper-Arndt had documented in an article for the *Frankfurter Zeitung*. During his annual late summer sojourn Eisner had hiked the 7 kilometers down from Westerland over beach, dune, and bog to interview the schoolmaster, the magistrate, the innkeeper, and the head of one of the five leading families. These five families shared equally the use of, and profit from commonly owned pastures and dunes. The rest of the island's inhabitants had long since partitioned their common lands; the old families of Rantum, descended from pirates and marauding salvagers, preserved the old system and were prospering by raising cattle and sheep, exporting hay to the mainland, and selling sea holly to Westerland's florists while their enterprising neighbors struggled.

Back at Christmas the Berlin publishing house S. Fischer had released in its edition of Ibsen's collected works a volume of his earliest writings. Its publication spurred Eisner to make good his commitment to Bloch to furnish an essay on the Norwegian by reviewing the new book. Eisner praised the translations of Ibsen's poetry but faulted editor Paul Schlenther for seeking in his introduction to discover in juvenile verse the profound motifs of later plays, since there was simply "no second example of a poet in steady ascent achieving perfection and timelessness with his last works of old age," namely, *Rosmersholm*, *The Master Builder*, and *Little Eyolf*. And in keeping with "our literary scholars' most ardent endeavor to confine poets to the impartial and independent, *pure* world of letters," Schlenther, "a genteel man of letters and court theater director," made no mention of Ibsen's leanings, but Eisner reminded the reader that in 1890 Ibsen wrote to the Social Democratic *Münchener Post* "that I, since I made it my chief purpose to depict human characters and human fates, have come to the same conclusions on certain points, without having consciously or directly intended it, as the socialist ethicists through their scientific research."

On 15 January 1903 the party organ's lead article documented a case of attempted bribery that revealed in embarrassing detail the curious inner workings of Berlin's security police.[33] A month after Krupp's funeral an editorial assistant at *Vorwärts* was approached by a character calling himself Deichmüller who claimed to be a brewer at Schultheiß and who wanted help finding work at the paper for a relation recently discharged from the military. He treated the assistant to several rounds at Aschinger's on Friedrichstraße and the Hops Blossom on Unter den Linden and steered the conversation to the role of *Vorwärts* in the Krupp affair. Although he was told that the paper had no vacancies, Deichmüller maintained contact with the assistant. At their next meeting, to which the suspicious assistant brought a coworker, Deichmüller flashed his wallet and proposed a second pub crawl for Saturday, 10 January. On that outing a woman at one of the taverns recognized Deichmüller and asked him what business a policeman had there. Undeterred, the mysterious patron set up a rendezvous for Tuesday evening at the subway entrance on Wittenbergplatz.

At the appointed time the assistant was met by Deichmüller and an accomplice, the shadow who for months had monitored comings and goings at the editorial offices. Deichmüller hurried his quarry into a waiting cab that took them on a roundabout route to Café Schiller near police headquarters. There they were met by Detective Diener—well known to the *Vorwärts* staff—who offered 30 marks every two weeks for information about individual editors, their activities, meetings of the party's executive committee, and what officials Wilhelm Pfannkuch, Alwin Gerisch, and Paul Singer did when they visited the Lindenstraße complex. These reports were to be sent to a post office box registered under the alias Reimann to Deichmüller, whom Diener addressed as Kröger. The assistant was then given 60 marks for his trouble. A loyal comrade, he promptly reported everything to his employers and turned the money over to them. At the end of the article recounting the sordid business appeared a block notice in boldface: "On deposit at our business office are 60 marks, paid to our editorial assistant on 13 January 1903 at the Café Schiller as inducement to breach of faith and betrayal of house secrets to the security police. The payer can reclaim them upon receipt of proof of his identity." For Eisner, a past victim of the "stoolie corps," the chance to expose the motivations and methods of its commanders was surely a measure of sweet revenge.

The twentieth anniversary of Marx's death afforded Eisner the opportunity to recapitulate systematically the party's theoretical fundament and consequent practical function. The banner article in the Saturday, 14 March, edition of *Vorwärts* was written in evident preparation for the coming electoral campaign.[34] For this solemn observance Eisner placed Marx in historical perspective as enunciator and elucidator of the mechanics of material history, who realized full well that the revolutionary rise of the proletariat was merely a stage of the dialectical process and, although an end in and of itself, not the end of social development, as the circumstances and relations created by the destruction of the old would yield in turn new, far different tensions. It was he who worked out "that the history of all previous societies is, in the final analysis, the history of relations of production and exchange, and that their development under the prevalence of private property expresses itself in political and social institutions as class struggle." Before Marx, wage laborers in capitalist economies were certainly aware of their shared position within bourgeois society, of their nexus of privation and misery, but as an amorphous mass they were incapable of effective, concerted action. Individually, their goals remained subsistence and, remotely, eventual escape from wage slavery by somehow accumulating capital. Collectively, they envisioned utopian socialist communes divorced from the greater society. Once again it was Marx who discerned the proletariat "as a class with distinct historical conditions for existence and laws of motion," who endowed it with an identity, imbued it with self-consciousness, and prescribed its purpose: "the conquest of political power for socialist revolution," a purpose that gave the propertyless currency and cachet for the first time.

The struggle for political power that would lead to revolution defined then the mission and tactic of the Social Democratic Party. Its Realpolitik, which pursued "only realizable goals . . . by the most effective means," was but "the initial stage of the action that will make it the politics of the ruling and revolutionizing proletariat." Recent developments, such as the French socialists' disappointing experience in the government, demonstrated that the reformist hope of transformation through legislation of existing state structures to socialism was illusory: "the brief dream of 'peaceful evolution' went to pieces blow by blow." And even as the party confirmed its true course, Social Democracy's most capable critics recognized the formidability of its philosophical underpinning. Here Eisner paid a compliment of sorts to a member of the Marburg faculty, Rudolf Stammler, citing him as one of "the more earnest among the bourgeois ideologues" who conceded that Marx's 'deeply grounded doctrine' was fairly unassailable.

Social Democracy's dual tactic, as Eisner had clarified in articles summarizing the party congresses at Lübeck and Mainz, certainly admitted parliamentary activity as part of the campaign to educate the masses and improve their lives, but it was no substitute for revolution, which by his wholly orthodox definition was the ultimate consolidation of political power, by all expedient means, that would create the dictatorship of the proletariat. He had argued repeatedly for greater electoral engagement, advocating taking the fight to the Prussian Landtag as well as the Reichstag. He firmly believed that the national elections of 1903, slated for mid-June, would bolster significantly the party's representation and influence. At the end of the 1902 party congress he already looked forward to the campaign as critical to socialism's rise. In its first headline of the new year *Vorwärts* proclaimed 1903 a "battle year," and Eisner's lead article recollected that in most all of the last year's local, state, and special elections "a serious decline of votes in favor of the existing order was coupled with the constant advance of the Social Democratic Party," and warned opponents that "the new year's electoral storm will shred the linen backdrop of their idyllic stage landscape."[35]

Eisner's sense of urgency, for all his professed confidence, derived from the inherent inequity of apportionment and the system of runoff elections. Since 1873 Germany had been parceled into 397 Reichstag districts, although the population had increased dramatically and shifted to urban centers. Now, thirty years later, several individual districts in Berlin alone—strongholds for the party—housed over a quarter-million voters, roughly ten times as many as in dozens of individual rural, Catholic or Conservative districts with the same representation as each of those in the capital. Because the party viewed elections as a means of spreading its message to every nook of the land, local branches in hostile districts were expected to field candidates even if defeat was certain. This willingness to mount incursions into exclusively agrarian and ultramontane preserves had established the SPD as Germany's single national party, but its real strength was, of course, in the industrial and mining regions. Election to the Reichstag required an absolute majority. If none was tallied, the top two pollers met in a runoff. As Eisner had witnessed in Marburg in 1898, regional and sectarian parties pushing constituent interests traditionally owned many a mandate. Social Democrats in runoffs in urban districts, their natural domain, generally faced Left Liberal opponents who also appealed to the bourgeois intelligentsia, an often critical bloc of swing voters. In short, the electoral system itself was virtually designed to preclude Social Democratic gain.[36]

The issues in the 1903 elections were Weltpolitik, colonialism, and the protective grain tariffs enacted the previous year by the Conservative, National Liberal, and Center bloc despite a concerted effort against them. *Vorwärts*, by Eisner's initiative and supported by the free-trade faction of the Left Liberal press, had prodded the party's Reichstag delegation to a dilatory tactic contrived to put off the final vote on the measure until after new elections. Through multiple amendments, protracted discussion of each minute detail, and insistence on roll-call votes, the Social Democratic members and a contingent of renegades from the Radical Party obstructed the proceedings—the first such slowdown in the Reichstag's history. Finally the Center introduced a measure, *lex* Aichbichler, to expedite voting on amendments by employing color-coded ballots and boxes. The tariff bill carried in December 1902, but the filibuster produced an unexpected result, having aroused unprecedented interest among the working-class electorate in the legislative process.[37]

Throughout the winter and spring *Vorwärts* attacked on all fronts. When the Reichstag met in early March to consider colonial appropriations, Eisner apprised readers of the jingoist agenda.[38] Lobbyists hung maps of Africa in the foyer of the Reichstag to instill in members "the patriotic enthusiasm necessary for approval," yet close inspection of the displays revealed that the coastal regions favored by German colonists were "the most dangerous, fever-ridden areas of all." Since too few European workers could endure the conditions, the planters had been compelled to recruit indigenous fieldhands, who all too frequently were driven by ruthless overseers. Now the planters and their backers wanted the authority to require natives to work the plantations and more troops to quell the unrest that would likely arise from the imposition of forced labor. Here Eisner connected the emerging hierarchy in the colonies to East Elbian feudalism, implying the servitude of Germany's own populace to Prussian agrarian, militarist, and expansionist designs: "Bondage beneath the fist of Prussian Junkerdom, brutal 'mastery' over defenseless slaves—that, then, is the latest aim of practical capitalist colonization in Africa!"

Three months before the elections Eisner recalled for voters the government's record since the last national elections in 1898 and urged them to reject in June the politics of imperialism, militarism, and protectionism. Social Democracy, he believed, had reached a juncture. "The great world-historical dispute between workers and exploiters, between socialism and capitalism will not be decided in this election, for it has already been decided, and the results of an election can neither validate this decision nor overturn it. The decision lies in the nature of things, in the necessity of economic development. . . . But in which forms, under what attendant circumstances, with what incidents this development will unfold—whether it will proceed by powerfully deliberate growth or finally reach its goal through violent struggle, having been thrown back and then advancing again—that is a verdict the world will await with bated breath."[39]

In the first week of April he informed the readership that of high priority on the next Reichstag's order of business would be military and naval appropriations and that supporters of imperial expansion were already agitating fiercely for an East Asian fleet that could challenge all comers. The German people, he declared, had it in their power to say no: "May they create a Reichstag in the coming elections that will deny reckless Weltpolitik . . . a new instrument to rush from one bloody and costly adventure to another."[40] Just over two weeks before the elections Eisner marked Pentecost by likening the vanguard of the workers' movement to Christ's apostles, driven by belief to change the world by changing men's perception of themselves. A scant band of persecuted devotees opposed the mightiest power on earth and won. "Their creed, which declined to recognize the Roman caesars' deity, was regarded as a doctrine of impudent revolution and lèse majesté in itself. . . . Above the battles for the

Reichstag is the battle for a new social order in which the moral teachings of the apostles can be practiced rather than merely preached."[41]

A week prior to the polling *Vorwärts* reminded its public that despite the party's best efforts to legislate that all elections be held on Sundays, the upcoming vote would occur the following Tuesday; workers were counseled to arrange with their employers for time off.[42] The morning of 16 June Eisner apprised readers that the polls would close at seven that evening and in his lead article reviewed the campaign and impressed the urgency of a strong showing.[43] The bourgeois parties, he wrote, cognizant of their dwindling appeal, shamelessly misrepresented themselves in order to attract voters. Rather than admit that their program aimed exclusively at the preservation of Junker privilege, the Conservatives reached out now desperately to small farmers and shopkeepers, whom they generally disdained and exploited. The Center concealed its desire to preserve the social order by keeping the state subservient to the church, touting instead its service to the 'common good' by mediating between the extremes of Left and Right. The National Liberal and Radical parties bandied the tired slogan of political freedom to the petite bourgeoisie whereas their true ambition was to free big capital from government restriction, workers' vigilance, and open competition.

A single party had the confidence in its program and constituency to make its appeal forthrightly. "Because Social Democracy represents the interests of the proletariat and in the proletariat the highest interests of the people and of humanity, it need not fear the numbers, it need not court the votes of those it will deceive and betray." On this day the oppressed everywhere looked to Germany, and the number of votes the party tallied would indicate both the political maturity and the potential of the workers' movement there. "The sum of socialist votes is the embodiment of Germany's national cultural heritage, which stirs the admiration and pride, not the envy and hatred of the proletariat of all nations."

That evening the *Vorwärts* editors gathered in eager anticipation around the same table at which they had fretted seven months earlier over the damage of the Krupp affair. As telegrams arrived reporting returns from districts across the nation, it became clear that the party's old guard, joined by hundreds of thousands voting red for the first time, had turned out in force to deliver a signal triumph—despite Wilhelm's megalomaniacal vow to "crush" whoever opposed him.[44] The SPD garnered over three million votes, nearly a million more than in 1898. In the capital Richard Fischer, Wolfgang Heine, Paul Singer, Robert Schmidt, and Georg Ledebour had won outright, and Leo Arons was to face a Left Liberal candidate in a runoff on Thursday, 25 June. Hamburg, Dresden, and Braunschweig also elected multiple Social Democratic deputies on the first ballot. But even more impressive were the nine unexpected mandates in predominantly rural enclaves where no socialist had ever won election.[45] And in Königsberg in East Prussia, a Conservative haven, Otto Braun forced the local favorite into a runoff, in which Braun would take over 40 percent of the vote. When the final ballot was tallied, Social Democrats had filled eighty-one seats, second only to the Center's hundred.[46]

Jubilant in the first flush of victory, Eisner hurriedly drafted the lead just before deadline. Borrowing a line from Wilhelm's adjuration to workers after Krupp's suicide to part ways with the party, he announced that Berlin's voters, 63,000 more than in 1898, had parted ways with the parties of reaction. In industrial regions of the Rhineland and Westphalia, Social Democrats had gained ground from the Catholics and in Württemberg from the Left Liberals. The Junker bread-gouging politics had come to grief. "If the rest of the night goes as it has up to midnight, then a world-change in German politics is taking shape. Germany is becoming the land of socialism." Then returning to the analogy between Social Democratic Germany and revolutionary France, he proclaimed: "Ours the Reich, ours the world!"[47] Until 03:00 the editors monitored returns. An extra edition slated for circulation at noon had to be assembled before 09:00. Toward dawn Eisner and Friedrich Stampfer broke for a walk before returning to their copy. They were accompanied by Antonín Němec, a comrade from Prague come to observe the election night bustle at Lindenstraße. Bone-tired but exhilarated, they strolled through the city streets with a copy of the morning edition, just off the press, in hand. A lone streetwalker on the prowl teased that the polls had long since closed, and at the Gendarmenmarkt they encountered a policeman who stepped from the shadows, saluted, and inquired guardedly: "How many do we have?"[48]

The following Sunday Eisner recounted in his column the mood of the election night and the next days.[49] Across Europe sympathizers were celebrating the party's showing in Germany. In Vienna and Prague extra editions of the socialist papers hailed the achievement. Red flags were hoisted in working-class quarters of Belgian cities. Class-conscious workers everywhere reveled in the moment. Or so one might think. Yet even in Germany there were Social Democrats who regarded the electoral success with dismay, fearing corruption by parliamentarism. To them Eisner's heady reportage and commentary gushed. Particularly offensive was the formulation "Ours the Reich, ours the world!" that transgressed against what Stampfer characterized as the prevalent "fanaticism of sobriety," which demanded stoical reserve and colorless text.

Soon the *Leipziger Volkszeitung* was deriding Eisner's "world change" and misquoting his prophecy as "We conquered the world!" Stampfer recalled the optimism of the moment. "Eisner's enthusiasm was understandable; the victory was intoxicating. To be sure, the party had no clue as to how it would someday win the final victory, and one hardly believed in the possibility of so total a Social Democratic electoral sweep that the monarchy, military, and capitalist society would capitulate without resistance. But the constant rise in Social Democratic numbers served equally to fill supporters with confidence in that victory and opponents with fretful anxiety."[50] In answer to the question of why the party had prospered in these elections, both Eisner and Stampfer believed that the filibuster against grain tariffs, an action propelled by *Vorwärts*, had galvanized popular support, an assessment shared by most historians. But Eisner thought that the Krupp affair also had worked to the party's advantage. Looking back, he wrote to Joseph Bloch on 2 September 1907 that "even today I consider the obstruction the one sensible thing we did, and together with the Krupp business it essentially swung the elections of 1903."[51]

Wholly in keeping with the final resolutions of recent party congresses, which held that in preparation for revolution the party would back legislation to ease the suffering and safeguard the rights of the proletariat, Eisner outlined in the lead of 4 July the "sociopolitical tasks of the new Reichstag."[52] Heading his list of legislative priorities were the institution of the ten-hour workday, greater regulation of working conditions for women and children, increased protection for workers in hazardous industries, extension of insurance benefits to all workers and their dependents as well as to the temporarily unemployed, and expansion of public-health initiatives.

The enthusiasm with which Eisner had greeted the party's electoral success and the ambitious agenda *Vorwärts* set for the new deputation irked Bebel, who was well aware of the significant increase in subscriptions to the party organ in Eisner's brief tenure and who resented his growing influence. Although Eisner had lavished praise on the party chairman—even to the point of the recipient's embarrassment—his independent bent of mind had defied manipulation by the old guard, an attribute strengthened by Ignaz Auer's constant succor. If the kaiser suffered from Caesarian megalomania, the chairman was certainly no less stricken with the delusion of papal infallibility. Seeing now Bebel's capacity for the "petty," Eisner resolved to be more critical.[53] Was he not Liebknecht's own chosen successor, Wilhelm Liebknecht who himself had schooled Bebel in socialism?

Historians of Wilhelmine Germany have tended to regard the elections of 1907, the referendum on German imperialism, as the watershed for Social Democracy, yet the seeds of the party's demise were sown in the summer of 1903 when its chairman, unable to negotiate success, initiated a purge, ostensibly to cleanse the leadership of impure ideological elements, but in reality to rid himself of perceived rivals. Bebel's intolerance of any divergence of opinion, no matter how inconsequential, from his personal views, would work its unholy poison and more than any single factor utterly doom the development of democracy as an organic process in Germany and disembowel on the sword of spite the party he had helped found. As his agents he chose precisely the most psychologically suspect personalities on Social Democracy's furthest anarchic fringe: the mercurial, malignant Franz Mehring and the displaced, disaffected Rosa Luxemburg.

Whereas Eisner endorsed an aggressive campaign of legislative reforms, he did not support Bernstein's suggestion that the party lay claim to a vice presidency of the Reichstag, an office its strength certainly merited but which required a visit to Wilhelm's court and the customary courtesy of a bow to the German emperor. Bernstein considered the gesture a meaningless formality, but most Social Democrats chafed at the mere thought of it. Through July and August debate on the issue escalated to diatribe. When Social Democratic voters from Berlin's Fürstenwalde district, hoping to prevent yet another convention feud, called upon Vollmar and Bebel to report at Dresden on the pros and cons of a Reichstag vice presidency, Bebel publicly accused them of advancing the revisionist agenda. The Fürstenwalder took umbrage in print and alluded to Chairman Bebel's paranoia.[54] Newly reelected deputy Wolfgang Heine then asserted that Bebel, abroad in the south, was poorly informed and had lost touch with the Berlin electorate.[55] Writing to *Vorwärts*, Bebel responded to the disenchanted local and Heine separately, charging both with conspiratorial motive but without presenting any grounds for his accusation.

Eisner expressed his thoughts on the desirability of a seat on the presidium in the lead of Sunday, 30 August.[56] He dismissed Bernstein's proposal as "the inscrutable impulse of a brooding party journalist." The belief that the office could further the legislative program was spurious but certainly no cause for the furor it had generated. Bebel, whom Eisner referred to here as "a man we all respect," unfortunately had only exacerbated emotions with his response to the Berlin critics. Party editors would perform a service to readers, Eisner appealed openly, by exercising their office "to be cooler counselors to intemperate contributors." Chronicling Social Democracy's historical electoral successes and setbacks, he reaffirmed the battle-tested tactic of balancing "demands of principle with claims of practical politics of the day, of the situation at the moment."

Among Eisner's papers at the Bundesarchiv in Berlin-Lichterfelde is a remarkable document, a letter written to Bebel on 30 August 1903 from Eisner's Boninstraße residence.[57] Addressed to Bebel's summer home in the Zurich suburb Küsnacht, the letter was never sent and remained sealed until read by Eisner's widow, Else Belli Eisner, on 17 September 1920. In his missive Eisner expressed his concerns for party unity. Neither Bernstein's ambitions nor Mehring's prejudices, he ventured, could damage Social Democracy in the long term. "But it does seem to me dangerous when the political party constantly loses itself in petty squabbling and by so doing strengthens that trade-union element, which uninfluenced by theories or leaders confines itself to so-called practical work solely from the requirements of its existence." Turning to the topic of a vice presidency, Eisner maintained that *Vorwärts* had sought to defuse the issue, but it simply would not subside. He personally believed that a vice presidency in and of itself was hardly worth the effort of the obligatory call at court, but he repudiated those, including Bebel himself, who opposed it on purely symbolic grounds, for "if the vice presidency were a question of life or death for us, we would not stumble over the thread of a formality." What did matter, to Eisner's mind, was which of the bourgeois parties controlled the presidium. A Left Liberal "could be of real service to us." He urged Chairman Bebel to take the high road at the Dresden congress so as to demonstrate to friend and foe alike that Social Democracy was ready to lead the nation.

Bebel wrote to Kautsky the same day, fuming that *Vorwärts* had shown its true colors, as evinced by Eisner's lead article, "which, on top of it all, is teeming with historical gaffes." He was incensed at Eisner's presumption that it was the function of a party editor to proscribe freedom of the press. Bebel urged Kautsky to intensify the offensive, especially against Auer, without regard for "stale friendship."[58] Before Eisner could post his letter to Switzerland, he found on his office desk the next day two official clarifications from Bebel on his dispute with Berlin's malcontents. Perturbed by Bebel's persistent irrational stance and confrontational tone, Eisner sought advice from Ignaz Auer and Alwin Gerisch before declining to print the chairman's remarks. He then wrote immediately to Bebel. "As long as the confidence of party comrades keeps me in my position, I cannot accept announcements that, in my firmest conviction, will surely have a discouraging effect on the masses of party comrades apart from the small circle of those who introduce and pass resolutions at the conventions."[59]

Infuriated at being admonished to silence by the editor of *Vorwärts*, who had been seconded by Auer and Gerisch, the party secretary and treasurer, respectively, Bebel turned to Franz Mehring, who was only too pleased to run the chairman's vituperations in his *Leipziger Volkszeitung* on 5 September under the title "Freedom of Expression in the Party."[60] Bebel then fired out a denunciation of *Vorwärts* to *Neue Zeit*, charging that Eisner had invented a version of party history to suit his fancy.[61] On 6 September Bebel wrote to Kautsky that he had received from Eisner "two heartrending letters that only showed me that the man is out of his element in the whole situation" and then confided that he was hatching a scheme to derail his rival's designs.[62] Bebel's plan was to demand that the press commission require Eisner to reprint the clarifications already published by Mehring.

Having read carefully Bebel's criticism in Kautsky's journal, Eisner responded to Bebel personally from his home on 8 September to dispel the chairman's delusion of infallibility and to protest Mehring's "reign of terror" in Leipzig. Papers to which Eisner had access while writing Wilhelm Liebknecht's biography in 1899 clearly refuted Bebel's version of events and confirmed his own: "Precisely *you* are in error and reproach us with 'fictionalizing.'" Eisner realized the hazard of his course but elected to proceed on principle. He confessed that Bebel's attack had left him despondent but resolved now to stand his ground regardless of the consequences. "If I am no longer wanted, that I cannot change—even though my life's purpose consists in the struggle for our cause. But I do sense that my nerves are not up to base insinuations and loathsome intrigues in the long run."[63]

In the sad realization that the party's chairman, within ten weeks of its popular zenith, had intentionally sown discord and division on the eve of the annual congress, Eisner reprinted Bebel's statements in *Vorwärts* on Wednesday, 9 September, prefacing them with a clarification of his own cosigned by editors Heinrich Wetzker and Wilhelm Schröder that refuted categorically Arthur Stadthagen's claim that the organ's editorial board was dominated by revisionist schemers.[64] On the same day Bebel, en route to the congress, wrote to Kautsky from Stuttgart before reading the paper that if Eisner refused to abide by the press commission's directive, he would demand retribution and promised: "In Dresden I will preach the most intense mistrust of all who come to us as academics and intellectuals unless they have proven by deed that they are party comrades as we need them."[65] On the eleventh, two days before the delegates were to meet, Eisner fully documented in *Vorwärts* his account of the events that Bebel had disputed, citing chapter and verse of the sources to which he had referred in his letter of the eighth.[66]

The party congress of 1903 afforded Germany's satirists a field day. In anticipation of the carnage, the Munich weekly *Jugend* (Youth) published an illustrated ballad titled "The Fratricide in Dresden," and when the delegates had adjourned, *Simplicissimus* followed with a cartoon in which a wild and disheveled Bebel, surrounded by the prostrate vanquished—Ignaz Auer, Georg von Vollmar, Paul Göhre—urges "And now, comrades, on to battle against bourgeois society!"[67] Recalling with chagrin the cartoon and the events it lampooned, Friedrich Stampfer wrote in his memoirs: "Thus the bourgeois intelligentsia regarded the Social Democratic Party after the Dresden party congress. The respect of June had turned to scorn just three months later. One began to foresee that the great party would dig its own grave through disunity."[68]

All that had been necessary, in Stampfer's judgment, for Social Democracy to win "everything" was to sway the intelligentsia.[69] To that end several prominent party journalists had contributed occasional articles to progressive bourgeois journals critical of the Imperial regime, mainly Maximilian Harden's *Zukunft*. In January 1903 Franz Mehring took to task the young economist Georg Bernhard in *Neue Zeit* for a piece in *Zukunft*. In the weeks leading up to the Dresden congress, Mehring denounced Bernhard, Berlin attorney Wolfgang Heine, new Reichstag deputy Paul Göhre, and Heinrich and Lily Braun as traitorous to the party for their collaboration on Harden's magazine.[70] Realizing that the radical camp intended to exploit the issue to bash as revisionists advocates of proactive legislation for the worker, Eisner had protested to Bebel in his letter of 8 September that in light of Wilhelm Liebknecht's articles for *Die Fackel* (The Torch), Karl Kraus's Viennese journal, the denunciations were farcical.[71] Sensing the mood of the moment, Eisner used the opportunity of a precongress meeting of party members from Berlin's Teltow-Charlottenburg district to draft a resolution pressing the congress to empower its Reichstag representation to positive engagement.[72]

On Sunday, 13 September, the day the congress opened, Eisner explained the resolution on the front page of *Vorwärts*.[73] Social Democratic deputies had never actually put forward bills in the Reichstag but rather had presented resolutions, which the government might consider. The Teltow-Charlottenburg comrades urged the party's deputies to author and present bills, drafts of which would be printed and made available at minimal cost to voters, that the constituency might monitor the proceedings. In addition to being the best means to achieve such goals as a standard workday, active participation in the legislative process would confront the majority with a dilemma: regardless of whether the bourgeois parties accepted or rejected the proposed bills, they would undermine their own class interests by either granting concessions to the workers or steeling the masses' will to overcome their opposition. As he had in the lead article of 4 July, just after the elections, Eisner included in the Teltow-Charlottenburg resolution programmatic reform of government finance, the penal code, the military, and public education in addition to expansion of workers' rights and benefits.

Bebel feared that the party's dazzling showing at the polls had strengthened the hand of those who supported reform legislation to improve workers' lives—an amelioration that would vitiate his rhetoric and loosen his grip on the party hierarchy. Mehring had provided him with suitable scapegoats, and Bebel succeeded in sidetracking substantive business at Dresden by excoriating for hours on end a handful of journalists whom he accused of subversion, disloyalty, and worse. But Bernhard, Göhre, and Heinrich Braun had not come to Dresden to be abused. In a coordinated counteroffensive Braun impeached Mehring's credibility by documenting his past as a mercenary foe of the party, then Bernhard read to the delegates a postcard written by Mehring to Harden in September 1892 professing his abiding friendship and scathing Bruno Schoenlank. Bebel sought desperately to defend Mehring and jeered various speakers, including congress president Paul Singer, who reproved the chairman for childishness. Göhre returned Bebel's epithets and pronounced him unworthy as a party chairman.[74]

Early on Wednesday, the sixteenth, Rosa Luxemburg wrote to Leo Jogiches of the sensation created by the revelations of Mehring's associations. "Yesterday Mehring was morally done in by Bernhard! The impression of the letter to Harden about Schoenl[ank] (that lout) was frightful. All workers are saying that only one course remains for M[ehring]: *to put a bullet through his head.* The continuation is coming today, and there will be still more scandals."[75] Indeed, Bebel's hectoring was not done yet. Turning to *Vorwärts,* he fulminated against its attempt to squelch his execrations and virtually insisted that only his appraisal of circumstances within the party, past and present, could be accurate. Although he maintained that Eisner, at thirty-six, lacked sufficient knowledge of the party's development to serve as its historian, he tempered his criticism of the chief editor: "You are an outstanding comrade and an exceptionally skillful journalist, but for these matters I would prefer another, as you are too young a comrade. . . . For that reason I would like for you to be displaced from that section of *Vorwärts* and confined to the section in which you serve the party most splendidly and can fully discharge your duties."[76]

Eisner chose to respond in his own venue to Bebel's screed once the congress adjourned.

His summation of the congress on 22 September diverged sharply from the panegyric of previous years.[77] "However high the renewed acknowledgement of the strategy for victory may be posted, reaching this goal, in our estimation, did not require such far-reaching debates as took place in Dresden, and the embittered vehemence of the feud is even less a necessary evil." The personal had supplanted the political to the detriment of the proletariat. Instead of discussing the summer's elections as "the preparation for systematic continuation of our agitation and organization," the congress had degenerated by design into a forum for rank character assassination. Two and a half days were squandered on the triviality of a few articles in nonparty publications, and Bebel's rambling "three-hour speeches" denied other scheduled speakers their allotted time at the podium. Agreeing with Wolfgang Heine's criticism from July, Eisner asserted that much strife and ill will could have been avoided had the chairman but forgone his lengthy vacation "far from the seat of the party leadership and the central organ" in the critical weeks after the elections when Social Democratic strategy needed to be discussed earnestly, openly, and in detail, for "at a distance one easily loses the proper perspective."

Rather than consolidating June's gains, August Bebel used the 1903 congress to orchestrate a witch hunt and show trial that belied the party's professed dual tactic, put to flight droves of newly won supporters, and sealed Social Democracy's fate. The party's rout in the elections of 1907, its impotence in August 1914, and fragmentation during the First World War were bitter consequences of his need, at age sixty-three, to assert himself as the indispensable and infallible patriarch. As surely as Wilhelm Pieck, inaugural president of the German Democratic Republic, was the rightful ideological heir to his literal schoolmasters Rosa Luxemburg and Franz Mehring, so too can the succession of Socialist Unity Party autocrats count August Bebel as their grandsire. Chancellor Bülow knew well how to press Bebel's performance at Dresden to advantage; before the new Reichstag he taunted that Russian despotism paled in comparison to the order Bebel would impose on Germany if given the chance.[78]

CHAPTER EIGHT

NEVER . . . A LESS FRUITFUL
SCHOLASTIC DEBATE:
INTRAMURAL STRIFE—EVOLUTION
VS. REVOLUTION (1903–1905)

U NDETERRED BY BEBEL'S HARANGUES at Dresden, Eisner resolved to maintain a centrist stance at *Vorwärts* befitting the national party's organ. Over the next two years his influence would rise to its prewar crest as he engaged in public debate with Kautsky on the nature and aims of Social Democracy, only to fall precipitately when he was driven from office in a purge orchestrated by Bebel, Kautsky, and Mehring. Never again would *Vorwärts* achieve the eminence or credibility it enjoyed under Eisner's direction.

The task at hand upon Eisner's return to the capital was the campaign for the Prussian Landtag, the first in which the party had determined "to participate experimentally in order to gauge how much success working people can achieve in an electoral system that makes a mockery of right and fairness."[1] By the byzantine system prescribed by Bismarck in 1867 to preserve privilege, candidates divided into three categories by the taxes they paid were to be chosen as electors by their class-based constituencies. These electors then would choose the representation to the lower house of the Landtag, the House of Deputies. All voting was by public declaration rather than secret ballot, and votes counted more or less, depending on the class of the voter. As a result of these constraints and Social Democracy's historic boycott, Prussia's largest political party had not a single representative in the Landtag. This year, though, after the phenomenally successful Reichstag campaign, Social Democratic candidates were standing in every district where there was some prospect of a mandate.

In his lead article of 4 October 1903 Eisner recapitulated the state of affairs in a feudal society surviving into the twentieth century and restated his critique of the "tragicomedy" of Prussia's liberal bourgeoisie.[2] "Prussia has remained a barbarian state hostile to education, where the churches flourish and the schools wither; where the greatest part of the rural populace languishes in intellectual and material bondage; where the administration reposes in a small, narrow-minded caste of ruling families, the justice system completely alienated from popular sentiment; where the citizens are still denied the most basic rights and the state as chief employer embraces the basest practices of rapacious enterprise and exploitation; where even the freedom of thought and research is forbidden and artistic creativity is subject to the police saber." Three-class voting had given the Conservative and Center parties, supported by the Junker squirearchy, an overwhelming majority in the Landtag, effectively disenfranchising not only the proletariat but also the bourgeoisie, who had long since bested their social betters economically. In districts where Social Democrats had no chance of success, the party was prepared to support Left Liberal candidates against their mutual adversaries, yet only a handful of bourgeois intellectuals welcomed collaboration. The great majority, of Eugen Richter's stamp, remained loyal to the crown in the delusion that they might somehow displace the Junker in the kaiser's affections and establish a bourgeois monarchy on the French model.

In the midst of the campaign two *Vorwärts* editors, Carl Leid and Julius Kaliski, were convicted of lèse majesté and sentenced to lengthy prison terms for their roles in publishing an exposé based on what may well have been, as Friedrich Stampfer surmised, a fraudulent letter, a hoax concocted to embarrass and discredit the paper.[3] No firm evidence has ever emerged, but given the attempts of the political police to infiltrate Eisner's staff after the Krupp affair, Stampfer's speculation is within reason. The episode had begun during the summer when *Vorwärts* came into possession of a fragment of correspondence bearing the letterhead of the crown prince's adjutant. As in any bureaucracy where rivals use expedient means to advance their causes, where stratification breeds contempt and jealousy, the German government had a problem with leaks: sensitive documents and memos lifted from desktops or fished from wastepaper bins occasionally found their way into the hands of socialist editors. Indeed, the regularity with which *Vorwärts* published these morsels confounded the incredulous and uninformed Conservative press.[4]

In this instance the script was recognized as the same from previously leaked communiqués that had proven accurate.[5] The anonymous author wrote here of plans for a stronghold to be constructed on Pichelswerder Island near Spandau, to which the kaiser might retreat if threatened by rebellion. Only a few miles to the north on the Havel lay the old Citadel, refuge of Prussian royalty during the Seven Years' War. As buffer to the proposed bulwark, the emperor's retinue and state servants were to inhabit the surrounding area, which would constitute a Reichstag electoral district unto itself. Ostensibly, the perceived threat stemmed from the recent surge of popular support for Social Democracy. Convinced that the letter was authentic, Eisner approved its publication. When *Vorwärts* disclosed on 16 August the scheme for a new, literal bastion of monarchy on Berlin's outskirts, the rival press for the most part treated the piece as satire, a flight of fancy as filler in the absence of hard news during dog days. The *Norddeutsche Allgemeine Zeitung*, however, regarded the design as a credible if ill-conceived court intrigue.[6]

Vorwärts stood by the story and once the kaiser's head of the civil cabinet, Hermann von Lucanus, categorically denied the allegations, made so bold as to print the names of the court circle implicated in the plan.[7] When the police raided the editorial offices in search of the pirated missive, a staffer rashly burnt it, destroying the one fast piece of evidence that could have been presented at trial, had it been securely concealed.[8] On 16 October the Third Criminal Division of the Prussian District Court rendered its judgment: nine months for Leid, four for Kaliski for impugning His Majesty.[9] Chief Prosecutor Dr. Isenbiel, recently cheated of certain victory by Frau Krupp's obstinance, had exacted a measure of revenge. Stampfer notes that Dietrich von Hülsen-Haeseler, chief of the military cabinet, resplendent in his general's uniform and makeup, mirthfully testified under oath that the *Vorwärts* reports were pure fabrication.[10] Some five years later, clad in a pink skirt and wreathed in roses, he dropped dead of a heart attack after performing a ballet for the kaiser at a party hosted by Prince Maximilian Egon zu Fürstenberg.[11] Indeed, several key witnesses for the state's case shared Friedrich Alfred Krupp's proclivity.

In retrospect Eisner firmly believed that the correspondence had been genuine and that, caught in their intrigue, the principals perjured themselves to avert further embarrassment to their liege.[12] To be sure, the idea of a defensible haven for an embattled monarch is historically the rule rather than the exception. What fails to tally here though is that the refuge would come replete with its own Reichstag district—the final tweak, as it were—as absolute rulers resorting to force of arms to preserve their regency rarely concern themselves with appearances of popular support or trappings of constitutionality. Stampfer's explanation is more plausible: that highly placed courtiers crafted a ruse. Judging by the key witnesses for the prosecution, the clever deceit appears to have been tailored by impassioned, vengeful men determined to redress Krupp's humiliation and death. Its perpetrators guessed that Social Democracy's organ would be unable to resist discovering a plot so insidiously reactionary.

After the verdict Eisner was impelled to admit publicly that two courtiers "who had been identified to us as cognizant of these plans," the crown prince's chief steward, Ulrich von Trotha, and court architect Bodo Ebhardt, had been wrongly implicated.[13] Rosa Luxemburg wrote to Eisner on 19 October to express support: "I do hope you have not taken the Kaiser Island business to heart. What a pity, though, that you did not duly lash the [Rudolf] Mosse paper [the Liberal *Berliner Tageblatt*] for its churlish gloating."[14] Although *Vorwärts* made use of the sensational trial and convictions in its agitational campaign for the Prussian Landtag and in its crusade against the lèse-majesté statute, the Kaiserinsel affair strengthened the hand of Eisner's critics.[15]

In the final days before the Landtag polling the party mobilized, dispatching members to hand out reams of leaflets at strategic locations and holding daily forums at which prominent speakers assailed Prussian plutocracy. Thursday evening, 5 November, Dr. Leo Arons, a physicist dismissed from his lectureship because of his affiliation with the Left, appealed to voters of the third district in the union hall on Engel-Ufer. Eduard Bernstein addressed an audience Friday evening at Wöllstein's Pub in the Adlershof suburb. Sunday morning the journalist Max Grunwald, former editor of the Erfurt *Tribüne*, spoke on the theme "The Landtag Elections and Their Significance for the Working Populace" at the Sports Park in Friedenau. That afternoon Georg Ledebour's talk at Witte's Beer Garden in Wilmersdorf followed a mass distribution of handbills.[16] On Tuesday, 10 November, *Vorwärts* requested that precinct chairmen telegraph results of balloting for selection of electors, but the lead article bespoke little hope: "If it proves that Prussia's strongest political party is incapable, despite all efforts, to win a considerable number of Landtag mandates, then the masses will have for the first time a proper conception of the grandeur of the electoral system in place in Prussia."[17]

The first round of voting, the selection of electors, was held on Thursday, 12 November. The next day *Vorwärts* reported early returns from across Prussia.[18] In Berlin's fourth district, which was apportioned a total of 1,525 electors, 488 Social Democrats, 867 Left Liberals (the amalgamation of Radical Party, National Social Union, and other progressive elements), and 29 Conservatives were confirmed as electors, whereas the great majority of voters had cast their ballot for Social Democrats. The second round, the election of Landtag deputies, followed on Saturday, 14 November. Although 2,300 of Berlin's 7,000 electors were Social Democrats, the party claimed not one of the city's nine mandates. To the reportage Eisner added his grim editorial. Deprived of its voice in the affairs of the Prussian state, the proletariat would seek other means to express its will: "The future will show in what forms the working class will continue this struggle."[19]

For five years Eisner had resolutely championed parliamentary participation—even in the Prussian Landtag elections—as the critical agitational component of Social Democracy's dual tactic. Days before the eleventh Reichstag convened in Berlin on 4 December, he sought to place November's disheartening setback and June's unprecedented advance in historical context. The twenty-three seats wrested from the bourgeois parties, it stood to reason, ought to prod the kaiser's government to sweeping reform so as "to blunt the revolutionary edge" of the whetted proletarian electorate, but Eisner saw no chance of that. For the next five years the majority, marshaled by Conservative Party leader Wilhelm von Kardorff, would likely continue to approve the budget, adopt protective tariffs, build ships, enlist soldiers, and levy taxes—"the fivefold standard by which the government measures a new parliament." Ironically, it fell to the workers' party, which "regards its work within the existing order merely as a prelude to far more consequential events," to drive substantive reform even while molding the future state. "The gulf separating the stymied future interests of the working class from its undeniable present interests is merely a figment of our opponents' imagination." The task of the party's new Reichstag delegation would be, as before, to strengthen democracy in preparation for the coming day.[20]

On Friday, 4 December 1903, the day the new Reichstag opened, Lisbeth Eisner gave birth in Groß-Lichterfelde to her fifth child, Hans Kurt, the last destined to survive infancy.[21] As an eventful year drew to a close, Eisner commemorated the liberal Prussian theologian, pedagogue, and essayist Johann Gottfried Herder at the hundredth anniversary of his death. In two articles that evince a careful reading of Herder's oeuvre Eisner summarized the thought of Goethe's early mentor and touted Social Democracy as the legitimate guardian of his legacy. The first, printed in arts supplement of *Vorwärts* on Thursday, 17 December, examined Herder's formative years, recounting his humble origins, the chance associations that afforded study at Königsberg, and the influence of his professors Kant and Hamann.[22] Particularly the latter, with his emphasis on the innate and intuitive, shaped Herder's conception of history and culture, leading him to the belief that literature was conditioned by the native language and heritage of its authors and thus grounded in popular custom. Imitation of foreign forms and styles, be they Greek, Roman, or French, was inevitably contrived and lifeless. In the oral tradition of the folksong, in the ancient Germanic and Celtic lays, in Shakespeare's natural disregard for the classical dramatic unities Herder perceived the poetic voice of the Northern peoples.

The second, longer article appeared as the paper's lead the next morning and took as its theme Herder's profound, enlightened sense of humanity, nurtured by Kant's tutelage and shared by the poets Bürger and Klopstock.[23] As "a proclaimer and servant of the great fraternal republic of the free and equal," Herder wrote initially in support of the revolution in France. His *Briefe zur Beförderung der Humanität* (Letters on the Advancement of Mankind) and *Ideen zur Philosophie der Geschichte der Menschheit* (Ideas on the Philosophy of the History of Man) shocked the sensibilities of the patrician Goethe, who upon scanning the latter work's chapter on forms of government, confided that 'with good reason not a word of it could be let stand.' Thus it was that the thinker who lamented in 1780 that 'the holiest rights of man are regarded as nothing and trampled under foot' by despotism and that 'even in enlightened Prussia the greatest slavery prevails' had never attained in Berlin the status of even Otto the Lazy, whose marble likeness graced the capital. But the greatest indignity to Herder's memory came at the hands of the bourgeois press, which now hailed him as one of their own: "Official Germany's celebration of the German classical writers is a desecration of corpses, and here too it must fall to Social Democracy to defend the intellectual heroes of humane liberalism against its degenerate window dressers."

Early in the new year Eisner turned his attention to Russia, examining Berlin's questionable cozy relations with St. Petersburg and the mounting tension between Russia and Japan. On Sunday, 3 January 1904, *Vorwärts* retaliated for the Kaiserinsel embarrassment by printing the names, addresses, salaries, and techniques of Russian secret police and their German operatives spying on and harassing Russian nationals residing in Prussia.[24] The Foreign Office secretary, Baron von Richthofen, had already been compelled to admit before the Reichstag that the government allowed Russian oprichniks to keep their compatriots under surveillance, but he insisted that those being watched were violent anarchists hatching plots against the tsar. The head of the shadowy security organization, addressed as "Excellency" by subordinates, was ensconced in a villa in a Berlin suburb where he was registered as an engineer under the name Harting.[25] His annual salary of 36,000 marks was "exactly as much as a Prussian minister's." A German hireling for 175 marks per month, Karl Wolz, lived at Sesenheimerstraße 4 in Berlin-Charlottenburg. Under the alias Hansen he frequented the Stuttgarter Square station, following his marks when they boarded trains, that he might discover their destinations and associates. A former sailor, Wolz was easily recognizable by scars on his forearms where tattoos had been cauterized. Wolz was tasked with keeping tabs on an influential intellectual residing in the Hermsdorf suburb north of Charlottenburg, whose return to Russia was of particular concern to the secret police. If the man could be arrested at the border, Wolz would receive 500 marks in reward. To learn as much as possible about his quarry, Wolz rented a furnished room near the Hermsdorf station for 30 marks per month. So good were the *Vorwärts* editors' sources in this instance that they knew that hapless Wolz had claimed 45 marks' reimbursement for the room, a tidbit that could not have pleased His Excellency.

There followed shortly a remarkably prescient two-part article outlining Russia's aims in the Far East and Japan's likely response.[26] The historical quest for a warm-water port, derailed by defeat in the Crimean War, had driven expansion to the east. The construction of the Siberian railway began in 1891, and soon European incursions into China prompted the Japanese to invade the mainland in order to secure the Korean peninsula and southern Manchuria. Japan handily defeated China, but Russia, supported by France and Germany, pressured Japan into relinquishing its acquisitions in favor of monetary reparations from the Chinese. Russia then occupied Port Arthur at the tip of Korea's Kwantung Peninsula to complement Vladivostok to the north. Were Russia to gain control of Korea, the two great ports would be linked and the Russian fleet, with stations along the Korean coast, would have won strategic control of East Asia.

Japan had used the indemnities exclusively to strengthen its military in preparation for a showdown with Russia. During the period of Russia's eastward push, "Japan transformed itself with exemplary speed from a hermetic feudal state culturally manifesting its specifically Chinese origin into a military and cultural state on the European model." In the last decade Japan's merchant marine had experienced more than a fourfold increase in tonnage, coal production had nearly trebled, and the nation's rail network had expanded from 1,621 to 4,025 total miles. Under no circumstances would the ascendant Empire of the Sun abide tsarist rule in Korea: war between the two, the analysis concluded, was presumably inevitable despite the United States' feverish attempt at mediation.

As he had memorialized Herder in December, Eisner had in February occasion to venerate Immanuel Kant. In the *Vorwärts* lead of Friday, the twelfth, the hundredth anniversary of the philosopher's death, and in Saturday's and Sunday's editions, Eisner hailed Kant's thought as seminal to modernity.[27] The three-part article, which he took care to initial as his work, constitutes one of his most significant writings on philosophy and reveals like no other the stations of his progress from left-leaning intellectual to committed socialist, begun at Marburg and completed in Plötzensee. In 1918 he declared in aptly scientific terminology borrowed from chemistry—which he had also studied in his cell—that this essay was no less than "an attempt to reconfigure the Marx-Hegel synthesis within the Marx-Kant compound, for in essence Marx belongs to Kant, in the line of the Enlightenment's great philosophers of the eighteenth century, however profoundly and decisively he . . . is influenced by Hegel."[28]

Drawing on Newton's investigation of the natural world and on Rousseau's thinking on humankind and society, Kant's epistemological and ontological construct laid the basis for objective inquiry and enjoined man to define himself through cultural achievement and aspiration. "Grounding the premises of thinking in empirical science, he simultaneously purged cognition of all supersensory metaphysics and metaphysics of all claim to scientific validity. He rubbed out religious mythology between science, from which it was banned, and human ethics, where it has no place." Disjoining belief from knowledge, Kant's skepticism became the secular creed of Western scholarship, anticipating both Nietzsche's reappraisal of morality and Marx's codification of historical determinism. By repudiating a supernatural source of order and salvation Kant simply redefined the human condition and gave man's destiny over to man. Ideology displaced faith in all discourse worthy of the name intellectual. As "conqueror of the metaphysical-mythological worldview," Kant consigned theological conjecture to the realm of imagination, "ideas about which nothing could be proven, for which he propounded the so grossly misunderstood 'Ding an sich.'"

Despite his provincial isolation in Königsberg, despite having to write under the Prussian censor, couching his thought in abstruse language, Kant emerged as the Enlightenment's perfector, exerting immense influence on contemporary thinkers and on the next generation, whose advances in diverse arenas created new disciplines and radically changed man's perception of himself and the world. Darwin, the botanist Matthias Schleiden, cofounder of the cell theory, and the physiologist Johannes Müller all proceeded from Kant's impulse. His spirit animates Schiller's writings on the aesthetic education of humanity and the plan for a universal history of man. Having studied with Cohen, Eisner emphasized here Kant's contribution to ethics. Rejecting divinely revealed and ordained morality, Kant declared that any legitimate moral code must derive from the reason of free men who willingly follow it. His categorical imperative transcended the Confucian "golden rule" of reciprocity, echoed in the New Testament, based on individual benefit. Kant's maxim demanded universal social utility, charging man to develop, to progress beyond self-interest. Accordingly, he also spurned aimless theoretical philosophizing as well as speculative "empirical" categorizations of randomly observed experience, with no underlying, unifying premise: 'Thoughts without content are empty, views without concepts are blind.'

In the context of his times Kant was the quintessential liberal republican, a relentless advocate of the French Revolution, even during the Terror, which he regarded as necessary to the consolidation of an ethical code of the free and equal. Like the bourgeois revolutionaries in Paris, Kant recognized the right of property with its attendant inequities even though he questioned the distribution of land whereby a seignior holding more acreage than he could work could compel others to serve him who jointly could have acquired their own considerable holding. In Kant's conception of the constitutional republic the independent citizenry— the self-sufficient, mature, male populace—would determine the laws by which society would be governed. That this class might unfetter itself from feudal constraints, Kant unabashedly advocated laissez-faire; indeed, he opposed Christian charity as a demeaning manifestation of patriarchal despotism that deprived the individual of dignity and subordinated him to the favor of an elite. Yet he realized that history was fluid and that the enlightened mores of each age would be dictated by circumstance.

Although claimed, as was Herder, by the German Center-Left capitalist press as a guiding light, "the classical thinker of liberalism," Eisner declared, "has nothing more in common with today's bourgeoisie." His mantle had passed to the proponent of scientific socialism. "If Kant conceived of his *Critiques* in essence only as a methodological framework into which all individual sciences were to be incorporated, then Marx fills the framework in the areas of history and economy, at the same time far surpassing Kant's meager intimations of that kind. He fixed the colossal multiplicity of historical experience in the granite structure of a unified system that neither strings together 'ideas' nor assembles mere 'facts' but rather discerns, interprets, and shapes the at heart revolutionary regularity of real events."

The conclusion of Eisner's essay welds Kant and Marx and elucidates how a cultural idealist schooled in Kant connected with the workers' party. "The resolution of a worldview striving for unity and certainty, embracing the whole man and the whole of humanity; the iron linkage of scientific knowledge with all political action; the fundamental conception of things; the conviction that a state based on reason is a realizable goal; the ethic of freedom and equality, which for all its idealistic ardor nonetheless stands solid and circumspect on the ground of proven facts, judging critically

without sighing sentimentality and tearful emotionalism; the unwaver-
ing cosmopolitanism that utterly scorns the sickly, opportunistic spirit of
bourgeois society mired in crassest self-interest, devoid of goals and ideals
yet tricked out in vain romantic finery: all these are the most basic traits of
international Social Democracy."

That the editor of a socialist daily for mass distribution to a proletarian audience would run so erudite a piece on so challenging a thinker
was an expression of sublime confidence in the receptivity of his readers
and their suitability to the high purpose of his dual masters. His critics
surely must have smirked at such unjaded optimism. When in mid-April
Eisner made editorial changes to Rosa Luxemburg's report on the trial
of the Russian anarchist Gerschuni, it was precisely Eisner's Kantian sensibilities she scathed in protesting his characterization of the fragmented
Russian Left: "the question of whether absolutism might be defeated
in Russia by the proletarian mass movement or by terrorist blows has
about as much to do with 'sectarianism' as Kant with socialism, if you
will permit me the comparison. . . . Stick to Saint Immanuel and earn
your bread honestly."[29]

In one of his annual articles commemorating the martyrs of the
March Uprising in Berlin and Vienna, Eisner returned to the transition
from bourgeois to proletarian revolution and commented on the current state of affairs from an historical perspective.[30] The bourgeois revolutionaries' belief in social equality born of innate human reason, he
wrote, defined a new age of man. With no real understanding of how
economic law prescribes political structure, no theoretical underpinning
derived from exhaustive study of past and present civilizations, the liberal
republicans operated for the most part intuitively. Cognizant of history's
mechanics and tendency, the Marxist workers' movement was revolutionary in and of itself without erecting the first barricade. Ironically though,
even while the now reactionary bourgeoisie expected the great, violent
upheaval any day, old-school incendiaries of the Left errantly regarded
Social Democracy increasingly as a reform initiative. "Never has there
been a less fruitful scholastic debate than that over evolution or revolution. . . . At no moment in world history have pent-up revolutionary
energies been greater than at present, and at no other moment than this
has it been less possible for the ruling class to trigger those energies prematurely by increasing acts of force." But, Eisner warned, there were
limits to ethical forbearance. "In any case revolution is not murder but
rather the struggle against murder; the revolution is truly not to blame if
that struggle must be waged at times by those barbaric means the masters
taught their slaves to use."

The first bright day of March after months of gloom that had affected him worse than usual filled the commuting journalist with desire to roam about in the sunshine: "Shimmering promise streamed over the broad plain out there in my quiet refuge." Dutifully, though, he boarded the train for the heart of Berlin and sat brooding in the overheated car on the dismal lives of women and children enslaved in their stifling dwellings by the contracted piecework of cottage industry.[31] When May Day finally arrived, overcast but mild, Eisner rose early to follow the festivities citywide. Riding the train from Lichterfelde-Süd past birch and fir forests, he was joined at each stop by workers turned out for union and party events. As the first of May fell that year on Sunday, the crush of celebrants was immense. Everywhere red pennants fluttered from windows, red carnations adorned lapels. Eisner made his way first to the Friedrichshain, where Bebel was to address construction workers at a nearby brewery. The cobblers rallied that morning at the Swiss Garden before their outing south to the Stralau peninsula between the Spree and Lake Rummelsburg.

Toward midday Eisner took the streetcar south to the cavernous New World Beer Hall on the Hasenheide at Rixdorf, where over ten thousand listened to the woodworkers' chorale and then a speech by Bernstein. Then traversing the city's north and east sides, he found pubs packed to capacity for concerts, cineograph screenings, puppet shows, and gymnasts' exhibitions. At six that evening from his vantage point at the Bock Brewery atop Tempelhof Hill, Eisner gazed out at "a forest of spread umbrellas" until a hailstorm chased the crowd. In Tuesday's edition of *Vorwärts* he reflected that one scene from Sunday seemed to underscore the rest: the sight of a few elderly women hunched with care, gilt hymnals in their trembling hands, diverting from the throngs of afternoon merrymakers into a dilapidated church, "representatives of a dying world that dared not demand its human due from life and hopes for it now from death."[32]

Japan's stunning rout of Russian forces in China was hailed by *Vorwärts* as a triumph of modernity over tsarism.[33] The report of Saturday, 18 June, stressed the tactical superiority of Japan's professional field commanders, all commoners, over St. Petersburg's court favorites, who had been outclassed at every turn. The Japanese military had proven itself under the most difficult circumstances: a war on foreign soil requiring timely naval transport of troops and heavy guns. After putting ashore at Inch'on, General Kuroki's First Army had driven toward Manchuria, stopping north of the Yalu to cover the landing of additional troops. To the south General Oku cut off Russian defenders of Port Arthur, and General Nodzu's Fourth Army defeated General Stackelberg's forces. The war, *Vorwärts* prognosticated, would ultimately hinge on control of Port Arthur and the fortunes of Russia's Far Eastern Fleet in the Yellow Sea.

Even while tsarist absolutism was "collapsing militarily in East Asia," the full scope of the Russian oprichniks' mission in Prussia and of Berlin's collaboration came to light in late June when nine German nationals were indicted by their government for clandestine assembly, high treason against Russia, and lèse majesté of the tsar. The prosecution had worked for over half a year to build its case; the defense was given less than three weeks to prepare for trial, slated to open on 12 July in Königsberg. The defendants, including a barber, two watchmakers, a master cobbler, an accountant, and a dispatch clerk at Vorwärts Press in Berlin, were charged with smuggling revolutionary texts into Russia. Among the writings were translations of Marx and Kautsky, Russian socialist journals published in exile, and anarchist tracts inciting the populace to acts of terror against the state. Early in January the Russian embassy, claiming legal reciprocity, had asked the German government to act on its behalf. Both the foreign and justice ministries had been more than willing to do St. Petersburg's bidding, for as Prussian justice minister Karl Heinrich von Schönstedt publicly asserted, when it came to combatting the Left, "Tua res agitur," which Eisner interpreted for his readers as "Russia's cause is Prussia's cause." The state prosecutor reported to Schönstedt, who in turn reported to the German Foreign Office, which communicated information to the Russian embassy.

The significance of the proceedings Eisner explained as inveterate class interest of Prussia's ruling elite, more immediately threatened by encroaching modernity than their counterparts in hopelessly benighted Russia. "Through all the vicissitudes of foreign policy the East Elbian caste of great-estate owners kept Prussia at the side of the Realm of the Knout. Russia has remained the mainstay of all European efforts at suppression." Eisner personally covered the trial in Königsberg, filing detailed reports and analyses of the arguments, issues, and sentences. The investigations had begun in September 1903 when the barber Max Nowagrotzki had received shipments of subversive texts in Russian and Latvian from a student in Switzerland. A police search of Nowagrotzki's home implicated two accomplices in nearby Memel on the Russian border. Correspondence found at their quarters led to the arrest of others, and further searches yielded bundles of the Russian socialist journal *Iskra* in the possession of Martin Kogst in Bajohren, which had been sent by Vorwärts Press in Berlin.[34]

The defense, led by Karl Liebknecht and Hugo Haase, shrewdly conceded that their clients had channeled socialist publications into

Russia—no German law forbade it—but disputed the spurious Russian claim to reciprocity as well as the legality and, by implication, morality of official Prussia's slavishness to Nicholas II. Turning the trial into a public forum on the evils of tsarist rule, they called witness after witness to testify to the state of affairs in Russia. Accounts of torture in Siberian prisons, bloody persecution of Jews, and the dire misery of the common people shocked the gallery.[35] In the midst of the proceedings Eisner broke from reporting testimony to critique Tolstoy's bold manifesto against the war on Japan. Even while Germans were on trial for smuggling subversive texts into Russia, Eisner wrote, Russia's great writer turned to foreign printers in his effort "to confront the tsar, grand dukes, generals, industrialists, plutocrats, and clerics with their crimes."[36]

The trial in Königsberg lasted two weeks. When the verdicts were handed down on 25 July, three of the defendants were acquitted of all charges. The stiffest penalty accorded the other six was a jail term of three months.[37] The bourgeois press generally echoed the claim by *Vorwärts* that the chief beneficiary of the government's efforts was Social Democracy. The *Berliner Tageblatt* denounced the trial as "a black page of Prussian justice." The *Frankfurter Zeitung* was equally scandalized: "A nice picture of German culture! Russian police informants are permitted to ply their mischief in Germany, upon whose denunciations Russian guests who have done nothing to Germany were expelled and in some cases even deported to Russia, that is, handed over. And to top it all off, in the end German citizens were subjected to a capital criminal proceeding for the monstrous crime of having helped smuggle Russian writings over into Russia. Please note that these writings were not prohibited in Germany nor is their transport to Russia of itself illegal."

The *Magdeburger Zeitung* added that although the abominable abuse of human rights in Russia was already well known, Germans "blushed with shame" at the revelation that their government was hand in glove with the tyrants. The Conservative *Dresdner Nachrichten* (Dresden News) bemoaned that Social Democracy, which "lives on the mistakes of its opponents," now had overcome the debacle of the Dresden party congress with the help of the state's incompetence at Königsberg.[38] As to comment on the trial in Russia, the censor had forbidden any mention of the proceedings.[39] Three days after the trial the Russian interior minister who had masterminded the sordid operation in Germany, Vyacheslav Konstantinovich Plehve, was assassinated in St. Petersburg in a carefully planned bomb attack carried out by a member of the Socialist Revolutionary Party.[40]

After the trial Eisner traveled with Comrade Schwarz of Königsberg, counsel for defendants Friedrich Klein and August Kugel, up the coast to the border area to see for himself the locale described by various witnesses. At the village Schwarzort they swam in the Baltic at sundown and then rested until midnight on a moonlit hill while gazing out on the shimmering water. The next morning they continued to once-bustling Memel, where Lithuanian farmers animated the old Fischmarkt, then on to Nimmersatt, "the northernmost place in the German Empire," haven to professional smugglers. At Hirsch Feinstein's tavern, the last on German soil, Eisner and his companion surveyed the clientele, types described in the courtroom days earlier. Crossing over into Russia, they were struck by the almost instant desolation: "The intensely worked, green Prussian countryside suddenly turned into a barren rolling grassland thick with boulders; it appeared that no plow had gone over these vast, empty marches, where even goats would have starved, since the Ice Age had brought these erratic blocks from the Scandinavian mountains."

At the customs station their papers were scrutinized while Eisner, acutely conscious of his Jewishness, read a seemingly endless list of punishable activities in Russia of which foreigners had to be aware. They were allowed to pass, but their camera was confiscated and a Cossack on bicycle followed them to the town of Krottingen, inhabited mainly by Lithuanians and Jews in a jumble of hovels. No newspaper was to be found anywhere. Almost everyone they encountered seemed introspective and joyless. "Only the young Jewesses standing before the houses were radiant, like a piece of the Orient: healthy, serious, of a melancholy-sensuous beauty." At the poorhouse the visiting Germans found a disquieting assortment of the indigent, crippled, blind, mad, and elderly. When they dispensed their remaining Russian coins to the inmates, the grateful recipients fell to the ground to kiss their benefactors' boots. A decade later Eisner confided that whenever he thought of Russia, it was images from Krottingen's poorhouse that came to mind.[41]

Over the next weeks Eisner assembled and annotated court transcripts, drafted an introduction chronicling Prussian-Russian relations, compiled press reports from across Europe on the Königsberg trial, intoned the moral in a brief conclusion, and added an appendix of related documents to produce a massive tome of well over five hundred pages. Published by Vorwärts Press, *Der Geheimbund des Zaren* (The Tsar's Secret Society) took its title from the statute against clandestine alliance, cited by the state prosecutor in charging the defendants.[42] The reader of Eisner's book could have no doubt as to who was in secret league with whom. Karl Liebknecht wrote a lengthy review for the 1 March issue of

Neue Zeit, in which he hailed the book as "a most arduous and commendable labor" that elucidated the issues and import of the trial as well as documenting the testimony. Eisner had "succeeded brilliantly" in conveying the politically charged atmosphere of the courtroom.[43]

The week before the Second Socialist International's sixth congress was to meet in Amsterdam, Eisner reviewed in two articles for *Vorwärts* the organization's history since its founding in Paris in 1889, examining chronic factionalism arising from national contexts of member parties— dissent registered chiefly in debate on tactics.[44] The pressing issue at Paris in 1900 had been "ministerialism," or whether a socialist might serve in a bourgeois government. The dispute was settled unexpectedly when delegates approved Kautsky's resolution affirming such service under certain extraordinary circumstances as a viable weapon of class struggle. The tactic, Eisner argued, varied by necessity from land to land and was determined in part by the prevalent form of government (Staatsform). "Freedom in the choice of tactical means increases with the growing consciousness of the masses, but the index of what is tactically permissible is no less dependent on the special national character of the class foe."[45]

What Eisner anticipated, a rehashing of the debate at Paris on Millerand's reform ministry, indeed occurred. Although he had emphatically denounced Millerand's concessions to French colonial policy, Eisner nonetheless approved in principle a socialist's entering a bourgeois government as consistent with Social Democracy's dual tactic if the workers' life could be significantly bettered by it. In a lengthy speech to the delegates Jean Jaurès, leader of the Parti Socialiste Français, defended Millerand and criticized German Social Democracy's 'impotence.' This time the majority sided with the Parti Socialiste de France, led by Jules Guesde and Édouard Vaillant, and condemned participation in the cabinet of a bourgeois government. On Sunday, 21 August, Eisner reported in his lead article that although the congress roundly rejected Jaurès's position, it recognized "with equal unanimity that errors are not sins and honest mistakes no crime."[46]

Eisner and Jaurès, cofounder of the newspaper *L'Humanité*, were related by intellect, erudition, and philosophical outlook, ideologically closer to one another than to their compatriotic comrades. "In 1904," Eisner later confessed, "as editor at *Vorwärts* I stood dangerously isolated, on Jaurès's side."[47] At Amsterdam Bebel had countered Jaurès's defense of Millerand by assailing the essentially plutocratic bourgeois republic as fundamentally opposed to the interests of the proletariat, a sentiment eagerly exploited by the German and French Right, who construed it as a Lassallean endorsement of 'social monarchy.' So great was

the hubbub in the Conservative press that Kautsky felt obliged to inter-
pret for the masses exactly what Bebel had meant by his remarks. In an
article dated 21 August, Kautsky explained for the readers of *Neue Zeit*
that Social Democracy considered a republic preferable in every instance
to a monarchy, as "class difference between proletariat and bourgeoisie is most sharply and clearly delineated in the republic."[48] He concluded that monarchy is strongest when the various classes hold each
other in check, which "can cause a monarchical government to take the
side of the proletariat against the bourgeoisie in certain cases." He then
denounced the perception that a bourgeois republic was more favorable
than monarchy to the masses as a "superstition" spread in the socialist
ranks by pernicious revisionism.

Eisner's initialed response appeared in *Vorwärts* on Tuesday, 30
August.[49] He acknowledged as accurate Kautsky's description of the
prevalent class interest of the bourgeois republic, but took issue with
Kautsky's assessment of the "muted nature of class conflict under monarchy" and with the the term 'republican superstition.' The objectionable
points could give rise to the misinterpretation that Bebel thought class
conflict to be less intense in a monarchy than in a republic—an opinion, Eisner insisted, "that Bebel of course does not and cannot espouse."
History documented that no ruling class tolerates a monarchy that does
not advocate its interests exclusively. From time to time the monarchical
government might see fit to play off one element of the ruling class against
another, but never would it favor the ruled over the rulers. "Conversely,
in democratic republics and constitutional, titular monarchies such as
England the ruling classes, in their internal squabbles regarding interests,
are compelled to entice the proletariat to their side through concessions.
. . . It contradicts all fact and turns the true relationship on its head to
claim that the purer and harsher form of class conflict exists in republics. In the bourgeois republic and related forms of government one seeks
to corrupt the worker with gifts, in absolute monarchy to intimidate the
worker with force."

To bolster his position, Eisner cited Bebel's article of 5 September
1903 in *Neue Zeit*. The next day, 31 August, Eisner assured Kautsky in a
personal letter that he shared the desire "to engage in science rather than
polemic" and explained that he intended to print Kautsky's response and
his rejoinder together. "I have a bad conscience," he confessed, "that by
so doing I misuse a bit the editor's privilege and frame your position less
favorably, for . . . the impression of the last piece, which I accord myself,
has a power all its own. But I think I can be fair to you too."[50] Indeed,
in that morning's paper Eisner had run an op-ed piece by one of his own

staff, Heinrich Ströbel, that sided squarely with Kautsky. Appended to Ströbel's remarks was Eisner's editorial nota bene that Kautsky himself had sent a reply, which would run in Thursday's paper.[51]

Publication was delayed by a day, that Eisner might draft the rejoinder. In his piece Kautsky charged that Eisner had cited Bebel's comments eristically out of context, imputing inconsistency where there was none. Kautsky clarified that by 'republican superstition' he had meant the belief that "there resides in the republican bourgeoisie a far greater inclination to further the liberation of the working class than in the monarchy and the monarchical bourgeoisie." It was the French republic, he pointed out, that had beheaded Baboeuf and massacred workers in June 1848 and May 1871, whereas the German monarchy, prompted by Bismarck, had implemented universal suffrage and workers' insurance.[52]

The public debate between the chief editors of Social Democracy's two most prestigious organs continued for another week with juxtaposed installments on 2 and 7 September. The image of Kautsky as a "narrow-minded petit tyrant" that his son later sought to dispel is starkly limned in Kautsky's reply and retort to Eisner's assertion and rejoinder, where open intellectual challenge is met with sneering scorn.[53] Even Bebel was alarmed. On Tuesday, 6 September, he wrote from Küsnacht that he had followed the dispute with dismay: "I am of the opinion that you are much too nervous and right away take things too seriously. You polemicize too much. . . . I would not answer *Vorwärts*, or in any case only very cursorily. I fear though that my good advice comes too late."[54]

Indeed, Kautsky had already drafted his second response, cast as a retort, from his home in Berlin-Friedenau two days earlier. He ended it by claiming that Eisner, by advocating Jaurès's cause, had contributed to the woes of the French party and sullied the international prestige of *Vorwärts*: "The whole, great reputation that *Vorwärts* enjoys among party comrades abroad, thanks to the importance of German Social Democracy, is pressed thus by its chief editor into the service of opponents of unity." To Eisner, the very man who over six long years had raised the paper from justifiable obscurity to make its reputation at home and abroad, the insult must have seemed the most despicable infamy. In disgust he remarked that the readership had to be dumbfounded by the degeneration of the debate, and that despite having compromised the party organ so terribly by raising the issue, he could discover no more proof in Kautsky's latest ramblings that monarchy was more disposed to the workers' movement than was the bourgeois republic. Accordingly, "any further requital on this point is superfluous."[55]

After reading the final exchange, Bebel wrote to Kautsky to commend him on successfully concluding the contest, as Bebel thought Eisner's parting comments weak and ineffectual.[56] But Kautsky had no intention of leaving off. Over the next four months he churned out a seven-part series in *Neue Zeit* under the title "Republic and Social Democracy in France." Moreover, he planned to have at Eisner and his supporters during the Bremen party congress. Apprised of his strategy and knowing well Kautsky's vapid style, Rosa Luxemburg, two weeks into a three-month sentence for lèse majesté, wrote from the Zwickau Jail on 9 September to offer her advice in frightful mixed metaphor: "I have no doubt that you will bash out Kurt, Georg [Gradnauer] and Co.'s so-called brains, but you must do it with relish and delight, not as some tedious intermezzo, for the public always senses the mood of the combatants, and the joy of the fight gives the polemic its ringing tone and moral superiority."[57]

On Sunday, the eighteenth, Eisner previewed the 1904 congress's agenda and opined that although the bourgeois press eagerly awaited another Dresden, this year's meeting would be quiet and productive.[58] Among the prominent issues for discussion were curriculum reform in the public schools and an agitational campaign to recruit Catholic industrial workers and the rural proletariat. The education question was particularly galling for the party, as the state schools were being operated for all intents and purposes as church schools, inculcating in students the fear of God and respect for the divinely sanctioned social order. Without naming them, Eisner pointedly admonished Bebel and Kautsky. "The time of the party congress is intended for the business of the whole party, and the larger the party becomes, the more extensive and involved its activity, the more so interest in the inclinations of individuals will naturally dwindle, even if these persons fall under the 'leadership' category."

That evening over three hundred delegates convened in the great hall of Bremen's Kasino, with an audience of well over a thousand from the local membership. In his opening remarks Bebel declared that the party had not splintered after Dresden and that he was confident it would hold together despite the sharply differing opinions for which the annual congresses served as a forum.[59] But the Bremen congress was, as Eisner had hoped, a working meeting rather than a bloodletting, with time even for a daylong cruise on Thursday out to Helgoland.[60] Reviewing the week's proceedings on Sunday, 25 September, he wrote with obvious satisfaction that the delegates had disappointed the bourgeois papers. The party had recognized school reform as a critical cultural mission that would demand a comprehensive campaign over a period of years. At Karl Liebknecht's

urging, who shared Engels's belief that there could be no revolution without first winning over the common soldiery, the assembly protested mis-
treatment of the rank and file by superiors but stopped short of endorsing
his call to agitate young men against the military before their conscription—a failing Eisner would soon revisit.[61] In the final session the report
on the International congress at Amsterdam ended with Bebel's affirmation of the efforts of Jaurès's party to mend the rent in French socialism.
"A year ago," Eisner editorialized smugly on the front page, "we were
compelled to subject the proceedings of our party congress to thorough
criticism in this space. If the course of the last year has fully shown the
accuracy of that self-examination, we are now happily in the position to
approve of Bremen's outcome."[62]

In the week after the congress the People's Free Stage of Berlin held
a general meeting the evening of 29 September. Eisner, who served with
Joseph Bloch, Robert Schmidt, and Friedrich Stampfer on the program
committee, was in attendance for Simon Katzenstein's lecture on "Crime
in Drama" and the executive committee's business report. Due in no
small part to Eisner's efforts, membership had grown to ten thousand,
and hundreds of new applicants had to be turned away for want of seating at the performances. In the last year the association had staged plays
by Bernard Shaw, Sven Lange, Ernst Preczang, Shakespeare, Lessing, and
Goethe. A poetry and concert series had been launched, after repeated
requests to the city administration, in the Bürgersaal of town hall. The
most recent offering featured Hugo Wolf's song settings of Mörike's
verse.[63] The cultural diversion and inspiration provided Berlin's workers
by the People's Free Stage was easily no less welcome to Eisner, whom
Stampfer credited in his memoirs as the driving force to the committee:
"The most indefatigable among us was Kurt Eisner. Here he was completely in his element, and often I had the impression—not just in the
Volksbühne—that he was by temperament more artist than politician."[64]

Reading at home on 10 October 1904, Eisner paused over a Left
Liberal paper's account of a dispute between Bernstein and Ruberrimus,
pseudonym of Ernst Heilmann. The *Freisinnige Zeitung* (Progressive
Newspaper) reported Kautsky had declared that Ruberrimus in this
instance merited a "kick in the seat." Eisner wrote immediately to Kautsky
in protest, as Count Bülow did well enough bashing Social Democrats
on his own. But beyond the issue of principle Eisner had a high opinion
of Ruberrimus and wondered at Kautsky's rebuke. "I know Ruberrimus
from the Königsberg trial. He was reporting on it there and accomplished
the enormous work alone with near superhuman devotion. Moreover,
I know that he was chucked out of his legal career because of political

activity: lectures at trade-union meetings." Eisner appealed to Kautsky to divulge the grounds for his scorn, as Ruberrimus was under consideration for appointment to the *Vorwärts* staff.[65] Kautsky responded by posting to *Vorwärts* his thanks to the host of well-wishers congratulating him on his fiftieth birthday.[66]

Kautsky rejoined his polemic with full force after Eisner wrote in early November on militarism and democracy in France. Eisner's piece examined the attempt by the French Right to topple the Combes government through an assault on its firmly republican defense minister, General André, for initiatives to democratize the officer corps. Notes compiled by one of André's informants on the the political reliability of various officers had been stolen and leaked to the press, and until Jaurès exposed the motives and methods of André's critics, it appeared probable that their smear campaign would succeed. When the government decisively won a vote of confidence in the Chamber of Deputies, the Conservative member Syveton set upon André, striking him repeatedly in the face with clenched fist. Its opponents dispersed and disgraced, the Combes goverment, Eisner observed, could continue its work, "which is, to be sure, thoroughly bourgeois and inadequate for French Social Democracy," toward liberalization of the French state.[67]

Kaustky immediately took issue, arguing that the fight against militarism had nothing to do with whether the officer corps was controlled by the feudal landed gentry or the commercial bourgeoisie; only the establishment of a people's militia would wipe away this preserve of elitism. The French republican military would be brought to bear against strikers as quickly as its predecessor. Kautsky faulted Jaurès for defending General André, who vehemently opposed socialism, and for preventing the collapse of a government that persecuted socialist schoolteachers. Precisely because Jaurès advocated ministerial socialism, itself a by-product of the Dreyfus affair, he could no longer advance the class interest of the French worker. But worst of all in Kautsky's view was that André's reliance on informants could be justified by the organ of German Social Democracy: "It is not our intention to polemicize here against Jaurès. What concerns us above all is the bearing of *Vorwärts*, which is enchanted by Jaurès and slavishly follows his lead."[68]

Marking that Kautsky had aligned himself with the most reactionary elements of French society, Eisner responded with a detailed rebuttal, the gist of which was that Kautsky in his theoretical ether and out of deep antipathy to Jaurès could not grasp the context of events in France and therefore missed the crux of the matter. Jaurès, Eisner maintained, had saved the Center-Left coalition from defeat at the hands of the proletariat's worst enemies—a defeat abhorrent to all who espoused democracy. "It is profoundly regrettable that Comrade Kautsky through boundless accusations makes it infinitely difficult for socialists of other countries to understand circumstances in France."[69] Kautsky fired back that he considered it pointless to try to reach an understanding with the editor of *Vorwärts*, as their opinions on French politics diverged too sharply for that. He conceded that he too would have voted in favor of the Combes government, as had Vaillant's revolutionary Parti Socialiste de France, but he reiterated that Jaurès had compromised all socialists by defending the use of skulking spies.[70] In his final comments Eisner declared that Kautsky's aversion to mutual understanding was his alone. "Kautsky was so often our teacher that we would have no reluctance to acknowledge it if he proved us in error."[71]

The Sunday before Advent, the day on which Germany's Protestant North commemorates the dear departed, Eisner elegized the last tender sprays of lilac, victims of the recent frost, and mused on the symbolism of winter's onset for humankind.[72] Perhaps he sensed that Lisbeth's difficult pregnancy at thirty-seven boded nothing good. And indeed the twins to which she gave birth, Angelus and Ruth, expired in the cradle on 29 December.[73] At what must have been for Kurt Eisner a moment of intense personal reflection on life's watersheds, his most inimical critics conspired tirelessly against him. To Bebel, Kautsky and Mehring, Eisner's resolutely centrist posture at *Vorwärts* had become more galling than the revisionists' most counterrevolutionary initiatives. Megalomaniacal and rash by definition, political extremists typically fancy that by laying waste to the middle ground they hasten the demise of their bitterest rivals. Somehow the spiteful triumvirate had lost touch with the reality that their bitterest rivals were hardly the reformists within their own party, much less the would-be mediators who strove to hold the fragmenting party together. Eisner later clarified the dynamic of the psychosis: "Governments divert attention from internal problems by channeling passions to external concerns. With parties just the opposite occurs: external impediments eat their way inward. Frustrated feelings of power over one's enemy turn into belligerence toward one's comrade. If I cannot topple a cabinet minister, well then at least I can bring down my friend Schulz."[74] Because Eisner had encouraged diverse points of view at *Vorwärts*, the plot against him found support among the very associate editors and correspondents whose careers he had advanced.

Correspondent Georg Ledebour, for example, evidently infuriated by *Vorwärts* and Bernstein simultaneously endorsing his call to action against Prussia's three-class electoral system, denounced the paper's intolerable "policy of glossing over differences" that succored Bernstein's designs.[75] Mehring too went on the attack, asserting that *Vorwärts*, "instead of being, according to its charge, the ideological backbone of the party, swings back and forth on every question of principle and has long since become a rudimentary organ for the political, scientific development of the party."[76] The day after Christmas Victor Adler wrote to Bebel from Vienna to express his concern at Mehring's execrable smear.[77] "No one anywhere," the Austrian Social Democratic leader counseled, "would put up with how FM. treats K Eisner, how the *L. Vlkz.* treats comrades in general." At the height of turmoil at the Dresden congress it was Adler who had convinced Eisner not to resign his office. Now Adler wondered why Bebel had ever allied himself with a rogue such as Mehring and warned Bebel of the risks: "Now you are exposed to the complete ruthlessness of this man for whom there is nothing at all to be spared, to whom truly nothing is sacred other than his own self-righteousness and vengefulness. . . . Better to have such people as adversaries than friends!"[78]

Hoping perhaps to begin the New Year with a less sullied slate, Eisner wrote cordially from his office to Kautsky on 4 January to ask his collaboration on a pamphlet Vorwärts Press planned for the hundredth anniversary of Schiller's death. Having been charged with editing the special issue, Eisner proposed that Kautsky contribute an article on "social stratification in the period of Weimar classicism." He reported that things were back to normal at home and closed with a warm greeting to Kautsky's household. Appended to the typescript was a note in Eisner's hand that he was "of course amenable if any other theme appeals to you."[79]

CHAPTER NINE

REVOLUTIONIZING MINDS:
THE SCORCHED MIDDLE
GROUND (1905)

EARLY IN 1905 THE SOCIALIST PARTIES of Europe fixated on events in
Russia. The strike in St. Petersburg in mid-January, led by the prison
priest Georgi Gapon, unexpectedly unified forces for reform from the
salon to the stable. As *Vorwärts* reported on the fateful Sunday of 22
January, 96,000 workers at 174 concerns in and around the capital had
struck in support of the workers' rights movement that had its impetus
in the dismissal of 4 workers from the Putilov Iron Works for belonging to a workers' association founded by Gapon the previous year. On
the fifteenth the dismissed workers' comrades unsuccessfully demanded
their reinstatement. The next day Gapon led a delegation of 84 workers
presenting much broader demands, including an eight-hour workday, a
minimum wage, double pay for overtime, improved sanitation, and election of a workers' council to help set wages and determine grounds for
dismissal. On 17 and 18 January workers struck to impress the urgency of
their grievances.

What had begun as an economic issue, Eisner noted with evident
satisfaction, had escalated to a political action. *Vorwärts* reported that
workers planned a demonstration march to the Winter Palace, where
they would present their grievances in the form of a petition to the tsar.[1]
Bourgeois intellectuals had met Saturday evening to urge Nicholas to
accept the document.[2] Ominously, he called for three regiments of cavalry
and a division of infantry to reinforce the garrison of 50,000 troops and
four regiments of artillery. Ignorant yet of what was already unfolding on
Bloody Sunday, the *Vorwärts* public read the correspondent's speculation
that bloodshed seemed inevitable.[3]

The next issue appeared on Tuesday, 24 January, with horrify-
ing details of the massacre in St. Petersburg.[4] History records that the
peaceful demonstration "was dispersed by troops with a cynical brutality

unusual even for Russia."[5] Commanded by Prince Boris Vasilchikov, the military formed a cordon on the square before the Winter Palace. The correspondent for the *Berliner Tageblatt* wired that shortly before noon a procession of at least 15,000 workers crossed the square, singing a hymn and bearing crosses and portraits of the tsar. At their head was Gapon, who advanced to hand the petition to an officer. Rebuffed, Gapon returned to the ranks of the workers, who moved forward toward the cordon. They were met with a withering fusillade that felled 600 in an instant. In the afternoon an assembly of 20,000 workers was attacked at the Moscow Gate and another 1,300 casualties inflicted. Cossack cavalry cut down marchers in the streets throughout the city. The *Tageblatt* reporter expressed stark horror at the massacre of the unarmed populace, with women and children "terribly maimed by saber cuts and horses' hooves" in the blood-drenched snow. The Russian government officially acknowledged 76 dead, 233 wounded.[6]

In his commentary on the reports Eisner remarked that neither cross nor the tsar's image had preserved the meek suppliants from their doom, and he asseverated with barely subdued moral rage that "St. Petersburg's Bloody Sunday must not be the end but rather the beginning of the revolution that liberates humanity from the ignominy of Russian absolutism."[7] On 9 and 10 February *Vorwärts* ran under the title "The Revolution in Russia" a two-part article by Rosa Luxemburg in which she argued that the spread of the uprising across Russia and its dominions, specifically Lithuania and Poland, indeed demonstrated that "the spontaneous, blind revolt of oppressed slaves" had given way to "a genuine political movement of the class-conscious, urban proletariat."[8] To the amazement and chagrin of the government, the slaughter at St. Petersburg touched off strikes and demonstrations of solidarity with the strikers across the empire, forcing the authorities to grant sweeping concessions.[9] Military defeat in Asia followed by rampant domestic unrest shook the foundations of the state and presaged its imminent collapse.[10] The concept of the mass strike as a political weapon of choice gained credence in Western Europe, alarming not only Germany's industrial capitalists, who feared for their power and profits, but also the trade unions' rank and file, who feared for their dearly gained security and benefits.

In joint observance of the March Revolution and the hundredth anniversary of Schiller's death, the People's Free Stage, at Eisner's importunate urging, sponsored the first performance of Beethoven's Ninth Symphony before a proletarian audience on 18 March 1905 at the Friedrichshain Brewery in Berlin.[11] It was no small feat, for even his fellows on the theater's board questioned the point of such an enterprise. Friedrich Stampfer remembered that Eisner had repeatedly proposed a performance of the Ninth. "We laughed. Where was the money to be found? And the suitable space? And the choirs? And the appreciative public?"[12] But the presentation proved so successful that a second concert was organized.[13] Eisner, himself an ardent pianist, explained the significance of Beethoven's symphony and its performance at the brewery. While he formed his great paean to human possibility, Beethoven was studying Kant. One quote in particular, recorded in the composer's notebook, underlay the meaning of the work: "The moral law in us and the starry heaven above us." The Ninth became the consummate artistic expression of the consummate social concept, articulating the pure revolutionary ideal, the self-realization of humankind as a unified whole above selfish desire, exploitation, and gain. "Moral law and starry heaven," Eisner wrote for the inaugural issue of Heinrich and Lily Braun's *Neue Gesellschaft* (New Society), "engender in the minuscule, miserable consciousness of man the creative, infinite consciousness of mankind, that knowledge and will ascend from the chaos of murky confusion to the principled order based on the dictates of reason." The nearly three thousand workers who bought their tickets and sat rapt in a packed beer hall demonstrated that the workers' movement had achieved its cultural class-consciousness.[14] After that initial performance in Berlin, Stampfer later wrote, the Ninth became part of the socialist repertoire. Seated at its performance on 31 December 1917 at the Free Stage's stately theater on Bülowplatz, he "listened while thinking more than once of Kurt Eisner and his splendid pioneer spirit."[15]

Russia's troubles in the Far East caused Europe's great powers to reappraise their foreign policy and alliances. The French government, in hope of safeguarding its colonial venture in Morocco, concluded accords with Italy, which had designs of its own in Libya, and with Britain, which wanted leeway in Egypt and the Sudan. In violation of an 1880 compact on Moroccan sovereignty, French foreign minister Théophile Delcassé chose not to consult with Berlin about his agreements with Rome and London.[16] Already in 1904 the German advocates of Weltpolitik clamored for their government to check French ambitions, even if it meant war. Heinrich Claß, founder of the Pan-German League, complained that Bülow was idly standing by as Germany's stake steadily declined. "On a level with Spain, we see ourselves cheated out of a holding to which we have just as much claim as does France—and all this despite it once having been proclaimed that no major decision might be made in the world without the German kaiser having a say."[17] Friedrich von Holstein, animus of the Foreign Office and an intimate of Field Marshal Alfred von Schlieffen, army chief of staff, was also spoiling for a fight, "aware that his country could hardly hope for a better opportunity to deal with France than it had in 1905," with Russia preoccupied and indisposed.[18]

Thus it was that Kaiser Wilhelm deviated from the itinerary of a Mediterranean pleasure cruise in March to put into port at Tangier, where he both assured the sultan of German support of Moroccan sovereignty and warned the French consul that Germany would not be denied its rightful place in the sun.[19] In Paris the Rouvier government teetered. Georges Clemenceau, in the newspaper *L'Aurore*, attacked Delcassé's miscalculations, as did Jaurès in *L'Humanité*. Eisner readily apprehended that the kaiser's bellicosity signaled a radical departure from Chancellor Bülow's Moroccan policy of the previous year, when France's activities in the crumbling sultanate were accepted as a stabilizing influence that could only benefit German commerce. However reluctantly, Bülow evidently had been swept up in the tide of imperialist fervor. "Since German trade interests in Morocco are not imperiled," Eisner wrote in *Vorwärts* on Sunday, 25 March, "there can be but two possible explanations for the kaiser's trip to Tangier and the attendant semiofficial hubbub: either one wants something serious or a show is being staged for those who delight in glitz."[20]

A week later Eisner sounded the alarm in earnest when Bülow announced that he would commence direct negotiations with the sultan. The chancellor's gambit proved grist for the jingoist mill in the rival capitals. "Through threatening notes and threatening speeches tensions are being incited between peoples who more than ever have the duty to cultivate their cultural harmony. The working class in Germany and in France, in particular, rejects out of hand the provocation of grave conflict over Morocco."[21] Through April the rhetoric of brinkmanship intensified. On the eighth *Vorwärts* reported that in London, where Germany's swelling fleet was regarded with utmost concern, Bülow's machinations were interpreted as a bid for access to deep-water ports on the Atlantic, a prerequisite for challenging Britain's admiralty.[22]

In the midst of what historians now term the first Moroccan crisis, Eisner took the opportunity afforded by Germany's centennial celebration of Schiller's legacy to examine the cosmopolitan, republican poet's flight from revolutionary engagement to aesthetic abstraction. That Schiller's incendiary drama *Wilhelm Tell*, glorifying the revolt of an oppressed populace against a tyrannical regime, ironically became the sacred text of militarist German nationalism, was in part his own doing. Reliance on the largesse of aristocratic patrons had tempered Schiller's early social radicalism with deferential sensibility. Although he penned *Tell* well after the French Revolution, he—an honorary citizen of the Republic—refused to acknowledge there or elsewhere the watershed event that realized the political ideals of *Kabale und Liebe* (Intrigue and Love), his youthful drama of revolution. Having graduated from firebrand to showpiece courtier-laureate, Schiller could ill afford to continue in the genre of topical tragedies of class difference; hence his refuge in philosophical treatise, history, historical drama. The clarion had gone mute at the decisive moment. "It was the tribute he unconsciously had to render petty-state German despotism from the social misery of a poor writer toiling laboriously to earn his bread, condemned to live by the favor of the very elements who in France went to the guillotine."[23]

The successful strikes in Russia stoked renewed debate on the general strike as a political rather than purely economic weapon, wielded to win and protect civil rights or topple regimes as well as to achieve better pay, benefits, and working conditions. At the congress of party-affiliated trade unions, held late May in Cologne, delegates jealously guarded their purview from encroachment by party theorists and politicos bent on expropriating the strike action to their ends. Following a report by Theodor Bömelburg, Reichstag representative for Arnsberg in the Ruhr, the congress resolved to reject "all attempts intending to prescribe a fixed tactic through propagating the political mass-strike," leaving the thwarted radikalinskis to fulminate against the antisocialist character of the socialist unions.[24] Rosa Luxemburg's correspondence from the first week of June indicates that the party's extremists were under considerable stress. She herself was meeting with Kautsky daily, Parvus looked "frightful," and both he and Luise Kautsky maintained that Bebel was seething, incoherent, and paranoid, attributing some perfidy to his friend Victor Adler.[25]

In answer to the Far Left barrage Eisner formulated a well-reasoned lead article, "Union and Party," to present a balanced view of the question.[26] To the radicals' contention that the two organizations were working at cross-purposes Eisner responded by citing with approval commentary from Nuremberg's *Fränkische Tagespost* that posited the two sides' positions as fitting and proper to their respective stations in the greater movement. "The best means of avoiding friction," Eisner wrote, "we see in being clear in one's mind about the different functions of the trade-union and political organization." The former historically concerned itself with relations between workers and employers. In this context it was logical that the unions, which collected and distributed the monies that sustained striking workers, wanted "nothing to do with the political mass-strike." The party, on the other hand, as political voice of the organized proletariat, had as its mission to educate the great masses as to their class interest and ultimate objective. The pure democracy of the trade unions, which subjected major decisions to a vote by the membership, was secondary to the party's long-term aim of building socialism, for "the goals of the proletarian movement do not culminate in democracy alone." The party then was perfectly within its rights to consider the general strike as a means of advancing the common cause. In the realization, he concluded, that whenever the party called for concerted political action, it was above all members of the unions who responded, Social Democrats of all stripes would do well to recognize and respect the place of both organizations in marshaling the masses.

But considering the general strike hypothetically was for Eisner by no means tantamount to supporting it, at least at this stage of his and Germany's development. Two weeks later he reviewed Henriette Roland-Holst's *Generalstreik und Sozialdemokratie* (General Strike and Social Democracy), for which Kautsky had provided a foreword hailing its clarity on "the most important practical question confronting us at present—the question of the sharpest weapon in the great decisive battles toward which we are moving."[27] Systematically recapitulating the debate and dissecting Roland-Holst's analysis, Eisner found fault with what he regarded as her central premise. He recalled for readers the historical opposition of leading socialists, citing Liebknecht's dictum that the 'general strike is impossible, and were it possible, it is unnecessary!' At its Bremen congress in September the party had rejected a proposal to take up the issue at Jena in 1905, and at the International congress in Amsterdam the previous August Roland-Holst's own Dutch comrades had successfully introduced a resolution condemning the general strike as 'impracticable' and warning workers against anarchist, prostrike propaganda aimed at undermining the patient organizational work of union and party to forge a unified power base.

Examining strikes in Sweden, Italy, Belgium, Holland, and Russia, Roland-Holst established categories: the solidarity strike, the anarchist general-strike conceived as a final showdown between labor and capital, the economic strike with political implications, and the political mass-strike called to confront or contain the bourgeois state. At issue from Eisner's perspective was the application to Germany, England, and France of occurrences in lands where the workers' movement was less mature and the circumstances less conducive to mass political revolution. "We believe the work-stoppage for political ends to be a weapon of the working class. It is not, however, a means that may be permitted to supplant, sidetrack, or in any way obscure the highest principle of the Social Democratic tactic, which to be sure is and remains revolutionizing minds, which, as our opponents have said, is lethal precisely because it makes use of laws and cannot be suppressed by laws."

A scant two years earlier the Social Democratic Party had claimed three million votes in the elections of 1903, a third of the electorate, establishing itself as Germany's most populous party. In the interim Chairman August Bebel, to all appearances, had done his utmost to fragment the unity that had produced so great a demonstration of common cause against the Wilhelmine state. To do his bidding Bebel turned to a brood of rarefied ideologues at odds with the mainstream rank and file and as often as not at each other's throat. Their efforts contributed to what Carl Schorske termed "the great schism" of the German Left, alienating hundreds of thousands of once fervent supporters and casual sympathizers alike. In the vacuum created by the rift proponents of Germany's imperial venture found a comfortable niche, coopting above all skilled labor weary of the constant discord of their comrade clarions.[28] The Russian revolution of 1905 and the ensuing debate in Western Europe on the general strike's application was the great catalyst to the polarization. Exemplary of the animosity is the advice of Otto Hué, editor of the *Bergarbeiter Zeitung* (Miners' Newspaper), organ of the miners' trade union, to the firebrand theorists to take their revolutionary fervor back to Russia "instead of propagating general-strike discussion from their summer resorts."[29] The gibe was meant for Luxemburg and Kautsky, who confessed sensitivity about his Slavic ancestry in a letter of 20 July to Victor Adler.[30]

Eisner recognized now that Social Democracy had reached a critical juncture. As chief editor of the party's voice, he determined to make his own voice heard in favor of inclusion and concerted action, not only within the German fold but between it and the workers' movement in France, Germany's most immediate likely enemy in a war over colonial expansion. In addition to its function as the party's central organ, *Vorwärts*, as the subtitle *Berliner Volksblatt* proclaimed, was also the people's paper of the metropolis. In Eisner's tenure, first as Liebknecht's acting editor in chief and then as managing editor, subscriptions had climbed steadily from 53,000 to 88,000.[31] Through his fruitful initiatives to update the paper's format, improve style, expand coverage, and overhaul operations, he had established close ties with key figures in the local party and won admirers nationwide and abroad. His work with the People's Free Stage and active participation in precinct meetings extended his influence in diverse milieux. Already under attack from Bebel and his minions, Eisner concluded that the moment to act on his convictions had arrived. Convinced that the party was dangerously divided over the general strike and indifferent to the very real threat of war with France and

England, he sought to refocus attention on the ruling states' machinations for imperial dominion in Africa and Asia.

Shortly after Bülow unexpectedly sent the Reichstag into summer recess on 30 May, Eisner received a letter from reliable sources in Paris who reported that the German government was planning mischief in Morocco and wanted no meddling from the people's elected representatives. "In Berlin," he recalled in September 1918, "no one knew—outside a narrow circle of Pan-Germans, high military brass, leading weapons makers and heavy industrialists—that something special was in rehearsal for the world stage." His French correspondents entreated him to apprise the German proletariat of the danger. Eisner proposed to local party officials that the French centrist Jean Jaurès be invited to Berlin to hold an address on the maintenance of world peace.[32] They readily agreed and charged Eisner with the correspondence. The French party reciprocated with an invitation to Bebel to speak in Paris.[33] In a letter of 27 June Jaurès gratefully acknowledged Eisner's initiative but warned that "the impression in France would be bad under the circumstances if the meeting were to be prohibited and I were deported from the country."[34]

On Saturday, 30 June, Luxemburg and Kautsky wrote jointly to Arthur Stadthagen that Eisner's "intrigue" and "coup" had to be countered by summoning the French radicals Jules Guesde and Éduoard Vaillant to speak as well.[35] The next day Eisner ran in *Vorwärts* a lead article titled "The Proclamation of World Peace," announcing that Jaurès, "at the urging and invitation of Berlin's party comrades and with the mandate of the French socialist parliamentary deputation," was to speak at noon on Sunday, 9 July, at the New World Beer Hall.[36] Likening the ruling states' chauvinist diplomacy to Russia's beloved drawing-room boardgame, Eisner contrasted international labor's straightforward strategy for derailing their designs. "While peoples are moved back and forth like the inanimate miniatures on a chessboard, this action of the German and French proletariat centers on a simple and modest proclamation of firm will that the proletariat of all nations are indeed united in opposition to the ruling class's wild feuds driven by special interests. . . . The Russian collapse has plunged all international relations into a raging torrent. Everything is in flux, everything uncertain. The chessboard on which diplomats were accustomed to playing undisturbed has fallen to the floor and the figures are a confused jumble. But precisely the Russian collapse shows that war, violence, and oppression, that the potentially all-consuming politics of world plunder . . . have no more currency."

Both Chancellor Bülow and Chairman Bebel noted with consternation Eisner's remarks. The Conservative press demanded that the government prevent Jaurès's talk. Prominent Liberal and Catholic papers, on the other hand, saw no harm in the visit of a highly regarded French politician interested in promoting peaceful relations. The *Frankfurter Zeitung* hailed Jaurès as a "moderate and tactful man" and pronounced any talk that improved understanding between the two countries as "a good thing under any circumstances." The *Kölnische Zeitung* would regard it as "not only unintelligent but also a sign of regrettable weakness," were Bülow to bow to pressure from the Right and ban Jaurès's appearance. Even the *Berliner Neueste Nachrichten* (Berlin Latest News) smirked that workers who understood no French should not be deprived of the pleasure of seeing a Frenchman.

But bow Bülow did. On Wednesday, the fifth, he wrote to the German ambassador in Paris, Prince Radolin, to forbid Jaurès's trip. The chancellor took pains to express personal admiration for Jaurès but declared that he would not allow Jaurès's appearance to serve the ends of the event's organizers, as stated in *Vorwärts*: to influence German foreign policy in such a way as to advance international class warfare. He cited specifically an article in *Neue Gesellschaft* that spelled out their intent: "The revolution dynamited the Russo-French alliance; now it is Social Democracy's historic duty to provide for the French Republic what it hoped in vain to find in the Russian rulers: protection from the provocations and overblown power-grabbing of Imperial German politics."[37] Friday, 7 July, *Vorwärts* called on its public to turn out in full force to hear Richard Fischer speak in Jaurès's stead.[38] Jaurès's response to the incident was printed in his paper, *L'Humanité*, beneath the title "The Fear of Socialism," an article that implied Bülow's hypocrisy in squelching the rally when his government touted peace as one of its own programmatic objectives. The ban, Jaurès hypothesized, stemmed from a perceived "professional encroachment on existing capitalist and feudal diplomacy."[39] The London correspondent for *Vorwärts* reported that the scheduled rally had aroused little interest there until Bülow's action created a "genuine sensation." The *Times* underscored the party's shrewdness in organizing the event and judged the chancellor's reaction an unwitting validation of Social Democracy's political clout.[40]

Sunday morning *Vorwärts* defied the government by printing Jaurès's speech in its entirety.[41] As if in answer to the wags at *Neueste Nachrichten*, Eisner noted that Jaurès himself had translated the speech into German. The text opened by relating Franco-German diplomacy during the recent Moroccan crisis to two locomotives hurtling headlong at each other in a game of bluff. Even if the one driver's reason asserted itself over bravado, the kinetic force of the train might be too great to stop, dooming the powerless and terrified passengers. Because the negotiations between the two governments were shrouded in secrecy, it was a mystery how disaster had been avoided at the last moment. It fell then to the international proletariat, to German and French workers acting in tandem, to brake the wild rush of the imperial powers toward inevitable confrontation. The task was enormously daunting because of the tensions and enmities inherent in capitalist society, "which the world's proletariat, with its still insufficient organization, its inadequate political power, is not yet capable of bringing under control with certainty." Jaurès also warned the ruling states of the risks of fomenting war, as the suffering arising from it would unleash revolutionary forces that could not be contained by advocates of nonviolent change. On the other hand workers could have no illusions about favorable outcomes, for war can breed fanatical nationalism, militarism, reaction, and dictatorship. Jaurès therefore counseled patience, organization, and greater cooperation between workers of both nations.

At noon six thousand workers filled to capacity the beer hall in the Nixdorf suburb, another twelve thousand packed into the garden. The local gendarmerie was backed by a detachment of a hundred municipal police from Berlin. Fifty uniformed police were on stage in the wings, and numerous plainclothesmen among the audience. The party faithful present had already read Jaurès's address when Eugen Ernst greeted them and warned of the presence of secret police: "Comrades, I ask you to be careful of what you say, so as not to be visited perchance with some unpleasantry." His adjuration did not dissuade the more disgruntled from shouting abuse at the police and Chancellor Bülow. Ernst then read a telegram from Jaurès proclaiming solidarity with German workers in their cause. Richard Fischer, a founding member of the party and a close associate of Eisner, followed with commentary on why the government so desperately wanted to prevent the rally and on the critical collaboration with comrades in France. He compared Jaurès's stance to that of Bebel and Liebknecht in 1870, when they opposed the Franco-Prussian War and the annexation of Alsace-Lorraine. Fischer then delivered a searing indictment of Weltpolitik, the government's definition of national interests, and ministers, by name, who left office to direct the corporations they had helped to immense profits. Citing Eisner's documentation of the Königsberg trial, he detailed the government's cozy relations with the tsarist regime. The assembly endorsed unanimously a resolution affirming world peace, hailing the Russian revolution, and rejecting Bülow's politics of obfuscation and repression.[42]

Eisner's initiative had proven a tactical masterstroke for Social Democracy—or so it seemed. If Bülow was embarrassed by Eisner's triumph, Bebel was positively incensed at being upstaged. Two months later he was still unhinged. During a meeting to address their differences he pointedly borrowed Eisner's chess analogy in a rebuke: "I will not allow myself to be moved back and forth like a chess figure by you."[43] In the last months of the First World War Eisner lamented the woeful lack of principled leadership that had doomed Social Democracy to the role of accomplice in the catastrophe. Bebel's scheduled talk in Paris fell through because of his own reluctance: "He was disinclined to projects undertaken without his involvement; indeed he liked to rebel against 'authorities,' provided that he himself was not the authority in question, in whom person and cause increasingly seemed one and the same to him. . . . Since those stirring weeks I knew that world war was bearing down like inescapable fate, ponderous, unnoticed, ineluctable."[44]

In the week before Jaurès's slated appearance, Eisner wrote for *Vorwärts* a critical appraisal of the published agenda for the Jena party congress, as determined by the party executive. Once again perfunctory reports and discussion of internal party matters took precedence over national and international issues of critical concern, despite repeated attempts by numerous Social Democratic constituencies to bring them to the fore. The ten-hour workday, electoral reform in Prussia, international relations in the wake of the Russian revolution, the new navy bill to expand the fleet and further Weltpolitik were questions that demanded emphatic position statements. Scheduled discussion of the general strike, Eisner argued, was well suited to consideration of Prussian suffrage, if time could but be found. Taking aim at Bebel, he declared that "unlike the bourgeois parties, Social Democracy is not a party of leaders whose moods and whims sway any number of followers this way and that; it is the party of the people with Social Democratic convictions who determine their political fate for themselves."[45]

The next day *Vorwärts* printed the dissenting opinion of three editors—Heinrich Ströbel, Heinrich Cunow, and Paul John—applauding Mehring's position that in light of the suspect elements swelling Social Democratic ranks in 1903, the party was required to devote itself at Jena to self-examination and reconfirmation of its Marxist stance.[46] Simultaneously Kautsky launched his campaign against *Vorwärts*, deploring its "pessimistic pronouncements on the Russian revolution."[47] The next week Kautsky ridiculed what he deemed Eisner's faulty understanding of Roland-Holst's book, classed the formulation 'revolutionizing minds' with Sancho Panza's flowery but meaningless ramblings, and scoffed at the proposal to address at Jena issues on which the party was unified and skirt debate on the general strike. "The unsuitability of *Vorwärts*, in its current form, to serve as leading organ on the party's internal questions has never before been as apparent as in this affair."[48] Kautsky was joined by Mehring in a well-coordinated offensive to seize control of the paper for the radical cause. On 11 July Mehring accused *Vorwärts* of siding with the bourgeois press by objecting to his smear of terminally ill Eugen Richter as a "knave even in dying." Justifying the epithet, Mehring wrote that "the Berlin comrades who read only *Vorwärts*" were ignorant by design of the circumstances and promised to address in due time its aspersions against the *Leipziger Volkszeitung*.[49] Horrified by the intemperance of their denunciations, Victor Adler implored Kautsky in a letter of 17 July to consider the damage that was being done to the party's public image: "I regard as utterly pernicious your entire tactics against *Vorwärts*—to the outside observer it appears that the party has nothing better to do than discredit its central organ and tear down the editors as idiots."[50] In reply Kautsky conceded that "whatever the *Leipziger Volkszeitung* prints is always construed even beforehand as malicious" but maintained that *Neue Zeit* was the proper forum for debate of the party's internal affairs. "You see my attack on *Vorwärts* as a breach of solidarity. . . . But when this most important party organ is given over to a band of ignoramuses and intriguers who increasingly stupefy the party, when all attempts at reform fail because this band, through their masterful intrigues, can bamboozle and paralyze in confusion those responsible for their oversight, then no other course remains than making it public. The current editorship is a cancer. If I cannot reform it, then nothing remains but to discredit it. That may be bad, but from the standpoint of solidarity too it is still superior to the infamous intrigues of Eisner, Fischer and Co."[51]

That week Kautsky had run Arthur Stadthagen's reproof of Eisner's desired agenda for the congress. All party publications, Stadthagen asserted, had the leeway, indeed the duty to present the Social Democratic perspective on Weltpolitik and any other current issue, as *Neue Zeit* and the *Leipziger Volkszeitung* had done so brilliantly. The annual congress's function though, by the party's bylaws, was to consider internal matters: "At any given time those questions touching party life have their roots to great extent in topical political relations." Continuing in the vein of Kautsky's Sancho Panza dig, Stadthagen intoned that "Social Democracy lives and fights grounded in reality, not in utopias."[52] Evidently, reality was best served by hypotheses on the general strike's future application in Germany. Rosa Luxemburg wrote warmly to Stadthagen on 25 July to offer congratulations on this crystalline logic.[53] Seeking perhaps to demonstrate his commitment to equitable reportage, Eisner evidently wrote simultaneously to Luxemburg in confidence to offer her the status of either economics editor at *Vorwärts* or, at the least, regular contributor. On Thursday, 27 July, she sent a hurried note to Stadthagen, requesting a meeting: "Kurt has sent me an important letter that we must discuss together. I am writing now to Cunow at the *Vorwärts* offices: he should come with Ströbel to the Dessau Garden after their copy deadline."[54]

In January Mehring had been called to account by local party officials in Leipzig for his feud with *Vorwärts*.[55] In his defense he maintained that they had charged him to edit their organ as "a clear paper of principles in the sense of Lassalle, Marx, and Engels and in opposition to all divergent tendencies." This, Mehring candidly told his directors, he could not do "without personal quarrels arising in the party that negatively affect your paper and the party too." The officials deemed his assessment too pessimistic and implied that squabbles might be avoided through greater restraint. On 5 August Mehring made good on his promise and rejoined the feud with a vengeance, running as his lead the article "On 'Good Tone,'" in which he complained of mounting recriminations against the *Leipziger Volkszeitung*. The latest round of protests, Mehring claimed, stemmed from Eisner's misleading review of Roland-Holst's book, which Kautsky had already fittingly decried as a "ragout of platitudes." Rather than engage its opponent in direct debate of the issue, the central organ lamented the appalling lack of "good tone."[56]

Eisner responded acerbically with a signed two-part article, "Of Bad Tone and Good Logic," exposing Mehring as an incorrigible libeler who routinely made use of character assassination in his attacks on comrades and colleagues. At the Erfurt party congress of 1891 Bebel's resolution demanding that internal criticism be objective, truthful, just, and ethical was accepted unanimously. Six years later at Hamburg Bebel inveighed once again against the spiteful, supercilious writing of some whose names he declined to speak. Now though, Eisner continued, wretched excess was permitted and thus encouraged, and anyone who protested was reviled by the guilty. "By this pattern the *L.V.* always has defended the right to bad tone, which it of course fancies as an exclusive right. . . . Whoever defends himself against this monopolistic right to bad tone is—and always this is the only argument advanced—philistine or sentimental, puling, sniveling, as squeamish as an old maid, a weakling, in short an idiot and blackguard to boot." Widening the scope of the critique, Eisner assailed the method of Mehring and his "clique," who invariably took the same line, leapt to each other's support when challenged, and heaped synchronized abuse on their critics. "Thus all the world is terrorized and intimidated by their organized defamation of outsiders and by the organized homage to their own greatness."[57]

On 16 August Mehring wrote that he had intended to ignore K. E.'s "literary antics" but numerous correspondents urged him to address "the entire *Vorwärts* question, which after all weighs on the party like an incubus." But his readers would need to wait until he concluded his explication of Roland-Holst.[58] Even before Mehring could commence with the indictment of the central organ, Social Democratic voters in Bochum, meeting on Sunday, 22 August, petitioned the party congress to condemn "the incessant bickering of a group of comrade journalists and not to allow the congress to become the arena for a personal literary dispute." Eisner hastened to second their resolution and pointed out that with the exception of two papers supporting the *Leipziger Volkszeitung* virtually the entire party press from every region of Germany had taken the same line against the polemic.[59] Nuremberg's *Fränkische Tagespost* was outspoken in its condemnation of Mehring's philippic, and Kassel's *Volksblatt* declared that whereas Kautsky's journal played no role in the rise of the Social Democratic press, *Vorwärts* led the way "thanks to the eminent journalistic talent of Comrade Eisner."[60]

Having returned from vacation in the Tirolean Alps, Kautsky resumed his attack that week. For confirmation of his own position Kautsky turned to Roland-Holst herself, who wrote that she was mystified by Eisner's interpretation of her work, for she too regarded the general strike as but one recourse and feared anarchist putsches. Kautsky repeated here his accusation against *Vorwärts*: "Its inability to assume a leading and productive role by objectively probing internal party questions, and its allegations, made time and again since Dresden, that these questions rise solely from literary vanity and spite put it increasingly at odds with those who regard these questions as vital to the party."[61]

Indeed, party circles in the capital had begun to consider relinquishing *Vorwärts* as its central organ in order to preserve the paper's function as the *Berliner Volksblatt*, the socialist voice of Germany's largest industrial center. At a meeting of Social Democratic voters in Leipzig's eighteenth electoral district, Paul Lensch, associate editor of the *Leipziger Volkszeitung*, asserted that the Berlin party's considerations demonstrated that the raging controversy was more than a heated personal disagreement. On Sunday, 26 August, Eisner's editor for party affairs, Heinrich Wetzker, remarked that Lensch was ill informed as to "why Berlin's comrades lay claim to *Vorwärts*."[62] That same day the *Leipziger Volkszeitung* printed the first of Mehring's nine lead articles titled "The *Vorwärts* Question."[63] Tracing the fifteen-year history of the party organ, Mehring developed the thesis that the dual function of *Vorwärts* and the peculiar organization of its editorial board were conducive only to the internal division and lack of ideological direction that had plagued the paper for a decade. As organ of both the Berlin party and the party as a whole, *Vorwärts* had two governing bodies: the local leadership and the party executive. Consequently, instead of proclaiming Social Democracy's revolutionary tenets, *Vorwärts* had conveyed the broad spectrum of opinion in the party, which, on issues as divisive as the general strike, was contradictory. Whereas other party papers, be they revisionist or radical in outlook, had what he termed a "majority editorship" and consistently represented a particular point of view, the *Vorwärts* editors argued various approaches to the same issue, with their managing editor having his final say on most everything. "There will be no end to the current disputes," Mehring declared, "until either no party paper is edited according to the old party principles or *Vorwärts* is given over to whom it rightfully belongs: the comrades of Berlin in whom the old party principles are as alive as anywhere else in the empire."[64]

Mehring credited the members of the party's executive committee with never having acted as "a kind of supreme censor" to the party press, but the result of their longstanding forbearance was that now the executive and the central organ were constantly at loggerheads, although *Vorwärts* was obligated by party statute to follow the directives of the executive.[65] Indeed, Mehring complained, supporters of *Vorwärts* illogically maintained that the composition of its editorial board should reflect differences of opinion in the party, for to Mehring's mind there could be no difference of opinion on either the duties with which the central organ had been charged by the Halle party congress of 1890 or the failure of *Vorwärts* to discharge those duties faithfully. As a result of this intolerable breach *Vorwärts* continually overvalued parliamentary participation and ineffectively criticized the capitalist-imperial opposition on ethical rather than empirical grounds. Mehring judged as inapplicable to socialist organization the notion "that the managing editor should more or less lord over his department editors as consummate genius and meddle from above in their specialities, which they generally understand much better than he."[66] By right of eminence in defining the Social Democratic Party's ideals, old and overworked Wilhelm Liebknecht had been designated editor in chief of the newly established central organ. At his death the party executive had withheld that title from his successor to signal that *Vorwärts* was to be ruled by a majority, and Eisner's position was to have been that of coordinator rather than commander. But because the Berlin leadership insisted on joint oversight with the executive, the executive's goal was thwarted, as "a frontline paper's ability to act can only suffer if it must answer to two masters."[67]

Because of the deplorable state of affairs at *Vorwärts* during the last years of Liebknecht's tenure, Mehring characterized Eisner as "far more a victim than perpetrator, far more to excuse than accuse," for despite the man's good intentions, his belletristic idealism was fundamentally incompatible with the requisite Marxist economic-political orientation of scientific socialism. In the *Communist Manifesto* Marx and Engels themselves inveighed against "the literary socialism so prevalent today at *Vorwärts*, which would liberate the working class by means of aesthetic sensibilities and ethical rationalizations."[68] In his concluding installment, nine days before the Jena party congress was to convene, Mehring suggested that "the evil be brushed aside with a gentle hand at the proper moment."[69]

In what he intended as his final word on the controversy, Kautsky too drew the pejorative comparison between the scientific socialism to which he adhered and the "sentimental socialism" that currently ruled *Vorwärts*. The basis of the former was a classically Marxist "economic-historical" orientation to politics, whereas the latter was rooted in "ethical-aesthetic thinking." Through exhaustive empirical study scientific socialists sought to fathom and illuminate "the relations between economics and politics." Conversely, sentimental socialists, "less concerned with understanding things than passing judgment on them," aimed at arousing "disgust at the immorality and ugliness of existing circumstances." Kautsky conceded that both ethics and aesthetics had their place in class struggle, for inspiring the masses to sacrifice and commitment, imbuing them with higher aspirations, but "wherever economic-scientific thinking is not dominant, assigning goal and direction to the agents of ethics and aesthetics, the two sides must come into conflict." Forging unified public opinion was of relatively little consequence for the class struggle when weighed against consolidating "unity of action," which scientific socialism allegedly effected in some way Kautsky failed to specify.[70]

With characteristic aplomb Eisner printed verbatim the diatribes against him and defended himself vigorously. On 2 September he ran the first of a seven-part series titled "Debates on If and But."[71] He began by pointing out that, contrary to Kautsky's claim that he had given Roland-Holst belated and short shrift, *Vorwärts* was the first Social Democratic paper to present a critique, and nothing more thorough had appeared in the interim. Rather than systematically refute Eisner's review, Kautsky had questioned the credentials of the *Vorwärts* editors and called for their muzzling. Alluding again to Mehring's clique, Eisner counseled that Kautsky "finally should accustom himself to speaking on his on account and at his own risk and not instantly drag up an imaginary affirming chorus to lend force to arguments." In fact, Roland-Holst's book had enjoyed a mixed and unpredictable reception, for whereas some trade unionists opposed to the general strike hailed the study as a veritable primer for their cause, Social Democratic voters in one electoral district interpreted it as a blueprint for seizing the means of production—a notion Roland-Holst herself regarded as anarchist folly. Eisner promised to revisit Roland-Holst's text, reveal how Kautsky had vitiated the party's debate on it, and clarify why the party's central organ could not be permitted to chase after "every Pied Piper."

In the next four installments Eisner, citing chapter and verse from Roland-Holst's work, laid bare its internal contradictions and logical inconsistencies as well as examples of Kautsky's selective reading. It was Kautsky, not he, who by pinning all hopes on a momentous day of reckoning and by devaluing the import of molding class consciousness through incremental conquest of political rights, engaged in idle, utopian speculation about the future with his dialectical sophistry. "Just what is it supposed to mean that the masses should discuss and study the general strike? Is one to teach them what striking is all about? The class-conscious worker already knows that. Striking means sitting idle, doing without, going hungry. Striking means unemployment and ostracism. Striking for political causes means in some cases jail, powder and shot as well! In the workers' movement the decision to stop work has always been the *hardest test* of solidarity and clarity of purpose, and no one should underestimate the quiet heroism that even the least economic struggle requires."[72]

In this philosophical joust against a consilient thinker, Karl Kautsky had overreached with invidious classifications that divorced the science of ethics from the workings of capital. Were that elusive moment to arise when material circumstances enabled revolution in Germany, Eisner declared, the long, cloistered study of economic conditions, which "virtually any accountant can do," would be meaningless if the will to act were wanting, and that will was born of moral resolve. "But firing passion is the thorniest problem of political education."[73] By implication that skill was hardly the forte of the brooding economists.

Throughout the summer of 1905 the party executive committee, the press commission for *Vorwärts*, Berlin's key functionaries, the chairmen and treasurers of Social Democratic voters' leagues from the capital's eight electoral districts, the local oversight commission, Brandenburg's commission for agitation, the party's Reichstag deputies and candidates from Berlin and its environs, and editors at *Vorwärts* met to consider the complaints against the central organ's editorship.[74] The executive committee at that time was composed of eight members: cochairs Bebel and Singer; secretaries Ignaz Auer, Hermann Molkenbuhr, and Wilhelm Pfannkuch;

treasurer Alwin Gerisch; and members-at-large Wilhelm Eberhardt and Robert Wengels.[75] On 2 August Kautsky wrote to Victor Adler to decry once again Eisner's refusal to act as mouthpiece for the executive. Kautsky further confided his own reservations about that body, "a council of old men who are so absorbed by office work and parliamentarism that they curse every expansion of their purview."[76]

Despite Bebel's efforts to pack *Vorwärts* with editors who would follow his lead—just as he had packed the executive committee—the deliberations exonerated Eisner and his closest associates from alleged mischief and malfeasance.[77] In retrospect Eisner erroneously believed that questions of the paper's governance had been laid to rest. "The executive made proposals for safeguarding the views of the minority, to which we voiced our agreeement. We ourselves declared our willingness, above and beyond what was proposed, to cede to the minority virtually all discussion of internal party questions. Moreover, we expressly agreed to possible further measures for expanding and augmenting the editorial staff, such as recruitment of a preeminent authority on economic matters."[78] At meetings on 1 and 8 September the party executive, the press commission, and the editors of *Vorwärts* reached an accord regulating relations between majority and minority. By mutual agreement, Heinrich Wetzker, who no longer wished to continue as editor for party news, would be replaced in that capacity and reassigned other duties.[79]

One of Eisner's chief critics at the time was Clara Zetkin, editor of *Die Gleichheit* (Equality), the party's feminist journal, and one of nine members of the national control commission. Like Kautsky, she too was dubious of the executive's ability to reconfigure *Vorwärts*. On 13 September she wrote to Kautsky that she was considering a public appeal to the party at large, even if it meant having to resign her offices.[80] At a meeting the next day, just three days before the opening of the congress, Eisner and Bebel clashed when Bebel bitterly assailed Eisner's initiative in July's peace demonstration as a usurpation of authority—a harbinger of greater ill.[81] At the final meeting of the press commission and the *Vorwärts* editors before the congress, hulking Heinrich Cunow lunged at Eisner, seized him by the throat, shoved him against a wall, and would have struck him in the face had he not been pulled away.[82] Now violence against comrades had become a means to press the radical agenda.

The two major issues the congress had to deal with were the general strike and a proposed restructuring of the party's organization. Ever the chameleon, Bebel imposed his protean slant, hailing and harassing the same individual or organization in one breath. Kautsky, for example, drew praise for having clarified the party's stance on the general strike, criticism for underestimating the significance of parliamentary participation.[83] It was suddenly as if Bebel had not treated as calamity the party's electoral success of 1903. That he would reverse himself secretly before year's end on the issue of general strike and then ardently deny the inconsistency at the next party congress evinces in equal measure his duplicity, mendacity, and lubricity.[84] With regard to organizational structure, elements sick of the "press feud" questioned the need for a central organ altogether and wondered why every party paper could not be charged with prominently printing the executive's pronouncements. Voters' leagues from six of Berlin's eight electoral districts, supported by comrades in Bremen, called on the party to dispossess itself of *Vorwärts* as central organ and return the paper to its true constituency.[85] The executive's annual report deplored the quarrels in the party press over differences of opinion, for "repeatedly comrades disdained objective discussion and crossed over into personal dispute," as if it were more important to enhance their own standing than to advance the interests of the proletariat.[86] The matter was referred to an ad hoc committee, the Commission of Fifteen, chaired by J. H. W. Dietz, founder of the eponymous Stuttgart publishing house.[87]

Otto Wels, chair of Berlin's press commission and delegate of the city's fifth district, the same group that had presented a resolution against Mehring's attacks, personally supported the minority editors at *Vorwärts*.[88] He took the floor on the first day of debate to speak in favor of the Berliners' joint motion to free *Vorwärts* from the onus of central organ, that they might have the same right to clear and forceful expression of their views as comrades anywhere else in Germany. "If, however, *Vorwärts* is to remain central organ, then there is no other recourse than for a secretary of the executive to sit permanently on the editorial board and immediately take a position reflecting the executive's view on every new issue that arises, or for *Vorwärts* to have an editor in chief again who, like Liebknecht, has the duty to take part in meetings of the executive."[89] Bebel answered that the Berliners had succeeded in placing four of their fellows on the *Vorwärts* editorial board, two of whom had gone over to the party's Right, swinging the majority in that direction. Bebel then declared that were he to be reelected chair of the executive committee, he intended "to redress the justified complaints that we fully share with Berlin's comrades and to consult on ways and means as to how the present untenable state of affairs—I emphasize that—can be remedied." On behalf of the executive and the control commission he urged with success that the motion be rejected.[90]

In light of the compromises reached after three months of negotiations, Eisner and political editor Georg Gradnauer, who were themselves delegates to the congress, were by their own account "taken aback" by Bebel's remarks. Eisner was dissuaded by executive cochair Paul Singer from his intent to clarify before the congress as a whole, once the Commission of Fifteen had concluded its work, the exact state of affairs at *Vorwärts*. Even before the commission met, Singer assured him that "no changes whatsoever are to occur in the editorial balance, even if strengthening the staff by the addition of an editor schooled in economics possibly does come into consideration."[91] Members of the paper's majority and minority, Kautsky, Mehring, and other concerned parties were called to meet with the commission.[92] In a dramatic session Heinrich Ströbel, seconded by Mehring, launched into a tirade, denouncing as "stupid, gallimaufry, contradictory to the ABC of Marxism" a definition of class struggle in an article authored by Eisner. When Eisner revealed that the offending passage was quoted verbatim from Kautsky, the room went quiet.[93]

Later that afternoon Bebel appeared before the commission, and rumors circulated that evening that he had announced that Heinrich Wetzker had been sacked or would be sacked shortly. The next day Eisner privately confronted Bebel, but he denied having said any such thing. Reassured by Bebel's denial, Eisner considered the matter closed.[94] The Commission found that with regard to the recent exchanges between *Vorwärts* and its detractors, the "spiteful manner of discussion impugning the personal and party honor of comrades" impeded programmatic agitation and merited categorical condemnation, but the controversy could not be regarded as a mere literary squabble, stemming as it did from "serious differences of opinion on substantive issues, especially those of principle." It urged that critiques of the party's program were best confined to the pages of *Neue Zeit*, the journal established for discussion of theoretical issues, and charged the press commissions with oversight of their papers' tone. Finally, the party executive was enjoined to mediate when necessary to enforce the recommended guidelines "while fully respecting free expression of opinion."[95] Eisner learned later that in closed deliberations one egregious instance of Mehring's conduct in the campaign against *Vorwärts* was "uniformly branded as baseness."[96]

Friday, 22 September, was reserved for Bebel's report on the general strike and consideration of his proposed resolution. For three and a half hours he droned on in the morning session, weighing the party's imperatives against those of its affiliated unions.[97] In the afternoon session Rosa Luxemburg then spoke in favor of the mass strike, deriding as fools, cowards, or traitors those "cautious, so-called Social Democrats"—calling by name here Robert Schmidt, Wolfgang Heine, and Karl Frohme—who

failed to recognize in the spontaneity of the ill-organized Russian revolutionaries that "the time our great masters Marx and Engels prophesied
has come, when evolution turns into revolution." Her impassioned, ven-
omous speech met with applause and jeers.[98] Although Bebel had vilified
Vorwärts for its refusal to toe Kautsky's line, his resolution in fact came
much closer to the position Eisner enunciated in the article "Union and
Party" and in the subsequent series "Debates on If and But," for Bebel
urged the "fullest use of the mass work stoppage" to counter assaults on
hard-won rights of enfranchisement and association or to win such basic
rights where they were yet denied. At the same time he emphasized the
need for greater political and union organization and charged the party
press with educating the masses in the most effective application of the
mass strike.[99] By advocating the general strike, but only in certain contexts and to specific ends in clashes with the state over workers' rights,
Bebel maneuvered between the radical theorists and the trade-union leadership, winning overwhelming approval for the resolution by a vote of
247 to 14. Both Eisner and Gradnauer sided with the majority.[100]

After the congress's concluding session on Saturday, Eisner drafted his
summary of the week's work for *Vorwärts*.[101] He came away from Jena convinced that progress had been made in three areas: organizational reform,
party-union relations, and tactical refinement. Although the Commission
of Fifteen ruled that the press feud was driven by sharp division on substantive issues and not, as Eisner had charged, by personal animosity, its report
corroborated and censured the barbed invective and dishonest aspersions
that he found so repugnant—a finding ratified by the congress as a whole.
"The sense and purpose of this resolution," he wrote, "is that the original, objectively valuable debate not degenerate into inane, repulsive literary bickering." He declared that the Commission was the proper forum
for considering the grievances, as its members' familiarity with the matter
enabled them to deal in substance rather than impressions.

That Eisner took Bebel at his word is apparent in the comment that
even though the Commission worked behind closed doors, there were
"no secrets" to be shielded from public discussion. Eisner regarded as
personal vindication the moderate resolution on the general strike. "The
party took up the mass strike as a weapon in its arsenal, just as predicted
and as we construed the question: as a possible, topical weapon for defense
against political disenfranchisement and for conquest of new political
rights. Therein lay the great value of this significant debate, in part in the
demonstration of unbending resolve to defend and increase our rights,
but also in the renewed affirmation of our tactic up to now to enlighten
minds, to inspire, to organize the masses, to forge discipline, and to work

on tirelessly in all areas of public engagement." For the moment Eisner believed that no provocation from its enemies would lead the party into reckless, anarchist adventurism.

After reading Eisner's summary, Kautsky too claimed victory in his assessment for *Neue Zeit* the week after the congress.[102] He hailed the Commission for recognizing that the essence of the dispute with *Vorwärts* was ideological and for recommending his journal as the appropriate venue for debate on internal matters. The strike resolution he welcomed as the congress's indispensable crowning achievement: "Were we to declare the mass strike an impossibility, we could not hold long to our past tactic, as reconfirmed at Dresden." How soon he was to be dispossessed of this conceit. That same week Luxemburg wrote to Leo Jogiches that he could ignore the "pitifully falsified" report in *Vorwärts*, for "Jena in its entirety is a mighty victory for us all down the line." Bebel and Kautsky were well pleased with her performance, indeed. Bebel acclaimed as 'maliciously beautiful' her execrations against their opponents. Mehring, on the other hand, she reported on 3 October, was ostensibly so distraught by the Commission of Fifteen's resolution that he was poised to resign his post at the *Leipziger Volkszeitung* and leave the party altogether, although she confided that his employers would welcome the departure—the likely reason for his pique.[103]

After the congress Bebel hurried to Essen to campaign in a crucial runoff election. He was joined by Luxemburg, who stood in for him at three rallies when he fell ill. She wrote to Jogiches on 29 September of her heavy workload and of Bebel's insistence that she provide as many as two articles weekly to *Vorwärts*.[104] Upon his return to the capital Bebel engaged in a series of closed meetings the first week of October to revisit issues of governance and staffing of *Vorwärts*. To the end of quelling his most formidable rival within the party, Bebel was bent on undermining Eisner's influence by any means, however devious and authoritarian. On Monday, 2 October, Bebel represented the executive at a meeting with the press commission and local party officials dissatisfied with the measures at Jena to strengthen the executive's control of *Vorwärts*.[105]

The next evening Kautsky fetched Rosa Luxemburg at her Friedenau apartment for dinner at his home, where he reported details of his meeting earlier in the day with the executive.[106] On Wednesday the press commission invited the *Vorwärts* editors to a meeting slated for the sixth.[107] Thursday, the fifth, Luxemburg received a letter from Bebel confirming the terms of the arrangement he had proposed in Essen: two lead articles of two columns weekly on the economic or political subject of her choice, with guaranteed acceptance as anonymous editorial pieces, unless she cared to initial them, and a sweetheart fee for each contribution. In the evening she went to Kautsky's residence to take counsel. He knew more details than Bebel had revealed in his letter of offer.

Luxemburg wrote the next day to Jogiches that Bebel planned sweeping changes at *Vorwärts*. "In addition to my collaboration, the 'reform' encompasses the creation of a solid majority of the left wing by firing two small fry and hiring two new editors." She took pride in having played so prominent a role in the shake-up, even though she was not "apparently involved in this scandal." Together she and Kautsky formulated a plan of action to consolidate the seizure of the party's central organ. They met at Cunow's the next morning to enlist his support for a pact of the radicals on the editorial staff to resign en masse if her articles sparked a row with either the other editors or the executive (even before she accepted Bebel's offer, Luxemburg was plotting with Kautsky to subvert him). Cunow was giddy with delight at the prospect of the confrontation that would throw *Vorwärts* into tumult. Luxemburg then wrote to Bebel that while she despaired of any real change as long as Eisner, Gradnauer, and Wetzker remained on board, she would accept the offer if she were assured of a permanent editorial majority of radicals. She confided to Jogiches that by February at the latest affairs at *Vorwärts* would be settled.[108]

On 6 October, the day of the press commission's scheduled meeting, none other than Paul Singer apprised Eisner that the executive intended "to deliberate and decide without the editorship's being present." The editors were excluded from the meeting they had been asked to attend that afternoon, and the executive imposed a gag order on the participants.[109] With Luxemburg's conditional acceptance now in hand, Bebel undertook to make good on his part of the bargain. He called for Wetzker's dismissal and denounced editor Julius Kaliski as a turncoat. Once Bebel had spelled out the terms governing Luxemburg's submissions, the press commission remonstrated that no reputable editor could be expected to accept articles sight unseen. Moreover, the commission objected to the dismissal of editors for departments that hardly figured in the paper's political stance.[110] The six editors of the majority—Eisner, Gradnauer, Wetzker, Kaliski, Paul Büttner, and Wilhelm Schröder—wrote jointly to the executive on 10 and 17 October to protest their exclusion from deliberations or even prior consultation, first on the grounds of socialist solidarity and common decency, then in the second letter as a breach of established right and custom within the party press. Citing their long official service to party and paper, they accused the executive of having appropriated the despotic practice of an entrepreneur, who "as master of the house directs every aspect of the enterprise."[111]

Bebel, Singer, Pfannkuch, and Wengels responded jointly in writing on Friday, 20 October, that the executive had and would continue to act within the guidelines of the party's organizational statutes, and they confirmed that the deliberations concerned changes to the central organ's editorial staff: "dismissals on the one hand, appointments of new personnel on the other."[112] The following evening Eisner handed Wilhelm Pfannkuch a letter of resignation signed by the six majority editors, which contained the two-sentence text of a notice that would appear in the Sunday edition of *Vorwärts* the next morning: "In response to a decision of the party executive, the undersigned tendered in writing their resignation on 21 October 1905. Consequently, they are to quit the *Vorwärts* editorial board on 1 April 1906."[113] On Sunday Bebel and Kautsky held a war council, and Kautsky then scurried to Luxemburg's Friedenau apartment for her guarantee that she would step up when called upon. She reported to Jogiches that Bebel originally had no intention of replacing Eisner, Gradnauer, or Wetzker, but now he was determined to compel the executive to accept the joint resignation and immediately terminate their employment, that an entirely new board might be appointed. She likened Bebel's plan to "forming a cabinet" of the Far Left and acknowledged that they would need show that they were fit to lead.[114]

On Monday the executive, the press commission, and the local Berlin hierarchy voted to accept the resignations. An announcement of the vote, with no advance notice to the six departing men, was printed Tuesday on the backpage of *Vorwärts*.[115] The same day Gradnauer posted to editors of various party journals for their "private information" copy of the correspondence between the *Vorwärts* majority and the executive.[116] Luxemburg crowed to Jogiches that Bebel's "palace revolution" was progressing nicely and that he had charged her with the central organ's lead for 1 November. She realized that it was her lot to bring some sense of clarity and style to what would be a staff of "miserable (but 'kosher') scribblers."[117] On Wednesday, 25 October, the executive forbade publication in *Vorwärts* of other papers' comment on the resignations. Eisner wrote immediately to apprise Gradnauer's addressees of the ban.[118] Thursday evening Kautsky fetched Luxemburg for a briefing with Bebel. "We sat and talked—or much more listened—for he spoke as ever 'all by himself' until eleven o'clock," she recalled for Jogiches. Bebel divulged that he had written to Julian Marchlewski, an old confederate of Luxemburg, Mehring, and Parvus, to enlist his collaboration.[119] Sunday morning Eisner awoke to read below the *Vorwärts* masthead that he and his colleagues Gradnauer, Kaliski, Schröder, and Wetzker were relieved of all duties at the paper, effective immediately, and Paul Büttner was demoted to proofreader.[120] At 10:00 that morning the executive, the press commission, and the retained editors met with the newly appointed editors and regular contributors: Georg Davidsohn, Wilhelm Düwell, Hans Weber, Luxemburg, and Marchlewski. Rosa Luxemburg came away from the meeting with a migraine.[121]

CHAPTER TEN

THE COMPLETE PARITY OF MY EXPERIENCES: FROM EXILE TO NUREMBERG (1905–1907)

WRITING TEN YEARS AFTER Bavarian head of state Kurt Eisner had been felled by an assassin's bullets, Austrian comrade and colleague Stefan Großmann eulogized him for the Berlin journal *Tagebuch* (The Diary) as "the most refreshing, brightest, most vital journalistic talent that ever worked in the Social Democratic Party." To attain that station, Großmann explained, Eisner had to rise above an organizational structure and culture that succored mindless mediocrity and worse. "Thus it is understandable that Germany's greatest party did and does not possess a single robust, readable, and truly read daily newspaper. . . . In the first decade of this century Kurt Eisner tried to make a great paper of *Vorwärts*. He might well have succeeded, had not an underground war been mounted against him one fine day, which no one who experienced it then can forget."[1] Accusations and denials were exchanged publicly and privately for a month after the purge, protests organized, old bonds dissolved, and new links forged.

Heinrich Braun, cofounder of *Neue Gesellschaft*, headed an influential group of party editors and journalists opposed to the radical agenda who, deploring the unsavory conspiracy and peremptory deposals, considered launching a strike of their own.[2] The summary cashiering was denounced by its victims as a lockout engineered by the party executive, a cry that resonated in the trade-union press.[3] In the final week of October Kautsky adamantly disputed the right of party journalists to bring to print personal political views that deviated from the party's official stance or that of their governing bodies. The dissident who "represents a view or represents it in a way contrary to the convictions of the organization" should be dismissed for the breach of party discipline.[4] The next week Kautsky ran in *Neue Zeit* an article by Georg Ledebour disparaging the actions of the six deposed *Vorwärts* editors as a "revolt of the literati." Ledebour claimed that in an organizational meeting of the Workers' Press Association at the Hanover party congress of 1899, Eisner, in his first year at *Vorwärts*, had advocated the journalists' strike as means of undermining a domineering press commission—a proposal that alienated the tried and true comrades among the audience. "I could not have dreamed then that one day a serious attempt would in fact be made at a writers' strike in the party, much less that it could appeal even temporarily to other party journalists beyond the circle of its originators." By placing personal and pecuniary considerations before party interests, the six intractable men of letters had shamefully betrayed the confidence of ordinary workers and repaid with spite the forbearance of their overseers.[5]

Eisner's response was as scornful as anything he ever wrote. Ledebour was neither misinformed nor confused about the circumstances and events he recounted but rather lying outright to advance the clique's ambitions. Eisner ridiculed and refuted Ledebour's allegations point by point while at the same time probing the dark psychology of privileged journalists who denounce rival counterparts as privileged journalists, just as the reactionary press had done to Marx and Engels. The belletrist's label that Ledebour applied to the six majority editors was equally suspect, for they included a turner, a cigar maker, and a typesetter, whereas the retained minority was made up of a former actor, an accountant, and an attorney. In fact, the literati commandeering the party were Ledebour's own set. He, Mehring, Kautsky, Luxemburg, and Stadthagen somehow rated as "German Social Democracy's elect," free to ply their mischief, besmirch their adversaries with any fabrication, and twist the intent of resolutions and proscriptions against them to their benefit—doing untold harm to the credibility of the Social Democratic press and to the greater cause. "As party comrades, in the interest of the party, we advocate a self-confident, principled, independent, informed, and capable professional class of party journalists. Any erosion of the standing and dignity of our writers is the greatest detriment to the party. . . . We have all reason to uphold the status of the intellectual leaders and educators of the masses, as befits a party that claims to be a party of science, an heir to classical philosophy. . . . If, however, writers themselves do their utmost to denigrate their own station, then Social Democracy has ceased to be a party of culture." As to Ledebour's version of the meeting at Hanover, Eisner countered that he was hardly at odds with the membership of the Workers' Press Association, as he was tapped to serve on its board. Its chairman, Adolf Thiele, having read Ledebour's claim, wrote to *Vorwärts* to deny that Eisner had proposed any such strike, but the new editorship declined to print the correction.[6]

Eisner submitted his answer to Ledebour on 7 November to *Neue Zeit*, asking that it be printed in the next issue.[7] The same day he wrote to his ally Richard Fischer, Reichstag deputy from Berlin's second district, that Bebel's most recent invective against him in *Vorwärts* was sheer invention, the product of a sick man suffering from "full-blown hallucinations."[8] That morning *Vorwärts* had printed a letter from Bebel accusing Eisner of attempting to undermine him first by flattery then by affront and of collaborating with the bourgeois press in a conspiracy against the party's leadership. "To those desiring to study more closely the disposition and opinion of my opponents, I recommend frequent visits to the Café of the West in Charlottenburg. The clan hostile to the party executive and especially to me convenes there to pour out their hearts amid the pricked ears of opponents and bourgeois journalists."[9] Joseph Bloch, eminent editor of *Sozialistische Monatshefte* and regular participant in the weekly Kaffeeklatsch, wrote immediately to Bebel to question his motive and judgment in making such pointed, false claims and to deny that any of the six former editors had ever been present at table. Further, he objected to Bebel's characterization of the clientele: "Whoever comes is welcome, and thus 'revisionists' and 'radicals' have spent many a congenial evening together there over the course of years."[10]

Eisner too responded personally to Bebel. In a letter of 10 November 1905 he stated that the new editors' distorted account of opinion on the purge in the party press already deprived him of the respect requisite to a rebuttal. "Only a certain sadness fills me that all our years of hard work endeavoring to maintain the reputation of *Vorwärts* as an absolutely truthful paper, honestly objective in party conflicts, has been utterly annulled in a few days." In quiet tone and measured language he charged Bebel with libel, abuse of power, wanton recklessness in directing the cabal, and incompetence in office since the party congress of 1903, when Bebel showed himself unfit to lead. "For me," he wrote, "Dresden was the collapse of a political and personal illusion." Irritated that Bebel sought to lump him with the revisionists, Eisner declared that as a matter of conscience he would readily acknowledge the association if it existed, but he refused to be misrepresented, never having had anything to do with either the revisionist crowd at the Café of the West, whom he had challenged repeatedly "without of course ostracizing them," or the radical clique at the Königgrätz Street Bowling Club with their hackneyed quotes from Marx, feigned erudition, and unassailable yet uncomprehending ideological piety. "But you know very well, Comrade Bebel, that I almost always went along with you, and whenever I deviated tactically, took up my place as a rule to your *left*."[11]

A week after submitting the article to *Neue Zeit*, Eisner inquired of Kautsky if it were to be printed in its entirety or rejected, adding that he hoped to expose "a few of the most malicious lies" being spread.[12] Kautsky determined to reject it, purportedly in hope of effecting a reconciliation between the two camps. Eisner replied angrily on 14 November that he intended to publish the article elsewhere, having seen no attempt at reconciliation by the editors of *Neue Zeit* or *Vorwärts*.[13] Denied the pages of the party's national organs as a forum, Eisner turned to Heinrich Braun, who ran it late November in his revisionist weekly, *Neue Gesellschaft*. It was a bold stroke on Braun's part, for Eisner characterized himself in the piece, as he had in the letter to Bebel, as a staunch opponent of Bernstein and his adherents.

Before month's end the six ousted editors packed off to Georg Birk's Munich press a manuscript titled *Der Vorwärts-Konflikt*, a white book of annotated correspondence, official notices, and reprinted articles pertaining to the struggle for control of the central organ. Categorized eighty years later by East German historian Dieter Fricke as a "veritable broadsheet of defamation against the revolutionary, Marxist forces in the party, targeting August Bebel above all," the compilation established Bebel's systematic deceit ad nauseam.[14] Its preface stressed the broader implications of the former editors' fate not only for their colleagues in the party press but also for an organization that professed democratic ideals of inclusion and transparency. A more pointed indictment of the executive's imperiousness took the form of an implied comparison embedded in the editors' explanation of their resignations: "How can editors of the party press still dare to attack without blushing the personal regime, the cult of authority, . . . hierarchy, and blind obedience?"[15] Obdurate in delusion and petty in ignominy, Bebel scoffed at the recriminations of "the noble six," although clearly he was stung by being likened to his royal complement, the personification of Prussian autocracy.[16]

Within months the radical triumph proved a Pyrrhic victory. However reluctantly, Bebel and the rest of the executive committee found themselves compelled to ratify the wisdom of Eisner's muchmaligned article "Union and Party," the catalyst to Kautsky and Mehring's campaign to unseat him. In Saxony political strikes staged against conservative assaults on workers' voting rights threatened to bankrupt the unions. In its meeting of 8 December 1905 the executive conceded that the general strike was impracticable under existing circumstances and had to be disavowed. On 16 February 1906 a secret accord was struck between the party executive and the trade unions' general commission, by which the executive agreed that the party would underwrite political strikes, which the executive would in any case officially discourage.[17] Under Heinrich Ströbel's inept leadership, the new editorial board at *Vorwärts* immediately began to crumble. In her first week Rosa Luxemburg confirmed Jogiches's observation that *Vorwärts* was sinking quickly to the level of a provincial rag. Of her colleagues she reported there was not a single journalist among them; they were all "oxen, and arrogant ones on top of it."[18] By the end of December she had resigned her position and fled to Poland.

These reversals of fortune presaged more momentous changes yet. In the national elections of 1907 targeted fringe voters turned from the party August Bebel had so deliberately polarized, casting their lot with Germany's imperial venture. Colonial expansion fed on nationalist fervor, bringing the nation into grave conflict with France and Great Britain. During the First World War radical Heinrich Cunow would undergo "a cataclysmic conversion to patriotism."[19] Kautsky turned on Mehring and had to be dissuaded by friends from publishing yet another tract excoriating a comrade.[20] And in November and December 1918 it was Otto Wels, Bebel's erstwhile stooge on the press commission, who as Ebert's commandant would crush Rosa Luxemburg and Karl Liebknecht's Spartacist Revolution in Berlin. Displaced and isolated in October 1905, Kurt Eisner persevered in his centrist line, campaigned tirelessly in print and from the lectern to revolutionize minds, and warned in vain of the inevitable outcome of Germany's course. After August 1914 he became a leading critic of the war and played a key role in galvanizing the opposition into a new socialist party. In January 1918, in decidedly revolutionary circumstances, he organized in Munich a general strike and was jailed for treason. Released nine months later, he marshaled the forces of revolution, proclaimed the Bavarian Republic, and became its socialist premier.

For a full year after his departure from *Vorwärts* Eisner weighed his options, determined not to yield the political middle ground in the party. The two leading publications of the party's revisionist wing bid for his collaboration. Prominent bourgeois editors came calling as well. Karl Kraus sought to woo him to *Die Fackel*, Vienna's scintillating satirical journal, an opportunity Eisner declined on ideological grounds. On 1 February 1906 he wrote to thank Kraus for his cordial and attractive offer and to justify the decision over which he agonized for some time. "In the first place, I believe that our outlooks deviate too greatly—I am after all, by party affiliation, a Social Democrat—that, even given your great tolerance, we could suffer each other at length. . . . In the second, and this is decisive for me, I harbor the greatest respect for our Austrian, particularly our Viennese comrades, whom you like to taunt from time to time. That is your perfect right, but it seems tactless to me to collaborate on a foreign journal that makes my comrades an object of its polemic."[21] Siegfried Jacobsohn too unsuccessfully solicited Eisner's collaboration on *Die Schaubühne* (The Stage), Berlin's theater review.[22] Buoyed by contract work and generous advances from sympathetic publishers, Eisner worked from home, churning out three books in short order, in addition to occasional articles for Braun's journal. J. H. W. Dietz, the Stuttgart publisher who had vied for Eisner's services six years earlier, issued a contract for a multivolume literary history. From 1 January 1906 Dietz paid monthly advances of 250 marks for the next year, showing charitable forbearance when no manuscript materialized.[23]

The 6 December 1905 issue of *Neue Gesellschaft* featured Eisner's seminal essay on the deficiencies of public education, a problem that would engage his interest for the next years and bring him once again into sharpest ideological conflict with his chief adversaries. "The Expropriation of Parents" was prompted by a bill pending in the Prussian diet to regulate school funding and teachers' salaries. Provisions in the bill required that Prussian public grammar schools be classed as Protestant or Catholic and that religious instruction be consigned to one confession or the other, effectively creating a system of publicly funded parochial schools. In the same number Braun ran an article by Pastor Paul Göhre clarifying what was at stake.[24] During his tenure at *Vorwärts* Eisner repeatedly focused attention on the woeful state of schooling for proletarian children.[25] The criticisms were validated independently by foreign scholars. American Thomas Alexander, professor of elementary education at George Peabody College for Teachers, studied the *Volksschule* (elementary school) before the First World War and found "that the Prussian is to a large measure enslaved through the medium of his school; that his learning, instead of making him his own master, forges the chain by which he is held in servitude; that the whole scheme of Prussian elementary education is shaped with the express purpose of making ninety-five out of every hundred citizens subservient to the ruling house and to the state."[26] Göhre confined himself to the issues of religious instruction, demanding its removal from the curriculum altogether.

Eisner launched a broader offensive. The propagandists of the Right, he wrote, reveled in frightful images of the future under communism. Infants would be taken from their parents nine days after birth, deposited in an assembly-line nursery, raised to automatons by soulless bureaucrats appointed to the purpose. The tenderest, noblest emotions would soon die out, the individual utterly dehumanized by mass-molding in service to the monolithic state. The future-state scenario, Eisner argued, paled in comparison to the present state of affairs, where the complete displacement of parents was already the stark reality. "In Prussia approximately six million children from age six to fourteen are delivered to a hostile drill academy that equips them with some requisite, meager skills but for the most part seeks to break them in a way stultifying and crippling to their own interests." Their parents, deprived of voting rights by Prussia's three-tiered electoral system, had no say whatsoever in the schools' organization, curriculum, standards for employment of faculty, or methods of instruction. Consequently, their children's inherent curiosity was blunted by rote memorization and catechismal repetition so that the values and superstition of the ruling class might be instilled into their dulled minds. What the Volksschule taught best was an attitude of subservience to one's betters. In the final analysis, Eisner reasoned, the problem was at heart another manifestation of inequitable franchise.

Feste der Festlosen (Feasts of the Feastless), an anthology of Eisner's articles on holidays, commemorations, and rites of passage significant to the proletariat, was published by Dresden's Kaden Press, complete with expensive plates, art *nouveau* woodcut flourishes, and elegant binding that bespoke the elevated cultural aspirations of its audience. In a review for the New Year's issue of *Neue Gesellschaft* Leo Berg wrote that what distinguished the book was its author's "yearning for the solemn, the festive, and the victorious in the worker's life after long struggle and toil, and the higher conception expressed here of the value of celebrations in life." Citing widespread opposition within the party fifteen years earlier to the People's Free Stage as a corruptive luxury, Berg hailed the wonders it had wrought and praised in particular Eisner's essay on the meaning of a Beethoven performance staged for workers in joint observance of Schiller's life and the March Revolution.[27]

For Vorwärts Press Eisner undertook a second edition of his biography of Wilhelm Liebknecht, supplemented by commentary on Liebknecht's stance on various tactical questions, passages from Liebknecht's unpublished writings and correspondence, and papers and photographs provided by the family. In mid-February Karl Liebknecht wrote to promise material Eisner had requested.[28] Eisner noted in his preface that his "return to the status of freelance writer" afforded him the leisure to revise the work that had been out of print for years. Its publication was slated to coincide with what would have been Liebknecht's eightieth birthday on 29 March 1906.

In light of Liebknecht's tutelage of Bebel, his successor as socialist icon, the new edition gave Eisner the chance to assess Bebel's failings in that office and, indeed, the need for an icon at all, since no one else had quite measured up to Liebknecht's stature: "It may be that the time of the individual, of heroes generally, is past, and that would be, in the final analysis, not just a necessary development but a fortunate one too" as labor strove to realize its collective potential. Accordingly, Eisner's appraisal of his predecessor and intercessor at *Vorwärts* was more balanced than before, and he openly confessed their differences of opinion, especially on the party's electoral boycott in Prussia. Although Eisner recognized that Liebknecht lacked organizational skills, left the details for others to work out, and had difficulty separating the personal from the political, he was nonetheless indisputably the stalwart of democratic socialism in Germany, and his great talent had been in forging unity out of shapeless discord. Targeting Bebel once again, Eisner concluded that of Liebknecht's many qualities, the greatest was his adroitness at defusing the divisiveness of factionalism. "This ability to forget all animosity and all antagonism at the critical moment and to serve only party peace, party unity—that made him in spite of everything, even inwardly, an indispensable party leader whose gift for consolidating became more important the more the party grew."[29]

The French government's exhaustive yellow book on the first Moroccan crisis had elicited a paltry rejoinder from Berlin in the form of a white book. Once Eisner had read excerpts from the French report in the press, he concluded, as he confided to Lily Braun on 17 January, "that this collection of documents represents not only the most compromising revelation of Wilhelmine politics that has ever come to light but also affords us the weightiest weapon against the ruling system."[30] Unable to locate a copy of the yellow book in the German capital—not even the members of the Reichstag had one—Eisner turned to the French ambassador Bihourd, who procured it for him in Paris.[31] Comparing the two versions of events, Eisner was convinced that in contrast to the "historically significant" French text, the German sham report, full of inaccuracies and distortions calculated to mislead, could have been compiled by "a chancellery clerk of average ability in an average hour," and proved that "after Morocco there is nothing credible in official German politics other than their own absurdity."[32] Horrified by so casual and inept an attempt to dupe the public, he used the report from Paris to write a detailed exposé of Bülow's chicanery. *Der Sultan des Weltkrieges: Ein marokkanisches Sittenbild deutscher Diplomaten-Politik* (The Sultan of World War: A Moroccan Genre Painting of German Diplomat-Politics) warned comrades and compatriots alike that German diplomatic intrigue and incompetence had brought Europe perilously close, "twice, perhaps three times, in the last twelve months to the brink of a war in which members of the proletariat were to be set at one another without knowing the reason and purpose."[33]

In a foreword written on 21 January 1906 Eisner praised French socialists for keeping the diplomatic corps in check, whereas the German party fairly abdicated its responsibility and abandoned foreign policy to the jingoists. Just as the problems with public education in Prussia stemmed, to Eisner's mind, from the disenfranchisement of the working class, so too was the stranglehold of the Prussian state on Germany's foreign policy a result of the de facto exclusion of Social Democrats from the diet whence the Junker influence on national life emanated. Three days later he wrote to Jaurès that it was his intent to follow Jaurès's example and incite the public to action: "The operation you performed on the Delcassés I am undertaking against the Bülows." He closed with the promise to tell Jaurès of his personal situation within the party when they met in Berlin, Paris, or Stuttgart.[34] Published by Kaden, Eisner's book generated sparse interest, sitting unsold in bundles at the publisher until world war ravaged Europe. By September 1918 it was sold out.[35]

Joseph Bloch, whom Eisner tried to enlist in his campaign, wrote on 29 January 1906 that his view of German foreign policy and the Morocco affair differed significantly from Eisner's and that it was "not very likely that your brochure will modify this standpoint essentially."[36] Eisner later attributed the indifference with which his efforts met to two factors. The press feud had damaged his credibility at a critical moment, and Social Democracy had for so long made the threat of war a cornerstone of its agitation that war's imminence and horror faded into the abstract, trivialized by the perpetual tocsin.[37] Nonetheless he threw himself into the effort. For *Neue Gesellschaft* he recapitulated the main points of his exposé in an article titled "Diplomats," quoting from the yellow book Bülow's truculent intimations to Bihourd, revealing how Germany curried favor with lavish cash payments to a parasitic despot, and documenting beyond question that the egregious clamor served only to isolate Berlin and weaken the nation's influence.[38] For the first time in his career Eisner took to the lectern. His initial talk on the Moroccan crisis met with a lukewarm reception at best. "From the first word I felt the passive resistance of the audience. Those were all things that lay far beyond their interest. And that someday there would be war, well, everyone had known that for a long time anyway. In any case there was still time to deal with it." He reckoned it as "a hopeless beginning."[39] That winter and spring he returned to the topic repeatedly in his pieces for *Neue Gesellschaft*.[40]

Heinrich Braun, who in the past had urged Eisner to leave the central organ and join the staff of *Neue Gesellschaft*, proffered now the status of regular contributor, but he and Eisner were at odds as to what the title implied. After Braun had returned an article on foreign policy that Eisner had deemed important enough to complete in the throes of the flu, Eisner wrote on 24 February that "'regular' contribution, for which you *recruited* me and which is the only arrangement to which I can agree, is of course a contradiction in terms if the 'regular' contributor cannot be assured of having at his disposal, regularly under all circumstances, the *necessary* space."[41] Three days later he expanded on his reservations, expressing wonder that Braun considered it a limitation of his prerogative as editor to reserve pages in his journal for those writers he had contracted to provide weekly articles.

Since 1893, Eisner wrote, he had never submitted an article to a weekly for which he served as regular contributor that the article was not promptly accepted. He was mystified by Braun's practice of rejecting solicited articles without citing any reason and noted the supreme irony of having his work spurned by revisionist and radical journals alike. "For me this outcome is especially unpleasant in that I no longer have any Social Democratic journal at my disposal and, if I want to voice myself in Berlin, must turn to bourgeois enterprises. On the other hand the positive in it is that my equilibrium as a party comrade is restored. I revel in the complete parity of my experiences."[42] In late March Joseph Bloch solicited for *Sozialistische Monatshefte* a critique of Kautsky's theoretical premises, but Eisner was in the midst of another book project.[43] Having reconciled himself to freelance work for the time being, he was content to be occasional contributor to *Neue Gesellschaft*, for Braun was in any case more receptive than Bloch to his views on Weltpolitik.

As he had done for the Schiller commemoration the previous year, Eisner composed an appreciation of Heine in observance of the fiftieth anniversary of the poet's death. Of Eisner's voluminous literary criticism, this essay rates among the most insightful and penetrating. The exile in Paris held a special fascination for one marginalized among his brethren. Heine's great contribution to German letters, Eisner declared, lay in the actualization of humane, artistic ideals through direct engagement with the momentous issues of his time—a commitment that in turn endowed his writing with matchless immediacy and its earmark scourging irony. Romantics and neoclassics alike had fled from the harsh reality of Germany's political immaturity to construct their own subjective habitats, "secluded forest brothers conversing with elves and gnomes in mystical moonlight" or initiates of "a Greek temple where, liberated from temporal gravity, they paid homage to the eternal, sacred ideal of humanity." The Jewish expatriate's refuge conversely was birthplace of the new order, his idol Bonaparte, flesh-and-blood executor of the Revolution, who crossed the Rhine to dash the underpinnings of feudalism. Synthesizing romantic individualism with neoclassical humanism, Heine found his voice and raised it against Metternich's reconstituted ancien régime. Hounded out of Germany for his trouble, he became Germany's foremost poet to the rest of the world. Noting that *Buch der Lieder* (Book of Songs) was the first German-language work to be translated into Japanese, Eisner reckoned as Heine's greatest honor that of having no monument to his memory on German soil, for a far worse fate than notoriety or obscurity was the cooption that befell Schiller.[44]

In the spring Eisner hammered away at the exclusive Prussian franchise in his articles for *Neue Gesellschaft*, tying police corruption, a spying scandal, and the expulsion of political refugees to Prussia's status as Western Europe's last refuge of barbarism and reaction—a status perpetuated only through restricted suffrage.[45] "Petition Nr. 70," an essay printed in the 6 June issue, is remarkable for its cogency and urgency in confronting Social Democracy with its unwillingness to act decisively to achieve a critical end.[46] Since the first of the year its leadership had summoned Prussian workers to four mass rallies against the discriminatory voting law. The Prussian members of the party executive had presented to the Prussian diet a petition demanding "universal, equal, direct, and secret suffrage for elections to the Landtag for all citizens over the age of twenty regardless of gender." The lower house declined to consider the petition; the upper house rejected it without debate.

Recalling how speakers at the rallies impressed on their audience the gravity of the initiative, couching it as a struggle for political existence, for democracy, for German culture itself, Eisner presented two courses of action, dispassionately arguing the expedience of each. The first was to ally with the progressive bourgeois parties committed to electoral reform. Were the party's legions to turn out in support of Left Liberals, "a cartel of the sort the Junkerdom has long feared," the system could be brought to bear against itself. The second course was wholly in keeping with the party's own stated policy, adopted with near unanimity at Jena. Having voted in favor of Bebel's general-strike resolution that called for its application to win equal political rights, Eisner now held the executive to its word, knowing full well that Bebel had already recanted. Eisner did not expect the party to call a general strike from above—he had long argued that would be counterproductive—but rather simply to support it once the masses had been moved to act by their distress. It fell to the unions to marshal their members and thrust them into action, to the party to clarify the historical circumstance, enunciate the political goals, and recognize the critical moment for full assault.

In January 1905 Eisner had agreed to write a book for Vorwärts Press, a general history of the nobility, but it was only after his departure from the central organ that he immersed himself in the project.[47] Once he had begun to mine the primary sources, a narrower focus and more ambitious goal emerged. He determined to treat the Prussian aristocracy's efforts to counter the French Revolution, the effects of which still blighted Germany's development as a modern state. "I wanted to show in the Imperial German and Prussian collapse of 1789 to 1807 how Germany lagged behind the great Revolution; how it tried to creep away, was chased down, and brought low; how even amid this catastrophe the nation made a beginning at embracing the most progressive European development—a beginning then voided by the military victory of the absolute monarchy and the feudal estate-owning class."[48]

The book's publication was to coincide with the hundredth anniversary of Prussia's crushing defeat at Jena (14 October 1806) and the Treaty of Tilsit (9 July 1807), by which Prussia ceded its lands west of the Elbe. Although Vorwärts Press commenced monthly payments of 250 marks on 1 April 1906, to run through 1 March 1907, totaling 3,000 marks, Eisner signed no formal contract until 2 July 1906. Its terms specified a first edition of five thousand copies for a work with the title "The Nobility: On the History of a Ruling Class," intended as a volume in the press's popular series on cultural history.[49] Galley proofs of the first chapter, on the rivalry between England and France, were issued that summer.[50] What came to print in January 1907 under the title *Das Ende des Reichs: Deutschland und Preußen im Zeitalter der großen Revolution* (The End of the Empire: Germany and Prussia in the Age of the Great Revolution) was substantially different in both scope and style from the works of the popular series.[51]

Eisner thought carefully about his approach to writing history for a proletarian audience. In keeping with his didactic imperative to shape minds to think critically, he rejected a narrative of events, a drama of dynastic rivalry, pitched battles, and court intrigues, in favor of a sweeping social history drawing on an array of primary sources—private correspondence, royal edicts, guild records, philosophical treatises, speeches, military directives, lyrics to drinking songs, official proclamations, press accounts, government reports, diary entries, poetry, economic statistics, casualty lists—linked by his introduction and commentary clarifying their significance. He provided detailed documentation so that readers who cared to look deeper into a particular aspect might undertake research projects of their own, for "education, intellectual independence, clear and free judgment, in short the strong character of the mind cannot be acquired through mere study and assimilation, however zealous, but only through one's own questing and grappling, and history offers the richest and most fruitful field for such endeavors." In that respect he warned his audience against the work of Germany's two most renowned historians of the day, Treitschke and Ranke, who from slavish class interest wrote in justification of the Wilhelmine state, appropriating both the moldy methodology and scraping deference of scholasticism.[52]

Eisner's review in the 27 June 1906 issue of *Neue Gesellschaft* of two books by Prussian officers indicates that he was thoroughly versed in the sources and well into the project. He judged General Colmar von der Goltz's *Von Roßbach bis Jena und Auerstedt* (From Roßbach to Jena and Auerstedt) an update of Lieutenant General Friedrich August Ludwig von der Marwitz's attempt in his memoirs to shift the blame for Germany's humiliation at Jena from the ineptitude of his Junker comrades in arms to the pernicious influence of the Enlightenment. Equally flawed was *1806: Das Preußische Offizierkorps und die Untersuchung der Kriegsereignisse* (1806: The Prussian Officer Corps and the Investigation of Events in the War), compiled by the Imperial general staff. By documenting the proceedings of courts-martial after the defeat, the work sought to rebut historical criticism that the Prussian command, as exclusive preserve of an inbred caste, was too ossified to recognize its failings. What the book proved beyond dispute, Eisner observed, was that the French officers, who had advanced on merit rather than lineage, were more willing to sacrifice themselves for their cause than were their Prussian foes. At Roßbach 650 French officers fell in ninety minutes, whereas 190 Prussian officers perished in the campaigns of 1806–1807, fewer than were cashiered.[53] As epigraph to his history, Eisner quoted Professor Kraus, Kant's successor at Königsberg, who attributed the superiority of the French army over all opponents to "the republican spirit retained from the times of enthusiasm for the rights of mankind, and conversely in the soul-killing demon of feudalism."

Eisner's central premise in *Das Ende des Reichs* is that the events in France that effected the collapse of the millennial Holy Roman Empire represented the second stage of a political and economic divide in European civilization and culture. Some nations crossed the divide into modernity, others hung in the cobwebs of a bygone era. The first nation to liberate itself from feudalism and to progress beyond an agrarian economy had been England. After the French bourgeoisie followed suit, England and France became capitalist rivals. When the French then exported their revolution on the Continent, the English allied with the feudal forces of reaction in order to stymie free economic development and attendant challenges to their "world monopoly of trade and industry." In the popular mentality the face of the struggle is the portrait of Napoleon, but his image had to be deconstructed, stripped of the overlay of myth.

> If one once grasps this most profound economic antithesis throughout the period of the great French Revolution, the ambitious, insatiable world conqueror, the cunning Corsican, the scourge of humanity, and whatever else Bonaparte may have been called in the English and Junker-tsarist legend disappears altogether. The French consul as well as the emperor appears as the hero of a desperate defensive struggle against the aggression of global British despotism, fighting for the economic development not just of France but of the European continent. . . . Yet even if every trace of the ambitious and perfidious world oppressor is rubbed out of the picture . . . , Napoleon is still nothing more than the revolutionizing precursor to bourgeois, capitalist-industrialist development on the Continent, not the revolutionary of world freedom, not the bearer and bringer of democracy.[54]

The implication was clear that only by fully understanding their moment in the continuum vis-à-vis their English, French, and Russian comrades could German workers effectively advance toward their end goal. For that reason the study of why Europe's states developed so differently was "the most vital issue of political engagement."[55] By any standard *Das Ende des Reichs* is an impressive achievement, a masterful feat prefiguring in many respects the historiography of Lucien Febvre, Marc Bloch, Fernand Braudel, and their Annales School. Half a century after its publication Professor Koppel Pinson, an ardent admirer of Treitschke and by his own word "one who finds liberal democracy, humanitarianism, and the ethical ideals of the Judeo-Christian tradition most congenial to his own frame of mind," drew on Eisner's book for his classic *Modern Germany* and recommended to his readers the "interesting material not available in the academic works on this age."[56] Georg Olms Press of Hildesheim marked the two-hundredth anniversary of Jena by reprinting in facsimile the second edition of 1907.

After packing off *Das Ende des Reichs* to the compositors in the fall, Eisner went back out on the lecture circuit. Over the course of two evenings, 23–24 November, he spoke in Kassel on Nietzsche's philosophy, contrasting its central tenets with the ideals of the workers' movement and examining evolving critical reception. In preparation for the talk he borrowed from Joseph Bloch the just-published study by August Horneffer, *Nietzsche als Moralist und Schriftsteller* (Nietzsche as Moralist and Writer).[57] Indeed, Horneffer's own public lectures the previous spring prompted the invitation for Eisner to speak and ensured a packed hall. The local *Volksblatt* ventured that the turnout vindicated the organizers' ambitious program of scholarly forums. On the first evening Eisner surveyed Nietzsche's life and works, then read passages from *Nietzsche contra Wagner, Der Antichrist,* and *Also sprach Zarathustra.* The second evening was devoted to a wide-ranging critique. Of the first the *Volksblatt* reported: "Lengthy applause followed the presentation by Eisner, long familiar to most of our readers as a brilliant writer and whom we came to know last night, to our surprise and delight, as a captivating speaker too. All theatricality, of which there was no lack in Horneffer, is foreign to Eisner's flowing, clear delivery. Depth of thought, sense of style, and richness of language shone in each sentence, on which the dense audience hung rapt."[58] The paper serialized the entire lecture in five parts.[59]

The respite from meeting a perpetual deadline had afforded Eisner time and opportunity to explore new venues for his talents, to tie up loose ends, and regain focus. But he certainly missed the ready forum for his views on the thorny problems confronting Social Democracy, most prominently the lack of a coherent foreign policy, exclusion from public life in Prussia, the inadequacy of workers' schooling, and the woeful inability of party leadership to achieve positive results. Having weighed attractive offers from a number of journals, Eisner settled on a return to running a party paper, one not subject to the dictates of the national executive. By October he had tentatively agreed to succeed once again the Austrian Adolf Braun, who was moving from Nuremberg's *Fränkische Tagespost* to the *Arbeiterstimme* in Vienna.[60] On 12 December Eisner wrote from Boninstraße 3 to Richard Fischer of his decision to accept the position of editor in chief at Nuremberg. There he believed he could show what might be accomplished, for he regarded the catastrophic decline at *Vorwärts* with horror: "The total incompetence of the editorship is a danger to the party." He shuddered at the central organ's incomprehensible positions and lamented that it printed crucial news a day or two behind the party press that subscribed to Friedrich Stampfer's correspondence.[61]

Established in 1871, the *Fränkische Tagespost* had grown over the last decade under successive editors Albert Südekum, Philipp Scheidemann, and Braun to become Bavaria's leading Social Democratic paper. Its twenty thousand subscribers, roughly a fourth of the *Vorwärts* number at

Eisner's departure in October 1905, significantly outstripped the readership of the *Münchener Post*.[62] Eisner was slated to take control in March.
In the interim he followed with justifiable concern the campaign before
the national elections of January 1907, continued to write for *Neue
Gesellschaft*, and entertained a commission from Joseph Bloch.

The fall 1905 Center Party Reichstag deputy Matthias Erzberger
had written anonymously a series of articles for the *Kölnische Zeitung*
exposing corruption in the colonial department of the Foreign Office.
Over the next year mounting criticism of Bülow's African policy, exacerbated by the saber-rattling over Morocco, culminated when the
chancellor asked the Reichstag for nearly 30 million marks to send fourteen thousand troops to quell a native revolt in Southwest Africa. The
Social Democrats joined the Center to vote down credits. Staking his
office on the gamble, Bülow dissolved the Reichstag on 13 December
1906. Confident of gaining seats, the party's deputies cheered as Bülow
read the dissolution order.[63] From the outset Bülow cast the election
as "a great test of whether Germany is capable of developing from a
European into a world power."[64] Branding his opponents unpatriotic,
he sought to woo the Left Liberals into a bloc against Social Democracy
and the Center, but the main thrust of the campaign was against Social
Democracy. Bülow wrote on 31 December to General Eduard von
Liebert, former governor of German East Africa and chairman of the
Imperial Union against Social Democracy (Reichsverband gegen die
Sozialdemokratie): "Although no other state has done more than the
German Reich for the present and future of its workers, for their material and intellectual needs, although the German workers are the best
educated in the world, millions of them nevertheless support a party,
either actively or as sympathizers, that seeks to revolutionize state and
society from the ground up. The German people must free themselves
from such pressure."[65] Seeing political advantage in joining Bülow's
reconstituted *Kulturkampf*, the Left Liberals abandoned their criticism
of colonial mismanagement and joined in the jingoism.

Eisner presented his commentary in the 26 December 1906 issue
of *Neue Gesellschaft*. Bülow's purpose, he ventured, had less to do with
mopping up the Hottentots than with impressing on the Reichstag that
its office was that of "Münzjuden," Jewish financiers, expected to bank-
roll cheerfully the emperor's schemes. If the tattered remnants of Eugen
Richter's party properly construed the situation, they would rush to the
aid of representative democracy against the government's assault. Noting
that the National Liberals and Left Liberals were now so debased as to
collaborate with their traditional archrivals, the agrarian Conservatives,

Eisner urged the Left Liberals' few politicians of conscience, namely, Theodor Barth and his associates, to defect. He concluded that it fell to Social Democracy to smash the nationalist bloc of the Reichstag in the coming elections, "which will determine if Germany sinks below Turkey politically as the last European ruin of Asiatic despotism."[66]

Six weeks later Max Schippel reviewed *Das Ende des Reichs* for *Sozialistische Monatshefte*, taking issue with several key points, such as the interpretation of Napoleon's foreign policy as a radical departure from that of the monarchy, but praising the work generally as "absorbing from start to finish, vibrantly written, its rich, nearly superabundant cultural-historical material assiduously compiled."[67] He overlooked what Eisner held to be the work's most significant contribution to the study of the period. In a letter of 6 February 1907 Eisner expressed his dissatisfaction to Joseph Bloch. "What annoys me in Schippel's critical remarks is not that he perchance contests the basic premise of my book—the English-French rivalry—but just misses it. . . . In the description of the revolutionary wars I certainly underscored the decisive role of England, which began to finance the wars once the realization set in that the Revolution was not destroying France's economic might but rather boosting it." Of far greater interest to Bloch, an unabashed admirer of Napoleon, were the insights into his hero's ambitions, achievements, and failings, for example "that Napoleon sought to secure the [Revolution's] democratic legacy by the means of the old, absolute state and foundered in his attempt for that very reason."[68] Whereas Bloch had little sympathy for Eisner's take on Germany's foreign policy, he valued Eisner's expertise in literature and understanding of the French and their historic revolution. Having solicited to no avail an article on Frank Wedekind the previous year, Bloch began now to importune Eisner for "an exquisite portrait of Napoleon's personality" for the *Monatshefte* and offered to send requisite sources.[69] Eisner agreed to make an attempt and asked for the studies by John Holland Rose, Paul Holzhausen, and August Fournier.[70] On the same day though that he posted his request for books Eisner began another project altogether. Between 19 February and 8 March 1907 he wrote the libretto to an opera, "Iferit," which he characterized as "fragments from youthful dreams returned, full of purity, devotion, and longing."[71] Composed for Toni Hendrich, Elisabeth's sister, the piece evinces the unraveling of his marriage.

The Hottentot elections, as they became known, were held on 25 January, with runoffs completed by 5 February. Although the Social Democrats gained a quarter-million popular votes and held their core electorate, they faired poorly in closely contested districts where in 1903 they had garnered support from unaffiliated workers and Left Liberal sympathizers. For the first time in seven national elections their percentage of the total vote declined. The Reichstag deputation was halved, sliding from 81 seats to 43 and from the second largest caucus to fifth, behind the Center (105), Conservatives (60), National Liberals (54), and Left Liberals (49).[72] Eisner had considered the victory of 1903 an unprecedented opportunity for Social Democracy to make the Reichstag a counterbalance to the chancellor and his cabinet and, by a legislative campaign of sweeping reform, to delineate more clearly the lines of battle in the ongoing class struggle. His optimism was ridiculed by a doctrinaire clique who convinced the party chairman to mount a protracted purge of precisely those moderates who held to the dual tactic of the Erfurt Program: practical and organizational work as preface to the rule of the proletariat. Having failed to eradicate revisionism, the party radicals of the moment—most prominently Franz Mehring, Rosa Luxemburg, and Karl Kautsky—aided by August Bebel, pursued a scorched-earth tactic against the party's middle ground, unwittingly effecting a fateful shift to the right, which by August 1914 would situate Social Democracy squarely in the nationalist camp and shatter the Socialist International. In the bleak winter of 1907 Bebel and Co. got what they had bargained for at Dresden: a cataclysmic drubbing that so relegated the party to the fringe of political life that its "leaders" hastened to repudiate their former positions, all the while adamantly denying their inconsistency.

The revisionists, who had always been more receptive to the colonial enterprise, called for an immediate reappraisal of the party's stance. Bernstein argued in *Sozialistische Monatshefte* that the polling's outcome was "the natural consequence of the spurious treatment that the colonial question has been accorded up to now in our ranks."[73] Richard Calwer pegged the higher wages of English and American workers to their governments' aggressive agenda of colonial expansion.[74] Kautsky lamely attributed the loss to the bourgeoisie's rising fear of socialism, fanned by the party's great gains in 1903 and the Russian revolution of 1905.[75] Even before the polling, though, he had moved closer to Bernstein to advocate a "purely cultural" colonialism by which "Europeans occupy an overseas land in order to bring their higher mode of production to its inhabitants."[76] Bebel, utterly incapable since 1903 of staking out a coherent, consistent position on virtually any question, had already hedged on Social Democracy's traditional opposition to imperialism nearly two years earlier. In a speech before the Reichstag on 29 March 1905, he declared the party's willingess to back Bülow's Morocco policy "in so far as its purpose was to protect German trade interests by guarding the sovereignty of Morocco against France."[77] Friedrich Stampfer records in his memoirs that the hardline radicals persisted in scoffing at any election result as inconsequential. "And yet there was no one in the party at that time who did not perceive that result as a crushing defeat. With good cause. Whoever did not read it in the election statistics could see it on the street. What had become of Berlin, 'red Berlin?' Huge crowds gathered and streamed through the streets in celebration of their victory. . . . We saw them again at the end of July 1914, when they shook their fists at those of us demonstrating for peace on Unter den Linden."[78] After reflecting on the results, Eisner presented his analysis in the 20 February issue of *Neue Gesellschaft*. His article took the title "The Case of Molkenbuhr," as Hermann Molkenbuhr, one of the party's most veteran politicians, was among the deposed deputies, having been unseated by an Antisemite nonentity.

Looking back to 1903, Eisner lamented the unwarranted fear on the part of "the party's most influential personalities" that the remarkable electoral gains would convert Social Democracy into a purely parliamentary movement. "Those knowing the history of Prussia's driving force in the German Empire were convinced of the virtually categorical impossibility of socialism, in however a diluted form, being suitable to govern, and they had to regard the party's internal discussions of program and tactic as a wretched excess, as a waste of time and diversion, even apart from their form." Bebel, himself leader of the parliamentary deputation, had railed at Dresden against a party-led legislative campaign for reforms, ceding the drafting of bills to the government's privy councilors. And it was precisely here where the party played into the hands of its bitterest enemies, for although the bourgeois critics constantly characterized Social Democracy as a purely negative force, their greatest fear was the positive work of which it was capable. Why else had the bourgeois Right redoubled its assault on unions? In fact, Eisner asserted, the enmity of the Right only increased, accentuating class interest and strengthening class consciousness, whenever Social Democracy achieved a tangible improvement in the lives of the proletariat. For that very reason Bebel's histrionics at Dresden would be laughable now, had they not been so damaging.

By repudiating the serious responsibility with which Germany's electorate had entrusted the party, Social Democracy showed itself incapable of pursuing effectively its own two-pronged attack on capitalist society. The glaring deficiency had been nowhere more evident than in its impotence in combatting the Prussian school bill the previous winter. While the bill was still being considered in the lower house of Prussian diet, the party's Reichstag deputation should have proposed a national bill to override it. "Our program," he wrote, "is brimming with the full-ness of immediate reforms, and we determine at least the degree of our standing in public opinion by the force and impression of our positive work, just as the Center boosted its influence primarily through its par-liamentary efficacy."

He warned that accommodating the bourgeois parties' program for colonial expansion was a veritable formula for failure, for no amount of concessions by Social Democracy would elicit reciprocity: "Or does some-one perhaps believe that the ruling squirearchy would be won over to our demands for the right of farm workers to unionize and for democratic suffrage in Prussia, if we would but be so civil and patriotic as to approve all military credits? Or would the industrial entrepreneurs warm to the eight-hour day and a high national property tax, if we were to swallow all the fleet and colonial bills?" The answers to these questions were, after all, the lesson of Molkenbuhr's defeat. Although Left Liberal intellectuals had made overtures to the party's revisionists, seeking to draw them into collaborative coalitions, the bourgeois parties had targeted the revisionist leaders for defeat because of their advocacy of positive work. Molkenbuhr, "Germany's foremost expert at present in the fields of social policy and cartels, the most circumspect and at the same time most resourceful coau-thor of all worthwhile social reforms, the master of productive criticism and positive work," had been marked for having made a difference.[79]

Eisner's move from Berlin to Nuremberg in March 1907 was fraught with the symbolic significance of a profound life change. His marriage had collapsed, but he perfunctorily weighed relocating wife and children to Bavaria's northern hub. He left behind in the Prussian and Imperial capital his dying sister, his gravely ill friend Ignaz Auer, and the woman he now loved. By midmonth he wrote to Toni Hendrich to tell of his circle of acquaintances, to thank her for visiting his sister, and to ask that she wire him when he should be at Martha's bedside for the end. He envisioned meeting daily at Café Kusch with his new companions—three teachers, a local toy magnate's son, and a single colleague—to bemoan their lot as "the only people in Nuremberg with intellectual needs." He dreamily projected a quiet, routine existence in the provinces. "I already see more or less how my future life will unfold. Work (long and hard), café, theater, and evenings in the presence of the beautiful proprietress of the Golden Post Horn, who was in Paris for three years and has had her portrait painted six times. Among the patrons is an old sculptor who sings folksongs to the guitar, wondrously gripping, with the inspiration of a hermit fortified by drink. In ten years I too might be singing there to the lute, a lonely fool." Eisner counseled Toni to safeguard his cards from the prying eyes of Friedrich Stampfer's wife, for Lisbeth was quoting passages from them in her letters to him. "I have nothing against Lisbeth's knowing everything, but it seems pointless to me in any case."[80] Two days later he wrote to Toni from Café Kusch: "My trust in you is the sum total of my life. I repose in it, feel secure in it, cast all my hopes in it. In you I have found sister and friend, and anyone as lonely as I have been all this time clings to such feelings."[81]

THE MOST GENUINE AND FRUITFUL RADICALISM: TAKING THE LEAD AT THE *FRÄNKISCHE TAGESPOST* (1907–1908)

MARTHA EISNER'S LONG SUFFERING came to end the morning of Friday, 22 March 1907. Her body was interred three days later at Weißensee's Jewish cemetery.[1] The same week Eisner wrote to Toni Hendrich's young son, Gerhard, of insomnia, enervation, and "dreams like rusty sawing."[2] Apprised of the family's loss, Joseph Bloch apologized on 8 April for having dunned Eisner all the while for the article on Napoleon when he scarcely had time to write the leads for the *Fränkische Tagespost*.[3] Readers had been informed in late February of the change of editors and were introduced to Eisner's range of capability by a detailed review of *Das Ende des Reichs* that appeared on the front page of 9 March.[4] Its author judged the book one of those watershed reappraisals that "bluntly and courageously counter the mindless or unconscionable fairy tales of official historical dogmatism."

Eisner's lead of 28 March, "The Danger of the Press," was a manifesto in the same vein, proclaiming the crystalline purpose and financial independence of the party press in contrast to the often veiled agenda and venality of its bourgeois rivals.[5] Even the official organs of the most reactionary parties and interests, he wrote, were innocuous compared with papers that feigned impartiality while taking the line of sponsors whose fortunes depended on the maintenance of status quo. Because these papers relied on revenue from subscriptions and advertisements, their reportage invariably conformed to the opinions of a vested clientele, the beneficiaries of the ruling state. "The frightful political immaturity and woeful political incompetence that still prevail in Germany are in no small part the effect of the bourgeois-capitalist semiofficial press." The Social Democratic press, on the other hand, was solely the enterprise of the party, and its profits were channeled back into the workers'

movement that begot it. "Free and independent, it serves only the socialist worldview, the liberation of the oppressed, truth, and education."
Thus through his choice of newspaper the citizen determined not only
his own future, but that of all mankind. With this appeal to Nuremberg's
populace Eisner launched his campaign to make North Bavaria the heart-
land of democratic socialism.

Two articles in the issue of 8 April evince Eisner's concept of the
rights and duties of ethical journalists. The first, "The Forbidden Joke,"
reported the trial of Olaf Gulbransson, cartoonist and editor for the
Munich weekly *Simplicissimus*, for having lampooned the self-serving
patriotism of Hamburg magnates Albert Ballin and Adolph Woermann,
trusted advisers to the kaiser and leading proponents of colonial expansion. Charged with libel under paragraph 187 of the German penal code,
Gulbransson was sentenced by the Hamburg court to three months'
imprisonment. "Every joke, every satire, every caricature," Eisner wrote,
"is by definition a knowingly untrue assertion if one takes them literally,
for their effect derives from exaggeration, a conscious departure from
reality. In this way every comic paper becomes a single, continuous felony,
and it is not even necessary to place, in addition to the kaiser, all the kaiser's friends under the protection of the lèse-majesté statute."[6] The second piece, "The Right of Criticism," defended a review that had drawn
fire from the Center Party for deriding wrestling matches staged by the
Apollo Theater. The Center's local gazette charged that the *Fränkische
Tagespost* insulted the good people in the audience and injured the theater's business. In reply Eisner argued for higher culture: "The press has
the duty of elevating public taste through the critique of public performances. . . . This moral interest appears to us not to be outweighed by
the business interest of the Apollo Theater."[7]

In the next day's paper an unsigned article, "The Cultural Work of
Women," parried a sensationalist assault on women's suffrage printed in
the Scherl syndicate's *Tag* (The Day).[8] The author of the socialist response,
nineteen-year-old Else Belli, deplored the persistent archaic mentality and
championed Social Democracy as the only venue for women who strove
to advance culture. Seven months pregnant and unwed, she would soon
figure prominently in Eisner's personal and professional life.

On Wednesday, 10 April, a telegram from Berlin reported the death
by stroke, earlier that morning, of Eisner's patron and confidant Ignaz
Auer.[9] At sixty he had been seriously ill for some time.[10] Later that day
Eisner wrote to Toni Hendrich that he planned to come to Berlin "to
bury the man who stood closest to me in public life, whom I loved most."
He asked that she meet him at the train station and that she not tell his

family of his plans.[11] On Thursday's front page Eisner eulogized Auer as a peerless leader and recalled their first and last meetings. The first had left him with the impression of an embittered cynic "who always sees the galled, the diseased, the base, who in disillusioned recognition of the all-too-human lost his faith." Only recently came the realization that the truest leader of a democratic party defies commonplace judgments: "His only means of power is his personal strength, his only security the trust that he enjoys, for which he must fight anew every day—often against dark flowing masses that shift and slide, err and falter; and at times against rivals who want to go other ways, if indeed they are not pursuing entirely personal interests."[12] It was a lesson Eisner would take with him to his own grave. He organized a memorial service for Auer on the twenty-fourth. Nuremberg's Philharmonic Orchestra performed the dirge from Beethoven's *Eroica*, "Siegfried's Death" and "Entry of the Gods into Valhalla" from Wagner's *Ring*, and Handel's "Largo." The Union and Toward the Light workers' choruses sang, and Eisner held the oration in a packed hall where members of Nuremberg's progressive bourgeoisie paid their respects together with the ranks of Social Democratic mourners.[13] Two days later Bloch sent Eisner the May issue of *Sozialistische Monatshefte*, dedicated to Auer's memory, with appreciations by the journal's regular contributors. "By no stretch," Bloch confided privately, "not even after his death, did Auer ever receive the least due he was owed by the party."[14]

The first run of *Das Ende des Reichs* had sold out in four months.[15] A second edition was printed, for which Eisner cast a brief foreword, noting the favorable critical reception in the party press and deathly silence of the rival bourgeois press, a shrinking from the truth, which "in the great world conflicts of the future will condemn bourgeois Germany to intellectual defenselessness and finally to material collapse."[16] Yet in the wake of the electoral defeat for which he was largely culpable, old Bebel had lurched precipitately to the right, asserting during the Reichstag's military budget debate of late April Social Democracy's support for a strong, efficient army along the lines of Scharnhorst's ideal citizens' soldiery. Bebel was seconded on this point by recently elected comrade Gustav Noske, future head of Ebert's bloody anti-Spartacist campaign of 1919, who declared that the party would defend the fatherland from attack as patriotically as the Conservatives.

Prussian war minister Karl von Einem heartily approved Social Democracy's new stance and pressed Bebel to rein in or drive out avowed antimilitarists such as Karl Liebknecht. Having already clashed with Liebknecht on the issue at the Mannheim party congress of 1906, Bebel now sought to silence him altogether by declaring that opinions expressed by party members not serving as Reichstag deputies were "in no way authoritative."[17] Weighing in quickly, Eisner counted it a great strength of French socialism that Gustave Hervé could oppose militarism as vigorously as Liebknecht and remain at the fore of his party. "With regard to the German party," he wrote in his lead article of 4 May, "it can be only useful if there are individuals in it too who make it their special purpose in life to combat militarism's dangers to culture in all its manifestations."[18]

By midmonth Eisner had installed Lisbeth and the children in a tranquil abode in Behringersdorf, an idyllic village situated east of town on the north bank of the Pegnitz, where, he informed Bloch, "mail is delivered but once a week, and then only in good weather."[19] His aged mother had helped the family settle in and was "getting along well for the moment with Lisbeth," he reported to Toni in Berlin, "and I do my utmost to maintain peace." On his birthday, 14 May, he had worn the shirt and tie Toni sent him.[20] He wrote to her on the twenty-second that he planned to begin a book, a series of letters to a female friend about socialism. "I would like to erect simultaneously a monument to the cause I serve and the woman I love." He promised that the first letter would be printed on her birthday.[21] Within two weeks Eisner proposed that they act on their mutual attraction and "live in one another as befits man and wife, so far as they want to be human." His marriage had run its course and was now an emotional burden, sapping all joy from life. Still he recognized his substantial obligations. "The instant I see the possibility of providing my family material security, I will loose the bond. I will and must do it, regardless of what becomes of the two of us . . . precisely in the children's interest."[22]

In the last week of May Joseph Bloch solicited an article on Hermann Cohen's logic and asked for titles of works on Cohen that might help him better understand the neo-Kantian master.[23] Amid a campaign for a strong Social Democratic showing in elections to the Bavarian Landtag, Eisner paused to reply at length. Eschewing the formulaic greeting of "esteemed comrade" in favor of a heartfelt "dear colleague" and forsaking his admittedly "wretched scrawl," Eisner took pains to type his warmest response. "Never yet to have written on Cohen I count among the worst sins of omission of my nefarious existence. I am aware only of an Italian monograph on C. He of course stands apart from the clique and for that reason is treated much as am I by the Leipzig vegetable-soup chefs of Marxism untinged by any ethical encumbrance and any kind of knowledge. Your best source for information might be Ernst Cassirer, adjunct professor at Berlin University. Or better yet contact Cohen directly, but do not forget to say hello from me. As long as I was in Berlin, I was always able to talk with him a few times each year. To have forfeited him and the [Felix] Weingartner concerts I reckon among the losses of my banishment."[24]

Bloch wrote back that his interest in Cohen stemmed from a personal conviction that "the future of philosophy is also that of mathematics and vice versa," specifically in the theory of diversity. He announced that he planned to visit Nuremberg in early June yet and hoped to call on Eisner that they might reminisce about mutual acquaintances in Berlin. He appended a postscript: "Using a typewriter is your most fundamental progress since joining the party and moreover an action that serves the public good."[25]

On election day, 31 May, Eisner joined the entourage of candidate Sigmund von Haller, a prominent physician, in an open automobile on a sally to nearby Erlangen and environs. Making thirty-three stops over a course of 166 kilometers, their novel transport scattered chickens and geese and drew out the curious of every hamlet. Affixed red and white placards bore the candidate's name and title, which the locals read as *der*. "THE Sigmund von Haller! arose the cry wherever the vehicle whizzed past people, THE Sigmund von Haller! became the campaign slogan of the entire district," Eisner recounted. Hours after the dust-caked party returned to Nuremberg, the telephone call came from Erlangen that Dr. Haller had been narrowly elected on the first ballot. Reflecting on the events of the previous day, Eisner realized that candidates stumping by train or on foot rarely reached the public not already committed to them. The car, on the other hand, afforded access to every diverse segment of the far-flung electorate, who stood in awe of the mechanical marvel and its mission in their midst.[26] After the humiliation of the recent national elections Social Democracy enjoyed a triumph in Bavaria, increasing their deputation in the Landtag from twelve seats to twenty, third to the Center's ninety-nine and the Liberals' twenty-five.[27]

In the last week of June the nation's attention was focused on the Munich trial of Carl Peters, the freebooter who lorded over German East Africa. A decade earlier he had been made to forfeit his governorship after atrocities against the native population were publicized in Berlin. Most shocking was that he had his black mistress and one of his servants hanged when they were discovered as lovers. Catholic missionaries decried German crimes in Africa, and finally Peters faced charges in Bavaria's capital just months after the Center Party had weathered the jingoist storm in the Hottentot elections. The trial was a symbolic showdown, for Wilhelm II had officially reinstated Peters and renewed his pension on behalf of a grateful nation. Despite mounting Social Democratic support for colonial expansion, the *Fränkische Tagespost* fiercely attacked both Peters and the interests that promoted him, proclaiming that the *Münchener Post* accurately judged Peters a gutless killer: "It is proven that he is a murderer, and there can be no further doubt that the familiar phenomenon of cruelty rooted in cowardice is at work in his case too."[28]

Eisner was present at the trial and reported his personal impressions. The sweltering courtroom was filled with fanatical champions of the Bülow bloc, who were positively titillated by salacious details of Peters's predatory liaisons, the stuff "one finds written by pimps in the margins of books in prison libraries." Refined ladies of Munich society hung on graphic descriptions of African sexual mores. The press correspondents were part of the spectacle. The Liberal *Münchner Neueste Nachrichten* assigned its Alpine specialist to the trial. Peters himself struck Eisner as a gaunt figure with a hawkish physiognomy and dull, menacing eyes: "the breed of that Prussian Age of Bismarck, . . . the lowest type ever produced by a degenerate ruling class." That this stamp of man—avaricious, brutal, debauched, depraved—was the agent of European culture abroad caused Eisner to wonder what a black man must think of the white man's nature. Indeed, the only *Mensch* among the parade of witnesses was the Catholic missionary, a man whose energy had been directed to influence people by his spirituality and intellect rather than by bribes and force. "Is it not a terrible sign of Germany's decline," the Jewish leftist asked his readers, "that clericalism, which forms the lowest level in nations of culture, represents a higher stage of development here than the bourgeois brood and the feudal horde?"[29] Peters was acquitted, left the country for London, and had his counsel file a libel suit against Dr. Georges Weill, Eisner's political editor.[30]

In July Eisner pressed two initiatives for greater democratization of critical Social Democratic enterprises. The one addressed the party's ill-conceived approach to workers' education; the other championed the creation of a self-governing central press bureau, to be run by the revived Workers' Press Association or a new organization established expressly for the purpose—and therefore not as a tool of the party executive or the press commissions. Both initiatives were vehemently opposed by the principal editors of *Vorwärts*, who owed their jobs exclusively to the favor of the executive rather than to any innate ability or accomplishment—as Rosa Luxemburg ruefully conceded during her first week on staff—and who themselves held appointment as instructors at the Party School in Berlin. The impetus to Eisner's critique of elitist education was the publication of a report by the Prussian Trade Ministry on vocational training in the United States. The report documented that in the year 1902, schools in 270 American cities required "manual training" in woodworking and metalworking as a complement to the academic curriculum.

In a lead article for the *Fränkische Tagespost* titled "A Step toward the Socialist Ideal of Education," Eisner hailed the American realization of Fourier's, Owen's, and Marx's pedagogical vision and deplored the prevalent attitude of German educators that practical familiarity with the lathe or anvil was beneath the dignity of a student at the gymnasium.[31] Over the next year he repeatedly contested the premise of the Party School, established fall 1906 in Berlin by the party executive as an institution for training gifted young functionaries as party leaders through a half-year crash course in economic history and theory, historical materialism, sociology, law, and related topics taught by Mehring, Luxemburg, Stadthagen, Cunow, and their clique.[32]

The critique of how news was gathered by and disseminated in the party press stemmed from the Social Democratic press workers' meeting in March, at which every ideological faction and the party executive were represented. The proposal for a self-governing central press bureau had been made there and prompted no objection from any quarter. At a summer meeting of the executive of the Workers' Press Association, of which Eisner served as second chair, the issue was raised as to whether party journalists had the same rights as other organized workers' collectives or whether their professional practices were to be regulated by an external bureaucracy. The party executive, the *Leipziger Volkszeitung*, and *Vorwärts* then joined forces in opposition to a self-governing press bureau. In late July and early August the *Fränkische Tagespost* and *Vorwärts* sparred repeatedly over the proposal, causing the Left Liberal *Fränkischer Kurier* to remark in what little esteem the central organ held Nuremberg's Social Democratic voice.[33]

At the general meeting of Nuremberg's Social Democratic Association in early August, Eisner voiced his concerns about the upcoming party congress in Essen. He recalled how after the electoral victory of 1903 the Dresden congress had become the most divisive in party history. At this year's congress, he observed, there could be little debate about the effect of the division, for "our increase in votes in the last Reichstag election in no way kept pace with the immense growth of the industrial population." Now, after a defeat as stunning as that past triumph, Eisner counseled against fault-finding and finger-pointing, since there were much greater tasks at hand. "What will we do," he asked, "at the outbreak of war of reaction against democracy or revolution?" And in continued support of Karl Liebknecht's stance, he declared: "Since Germany is in itself the military state, German Social Democracy has the responsibility above all to lead the fight against militarism." At the close of deliberations on 9 August the association elected Martin Treu, Max Haugenstein, and Eisner as its three delegates to the Essen congress.[34]

A week later Bloch disingenuously congratulated Eisner on his election.[35] Three months earlier Bloch had confided to Karl Leuthner, a favored contributor to *Sozialistische Monatshefte*, that Eisner's defiance of Bebel's concessions to militarism were disconcerting but not surprising. "I have always regarded it as a regrettable misunderstanding that Eisner is lumped in with the revisionists, from whom no less than everything separates him. . . . (There are some things I find appealing, for example his view and admiration of Napoleon's personality, though I reject his political conclusions. Just as it is my fast rule never to print anything political by Eisner. Once many years ago I made an exception. Hardly again. Precisely because I like much about Eisner, I regret that he has gotten into politics, which is bad indeed for both.)"[36] A committed nationalist, Bloch generally supported Germany's colonial policy and military. Fearful of Eisner's influence in the South, Bloch aimed to counter it. In advance of the congress of the Socialist International in Stuttgart in mid-August, he dedicated an issue of his journal to combatting anticolonial and antimilitarist sentiment.[37] To that end he solicited from Leuthner an article that would "prepare a thorough end to the ethical-aesthetic visionaryism that foments revolution from editorial desks and proclaims antimilitarist general strikes."[38]

The Stuttgart congress of the International convened on Sunday, 18 August, and concluded the following Saturday. On the eve of the opening ceremony Eisner filed his first reports for the Nuremberg readership. He had long looked forward to a meeting with Jaurès and hoped for adoption of Hervé's resolution to "answer any declaration of war, from whatever side it might come, with . . . strike and insurrection."[39] Hervé's resolution went beyond that backed by the majority of the French delegation, which called for joint action to prevent war by every means yet paid homage to the legitimacy of national defense. The German delegation, led by Bebel, fought furiously to weaken the French resolutions and preclude discussion of the general strike in any context. The delegations from eastern Europe, marshaled by Rosa Luxemburg, offered a compromise amendment that closely paralleled Eisner's position in the 1905 article "Union and Party." The amendment called upon workers of the belligerent powers to make use of the most appropriate means, "which will necessarily vary according to the sharpness of the class struggle and the general political situation," to prevent the outbreak of war. Once a war had begun, the workers were enjoined "to exploit with all their might the economic and political crisis created by the war to arouse the population and to hasten the overthrow of capitalist rule."[40]

Lenin noted in his journal with disgust the smug contempt in the German assault on Hervé.[41] Although Bebel, Vollmar, and Eduard David did their utmost to undermine the International's resolute opposition to militarism, war, and colonialism, they found themselves outvoted in the plenary sessions. In his summary article Eisner welcomed the resultant clarity of the proclamations against imperial adventurism and foreboding hostility between bourgeois states locked in competition for plunder. Particularly gratifying to the slighted author of *Der Sultan des Weltkrieges* was the Saturday's ringing declaration of socialism's commitment to peace: "Here finally for once one could experience the most genuine and fruitful radicalism."[42] Following the congress Eisner hosted Jaurès and his comrade Albert Thomas for a two-day sojourn in Nuremberg. The transplanted Berliner delighted in serving as tour guide to the Germanic National Museum, St. Sebaldus, and the Golden Post Horn, a tavern frequented by the painter Dürer, champion of Renaissance humanism. In September 1918 Eisner would recall in his bleak cell at Munich's Stadelheim Prison how the editor of *L'Humanité* reveled in the experience of Franconia's medieval jewel.[43]

If Luxemburg had been compelled by circumstance toward Eisner's tactical position of 1905, Eisner had moved closer to hers, as he detailed in a remarkable letter of 2 September to Joseph Bloch, the most candid statement of his political philosophy he ever formulated.[44] The letter was written in response to Bloch's private accusation that Eisner played both sides. Eisner began with the disclaimer that his refusal to affiliate with either camarilla within the party had set him at odds with both and often brought him into conflict with his "best personal friends." What followed was a forthright rebuke of the revisionist agenda and bearing at the congress, echoing Lenin's critique. "You 'revisionists' . . . demand nothing but tolerance for yourselves and then become intolerance personified toward others whenever you think you have the upper hand. It was absolutely revolting how the revisionist clique at Stuttgart made a show of their satisfaction that Karl Liebknecht—over whom hangs the danger of imprisonment and the certainty of loss of office—was not even proposed for the military committee even though he, as a specialist in the field, would have had to be named to it. If ever, God forbid, you win control, the *Vorwärts* conflict would repeat itself in an even more repulsive way." Eisner then passed harsh judgments on two of Bloch's favorites, calling Richard Calwer, the party's chief advocate of colonialism, "a self-opinionated driveler" and characterizing Georg von Vollmar as conniving and duplicitous for secretly urging Hervé's expulsion from the French party at Stuttgart, then denying that he had done so. Bloch himself, Eisner declared, was so woefully naive "about actual political process" that he gave credence precisely to those already exposed as mountebanks.

Having voiced his opinion on Bloch and his set, Eisner than turned to his own position and asserted with unblinking frankness:

> Observing and adapting to the flow of politics and then practically applying what comes from that seem to me the unconditional prerequisite of every politically active man. Since the beginning of my public activity I have not vacillated in my views. . . . In fact, I have changed in but one regard. Since the days of the Morocco affair, when I was compelled to recognize our complete impotence, and since the shameful collapse of the Prussian suffrage movement, I have been ardent supporter of that action you deign to deem part game, part delusion. I am convinced that not only will we be unable to avoid violent conflicts but that there is greater future value in bloody defeats than in all of our busy idleness. We will not be spared our revolution. We will not have it better than the English, French, or Russians. And thus I am not just for the mass strike but also for taking to the streets. If I bore the responsibility for such undertakings, I would take it upon me without any hesitation, with all the consequences. You may oppose this conception, but you cannot dispute that it proceeds from an entirely unified, considered system of action that does not discount practical work, nor does it spurn any means, whether compromise or revolution. It is the view of Jaurès too, whose opponents reproach him, just as you do me, for contradictions. For that reason I am, for example, on military and suffrage issues "ultraradical," as on colonial and union issues, and on issues of ministerialism or even budget approval "ultrarevisionist." That both camps are annoyed because of it, that they do not know where to begin with me is as vexing for them as it is unpleasant for me.

He closed with a jest, threatening to punish Bloch if he did not mend his ways—by forsaking the typewriter and returning to longhand.

Eisner departed Nuremberg early for Essen in order to attend a two-day meeting of the Workers' Press Association before the party congress was to convene Sunday evening, 15 September 1907. On the fourteenth the *Fränkische Tagespost* ran as its lead Eisner's reflections on the challenges before the congress delegates. He declared with due gravity that the deliberations at Essen would be scrutinized worldwide in light of the Germans' conservatism at Stuttgart. Whereas the International had embraced a "socialism of action" three weeks earlier, the host party had isolated itself. German Social Democracy's retrograde slide was reflected, Eisner wrote, in the opposition to a central press bureau. An ossified party executive insisted on control over a flagging, crucial operation in which it had no expertise. "On this question, which is solely a question of technical organization of the party press, spuriously extraneous factors have been introduced, and the technical question has been turned into an issue of dogma."[45]

The same day the article appeared, Eisner was already embroiled in debate at the Workers' Press Association meeting, staunchly opposing the attempt by Heinrich Schulz of Berlin to dissolve the association. On Sunday Eisner offered his comprehensive proposal for the central press bureau. To illustrate the need for the office, he compared the party press's coverage of Interior Minister Posadowsky's resignation, announced on Saturday afternoon, 22 June, with that in the bourgeois press. The next day *Vorwärts* ran a brief lead on Posadowsky's departure, Hamburg's *Echo* put out its own notice, and the other Social Democratic papers that had received Stampfer's correspondence in time simply reprinted his article. In contrast, the bourgeois papers nationwide independently presented detailed report and analysis. Even by Monday some party dailies had yet to make note of a political development of import to their readers. "If we want to influence current events," Eisner told his comrade colleagues, "consider what it means if we print our news and opinion later than the bourgeois press."

Having worked for the Herold News Agency and as an editor for both bourgeois and party papers, Eisner certainly understood better than most the imperatives and exigencies of gathering and printing news. His plan called for a headquarters in the capital, with a branch office in the Ruhr or southern Germany. The press bureau would compile news releases for daily dissemination, transmitting urgently topical reports by telegraph and telephone. The governance of the press bureau he entrusted to a biennial conference of the party executive committee, the control commission, fifteen representatives from the Reichstag deputation, two members from each editorial staff, the executive committee of the Workers' Press Association, five freelance journalists, five party secretaries, ten business managers, and ten representatives from the press commissions. The conference would elect the staff of the press bureau from a list of ten candidates nominated by vote of all party editors. Eisner envisioned as the bureau's critical function the reportage of the underlying political significance of news items so as "to enable editors outside the capital to fight effectively against opponents, to coordinate actions, and to marshal them uniformly along the entire line of the party press." The association forwarded its recommendations to the party congress's program committee.[46]

The Essen party congress began that evening. On the second full day of deliberations Eisner entered the debate on militarism. Freed of the constraints of his past office as chief official commentator, he lashed out at Bebel and Noske for April's patriotic bootlicking in the Reichstag after the Hottentot elections. In their eagerness to appease bourgeois public opinion, they exacerbated international tensions, exposed French socialists to criticism from their opponents, and aroused suspicions of socialists worldwide as to the German party's commitment to peace. "International relations at the time were fraught with considerably more peril than Bebel thinks. . . . Whenever the bourgeoisie can say vis-à-vis foreign countries 'Even the proletariat is on our side,' the danger of war is present."[47]

The party executive and the control commission, determined to keep the press on a short lead, offered their own proposal for a central news service based in Berlin. By their schema staffing and governance of the press bureau were the purview of the party executive, assisted by an advisory board of five editors, whom the party leadership would select annually.[48] In his report to the party congress on Thursday, 19 September, Hermann Müller, a member of the party executive, conceded that Social Democracy indeed lagged far behind its rivals in transmitting news and that a central news service was badly needed. During Friday's discussion of Müller's report and the executive's proposal, Adolf Thiele, chair of the Workers' Press Association, protested that no provision had been made to syndicate the reports of foreign correspondents, and he argued to no avail that the advisory board should be chosen by members of the press rather than by political functionaries. The executive's proposal was approved by large majority.[49] Eleven years would pass before Eisner could fully grasp that the party executive and press were equally incidental in moving the masses to concerted action.

A stroll's distance from the drab Maas Beer Hall where the delegates met was a tidy neighborhood of uniform cottages situated in lush gardens, each "a little realm unto itself." Here Eisner reconnoitered at his leisure Altenhof, a retirement community created by Essen's chief employer, the Krupps, for workers worn out by decades in the foundries. In this verdant oasis the air was remarkably free of the acrid soot that blighted the environs. After a lifetime in squalid tenements of the workers' quarter, the residents of Altenhof spent their last days in a veritable earthly paradise, or so it seemed. Yet the inhabitants whom the curious visitor encountered on his walk through the grounds were like ghostly shells, "pale, gray figures shuffling along the spotless streets with a blank look, tired and indifferent." The one man with whom he spoke at any length, an amputee with multiple images of his patron displayed throughout his abode, proved as dishearteningly simple and servile as a Russian peasant, so much so that Eisner left downcast at the spectacle of "a cemetery of the living," whose bodies and minds had been used up before death delivered them from their sad state. "Someone who has spent twenty years working the blast furnace," he observed, "is no longer a man conscious of his existence."[50]

After the congress Eisner did not return immediately to Nuremberg but journeyed up the Rhine to Mannheim, where he was slated to hold a series of lectures on Napoleon. In a letter to Joseph Bloch two months earlier he had promised to send the long-awaited essay once he had scripted the talks.[51] Sunday evening, 22 September, he wrote from the Darmstädter Manor Hotel in nearby Heidelberg to Toni Hendrich to assure her that it was not his passion for her that maddened him.[52] The content of a missive penned three days later suggests that their relationship was in flux: "If Lisbeth endeavors to provide a friendly home for you with us, I shall forgive her everything and endeavor to make her happy. I will desire no more then and be content if you trim my hair each month as you did in the old days."[53]

Back in Nuremberg the last week of September, Eisner reflected on the proceedings at Essen. The congress was to have launched the national election campaign, but the new Reichstag was long seated before the first gavel fell at the Maas Beer Hall. In the knowledge that Nuremberg had been tabbed for the 1908 congress and that he would have a significant role to play in its success or failure, Eisner chose to regard Essen's dubious results philosophically. On the issue that affected him most immediately he wrote: "The establishment of a press bureau, which appeared impossible after the unpleasant debates in the party press, was ultimately accepted with next to no discussion in a form that can be either fruitful or useless, depending on the spirit guiding its operation; in the end everything will hinge on the persons who are prepared to take on this delicate and daunting assignment."[54] Friday evening, 27 September, Eisner joined fellow delegates Max Haugenstein and Martin Treu at the Golden Rose Tavern to brief the membership of Nuremberg's Social Democratic Association on the outcomes of the Essen congress.[55]

World war crept closer in late October when the German high court sentenced Karl Liebknecht to eighteen months' imprisonment for having had the temerity to assert as an attorney that the authority to declare war should reside in the nation's elected representatives, not in the monarch.

"Is the circle around Him," Eisner exclaimed acerbically to the reader-ship of the *Fränkische Tagespost*, "are Eulenburg, Moltke, Hohenau not really better suited to decide on war and peace than the millions of the German people!"[56] The character of the three named associates of the kaiser was broadly suspect, as each had been tainted by persistent accusa-tions of homosexuality. Eisner's worst fears of ascendant Mars, the stress from a defunct marriage, general disappointment with the party's state were all compounded by the onset of winter, ushered in by cold rains thick with soot. "The coal dust itself, it seems, has transformed into rain, and this coal-rain will never end, never! . . . Worries fall with this black rain straight into my soul. The fear of winter seizes me."[57]

Among Eisner's cataloged papers at the German Federal Archive in Berlin-Lichterfelde is a revealing testimony to his emotional state the year of his resettlement from the capital to Bavaria. A file folder dated 1907 contains a literary work, the purported journal of a forty-year-old intellec-tual in a troubled marriage.[58] The setting has been changed to the 1890s, yet Eisner signed his own name to the piece rather than employing one of his pseudonyms. Printed and distributed for serial publication by *Das sozialistische Feuilleton* (The Socialist Arts Pages), a syndication based in Frankfurt am Main, *Sinnenspiel* (Play of the Senses) is a fictional articu-lation of very real disillusionment and desire. The entries chronicle the midlife crisis of Paul, a doting father at odds with his wife, Klara, to whom he still feels a strong attachment. Sent by his doctor to a sleepy seaside resort for three months' rest, Paul attributes his nervous exhaustion not to overwork but to fundamental differences of interest and outlook with Klara. "On questions of art we are of one mind, and our best moments are when we return home from the theater, concert hall, or painting exhi-bition lively exchanging our opinions. But she cares nothing for politics and just as little for dry science, and precisely these constitute the heart-beat of my existence." Through his first-person narrator, Eisner deftly charts the stations of alienation of affection. Paul readily confesses his part in the process: "I behaved coolly when I felt that way, and if something about my wife displeased me, I showed it in every word and gesture."

At the resort Paul concludes that the initial youthful attraction to a girl stems from the curiosity, conditioned by mores of dress, as to how she might look in her nakedness—a fatal curiosity that joins partners who are ultimately incompatible. "And once we have had our look, then the misery begins, then we discover her soul and realize that two people who will remain eternally foreign to each other have forged themselves to each other for the sake of corporal sentimentality." To regain his lost vitality, Paul determines to re-create the passion of youth by fixing on a desirable woman and giving himself over to an imaginary affair with her: a physically pure, lascivious pursuit of the mind, calculated to heal the heart. And indeed he finds his object of desire in the teenaged daughter of an acquaintance. But even while Paul wallows in his fantasy, Klara, back at home with the children, engages in a real affair with a younger man whom Paul regards as an intellectual inferior. Paul suspects from Klara's confused letters that she has been unfaithful. Upon his return she confesses, and he insists on an amicable separation, knowing despite his insincere assurances to the contrary that he will never see her again.

In November Eisner had occasion to act on his regret, expressed to Bloch six months earlier, at never having treated Hermann Cohen. Publication of the second edition of *Ethik des reinen Willens* (The Ethics of Pure Will) by Berlin's Bruno Cassirer Press prompted a three-part review for the *Fränkische Tagespost*, which Eisner provocatively titled "The Ethics of Socialism."[59] He began in defense of Marxism's historical aversion to moral idealism. "An attempt to ground and consolidate socialism in ethics will meet with justified doubt in socialist circles. Not without reason have ethical pretensions been discredited in our age. Moral cliché lost all currency; one learned by experience that the lofty promises it always arrogated to itself were simply incapable of taking root in reality and soon only served to gloss over the inner hollowness with gleaming and blazing words or even to obscure the infuriating injustice of the times with idealistic declarations. No wonder that proletarian socialism looked about for other, more solid supports than philosophical ethics were able to give it." The philosopher's place, he argued here, was not like that of sociologist or economist to quantify hypotheses empirically through research but rather to unify and systematize thought by constructing a framework of rationally derived cultural values and modes of inquiry. Yet the import of Cohen's undertaking for Social Democracy was indeed practical, for despite the healthy skepticism of scientific socialism toward the study and application of ethics, it was undeniable that the party took distinctly moral stands on any number of issues. "It by no means consigns every diverse question to the domain of social economy but on the contrary freely and unwaveringly makes moral demands for their own sake. For it virtue has its own right." Distinctly immoral, in contrast, were the motivations of the ruling class, which never shrank from fomenting social calamity and misery if its interests were served by such.

In related articles Eisner attacked the Prussian Junkerdom's malign influence on both Germany and Europe. Prussian politics, "a school for the ruthless deployment of power," was illustrative of the boundless avarice and arrogance of privilege, impoverishing the populace, crushing whole cultures, provoking international strife, threatening national unity itself, if necessary, in order to sustain the feudal hierarchy. Yet the ultimate mischief eroded even the ruling state's preserve: "Every declaration of war signifies in a certain sense a proclamation of anarchy. . . . To pit the masses against themselves is ancient history. The new age, however, will begin with the masses wielding their power for themselves."[60] Two days after he admonished in print Prussia's masters, the *Fränkische Tagespost* informed its readers on Monday, 2 December, that Carl Peters, whom Eisner had characterized as the personification of Prussian corruption and brutality, had won his case against the paper and that Georges Weill was fined 400 marks for libel.[61] Two weeks later Eisner ran as his lead a comparison of the German standard of living with that in other industrial nations.[62] Drawing figures from the just-published *Vierteljahrshefte der Statistik des Deutschen Reiches* (Statistical Quarterly of the German Empire), he laid out how workers' wages lagged far behind those of comrades abroad and how the German citizenry's buying power was diminished by exorbitant tariffs on staples. "Thanks to agrarian policies under Prussian Junker control Germany is currently by far the world's most expensive country."

Amid so much disheartening circumstance the Social Democratic press remained a beacon in the gloom. At the end of his first calendar year in Nuremberg, Eisner apprised *Tagespost* subscribers of the paper's operations, its plans for growth in 1908, and its burgeoning influence in North Bavaria. It had assembled an experienced staff who reported on the broad spectrum of politics and economics, party and union, the women's movement, and international affairs. The latter in particular, neglected as it was by the German press as a whole, had become a specialty: "Our reportage in the area of foreign policy has repeatedly provided the public a deeper knowledge of obscure dealings." He alluded to Friedrich Stampfer, the paper's correspondent in Berlin, who kept the editors informed on the most recent occurrences by telegraph or telephone. The feuilleton, meant to educate while entertaining, had been expanded in volume and scope. In the coming year Eisner promised a fundamental restructuring of the paper. Moreover, the entire enterprise was to move into its own building, space that would afford much-needed technical upgrades. To strengthen their own voice, he appealed to the loyal clientele to combat the self-proclaimed 'independent' press, which relied in large part on subscriptions from a proletarian audience. The party press had achieved great things, schooling the masses in vital critical thinking and effective political activism. Those workers who apathetically took their news from suspect sources unwittingly undermined their own development, for "political indifference is intellectual alcoholism."[63]

Indeed, competition between the *Tagespost* and the *Kurier* intensified in the new year. On Saturday morning, 11 January, editors Georges
Weill and Paul Schlegel appeared before the assessor's court in a libel suit
brought by Sigmund Mohr, or "Cato," of the rival newspaper. In four
articles Mohr, on the basis of his "town-hall snooping," had been derided
as a "scrounger," "hack," and "lackey." Eisner and fellow editor Georg
Gärtner were summoned to testify.[64] In this instance the court meted out
jail time, a sentence that even the Center Party's organ, the *Nürnberger
Volkszeitung*, deemed excessive: "The harsh sentence—one had expected
a fine at most—caused something of a sensation in the courtroom and
serious headshaking among the local populace."[65]

More sallies against the Prussian hierarchy evince the inclination to
greater Bavarian autonomy that Eisner would assert a decade hence as
head of state. In mid-October 1907 he had authored a two-part centennial commemoration of statesman Theodor von Schön's call for the
free trade of land, a pronouncement state-appointed historians cited
as emancipating the peasantry from the last vestiges of serfdom. "In
reality," Eisner clarified, "this edict initiated then the Prussian Junker
emancipation that so thoroughly loosed the peasants from the soil that
they retained not even the illusion of ownership but became propertyless agricultural laborers." The resultant consolidation of East Elbia's
great estates buttressed the feudal order so fateful in Germany's persistent retardation.[66] Now in mid-January he renewed the campaign
to impress on his readers the threat posed to their interests by a caste
essentially at odds with the twentieth century, for whom the relative liberality and greater communality of Bavaria were anathema. The Junker
tradition of controlling every aspect of their subservients' lives was
utterly unfazed by European cultural progress. "Patriarchalism still runs
in the blood of the Prussian state; the claims of modern liberal development have touched it only superficially, and today we have reached the
point where the fate of the German Empire will be decided: whether it
goes the Prussian way to the monocapitalist, patriarchal slave-state or
the German way to Social Democracy."[67]

A review of Friedrich Meusel's biography *Friedrich August Ludwig
von der Marwitz*, on a Prussian aristocrat during the Napoleonic wars,
provided Eisner opportunity to reiterate the benightedness of the North
and to champion suffrage reform.[68] "No one will ever become clear
about the necessity and possibilities of the Prussian voting rights movement who does not understand the nature of the Junkerdom. . . . One
hundred twenty years after feudalism's historical death, which occurred
with the outbreak of the French Revolution, . . . that same feudal nobility

is today unchanged in its nature, colossally strengthened in its political and economic power, still lord over German development." He moved closer to a declaration in favor of separatism in his lead of 25 January, "Bend or Break."[69] Contrasting the South's democratic franchise with the weighted three-class balloting in Prussia, he concluded that national unity hinged on uniform voting rights. "If Prussia retains its electoral system, which preserves the Junker military state, Germany will either fragment or—what is more likely—the Prussianization of Germany will be completed formally as well. The governments in South Germany know, of course, from many long years' experience the ever more threatening difficulties that Prussia will present them."

The article on Napoleon that Eisner had promised Joseph Bloch months earlier had never gone out. Bloch wrote on 1 February to goad him by warning that the publishers who lent the requested books had lost all patience. He added that an article in *Sozialistische Monatshefte* would revive Eisner's national fame, which had flagged since his sphere of activity and ambition was evidently reduced now to the South German provinces. Bloch mentioned that he had heard of the many speaking engagements and tireless agitation from Albert Südekum, Reichstag deputy and since 1901 publisher of the journal *Kommunale Praxis* (Communal Practice), but Bloch urged him to more fruitful pursuits. "You simply have to get back to writing. The profession of itinerant speaker certainly has its attraction. And if one, as you have, gives eighteen talks in fourteen days, . . . one can surely soon reach dizzying heights on the political stepladder. But I mean better by you. I want you yourself to be known beyond Rothenburg."[70] On each count Bloch's appeal fell on deaf ears.

CHAPTER TWELVE

SO SUSPECT A HERETIC, AS SURELY I AM: NEW BEARINGS IN NORTH BAVARIA (1908)

I N LATE FEBRUARY 1908 Eisner relished his immediacy in Germany's Catholic South to *Karneval*, the week-long festival of wanton indulgence preceding Lent. For one long fascinated by the spiritual and psychological affects of holidays, the bacchanalian abandon heralding spring and the rebirth of the natural world spoke to a troubled soul poised to slip the emotional confines of his stagnant marriage. Both the packed schedule of lectures, which Joseph Bloch regarded as suspect, and the effort to broaden the scope of his political pursuits were symptomatic of Eisner's need to redefine and reinvigorate himself by venturing out from his home in Behringersdorf and his office at Luitpoldstraße 9. Direct personal contact with the working-class public, a diversion he savored during Paul Bader's campaign in Marburg fifteen years earlier and for which he carved out time in Berlin, afforded welcome respite and inspiration.

At *Vorwärts* Eisner wrote an annual observance of the March Revolution of 1848. This year, having had the opportunity to witness the pre-Lenten merriment in Munich, he related the life force of Karneval to revolution itself. "Being loosed from all constraints, leaping exuberantly over all barriers are common to the forceful stirrings of head and heart. Life itself enters into all its power. Nature and natural law triumph. Races such as the French, who engender not only new constitutions, new social order, but new dances as well, who die for freedom with grape leaves in their hair, whose mass will finds joy's rhythm and desire's dynamic in the yearning for freedom, can never be completely oppressed." On the Saturday and Sunday before Ash Wednesday the citizenry of Bavaria's capital were caught up in the riot of ecstasy, class distinctions obscured by the celebrants' masks. Awed by the spectacle and its sociological context, Eisner noted particularly the colossal business done by the city's pawnbrokers during the festivities—"What does man need when freedom's intoxication lays hold!"—and the disproportionate number of births each year in November, nine months after the mass "affirmation of life."[1]

Six months before the Social Democratic Party was to hold its 1908 congress in Nuremberg, the *Fränkische Tagespost* announced that key logistical arrangements had been finalized. The opening ceremony on Sunday, 13 September, was to be held at the municipal banquet hall, which accommodated eight thousand guests. The sessions would take place in the rented Hercules Velodrome.[2] The local Social Democratic Association publicized a prize competition for the design of a picture postcard linking the coming party congress with the historic meeting of workers forty years earlier in Nuremberg's town hall.[3] Eisner certainly planned to utilize the moment when the party assembled in his new preserve as a critical opportunity to reassert his vision. A year now into his tenure as editor in chief, he had consolidated his position through undeniable dedication and diligence and had succeeded in recasting the *Tagespost* to advance his political agenda. London correspondent Max Beer, whom he privately lauded as "the party's *only* expert in foreign policy," reported on European affairs and international relations, with special emphasis on Germany's imperial adventurism.[4] Hulda Maurenbrecher covered women's issues from the theoretical and practical perspective. Julius Kaliski, Eisner's embattled confederate at *Vorwärts* and confidant in the capital, provided a syndicated column on economics, and Hugo Lindemann, a close associate of Südekum, contributed a regular review of practical local initiatives nationwide.

At Social Democracy's biennial regional meeting in Würzburg the weekend of 24–25 April, Eisner determined to press for a more activist role yet for his paper and its constituency. One of ten delegates elected from Nuremberg's Altdorf district, he had high hopes for the conference in promoting greater consciousness among North Bavarian workers of their potential in national cultural development. As South Germany's rapidly growing industrial base, the region might form a counterbalance to reactionary Junker influence: "If the South becomes industrially competitive with Prussia, South Germany's democratic propensities will gain an altogether different significance as immediate means to power against the feudal barbarism of the East and North."[5]

Late Saturday evening at Würzburg the delegates were locked in a discussion of the function of the *Fränkische Tagespost* and its announced reorganization. A delegate from Rothenburg complained of insufficient regional coverage and lamented that party officials had resorted to placing notices in bourgeois papers to inform comrades of events. He called for a weekly supplement devoted to regional affairs or a daily section for each electoral district. Eisner in turn asked the assembly to reject the proposal for a weekly supplement and promised more thorough coverage with the changes at the *Tagespost*. He then put forward a proposal of his own to make workers' education a central mission of the party. Younger workers, he asserted, had been ill-prepared by the Volksschule to assimilate even what they read in their newspapers. Whereas the rival Center Party commanded a virtual army of chaplains paid by the state to miseducate schoolchildren, Social Democracy had failed to recognize that the effort to equip the masses with the knowledge and skills requisite to informed, critical thinking had to be as thoroughly organized as its union operations and political initiatives. Summarizing his comments, the *Tagespost* wrote: "In North Bavaria we should start to enlist people to pursue educational endeavors exclusively. Our opponents will be vanquished sooner by positive learning than by polemic."

Albert Südekum hailed Eisner's proposal for a Social Democratic shadow ministry of education, noting that Eisner's herculean feat of holding twenty-three lectures in two months simply could not be sustained by any single individual as a part-time pursuit in addition to his regular, vital work. Südekum promised to place at the disposal of the contemplated North Bavarian education center his well-stocked traveling library. Martin Segitz, the Reichstag deputy for Fürth, also spoke in support of Eisner's proposal but voiced concern at the estimated expense, between 5,000 and 6,000 marks, of engaging a professional pedagogue and suggested that the motion be referred to the regional executive committee for further consideration. In tabling the motion, regional secretary Max Walther expressed the hope that "with the rise of the *Tagespost* it might be possible in the near future for the Franconian Publishing House, in concert with the party, to finance such an educational enterprise."[6]

In conjunction with his Würzburg campaign Eisner systematized his thinking on proletarian education in the essay "Communism of the Intellect" for the May issue of *Dokumente des Fortschritts* (Documents of Progress), an international review published in multiple languages.[7] He began by underscoring the autodidactic imperative of workers' learning. In the earliest stages of organization, the ambitious went to school to Lassalle and Marx, the first two German thinkers to address themselves to the common man. Indeed, the law itself held as treason any effort to elevate the aspirations of labor. Fichte drew on Pestalozzi for his *Reden an die deutsche Nation* (Addresses to the German Nation), "a propaedeutic for a communist polity," parts of which had only recently come to print. Rife was the rationalists' view that precisely the harshness of life rendered the fourth estate receptive to scientific thought that challenged the presuppositions of status quo. Just as the bourgeoisie outstripped the feudal aristocracy in letters, accomplishment, and wealth, so too had the proletariat determined, despite exclusion from schooling and property, to overhaul the new rulers through the superior "*morality* of intellectual disposition." The results were historic. "The basic conception of education as potential public property," Eisner declared, "has been established beyond any doubt through the development of Social Democracy's cultural work." In support of his claim he cited the niveau of the party press, the monographs disseminated in huge runs by its publishing collectives, the benchmark productions staged by its people's theaters, and the political idealism of its members, who devoted themselves to the life of the mind, attended lectures, and met to discuss the broad scope of thorny social issues after having put in a full day's exhausting work. "Indeed, party and union have created something like a pedagogical province in which the proletariat is educated for its historical mission."

Turning to the problems and deficiencies that nonetheless plagued Social Democracy's noble venture, Eisner confessed that those engaged in the effort inevitably felt overwhelmed from time to time by the enormity of the task and the gap between the real and ideal. The moments of despair though were best dispelled by a brief diversion into the insipid bourgeois or university milieu. The first ranks of comrades moved haltingly in their self-education from abstract to concrete, from theory to practice; individual progress kept pace with that of the fledgling movement as a whole. The new guard, in an era of empowerment, was confronted now with a bewildering array of fully developed concepts, attendant terminology, and facts and figures. "Today's newspapers, addresses at meetings, brochures and books too, even the simplest public lectures meant to educate invariably assume a level of knowledge that the young worker has not attained. Often a single foreign word, which he cannot fully grasp because of a lack of language training, presents endless difficulty, and the shaky understanding accustoms him to arguing in words and phrases instead of confidently reconstructing concepts." With little leisure and few resources on which to draw in his mammoth undertaking, the young worker struggled for mastery of the basics.

On his forays into the hinterland Eisner had seen firsthand in his audience the criminal, stupefying effects of the Volksschule, which existed solely to impress subservience and impede independent thought by "filling minds with religious and historical legends." Whereas the state employed legions of pedagogues to ready a few thousand elite for self-perpetuation, the millions went to rack and ruin. Only a single student from the working class was admitted to study law each year at Prussian universities, and the institution of university extension, so prevalent in English-speaking countries, was unknown in the land of Schiller, proclaimer of universal fraternity. For that reason the party resolved at the Mannheim congress of 1906 to redress the frightful imbalance of opportunity. The Prussian state responded with a statute limiting assembly: only those workers eighteen or older were permitted to attend political meetings. From age fourteen, when pupils left the Volksschule, until eighteen, three million workers were prohibited from learning in the one institution that promoted their interests. "No civilized state is as distant from the communism of education, that prerequisite of every real nation, as is Germany."

In the great industrial centers of Germany the proletariat's effort at self-education through the offices of its political party and unions had achieved conspicuous success, but beyond these strongholds of progress, despite the diligence of well-intentioned volunteers, who were themselves inadequately prepared, the situation was generally pathetic. One needed only to hear a workers' chorus or orchestra in an outlying town to understand the problem. Yet gifted young artists, teachers, and scholars languished unemployed in the capitals while a nation clamored for their services. Here Eisner appealed to these talented, disaffected young people "to go out among the workers as simple workers with no ambition other than to accomplish what they could with their abilities out of pure will to commonality." What was at stake was the viability of citizenry. "The misery of German politics, the exclusion of the populace from controlling its own destiny, the political pallor and immaturity of the German nation, the petit-bourgeois indecision and spinelessness of a people who never wrested democratic self-determination are rooted in the inequality of basic education, which has divided not just men but intellect and will, thought from action."

In May the *Tagespost* serialized Gorky's *Mother* in its feuilleton, reviewed six lectures on Beethoven held in Nuremberg by the Munich professor Hermann Ludwig von der Pfordten, and displayed in its show window a forty-volume library of works selected specifically for a proletarian audience. On Sunday, the thirtieth, the *Tagespost* announced that construction of the paper's new headquarters was nearing completion and that changes were coming with the move. Additional staff had been engaged, an entertainment supplement was to appear five days each week, and a weekly educational supplement would "introduce the masses of people to higher learning according to a unified plan in systematic progression." *Der Volksbildner* (The People's Pedagogue), as the supplement had been dubbed, was designed for filing as a handy reference guide, a workers' encyclopedia of sorts in installments.[8] On 23

June Nuremberg's Social Democratic organ could report that its subscriptions had risen to 22,500, making it by far the most read political newspaper of North Bavaria.[9]

Nearly three years after his departure from *Vorwärts* Eisner was prompted by the Prussian Landtag elections to revisit the circuitous course and perverse psychology of internal party politics. In 1903, after Bebel's volte-face, Social Democracy ended its historic boycott and fielded a slate of candidates. Despite posting the second greatest number of ballots of seven contesting parties, the SPD won no representation, the result of weighted voting. In July 1908, however, seven Social Democrats, led by Karl Liebknecht, were seated in the Landtag, an invaluable new venue for agitation and propaganda. Eisner observed the occasion by recalling his isolation early in his career at *Vorwärts* precisely for advocating participation in Prussian Landtag elections, "my first act of high treason against the party line." What ten years of intramural debate had taught him was that all too infrequently issues were decided "on the basis of what has been written or said, not on the basis of who wrote or said it."

Just as had occurred after the national elections of 1903, a clique marshaled by a Berlin editor had turned on their comrades who regarded electoral success as success and denounced them as revisionist opportunists hand in glove with bourgeois liberalism. The clique still failed to grasp the significance of the Prussian elections, which conclusively dispelled contradictory elements of the party's tactic: "The success has ended forever that policy of demonstrative inaction, which was hotly and bitterly contested for decades." Eduard Bernstein had been the first to recognize the value of a campaign for the Prussian Landtag. Although Eisner acknowledged his longstanding differences with Bernstein, he hailed him here for pressing the issue and observed that among the seven new Social Democratic deputies were the most vocal past critics of Bernstein's visionary demand that the party vie for the seats they currently held. As late as winter 1906 the lead article in *Neue Zeit* preached against the Landtag campaign, which Social Democrats, save the odd "complete fool," universally regarded "as one of our finest accomplishments and as the source of new hopes and future victories." It was often the case, Eisner remarked, that the originator of an idea must see it brought to fruition by epigoni. He who served the good cause had to inure himself to every slight, expect no gratitude, and simply persevere for the sake of the cause.[10]

At the Nuremberg party's midsummer meeting Eisner championed his education platform as he had in April at the regional meeting in Würzburg. The henchmen at *Vorwärts* attacked his ideas as an assault on the Party School in Berlin and impugned his motives, asserting that the pure Marxism taught at the academy materially impeded his fore-most desire to return to Berlin and reclaim the editorship of the central organ! Berliners well schooled in Marxist orthodoxy, Eisner quipped in summarizing the detractors' stance for his North Bavarian readers, "would never again put up with so suspect a heretic, as surely I am." He then went on the offensive. As *Vorwärts* had ignored every objective argument he had advanced in his critique of the party's education policy, he responded now by ridiculing the concept of an ideological catechism to enlighten the mind. "If the Party School were in fact a drill academy for an orthodox instructional slant, I would indeed become a genuine opponent of the undertaking, for it makes no difference whether cleri-calism is tinged socialist or centrist. If I thought that the teachers at the Party School were selected not for reasons of ability and character but for proper outlook—as in Prussian state government and adminis-tration—I most certainly would . . . battle openly by every means such corruption and party careerism."

The 60,000 marks spent the past year on the Party School would yield greater returns in a broader venture, one that aimed to further the intellectual aspirations of the rank and file, to equip them for lifelong self-education rather than to incubate functionaries in the image of the academy's patrons. "We should renounce molding an elect band of party leaders through half-year courses in Berlin and turn instead directly to the masses of the party yearning to learn. And since these masses can-not take off half a year and go to Berlin, the Berlin Party School must come to the masses." Far more productive and cost-efficient, Eisner urged, was a decentralized approach, by which locales nationwide would engage competent pedagogues to offer courses of instruction on Sunday afternoons for all those interested, including party and union officials in need of training in administration. The Berlin comrades, with their wealth of resources, could establish their own permanent school, if this model appealed to them, but other schemata were better suited to the needs of the populace outside the capital. The choice at hand was a question of "breeding an elite or educating the masses."[11]

As Social Democracy's leadership made ready for September's con-gress in Nuremberg, Eisner pressed his agenda to expand the Bavarian organization's influence in national party politics as counterbalance to Berlin and Leipzig. The upcoming vote on the government's budget in the Bavarian Landtag occasioned a reconsideration of the Lübeck resolu-tion of 1901, which enjoined state deputations to toe the party line and reject proposed term budgets as a matter of course, unless extraordinary circumstances militated for approval. On 21 August 1908 Eisner wrote to

Konrad Haenisch, editor of Dortmund's *Arbeiter-Zeitung* and vocal critic of a "separate path" for the party in Bavaria.

> You know absolutely nothing of our conditions. If it were really so simple to explain every political situation with two woolly formulas then any imbecile could set policy. What is remarkable is that precisely you historical economists fail so utterly when it comes to applying your theories and instead of explicating begin to cry ethics. Otherwise you would have to know why at present, in Bavaria in particular, our situation in relatively favorable. It is for once the small states' fear of the growing political and economic predominance of Prussia. Here one wants to live in peace, even with the proletariat. More important yet is the following fact: Bavaria is on the brink of massive industrialization and growth of the proletariat. Social Democracy alone represents the progressive tendencies in this development. A ministry composed solely of professional civil servants, such as that now at the helm, is by nature much more disposed toward us, just from a kind of purview of charge, than toward the bourgeois parties, which only represent their own interests and not the tendencies of economic development, especially not in petit-bourgeois and agrarian Bavaria.[12]

In signed leads of 28 and 29 August titled "Four Questions" Eisner cast the logical argument for an affirmative vote in Munich's Landtag, prefacing his construct with the observation that aside "from all passions, from the personal, from overt and covert motives, from the power structure and its needs," there was something about the way this question had been addressed over the years that hampered any satisfactory resolution. He therefore proposed to treat it as an exercise in logic, for "like all political discussions in our party, debate of the budget issue suffers from a lack of systematic preliminary examination, of prior definition and clarification of terms, of precise formulation of the question and articulation of content."

Whereas theory, he reasoned, provided both the party's framework for conceptualization and general guidelines for consequent action, it could not prescribe a response to every exigency. Politics, on the other hand, required principled, informed, willful decisions from the leaders of mass constituencies. If each decision were dictated a priori by an ideational code of conduct, then all party offices from the executive committee to editorial staffs could be filled by lottery among its six hundred thousand members. With regard to term budget votes, the party's position was rife with inconsistency. Rejection of the budget as a symbolic rejection of the class state, when on all other days of the session the party approved credits for legislation it supported, was an empty gesture and worse: "the dangerous education to irresponsibility, dulling all political consciousness." Beyond Prussia and Saxony, state constitutions allowed for the development of democratic institutions. In Bavaria, where the party's representatives helped determine the allocations, pro forma rejection would permit the government to operate by the previous budget, "infinitely worse than that on which we now collaborated." In a state such as Bavaria, a repudiation of the budget remained an option if the party's deputation, convinced of a reasonable prospect of success, sought to incite a revolutionary conflict that might usher in "a new era in Bavaria for the good of the entire nation." The operative principle should be that the party's state deputations vote in minority exactly as they would if they held a majority. Logical and ideological consistency required that if the party invariably rejected term budgets as a protest against the ruling state, it was also obligated to abandon all parliamentary participation and confine itself wholly to syndicalist tactics.[13]

Joseph Bloch wrote from Stuttgart to say that he was "for once completely in agreement" with Eisner's stance.[14] On 30 August, the day after the second part of the article appeared, Victor Adler protested in a letter to Bebel the obsessive persecution by *Vorwärts* of Eisner, who, in part because of the personal affront done to him in Berlin, had now "gone mad" in Bavaria's more tolerant political climate and mistook the relative weakness of its state for beneficent liberality.[15] The next day Julius Kaliski reported gleefully from the capital that the party bosses were alarmed at the new resolve of the Bavarian organization. "They are systematically planting the idea here that only you, you alone, have induced the decision of the deputation. The demonic influence of Eisner! You in Nuremberg . . . are the surest defense against Prussian distortion."[16] At the same time a police agent in Berlin reported to superiors that there indeed existed a "so-called Eisner Group" of Social Democratic editors at the *Dessauer Volksblatt, Bochumer Volksblatt, Solinger Arbeiterstimme, Offenbacher Abendblatt,* and *Mainzer Volkstimme* who cast their lot with him through "thick and thin."[17]

In an attempt to weaken Eisner's influence Karl Kautsky resorted to sheer sophistry, his proven weapon of choice. He claimed to present in *Neue Zeit* a comprehensive analysis of disparate political and economic development in the German North and South.[18] Eisner rose to the challenge, ridiculing Kautsky's intent, method, and conclusions. In four signed leads titled "Advanced East Pomerania" he exploded the mythology of Kautsky's, 'economic-historical' sham science.[19] The proof of every theoretical law, Eisner declared, was to be found in its application. If the theory was not borne out by reality, either its conceptual premise was false or it had been misapplied to the phenomenon it purported to explain. With Kautsky's most recent article it was a question of both. According to the "authoritarian party academic," Eisner wrote, Prussia was more economically developed than Bavaria and thus reflected a more advanced stage of class conflict—the shape of things to come in Bavaria, where the current greater democratization was simply the result of a less advanced economy. By Kautsky's model, tensions in the South had not yet 'come to a head.' What Kautsky conveniently ignored in Marx's prognostication of the ineluctable immiseration of the proletariat was that the workers' movement itself had broken the chain of events Marx foresaw. Nevertheless, Eisner asserted, although the organized proletariat had bettered its own lot in the sixty years since the *Communist Manifesto* came to print, tensions between labor and capital had grown, not because the oppressed had nothing to lose but their chains but, to the contrary, because their capitalist masters felt increasingly threatened by the workers' mounting class consciousness, solidarity, and economic and political leverage.

Kautsky failed to take into account that it was the feudal structure of agricultural East Elbia, not the economic might of industrial Westphalian industry, that drove Prussian politics. Moreover, Eisner charged, Kautsky had used statistics from 1895 to justify his claims, although the figures from 1907 showed that in vital categories such as population growth and density, miles of railway, and productivity of acreage under cultivation Bavaria was significantly more developed than East Elbia. Belying Kautsky's construct yet further was that precisely in England, the most industrialized nation of Europe, all classes of the citizenry enjoyed greater freedom, whereas in Russia, the least industrial, the most oppressive conditions still prevailed. Eisner closed his series by reminding readers that Kautsky had taken a similarly errant position on the general strike before the party congress at Jena. Whereas Kautsky considered the general strike the silver bullet for felling capitalism and class society with a single shot, Eisner treated it as a useful tactic in the party's ongoing political struggle. "While we were still quarreling over the difference before the members of the Jena Commission, the resolution affirming my view had already been printed, and Kautsky fell in line." Now Kautsky overvalued symbolic rejection of the budget, and once again he was polemicizing against his opponents.

On Saturday, 12 September, the day many delegates arrived for the party congress in Nuremberg, Eisner showcased his paper's vitality with a much expanded issue. Although his lead article proclaimed as the congress's crucial mission the defeat of the Bülow bloc's campaign to impose Prussian dictates on the rest of the nation, much of the rest of the issue was devoted to the local effort to further workers' education. "The organization of education in North Bavaria has come to life now and begun its work," began the report, which listed the officers in the enterprise and presented a tentative schedule of events for the next two quarters. Trade-unionist Georg Bohl and Eisner served as chair and vice chair of the steering committee, respectively. Dr. Max Maurenbrecher had been engaged as the professional pedagogue. Through the fall he was to hold lecture series on Lassalle, the rise of cities, and the world of Christ's time. Outside of Nuremberg and Fürth single lectures were planned in half a dozen prominent towns and a score of hamlets from Ansbach to Zirndorf. Maurenbrecher was also to conduct reading and discussion groups on Sunday morning for more advanced learners, Sunday afternoon meetings for young people, and special sessions weekday afternoons for unemployed workers. Guided tours of museums, natural science fieldtrips, plays, concerts, art evenings, and a folk-festival gala complemented the lectures and discussions.

In the second quarter, January through March, Maurenbrecher would offer a weekly lecture on social stratification in Germany, Georges Weill a five-part series on trade policy, and Eisner would give four talks on Marx, two on Goethe. *Der Volksbildner* was to be launched 1 October as a weekly supplement to the *Tagespost*, with planned series on topics as diverse as basic political concepts, general socialism, national economy, geopolitics, physics, botany, astronomy, and German cultural history.[20] Maurenbrecher outlined his priorities in an essay titled "Workers' Education," which would prove immediately controversial.[21] "What we need for the masses of party comrades," he wrote, "is not 'theory of socialism' or 'teachings of our masters' or however else these formulations run, but rather facts on the basis of which they are compelled to draw conclusions."

On the first full day of the congress Heinrich Schulz, in his report as chair of the education commission, took pointed exception to Maurenbrecher's "grotesque" assertions, which Schulz, himself a teacher at the Party School, deemed antithetical to the party's most cherished principles of mass education. If workers had no need of theory, he asked sarcastically, why then did their teachers, other than to preserve their intellectual superiority over ignorant plebeians?[22] This was hardly the beginning for which Eisner had hoped. Later during the afternoon session he sought to clarify the tenets of the education initiative in Nuremberg, an undertaking to redress the failings of the Party School's approach. The academy's mission of training thirty handpicked comrades as functionaries through a six-month curriculum by no means addressed the education of the masses, nor were these thirty graduates equipped in any way to transmit what they had learned to others. "When one reads that Party School pupils who have just enjoyed half a year's instruction then straightaway present a series of twenty-some lectures on value theory, it shows, in my opinion, an insufficient appreciation of the difficulty of learning and above all an insufficient respect for the teaching profession in the proletariat." His comments were greeted by both applause and hissing.[23]

Far from denying that the Party School catered to the elect, Rosa Luxemburg rose to avow that as a member of its faculty "I could not wish for any better elite corps." In contrast to Eisner and Maurenbrecher's view, what workers needed most was precisely the theoretical perspective that promoted systematization of their practical knowledge. "If anything has convinced me of the necessity of the Party School, of the dissemination of the understanding of socialist theory in our ranks, it is Eisner's critique." Now her supporters dutifully lined up to take their turn. Max Grunwald of Berlin attacked Eisner and Maurenbrecher as "aesthetic literati of bourgeois stamp." Wilhelm Pieck of Bremen, Luxemburg's prize pupil, claimed that Eisner's conception of proletarian education was a clever ploy to strengthen his perverse influence on ill-schooled workers, "to take them down paths that do not lead to the conquest of political power but rather . . . place the masses at the disposal of particular right-leaning Social Democrats and left-leaning Liberals for their social-reformist aspirations." The future Stalinist puppet who would return to Berlin from Moscow in 1945 to bring the German proletariat under a new yoke denounced Eisner's charge of elitism as "demagogic."[24]

Eisner answered with a quote that touched both Pieck and Luxemburg. "The workers themselves, when they . . . give up work and become writers by profession, always do damage 'theoretically' and are ever ready to follow the muddle-headed of the alleged 'scholarly' caste." Its author was not Max Maurenbrecher but Karl Marx, another intellectual of bourgeois heritage, rebuking the Berlin anarchists. Pieck's declaration, Eisner continued, that comrades at odds with the Party School's approach had no business in the party was proof that his charge of elitism was justified.[25]

Karl Frohme's resolution urging greater latitude for state deputations of Württemberg, Baden, and Bavaria in considering their governments' proposed budgets further demonstrated the North-South divide and the revolt against the Berlin-Leipzig axis. The motion was defeated by a vote of 216 to 160, with nearly 43 percent of the delegates conditionally supporting approval of annual expenditures proposed by state governments.[26] Soon the South Germans would break with the party line and, like their English comrades, vote to approve term expenditures favorable to their constituencies. Eisner's editorial on the congress's outcome reiterated the necessity of a new line recognizing the demonstrated efficacy of different tactics in different regions: "Indeed, the attempt by a certain camp to dictate by compulsory decree another political course for party comrades in South Germany has miscarried completely." It would have been far more prudent, he judged, to have devoted the time wasted on the budget debate to a serious discussion of foreign policy.[27]

Friday, 25 September, the *Fränkische Tagespost* announced that the paper's operations would shift on 1 October to its own new building on Breitegasse. With the change of address readers could expect improvements: two new supplements were to complement the party's national illustrated weekly, *Neue Welt*. *Die Furche* (The Furrow), a daily entertainment section, would contain stories, serialized novels, poems, sketches, and the like. Slated for the inaugural issue was the first installment of Upton Sinclair's *Metropolis*, its first printing in Germany. The weekly *Volksbildner* would support North Bavaria's Social Democratic education initiative through a series introducing diverse fields of knowledge to its mass proletarian audience. Despite expansion, the monthly subscription price was to remain 70 pfennige when two Miriam cigarettes cost 5 pfennige, a pound of Helgoland cod 35 pfennige, lunch at Carl Brecheis's wineroom 80 pfennige, a derby hat RM 2.50, and a pair of men's shoes RM 4.80.[28] At the Hercules Velodrome on Wednesday evening, 30 September, Max Maurenbrecher held the first lecture sponsored by the local party's education committee. The general public was invited and no admission charged to hear his talk on the topic "Workers and Education."[29] In the next day's *Tagespost* the format changed from four columns per page to three, with noticeably clearer print. The first *Volksbildner* included pieces on the economy of the first-century Germanic tribes by Wilhelm Hausenstein and on fundamental political concepts by Friedrich Stampfer.

Joseph Bloch wrote the same week to congratulate Eisner on the new format and the supplements but urged him to darken the print.[30] Nuremberg's Catholic *Volkszeitung* marveled at the resources Social Democrats committed to their press. The rival paper reported that the local party had spent a quarter-million marks for several buildings on Breitegasse, then had them demolished to make room for the modern structure to house their press and newspaper. The new facility was reputed to have cost 850,000 marks, bringing the total outlay to well over a million. "The paper, the *Tagespost*, appears in a comfortably handy format, with a sumptuous layout now and a wealth of content that any three people would be hard pressed to digest."[31]

The Catholic clergy of provincial Franconia were less charitable in confronting the party's advance, as Eisner experienced when he spoke on "the religion of socialism" at the first Social Democratic meeting ever held in the village of Abenberg. He later recalled that the parish priest "preached fanatically at church beforehand and afterwards against me." The meeting's audience, however, proved both attentive and receptive. Eisner began his talk with purely anthropological observations about the origin of faith. "If we move from individual religions, we discern generally that *all old religions stem from three roots: from man's powerlessness over nature, from the defenselessness of the individual in the given social order, and from mortal fear of death.*" As observation and knowledge became science, however, natural phenomena formerly regarded as divine omen or retribution were demystified, codified, even harnessed for man's benefit. Reason enhanced the popular sense of dignity, justice, and commonality. The oppressed gradually rejected their lot as divinely ordained. The old beliefs in passive acceptance, endless sacrifice, and rebirth in a better place were superseded by a modern faith in man's ability to understand the world, to effect change, to improve his circumstance. Socialism, Eisner declared to the congregation, was that new faith that unified all knowledge, conscience, and creativity. When some days later the priest used a graveside service for another tirade, the flock rose up and their shepherd was reassigned by his bishop.[32]

At the moment of his newspaper's glory Eisner found himself under personal attack from local comrades aligned with the party executive in Berlin. In early October delegates to the party congress reported to the membership in public meetings. Georges Weill lamented that at a recent forum in Selb a delegate announced that efforts were underway in Nuremberg to oust Eisner from his job. Weill singled out the Nuremberg attorney Max Süßheim, an opponent of Eisner's position in the budget debate, for disparaging his year-and-a-half tenure at the *Tagespost* as a 'regrettable' phase of development.[33] In league with Süßheim were *Tagespost* business manager Karl Fentz and Landtag deputy Sigmund von Haller, both of whom sought to distance the party in North Bavaria from that in Munich, the stronghold of reformists around Georg von Vollmar.[34] Regional party secretary Max Walther confirmed at Friday's meeting that there was an organized effort to force Eisner out, then spoke in support of the leadership at the *Fränkische Tagespost*. Comrade

Baumgartner deplored the cabal against Eisner and hailed the improvements he had made. The disgraceful conspiracy had arisen, Baumgartner alleged, simply because the critics could not abide the paper's editor personally.[35] Soon enough there would be more grist for their mill.

The third issue of the *Volksbildner* began with the first of the letters on socialism that Eisner had planned to dedicate to Toni Hendrich.[36] Now, however, having come to the decision to leave Lisbeth, he directed his anonymous remarks to his wife in a public declaration of personal and philosophical estrangement. The initial missive makes clear that its author has taken final leave of his longtime partner and wants to record the grounds for his departure. After many years together he finally realized that her indifference to his social and political ideals derived from a stark, supercilious aversion to the masses. The epiphany came on an outing in the mountains, where the detached desolation of life prompted the author to reflect aloud on the welcome hustle and bustle of the city, with its "arclights and streetcars," the triumph of man's will over the vast wilds. When he lauded the collective consciousness that animates the urban proletariat, his partner's hesitant yet candid response confirmed his worst suspicions: "I hate people crowded together; they are mean, filled with vile desires and degenerate instincts, hopelessly dependent in a thousand ways. . . . I do not believe that these people want to be redeemed or that they can redeem themselves. Their souls are poisoned, like the air they pollute with their work." Shaken, the author senses that he was never a partner in a true marriage but merely the housemate of a distant woman who regards his cherished tenets as delusions.

Eisner had evidently confided his misery to Hulda Maurenbrecher. Just after the first of the *Sozialistische Briefe an eine Freundin* (Socialist Letters to a Female Friend) appeared in the *Volksbildner*, she treated marital incompatibility in an article for the *Furche*, sympathetically depicting her colleague's anguish and defending his actions. "Among proletarian marriages there are many that bear this curse: that the husband's interests and intellectual engagement grew extraordinarily through his introduction into political life or union activity whereas the wife in the best years of her development, always bound up in, and completely occupied by household and children, lagged far, far behind the husband."[37] Eisner moved from the house in Behringersdorf to Nuremberg's Hotel Schneider near the editorial offices of the *Tagespost*.[38] Under fire from critics of his Bavarian politics and at another personal crossroads, he tendered his resignation as the paper's editor, effective 1 April 1909, and received acknowledgment on 28 October that commissioner Sigmund von Haller had been duly apprised of his decision.[39] Haller wrote to Eisner on 30 October that he wanted to meet with him to discover the reason for the resignation, which he claimed to find most disappointing. Illness, however, precluded travel and any immediate resolution.[40]

In November Eisner began paying Lisbeth monthly child support of 336 marks, payments he would continue until mid-1915.[41] Six subsequent installments of the *Sozialistische Briefe* ran through the first month of the new year.[42] In them Eisner cataloged his irreconcilable ideological differences with Lisbeth, whose worldview he reckoned as naive and hypocritical. She whose childhood poverty had driven her to the brink of prostitution nonetheless regarded herself as superior to others no less destitute. Despite her daily reliance on the conveniences of modern society, she professed a yearning for simple farm life, which, he argued, is frightfully idealized and frequently threatened with doom by the demise of a single cow. She valued the lessons of a plain folksong over those of an exhaustive scholarly tome with expansive digressions documented by minute footnotes. The science in scientific socialism left her cold. Preferable were the old virtues of love, compassion, and pity—virtues that taught us to clothe the naked, feed the hungry, and accept martyrdom yet somehow failed to prevent continual exploitation and violence.

Eisner's newfound passion—and cause of rising tensions at the editorial offices on Breitegasse—was Else Belli, a twenty-one-year-old *Tagespost* staffer with a party pedigree. Her father, Joseph, had been lieutenant to Julius Motteler in running the Red Field Post, Social Democracy's illegal news-distribution network during the period of exile under Bismarck. Born 29 October 1887 in the Hirslanden quarter of Zurich, Else Belli moved with her parents to Stuttgart, where her father began work in 1890 as business manager of J. H. W. Dietz's publishing house.[43] In Württemberg's capital she was a pupil of the famed teacher Wilhelm Seytter, author of an imposing local cultural history, *Unser Stuttgart* (Our Stuttgart), still cited a century after its publication in 1903.[44] Two of Dietz's authors, Clara Zetkin and Anna Tomaszewska Blos, encouraged Belli's intellectual development. Zetkin was editor of *Die Gleichheit*, the party's fortnightly women's journal, to which Blos was a regular contributor. The latter, whom Belli regarded as "schoolmarmish," pushed her toward university, but Zetkin gave rein to her desire for experiential learning.[45] Belli's story "The Fugitive" came to print in *Die Gleichheit* two days after her nineteenth birthday.[46] A photo from 1906 shows a lithe, dark beauty in the costume of a fado chanteuse, displaying a mandolin on her lap. Her beguiling melancholy gaze seeks out the viewer's eye.[47]

Else Belli's literary ambitions were sidetracked by an affair with Hermann Otto Bach, a Stuttgart bourgeois five years her senior. Relocated by her father to Munich, Belli gave birth there at age nineteen to a daughter, Freia, on 6 June 1907.[48] Late into the pregnancy she was writing on women's issues for the *Tagespost*.[49] Through the intercession of her patrons Belli was employed as a secretary at the Party School in Berlin.[50] In January 1908 she reported for *Gleichheit* on the stenographers' and typists' associations bankrolled by the Berlin typewriter firm Glogowski to keep young women from affiliating with a union that represented their interests rather than those of their employers.[51] She was allowed to audit lectures, but her flirtations and romances, including a liaison with Arthur Stadthagen, became scandalous, prompting Franz Mehring to effect a ban on all auditors.[52] By autumn she was under Eisner's wing, filing reports for the *Tagespost*. In October she covered a performance by the dancer Rita Sachetto at Nuremberg's Municipal Theater. Eisner had chosen not to attend and sat in the Golden Post Horn. During the performance's intermission Lisbeth Eisner, accompanied by trade-union secretary Helene Grünberg, angrily confronted Belli about her relationship with Eisner. Belli fled the theater and sought out her new mentor at his tavern. As they sat together, she asked him if he might take her on as his personal secretary were he to quit his post over the budget squabbles with Fentz.[53]

With his newspaper's renaissance under way and its influence growing, Eisner continued to work at a torrid pace. On Saturday, 14 November, the *Tagespost* declared in an editorial introduction to Dr. Südekum's article "Community Democracy" that the paper would be placing greater emphasis on municipal politics and governance, as the local party anticipated a major victory in the upcoming elections for the Nuremberg town council.[54] The same issue contained a full-page notice on the expanded services offered by the party's Franconian Publishing House and Printing Operation, Ltd. in its new facilities. The thoroughly modernized operation with its state-of-the-art rotary presses could turn out everything from custom stationery to full-color catalogs. A bindery, bookstore, and full subscription service were all part of the enterprise. An extra edition the same day included detailed illustrations of the compound at Breitegasse 25/27 and Frauengasse 12. On the following Saturday the *Tagespost* urged its constituency to the polls on Monday to support fifteen Social Democratic candidates for the town council. For the first time the party was assured of representation, the electoral system of proportional representation having been mandated by Bavarian law.[55] On Wednesday the paper reported that the party had claimed ten of twenty seats on the council.

Subject now to mounting political, professional, and personal abuse in Nuremberg, Eisner explored his options, but the paramount consideration was to maintain his relationship with Else Belli. The first week in December the governing board met with *Tagespost* officials to review grievances with the editor in chief. At issue was Eisner's having his favorite on the payroll. He defended Belli's collaboration as "thoroughly justified *objectively*" and asserted that those in a position to judge were in complete agreement that she was "one of the strongest literary talents of our party," but he sought to quell the criticism and "end all the gossip" by assuring Haller that Belli would leave the staff by 1 January 1910.[56] Karl Fentz wrote to him 6 December unequivocally: "With regard to our conference yesterday as to Fräulein Belli's collaboration at our *Fränkische Tagespost*, I inform you that now as before I hold to my view, which Comrades [business manager Konrad] Dorn, [party secretary Martin] Treu, and [stonemason Johann] Merkel share too, and in the name of the Publishing House reject any collaboration of the said Fräulein at our paper from today on."[57] A compromise was reached whereby Belli left Nuremberg but continued to contribute occasional freelance pieces.

For the rest of the month Eisner subordinated personal frustrations to productive work. The election of Engelbert Pernerstorfer as vice president of the Austrian Reichsrat, as reported by the *Tagespost* correspondent in Vienna, was the lead article on Friday, 11 December. In two years the Austrian Social Democratic faction had swelled from eleven to eighty-nine deputies to become the second largest of the house. In the first session of the new term the Austrian Party laid claim to its rightful place in the presidium.[58] A week later, prompted by revelations that the kaiser had been prohibited by his chancellor from granting further interviews after divulging state secrets to an English reporter, Eisner explored the question of "how monarchies come to an end." Whereas the English, French, Serbs, and Portuguese had dispatched unsatisfactory rulers with gruesome finality, the Norwegians recently informed their king by registered letter that they no longer required his services, and the Turks deprived Sultan Abdul Hamid of power while allowing him to retain his title and harem. Noting that some of the fifty-odd Hohenzollern castles maintained by public monies were being advertised for sale, Eisner ventured with tongue in cheek that the end of German absolutism would come via liquidation as an unprofitable asset.[59]

Late Christmas Eve Eisner boarded a third-class car of the train to Munich en route to Dachau, the art colony northwest of Bavaria's capital where Else Belli lodged now at the Hörhammer Guest House.[60] In transit through the night he doubtlessly pondered his life's new course. Well in advance of the 1912 elections he was being touted in Dessau-Zerbst's Anhalt 1 Reichstag district as the party's nominee.[61] His nomination was spearheaded by Heinrich Peus, editor of the *Volksblatt für Anhalt*, who himself had represented Potsdam 8 in the Reichstag from November 1886 to December 1906. Both men had served as officers of the Workers' Press Association.[62] As enticing as the possibility of returning to Berlin with a legislative mandate must have been, Eisner still held out hope that Nuremberg's hierarchy might yet be swayed to honor his vision for the *Tagespost* and entrust the hiring of staff to him.

CHAPTER THIRTEEN

DEAR LITTLE WHORE: PERSONAL AND PROFESSIONAL TURMOIL (1909)

B ACK IN NUREMBERG after his brief holiday respite in Dachau, Eisner ran the usual year-end retrospectives in the *Tagespost*. Pride of place was accorded Georges Weill's two-part article on Germany's woeful foreign policy in 1908, citing in particular the kaiser's *Daily Telegraph* interview and the "one defeat after another" that national prestige suffered from Bülow's inept meddling in Morocco.[1] Tuesday, 5 January, Eisner drafted a proposal to Vorwärts Press in Berlin. His resolve "to withdraw from all editorial endeavors" and to devote himself to literary pursuits was impracticable at present, but he would devote "every spare moment" to the multivolume overview of world literature he had been invited to provide. He ventured that the undertaking would attract considerable interest, as no "cultural-social history of literature" existed. In addition, he was working on a history of the nobility and planned a continuation of *Das Ende des Reichs*, a project he had discussed with Comrade Bernhard Bruns. The latter he could deliver by 1 July 1912. Moreover, he had made considerable progress on a study of Fichte, a project that had occupied him for some years already, and he would gladly forward copy of the lecture series on Marx he was to present in the spring.[2]

That night Eisner wrote to Belli from his room at the Schneider Hotel that he intended to meet with his wife the next afternoon to finalize some arrangement. Lisbeth wanted to leave Nuremberg, and he thought that she would do well to relocate to a small town such as Jena. "I will renounce everything, even the children. I know now that they love me but will go with their mother." Once his family vacated the field, he saw no reason that Belli should not be with him in Nuremberg. "Then in a few months I shall present the people with the choice of losing me or having me and you." He announced that he would arrive in Munich late Friday afternoon and asked her to take the train from Dachau to meet him at the main station. They could then ride back to Dachau together, "where we might hope to find a nest for us two." On the twenty-sixth he would begin a tour of the electoral district in Dessau, but would visit her the weekend prior to departure. He closed by imagining that they were together. "And now I take you into the nice, warm, clean bed and entangle myself in your downy legs."[3]

Three Kings' Day, 6 January, Belli wrote to him that the smell of burning incense in the guest house the previous day had fuddled her senses. In the night she had erotic, vampire dreams of holding his head in her hands, drinking his blood, and bathing her breasts in it. Her closing was equally explicit. "You, my Greek, fare well. I kiss your hand and let it bless my womb."[4] On the seventh Eisner penned a postcard from his office. Lisbeth was accosting him daily at work and was capable of "every nastiness." He had urged her to seek a divorce and relocate to Erlangen, where he might visit their children. He threatened to "disappear from Nuremberg one day without a trace" if she did not comply. As to Belli's most recent submission, neither Weill nor he was impressed. He promised to discuss the manuscript's failings—"too little conception, too novelistic, too much wild fantasizing"—when he returned to Dachau the next day.[5]

The *Tagespost* reported on the nineteenth that the local trade unions had published an expansive catalog of their Central Library's collection of 4,500 volumes. In addition to works on "history and culture, geography and ethnography, natural science, law and government, national economy, sociology, socialism and Social Democracy, engineering and technology, philosophy and religion, pedagogy, and art" the collection boasted a full complement of German literary classics. Comrade Scheid from Munich had organized the library's holdings along the lines of Hugo Heimann's Workers' Library in Berlin.[6] Earlier the same day, just after midnight, Eisner had written to Belli from the Kerzinger Café on Luitpoldstraße. Exhausted from a public lecture in a village 8 kilometers west of Nuremberg's heart, he despaired of any positive effect. "I have just come from Zirndorf, where again I hung on the cross for an hour and a half, possessed by the delusion of educating people about politics and yet riven simultaneously by the knowledge that it is a delusion."[7] The next day he reported to Belli that he had gone to Behringersdorf to retrieve some books. His children had flocked to him until Lisbeth's plaints caused them to shrink back, wailing. "In vain I have tried to induce L. to file for legal separation. She is a force of nature, unmoved by reason. She is destruction, elemental devastation. . . . What am I to do? Even the shrewdest and bravest man is helpless and defenseless in such a case."[8] In the final installment of *Sozialistische Briefe an eine*

Freundin, printed in the *Volksbildner* the fourth week of January, Eisner concluded his unsigned missive to his unnamed wife with the declarations that he would never write to her again and that he was confident a new partner would come to him, one whom he would nurture and cherish until death—*bis in den Tod*. He was already closing his letters to Belli with the phrase.[9]

Just before his trip to Dessau to meet the electorate, Eisner went to Berlin to hear the Prussian Landtag debate the proposed change from three-tiered voting to universal suffrage for election of its members. Without the required entrance pass he bluffed his way past a police cordon and doormen by casually proclaiming himself "press" and took a seat in the gallery. There he spoke briefly with the brother-in-law of Dr. Oskar Bie, editor of *Die Neue Rundschau* (The New Review), and asked him to relay the message that he would soon submit the manuscript of a novel. "So now," he wrote to Belli on the twenty-fifth, "you just need to write the novel. If I send it off, it will receive special consideration."[10] The following day he posted a card from Dessau to tell her that their romance was the talk of the capital. "All Berlin was buzzing about the 'affair.' The *casus belli* joke made the rounds."[11] On Wednesday, 27 January, he composed a longer letter from Dessau's Golden Purse Hotel with the greeting "dear little whore of my fate!" In Berlin rumor had it that the Reichstag might be dissolved and new elections held. "It is conceivable that in a few weeks I could be a Reichstag deputy and ride through Germany first-class." Turning serious, he repined that no one he had met was well disposed toward her. "Write your novel, Els, the novel of the woman who immediately upon her first step beyond the confines of family amorally and unsentimentally discards all feeling for convention and society's prejudices."[12]

Eisner spoke the next day at a rally in Dessau, where he denounced Anhalt's state secretary, Hans von Dallwitz, as an unabashed champion of Junker interests "who in the Prussian House of Deputies once voted against the great cultural work of the Central Canal" as a threat to squirearchy monopolies. His ilk would topple Bülow and indeed Wilhelm himself if the government backed Landtag electoral reform or estate and inheritance taxes. Were the Reichstag to be dissolved, Eisner declared, the party must press for both. He ended his appeal with a rhetorical flourish: "All our strength, all our sense, all reason, all industry and effort we will commit to realize this our program. Not so as to mobilize for death, to arm for destruction, to bring about the greatest possible mutual slaughter do we pursue our program but rather to create life. We must seize our goal with the utmost ardor. The people should govern: that is our national honor. We fight for labor against exploitation, for freedom against oppression, for the people against caste and the personal regime!" The *Volksblatt für Anhalt* reported in a front-page article that his remarks were received with thunderous applause.[13] Friday evening Eisner wrote to Belli from his hotel in Dessau that he was celebrating a great victory. "My candidacy seems certain and a success in the elections not out of the question. Then I would have to live half the year in Berlin, but I hope not alone."[14]

The return trip to Nuremberg must have seemed a descent into the valley of the shadow. Back in his office, which he had come to regard as the "iron maiden," Eisner found that the rumor mill had operated at full tilt in his absence. He suspected Max Süßheim of concocting the tale that he had skipped town, leaving his family destitute. The suspicion was widespread that he was ghosting Belli's submissions to the *Tagespost*, and Fentz had attempted to scale back the honorarium she was to be paid. Lisbeth was no longer inclined to leave Behringersdorf. Her attorney, Dr. Aal, informed Eisner that his confession of having committed adultery was insufficient for the court. But if Belli testified that she had slept with him, they would be unable to marry in Germany.[15] In despair Belli accused Eisner of regarding their relationship as a continuation of his experimental dalliance with Toni Hendrich. He confessed that his attraction to Lisbeth's younger sister indeed had been "an attempt at escape to freedom," but protested that the bond with Belli was genuine and essential. For him she represented Goethe's indispensable 'eternal feminine.'[16] He disclosed that Sigmund von Haller planned to move to Nuremberg in April and wanted to join the editorial staff at the *Tagespost*. Eisner had in mind a quid pro quo: Belli must be brought back to Nuremberg. That failing, he would join her in Dachau, where together they might put out a syndicated feuilleton.[17]

Anticipating every eventuality, Eisner refreshed his idiom in theater criticism. In an article for the *Tagespost* he went to some lengths to clarify why class-conscious workers should regard the theater as anything other than a leisure pursuit of the privileged. In the past, he wrote, the "contradiction between my artistic and social-political conscience" left him loath to pan poor acting, as the disapproval served only to strengthen directors at the expense of their underlings in a brutal capitalist enterprise. "Whoever works on the stage is a wage-worker, nothing else, a proletarian with even fewer rights than most." He praised the recent pamphlet *Theater-Elend: Ein Weckruf* (Theater Misery: A Wake-Up Call) by Dr. Maximilian Pfeiffer, Reichstag deputy for the Center Party, who despite his affiliation had emerged as "an expert, relatively impartial, warmhearted advocate for art and artists."[18] Monday, 8 February, Eisner posted a card to Belli to say that the *Münchener Post* was providing them with theater tickets for Saturday evening.[19] Belli wrote the next day and again on the tenth to assure him of her love. She relished an evening on the town and recalled when they sat together in the Luitpold Café recently, "how rich, how happy I am, we are!"[20]

Struggling to finish a two-part article on Darwin, Eisner felt over-burdened and stretched thin.[21] Lisbeth came to town on Thursday to inform him that she intended to move to more expensive lodgings and would keep all their furniture. His colleague Fentz kindly suggested that he move some of his books to a secluded room in the editorial offices. Eisner placed an ad the same day for two unfurnished rooms.[22] After the theater weekend with Belli in Munich, Eisner settled into the third-class car, wrapped himself in a borrowed blanket from the Hörhammer Guest House, and dozed on the crawl back to Nuremberg, a slow begin-ning to an eventful week.[23] At the just-concluded conference of the Social Democratic Voters' League (Sozialdemokratischer Wahlverein) in Anhalt's first district, fifty-three delegates and officials had unanimously approved Eisner as their nominee for the Reichstag. Georg Könnecke informed him from Dessau that his four appearances there at the end of January had universally impressed the party regulars. Heinrich Peus requested that Eisner send him his writings and some biographical tidbits, as "people want to know things like that."[24] The *Tagespost* reported the nomination on Monday, 15 February, in a single sentence.[25]

From his Berlin sources Eisner received confidential word that the editors of the *Vossische Zeitung* had acquired documents implicating Rosa Luxemburg as a Russian police agent, a revelation rendered more cred-ible to him by her release from a Warsaw prison in the summer of 1906. He shared his thoughts with Belli. "If this information is confirmed, Judgment Day will have come at last for the despoilers of the party who laid waste to German Social Democracy. My old assertion would be con-firmed too that the police are behind all the ruinous party scandals. Rosa was and is Karl Kautsky's intellectual controller; she works in tandem with Franz Mehring (who has been suspicious to me for years): stirring up discord was their true mission. . . . She misapplied Marxism so as to deprive the party of any possibility of a positive influence. She is the soul of the intellectual drill academy known as the Party School."[26] Within a week Eisner learned that the allegations could not be verified, yet he had no doubt they were true. But by then he had problems of his own. Questions about his personal life threatened his viability as a candidate for the Reichstag, and he had been called to account. "I wrote to the people," he apprised Belli, "that I refuse on principle to disclose publicly information about my private relationships; in confidence, though, I told them the truth, which I proudly profess."[27]

At the end of the month Eisner arranged to rent the room offered by Karl Fentz. Above it was a roof garden at his disposal, all for a most reasonable 15 marks per month, including heating and lighting. Eisner determined to shelve his library in his editorial office, believing that book-lined walls would render the space "more dignified." Having settled accounts with the Schneider Hotel, he moved on Thursday, 10 March, into the new abode, "a proper bachelor jumble . . . without a trace of what one calls artful interior decoration." He apprised Belli bitterly that Lisbeth insisted on keeping his piano "even though no one there plays." He was already paying 800 marks' annual rent for the house in Behringersdorf, and her new residence was to cost nearly double that.[28]

On consecutive evenings in mid-March Eisner held two public lectures in Nuremberg on Goethe's *Faust*, the drama of an aging intellectual's attempt to reclaim life through love.[29] The day of the second lecture his lengthy review of a performance by the nude dancer Olga Desmond at the Apollo Theater was prominently featured in the *Tagespost*. Although the local police required her to wear bathing bloomers and "a kind of bandage" over her breasts, she succeeded in conveying the sensuality of the human body.[30] As winter turned to spring Eisner had motive to meditate on physical attraction, emotional commitment, and new life. On 7 April he composed for Belli a Petrarchan sonnet commemorating her pregnancy as a rite of spring and his own rebirth.[31]

Eisner's four planned lectures on "Karl Marx and His Worldview," scheduled over the course of nine evenings at the end of April, were postponed until the fall because of the speaker's "indisposition."[32] But by the eve of May Day he mustered his rhetorical skills to remind the celebrants that German workers had not yet achieved what their comrades had in other industrial societies. "Where in the world might there yet be another personal regime! Where could the dual alliance of Junker and priests still decree, as if we were living in the age before 1789, what the masses of people have to pay in taxes and how they are to pay them! Where on earth would it still be possible not to have implemented democratic suffrage in a country with compulsory military service! . . . Prussian Germany has never been anything other than a military and police enterprise. The horrid militarization of European civilization can be put down mainly to the nature of Prussian-German politics."[33]

Precisely this aversion to Prussia's influence on German foreign policy clashed with Joseph Bloch's nationalist socialist agenda. Indeed,

Bloch regarded as wholly positive Bülow's play to supplant Wilhelm as chief author of state initiatives in international affairs. In a letter of 19 November 1908 Bloch had solicited from his Austrian confederate Karl Leuthner an article for *Sozialistische Monatshefte* to legitimize German national interests as articulated and pursued by a genial man of vision. "The truth is that ultimately I would have no great objection to a personal regime in foreign policy if the individual in charge himself inspired sufficient confidence in his talents. For after all, foreign policy cannot be formulated in parliament; there must of course always be a great personality in whose resolve it coalesces."[34] Had Bloch's copious correspondence with his protégé fallen into the hands of their adversaries, the editor of *Sozialistische Monatshefte* surely would have faced the same kind of accusations made against Rosa Luxemburg by the *Vossische Zeitung*, for by providing Leuthner with detailed appraisals of party comrades' personal strengths and weaknesses, allies and enemies, by coaching him to play off one individual, faction, or newspaper against another so as to subvert socialist opposition to Berlin's expansionist strategy, Bloch certainly appears to fill the bill as agent provocateur for the Pan-German League.

In mid-December Bloch praised Victor Adler for championing a 'strong Austria' as a deterrent to war and impressed on Leuthner the necessity of undermining the position of Eisner and Stampfer, whose constant assaults on the ineptitude of the Foreign Office strongly influenced the party press and Reichstag deputation.[35] Now, four months on, Stampfer telephoned Bloch on 20 April to express indignation at Leuthner's assertions in the article "Master Race and Slave Race," where Leuthner alleged that "the Clubs of the Harmless who influence in large part public opinion in Germany" were undermining legitimate national interests in favor of British and Russian imperial designs.[36] Bloch wrote to Leuthner on 29 April that his "polemic against Eisner is completely justified," but referred him to an article by Berthold Heymann in the *Chemnitzer Volksstimme* that was complimentary of Eisner and condemned smear campaigns against party comrades.[37]

On Wednesday, 5 May, while Eisner hiked the countryside on vacation, Georges Weill ridiculed "the great Prussian patriotism of Austrian comrade Karl Leuthner," who decried the *Tagespost* as a corrupt tool of Germany's rivals and, recycling Kautsky's gibe echoed privately by Bloch, branded Eisner a feuilletonist out of his depth in international politics.[38] The offending piece, just published in Bloch's journal, was the article "Relearning," in which Leuthner admonished Social Democracy to forswear criticism of the German government's Weltpolitik.[39] In a caustic, signed article Eisner responded from the trail. "Forever and a day Comrade Karl Leuthner, living in exile in Vienna, the world's only Prussian by choice—we others are at worst Prussian by necessity—has been hawking in *S.M.* poor copies of Hohenzollern metaphysics à la Treitschke as unlearned socialism." Now, Eisner sneered, Leuthner was promoting joint German-Austrian imperial adventurism, an enterprise that German socialists could regard as nothing shy of absurd, for if Bülow's reckless rush into Morocco had no appeal, Austro-Hungarian foreign minister Aehrenthal's designs on the Balkans had even less. Leuthner's aberrant position, so divergent from mainstream party sentiment in either Austria or Germany, served a single purpose: the editorial imperative of *Sozialistische Monatshefte* to further "cooperation of German Social Democracy with Left Liberalism" by minimizing fundamental ideological divides, especially on foreign policy.

Eisner closed his piece with a bitter aside. "Leuthner does me personally the honor of calling me a gifted feuilletonist and comical weekly serialist. I do not know if I justify this high praise of having the gift for one of the most difficult and valuable literary fields. But I do know that an ambition not to be taken seriously, however well rewarded, never leads to the success of having a comic effect."[40] Upon reading Eisner's article, Bloch queried Leuthner in a letter of 14 May why he had characterized Eisner as an expert feuilletonist at all. "I know of course that it is the general opinion, but . . . I at least have little regard for this talent of Eisner's either. In essence everything is just empty word play, devoid of any real humor, much less a perceptible perspective. Everything is intellectual in the negative sense and just simply words. To me Eisner in his entirety is nothing but [Moritz Gottlieb] Saphir in modern dress. . . . At heart his literary output is the same as his politics: mere word combinations in lieu of concrete conception."[41] Yet Bloch evidently considered Eisner's conception of foreign policy coherent and compelling enough to move the party rank and file in ways Bloch regarded as detrimental, and in Max Beer, London correspondent for the *Fränkische Tagespost*, Eisner had found a kindred spirit. Accordingly, Bloch directed Leuthner to single out both men for repeated attack.[42]

In mid-May Eisner wrote to Georges Weill from Karlsruhe that Fentz had not yet paid him 55 marks he was due for two articles for the *Furche* and he had no means of settling his hotel bill or buying his train ticket back to Nuremberg. "More than ever," he confided, "I yearn to be completely free and disappear. I won't take being a coolie much longer."[43] He returned to man a post he regarded as increasingly embattled and undesirable. On 7 June he reported to Else Belli another disagreeable meeting with the press commission and vented the suspicion that Adolf Braun, eager to return to Nuremberg from Vienna, was working behind the scenes to undermine him. Weighing his resignation and a decisive change of course, Eisner asked earnestly for Belli's counsel. If she assented, he would give ninety days' notice on the first of July. "I could be with you starting 1 October, but we could all perish together. For I do not expect that I would continue then to write for the *Tagespost*, and you would lose your chief source of income as well. We stand before a difficult decision. Are you prepared to suffer want and woe with me and, if it must be, even death? And would you work to help me support my poor children too?" He appended an appeal to ask her father to inquire of Dietz in confidence if the contract for the history of literature, issued three and a half years earlier, was still valid.[44]

The quarrel with Bloch and Leuthner intensified. Bloch wrote to Leuthner on 1 June to register his dismay at Beer's fundamentally Internationalist view, expressed in a recent article, that it made no difference to German workers whether their lords were German, French, or English. "It is a scandal," Bloch fumed, "if such a thing can be said in German Social Democracy without contradiction."[45] Despite their public disagreement Eisner came to Bloch's defense when *Vorwärts* and the *Leipziger Volkszeitung* smeared him for publishing *Sozialistische Monatshefte* with the financial assistance of bourgeois benefactors. The *Fränkische Tagespost* reprinted a clarification from the *Münchener Post* that the party leadership had never declined funds from bourgeois sympathizers eager to further the socialist cause. Eisner reiterated that however ardently the *Tagespost* opposed the recent tendencies of the *Monatshefte*, there could be no doubt about Bloch's integrity or the quality of his publication, which was unsurpassed by another Social Democratic organ. "And moreover it is generally known in the party that the publisher is precisely the most disinterested editor in the entire party and takes no personal advantage from his great work. When it is said of this very man, who has certainly committed serious errors from the party's political perpective, that he is a scoundrel who sold out to our rivals, is bribed by them to deliver up the party to the bourgeiosie via his journal, to which virtually all leading party comrades contribute, much greater damage is done to the party by such deplorable tactics than by even the most objectionable articles of the *SM*."[46]

Bloch nevertheless complained bitterly to Eisner on 14 June that the *Tagespost* had ranged itself with the likes of *Vorwärts* against the *Monatshefte* and that Eisner's "anti-German" stance on foreign policy was "ruinous" for the party. "If I may give you one piece of advice," Bloch appealed, "it is this: rein in the reactionary zeal of your colleague Beer a bit."[47] Eisner responded the next day to underscore their differences on crucial questions, to hail Beer as Social Democracy's supreme authority on foreign policy, and to question Bloch's reliance on his Viennese protégé. "I regard Leuthner—from the start actually—as a crank."[48] And in truth *Vorwärts* had seconded Leuthner's critique of Beer.

Beer himself addressed his critics in a piece for the 21 June issue of the *Tagespost*. "Since my main concerns are to clarify international politics through hard facts and conclusions drawn from them and to work for pure internationalism within the workers' movement, I welcome every opportunity to discuss foreign affairs." What follows proved cannily oracular. The tensions between Germany and England, he asserted, were genuine, and the only recourse for the proletariat was to resist the nationalist appeals of the parties that stood to benefit from the mounting conflict. The enmity of the central organ's new guard for the editor of the *Tagespost* had caused them to use Eisner's former pseudonym, Joc, to characterize Beer's views frivolously as a joke, but the threat of war was direly grave. Beer drew an analogy to the early Christian church. Its unity was undermined by particularism until Paul decreed that there could be no distinction between Jews and Greeks, for they were all just Christians now. "And so should it be in socialism too: neither Germans nor Englishmen but just socialists striving for democratic freedom and socioeconomic fraternity."[49]

The first week of July Eisner was in sweltering Berlin, where he felt overwhelmed by the noxious odor of sweat and petrol fumes. He looked forward to seeing Else Belli the following Wednesday and wrote to allay her concerns about an onset of night terrors. "It means nothing," he counseled. "Still, you should concentrate what little energy you have in your waking hours to ridding yourself of all life's fears. There is simply no point to dreading its vicissitudes and dangers. This banishing of fear is perhaps the only productive moral demand."[50] Six months pregnant with "Baby Wolfgang" and her career dependent on Eisner's support, Belli had ample cause for troubled sleep, and Eisner certainly had worries enough of his own to dispel. He divulged to Belli on 29 July that Sigmund von Haller had called a meeting of the press commission's board to deal with Eisner's 'personal affairs.' The next day, though, he apprised her that by the meeting's end "the enemy lay writhing on the floor." Indeed, Karl Fentz had offered to manage Eisner's payments to Lisbeth in Behringersdorf and proposed laying aside the children's tuition in advance, deducting it each month from his salary. Eisner readily assented. "I have never had it so good," he confided to Belli, "to be relieved of all these nasty details."[51] The same day, 30 July, Belli noted for him her impressions of his stern, serious look in youthful photos. "As a young man you are most strange to me. You are completely different now, gentle and kind as only a man of your maturity can be." His ironic vein had once caused her to suspect that he might regard women with contempt, like the villains in his book on Nietzsche. How gratified she was to have erred in that judgment.[52]

From his myriad annoyances Eisner found escape in public appearances in East Bavaria's hamlets. There the Social Democratic Party was gaining support by assailing tax increases on beer, brandy, coffee, tea, and cigars backed by the Center and Conservatives in lieu of the inheritance tax proposed by Chancellor Bülow, who retired when it became clear that he no longer held sway over either the kaiser or the Reichstag's bourgeois parties. In the midst of the campaign the *Tagespost* reported that Georges Weill had spoken in Gunzenhausen, Max Süßheim in Neumarkt, Max Walther in Schwarzenbach an der Saale, Josef Simon in Oberkotzau, and Eisner in Marktredwitz and Mitterteich, where he drew crowds of six hundred and four hundred irate citizens, many of whom had traveled from their farms.[53] "After the Nuremberg mess," Eisner wrote to his lover on 2 August, "my agitation tour in darkest Germany was a salvation. Speaking to these simple people, one feels anew the warm blood of the great cause coursing."[54] And indeed the party was making inroads. Between 1 January 1908 and 1 July 1909 its membership in North Bavaria had grown from 26,566 to 30,394, driven in part by holding 625 public meetings and distributing hundreds of thousands of fliers.[55]

To improve his and Belli's personal finances, Eisner sent to press the last day of July his translation of Guy de Maupassant's "Boule de Suif," vetted by the bilingual Georges Weill.[56] The piece was slated for publication in installments in the *Furche*, but Eisner was confident that it would be syndicated in the party press.[57] "Let us hope," he wrote to Belli, "that we earn something from it that I can put part into the till for my dear, good Wolfgang."[58] Joseph Belli wrote to Eisner from Stuttgart in mid-August that Clara Zetkin, in response to a query from a female comrade in Nuremberg, had vouched for his daughter's contributions to *Gleichheit*. He urged Eisner to continue to encourage her productivity: "Else should work, show that she is worth something, and then there will be peace."[59] The royalties from their articles trickled in. The last week in August Eisner instructed Belli to acknowledge receipt of 34 marks from Adolf Müller, editor of the *Münchener Post*, and her short story "The Great Angler" was printed in the 31 August issue of the *Furche* under the pseudonym Speranza, feminized form of Eisner's own alias from his days in Marburg.[60]

Despite Eisner's most recent dispute with *Sozialistische Monatshefte*, he wrote to Joseph Bloch on 24 August that an article on Kant forwarded to him for review was not worth the while. "Fortunately the author is not a party comrade, otherwise he could provoke a debate in Leipzig over the Kantian revisionists." Eisner reported that he had recently given a two-and-a-half-hour talk in Dessau expounding his theory of practical work, but the press account was sadly deficient. "Perhaps I will have the opportunity to present the lecture somewhere else, and then a stenographic record would serve as the basis for fruitful discussion."[61] He was alluding to the party congress set to convene in Leipzig, stronghold of his most implacable critics. In the relative calm before the storm Eisner interspersed his political pieces for the *Tagespost* with cultural offerings in an effort to maintain some personal equilibrium. On Thursday, 26 August, a commentary on Eduard Bernstein's quarrel with *Vorwärts* over pay for his submissions was paired with a review of two productions of Max Reinhardt's far-flung Artists' Theater. In the first article Eisner clarified that during his tenure at *Vorwärts* he held to Wilhelm Liebknecht's policy of sustaining all party contributors, regardless of viewpoint. Presenting the spectrum of Social Democratic opinion was, after all, the function of the *central* organ. Accordingly, despite his "occasionally most emphatic criticism" of Bernstein's articles, he nonetheless welcomed continued collaboration. "This conception of editorial professionalism . . . assured that no clique, no isolated entity could perchance emerge, no quiet, shady (and therefore all the more effective) boycott of particular persons and groups could be exercised."[62]

In the theater review Eisner compared Wednesday evening's performance of Shakespeare's *Midsummer Night's Dream* at Nuremberg's Apollo Theater with the same company's 1908 staging of *Twelfth Night* in Munich. Although he took issue with the commercial nature of Reinhardt's super troupe, "something like a theater trust," which rented multiple playhouses simultaneously across Germany, he applauded the stark, minimal sets of the Munich production, a far cry from Reinhardt's cluttered naturalist interiors of old. The pared-down décor, subtly shaded surfaces, and subdued costumes wondrously heightened the effect of the spoken word. No curtain marked a change of scenes, rather "goblins with swaying lanterns slip across the stage" in the dark to rearrange the few props to the strains of a Humperdinck melody. In particular Eisner praised the tragicomic genius of the actor Hans Waßmann as Sir Andrew Aguecheek, whose portrayal of bumbling men of power rendered them all too human. But it was above all the modern staging that produced the greatest effect. "Imaginative suggestion replaces naturalistic imitation, which in any case is still just tempera on card-board, thereby affording the inventive artist opportunity to create the comic and caricature directly on set."[63]

Friday at dawn Eisner was among a group of dignitaries, journalists, and aviation enthusiasts assembled on the outskirts of Nuremberg to wit-ness the approach and docking of Count Zeppelin's *Reichsluftschiff ZIII* (Imperial airship), purchased the previous year by the German Army. The sight of the gleaming leviathan gliding through half light toward rapt spectators filled him with awe. In his report for the *Tagespost* he hailed the craft as an embodiment of indomitable human spirit: "the dedication of intellect to an idea, the energy of steadfast, sacrificial determination undeterred by malicious yapping and shrinking cowardice." That night he scribbled a postcard to Belli to say that he had spent the entire day watching the aerial maneuvers and that he intended to go back out for more before daylight.[64] The next week he wrote to her on Thursday, 2 September, that the dirigible had flown back over Nuremberg once more. "For some time I watched it pass and let it cheer my soul after all the nonsense and nuisance of our mundane existence, of which yesterday's meeting for the party congress gave proof again."[65]

In the midst of his campaign for a Reichstag seat Eisner had to regard the Leipzig congress as a bully pulpit where he might preach the politi-cal agenda of intense practical engagement, the improvement of work-ers' lives and status in preparation for the decisive assault on Germany's state structure. On the day before the proceedings he reminded *Tagespost* readers of the party's debacle at Dresden and underscored the urgency of concerted, positive action. "Once before in a year of brilliant victories we held a party congress in Saxony that bore much of the blame for the sub-sequent stagnation. . . . It would be a fateful error if the party congress, instead of acting, were to effect long debates on one or another more or less frivolous question." The pending national insurance statutes, he argued, presented an ideal venue for meaningful contribution.[66]

On the second day of deliberations Eisner made good on the plan, revealed three weeks earlier to Joseph Bloch, to repeat for a stenographer his theory of practical work. Attending the congress as representative of his Dessau electorate, Eisner presented his ambitious parliamentary ini-tiative as resolution 268, seconded by nineteen comrades. Its wording specified that the national delegation would be "authorized to draft and introduce in the Reichstag an action program of topical legislative projects . . . that embody the creative will of Social Democracy and the proletariat and are so framed as to be readily practicable, even in bourgeois society." The consolidation of labor law as well as reform of the military, school system, tax structure, criminal code and courts might all be addressed systematically by the campaign. For assistance in drafting their bills Eisner envisioned that the party's deputies would formally solicit counsel from extraparliamentary experts.[67]

The debate in that morning's session over national tax code reform, Eisner remarked, would not have occurred if all comrades truly understood that 'practical work' meant that "the party can demand this and that in the present situation . . . to free the great mass of the population from crushing burden." There could be no question as to whether the party should favor direct over indirect taxes, for the slogan 'For this system not one man, not one penny!' was meaningless unless Social Democracy really could block all funding. His audience was well aware that direct taxes, unlike those collected by third parties for the government—sales and exise taxes, for example—were apportioned by the citizen's ability to pay.

To shouts of approval Eisner declared: "I say that more would be achieved for the fight against militarism, fleet-building, and Weltpolitik if we were to bring about so much as the rudiments of direct taxation in the nation than if we give the greatest speeches and say no a thousand times. The moment we succeed in implementing direct taxation in the German Reichstag is the beginning of the end of this system." For once the constituencies of the bourgeois parties realized that through direct taxes they would have to foot the bill for the lavish spending projects of the interest groups supported by their leadership, these voters too would lose their enthusiasm for imperial grandeur. Anticipating criticism, Eisner asserted emphatically that his proposal was neither concession nor compromise but rather "a systematization, an augmentation, or, to make use of the word, a radicalization of parliamentary work."[68]

In the ensuing discussion members of the Reichstag defended their votes on various tax bills as principled opposition to the state. Leopold Emmel protested that the German government itself had made no concessions to Social Democracy that might prompt the party to change its tactic. He characterized Eisner's direct-tax proposal as favoring "the lesser evil," which was in any case still an evil.[69] Paul Singer regarded even the slightest accommodation of their opponents' interests as a tactic "unsuitable to, and unworthy of our party," the first step down a slippery slope.[70] Georg Ledebour ridiculed Eisner's resolution as a "a new bourgeois code of law on the basis of the materialistic conception of history." He quipped that any deputy who cosponsored the resolution should be charged with working out the details, for "any such capacity for work would be extraordinarily valuable."[71] To peals of laughter from the audience Eisner closed with a final rejoinder: "If Ledebour, given his subjective mistrust in the human capacity for work, already considers this effort impossible, if he believes it will take centuries, then I am sadly, reluctantly obliged to forgo our counting on the valuable collaboration of a Ledebour in the still somewhat ongoing work of forging a socialist society." Despite his winning the repartee, the resolution was rejected when the vote was cast minutes later.[72]

On Wednesday, 15 September, the day of the vote, Eisner wrote to Belli that he was fed up and had no more desire to take part in the proceedings, especially in light of the evident generational divide in the party. Moreover, he had learned that Dietz consigned the history of literature to Franz Mehring, all the more disappointing in that Eisner had confided to Dietz that he would resign from the *Tagespost* to take the assignment.[73] Exacerbating the pique was a comic paper circulated at the congress by the *Leipziger Volkszeitung*, which lampooned his preoccupation with foreign affairs and constant 'war prophesying' (while the German and Austrian general staffs were secretly collaborating to refine the Schlieffen Plan).[74]

Upon his return to Nuremberg Eisner presented for the paper's readers a sarcastic, scathing assessment of the congress that reflected his disenchantment.

> After all manner of confusion German Social Democracy arrived again at complete unity and clarity: that is the positive outcome of the Leipzig party congress. Present German politics surely lead the way we must go. Tactical problems that occupy and menace the proletarian movement in politically progressive lands, in democracies and bourgeois republics, do not yet exist for us who still have to fulfill every political requirement of modern development. Therefore our discussions have often been nothing more than debates over the future or past, about theoretical possibilities rather than immediate realities. This general German tendency to political discussions about eventualities is so strong that we ourselves, even once critical decisions have already been reached, reduce the accomplished act to a posed hypothesis never again to become reality and then quarrel about it.[75]

And indeed at a meeting held on Friday evening, 24 September, to brief the local membership on the proceedings at Leipzig, Eisner was called upon to justify his resolution once again. In his recapitulation he noted that Social Democracy had borrowed the rallying cry 'not one man, not one penny' from the bourgeois revolutionaries of the last century.

Donning the logician's mantle, he argued that if the party truly espoused that sentiment, it would be obligated to boycott all parliamentary participation, for any accommodation of the system amounted to collaboration. When the Reichstag considered the fleet bill of 1905–1906, the party's deputies had demanded direct taxes and voted in favor of the inheritance tax. Resolution 268 sought to regularize and facilitate Social Democracy's long-accepted parliamentary work, for its functionaries and union officials could surely address the interests of the working class better than the government's privy councilors. To the good, Eisner allowed that he was encouraged by the debate at Leipzig, which occurred without reference to radical and revisionist camps. He urged those present to mind the greater goal, citing the dying words of the French aviator Ferdinand Ferber, killed two days earlier when his airplane crashed: "How ludicrous to fly so low; I must fly higher in the future."[76]

CHAPTER FOURTEEN

TO FIND A LOST LIFE: FROM NUREMBERG TO MUNICH (1909–1910)

I N THE FINAL WEEKS OF HER PREGNANCY Else Belli moved into a neat, two-storey house acquired by her father in a quiet southwestern sub-urb of Munich.[1] The residence at Lindenallee 8 was situated at the edge of the vast Forest Cemetery in Großhadern, twenty minutes by tram from the city's hub. As much as Eisner would have liked to be with her, he was beset by press deadlines, speaking engagements, professional affronts, political squabbles, and personal anxieties in the North. On 1 October 1909 he wrote from Nuremberg, concerned for his estranged wife's state of mind. "If I had the money, I would send Lisbeth to Pastor Blumhardt in Bad Boll for a few months. In such surround-ings her devastated soul could recover perhaps, and she might finally come to grips with the inevitable." He worried too that the strike at the Ferdinand Wolff confections factory, for which the local party was responsible, might turn ugly. His level of involvement was such that he could "think of little else," but other woes soon arose.[2] In midmonth the Spanish educator Francisco Ferrer, founder of the secular, egalitarian *Escuela Moderna*, was executed by firing squad at Barcelona's Montjuich Fortress in the aftermath of the "Tragic Week" riots.[3] Protests erupted across Europe. The *Fränkische Tagespost* announced on Saturday, the sixteenth, three days after Ferrer's martyrdom, that Eisner and Georges Weill would address the German Center Party's shameful endorsement of "this eruption of medieval benightedness and barbarism" at separate demonstrations the following day.[4]

Sunday morning Eisner spoke to a packed house of solemn mourners at the Saxon Manor Inn on Neutorstraße. Afterward he had walked out to the Forest Café and emptied his purse for a cup of tea. He planned to spend the evening "utterly alone and destitute" at his office poring over Ibsen's just-published literary remains. Worse than poverty and solitude was the current rumor that his personal circumstances were causing him to neglect his work. "When Haller insinuated the like yesterday," he wrote to Belli, "I declared that for one year I have enjoyed the happiest and most productive period of my life. When I was completely shattered two years ago and on the brink of suicide, my editorship was extolled. . . . O holy stupidity!"[5] In the next week he spoke before a crowd of forty to fifty thousand at the burial of a worker killed during the strike and then, despite suffering from the effects of ingesting impure water, to the largest party rally ever held at Regensburg.[6]

Unable to sleep, Belli complained the night of 28 October of growing discomfort. She had laid out clothing and a blanket that day for the new baby and explained to her two-year-old daughter, Freia, that she might expect a brother.[7] Two days later Joseph Belli telegraphed Eisner at the Wettin Hotel in Dresden that Else had given birth to a daughter.[8] That evening Eisner sent his greetings: "I kiss your hand tenderly and imagine what Ruth, Little Wolfgang's older, most reasonable sister, might look like."[9] Concerned that their penury was affecting Else's emotional state, he wrote Friday that he would arrive in Munich the next evening with ham and cheese and that his series of lectures on Marx, postponed from the spring to late November and early December, should yield something for her.[10]

The same Friday the *Tagespost* reported that Nuremberg's Center Party had held a meeting to justify Francisco Ferrer's death sentence by a kangaroo court-martial. Only a fraction of those in attendance were sympathetic to the two clerics who spoke, for Social Democrats had mustered in force to confront the Catholic apologists. The second of the featured speakers attacked Social Democracy as a godless party controlled by Jews. Present as chief agitator was Eisner, who in the open discussion characterized the Center Party as a ruling-state tool for the oppression and exploitation of all workers regardless of their faith. He clarified that among Social Democracy's cherished tenets were the separation of church and state and the recognition of religious faith as a strictly private matter. A number of clergymen, he pointed out, had found their way to socialism in Germany as well as England. Turning to the question at hand, he reminded Catholic workers in the audience that the Center Party's leading paper had censured the Maura government's reign of terror in Spain before Ferrer's death. As Eisner spoke, Georges Weill presented the chair a resolution condemning both Ferrer's execution and the Center's support for the Maura government's henchmen. The chair's refusal to bring it to a vote triggered a mass walkout.[11]

The imminent departure of Weill from the *Tagespost* was announced in mid-November. He had resigned his position as chief political editor to return home to Strasbourg to stand for the Reichstag in Metz, Alsace-Lorraine's fourteenth district. His successor was to be Richard Bernstein, contributor to the Social Democratic monthly *Der Kampf* (The Struggle), a Viennese publication edited by Otto Bauer, Adolf Braun, and Karl Renner.[12] Apart from his lover and child, and with his friend and chief ally moving on, Eisner explored once again his professional options and new channels of income.

At another turning point in his life, while incarcerated at Plötzensee years earlier, Eisner planned to syndicate to Left Liberal journals his reflections on the workings of the Reichstag. Now he envisioned a syndicated feuilleton for the Social Democratic press. He was already producing the like for the *Tagespost* with the *Volksbildner* and the *Furche*. He announced the enterprise in a letter of 17 December to a targeted group of party editors nationwide, declaring that the undertaking grew out of his long experience in assembling arts supplements for well-funded journals. Knowing that papers serving smaller readerships relied on various comrades' correspondence services for their supplements, he readily acknowledged the quality of his competitors' publications but maintained that "a syndication reflecting all facets of cultural life and fostering all forms of the specialized arts section is lacking." Beginning in January 1910, his *Arbeiter-Feuilleton* (Workers' Feuilleton) would provide weekly a topical, comprehensive offering from which the editors might select individual pieces or print in its entirety. He enclosed a preview sample anchored by his own rigorously documented article on the mirror industry in Bavaria, which he billed as suitable for "the broadest public."[13]

"The Eternal Workers" drew on impressions of misery formed while Eisner traced the stages of manufacture from the glassworks in the forests of the Upper Palatinate along the Bohemian border to the mercury-coating plants in Fürth. In September he had visited the town of Neunburg vorm Wald and observed whole families engaged in grinding and polishing glass plates. Housed literally on the factory floor, as many as eight families slept amid the machinery and barrels of rinse water, for the grinding blocks ran day and night and required constant adjustment. The red dust of the iron oxide polishing agent coated everything and choked the air. Legal proscriptions against child labor were generally ignored, fatal accidents attributed invariably by management and their insurance companies to workers' negligence. Endless work shifts alternated with mandatory unpaid 'vacations' lasting weeks on end whenever rain or drought adversely affected the water-powered mechanisms. The most skilled laborers earned 15 marks per week, while managers contracted by the absentee owners to oversee operations pocketed 250 marks. Although

Social Democracy had penetrated the region, the Center Party still held sway. The workers were told by their priests that it was their lot in life to supply the 'Mirror Jews' of Fürth with the polished glass plates for a pittance. Once the finished plates were delivered to Fürth for the mercury backing, the fine work was done mainly by women, who suffered a variety of debilitating ailments from exposure to the poison. Surely no product, Eisner concluded, reflected the monstrosity of capitalism better than the shimmering glass of narcissistic indulgence.[14]

Friday night, 17 December, he reported to Else Belli that he had worked until 02:30 that morning to post the *Arbeiter-Feuilleton* announcement. The production costs had taken his last pfennig.[15] The piece on the mirror workers ran Christmas week in the *Furche*. The final issue of the *Volksbildner* appeared at the end of the month. With the beginning of the new year it was subsumed into the *Furche*.

Saturday, New Year's Day 1910, Eisner posted to fellow editors notice of fees for printing material from the first regular issue of the *Arbeiter-Feuilleton*: 5 marks for individual articles in their entirety, 3 pfennige per line for briefer offerings. He requested payment for whatever they had chosen to run from his trial edition, "in the case it might not yet have been sent," and apprised that only the next number would be handwritten copy; successive issues would be typed.[16] Monday he sat in a meeting of Nuremberg's press commission, chafing at lost time.[17] Later that day he dashed off a letter over dinner at Hotel Schneider to prompt Belli to have her submission to him by Friday. "You *can* work now," he chided, "so you *must* work now." He despaired of putting out as full an issue as he had planned, even if they worked together all day Sunday on it in Munich. He hoped to arrive Saturday with the proofs. As to positive developments, the press commission had unanimously approved the addition of Martin Segitz, his own choice, to the editorial staff of the *Tagespost*, over objections from Haller and Fentz. And Friedrich Stampfer's wife had telephoned from Berlin to ask how she and Ruth were faring.[18]

In midmonth Eisner began a serialized critique of Hermann Oncken's fourteen-hundred-page biography of Rudolf von Bennigsen, leader of the National Liberals. Divulging hundreds of confidential reflections from Bennigsen's unpublished correspondence and personal papers, Oncken afforded extraordinary insight into the often sordid political machinations attendant to German unification and Bismarck's reign of terror over the North German Confederation, the Reichstag, and a succession of Prussian monarchs. In this endeavor Eisner returned to writing history, a congenial medium, as he had shown with *Das Ende des Reichs*. The ten installments of the critique appeared over the next five months in the *Arbeiter-Feuilleton*, constituting a neatly synthesized interpretive essay on the course of events of the half century from the Revolution of 1848 to Bennigsen's dismissal as president of the Prussian province of Hanover in 1897 for having supported increased civil liberties. Although Eisner's main concern in the essay was to trace the Liberals' abandonment of every core ideal in exchange for a semblance of power in the Prussian-German nation, his patent secondary aim was to condemn Bismarck's Machiavellian statecraft.

The first two parts of "Bennigsen: The Tragicomedy of German Liberalism" circulated in the second issue of the *Arbeiter-Feuilleton* and ran in the *Furche* 18 and 19 January.[19] Eisner hailed Oncken's work as "a first-rate source for German party history" and paid respects to Bennigsen himself, whom he found more appealing than Bassermann and fellow political businessmen who inherited the party leadership. "He, in contrast, had something of a cultivated European politician; he had knowledge, ambitions or rather aspirations guided by ideals; and at times even a high-mindedness and finer intellectual sensibility nurtured by diverse cultural riches shone through his wan and a bit jaded rhetoric."[20] As a student of law at Heidelberg he steeped himself in authors writing 'about current social relations, especially about easing the sad lot of the working class.'[21] He joined the Hanoverian civil service, yet in 1848, at age twenty-three, his sympathies were republican, even socialist in the wise of Lamartine and Louis Blanc. Present that summer in the gallery for the proceedings of the National Assembly at St. Paul's Church in Frankfurt, he advocated constitutional monarchy as a transition to democracy, but the Prussian king's refusal of an emperor's "crown from below" in April 1849 and the bourgeoisie's paralyzing fear of red anarchy dashed Bennigsen's hopes.[22] He returned to his post embittered and cynical, withdrawing eventually from public life altogether until the fight for a constitution thrust him to the fore of the bourgeois opposition to the reactionary government of Wilhelm von Borries.

In successive installments Eisner chronicled how, once Wilhelm I had succeeded Friedrich Wilhelm IV, Bennigsen and Johannes Miquel founded the National Union in 1859, seed of the National Liberal Party, to combat conservative, Catholic Austria's domination of the German Confederation and to promote a 'Small German' national state led by Prussia. "The ascendant bourgeoisie," Eisner commented, "needed national unity for economic purposes."[23] The ideal of political freedom was thus subordinated to that of consolidation. When three years later Bismarck was named the Prussian chancellor, the National Union became his instrument for German unification on his terms. When he provoked a war with Austria in 1866 over Schleswig-Holstein, Hanover backed Vienna and became a Prussian province upon Berlin's decisive victory at Königgrätz. From then on Bennigsen pursued a Realpolitik of accommodation, advancing National Liberal Party influence even while abandoning its professed core values. As chair of the party deputation in the Prussian House of Deputies, the Reichstag of the North German Confederation, and the Reichstag of the German Empire, he served as means to Bismarck's ends until Bennigsen's opposition to the antisocialist law and protective tariffs disjointed their collaboration. He ended his political life as president in chief of Hanover, having been named to that office by Wilhelm II, grateful for his contributions to the Prussian-German Empire.

Despite their early demands for popular sovereignty, legal equality, constitutional guarantees for rights of expression, assembly, and affiliation, German Liberals were at heart, Eisner judged, "loyal subjects" whose wealth and education set them at odds with the masses of the truly oppressed.[24] To gain meager concessions from remnants of the ancien régime yet ensconced in Prussia-Germany, Bennigsen and his associates were ever willing to represent themselves as the bulwark protecting property and privilege from "the revolution that others might make if the wishes of the moderates—who themselves certainly neither would nor could make revolution—were not granted."[25] On the other hand Bismarck, whom Eisner regarded as "the most intelligent" of the Junker, passed himself off to the Liberals as moderator of "the wild men of the feudal world." Through his skillful manipulation "it became German liberalism's function to rescue the conservative cause from the Conservatives, the Junker way of life from Junkerdom." As their own ideological agenda was increasingly relegated to the realm of the future, Bismarck referred to the Liberal leaders dismissively as 'the crown prince's ministers.'[26] Still, Bennigsen had recognized that the workers' movement had brought politics in Europe to a historical turning point, the crossroads of social progress and violent anarchy.

Eisner takes every opportunity here to underscore his archvillain's perfidy. Historians have long suggested Bismarck's complicity in the alleged assassination of the deposed Bavarian king Ludwig II, whose perplexing death on the shores of Lake Starnberg in June 1886 smacks of criminal conspiracy. Ludwig's personal debts from lavish spending on the arts and architecture threatened the economic stability of the Bavarian state and undermined Bismarck's national military budget. Eisner goes a step further by implicating Bismarck in Max Hödel's failed attempt on the life of Emperor Wilhelm I in May 1878, impetus to the reintroduction of the antisocialist law, which the Reichstag, at Bennigsen's impassioned urging, had rejected once before. Hödel, generally characterized as "half-witted" or "half-crazed," fired multiple pistol shots from close range as Wilhelm and his daughter rode past in an open carriage on the crowded boulevard Unter den Linden, yet no one was hit.[27] "In this game of intrigue from 1877/78 Hödel's assassination attempt is so perfectly timed, so on cue as in a comedy, that to deem it coincidence would demand belief in miracles. One cannot be rid of the suspicion that the pistol, in all probability loaded with blanks, was put in the hand of the Christian Social dupe by those who required the assault. . . . The 'danger of Social Democracy' emerges at the precise moment when the terror was desired."[28]

Of particular interest in Eisner's essay are his judgments of Bismarck's efforts to negate the progressive influence of South German states in both the North German Confederation and the German Empire. After 1866 the Blood and Iron Chancellor rattled the Prussian saber at France whenever liberal forces marshaled for expansion of constitutional rights and guarantees. "Bismarck's politics of securing domestic dynastic-Junker hegemony through foreign imbroglios culminated in the Franco-Prussian War."[29] The diabolical stratagem hinged on his goading Napoleon III to war in the belief that the South would ally with Paris to cast off Berlin's yoke.[30] The march on the French capital was merely one thrust of Bismarck's greater campaign to divide and conquer the bourgeois opposition at home. "Crossing the Main on the way to German unity served the singular purpose of extending Prussian autocracy to the South."[31] To liberate the South then from East Elbian domination, Eisner, as head of the Bavarian Republic, contrived the converse by seeking an alliance with France against Prussia.

Having spread himself beyond thin and fretting over finances, Eisner was prostrated by influenza in late January. The lingering physical misery bred depression. Isolated and targeted, he was living now in a room of Bernstein's ground-floor flat on Wodanstraße.[32] On the twenty-first Eisner wrote to Belli that he felt as utterly alone as "an old tramp" and speculated that he might well succumb without anyone being aware of his demise. His son Reinhard had paid a visit, but only to deliver Lisbeth's demand for more money. That night he determined that he did not have the luxury of being sick any longer, that he would pull himself together and go back to work.[33] Vain hope. The next day Lisbeth herself came to call and implored him to move back home where he could be cared for. When he quietly but firmly declined, she pronounced him 'completely mentally ill' and left in a rage. Lack of money precluded medical treatment, but he expressed to Belli confidence that he was hardy enough to pull through even without it. "Frau Lisbeth need not worry yet that I might die and deprive her of her precious money."[34] Belli wrote on 22 January that their daughter was thriving at her breast and had been told that her father was "the poorest man in the world."[35] Lisbeth now directed Reinhard to write to Belli to accuse her of plunder. Informed of it, Eisner prescribed a response: "I am not angry with you, but you are old enough to realize how such rudeness wounds and vexes a man like your father." When the boy returned to Wodanstraße, Eisner sent him away with the warning that he would disown him if there were another offense.[36]

Partially recovered and more conscious of mortality than ever, Eisner boarded the train to Berlin to see his mother and to renew critical acquaintances. He took her to luncheon at the elegant Kempinski Wine Rooms in Charlottenburg and called on Lily Braun the next day.[37] Returning to work in Nuremberg, he felt listless and was given to moments of gloom. "I still lack spark," he wrote to Belli on Wednesday, 2 February, "and sometimes it seems that I might expire gently in peace with all my poor unborn and unfinished works, nevermore hear Beethoven, and never see you and our Ruth again. It would grieve me a bit not to have attained a Blüthner piano and a few quiet years together with you." He urged her to eat better and get more fresh air.[38] On the fifth Karl Fentz demanded that Eisner return the key to the storage room he had been let at the *Tagespost* complex on Breitegasse and that he clear the editorial office of his private library, "as we can no longer abide its being completely trashed by this mess."[39]

August Bebel's reminiscences, just published by Dietz in advance of his seventieth birthday, generated glowing reviews throughout Germany. The *Tagespost* acclaimed the book in its lead of 5 February as detached reflections on a tempestuous life by a great man gone from driven by history to driver of history. Privately Eisner damned it as "a wretched, philistine book" appealing to the audience Bebel merited. "He has a brilliant *bourgeois* press! Now then is it suggestion or more: elective affinity? It really belongs in the bourgeois parlor, at hand to teach bourgeois children nicely how through industry, frugality, and strong moral values a poor orphan can eventually become a highly respected fellow citizen and well-off man of means. How gigantically in contrast towers Liebknecht's figure . . . , how powerfully Ignaz Auer's proletarian pathos. I gradually understand how the party has now come to be just a solid business venture with Bebel and Singer."[40] In Berlin the Party School's celebration of Bebel's birthday on the twenty-second ironically underscored Eisner's assessment. Before the day's lectures commenced, Franz Mehring addressed the chosen, the proletariat's privileged elite, hailing the party chairman as a key founder of the enterprise, reflecting on the lessons they might learn from Bebel's own hard-won education, and urging them to emulate his exemplary rise.[41]

Circulation of the *Arbeiter-Feuilleton* resumed with a note that the interruption stemmed from the editor's illness. The third issue's offering included five dark vignettes signed with the familiar pseudonym Kesr: "The Swindler," "Indecency," "The Murder," "The Willing Sacrifice," and "A Lieutenant and Ten Men."[42] He apprised Belli on 10 February that Stuttgart's *Schwäbische Tagwacht* (Swabian Daily Watch) had run its first selection from the *Feuilleton*, her seasonal piece "Shrovetide Plays." He urged her to make use of the book on gardening that he had posted to her the previous day. Complaining of languor and cheerlessness, he envied her situation: "It is splendid to be free, secluded, and absorbed in work."[43] Under the pen name Zero, reflecting the consciousness of his state of flux, Eisner began a string of sonnets. In "Demise of Dust," dated 16 February, he employs the imagery of a comet's disintegration to convey the free fall of changing course.[44] On the following Sunday afternoon his four younger children—Ilse, Hildegard, Eva, and Hans—came to his residence at his invitation, and they all went for a walk despite his lingering symptoms. That night he was up late composing a sober assessment of Bebel's career. "The writing is dreadfully hard for me," he confessed to Belli. "What all has been scribbled about the man is absurd. . . . Marx, Lassalle, Liebknecht—no one amounted to as much."[45] The *Tagespost* commemorated Bebel in a marginally tempered panegyric on Monday, focusing on the festivities in his honor. "Not in solemn pause and contemplation," it opened, "does the proletariat celebrate now the man who, as the last from the heroic age of socialism, embodies its political history and social self-consciousness."[46]

Increasingly distraught at the prospect of her husband's departure from Nuremberg, Lisbeth Eisner sought to enlist an accomplice to go with her to Munich to assault Else Belli. When report of the plan came to Eisner, he cautioned Belli to lock the house and to familiarize herself with his revolver.[47] In the next days he had more yet to contend with. Between 1908 and 1909 the *Tagespost* enjoyed a RM 12,000 increase in subscriptions and advertisements, yet the balance had gone from a RM 37,000 profit to a 15,000 loss. At the 24 February meeting of the press commission Eisner attributed the downturn to Karl Fentz's mismanagement. Fentz in turn demanded Eisner's dismissal. The commission elected to postpone a vote on the motion. "Thus I will beseech the gods," Eisner wrote the next day to Belli, "that the press commission might be so idiotic as to send the party press's best editor packing. Then I *will be compelled* to go, have no responsibility, have breached no duty, and could begin the struggle for a worthy existence at your side in good conscience."[48] On 28 February Eisner was informed by letter that his library and furniture had been placed in storage, the expense of which, RM 14.40, was being docked from his pay.[49] The same day Hermann Wallfisch, business manager of the *Dresdner Volkszeitung* and Kaden Press, wrote indignantly to Fentz to protest his outrageous behavior. "In my twenty years in the profession I have never heard of one employee demanding that another employee in the same firm be sacked. . . . See to it that you recover your former composure and coolheadedness and come to an understanding with Eisner. He is, to be sure, a complex character, and I concede that it might not always be easy to deal with him. But the Eisners of the party are damned scarce, and you won't find many with his decency, reliability, with his enormous diligence, and with his passionate love of party."[50]

Albert Südekum, Nuremberg's Social Democratic deputy to the Reichstag, recorded in his journal on 5 March that he had been summoned to a meeting of the *Tagespost* directorate on the thirteenth to resolve the conflict. Südekum insisted that no decision be made before a hearing could be scheduled with Eisner and Fentz.[51] The invitation to address the directorate on Maundy Thursday, 24 March, only annoyed Eisner, ready now to make a clean break and booked to appear at party events in Nuremberg, Frankfurt, and Schweinfurt.[52] Concerned about the status of his Reichstag candidacy, he wrote to Julius Kaliski in Berlin on the eleventh: "It occurs to me that Dessau has not summoned me to a rally since August of last year. Might any of you have heard why? I know that some are working against me there too. In the end I shall lose this divine good fortune as well." He likened his situation in Nuremberg to that at *Vorwärts* in 1905, with his present opponents recyling Bebel's past accusations. Certain of the outcome, he took a decidedly fatalistic view of his lot. "Thus this time, Kali, I shall be thrown out a stone-dead man. Time will tell if I can come back to life yet again. . . . I am calmer, cooler because I have no more illusions to lose."[53]

Wednesday evening, the sixteenth, an audience of fifteen hundred assembled in Nuremberg's Hercules Velodrome to remember the March Revolution. Beethoven's third *Leonore* overture prefaced Eisner's talk on Ferdinand Freiligrath, transformed by the events of 1848 from favored poet of King Friedrich Wilhelm IV to laureate of the workers' movement. A performance of *Eroica* by the Philharmonic Orchestra, recitations of Freiligrath, and two chorales rounded out the program, which had been organized by the local party's education committee.[54] Having determined that the time had come to force the issue of his release, Eisner tendered his resignation as editor of the *Tagespost*, effective 1 July. Among his papers at the German Federal Archive in Berlin-Lichterfelde is an undated draft announcement that he and the directorate had reached an "amicable agreement"; in the interest of both parties he was stepping down in good standing to fulfill contractual obligations for book-length projects due in the next two years.[55] Notice of Eisner's planned departure appeared in the paper on Saturday, 19 March. The next day he wrote to Belli that opinion was decidedly against Fentz and the directorate, so much so that they might try to retain him. "But I will guard against that," he assured.[56] At the Maundy Thursday meeting Südekum, who favored retention, negotiated a settlement encouraging Eisner's continued collaboration as regular contributor.[57] In a spring sonnet titled "Resurrection," disseminated by the *Arbeiter-Feuilleton*, Eisner expressed his sense of liberation and rebirth with a sanguine tercet:

> A butterfly flutters bright on yellow wings,
> in all the heights a seeking singing rings.
> The distant flows into my thirsting soul."[58]

A letter of 31 March to Belli echoes the sentiment: "In your young spirit I hope to find a lost life. You are to be my own self."[59]

An invitation to speak at Dessau did indeed come. Eisner was called to appear Easter Sunday, 27 March, at a mass demonstration for universal suffrage in Prussia. His concern, however, at waning local enthusiasm for his candidacy proved well founded. On Tuesday after the demonstration Peus entreated Eisner to return the following Sunday for another engagement. "Several among the leadership here believe that you are not making your voice heard. Some wanted Liebknecht, Ledebour, and the like. I adamantly insisted *it is a matter of honor that you speak*. Through that you must become known to the thousands." Rudolf Breitscheid, an ally of Ledebour, was to share the rostrum.[60] Unwilling yet to concede to rival comrades, Eisner shuttled back to Dessau, then hurried on to Berlin to confer with friends.[61] Saturday, 2 April, he wrote to Belli from Dessau that his successor at the *Tagespost* was to be Wilhelm Herzberg, editor of the *Pfälzische Post* in Ludwigshafen, "a thoroughly decent sort but no dazzling performer."[62]

Two weeks later Eisner received a letter from Dessau requesting that he address pernicious rumors that he had fathered a child by his lover, that he had been dismissed from the *Tagespost* for misappropriation of funds, that he spent half his time with his lover in Munich, that he had let his lawful wife and children go hungry. "I know that I belong to the reviled, the cast aside," he confided to Belli. "I certainly did not court the Reichstag nomination in Dessau, nor is it of any personal consequence. I accepted it simply because I was asked. If I lose it now though, if it can be wrested from me, then the door is open to every defamation, and I shall be swept away by the maelstrom." His only recourse, he ventured, was to remain constant to his work, to her, and to the dictates of conscience.[63]

On Sunday, 24 April, Eisner embarked on a week-long speaking tour of Baden, with scheduled appearances in towns along the Rhine, including Strasbourg, Rastatt, and Karlsruhe. Tuesday in Strasbourg he took time out from giving talks and filing articles to dine at the home of Georges Weill.[64] The following Monday he was back in Nuremberg to address an assembly of metal workers on the topic "The Culture of the Workers' Movement." The evening after May Day observances the crowd at the Becken Garden Beer Hall was large and spirited. Tracing the history of labor from slavery in ancient Greece through the Luddite rebellion to Australian workers' current campaign for a six-hour day, Eisner framed the mission of the workers' movement as the pursuit of a worthy, productive existence. In Germany, where only women enjoyed the legal protection of a ten-hour workday, much was left to achieve. Labor's purpose, he continued, should be neither the creation of capital assets nor the material sustenance of the individual worker but rather the cultivation of humane, communal values that refine society as a whole. "When we ourselves demand more from life, we advance culture. Thus every reduction of the workday, every improvement of wages and conditions represents cultural progress, for we gain time for ourselves and release from anxiety." The *Tagespost* reported that his remarks were greeted with long applause.[65]

Three days later Südekum met with Eisner and Herzberg in Berlin to discuss the transition of leadership at the paper. Eisner repeatedly denied inciting his supporters to insurrection. Realizing now that he was about to take up residence in a hornets' nest, Herzberg sought to inform himself about the conflict and agreed to take counsel with Südekum when in doubt. In mid-June Südekum presided over a joint meeting of the *Tagespost* directorate, the press commission, and local party officials in Nuremberg to smooth the rift over Eisner's departure.[66] Eisner wrote to Belli on 23 June, however, of ongoing recriminations against those staffers closest to him. "All of it fills me with such disgust that I am quite nearly paralyzed physically and mentally, almost incapable of work."[67]

Belli was busying herself with preparations for his arrival in Munich, converting a room into a library for him. Her father had come from

Stuttgart to do household chores and assist with the children, which allowed her time to play the violin each day and plan an article for *Gleichheit*.[68] In the midst of packing his belongings Eisner dashed off a postcard on Tuesday, 28 June, urging her to remain vigilant, for Lisbeth was plotting bloody vengeance.[69] Accompanied by Richard Bernstein, he went to Lisbeth's residence later that day to take his leave, a visit that ended with "a wild madhouse scene."[70] On Kurt Eisner's last day as editor in chief at the *Fränkische Tagespost* Albert Südekum wrote from Berlin to thank him for his efforts in Nuremberg, to bid him a fond farewell, and to invite him to write for *Kommunale Praxis*, offering 20 marks per article.[71]

CHAPTER FIFTEEN

SOMETHING OF A PARTY
OFFIZIOSUS IN BAVARIA:
POLITICAL EDITOR AT THE
MÜNCHENER POST (1910–1911)

A S EISNER HAD SURMISED PRIVATELY, his candidacy for Dessau's
Reichstag seat was effectively doomed. Friday, 1 July 1910, Heinrich
Peus appeared in Nuremberg to investigate firsthand the rumors of professional dissolution and personal dissipation. Adolph Hoffmann, whom
Eisner counted among the ruinous "Berlin clique," had offered to stand
in his place. Confronted by Peus with what Karl Fentz and Max Walther
had said of him, Eisner resisted the impulse to withdraw on the spot and
remarked coolly that Peus would have done better to speak with people
"other than scoundrels." After interviewing members of Eisner's camp,
Peus returned to Dessau incensed at Fentz's willful misrepresentations.
Eisner went first to Berlin then to Dessau to shore up his campaign,
but the damage could not be undone.[1] On 5 July Peus met with Albert
Südekum in Bitterfeld to assess the sustainability of Eisner's candidacy.
Once Südekum had voiced his opinion, Peus proposed Julius Kaliski
in Eisner's stead. Südekum suggested Wolfgang Heine. Heine visited
Südekum on the eighth and consented to stand.[2] One month later the
Social Democratic Press Bureau in Berlin announced that a "change of
his professional and personal circumstances" impelled Eisner to resign his
candidacy in favor of Heine.[3]

Resettled in the Bavarian capital with Else Belli and their infant
daughter, Kurt Eisner at age forty-three struck out in new directions.
Although he continued to speak at party functions near and far, Eisner
channeled rejuvenated energies into his freelance writing, fresh family life,
and a position on Adolf Müller's editorial staff at the *Münchener Post*.
The change of scene restored him. He resumed professional contact with
Joseph Bloch and Heinrich Braun and immersed himself in South Bavarian
activism. Bernhard Grau observes that "astonishingly soon Eisner fell in

step again and found his place in the political and social life of the city and the local party organization."[4] Gone was the despair he had confessed to Kaliski just three months earlier, dispelled the inability to work that had plagued him in the final days at his desk on Breitegasse. In a letter to Social Democratic newspaper editors he outlined an expansion of the *Arbeiter-Feuilleton* to provide reviews of books and journal articles of topical interest.[5] Just over a week after arrival in Großhadern he apprised Bloch on 15 July that, far from suffering from the exhaustion of ordeal, he was experiencing "an astounding zest for work" born of newfound freedom.[6] Doubtless with tongue in cheek Bloch wondered in reply if the long-awaited article on Napoleon were done and then asked if Eisner might furnish an article with the title "Anatole France as Socialist."[7]

But Eisner was pursuing his own projects at the moment and required assistance from Belli, whom he asked to clear her schedule a few days each week "for dictation and copying."[8] On 17 July he scratched a postcard to Braun, now organizing an anthology on Napoleon for the Berlin press Morawe & Scheffelt, to report that he had begun outlining his essay that day and to propose to translate part of Louis Napoleon's *Des idées napoléoniennes*. He added that he would soon acquire an Underwood typewriter, a boon to all of his correspondents. He had spoken the previous day with Wilhelm Hausenstein, who also was set to draft something for Braun's planned volume.[9] On another front Eisner planned to file syndicated reports from the fifty-seventh general meeting of German Catholics 21–25 August in Augsburg and from the International Socialist congress 27 August–4 September in Copenhagen.[10]

Despite the havoc of unpacking his books and files, both he and Belli worked prodigiously to put out replete issues of the *Feuilleton*. For the mid-July edition he demythologized the artificially cultivated saintly image of Prussia's Queen Luise on the hundredth anniversary of her death, documenting her as a sycophantic "femelette," naive meddler in affairs of state, and petty schemer whose overriding concern was to safeguard ruling-house privilege from Napoleon's assault.[11] Belli contributed a fictional tale of a young woman's self-liberation from her artistic but domineering husband and likely authored a commentary, though signed "—t —r" so as to drive marketability, on the fatal shooting of the Stuttgart court diva Anna Sutter by a former lover, conductor Aloys Obrist, who then turned his Browning pistol on himself.[12] In keeping with the severance agreement negotiated by Südekum with the *Fränkische Tagespost*, Eisner's treatment of Queen Luise appeared in the *Furche* on 19 and 21 July. His review of Hungarian choreographer Ernst Matray's ballet pantomimes ran on the theater and arts page of the *Münchener Post* on 10 August.[13]

In conjunction with the Catholic meeting in Augsburg, the *Arbeiter-Feuilleton* offered editorials on an array of church doctrine and policy. One essay deplored the mandatory celibacy of priests as a medieval relic, a perverse institutional hypocrisy contributing in many cases to "pathologically heightened sensuality" and ultimately to criminal abuse of their spiritual office.[14] Another briefly noted that Defoe's *Robinson Crusoe*, one of the "dozen books of world literature . . . that have truly entered the collective consciousness," had been judged by a Jesuit priest as suitable reading for young people only after 'rigorous editing.'[15] Censorship is the theme of Belli's story "The Realm of the Mute" as well, in which a dwarf presents the king with a machine that snatches tongues from heads.[16]

Eisner's reports from the congress of the Second International in Copenhagen give voice to renascent exuberance after the emotional trial of his abortive Reichstag campaign. There he reveled in the egalitarian society of the Danish capital, "prelude to the social republic," where the nine hundred delegates met in the baroque palace of Schiller's patron Count Schimmelmann, its walls bedecked for the occasion with red banners. Soldiers amiably joined the parade of workers, the police belonged to a union, and the Social Democratic unions, in a symbolic statement of their standing in the community, had commissioned sculpture that adorned the modern town hall's entrance. Among the cosmopolitan mix of languages, minds, and personalities Eisner renewed his acquaintance with Jean Jaurès and rediscovered the "endless laughter of life" in jovial gatherings after the day's deliberations. No laughing matter, however, was the pressing, contentious issue for the Copenhagen congress, just as it had been three years earlier at Stuttgart: the necessity for prescribed, concerted action to prevent or end a war. And once again the Socialist International was riven by national party interests. At the closing reception in the resplendent town hall Jaurès, pressed to speak by members of the German delegation, rose and chillingly foretold a coming bloodbath that would usher in the new age of man.[17]

At noon Monday, 5 September, Eisner boarded the train to return home. He was already planning to cover the national SPD congress, set to begin on the eighteenth in Magdeburg. There he anticipated seeing Adolf Müller, evidently to cement Eisner's regular collaboration on the *Münchener Tagespost*.[18] *Der wahre Jacob*, the party's popular semimonthly arts and entertainment journal, had subscribed to the *Arbeiter-Feuilleton* Copenhagen issue, assuring greater exposure for the venture.[19] Circulated to coincide with the opening of the party congress, the mid-September issue featured Eisner's advice to the delegates in "Magdeburg Sauerkraut" under the byline Kesr.[20] Here Eisner drew on long experience to offer counsel in piquant snippets: "Before you go to the party congress, draw up a list of participants you can stand and those you cannot. Always vote with latter and good decisions will ensue. . . . It is a misfortune for a speaker to present clear arguments; his opponent considers it a singularly outrageous nuisance. . . . Moral indignation is the mind's trick to save itself having to think. The single word 'Schweinehund' has had more effect than all philosophy and science combined. . . . Only that discipline is revolutionary the practice of which demands risk and sacrifice."

"Magdeburg Sauerkraut" ran in the 18/19 September edition of the *Münchener Post*. Thereafter Eisner's work—articles on politics and economics, reviews of books and performances, reports on debate in the Bavarian Landtag on Prannerstraße—significantly enriched Müller's paper, enhancing particularly the standing of the feuilleton in Bavaria's cultural center.[21] Eisner joined Martin Gruber, Paul Kampffmeyer, and Max Kratzsch on the editorial staff.[22] Although his special preserve was the arts page, his diverse contributions addressed the spectrum of public life. Charged by the party executive for Bavaria with covering the Landtag sessions from the press gallery, he provided cogent summaries rather than the customary stenographic record of speeches.[23] For the next few years Eisner served as Müller's indispensable lieutenant, for in addition to functioning as editor in chief of the *Post*, Müller was a key tactician of the Social Democratic deputation in the Landtag, directly concerned with Eisner's reports of the proceedings.[24]

Their pairing was congenial and mutually beneficial. Like Eisner, Müller had studied at university before turning to journalism and socialism. Both men had begun their careers at Berlin's Herold News Agency, an experience that imbued them with a distinctly international viewpoint.[25] More recently they shared the vision for a Social Democratic education campaign to uplift the masses rather than germinate a proletarian intelligentsia in a hothouse of Marxist theory. The same measures Eisner and Maurenbrecher implemented in Nuremberg—systematic introduction to diverse academic disciplines, progressive training in critical thinking, public lectures on topics of broad interest, rich cultural offerings—were championed by Müller and Kampffmeyer in Munich.[26]

Now Müller was the party's highest paid editor, earning 6,000 marks annually, more than had Eisner at the *Fränkische Tagespost*, 1,000 more than Kautsky at *Neue Zeit*. Eisner's pay as an associate editor would figure at 4,000 marks each year, supplemented by income from the *Arbeiter-Feuilleton*.[27] At this stage in his life, after turbulent tenures in Berlin and

Nuremberg, Kurt Eisner was content to have regular work as Müller's subordinate, all the more so since Müller had reined in the press commission by effecting regulations requiring approval of the local Social Democratic Voters' League for virtually any measure limiting his authority over personnel, purview, or publication of the *Post*. "With that the press commission was checked," writes Müller's biographer Karl Heinrich Pohl. "Then it was thoroughly disenfranchised by the election of [Sebastian] Witti, a close political ally of Müller and Vollmar, as its chair."[28] Thus loosed temporarily from the burdens of leadership and at some remove from the personal turmoil to which he was subjected in Nuremberg, Eisner fairly luxuriated in the new post, the productive creative partnership with Belli, and a private life at their home on Lindenallee, however great the demands to provide for two families.

On Sunday, 25 September, Eisner wrote to Heinrich Braun that he had been unable to finish the promised article before the trips to Augsburg and Copenhagen, as he had to "win bread for a great many heads each day in addition to that."[29] Three weeks later he sent out his treatise on Napoleon's German policy with a note reaffirming the interpretation advanced in *Das Ende des Reichs* as the "only possible one."[30] That fall Eisner produced a special issue of the *Arbeiter-Feuilleton* commemorating the centenary of Berlin University, founded through the offices of Wilhelm von Humboldt, "the only intellectually significant and free-thinking Prussian minister of education."[31] The commemorative issue was followed by a documentation of tuberculosis twenty years after Robert Koch's vaccine and an appreciation of Tolstoy's gospel upon his death at eighty-two on 20 November.[32] An article on the growth of American cities contrasted their footprint and character with those of Old World towns where defensive walls necessitated cramped quarters and narrow alleys that precluded modern transit systems and skyscrapers.[33]

In reports for the *Münchener Post* Eisner attacked the Center Party for routinely concocting outrageous fabrications against Social Democratic officials and initiatives. "This is precisely how the Center and its press do battle. . . . They lie like the devil and deceive as a matter of principle."[34] Early in December he reviewed Dr. Marie Bernays's exhaustive study of the spinning and weaving industry in Mönchengladbach, the Center's hub for antisocialist propaganda, and expressed admiration for her methodology and conclusions. To gain greater insight into the lives of her subjects, the young sociologist had worked in one of the mills for several weeks. Although she held her colleagues' spirituality for the one uplifting element of their existence, her carefully compiled statistics and documentation of the workers' cultural milieu gave lie to the Catholic pamphleteers who claimed that the church's social policy had profoundly bettered the lot of labor. "In facts and figures Marie Bernays's book unintentionally depicts the cultural devastation that capitalism brings about in its supremely Christian, boundless, and unbridled way in the Center Party's domain."[35]

Joseph Bloch wrote to Eisner on 10 December to solicit an essay on "a prominent personality of significance to us (but preferably an artist or scholar)" for inclusion in *Sozialistische Monatshefte* in the new year.[36] Eisner offered to portray Marie-Joseph Chénier on the hundredth anniversary of his death.[37] Bloch readily accepted, although he professed little enthusiasm for the choice, then chided Eisner for having submitted "a very fine article on Offenbach" to the journal of the People's Free Stage rather than to his serial.[38] At month's end Bloch gushed at what Eisner sent him: "It is exactly what I wanted—Chénier not as an independent artistic personality but rather as a reflection of a great period."[39] Indeed, Eisner feted "the dramatist of the Revolution" in multiple essays. The one for Bloch presents a detailed analysis of Chénier's themes in the context of his political career, which set him at odds with his monarchist brother, the poet André Chénier, who went to the guillotine in 1794. Another article, less academic, was circulated in the *Arbeiter-Feuilleton* and included in Eisner's *Gesammelte Schriften* (Collected Works). Here Joseph Chénier's humanist outlook comes to the fore. Both pieces dismiss his form as utterly conventional in its classical unities and neat alexandrines. What Eisner esteemed in Chénier, beyond his ethical grounding and enlightened mind, was the immediacy of content, the continuation on stage of ardent social debate for a vocal audience of *sans-culottes* directly engaged in the great upheaval. How different was Germany's theater of the time, where revolutionary passion raged only "from the orchestra pit to the wings."

The man whose *Charles IX, Henri VIII, Jean Calas,* and *Caïus Gracchus* enunciated the Jacobin creed reluctantly voted for the king's execution in the Council of Five Hundred but later broke with the radicals to denounce the Terror as irrational and dehumanizing. Despite his credentials as member of the committees of public education and safety, Chénier drew the wrath of the anarchist Montagnards with *Law Not Blood* and lived under proscription and threat of death until Robespierre's head dropped into the basket. Joseph Chénier's politics were his art. "The oneness of the writer and the politically active man, which is the pride of French literature from Voltaire and Rousseau to Zola and Anatole France, also forges the link between drama and contemporary history."[40] It was a model Eisner himself would follow in a few years from a prison cell.

From eighteenth-century drama for the masses to the mass medium of film, the Eisner-Belli publishing concern provided clients with abundant cultural offerings. The 31 December 1910 issue of the *Furche* printed "The Cinematograph in the School," in which Belli, under Eisner's initials, hailed motion pictures as a promising didactic tool to supplement text and lecture, chase monotony, and animate learning. "Every school has a larger hall, many a physics laboratory that can be readily darkened. I can imagine a 'movie afternoon,' as someone writes in the *Zeitschrift für Jugendwohlfahrt* (Journal for Youth Welfare). . . . I see a long line of cheerful, excited children streaming into the hall where a giant screen signals hours of delight. What seemed so incomprehensible earlier that morning becomes clear to them then: they see before them the silkworm's metamorphosis, almost smell the tropical flowers, almost hear the strange tongues of native peoples."[41]

Early in 1911 the enterprise expanded to the New World. On 16 January the *New Yorker Volkszeitung*, German-language organ of the Socialist Workers' Party of North America, ran Belli's story "Pink Fluff" with Eisner's byline.[42] Surely readers well familiar with the work of the cultivated man of letters would have wondered at the style and subject matter of certain pieces. The arrangement by which Eisner fronted for her, allowing her to submit her work as his, virtually guaranteed publication and generated income for the family, trumping considerations of both authorial ego and personal brand. His myriad speaking engagements and titanic workload no doubt hindered his production for the *Arbeiter-Feuilleton*, and since she had honed her skills under his close tutelage, her ghosting for him was mutually acceptable. Their partnership realized the collective ideal in this wise and others. Belli opened her home to his children from Nuremberg, and once she and Eisner could legally wed in May 1917, he claimed Belli's older daughter, Freia, as his own. When Eisner drafted his will in March 1911, he named Belli sole heir to his "fortune, property, and rights," but enjoined her to distribute monies equitably to Lisbeth Eisner and her children.

Specifically, the 5,000 marks from his life insurance policy with Victoria was to be divided equally between his two families. He appealed to the chair of the Workers' Press Association to award half the benefits due upon his demise to Belli and her children, regardless of their common-law relation to him. He directed that Lisbeth retain all household furnishings in her possession but left his extensive professional library to Belli with the expectation that she would not disperse it but rather donate it eventually to the Vorwärts Workers' Education Association in Munich. A third of all royalties from past and future publications was consigned to his children from the first marriage. As his literary executor, Belli was to seek counsel from Friedrich Stampfer, Julius Kaliski, and Georg Gradnauer with regard to publication or republication of his writings. In a separate paragraph Eisner bade her do what she might for his offspring should the need arise. "That I must be apart from my children Reinhard, Ilse, Hilde, Eva, and Hans and have no influence on their intellectual and moral development fills me with deep sorrow." He presented the document to Belli for safekeeping.[43]

Why Eisner saw fit to prepare a will at forty-three is in large part a matter of conjecture, but he had already expressed concerns to Belli. The bout of influenza that laid him low the previous winter gave cause to meditate on mortality. His long-fought campaign against the Center Party, to which Hermann Cohen urged him nine years earlier, had won new enemies in Munich, the virtual Rome of South Germany's overwhelmingly Catholic population. And in March 1910, a few days before he was to speak at a huge protest rally in Dessau, he did indeed "bequeath by testament" to Belli his library should he "fall victim to some police saber."[44] In February 1911 Eisner had been called upon to address meeting after meeting in Saxony—"thirteen in twelve days," he wrote from Chemnitz on the sixteenth—taxing even his immense energies to the point of exhaustion. After one of the meetings a miner remarked that Eisner's articles had caused him to picture the author as a strapping, robust young comrade. "The man almost wept with regret as if I already lay in my grave."[45] On the way there Eisner had stopped in Nuremberg to visit his children. After half a year in Munich he took pleasure in their change. Reinhard, the troubled youth so willing to do his injured mother's bidding a year earlier, had matured into "a powerful worker type, strong, self-confident, and good-natured." Ilse now bore a pronounced resemblance to her aunt Toni in both appearance and manner. Lisbeth asked if he would still be legally bound to support her if she remarried. When he told her no, she announced she would likely content herself with an affair (which would prevent him from wedding Belli).[46] Although Belli still enjoyed her hale father's support, Eisner clearly wanted to ensure her independence. In any case the will legitimized her claim to the lion's share of his material assets.

In addition he still feared Lisbeth's potential for violent confrontation. In January he had written for the *Arbeiter-Feuilleton* a personal commentary on a tragic case, the murder of the head of the Nuremberg Girls' High School, Dr. Herberich, in April 1910 by his wife, an outspoken suffragette who alleged domestic abuse. For shooting her husband in the heat of an argument, she was sentenced to four and a half years' imprisonment.

"I knew both people undone in this marriage scandal," Eisner remarked. "Both became victims." He admired the headmaster as a superior pedagogue with broad intellectual interests and pursuits, a Shavian, unbiased and judicious, articulate and socially adept. Frau Herberich, on the other hand, he characterized as shallow yet ambitious, painfully conscious of her subsidiary standing, volatile, tactless in discourse. Ill-paired though they were, her husband knew full well that if they were to divorce or even to separate, he would forfeit his job. Consequently, they quarreled privately, vehemently, in a conventional bourgeois marriage of convenience. In such a soulless union between increasingly incompatible parties, Eisner ventured, "anything is possible, *anything!*"[47] Although he had quit a dysfunctional marriage, he remained acutely aware of the threat his lawful wife's vindictive urge posed to his new life.

The prospect of being victimized by the police and courts, with which Eisner had ample experience, was a constant for opponents of the regime. Early in 1911 a perjury sentence that had sent seven Ruhr miners to prison in 1895 was overturned. The convicted were leftist activists whose leader, Ludwig Schröder of Dortmund, was assaulted by Gendarm Münter at a union meeting in Herne-Baukau. Münter brought suit against a miners' newspaper that reported the incident. At trial Münter testified that Schröder had attacked him. Schröder and the six witnesses who disputed Münter's testimony were charged with lying under oath. The court in Essen heard the case in August 1895 and meted out the maximum sentence, a combined total of nineteen years' detention. Schröder's attorney, Dr. Victor Niemeyer, worked tirelessly for redress, documenting Münter's history of alcoholism, brutality, and conscious misrepresentation. When the court reversed itself, several of the principals were long dead, including Münter. The others had been broken "in body and spirit" by their incarceration.[48]

Eisner's commentary appeared under the pen name Venturus in *Pan*, the avant-garde Berlin journal edited by Paul Cassirer, Wilhelm Herzog, and Alfred Kerr. In the absence of a constitution declaring the inalienable rights of the citizenry, he wrote, "Prussia is still ruled by the same provincial law in which Friedrich the Great's scholars practiced the art of Prussian jargon to disguise the dictatorship of force (state expediency) with liberal legal phrases." Expediency was determined by the kaiser or his agents, chief of whom were the police, whose paramount duty was to preserve the state. The state in turn vested the police with authority to render and impose a death sentence *stante pede* by means of saber or pistol. If called on to appear in court, the policeman, like all uniformed personnel, enjoyed privileged credibility: his oath trumped that of any civilian, a quaint remnant of feudal class law. Thus the lives of seven upright men could be wrecked by an unconscionable, professional thug in state service.[49]

In March the *Arbeiter-Feuilleton* printed the first installment of Joseph Belli's *Die rote Feldpost: Erinnerungen aus der Zeit des Sozialistengesetzes* (Red Field Post: Reminiscences from the Time of the Antisocialist Law), in which he recounted the smuggling operation by which newspapers printed by Social Democratic exiles in Switzerland were illegally disseminated throughout Germany. The series ran through the summer and was published in book form by J. H. W. Dietz the following year.[50]

Toward the end of March Eisner turned his attention to Alsace-Lorraine. Since its annexation to the Reich in 1871 the territory had been under Prussian rule. In response to mounting popular demands for a constitution and full statehood, the German government made concessions. At the urging of the Prussian Ministry of the Interior, the kaiser granted a constitution, effective 31 May, recognizing Alsace-Lorraine as a junior state with an appointed governor, establishing direct election of a Landtag, and allowing for a limited voice in the Federal Council (Bundesrat). In the midst of the deliberations Chancellor Bethmann-Hollweg registered his irritation at the upstart demands with the quip "politics are the art of the possible," prompting Eisner to reflect on the true political pretender in the twentieth century. After all, for peoples steeped in republican tradition and values, the feudal cast of the Prussian-German Empire was perversely necromantic. "Our governing statesmen, however," he wrote, "are buffoons from the past who want to preserve a bygone era when all the seeds of the future have already sprouted." Bethmann and his like could not be counted as serious politicians because they were incapable of grasping the historical dictates of the modern age. "All human development is leading to democracy and socialism, to the free political and economic self-determination of the whole. That is the possible because it is the necessary."[51]

The day after the First of May demonstrations Heinrich Braun thanked Eisner for bringing his colleague Paul Kampffmeyer to author a column on factory inspections and labor relations for Braun's new journal, *Annalen für soziale Politik und Gesetzgebung* (Annals for Social Policy and Legislation). He asked if Eisner might consider providing a similar critical survey of social conditions.[52] But Eisner was busy with other projects, one of which was his expansive review of the second part of Lily Braun's autobiographical novel, *Memoiren einer Sozialistin: Kampfjahre* (Memoirs of a Socialist Woman: Years of Struggle). The critique appeared in the 19 May issue of the *Münchener Post*.[53] He began with an intimate observation of how she had changed of late, her face reflecting the inner peace of one who had achieved clarity after long trials and relentless persecution. In a recent conversation, he divulged, she had expressed particular enthusiasm when "I told of my ever firmer conviction, arising from the experience of my 'educational lectures,' of how greatly the masses hunger for a positive, all-encompassing, uplifting worldview, for a vital religion of socialism that simultaneously embraces faith and knowledge, movement and goal, feeling and will, thinking and acting, the prosaic practical work and the idealistic future yearning." He was gratified to find that her book ended with a call for just such a vibrant, unifying secular creed over and beyond the cogitations, deliberations, and promulgations of a professional party elite.

The novel recalls events momentous and mundane, from the London women's congress of 1899 to the Berlin suffrage demonstrations of 1910, shedding new light on the contentious party congresses at Mannheim and Dresden, Reichstag election campaigns, the mechanics of grassroots organizational work, and the dynamics of intramural rivalry. Eisner hailed the candor of her revelations of sexuality, faulting only her delicate style when treating what he regarded as universal human ken and, as such, an inherently socialist issue. From her first affiliation with Social Democracy, the daughter of a Prussian general was suspect to her chosen comrades as ambitious and domineering. Never having won their full confidence left her embittered for years. Drawing on his long acquaintance with her and on his own occasional status as pariah, Eisner tracked her progression from injured outcast to serene sage secure in the knowledge that the cause itself is greater than all idiosyncrasy. He appreciated the recognition that the source of her anxiety lay in the conflict of commonality versus self, discipline versus desire, party versus personality. Once one lost oneself in the cause, self became inviolable. Later that summer Heinrich Braun lamented the reception of his wife's work. "Apart from your review and maybe one or two of the hundreds that have appeared, what has been written about the book thus far is wretched rubbish."[54]

A quarter century after the death of Ludwig II the Bavarian press and public perfunctorily observed the anniversary of their former king's pathetic demise. Had he lived, he would have turned sixty-six in June 1911. In a six-part series titled "After 25 Years" Eisner examined how fundamentally Bavaria had changed in the interval. So great was the difference that he ventured this would surely be the last sentimental commemoration of the Swan Knight, the romantic so add odds with his age, for future generations simply would have no understanding of his dreamily escapist mindset. Technological innovation was changing the world daily: flights of fancy had become reality, the swan-drawn caique superseded by motorized aircraft. Statistics on Bavaria's economic development since 1886 documented steady industrialization, a concomitant decrease in birthrate and infant mortality, and rise in longevity. Whereas Bavaria remained Germany's largest and most productive agricultural state, land ownership, unlike in East Elbia, was increasingly decentralized, passing from great estates to small farmers. Expanding transportation grids, telephone connections, and postal delivery put an end to the isolation of remote farmsteads. The social and political institutions lagged behind other development, but in these realms too progress could be reckoned. Twenty-five years earlier the Social Democratic Party was an outlaw organization. Now it alone, he declared, "draws the inevitable conclusions from the economic facts: only democratization and socialization can marshal and mold the colossal economic forces of the present."[55]

A conspicuously archaic institution was the Reichsrat (State Council), upper house of the bicameral Bavarian parliament, which Eisner profiled in "The High Seats," so titled because their gradation, from wooden perch to cushioned armchair, reflected the relative status of the occupants, from bourgeois cabinet minister to hereditary nobility. The scions of rapacious robber barons were now entitled to appropriate by legislation spoils that their forebears wrested by sword, dagger, or marriage. In the twentieth century the pillage and plunder occurred legally through protective tariffs, inequitable taxation, and wage slavery. In this venture the ancestral lords of the Reichsrat were abetted by the Center Party, which worked hand in glove with the gentry to maintain conditions so necessary to the survival of the church and its political advocates. As Bishop Anton von Henle of Regensburg had remarked the previous year in Council upon defeat of a bill mandating a 5 percent income tax, "Menial must remain menial!"[56]

On 1 July 1911, on orders from the kaiser himself, the gunboat *Panther* anchored at Agadir on Africa's northwestern coast, joined shortly by two more German warships, and the second Moroccan crisis was up to full steam. Forty days earlier French troops had occupied Fez, purportedly to quell a rebellion against the sultan and safeguard Europeans in the capital. In the belief that France, contrary to the Algeciras Treaty of 1906, intended to strengthen its hand in Morocco, Chancellor Bethmann's secretary of state, the gruff Alfred von Kiderlen-Wächter, demanded concessions in French Congo to ringing applause from the colonial lobby and jingoist press. That Paris spurned his gambit was bad enough for Germany's prestige; far worse was that London regarded Berlin's unannounced naval display as an intolerable affront and consequently stepped

closer to the French. Kiderlen urged the kaiser to war, but Admiral von
Tirpitz convinced Wilhelm that the navy had too much to lose. The
German government backed down in humiliation. On 4 November it
agreed by treaty to quit Morocco. As a sop France ceded a sizable patch
of wasteland in Central Africa, and thus the First World War was postponed for a bit.[57]

From the onset of the confrontation the *Münchener Post* sounded
repeated alarms. The lead of 4 July warned of another German adventure
in Weltpolitik that might test "the international proletariat's battle-read-
iness."[58] The next day a front-page article speculated that the Prussian
Landtag had been dismissed the previous week so that the government
might once again pursue mischief abroad without parliamentary interfer-
ence from any quarter.[59] On 8 July the lead summarized Jean Jaurès's
interpretation, published in *Vorwärts*, that Germany's show of force was
calculated to bring the French to the bargaining table. There Bethmann
evidently hoped to win lucrative African territory by diplomatic coup.
Where the provocation had succeeded wildly, Jaurès told his German
comrades, was in inflaming anti-German sentiment among his compatriots.[60] Throughout July the *Post* decried the Moroccan action and its supporters. On the thirtieth Eisner thoroughly refuted the claim of colonial
lobbyist Albrecht Wirth that German industry would soon grind to a halt
without iron ore from Morocco, displacing millions of workers. With no
factual documentation Wirth asserted that Moroccan ore reserves were
ten times their estimated value of 100 million marks. Had Wirth bothered
to peruse the statistics, Eisner rebutted, he would know that Germany
was already spending well over 100 million marks annually to import iron
ore. "Therefore the arithmetic reveals that the Moroccan iron billion figure, equally impressive and fantastic, would be less than nothing. Even
assuming that the reserve were that great, that it could be mined and
brought to Germany in its entirety, thanks to the acquisition of Morocco,
this supply too would be consumed in less than a decade, in less than five
years if indeed German iron reserves were exhausted."[61]

The *Post* ran on 8 August Eisner's "Diplomatic Understanding," four
fictional conversations between key figures in the crisis. In the first satire Kiderlen and France's ambassador to Germany, Jules-Martin Cambon,
find common ground in their exaggerated sense of self-importance. In
the imagined negotiations Eisner targets intentional obfuscation of events
by the governments and their allies in the press—August Sperl and the
Parisian daily *Matin* are mentioned by name—as well as any accord that
would give rise to future rivalry and conflict.[62] Two days later the Social
Democratic Party's executive committee issued its strongest denunciation

of the feverish warmongering.[63] Monday evening, the fourteenth, Wolfgang Heine spoke on the theme "Weltpolitik, World War, and Social Democracy" to a crowd at the Munich Kindl Beer Hall.[64]

Eisner revisited the culpability of Germany's bourgeois press in "The Public-Opinion Business," a clever, barbed essay published in the 16 August issue of *Pan*.[65] At the recent meeting of the national press association in Eisenach its chairman underscored the moral obligation to uphold journalistic integrity and incorruptibility. "Thus," smirked Eisner, "the heroic, ethical defiance of people who seethe with indignation at demands no one makes on them, who cannot be bought because there are no buyers." Of their own accord, uncritical and unquestioning, the German press already championed the dubious colonial enterprise gratis and swayed the misinformed to sell their birthright for a mess of pottage. The obsequiousness was baffling. "If Mannesmann Brothers, with the mobilization of German world power, were to succeed in gaining access to iron-ore mines in Morocco, it would be of course an immense gain for them. . . . But what interest does the German journalist have in a corporation's supply concerns?" Were he himself to propagandize for the colonial venture, Eisner proclaimed, he would enhance the status of the German press by charging a handsome fee: at least 1,000 marks for anything for Kiderlen, 5,000 for Mannesmann. When he was arranging his papers a few years later, he appended a note to the article, marking it "document from the incubation period of the world war."[66]

The wretched state of the German press figured in Eisner's essay on the satirist Jonathan Swift for the 7 September issue of *Sozialistische Monatshefte*.[67] With the end of censorship in England in 1693 the free press flourished. London alone boasted eighteen newspapers within a decade, and "one could print in England what would still be punished a century later in Germany on the gallows and wheel." The once-lowly journalist wielded immense political influence through public discourse, and the nation, liberated from the strictures of both absolute monarchy and Cromwellian puritanism, began its rapid ascent to world power. In the new age of unfettered scientific inquiry Newton codified the laws of physics, English philosophers addressed human happiness, and national economists studied social relations. In Swift's heyday, Eisner wrote, "every politician, every statesman is in some capacity a writer, journalist, scholar too, and every man of letters is in some wise also a politician."

In early September Eisner criticized colonialist demands for the partition of all Morocco into zones for exploitation by designated European powers. Southern Morocco, coveted prize of the Pan-German League, was inhabited by three hundred thousand Berber warriors eager to wage jihad on any invader attempting to plunder their land's resources. For the sake of private profit, a coterie of venture-capitalist freebooters would demand the protection of a sympathetic military command, whose forces' incursion would generate renewed conflict with France and Britain. "In the last decade the current German colonies cost us 500 million more than they yielded. . . . Germany itself remains among the poorly developed lands. Every cloudburst wreaks colossal devastation because our watershed network is still in its infancy. Every summer month without rain parches the fields because irrigation has yet to be introduced. From the tidal shallows we could win fertile farmland for countless people, but for that there is no money! . . . Of Germany's 54 million arable hectares 6.2 million are fallow or barren; in France, with the same agricultural acreage, only 3.8 million are unused." Had the monies squandered abroad to further Wilhelm's Weltpolitik been spent mindfully at home, Eisner argued, the fatherland would be a veritable Eden.[68]

In the midst of the peril the party congress took place 10–16 September in Jena. Eisner attended as a correspondent, filing reports to the *Post* and his various subscribers. On the eve of the first session he encountered Bebel, and the two dear antagonists chatted in passing.[69] Jaded by long experience, Eisner confided to Belli on the eleventh that Victor Adler's address alone broke the monotony of opening formalities. "Then everything went back to being dull and trivial." The business as usual included Rosa Luxemburg's charge that the Social Democratic leadership had been lukewarm in its condemnation of the Moroccan episode, an assertion with which he agreed, yet his approval was dulled by cynicism. "Rosa, that shrewd, spiteful creature, flaunts her intellectual superiority to the entire party executive and for once is right; precisely for that reason she is being deserted by everyone now." His top priority was to be productive enough that he might return to Munich with funds for a two-day vacation in the mountains with Belli.[70] Leisure time had become an extravagance, encumbered as he was with manifold duties. At the end of the month Eisner explained to Heinrich Braun the delay in getting copy to him: "I am now something of a party *offiziosus* in Bavaria and completely overwhelmed by it."[71]

Perhaps the chance casual conversation with Bebel, the chairman's ringing indictment at Jena of the latest eruption of Weltpolitik, and the knowledge that the old man was flagging moved Eisner to a more charitable review of the second volume of the reminiscences. The critique, which appeared 3 and 4 October in the *Post*, applauded Bebel's evident desire to deemphasize his influence on the party's growth during and after the years in exile. This narrative reserve Eisner deemed fitting, for any committed Marxist would concur that the movement molded the man, pushing him to the fore rather than following his lead. August Bebel was the personification of a collective will. "Previously it was only individuals, a few, who were steeled to heroism by trial; now the masses themselves were schooled to be the hero. Unshakable, sacrificial determination became the German proletariat's permanent inheritance from Bismarck's politics. Thus something greater was allotted to the little master turner from Leipzig than to all other secular leaders: his life, cause, work, and future became one."[72]

On 5 October and again on 28 November Eisner examined relative German and French reactions to the Moroccan crisis, referring first to an article by Camille Pelletan for *Matin* and then to a monograph by Pierre Felix, an infantry officer whose views were attracting considerable attention in Paris. In Germany rumor of war had prompted a run on the banks and attendant financial chaos. The German people, Pelletan observed, had reason to worry while the French remained calm, a difference he attributed to their respective state systems: republic versus monarchy. "France knows itself master of its fate; it need not fear that a government it controls could plunge it into a chance war against the national will. . . . Germany did not enjoy the same confidence because it does not have the same constitutional guarantees." Given as he was to rash rhetoric and provocation, or "tom-tom politics," Kaiser Wilhelm was an undeniable threat not just to his own subjects, but to all Europe.[73] Captain Felix took a decidedly proactive stance to the German threat. Written when the ink of the Morocco-Congo Treaty was still damp, his *Et maintenant? Le désarmement ou la guerre!* argued that what had deterred Berlin was the predominant British fleet—a deterrent that crescent German naval might would soon void. The time for decisive action was at hand. Either the European powers must agree to disarm, maintaining only an international force of a hundred thousand men and four cruisers for mutual defense, or they would eventually fight an unimaginably devastating war.

Eisner agreed with Felix's assessment of Germany's aims and a European war's consequences, but he had no confidence in bourgeois governments and their diplomats to prevent the cataclysm. The most effective army for preserving the precarious peace was the international proletariat mobilized in common cause. "The catastrophe lurks at the threshold. The danger is greater than ever. Social Democracy alone is peace." The first test would be the naval expenditures bill scheduled for consideration by the new Reichstag. By tying all military funding to an income tax, the party could derail the imperial juggernaut.[74] As he had written in *Pan* three months earlier: "If the article is incorporated into

288 ♦ Something of a Party Offiziosus in Bavaria

the German constitution that a sufficient war tax on the income, assets, and inheritance of the wealthy comes into effect at the moment of mobilization, then rest assured the world peace conferences will become superfluous and the Court of Arbitration at The Hague can be converted into a casino, cinema, or ice-cream palace."[75]

In waning autumn Eisner memorialized Heinrich von Kleist, the conflicted Prussian playwright who a hundred years earlier had shot himself on the banks of Berlin's Lesser Wannsee. In his brief life could be read the tragedy of a gifted misfit, a Junker with cultural aspirations who in the end could not escape the dual curse of class and convention. The man who infused Greek dramatic form with Shakespearean vitality, whose works "set tranquil Weimar classicism ablaze" died in destitution and despair, much of his best work, "tragedies of fate on the anarchic personality," yet unknown. At fourteen Kleist began his military career, as befitted young men of his station. But after seven years he resolved to 'leave a position in which I was incessantly martyred by two absolutely contradictory principles, ever in doubt whether to act as a man or as an officer.' Study of Kant and Rousseau, restless travel to France and Switzerland, a broken engagement to the daughter of a Prussian general, financial insecurity, failed literary attempts, a breakdown left him without prospects. Reduced to dependence on royal favor, the former cosmopolite turned to patriotic paeans against Napoleon. His last play though, *Prinz Friedrich von Homburg*, draws on his earlier dilemma. By disobeying the king's order, the dreamy prince leads his troops to a great victory for Prussia— and faces a death sentence for breach of discipline. Eisner pronounced it Kleist's final "protest against all things Prussian, the poet's foreboding acknowledgement that he would die of it."[76]

Kurt Eisner at thirteen. Photo by Oscar Roloff, Berlin.
SAPMO-BArch, BildY 10/200/91 N.

The Eisner family: Emanuel seated *center*, Hedwig standing *top right*, Martha seated *right*, Kurt, seated *far right*. Photo by Fritz Leyde, Berlin. SAPMO-BArch, BildY 10/213/91 N.

Kurt Eisner and Lisbeth Hendrich. Photo by J. Müller, Eberswalde.
SAPMO-BArch, BildY 10/210/91 N.

Kurt Eisner, 28 May 1893. SAPMO-BArch, BildY 10/204/91 N.

Lisbeth Eisner with children, Reinhard *right*, Ilse *left*, Hilde. Photo by W. Küpper, Marburg. SAPMO-BArch, BildY 10/208/91 N.

"Get up! That's no couch!" Kurt Eisner's drawing for the
"Plötzenseer Bilderbuch," *Der wahre Jacob*, 22 October 1901.

1902 Party congress in Munich. Kurt Eisner standing *second from right* behind Georg Ledebour. SAPMO-BArch, BildY 10/10717 N.

Feste der Festlosen

Hausbuch weltlicher Predigtschwänke

von

Kurt Eisner

Verlag und Druck von Kaden & Comp., Dresden, Zwingerstraße 22.

Title page for *Feste der Festlosen*, 1906.

Adolf Braun and Kurt Eisner in the editorial offices of the
Fränkische Tagespost. Photo by J. Muscat, Nuremberg.
SAPMO-BArch, BildY 10/211/91 N.

Kurt Eisner. SAPMO-BArch, BildY 10/205/91 N.

Lindenallee 8, Großhadern, on the outskirts of Munich. CJA 6.4/70/7/2.

Kurt Eisner preparing to speak at a party rally in Dresden on
17 April 1910. SAPMO-BArch, BildY 10/206/91 N.

DAUERKARTE

HAUPTKARTE

№ 1412

Für Herrn Kurt Eisner

Nicht übertragbar. Zum beliebigen Besuch der Bay=
rischen Gewerbeschau 1912 in München während der fest=
gesetzten Besuchszeit mit Ausschluß derjenigen Veranstal=
tungen, welche ein Sondereintrittsgeld erheben. Bei Verlust
wird die Karte nicht erneuert. Mißbrauch der Karte hat
deren Einzug und gerichtliches Einschreiten zur Folge. —

Eigenhändige Unterschrift:

Press credential for the 1912 Bavarian Trade Fair.
SAPMO-BArch, NY 4060/1/187-188.

Munich Press Ball, March 1913. *Left to right*: SPD Landtag member Adolf
Köster, Frau Köster, Kurt Eisner, Else Belli, attorney Adolf Kaufmann. Photo
by W. Hammer, Munich. SAPMO-BArch, BildY 10/212/91 N.

Lindenallee tea with Raoul Heinrich Francé, Ruth, Ilse, Kurt Eisner, Else Eisner, Annie Harrar. SAPMO-BArch, BildY 10/203/91 N.

Kurt Eisner in January 1918 before his arrest. Photo by
Germaine Krull. SAPMO-BArch, BildY 10/10668 N.

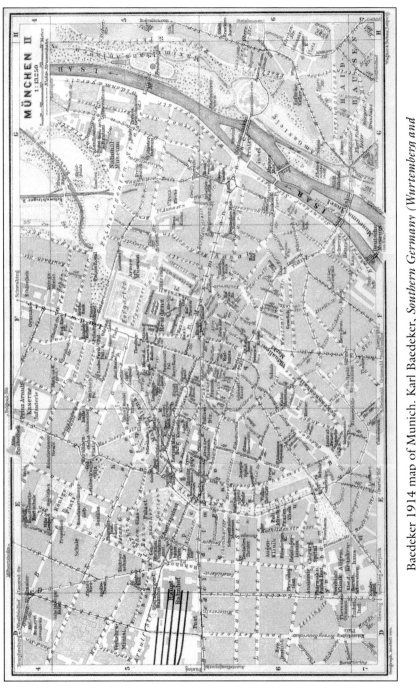

Baedeker 1914 map of Munich. Karl Baedeker, *Southern Germany (Wurtemberg and Bavaria): Handbook for Travellers*, 12th ed. (Leipzig: Karl Baedeker, 1914), 245.

"Excellency Scheidemann 1918," drawing by Kurt Eisner. BayHStA (Bayerisches Hauptstaatsarchiv München), MA 1027/75.

Für Freiheit und Recht!

Kurt Eisner
Bayerischer Ministerpräsident

"For Freedom and Justice! Bavarian Prime Minister Kurt Eisner." Postcard
printed by Ludwig Welsch Press, Munich, circulated 17 November 1918.

Felix Fechenbach, Kurt Eisner, Dr. Friedrich Muckle in
Berlin for the *Reichskonferenz* of 25 November 1918.
Süddeutsche Zeitung Photo / Alamy Stock Photo.

Else and Kurt Eisner, Hans Unterleitner on the way to the Provisional National Assembly. SAPMO-BArch, BildY 10/2591/67 N.

Cabinet ministers Hans Unterleitner, Edgar Jaffé,
Erhard Auer. SAPMO-BArch BildY 10/314/92 N.

Impromptu shrine erected on the site of Eisner's assassination,
21 February 1919. SAPMO-BArch, BildY 10/2238 N.

Kurt Eisner 1919. Photo by Robert Sennecke.
SAPMO-BArch, BildY 10/10575 N.

CHAPTER SIXTEEN

AT PEACE WITH MYSELF: RESETTLING INTO FAMILY LIFE (1912–1913)

T
HE REICHSTAG CAMPAIGN OF 1912, Wilhelmine Germany's last national
election, was hailed as a great victory for the Social Democratic Party
and a resounding defeat for Weltpolitik. Winning four and a quarter million votes on the first ballot, over a third of the immense turnout, the
party eventually claimed 110 of the 397 seats after runoffs, a gain of 67
from the 1907 debacle, 19 more than the second-place Center Party. For
the first time since the founding of the Reich, Social Democrats were the
dominant deputation, having won 27.7 percent of the mandates. In the
days leading up to the first polling on Friday, 12 January, Eisner and fellow functionaries fanned out across South Bavaria to rally the rank and
file. On the morning of the sixth he spoke in Prien, later the same afternoon in Endorf, and the following day in Kolbermoor.[1] On the eve of the
election the party's two candidates in Munich, Sebastian Witti and Georg
von Vollmar, addressed crowds at beer halls in their respective districts.[2]
The banner of Saturday's edition of the *Münchener Post*, circulated late
Friday afternoon, urged readers to the polls yet before the 19:00 close.

In its combined Sunday/Monday issue the *Post* reported the heady
results. Vollmar had been reelected in Munich's second district; Witti
was in a runoff with Left Liberal Georg Kerschensteiner in the first.
Nationally, Social Democratic candidates appeared to have won 67
districts outright and advanced to the second round in 120 others. In
runoffs in which no Social Democrat remained on the ballot, the party's voters were poised to sway the outcome to best advantage. The
lesson, Eisner wrote, was clear: "Whoever allies himself with Prussian
Junker reaction is forever lost." The Black-Blue Bloc of Center and
Conservatives was smashed.[3] Furious agitation preceded the second
round of balloting. On the seventeenth Eisner targeted proponents of
protective agricultural tariffs and low wages.[4] On the twenty-third an

editorial on the Reichstag's role in international affairs demanded the "democratization and parliamentarization of foreign policy" in the wake of Bethmann's near-disastrous Moroccan caper. "With the same decisiveness as before but with greater strength now, Social Democracy will oppose every criminal attempt to plunge the nation into war without the knowledge and against the will of the people."[5] When the final tallies were done, Witti lost narrowly to Kerschensteiner, who benefitted from Center Party support; Eisner's former Nuremberg associate Georges Weill won his race in Metz; and Wolfgang Heine, Eisner's replacement in Dessau, was elected in the party's sweep of Anhalt's two districts.[6]

In Bavaria's Landtag elections of February 1912 the Left and Center-Left parties collaborated to advance joint interests. In an effort coordinated by Adolf Müller and Erhard Auer, Social Democrats joined Left Liberals, Liberals, the German Peasants' League (Deutscher Bauernbund), and the Bavarian Peasants' League (Bayerischer Bauernbund) in a common front, the Red Bloc, against the Black Bloc of the Center, Conservatives, and Agrarian League. The Red Bloc's main goals were to supplant the Center Party in the second chamber, to expand electoral reform via proportional representation, and to declericalize the public schools and civil service. Although the Social Democrats and their allies took 50.7 percent of the total vote and significantly increased their representation, the Center won 87 of the 163 seats to retain control of the Landtag. The government of Clemens von Podewils-Dürniz was dissolved, and on 9 February 1912 Prince Regent Luitpold, in a nod to parliamentary authority, asked Georg von Hertling, chair of the Center Party's Landtag delegation, to form a cabinet.[7] In the last year of the First World War he would become the penultimate chancellor of Imperial Germany.

Just after Bavaria's Landtag elections Eisner observed the hundredth anniversary of the birth of Charles Dickens, the great serial chronicler of gaudy and gritty life in industrial England, with a two-part article for the *Post*.[8] At month's end Eisner was in Berlin, where he, Friedrich Stampfer, and Wilhelm Herzog went out one night on a Dickensian mission to document for a human-interest story the state of the old vice dens. "It was very comical," he wrote to Belli. "Vice was prohibited by the police in some places, out of business in others. So we sat in some café until morning, philosophizing on literature and women's issues."[9] His *Arbeiter-Feuilleton* continued to prosper nonetheless. Leo Kolisch contributed accounts of travels in South America. Julius Zerfaß filed reports and provided fictional pieces, poems, and essays. Else Belli's work, mainly vignettes based on observations of children, appeared in every issue under her own name, initials, or the pseudonym Speranza.

At the end of March Joseph Bloch asked if Eisner might consider taking over the column "Intellectual Impulse" for *Sozialistische Monatshefte*. "Comrade Hausenstein, who was writing it, is ready to give it up as he is pursuing entirely different topics now."[10] But Eisner was no less engaged with manifold projects than Hausenstein. In April the *Arbeiter-Feuilleton* called for republication of Joseph von Görres's *Das rote Blatt, eine Dekadenschrift* (The Red Page, Journal of a Decade) from 1798, "one of the greatest rarities of the book trade." Before Görres became a fanatical ultramontane, he had been an equally fanatical republican, advocating the secession of the Rhineland and alliance with France. Despite Görres's later service to the cause of reaction, his early writings were "among the strongest testimonials of German revolutionary spirit."[11] The next month Eisner's article "The Philosopher of Social Enthusiasm: At Fichte's 150th Birthday" appeared in *Sozialistische Monatshefte*.[12] Supremely erudite yet perspicuous and cogent, the essay masterfully synthesizes German thought since the French Revolution and evinces why Bloch offered Eisner the regular column.

As young men Fichte and Görres had much in common until the latter fell away into reactionary religiosity. In contrast, declared Eisner, Fichte "belongs to the wholly isolated figures of our classical age who, defiant and upright, go their own way." His path took him to Kant, but whereas Kant's grounding was in mathematics and science, Fichte's concept of subjective idealism drew on social ethics. His highest reality and ideal was the absolute I, or self, which embraced collective identity. That collective, eventually enunciated in *Reden an die deutsche Nation*, was defined by an emerging popular consciousness of a higher social order superseding the boundaries of principalities and the dictates of their rulers. Post-Holocaust scholars such as Isaiah Berlin and Robert Nisbet regarded Fichte as a founding father of national socialism, but Eisner had a different read twenty years before the birth of the Third Reich: "Fichte's fundamental idea can be expressed most simply now: his absolute I, his god, is nothing other than democracy and socialism as operative goal-principle, to be attained by the enthusiasm of engaged belief in this end." This secular faith in concerted reason to construct an ethically based society advanced the German Enlightenment to its zenith, for Hegel's dialectical synthesis was merely the conditional amalgam of conflicting forces' gains, or reason's 'ruse': divine providence in the guise of human progress. Little wonder then that Ferdinand Lassalle had "discerned the spirit of the workers' movement in Fichte."

Had Fichte been born English, Eisner surmised, he might have become a leading statesman rather than an embattled academic. In

England's freer air thought had more direct application to life. "English philosophy is worldly wisdom; German philosophy is a world unto itself apart from life." German thinkers' extreme introversion, their absorption with ideal schematics resulted from their inability to shape public life in a police state. Although Fichte overcame his fellows' impulse to obscurantism, his influence was no greater, even among those regarded as Germany's most cosmopolitan minds. His obdurate atheism and republicanism were deemed tactless by Weimar's court aesthetes, who conspired to drive him from the professorship Kant had helped him secure at Jena. Fichte's appointment at Berlin University derived from the state's misunderstanding of "his brand of patriotism," which was rooted in national education, not Prussian particularism. By the end of his life he had given up writing, contenting himself with his lectures. His premature death, five hundred days before Napoleon's defeat at Waterloo, likely "spared him being locked in a prison or driven into exile or even succumbing to intellectual-moral atrophy," as had Görres.

The cavalcade of illuminati continued with an appreciation of Rousseau on the two-hundredth anniversary of his birth and a personal tribute to Hermann Cohen on his seventieth birthday. More than any of his contemporaries, Eisner wrote for the 29 June issue of the *Post*, Rousseau shaped the thinking of the Age of Revolution, which found its first expression in the constitution of the United States. "The mind of this unhappy and restless, pathologically burdened, singular man spilled into the cultural consciousness of all humanity and in our own time gave rise to yet another secular pilgrim in Tolstoy."[13] The next week Eisner lauded Cohen, in the final days of his last semester, as Marburg's beacon, the only senior professor at a Prussian university who had remained Jewish, Germany's greatest living philosopher. Looking back on their relationship, Eisner gratefully acknowledged the neo-Kantian master's impact on his own life. "Never before had I met anyone who made such a lasting impression on me. Later, when I went other, at times unfamiliar ways, I found some, to be sure, to whom I felt bound by respect, men such as Ignaz Auer, Victor Adler, Jaurès. But only one ever exerted intellectual influence on the essence of my being: Hermann Cohen, the molder of men. And in all the tumult and storms of life the wistful memory of my time in Marburg remained vibrant."[14]

The pieces on philosophers were followed by an essay treating drama and the dramatist's milieu. That the spark of literary genius ignited at all, flared up, and shed light in many a dark corner of the planet was something of a mysterious quirk, wrote Eisner. That any play ever actually came to be staged was mere fortuity. "Drama transforms a scrap of chance into coherent necessity; it organizes the accidental. But drama itself is a product of blind chance from the moment of its conception up to its coming to life in the world." Disputing the platitude that genius is born of distress, he asserted that it, like any creative talent, had to be nurtured socially. Otherwise, the East Elbian peasantry would have sired a race of artists and scholars, and droves of wealthy merchants' cultivated sons never would have pursued belletrism as their calling. Once the playwright's work was done, its production depended on a host of compradors: publishers, impresarios, directors, thespians, critics, cliques. The poet's triumphant struggle to convert inspiration into invention was all too often voided by mundane commercial considerations. One popular movement, however, was imposing order on chaos across Germany now: the People's Free Stage that Eisner had first championed some two decades earlier. The collectivization of a public for pure theater "irrespective of any financial success" had freed art from market constraints and regularized great stagecraft. This cooperative, communal venture prefigured "the future state."[15]

In sharp contrast to the constructive influence of the Free Stage was the effect of Munich's satirical journal *Simplicissimus*, haven to those cultivated bourgeois sons unsuited to the family business or practice. One of their own, Frank Wedekind, had written a play in 1908 that savaged his fellows. Its performance by Munich's Comic Theater in August 1912 prompted Eisner to reprint his original review of the text. The new production confirmed that *Oaha* was "a literary catastrophe," "hopelessly stupid," "the tragedy of a fragmentary talent." Eisner paid due homage to the ruthless wit of the *Simplicissimus* set of self-avowed, apolitical radicals in ridiculing Wilhelmine Germany's faults and failings, but he faulted their failing, so evident in Wedekind's case, to raise anything from the rubble of wreckage. So brilliant in other respects, the magazine offered no direction to its public. "This imp knows nothing sacred on earth; that is his strength. But then he can produce nothing new or sacred; that is his sterility."[16]

Although fifteen thousand workers turned out in foul weather for the opening ceremonies of the party congress at Chemnitz on Sunday, 15 September, "the bosses spoke not a word," Eisner wrote to Belli the next day from the City of Gotha Hotel, "that moved heart or even mind." He gave his blessing to her proposed visit, while in Berlin for a few days, to Franz Mehring and asked that she greet his bitterest detractor for him. "The man has been so maltreated by his own clique as to have atoned for all his past, present, and future sins."[17] Having been commissioned by Dietz to chronicle the watershed year 1813, Mehring had recently sought to reestablish contact with Eisner, who at the behest of the party executive had worked on the same topic for some time.[18] Indeed, in July he had circulated in the *Arbeiter-Feuilleton* the first installment of a serialized history of Napoleon's Russian debacle one hundred years earlier.[19] The slight by Dietz would have vexed him more in the past, he admitted to Belli, but long experience with snubs, insults, and taunts from supposed comrades had left him philosophical. Now, when initiatives for which he had fought in obscurity and opprobrium had become party policy, he reveled quietly in triumphs others claimed as their own. "I am at peace with myself (with you), and my passion is that you too may learn the same and prevail. Getting free of vanity, malice, and self-pity leads to life."[20] That night, after the congress's first full sessions, Eisner joined Julius Kaliski in celebrating Georges Weill's thirtieth birthday at a pub, where the two seniors sat talking at a corner table well after midnight.[21]

On 18 October, the hundredth anniversary of the first volume of Grimms' *Kinder- und Hausmärchen* (Fairy Tales), Eisner underscored the political significance of the publication, which, speaking with the voice of the common folk in a time of fragmentation and foreign domination, aimed at the resurrection of an essential, national consciousness rooted in trial, perseverance, and deliverance. He lamented the decline of the oral transmission of popular heritage and culture from one generation to the next. The days of the grandmother seated by the hearth, a rapt audience of youngsters at her feet, were long past. Like the hearth itself, the tradition was dying out. "We no longer tell our children stories, old or new. The blaring metropolis renders us mute. The objects and occurrences of our industrial existence's prosaic perspective have no immediate connection to the old tales' imagery. Thus the Grimm tales today are for us just something like the flower pots that call to mind nature's colors in the desolate tenement house."[22]

A month later Eisner was on an extended speaking tour, scheduled for multiple appearances in Dresden and then two days of talks in Basel. From Dresden's familiar Wettin Hotel he wrote to Belli of disquieting loneliness and detachment. "I am speaking daily to attentive people in ice-cold halls. They seem satisfied with me." For company he accepted the invitation from members of the metal workers' union to join them over beer until past three in the morning.[23] Saturday evening, 16 November, he attended a performance of Tchaikovsky's *Eugene Onegin* at Dresden's Royal Opera. Absorbed in reflections on his audience of the past days, he composed on the playbill a poem describing the challenge of awakening minds to critical thought amid the din and joviality of a beer hall.[24] The meetings were wearing him down. "Saxony," he recorded privately, "exhibits the condition of an old socialist proletariat grown weary and almost indifferent again." The next day he and former *Vorwärts* colleague Georg Gradnauer called on Franz Diederich, editor of the arts section of the *Sächsische Arbeiter-Zeitung*, at his home in the northern suburb Hellerau. Eisner hoped to enlist him as a contributor to the *Arbeiter-Feuilleton*, but his report to Belli centered on Diederich's personal life. Two years older than Eisner, Diederich had left a failed marriage for a woman half his age. The unlikely couple and four young children lived in a cottage with books lining every wall. Despite precarious finances, "they *too* seem to have found their happiness." On Monday Eisner's mother came to Dresden to be with him until his departure Saturday night. He was touched by her longing and devotion. The evening of her arrival he wrote to Belli that he was canceling the trip to Basel to return home.[25]

The Christmas issue of the *Arbeiter-Feuilleton*, circulated on 9 December in typed, mimeographed copy to past and potential subscribers, included Wilhelm Hausenstein's essay "The Democratization of the Christ Child," topical pieces on Germany's coal supply and how war would impact proletarian families, and a new column by botanist Raoul Heinrich Francé, head of Munich's privately funded Biological Institute, which offered courses for the general public. In a cover letter Eisner announced that the *Feuilleton* would continue in the expanded format at new, graduated prices in accordance with Workers' Press Association guidelines. Francé's work would bear the pseudonym H. Falkenfels.[26]

The success of the party's electoral tactics of 1912 in Bavaria—policy Eisner had pressed since his appointment as editor of *Vorwärts*—prompted him to urge yet again the Prussian SPD to back Left Liberals in Landtag districts where Social Democrats had no hope of success. Only the end of Conservative and Center control of the Landtag could effect the equal suffrage that would afford the working class its due. And yet again a socialist Realpolitik in Prussia remained a pipe dream. Delegates to the regional party congress of 6–8 January 1913 at Berlin's Union Hall, among them a number of Eisner's old antagonists, obdurately embraced Social Democracy's impotence in the Prussian Landtag. Supported by Heinrich Ströbel, Paul Hirsch opposed Eisner's motion, which was defended in turn by Eduard Bernstein. The united front, Bernstein argued, had proven highly effective against the Black-Blue Bloc in Bavaria. "And here too I consider a like tactic the only way forward."[27]

The 11 January issue of *März* (March), Munich's progressive bourgeois journal for culture, featured two essays by Eisner on Bavarian politics. In the first, under the pseudonym Houyhnhnm from Swift, Eisner sought to read Georg von Hertling's agenda for Bavaria in the former philosophy professor's academic writings. Those who had been schooled in philosophy were naturally wont to wonder how their fellow might now actualize his cherished ideation. To be sure, it was altogether fitting that a philosopher should lead the government, a sentiment as venerable as Plato himself, but to transform the life of the mind into statecraft was immensely challenging at best. "Previously too ministers were occasionally dubbed philosophers, but only to indicate by this epithet that they were none too adept in office."

Examining Hertling's publications, Eisner found essays on Aristotle's conception of the soul, Descartes's bearing toward scholasticism, and Locke's quarrel with the Cartesians. But what proved most revealing as to Hertling's own political imperative was an article that appeared nearly a quarter century earlier, "Darwinism: An Intellectual Epidemic." Here the Catholic ethicist argued that the notion of man created in God's image was more fundamentally abhorrent to material philosophy than that of descent from apes via natural selection of species. Rejecting 'the pathological struggle of God-fleeing reason, aided by modern science, to efface every trace of the omniscient and omnipotent Creator's indelible stamp on His creation,' Hertling posited a divine 'lex aeterna' to be construed and enforced by the faithful. Having been elevated to his position of temporal power by Prince Regent Luitpold, Hertling typologically regarded himself simply as the agent of higher will, a proxy servant of the Almighty both literally and figuratively. So despite his vow to be a nonpartisan executive, Hertling harbored an irreconcilable disdain for the nonclerical parties.[28]

The second essay, initialed K. E., bore the title "The Nationalization of Minds." Here Eisner lampooned Hertling's bid to manage public opinion through a Prussian-style state newspaper, the *Bayerische Staatszeitung* (Bavarian State Newspaper), the first issue of which was in the works. Bankrolled by a few of Hertling's closest cronies, edited by Philipp Frick, and printed by Mosse Press, the Bavarian government's new organ was to draw on official utterances of ministers, diplomats, and civil servants at every level to underscore the wisdom and legitimacy of the "clerical-feudal worldview." Publication of the first issue, slated for New Year's Day, had been delayed by protests when the *Münchener Post* made known that all other papers would be compelled to dispense with channels of public information other than the *Staatszeitung*, as it alone would have proprietary right to all news of state affairs. What, Eisner wondered, would be the state paper's stance on freedom of expression in art, given Frick's recent fulminations against nudity in the work of Bavarian painter Wilhelm von Kaulbach? Would subscription be compulsory for teachers and clergy? Eisner clearly relished the irony that the self-avowed nonpartisan Hertling sought now to recast Bavaria in Prussia's authoritarian image by undermining the free press.[29]

Eisner turned to *März* too to answer critics of Bavarian Social Democracy's tactic and to expose the Center Party's strategy for returning control of the Reichstag to the Black-Blue Bloc. In "A Military Program of the Left," published anonymously in mid-February, he argued that the upcoming military funding bill presented a unique opportunity for Social Democracy and Left Liberals to forge an unassailable majority and prevent a repeat of the Hottentot elections debacle of 1907.[30] The joint chiefs of staff were pressing for introduction of compulsory service, a measure that would inevitably democratize the armed forces. The party had long advocated a citizens' militia in place of the professional soldiery. In exchange for Social Democratic support for credits, Eisner urged, the government and high command could be expected to meet three conditions: a one-year term of compulsory service; direct income, estate, and inheritance taxes to cover the costs; and an end to the proprietary officer corps, to be replaced by promotion from the ranks. Banking on the socialists' historical opposition to the spending bill, the Center planned to join them so as to force a call for new elections—and then wage a nationalist campaign against them. But circumstances had changed. Recognizing "that Russian expansionism currently poses the greatest threat to the peace of Europe," the party was prepared to defend Germany from tsarist designs.

On this question Eisner had been swayed, as he later documented in his prison journal from 1918, by the revelation of Adolf Müller, mysteriously privy to official intelligence, that Russia planned to attack Germany. At Müller's express urging he had already begun warning of the danger the previous November. The article for *März* was intended to effect new political alliances, to discourage the hawks of St. Petersburg, and to suggest the quid pro quo of approving military spending in exchange for desired reforms. "I foresaw that in the case of a war provoked by Russia, German Social Democracy—true to the old democratic motto Against Tsarism!—would advocate the war, and I wanted to avert in advance the party's precipitate, zealous switch from the policy of Not One Man, Not One Penny! to that of Every Man, Every Penny!"[31] Having done Müller's bidding would become one of his greatest regrets.

As busy as he had ever been in his career, Eisner was filing diverse reports for the *Münchener Post* and other party papers, putting out his syndicated feuilleton, and contributing to eminent bourgeois journals for arts and politics. The book division of Vorwärts Press anxiously awaited his long-promised second volume of *Das Ende des Reichs*, demand for which had been nothing short of "colossal." Indeed, if he might be moved to deliver the manuscript, a second edition of the first volume was planned.[32] But after Dietz had opted to publish Mehring's book on the aftermath of the Napoleonic wars, Eisner evidently considered himself a free agent. Wilhelm Herzog, who briefly assumed the editorship of *März* in 1912, counted Eisner among his closest associates. He admired Eisner's sweeping intellect and erudition, critical judgment, and valiant will. They met for coffee in the baroque Hofgarten off Odeonsplatz. "He always came with a bundle of books under his arm. Here we talked, often for hours on end, about developments in politics, literature, art, and the theater."[33] For the first time in years Eisner seemed to his friends settled and at peace. Looking back, Wilhelm Hausenstein noted that he devoted more time to the piano and took greater care with his personal appearance.[34]

In essays for *Die Neue Rundschau* Eisner critiqued the new mode of motion mechanics and 'scientific management' implemented at Pennsylvania's Bethlehem Steel Works by Frederick Winslow Taylor and championed in Germany by Professor Ludwig Bernhard of Berlin. By determining with exacting precision the most efficient, economical means of shoveling coal, lifting a load, or laying brick, the Taylor System increased the worker's output fourfold at a wage 50 percent higher than before and, theoretically at least, assured the consumer a lower price commensurate with the enterprise's lower costs of production. In actuality capitalist greed, Eisner asserted, would invariably dictate price-and-wage-fixing and ultimately void any projected gain for workers or consumers.[35]

The *Arbeiter-Feuilleton* observed the thirtieth anniversary of Marx's death with a special issue including excerpts from his unpublished papers and Eisner's essay "Marx's Conception of Art," which revisited the debate on what constituted genuinely proletarian literature. Whereas any number of Marxists held that the schema of historical materialism could be applied to art, Marx himself denied it "with such compelling clarity and transparent simplicity that here at least one should be safe from any perverse interpretations and designs." Nonetheless, the skewed applications persisted, one of the most popular of which maintained that because the bourgeoisie was in decline, so too must bourgeois art be decadent and inferior. Why then was the verse of monarchist André Chenier still sublime poetry and the drama of his Jacobin brother wan verbiage? Citing the introduction to the notebooks on political economy begun in 1857, Eisner showed that Marx recognized full well that golden ages of art bore little relation to the contemporary social and economic stage of development, that Homer's immortal epics and their heroes could scarcely have emerged in the age of gunpowder and the printing press, yet their power to move the human soul was undiminished after millennia. The *Münchener Post* ran the signed essay on 15 March.[36]

Joseph Bloch wrote just after the May Day demonstrations to prod Eisner for an essay on Percy Shelley.[37] The Shelley article had to wait, for Eisner temporarily assumed the duties of chief theater critic for the *Post* the first week of June, writing reviews almost daily in some weeks. That month he treated performances of Büchner's *Leonce und Lena*, Knut Hamsun's *In the Grip of Life*, Ibsen's *Rosmersholm* and *Ghosts*, Chekhov's *Uncle Vanya*, and Shakespeare's *Antony and Cleopatra*. He hailed the visiting Düsseldorf Playhouse as "the most cultivated" in Germany simply for staging Büchner's comedy. When typhoid fever claimed the life of the twenty-four-year-old playwright in 1837, Eisner wrote, "German theater's best hope" was buried with him in Zurich. "We have but one revolutionary drama in German literature, the volcanic eruption titled *Dantons Tod* (*Danton's Death*), and we have but one comedy that rates as a poetic work, Büchner's *Leonce und Lena*."[38] Hamsun's new play demanded the actors' highest skill, for "the representation of physical routine, which must not be reduced to insignificance by endless references, nor on the other hand all too robust, has to intimate the concealed secret of its meaning."[39] *Uncle Vanya* had failed a few years earlier in Berlin because the audience confused bombast with high drama and thus utterly missed his "drama of the life vainly striving to be a drama itself." The production by Munich's Royal Residence Theater was so "consummately perfect" as perhaps to fix Chekhov's masterpiece in the German repertory.[40]

At the same time there was drama enough in Eisner's own household. On 2 June 1913 Joseph Belli expressed concern for his daughter's welfare in a detailed letter. "Else writes to me that she can no longer endure the degrading circumstance in which she is compelled to live without being completely broken down physically and mentally." Specifically, Lisbeth's campaign of defamation continued unabated from Nuremberg, and worse yet, Eisner's children, visiting their home on vacation, repaid Else's hospitality by spreading the rumor that Ruth had been fathered by an architect in Dachau. Moreover, Lisbeth's chronic extravagance was utterly ruining them. "How can you possibly think that a woman should have the tranquility and strength to want to work who year in, year out is anxious whenever the garden gate opens that another debt collector has come!"[41] Freia Belli, Else's eldest daughter, later documented that her mother was so distraught by Lisbeth's vindictiveness that she wanted to leave Eisner, fled to Stuttgart, and had to fetched back to Munich.[42]

The domestic crisis checked, Eisner plied his critiques for the *Post* throughout the summer. On commission from the Bavarian SPD he began work on a handbook for voters, in which he intended "to represent the decisive influence exerted on state politics in general by the Landtag deputation's persistent work since entering the parliament." In a letter of 1 August to Georg von Vollmar he outlined his plan to produce "not just a reference work for agitators but a text and manual for the general public as well."[43] The party made regular advance payments to sustain his effort.[44]

When August Bebel died of a heart attack at a Swiss sanatorium on 13 August, Eisner traveled to Zurich for the funeral, then used a review of Fritz Brupbacher's study *Marx und Bakunin* to offer his sober respects, declaring Bebel "the leader of the proletarian International who exerted the most decisive influence on the politicization of the socialist workers' movement." Circulated in the *Arbeiter-Feuilleton* on Friday, 22 August, the piece ran in the *Münchener Post* the following Sunday and Tuesday.[45] The party congress of 1913, held 14–20 September in Jena, paid elaborate tribute to Bebel, yet there too grief was tempered by exigency. Citing "deep dissatisfaction in the ranks," Rosa Luxemburg called for "fresh air in our party life."[46] In that spirit Eisner wrote to Franz Mehring on the nineteenth to discuss their concurrent projects on Marx and to propose that they "settle the old personal quarrel."[47]

Despite the midsummer tumult Eisner made progress on multiple fronts. Announcement was made the last week in August that the *Arbeiter-Feuilleton* had subsumed Anton Fendrich's long-running syndicated hiking column *Schauinsland* (A Look into the Country), affording subscribers additional material for their papers.[48] The promised essay on Shelley appeared in the 11 September issue of *Sozialistische Monatshefte*. Eisner ranged the author of the sonnet "Ozymandias," that sublimely sardonic meditation on absolutist delusions of grandeur, with Georg Büchner, youthful heirs to the late Revolution's patrimony. "Shelley's life is dedicated to the proclamation of the democratic republic, of the future socialist state, of the freedom of personal development at a time when ruling England sent all Europe to war against Napoleon as mercenaries of its rampant capitalism and, unchallenged after his defeat, won the world for its industry even while brutally crushing the desperate outbursts of starving workers at home." Coupled with an overview of Shelley's work was an appeal for a complete edition in translation, a project worthy of one of the Social Democratic publishers.[49]

In mid-September the *Arbeiter-Feuilleton* celebrated Germany's neglected naturalist poet and playwright Arno Holz with a special issue including his early manifesto "The Language of Life" and Eisner's review of the ponderous tragedy *Ignorabimus*, published the previous spring, on the limits of scientific knowledge.[50] Eisner championed the play—despite its immense length, rank style, and minute stage direction—as *"the richest work intellectually and most ardent dramatically in German literature of our age."* Holz had set himself a formidable task, for it was difficult even "to conceive of how, for instance, an author might represent on stage the theory of relativity, which undermines the firmest foundation of certainty." In light of what Holz had undertaken, Eisner questioned the nomenclature of modern theater. "Since the Greek tragedies all great dramas are dramas of fate, and precisely those that call themselves such are not that at all but in truth dramas of chance hinging on some inane coincidence. The destiny of the sexes, social and political constraint, the inescapable compulsion of character: in short, fate elevates diverse circumstance to the level of urgency that is the stuff of drama. In *Ignorabimus* science is the fate, the struggle for knowledge is the tragic." That no theater had taken interest in it was shameful. Surely if audiences were willing to endure five hours of Wagner's *Götterdämmerung* in the mythological past, time could be found for a modern masterpiece treating the hopes and fears of the present.

Just after the party congress Eisner wrote to Else Belli from the Park Hotel in Mannheim to check on her progress with the next edition of the *Feuilleton*. He had gone to Baden to speak at meetings before the Landtag elections. Wednesday, 24 September, he noted that he had addressed crowds of 350 and 385 and planned to accompany Ludwig Frank, Reichstag deputy from Baden's eleventh district and candidate for the Landtag, to a rally later that day. The previous afternoon he had visited Heinrich Harpuder and his wife, who were making monthly payments of 50 marks on an "absolutely magnificent" Steinway grand piano. Eisner reported broader demand for his Landtag reports and groused that he saw less point to the agitational tours that took him away from home.[51] Five years earlier Joseph Bloch had urged him to concentrate on his writing. In March 1912 Bloch had offered a regular column in *Sozialistische Monatshefte*. Now, toward the end of 1913, Bloch once again sought to woo him as a featured contributor, on the same footing with "a few other of the most important collaborators" who provided pieces by agreed schedule. In his case Bloch proposed one article per quarter.[52] Still Eisner declined to commit.

The impetus to new party life for which Rosa Luxemburg had called at Jena came in the form of another military misadventure inflaming anti-Prussian sentiment nationwide. Earlier that summer Philipp Scheidemann had clashed with Bethmann in the Reichstag when the chancellor demanded that opponents of "militarism" define the term. Did Social Democracy oppose the army, the guarantor of national security? "Scheidemann, though, instructed the curious chancellor" the *Münchener Post* reported on 1 July, "that militarism is not 840,000 men but rather a system. . . . And because Social Democracy is a friend of the army, that is, of the people's sons serving in the army, it is therefore an enemy of militarism!"[53] Now it was the turn of militarism to define itself. On 28 October nineteen-year-old lieutenant Günter von Forstner, posted with the Ninety-Ninth Infantry Regiment in the Alsatian town of Saverne, advised recruits to "cut down" any civilian who accosted them there and offered a bounty of 10 marks to those who felled such a troublemaker. Forstner used the epithet "rowdy" for an Alsatian citizen, a slur playing on the native's dissatisfaction with the subservient status of the long-occupied territory in the German Reich.

The lieutenant's remarks were divulged to two local newspapers, and their detailed reports triggered mass protests. Forstner was confined to quarters for less than a week. When the civil authorities declined to subdue lawful protests, Colonel Ernst von Reuter threatened imposition of martial law. On 28 November he ordered his troops to disperse a demonstration. After being herded through the streets, nearly thirty townspeople were illegally detained, among them several court officials who were simply caught up in the crowd. Reuter made good his threat and suspended civil authority. Soldiers ransacked the editorial offices of one of the papers, marched through Saverne with fixed bayonets, and set up machine-gun emplacements. Three days later Lieutenant Forstner slashed with his saber a journeyman cobbler who heckled him on the street.

Ignoring official protests of various German civil authorities in Alsace-Lorraine, the kaiser and his chancellor defended the military's excesses as justified. The Left Liberals, National Liberals, and Center joined Social Democrats in the Reichstag in ringing condemnation of "military dictatorship." In an address to the deputies Prussian war minister Erich von Falkenhayn blamed the press for the controversy. On Thursday, 4 December, the Reichstag voted overwhelmingly to censure Bethmann, the first such vote in its history. Making use of the opportunity to challenge Prussian autocracy, the SPD mounted protest rallies in seventeen cities across Germany the following Sunday. Despite the parliamentary flap and widespread public ire, the army emerged unscathed and, indeed, reinvigorated from the imbroglio. Exonerated by court-martial in Strasbourg, Colonel von Reuter was then decorated by Wilhelm II. In London the *Times* pronounced the final verdict on 12 January 1914: "In Prussia the army is supreme and, through Prussia, the army rules Germany."[54]

CHAPTER SEVENTEEN

THE POWERLESSNESS OF REASON:
THE WORLD WAR ERUPTS (1914)

IN THE WAKE OF THE SAVERNE episode Eisner clarified the historical basis for the Prussian soldateska's absolute impunity. The secret cabinet order of 1820, issued by Friedrich Wilhelm III to enforce Metternich's Carlsbad Decrees against liberal student nationalism, authorized military commanders to declare a state of siege, impose martial law, and act on their own initiative to reestablish order if, in their judgment, civil authorities were slow to quell unrest. Wilhelm II reiterated the directive to his general staff in March 1899. This single dictate then was the covert constitution of Prussian Germany, preempting the "utter shambles of inchoate statutes" that ostensibly defined the rights of the citizenry. Thus it was that on German soil a "boy in a lieutenant's tunic" could terrorize a town's populace and prompt his colonel, a "fanatic born of military inbreeding," to follow suit. The conflicted bourgeoisie was ill disposed toward lasting protest, "for in the end the liberal citizen is himself a reserve lieutenant, and his son perhaps even a cadet officer too!"[1] It all boded ill for Europe's peace.

On through the winter of 1914 Eisner's theater reviews for the *Münchener Post* were a mainstay of the paper's cultural offering. Constantly astute and incisive, the pieces stand out from those of his colleagues and roundly justify Hausenstein's judgment that "they were splendid."[2] Both the famous and the forgotten have here their monument. Karl Rößler's popular comedy *Rösselsprung* (Knight's Move), which the Munich Playhouse premiered on 17 January, Eisner panned as predictably formulaic, the vacuous fluff of "beautifully dressed ladies and elegant gentlemen in a loquacious state and decorative frame," report of which struck him as more suited to the business page than the arts section.[3] By contrast he commended the Royal Residence Theater's resurrection of *Das vierte Gebot* (The Fourth Commandment) by Ludwig Anzengruber, a profound work neglected in favor of box office successes that betrayed "the total wretchedness of the German theater, its direction, and its audience."[4] High praise was accorded the Chamber Players' first German presentation of *The Wolves* by Romain Rolland, in Wilhelm Herzog's translation, on 4 March. Moved by public debate of the Dreyfus affair, Rolland had written the play in 1898 but set it in 1793 against the backdrop of the emergent Terror. "In this revolutionary drama Romain Rolland touched on the deepest tragic problem that rocks humanity time and again on its dark course through the millennia: the powerlessness of reason when the elements, the catastrophes rage."[5]

Hermann Stenz, an SPD functionary who had attended Eisner's most recent lecture in Mannheim, wrote to him in midmonth that Viktor Chernov, a founder of Russia's Socialist Revolutionary Party and editor of its journal, knew Eisner's work well and sought to solicit from him an article titled "German Democracy's Present Struggle against Absolutism in Light of the Saverne Affair."[6] Chernov's interest evinces the unease of keen observers at autocracy's predilection for apocalyptic caprice in the face of extinction. One of the oddly persistent myths about Europe's lurch into the First World War, perpetuated for decades by historians and novelists alike, is that it was somehow unexpected, a bolt from the blue, yet only the deeply deluded could deny that hostilities were imminent. Two Moroccan crises, both spawned in Berlin, had lavishly set the stage. The Schlieffen Plan and corresponding strategies in Austria and Russia defined the imperatives not of national defense but of territorial aggrandizement. Privy councilors and general staffs schooled in the objectives and successes of Bismarckian warfare misapprehended new realities. Ailing, failing political structures and their trappings were ripe for doom. Of the crowned heads Tsar Nicholas alone seems to have realized that the military posturing and stockpiling "will lead to the very cataclysm it seeks to avert."[7] Rippling anxiety was reflected in Social Democratic agitation. Saturday evening, 21 March, Rosa Luxemburg spoke at Munich's Kindl Beer Hall on the theme "Militarism and Civil Freedom."[8]

Concerned at the bourgeois newspapers' disproportionate influence on public opinion, particularly in the realm of foreign policy, Eisner framed his most systematic critique of the German press in a three-part article expounding grievances he had long aired to colleagues of the Workers' Press Association. The great weakness of the bourgeois news trade, he wrote in "Press Problems," was for the most part its very nature as a commodity of monied interests: it served a clientele, not an ideal. And yet there were bourgeois papers that had achieved wide readership and international prominence through the excellence of their reportage and analysis. Curiously, the ruling Conservative Party's gazettes were shabby enterprises with scant circulation. So too were the Center Party's papers in Bavaria all small productions with little genuine influence on public opinion. "Consequently the significance of the press," he concluded, "hinges solely on its journalistic qualities. . . . No newspaper can be based on serving party function alone."

In the past Social Democratic papers were mainly vehicles of propaganda. For months Engels had filled the pages of *Vorwärts* with his *Anti-Dühring*. Now, despite their conscious transition to actual newspapers, party organs still engaged in preaching Marxist theory to the choir. And although they had upgraded their equipment and woven mass distribution networks, they still relied on piecemeal correspondence services for their sources, having failed to consolidate a central news bureau. Conversely, the 'independent' bourgeois papers were uniformly and dangerously dependent on the government itself for international news. "Wilhelmstraße in Berlin directs the entire foreign policy of the bourgeois German press and only occasionally shares its dominion with the publicity machine of Krupp and other arms makers, who with the help of certain publishing concerns stoked the fire of world war during the recent Moroccan crisis, counter to the efforts of the government." Because these papers were controlled by shareholders, the considered judgment of their political editors—all private employees beholden to a corporate board—figured but little in what came to print. In this sense even the best bourgeois papers were venal and therefore inherently corrupt operations.

In contrast the party press was the "freest on earth," serving only the cause of "political and economic enlightenment" rather than manipulating public opinion so as to drive private profits. "In the many years of my Social Democratic editorial activity," Eisner attested, "I have indeed had to endure some not very pleasant conflict, but never did the party comrades whose confidence I enjoyed make even the slightest attempt to influence my convictions." Yet there was need for organizational improvement. Press commissions, "a thoroughly necessary and useful institution," existed to ensure that papers met the readers' needs, yet all too frequently overbearing commissioners with no experience in the trade sought to micromanage proven editors. Here Eisner urged that the commission chairmen should have the requisite background in both journalism and business to discharge their office competently. By the same token, most editorial staffs had a true leader—whether designated editor in chief or not—who by virtue of knowledge, talent, and experience presided by general consent over the collaborative. Reflecting, no doubt, on his tenure at *Vorwärts*, he maintained that the leading light should be accorded "decisive influence on the composition of the staff" when personnel changes occurred. A glaring deficiency of Social Democratic editorial staffs in general was the lack of expertise in the interlocking mechanics of capitalism. "No party paper should be without an editor or colleague assigned to cover all financial, industrial, commercial, agricultural enterprises within the paper's range of distribution." That specialist might then effectively advise unions on coordinating their actions and provide a more practical critique of the system.

Turning to criticisms of content, Eisner enjoined party editors to resist the impulse from some quarters to restrict the scope of their papers to club bulletins for parliamentary or union officials. The constituency had to remain the broad spectrum of the economically exploited, the politically oppressed, and those idealists determined to effect social justice. If anything, the papers should expand their content to appeal to a wider public and should engage business managers committed to constant growth. He cited the replete feuilleton as a critical means of winning new converts among bourgeois readers dissatisfied with business dailies that placed line limits on cultural reportage. The eminent theater critic called for fewer reviews of stage productions, "provocatively capitalist ventures," and more of creative and scholarly literature, to which workers had greater access. More space too should be accorded to classified ads, both to offset subscription prices and to draw proletarian women who were turning to rival bourgeois papers to locate and post used household items for sale.[9] The critique won immediate praise in some quarters. "Did you read Eisner's excellent article on our press in the *Chemnitzer Volksstimme*?" Albert Südekum queried Erhard Auer in a letter of 18 April. Two months earlier Südekum had proposed Eisner as the Bavarian correspondent for a new party syndication, the thrust of which was to be "informative" rather than "polemical." Under consideration for editor in chief was Eisner's friend Georges Weill.[10]

Easter week the Munich Chamber Players performed Friedrich Hebbel's tragedy *Herodes und Mariamne*. In his review for the *Post* on Sunday, 19 April, Eisner underscored the play's historical import. Hebbel recast Flavius Josephus's first-century account of passion, political conspiracy, tyranny, fatal impulse, and crushing regret to reflect the epochal shift from ancient to modern, from classical antiquity to Christianity. Eisner deemed Hebbel the precursor to Ibsen and dubbed his Jewish heroine "both the last Maccabee and the first Nora."[11] Consciousness of the moment increasingly pervaded Eisner's thought and work. Saturday, 30 May, he attended a reception at the Whitsuntide festival of the Bavarian Workers' Choruses in Munich. Inspired by hope's glimmer in face of doom, Eisner inscribed the program with an impromptu poem, "Prelude," the last lines of which read

In dark woes' haze
the dawn of freedom
sings through our days.[12]

The thunderhead's clap came the next month in the form of two muffled pistol shots fired by a young Bosnian Serb intent on liberating his compatriots from foreign rule. The freedom Eisner envisioned in his verse was years off yet, but the murder of Archduke Franz Ferdinand and his consort that Sunday noon, 28 June, in Sarajevo touched off a global war that swept away the German, Austrian, and Russian monarchies. In the protracted struggle for power after Germany's defeat Kaiser Wilhelm's successor would be a Social Democrat who lost two sons in the carnage, and Kurt Eisner, himself a head of state, would be slain by a hateful, callow gunman of privileged station. In the month-long prelude to Austria's declaration of war on Serbia, few close observers of international affairs knew the scope of agreements and strategies that would draw the Continent into what appeared to be a localized albeit grave conflict. "Secret plans," British military historian John Keegan notes, "determined that any crisis not settled by sensible diplomacy would, in the circumstances prevailing in Europe in 1914, lead to general war."[13]

For weeks following the assassination of the heir to the Austro-Hungarian crown, consternation reigned while covenants between Triple Alliance partners Germany, Austria, and Italy, and those of Triple Entente states France, Russia, and England were feverishly invoked in various chancelleries, foreign offices, and headquarters. Yet there was little surprise at the shooting itself. Vienna had moved forcefully against separatist aspirations of the Dual Monarchy's ethnic minorities. Franz Ferdinand, inspector general of the army, was the royal champion of modernization and expansion of the Austro-Hungarian military. He had traveled to Bosnia on invitation from General Oskar Potiorek, the provincial governor, to oversee summer maneuvers. The archduke's presence was a goad to the empire's malcontents. On 30 June the *Münchener Post* pronounced the killings tragically inevitable, "a somber reminder previously proclaimed to no avail on every page of world history that the rulers' politics of force arouse hotheads to desperate acts."[14]

The international press agreed that the gravity of the crime was magnified by its impact on Habsburg succession.[15] The crisis was escalated the first week of July by implication of the Serbian high command as sponsor of the killer and by announcement of the pan-Slavic union between Serbia and Montenegro. The German general staff, convinced that conditions were favorable for a quick, decisive war against Russia and France, welcomed the pretext for confrontation. By midmonth Austro-Hungarian foreign minister Count Leopold Berchtold and chief of staff Conrad von Hötzendorf, assured by Kaiser Wilhelm's personal pledge of German support, were urging Kaiser Franz Josef to war. He and Count Istvan Tisza, the Hungarian prime minister, were more cautious in light of the precarious balance of ethnicity in the Dual Monarchy and the influence of its Slavic minority.[16] Thursday, 23 July, the *Post* reported that Berchtold had presented Franz Josef the draft of an ultimatum to Belgrade demanding prosecution of all conspirators, a ban on organizations hostile to the Imperial presence in Bosnia, and more rigorous policing of the border.[17] Two days later the lead article speculated that Austria was determined to force Serbia to war.[18]

That same day the Social Democratic Party executive in Berlin called for mass demonstrations against German involvement in Austria's fight with Serbia.[19] The hawkish screech was now deafening. Saturday afternoon in Munich crowds gathered before the newspaper office hoardings to await the latest news. Reports were posted just after 19:00 that the Serbian government would acquiesce in Vienna's demands. By 20:00, however, more ominous dispatches were cheered by rowdies.[20] Belgrade's resolve had stiffened upon assurance of the tsar's support; the official response rejected the critical proviso of direct Austrian participation in the investigation of the conspiracy. Vienna broke diplomatic relations, and Serbia mobilized its army.[21]

Social Democratic officials in Munich scheduled a "peace proclamation" rally for Monday evening, 27 July, at the cavernous Kindl Beer Hall with Kurt Eisner as the featured speaker.[22] Because, however, the *Münchener Post* had itself become the target of chauvinist demonstrations and threats, the party leadership urged Eisner to feign illness that the rally might be canceled. He adamantly refused and spoke as scheduled to the thousands in attendance on the prevalent "threat to freedom of conscience" posed by nationalist fervor.[23] But instead of laying blame on Habsburg aggression, Eisner faulted tsarist expansionism for the Serbian provocation. "I was the only speaker in the hundreds of Social Democratic protest meetings at the time," he noted, "who castigated not Austria but Russia." He argued that if Germany, France, and England refused to be drawn into conflict, Russia would be thwarted and culture preserved. If, however, Russia moved against Austria-Hungary, German socialists must be prepared to take up arms, "for none of us wants Cossackdom to rule Europe."[24] In November 1916 Eisner wrote in retrospect that he was convinced—contrary to the vast majority of Social Democratic Party officials—that Serbia, not Austria, was the aggressor, "and to be sure as the instrument of Russia, which held that the time had come to set fire to Europe."[25] His resolution to check tsarism was approved with but one negative vote.[26] Nonetheless he had no delusions about the ultimate destructive force about to be unleashed. "No matter how it ends, war—especially a European war today—is a calamity, destroying victor and vanquished."[27]

On the day of the rally at the Kindl Beer Hall, 27 July, Eisner's impressions of feverish bellicosity among Munich's bourgeoisie appeared in three dramatic sketches for the *Arbeiter-Feuilleton*. In the first—based on an incident at the Café Fahrig, wrecked by a nationalist mob Saturday night, 25 July—a hotel restaurant band plays sentimental favorites while patrons discuss the likelihood of hostilities. A drunken clerk, a snide student, and an incensed couple vocally agree that the Serbs must be schooled in civility. When word comes that war has been declared, the jingoists demand the national anthem, then assault a foreign guest who declines to sing. The hotel manager's intervention touches off a melee. Tabletops, lamps, and windows are smashed to the strains of "Deutschland, Deutschland über alles!" The police arrive to find the establishment in ruins. The rioters have fled without settling their tabs.[28]

Having returned from a North Sea cruise, Kaiser Wilhelm studied Belgrade's answer to the ultimatum on Tuesday morning, 28 July, and declared to his staff that there was no further cause for war, as the remaining differences could be easily resolved through diplomacy. War Minister Erich von Falkenhayn, livid with rage at the suggestion, intimated a military coup against Wilhelm. Counseled by Falkenhayn and chief of staff Helmuth von Moltke, Bethmann pressed the Austrians to act before British foreign minister Sir Edward Grey's peace initiative might gain traction. Austria-Hungary indeed declared war on Serbia. Count Berchtold informed the Serbian prime minister via telegram.[29] That afternoon Adolf Müller apprised Eisner that sources in the Bavarian War Ministry had divulged in confidence that Germany would mobilize by week's end. Eisner in turn telephoned the party executive in Berlin and Ernst Heilmann, editor of the *Chemnitzer Volksstimme*, with the news. His disclosure met with incredulity. After repeatedly requesting confirmation, Heilmann put out an extra edition. Wednesday, 29 July, Tsar Nicholas ordered full mobilization of Russian forces. At Müller's request Eisner asked Heilmann to lobby for approval of war credits.[30]

That night Austrian gunboats shelled Belgrade from the Danube. The next evening party executive cochair Friedrich Ebert and treasurer Otto Braun departed Berlin for Zurich with the party coffers, fearing imminent arrest of the Social Democratic leadership, general outlawry, and another lengthy exile. Interior Ministry staff, however, assured party trade-union officials that the government was counting on labor organizations to help provide critical social services in wartime.[31] On Friday, 31 July, some party papers printed Friedrich Stampfer's proclamation, with explicit reference to the kaiser's past gibe, that "when the fateful hour strikes . . . , the 'rogues without a fatherland' will do their duty and in no way be outdone by the patriots."[32] The party executive perfunctorily dispatched Hermann Müller to Paris for consultation with the French socialists, but the die was already cast.[33] Before Müller could meet with his hosts, the Second International suffered a monstrous blow. Jean Jaurès, France's most prominent pacifist, was shot to death at his regular Montmartre café while dining with Pierre Renaudel, Georges Weill, and other comrades: two bullets to the back of the head at close range. The assassin, Raoul Villain, was a rabid revanchist who yearned for the Germans' ouster from Alsace-Lorraine.[34] The fallen hero's fateful Copenhagen prophecy of September 1910 was to be borne out in full.[35]

The German declaration of war with Russia came on Saturday, 1 August. That evening Kaiser Wilhelm, assured of Social Democratic support, spoke from the balcony of Berlin's Royal Palace to thank his former adversaries, forgive them their past trespasses, and welcome them into the fold. "I know no more parties, no more creeds," he proclaimed. "Today we are all German brothers and only German brothers."[36] The next day the Social Democratic trade unions forswore all strike actions.[37] The party's Reichstag leadership voted 4–2 to recommend approval of war credits, with David, Richard Fischer, Molkenbuhr, and Scheidemann affirming, Haase and Ledebour dissenting.[38] The Reichstag delegation followed suit 92–14 in caucus on Monday, 3 August.[39] Late that afternoon Germany declared war on France, alleging that French aircraft had bombed stretches of railway near Nuremberg the previous day. The French were mystified by Berlin's claim. The Reichstag's formal vote on war credits occurred Tuesday afternoon. In his address to the members Bethmann repeated the fabrication of a French aerial attack.[40] Social Democrats unanimously supported the funding measure. Even before the formal approval, the Schlieffen Plan had been activated. Intent on skirting formidable French defenses, German troops marched on neutral Belgium that morning in a push toward Paris. Honoring its guarantee of Belgian neutrality, Britain entered the war against Germany.[41]

On 3 August, the same day the *Münchener Post* eulogized Jaurès as "a victim of chauvinism," the German Foreign Office released its *Weißbuch* (White Book), an annotated compilation of documents intended to place blame for the war on the Entente.[42] Eisner's own tribute to Jaurès appeared on the front page of Tuesday's *Post* before he read the *Weißbuch*. The "martyr for world peace," he wrote, had agonized over the logical inconsistency of republican France's alliance with tsarist Russia and worked incessantly for French-German reconciliation. At this dark hour it fell to Germany to advance culture by crushing the Russian autocracy. "Now the German proletariat has to destroy the archenemy of European civilization; as Germans, as democrats, as socialists we take up arms for the just cause."[43] The same day his perusal of the *Weißbuch* shook that conviction and eventually "aroused my strongest suspicion . . . that the World War, as a western problem, was a continuation of Germany's aggressive Morocco strategy." When he learned of the tsar's proposal of 29 July, communicated by telegram to Berlin, to have the scheduled Third Hague Peace Conference mediate between Vienna and Belgrade—an overture the *Weißbuch* conveniently omitted—Eisner concluded that Germany had deliberately sabotaged potential diplomatic solutions in order to pursue conquest. Gradually he realized that he had been duped and manipulated "by the systematic, well-hatched intrigue of a socialist long hand in glove with the government!"[44] The evening of 4 August a handful of opponents to the *Burgfrieden* (domestic truce)—Wilhelm Pieck, Franz Mehring, Julian Marchlewski, Ernst Meyer, Hermann and Käte Duncker—met at Rosa Luxemburg's Berlin apartment to determine a plan of action. They proclaimed their stance in a letter printed the next month by newspapers in Switzerland. It was signed by Liebknecht, Mehring, Luxemburg, and Clara Zetkin.[45]

Eisner's relationship with Adolf Müller disintegrated rapidly. Eisner accused Müller in a letter dated 8 August of both betraying his trust and intending to marginalize him.[46] The German invasion of Belgium and the grotesque metamorphosis of the Social Democratic Party "at once from radical sworn enemies of bourgeois society into the most repulsive flag-waving patriots" swayed Eisner toward the opposition.[47] Paul Lensch, Heinrich Cunow, Konrad Haenisch, and Alexander Helphand—principals of the clique that had reviled him as a reformist accommodating the state—became so enraptured by their newfound nationalism as to be branded "social chauvinists" by East German historians.[48] In his patriotic exultations Haenisch seems a character lifted from Eisner's dramatic sketch of 27 July, immensely relieved that he might "join in the swelling fight song with full heart, clear conscience, and without the least fear of being a traitor for doing so: 'Deutschland, Deutschland über alles!'"[49] The past tirades against the party's accepting a Reichstag vice presidency because of the obligatory bow to the kaiser were rendered farcical now by the full prostration before the crown.

Evidence of Eisner's change of heart can be read in the 16 August edition of the *Arbeiter-Feuilleton*. In an essay comparing the alliances of 1914 to those of a century earlier, he justifies the blood sacrifice of Europe's workers as necessary to redress the "cleft between Germany and France created by the reactionary powers and the hundred-year intimacy between Prussian-German Junker politics and Russian tsarism." Pitted against each other by ruling-class statecraft, socialists in their various uniforms were fully conscious that their end goal was "the final reconciliation of Europe's civilized peoples." Eisner hailed Jaurès, who resolutely promoted peace between France and Germany, as "the best man in Europe" and printed his translation of an excerpt from *Histoire socialiste, 1789–1900*. The act of rendering a sacred text was therapeutic. Jaurès, he felt, as he related in the preface, "is once again walking beside me, into a brighter age."[50]

The freedom of conscience Eisner had professed to enjoy in the Social Democratic Party was suddenly in short supply. Opposition to the Burgfrieden he had helped forge at Adolf Müller's prompting came at a price. Among Eisner's papers in the Federal Archive at Berlin-Lichterfelde is a notice of 1 September 1914 from the editors of the *Münchener Post* rejecting his submission for objectionable content. Penciled in the margin in Belli's hand is the terse commentary "party censorship."[51] In her unpublished autobiographical novel Else Belli recounts how for several days Eisner sat at home playing the piano when he should have been off to the editorial offices. When she asked why he tarried, he simply sat quietly. Realizing then that he had been sacked, she seethed with rage against Adolf Müller and Erhard Auer. "It's true, isn't it? After all the comrades have jumped in with their Chief Comrade Willy, who knows no more parties, you stand in their way."[52] Dismissed as political editor for the *Post*, Eisner was retained as the chief theater critic in a political climate he characterized as "adverse to theater." At a time when universal drama born of human suffering and yearning—works such as Tolstoy's *Light Shining in the Darkness* or Strindberg's *Dream Play*—might have provided solace and sustenance, German producers were staging Biedermeier comedies.[53] As the German Army pushed into France, casualty lists began to run daily. The rash Lieutenant Forstner, progenitor of the Saverne affair, was killed in action 1 September near the village of Dannevoux, just west of the Meuse in Lorraine. Two days later Dr. Ludwig Frank, forty-year-old Social Democratic member of the Reichstag from Mannheim, fell at Nossoncourt near Baccarat.

Compelled by financial necessity, Eisner applied to Kurt Baake's Social Democratic press service for assignment as a frontline correspondent with the Sixth Army, under command of Crown Prince Rupprecht of Bavaria. "I wanted to experience the war firsthand and only report what I saw," he recounted in 1918. The request was endorsed by the party organization in Munich but blocked in Berlin by Hugo Haase, ever suspicious of Eisner's motives.[54] For the third time in his career he was trekking into the wilderness. He bitterly recalled his alienation by the party's newborn fanatical patriots, who hung maps on their walls and gleefully tracked the German offensives, who scoffed at protests over violation of Belgian neutrality and atrocities against civilians. "By mid-September 1914," he wrote, "I came into the most wrenching conflict with my best friends over it. I shall not forget how shocked they were, for instance, by my remark 'A Belgian worker is still dearer to me than a Prussian Junker,' so much so that they wanted to construe it as nothing more than a bad joke." Victor Adler, whom he encountered in Berlin, angrily rebuked him for accommodating the aspirations of Germany's enemies.[55]

A desperate stand by the French and British checked the German advance at the Marne. The significance of the stalemate, Eisner recalled in December 1918, was carefully concealed from the nation: "By shattering the German plan of attack, this battle six weeks into the war decided its ultimate outcome."[56] On the eastern front General von Hindenburg's army failed to encircle Russian forces in the battle of the Masurian Lakes.[57] Saturday, 19 September, Eisner visited a military hospital in Berlin, where captured French, Belgian, and Russian wounded were among the patients.[58] His disillusionment soured an opportunity to return to the capital, for the party executive, despite Haase's animosity, was considering Eisner for the editorship of a Berlin publication, presumably the family-oriented newspaper planned for national distribution on which Philipp Scheidemann reported to the party's advisory board (Parteiausschuß) on 30 June.[59] The negotiations with the executive were to take place on Monday, 21 September. In anticipation of the meeting Eisner attempted to telephone Belli repeatedly on Saturday but the lines were jammed. He wrote to her that afternoon that he faced a difficult decision. Every instinct signaled that a move to Berlin was "suicidal" under the circumstances. Still, he was intrigued by the possibility. "They appear to have big things in mind. I do not want to remove myself from the discussion. . . . I will consult with you about it in earnest then and, despite our existence being very much up in the air at present, I think I will say *no*."[60]

For his part, Adolf Müller, having proven his reliability to the government, was enlisted as a secret agent and special emissary of the Bavarian and German foreign offices. From September on he was virtually lost to the party, prompting Georg von Vollmar to complain to Wolfgang Heine on 19 October of the void created by Müller's absence.[61] Making use of his remaining daily forum, Eisner embedded in theater reviews his historical perspective on the war, a tactic not lost on his readers.[62] In a critique of the Chamber Players' performance of Heinrich Lee's *Grüne Ostern* (Green Easter) he noted a growing sense, even among lesser dramatic lights and the worst francophobes, of what Kleist had failed to grasp in his time: that Napoleon, "undone by the titanic attempt to defend and nurture the European continent's culture against English world power and Russian barbarism," was truly a tragic hero and that "Europe's catastrophe was rooted in the War of 1813."[63] Joseph Bloch had ardently thrown *Sozialistische Monatshefte* behind the war effort. In a letter of 14 October he asked Eisner to rush him a piece arguing that Germany must realize Napoleon's thwarted ambition to break England's sea power: "The main thing for me is the consistent historical proof that the current war is England's war, the direct and consequent continuation of its policy."[64] But Eisner had been too thoroughly repelled by Berlin's role in the two Moroccan crises to take up Bloch's cause, and he was now increasingly convinced that Germany was the aggressor in both east and west. Continental culture was driven by France and Germany. Any lasting European peace would require that the joint enmity rooted in Napoleon's conquest and Bismarck's Franco-Prussian War be supplanted by a Franco-German alliance, a new order based on popular mutual understanding. Redress of ingrained mistrust demanded a clarion disavowal of the mores of imperialism. Instead of vilifying France's closest ally, he began casting a lengthy article on international law, the slant of which was distinctly anti-German.

His intent, stated in the preface, was to clarify events obscured by "scholars of international law who believe it their duty now, on the basis of individual nationality, to deny or palliate their own countries' violations of that law and to allege and prosecute those of enemy states." The Hague Peace Conference of 1899 and 1907 had mandated conflict resolution through mediation and, that failing, proscribed military attacks on defenseless civilian targets. Ironically, the progress toward regulating warfare was effectively voided by partisan legal theorists who applied to international law the criminal code's right of self-defense condoning deadly force. It was therefore imperative for every combatant nation to brand the enemy as aggressor in order to fight without restrictions of compact or conscience. This need begat in turn outlandish pretexts for attack, such as Bethmann's patently false claim that a French plane had bombed a train line near Nuremberg on 2 August 1914, the day before Germany declared war on France. Indeed, even the invasion of neutral Belgium could be justified as a preemptive act of self-defense, for as Herbert Kraus, lecturer in international law at Leipzig, argued, a frontal assault of French fortifications would have been self-destructive.

On the other hand, armed civilian resistance against an occupying army, expounded by Clausewitz as the ultimate national self-defense, nullified injunctions protecting towns from shelling and legitimized harsh reprisals. Military commanders stressed their obligation to protect uniformed troops from sniping and ambush by the populace. "The irreconcilable antithesis," Eisner observed, "is that . . . [whereas] international law proclaims rules of warfare, the soldier is guided by martial expedience." As culpable as the legal apologists, he charged, were yellow journalists who demanded gruesome retaliation for alleged atrocities by hostile forces. A major German paper, for example, proposed that captured English officers be used in the trenches as shields against their compatriots' dum-dum bullets. Such exhortations to cruelty inflamed base emotions and piqued bloodlust when "the organs of public opinion in every country have yet a higher duty . . . to clarify perceptions of international law's virtue and provisions." The essay appeared in two parts in the December and January issues of *Der Neue Merkur* (The New Mercury), a new bourgeois monthly edited by Efraim Frisch.[65]

On Christmas Eve the *Münchener Post* reprinted as its lead an open letter to the Parisian *Figaro* from Georges Weill, Eisner's closest colleague at the *Fränkische Tagespost* and Reichstag member from Metz in Alsace-Lorraine. Since August he had been missing. Attempts by the party executive to locate him were futile. Weill, as his letter to *Figaro* revealed, had kept silent to protect his elderly parents in Strasbourg. Having relocated them to safety, he announced now that two days after Germany's declaration of war on France he had enlisted in the French Army. The party leadership pronounced its sharpest condemnation on the act of conscience by which "he of course removed himself from the Social Democratic Party and the Reichstag deputation."[66] In what he labeled "an unwritten letter" Eisner told Weill that no one had the right to revile him. "Decisions such as those you have dared to make are justified by history." Indeed, many good Germans had joined the French cause during the Revolution, and many had bolted Napoleon's army to fight for Germany. "By the same token," Eisner wrote, "your decision also ratifies *our* right—that of *German* Social Democrats—to defend our fatherland, the duty we have particularly as socialists."[67] As disillusioned as he was by the *Weißbuch* revelations, the war fervor of his comrades, and the high command's tactics, he still dreaded defeat by Russia above all else. Eisner was nonetheless sickened by the slaughter of Russians on the eastern front. On Christmas Day he contrasted the sublime holiday program of the Munich Chamber Players, featuring Otto Falckenberg's nativity play in Bavarian dialect, with a bloodthirsty hoarding placard cheering the heaps of enemy dead on the eastern front, a barbaric tribute of which history, he reckoned, would surely make note.[68]

CHAPTER EIGHTEEN

WRETCHED SUPERFLUITY: DIVIDED LOYALTIES (1915–1916)

O N NEW YEAR'S DAY 1915 Eisner reviewed for the *Post* Eugen Kilian's curious minimalist production of *Much Ado about Nothing* at the Royal Residence Theater. Although Eisner praised the comic genius of Albert Steinrück in the role of Dogberry, the lightning repartee of Mathieu Lützenkirchen and Emma Berndl as Benedick and Beatrice, and the exquisite charm of Berta Neuhoff's Hero, he questioned the stark sets and absence of orchestra, particularly in light of the court theater's profitability before the war, undiminished state funding, sustained attendance, and cost savings from a program truncated by two days a week. This "strategic financial retreat" unwarranted by actual necessity deprived personnel—carpenters, costumers, musicians, and stagehands—of much-needed income in a time of need. The issue exceeded the aesthetic considerations of stagecraft: "Ultimately it would be of sociopolitical value at the moment to expend something on settings and thereby support callings on which the war's economic burden weighs more heavily."[1]

At midmonth the commanding general of the Eleventh Army Corps at Kassel banned publication of the Social Democratic *Volksblatt* of Gotha for repeated transgressions against the censorship policy.[2] For the most part, though, party newspapers blithely acquiesced in the Burgfrieden. On the sixteenth Eisner used his review of Ludwig Biro's comedy *Der letzte Kuß* (The Last Kiss) to call attention to the acerbic critique of the hawkish press by Biro's Dual Monarchy compatriot Karl Kraus. For months following the Sarajevo assassinations Kraus suspended publication of his Viennese journal, *Die Fackel.* On 5 December 1914 it reappeared with the essay "In This Great Time," scathing the bombardment of cathedrals, submarine warfare, military manipulation of the media, cultural war-profiteering, and the complicit journalism that he deemed "the most murderous weapon of all." Indeed, the horrors of combat paled in comparison to "mankind's intellectual self-mutilation by its press." In one brilliant sentence Kraus registered his full scorn: "In the realms of impoverished fantasy where man perishes from mental starvation without feeling the pangs of hunger, where pens are dipped in blood and swords in ink, what cannot be imagined must be done, but what can only be imagined is unspeakable."[3]

In Berlin the party executive warned now of false reports in the foreign socialist press of growing dissatisfaction among German comrades. The 9 January issue of *L'Humanité*, for example, claimed that "the spirit of opposition is making progress in the ranks of organized Social Democracy."[4] Displaced as contributing political editor at the *Münchener Post*, Eisner still found venues for his writings on the war despite both internal and external censorship of the party press. The *Chemnitzer Volksstimme* had prominently featured his work before the war and served for awhile as Eisner's most reliable forum until heightened disagreement with its editor, Ernst Heilmann, over questions of neutrality and submarine warfare derailed that arrangement.[5] On 29 January 1915 the *Volksstimme* ran in its supplement Eisner's piece comparing the relatively mild press censorship in Bavaria with the more stringent regulation imposed by Prussia.[6] Soon he was embroiled in ongoing disputes with various military censors and isolated by comrades who maintained the disciplined accommodation mandated by the party leadership. Whereas Eisner himself, as his Christmas letter to Georges Weill shows, vocally supported German workers at arms against tsarism and its allies, he was increasingly critical of the government and high command's objectives and tactics.

On the other hand some Social Democrats believed that their service to the German cause would stand the party in good stead after the war, enhancing its credibility among the progressive bourgeois electorate. Army private Erhard Auer, first secretary of the Bavarian SPD and Adolf Müller's close associate in the Landtag, represented this view in a letter of 17 September 1914 to Georg von Vollmar: "The political situation for our party is excellent, we just have to take great care that our supermen (Übermenschen) don't muck it all up."[7] Wolfgang Heine too, beneficiary of Eisner's shelved Reichstag candidacy two years earlier, urged solidarity in a tract titled *Gegen die Quertreiber!* (Against the Trouble Makers!).[8] Eisner responded directly to Heine on 11 February with an extraordinarily prescient personal letter that has since been cited as the clearest statement of his break from the party line. He wrote privately because he thought it "harmful to polemicize publicly now about the party's stance," although it filled him with indignation.

He still believed what he had told the crowd at Munich's Kindl Beer Hall on 27 July—that Social Democrats were obligated to answer the call to arms—but defense of their native land in no way entailed support for the German government's own expansionist aims. Through their inability to separate necessary evil from wholehearted endorsement, Heine and his fellows, Eisner charged, had made Social Democracy "a proletarian appendage of the National Liberal Party." The joyful collaboration with Germany's Prussian militarist regime had severely compromised the party's standing in the International. "What reason do we have to defend the government policy, the imperial adventurism of a ruling class that before August 1914 treated Social Democrats as inferior citizens?" That Germany, as Heine continued to argue, was engaged in a defensive war was patently false. In fact, as careful study of the available documents revealed beyond any doubt, this was a war of German expansion at France's expense, a continuation of the disastrous Weltpolitik that had twice before led to the brink of world war over Morocco. Since Britain remained too powerful to topple, Berlin had consciously determined to crush France as an intermediary step. Defeated France would be forced to cede its colonies, which would provide bases for the German fleet in the final showdown with Britain.

"I am convinced," Eisner wrote, "that if the German plan of attack had succeeded in September—we indeed turned our weapons on the west and abandoned the east to the Cossacks—if we had crushed France then, we would have immediately sought to make peace with Russia." The great miscalculation, born of delusional wishful thinking, was that Britain would remain neutral. Eisner himself believed that the war would end badly for Germany. He realized that his was not a popular view but also that it was imperative for Social Democracy, if Germany were defeated, not to be identified too closely with the masters whose conduct of the war had already offended the sensibilities of the world. Although the International made no reproach of the party for joining the fight, "we do stand accused of behaving like agents of '*le* Kaiser.'" The party had failed to protest German forces' brutal breaches of international law and, worse yet, party officials had either denied evident atrocities or spoken in defense of such tactics. "This, above all, this positive assumption of shared guilt, is what isolates us in the entire International." For its unwillingness to speak out against wrongs, to stand up to fanaticism, Social Democracy would, he warned, be held accountable and forfeit influence. Eisner apologized for the length of his letter and closed cordially with a rationale for his passion: "In the wretched superfluity to which I am condemned, I feel even more keenly the duty not to abet mischief through silence."[9]

For having urged German workers to refuse to fight, Rosa Luxemburg began serving a year's sentence on 18 February 1915 at Berlin's Women's

Prison on Barnimstraße.[10] Increasingly deprived of print forums for his political commentary, Eisner committed the *Arbeiter-Feuilleton* to the campaign of discovery and dissent, blurring the distinction between cultural offering and topical editorial. The 22 February edition, for example, included his piece "On the Psychology of World War," followed in mid-March by his unsigned "historical observation" on Marx's explicit denial in the *Communist Manifesto* of a proletarian national identity within the bourgeois state.[11] Only by winning political supremacy could the proletariat ever 'constitute itself as a nation.' Marx's language, Eisner argued, was unambiguous: "to defend the fatherland in this sense means first off to *create* a fatherland by liberating it from class distinction and oppression."[12] In the same issue he observed the tenth anniversary of the historic performance of Beethoven's Ninth Symphony by the People's Free Stage in Berlin, the first for a working-class audience. Now he urged organized labor to reprise the Ninth across Germany for solace in a trying time. The great "work of the age" had come of its creator's own darkest hour. Excluded by deafness from regular social intercourse, Beethoven celebrated in music the intrinsic brotherhood of man despite cruelly imposed barriers. Certainly Eisner's own isolation within the party and that of German Social Democracy within the International weighed heavily on his mind.[13]

Similarly, the arts reviews for the *Münchener Post* served double duty. Sunday, 31 January, Eisner attended Julius Bab's "astutely reasoned" lecture touting Heinrich von Kleist as the premier national poet. In the 2 February issue of the *Post* Eisner examined the premise that Kleist's struggle to reconcile his Prussian-Junker militarist upbringing with his pronounced aesthetic idealism anticipated the uneasy synthesis of Bismarck's Germany with that of Goethe and Beethoven. Bab contended that Germany's present enemies regarded these two components of the national identity as mutually exclusive and thereby misapprehended a unique virtue. Eisner denied it. Foreign observers, he countered, readily posited the peculiar amalgam in their adversary's collective psyche; they simply had difficulty understanding how Germans could reconcile inherently incompatible attributes. "And precisely that mixture is winning foes for us abroad."[14] And to the Berlin impresario who wondered if it were permissible now to stage Shakespeare he responded on 14 March with a question of his own: "Do we not have to play Shakespeare if humanity is to find itself again?" He recommended that anyone who doubted it should see Rudolf Schildkraut as King Lear at the People's Theater in Munich, whose masterful interpretation embodied "that immeasurability of desperate world-wrecking, the tragedy of delusion of power."[15]

The realignment of the Social Democratic Party did afford Eisner an unlikely venue for publication in *Neue Zeit*, still edited by former friend-turned-enemy Karl Kautsky. Some of Kautsky's closest allies in the campaign to oust Eisner from *Vorwärts* were now ardent supporters of the German War Ministry, and Kautsky himself had been taken to task by the party's advisory board for the stale format and narrow perspective of the theoretical organ. Kautsky alleged that *he* was the target of "a conspiracy of the party's utmost left wing."[16] Ironically, at the moment the party as a whole lurched to the right, Kurt Eisner was bearing hard left from his customary centrist course. But instead of assailing his comrades' giddy enthusiasm for Burgfrieden and conquest, he focused the *Neue Zeit* piece, "Driving Forces," on the organization he held responsible for the war. The article came to print in the 23 April edition.

Under the direction of its president, Dr. Heinrich Claß, the Pan-German League had become the veritable engine of imperial expansion, forcing the state's hand in its dealings with colonial rivals. Indeed, the Pan-Germans constituted a de facto government more resolute and effective than Berlin's officialdom. Yet neither the Reichstag nor the press apprehended the League's extraordinary purchase in effecting its agenda, although its spokesmen had argued again and again for the necessity of war if Germany were to survive as a sovereign nation. Despite the prominence of many of those spokesmen in the Prussian aristocracy and military high command, the League's parliamentary and media critics routinely dismissed it as a fringe organization to be excluded or perhaps manipulated at will. Hence the widespread incredulity and sense of being swept up in a rogue tide when the near-farcical, royal double murder at Sarajevo escalated to apocalyptic bloodletting. "For about a decade," Eisner wrote here, "I have attempted with no success whatsoever to make known the political significance of that coalition with the corporate name Pan-German League advocating for a greater Germany." Although it operated as a patriotic front, the League virtually embodied "the play of driving economic forces" in shaping foreign policy, accomplishing more than all of the political parties combined.

Citing the impetus to both Moroccan crises, Eisner detailed how the League's *völkisch* (national) patriotic cant was merely window dressing. "The real goal is the acquisition of German colonies where German farmers can plant, that provide us raw materials for industry and need German finished goods in exchange. That is the 'secure market,' the dream of Germany's export industry." To establish these colonies Germany had to strengthen its position in Europe militarily through compulsory service and unbridled expansion of the fleet. Little wonder then that executives of so many of the League's offshoots and affiliates—the various interest groups of capitalist enterprise—were retired generals and admirals. The Pan-German message was spread by its own press and an army of academic propagandists who appeared "like snails after a thunderstorm" to offer commentary to leading bourgeois papers whenever tensions flared over another egregious excess of Wilhelmine Weltpolitik.

Anyone, Eisner insisted, who had followed the League's long, carefully coordinated, well-financed campaign for martial confrontation with the Entente powers knew full well that hostilities would ensue as soon as a fitting pretext arose. And yet so many government and party officials were caught unawares and seemingly paralyzed by the process set in motion at Sarajevo. This he knew from personal experience, for when those who understood what was afoot and warned of imminent danger, the 'leading' public figures pronounced them mad. Now for *Neue Zeit* Eisner quoted speeches and articles of Pan-German propagandists from January to December 1914 to document his allegations. General Konstantin von Gebsattel, Professor Richard du Moulin-Eckart, Admiral Alfred Breusing, Major General August Keim, and Professor Franz von Liszt urged the populace first to prepare for the inevitable struggle that would decide Germany's fate, then to persevere until sacrifice yielded victory or destruction. For as Dr. Moulin-Eckart uttered in April 1914, "if Ragnarök, the twilight of the gods, were imposed on us, then better in raging battle than in languishing invalidism."

With Germany now locked in the fight for which the Pan-Germans had long spoiled, it was imperative, Eisner argued, that Social Democracy establish its own distinct war aims and exit strategy lest the proletariat be dragged into the pit dug by their doomed erstwhile lords. "Those who persist in demanding, even in wartime, that the words with which they are bombarded should have meaning must recognize that every call to perseverance ceases to be an empty phrase only when the objective to be achieved is clearly stated. Then too the military situation to be interpreted as 'victory' depends on the objective." Although he despaired for the moment of the party's willingness to break ranks with the unabashed imperialists, he knew that breach was ordained.[17]

His article had its effect. The association New Fatherland, an organization founded in November 1914 to promote European peace, link domestic and foreign policy, and end "the present system by which some few may determine the weal and woe of hundreds of millions of people," promptly reprinted "Driving Forces" as the fourth in a series of pamphlets advancing its cause. Among the members and affiliates were the physicist Albert Einstein, journalist Hellmut von Gerlach, economist Lujo

Brentano, novelist Romain Rolland, and Eisner's Marburg acquaintance Ferdinand Tönnies. The first two thousand copies sold out quickly, and a second edition of three thousand was printed.[18]

A pamphlet on yellow journalism by the economist Karl Bücher and the press reaction to the sinking of the *Lusitania* by the *U-20* on 7 May impelled Eisner to exhort his comrades to uphold truth as the ultimate imperative in reporting on the war. Bücher's *Unsere Sache und die Tagespresse* (Our Cause and the Daily Press) condemned biased, sensationalist reportage not just in the enemy camp but to a lesser extent in German papers as well. He despaired at reading in foreign tabloids patently concocted, hateful accounts of German atrocities in the frontlines yet noted that even the soldiers in field gray protested some German journalists' debased vilification of Entente troops. Conversely he lauded the Social Democratic press, which for the most part had maintained a high standard of objectivity. He held that it was of utmost importance that reportage be factual rather than factional. To elevate professionalism, Bücher proposed a detailed academic curriculum for aspiring newspapermen, the basis for the journalism department he established the following year at Leipzig University, the first in Germany.[19]

Although Eisner duly credited Bücher's "good-natured professorial admonition to stick to the truth," he took pointed exception to the assertion that the German bourgeois press was in any way less culpable than its counterparts abroad. As evidence he cited the unapologetic jubilation of press accounts in Berlin, Munich, and Leipzig at the *Lusitania*'s fate, with nearly twelve hundred civilians drowned. The gloating confirmed how fully the nation's press corps abdicated its most sacred trust. Having forsaken all critical reserve, it now functioned as a tool of state, blissfully inured to the strictures of censorship. "Never," Eisner warned, "may the press allow its freedom of expression to be taken, and the more immediate the fateful hour of nations, the more we require the assurance, clarification, and direction that derive from incorruptible ambition to truth." In the absence of institutional leadership in this arena, it fell to the public "to liberate itself from the devastating influence of the sham press, to uphold the critical judgment and sense of truth that its newspapers deem incompatible with national obligations." The article was published in May by the *Essener Arbeiterzeitung* under the title "The Press in Wartime."[20]

General Egon von Gayl, deputy commander of the Seventh Army Corps in Westphalia, condemned Eisner's piece for undermining national unity and military interests by reviling that majority of German papers ceding their divergent viewpoints for the greater good of the fatherland. Gayl urged patriotic editors not to dignify such perfidy with further comment.

Eisner responded by writing to him directly yet carefully couching the answer in the subjunctive. "I would have to reject the deputy command's declaration in form and content as offensive and insulting, and since it is directed against a known spokesman of Germany's largest party, to charge breach of the Burgfrieden as well, if I did not have to fault myself for the failure of my own poor powers of written expression . . . to convince the deputy command not just of the purity of my intentions but also of the truth of my views." Gayl chose not to reply.[21]

Since the first months of the war Eisner had been exposing the hyperbole and hypocrisy of the "sham press." The shameless denigration of enemy combatants as cowardly and inept, he pointed out, became immensely problematic when the inept cowards withstood every German assault.[22] And upon report after report claiming that three-quarters of the hostile force had been killed or wounded in another rout, one had to wonder eventually at the math. "Thus in the course of the war," he observed in late October 1914, "such a remarkably tenacious race is gradually killed off by easily fifteen or twenty quarters and still keeps marching on."[23]

On Tuesday, 1 June, Eisner wrote from Munich to Else Belli, with the children on an extended visit in Stuttgart, to report good progress on a collaborative article with Frau Simmel but complained of sleeplessness for which he was taking the soporific Baldrian.[24] He was out late every night at the theater and up early to draft and file the reviews for the *Post*.[25] A week later news that British aircraft had bombed a dirigible hangar near Brussels filled him with anxiety. Recurring nightmares kept him up.[26] Shortages were stretching an already tight budget. The rising price of dogfood, 65 pfennige for a pound of milled oats, caused him to turn to a friendly waiter at the Excelsior Hotel, who saved table scraps for their ailing Juno.[27] On the twelfth Eisner received a letter from Arno Holz, on the verge of ruin in search of a publisher for his latest work. Ever Holz's champion, Eisner asked Belli to appeal to her father to speak with Dietz. "Could German Social Democracy not perhaps do something in return for a poet who was once quite aligned with it?"[28]

Having drawn the ire of the censors, Eisner himself found it even more difficult to bring his work to print. Circulation of the *Arbeiter-Feuilleton* waned as editors skittish about paying for articles that might incur penalties against their journals "canceled subscription one after another."[29] In mid-July he sent a submission to *Neue Zeit* with a grim admission: "To no avail I have tried to publish the enclosed article in the party press."[30] Earlier in the month Eisner had paid tribute in the *Arbeiter-Feuilleton* to the Czech reformer Jan Hus, whose martyrdom on

6 July 1415 still served as inspiration to the persecuted. Having taken up Wycliffe's banner against the corrupt papacy, Hus incited the populace to resist their exploitation for Rome's gain. He grounded his critique in Scripture and awoke in his Bohemian compatriots democratic and nationalist aspirations that shook the ruling houses. By order of the Council of Constance he was burned at the stake for heresy. Offered his freedom if he would but recant, Hus resolutely chose an excruciating death rather than betray truth. Battlefield bravery so celebrated through history as ultimate valor paled in comparison, Eisner declared, to heroism in defense of conscience. "This spiritual and moral service to truth ranks above all life, for it is prerequisite to a life worth living."[31]

Of special significance to Eisner in this bleak time were the Munich performances of Strindberg's plays written after the Inferno crisis, when the dramatist "took vengeance through art on what nearly strangled him."[32] In a February review of *The Pelican* Eisner had deromanticized the notion of heroic defeat in a lost cause. Whereas Wagner's epic vision of doom, proclaimed by thunderous orchestration, was conjured up in full martial panoply from Teutonic lore, Strindberg couched his *Götterdämmerung* in clipped syllables of speech accompanying the prosaic routine of contemporary life. The true poet is "he who can conceive and shape the mythos of his age by consolidating all its perceptions and thoughts, its language, forms, and substance."[33] Melodrama was woefully passé in the time of trench warfare. In May the Chamber Players staged the overdue German premiere of *The Ghost Sonata*, seven years after its debut in Stockholm. With its surreal plot, living-dead characters consumed by despair, and household history as a web of lies, Strindberg's late masterpiece mirrored the tragedy of current European life. In his critique for the *Post* Eisner deemed the play's surrealism "heightened reality" and likened the work to St. John's Revelation, "that darkly glowing book, which with its mystical force of longing has the power to raise great souls from despair."[34]

Monday, 13 September 1915, Eisner confided to Kautsky that he had been working for some time on an article titled "Freedom of the Seas," which he hoped to post to *Neue Zeit* in short order. "It is high time to bring an end to the ignorance in the party on this issue—as shameful as it is grotesque—which manifests itself even in official proclamations of the highest authorities."[35] Kautsky responded that he welcomed the submission but disclosed that from 1 October *Neue Zeit* would be printed again in Stuttgart and subject to internal censorship.[36] The implication was daunting. Otto Geithner, editor of the *Gothaer Volksblatt*, sentenced to three months' confinement for an article deemed critical of the kaiser, had just been released from prison and assigned to an army unit.[37] His paper, one of few that subscribed to Eisner's critique of the party leadership, had been banned by the military censor since February 1915.[38] For her antiwar agitation Clara Zetkin was awaiting trial for treason in a cell in Karlsruhe.[39]

Increasingly proscribed from the party press, Eisner once again struggled to stay solvent. In a letter of 1 October he confronted Joseph Belli for upsetting Else by lamenting their hand-to-mouth existence. Citing her chronic bouts of depression and frightful self-destructive impulses, he pleaded with the elder Belli to address any concerns directly to him. "You have no idea to what extremes Else can go in her distressed moments." He went on to clarify that the considerable personal and political consequences he faced upon leaving his wife and family for her were worthwhile because his nurture had saved her from herself. He expressed gratitude for the comfortable home her father had bought for her but confessed that he personally had preferred a more modest farmhouse in the country, which they themselves could have afforded. The commission to file Landtag reports had necessitated engagement of additional staff for the *Arbeiter-Feuilleton*, an unanticipated expense, but otherwise, even after the beginning of the war, they had managed to stay afloat. "It is true that we often have no money for days on end, but the cause is not lack of earnings but rather the irregularity and arbitrariness of honoraria payments." Should Joseph Belli make good on his threat to curtail support so as to part them, "it would be hard for us, but we would still endure because even then we would not lose each other."[40]

More unsettling than his personal circumstances was the state of Social Democracy. Friday, 3 December, Eisner unburdened himself at length in a letter to Kautsky. "At present it is not possible to speak the truth openly, so I will ease my conscience by this means," he began. Most of the party's members of the Reichstag, Eisner charged, were now complicit with the government he held responsible for the war, spurning every peace initiative embraced by the German proletariat. Just as Chancellor Bethmann had been driven by the hawkish clamor of special interests to acquiesce in a war he opposed, he was now hostage to the annexationist demands from every bourgeois party and elements of the Social Democratic majority. Eisner considered this the critical juncture for the party's dissidents in the Reichstag—the only Germans in whom the international proletariat retained confidence—to enunciate a peace proposal of their own. Invoking party discipline for the sake of unity, the majority faction contrived to silence their comrade critics. "Humbug!" Eisner answered, "At the moment there is more at stake than the superficial, formal unity of a social democratic party whose leaders are in large part no longer social democratic." Given the censorship of the press, the Reichstag was the only remaining forum where divergent opinion could be publicly voiced and heard. Besides, the deep division within the party was common knowledge. By speaking out against annexations, the opposition could promote peace without questioning the universally acknowledged right to national defense. There was more to gain than lose, however vehemently the majority faction objected. "Discipline can never be a pretext for relinquishing the profession of one's convictions." He concluded by urging Kautsky to make use of the missive as he saw fit.[41]

In successive issues of the *Arbeiter-Feuilleton* Eisner anonymously questioned Bethmann's persistent attempt to blame England for the outbreak of fighting in August 1914. The chancellor was wont to assert that there would have been no war had London firmly declared its neutrality, a claim Eisner countered with logic. "Only if one already regards the Entente's guilt as *proven* can one consider England's hesitance to declare neutrality as conducive to war. For if one were to accept (and the unbiased critic must indeed hold *both* results of his investigation for equally possible!) that the Central powers were resolved to fight, then conversely a declaration of neutrality, or even the mere *possibility* of England's neutral stance, must have had the effect that the Central powers, freed of their concern about England's intervention, then began the war straightaway."[42] A review of the published diplomatic documents incontrovertibly established that the German government knowingly misled the Reichstag on 4 August with a false version of events, prompting the declaration of war on Russia, and on this basis the people's representatives approved war credits.[43] Eisner's bitterness at the subterfuge was compounded no doubt by the memory of his own unwitting complicity, having trusted Adolf Müller's judgment.

Light shone in the dark on 21 December when twenty Social Democrats voted in the Reichstag against the fifth war-credits appropriation. Twenty-two more absented themselves rather than support the measure. The opposition was led by Karl Liebknecht, who had cast the sole vote against renewal of funding on 2 December 1914, inciting a furor over his breach of vaunted party discipline. Otto Rühle joined Liebknecht in rejecting the third military appropriations bill on 20 March 1915, and five months later thirty-two Social Democrats, Rühle among them, demonstrated the growing opposition to the war by leaving the hall while Liebknecht once again voted no. The eighteen Social Democrats who voted with Liebknecht and Rühle in December 1915 were members of the Haase-Ledebour Group. To be able to join freely in the opposition,

Haase, at Friedrich Ebert's insistence, had resigned the previous day as cochair of the party's Reichstag deputation. The wedge driving the Social Democrats' division was the German nationalist demand for territorial concessions as a condition for peace talks—a demand supported by the social chauvinists.[44]

In the minutes before the Reichstag vote Ebert and Friedrich Geyer addressed the assembly. Citing the determination of Germany's enemies to gain total victory, Ebert affirmed the absolute necessity of unified national defense but rejected expansionist war aims of both sides, for they would inevitably spawn future conflict. To enthusiastic applause of the bourgeois parties he endorsed the new credits. Geyer then rose to speak for the Social Democratic minority. Decrying the "military dictatorship that ruthlessly suppresses all efforts at peace and seeks to stifle free expression of opinion," he charged that continuation of the war served no end other than the destruction of culture. Precisely the annexationists, in Germany as well as abroad, were the greatest hindrance to peace negotiations. Accordingly, he and his nineteen fellows would vote to derail the war machine.[45]

Tuesday evening, 28 December, Eisner attended the world premiere of Strindberg's *Advent*, staged by Otto Falckenberg's Chamber Players, a post-Inferno morality play in which corrupt officialdom, condemned to hell, must recognize its wickedness in order to be purified. The performance, anchored by Emilie Unda as the judge's wife, Eisner pronounced a tour de force, but he fretted that Strindberg's "religious conversion" was misunderstood. Far from submission to a perceived divine design, his was a profession of faith in "all the scientific, economic, technological, organizational progress of the modern world" to transform and elevate humanity. Like Rousseau's, his was a social creed, indeed a "socialist confidence in the future, ethically conceived, early Christian in character, yet by no means romantic-reactionary." The Chamber Players' achievement under Falckenberg, even on a small stage with antiquated equipment, prompted Eisner to ask when it might be possible to construct a modern theater in Munich, nothing grandiose but rather simply refined and up to the state of the art.[46]

For his traditional New Year's retrospective and prospective Eisner chose a form utilized from Plato on to guide the reader to a reasoned conclusion. Titled "Collapse! A Conversation at the Turning Year," the didactic dialogue pits realist against visionary. The latter speaks with Eisner's voice in a debate on the collapse of capitalism. The realist maintains that in seventeen months of war capitalism has shown its renewed vigor: the factories are running at full capacity and unemployment is nonexistent. The symbiotic resilience of an economy and state based on greed is indisputable: "In the nation's most critical hour of need, capitalism demonstrates its colossal might to lend on its own security and future." The visionary counters that the war-profiteers' dream come true is a nightmare for the populace as a whole, a garish illusion of prosperity that will vanish when peace comes. While the creditors grow fat, the masses will scrape for generations to repay the national debt and interest. What the realist hails as triumph, the visionary derides as collapse. Their inability even to agree on a definition of terms is symptomatic, the visionary asserts, of the disintegration. The blurring of meaning, of moral absolutes is consistent with the breakdown of an order no longer viable. To millions upon millions the catastrophic war was unthinkable in the twentieth century, yet the ruling elite of Europe's feudal states succeeded in manufacturing it. Knowing now that the unthinkable has a life of its own, the visionary commits to forging a new world. "Never again will I let myself be appeased, silenced, stopped. No sacrifice can be too great. . . . The time for daring has come!"[47]

Economist Rudolf Breitscheid, formerly a regular contributor to Friedrich Stampfer's *Pressekorrespondenz*, shared Eisner's critique of the party's Burgfriedenspolitik. In May 1915 Breitscheid and his wife, Tony, launched their own syndication from Berlin, the markedly pacifist *Sozialistische Auslandspolitik* (Socialist Foreign Policy). For their publication Eisner prepared a series of articles on the French socialists' congress of December 1915, animated by the call of Marx's grandson Jean Longuet for his fellow *Chambre* deputies to urge their counterparts abroad to join in a peace initiative.[48] On New Year's Day 1916 Liebknecht's closest allies, known as the International Group, met in secret at his Berlin law office to consider Rosa Luxemburg's "Statement of Principles on the Mission of International Social Democracy," composed in her prison cell, as the basis of their program against the Burgfrieden, its adherents, and the war itself.[49] Her manifesto reiterated the primacy of the international proletariat over all national allegiances and demanded the immediate resumption of class war in the warring states. By wholeheartedly subscribing to imperialism, the party leadership in Germany, France, and England had exploded the Second International and immeasurably strengthened the ruling states' domination over workers everywhere. In light of this "treason against the most elementary principles of international socialism," she called for a new organization to lead the revolutionary masses.[50] The statement, amended by committee, was printed in a newsletter on 3 February. After the collective pseudonym of the editors, the newsletter eventually took the title *Spartacus*, and the International Group came to be called the Spartacus Group.[51]

The first week of January 1916 Eisner posted to *Neue Zeit* an article titled "On the Theory of Approving War Credits."[52] In support of
the soldiers fighting for their lives he argued for renewal of funding but
explicitly divorced defense of the troops from "the most brutal war of
conquest" waged by the government and high command. "If, however,
the funding vote becomes a symbol of struggle against the government
and the system—and increasingly it has become such in the course of the
war—then the emphatic rejection of credits becomes the first and most
obvious duty."[53] The entire piece was struck by the censor.

Tuesday, 11 January, Friedrich Ebert was elected cochair of the Social
Democratic deputation in the Reichstag, joining Scheidemann in Haase's
place. The next day the caucus acted on Carl Legien's motion and voted
to expel Karl Liebknecht from its ranks.[54] On the same day Erhard Auer
apprised Eisner that the party executive of Bavaria required that he repay
3,850 marks of advances for the voters' handbook he had failed to submit once the war began.[55] Two weeks later Eisner wrote to Kautsky that
the series for the Breitscheids had been banned by the censor, effectively
undoing the "one attempt made to date to square things with the French
party."[56] Ebert desperately hoped to keep Eisner and Bernstein, whom
he regarded as both moderates and key pacifists, from going over to the
opposition altogether.[57] But the great split in German Social Democracy
was imminent.

Eisner already had a following among the party's Munich youth group,
a formal organization for those from eighteen to twenty-three years of age,
some of whom were recovering from wounds suffered at the front. "The
experience of the World War and the opposing views within the party were
reflected in the youth group's discussions," Felix Fechenbach recounts.
A frequent speaker at their meetings was Kurt Eisner, whose precepts of
ethical socialism, presented in the memorable talk "Political Will in World
History," strongly appealed to the idealism of the audience. The Christmas
program he organized for the group in 1915 was particularly inspirational,
linking celebration with struggle. The local party leadership moved to reestablish control by changing the older age limit to twenty-one, thus forcing
out the most radicalized members.[58] Eisner detailed his dilemma to Joseph
Belli. "It appears as though at present everything is conspiring against me.
And this time it is dead serious. . . . I have here a large and growing following for my *intermediary* position in the party strife that is raging as hatefully
here as elsewhere. There seem to be some fanatics among the trade-union
officials who want to render me void."[59]

On 14 February, sick and listless at home, Eisner penned a note
to Kautsky to comment on German Social Democracy's woeful

fragmentation. He worried about the immediacy and authenticity of the reports he received on Haase's statements. "The most momentous thing," Eisner ventured, "would be for all elements of the opposition to unite on a *positive plan of action* for the *whole party*."[60] It was not to be. The following day the centrist Haase-Ledebour Group resolved to cease all further collaboration with the Spartacus Group for having willfully fragmented the opposition. Rosa Luxemburg, released from prison on 18 February, welcomed the rift as "a great step forward in clarifying, strengthening, and differentiating minds."[61] On 19 March the Spartacus Group convened again in Berlin, reaffirmed Luxemburg's manifesto, and called for socialist deputies in every warring state to reject categorically all war funding "regardless of the military situation," to agitate relentlessly in their parliaments against imperialism, and to rekindle the masses' international solidarity and opposition to war.[62]

The first opportunity presented itself the next week when the German government's request for emergency credits came to a vote in the Reichstag on Friday, 24 March. To shouts of derision from the bourgeois parties and the Social Democratic majority, Haase grounded the opposition's stance in the growing suffering of the German people and in the unwillingness of the government to make peace despite the relatively advantageous circumstances. "If it were solely a question of preserving the territorial integrity of the nation and the independence of our people, we could have likely already achieved peace. . . . Instead, ever louder are the voices claiming as the war's goal the expansion of our world power, the attainment of world dominion."[63] Liebknecht, Rühle, and eighteen members of the Haase-Ledebour Group, including Eduard Bernstein, voted no; fourteen other Social Democrats walked out in sympathy. Within hours members of the Social Democratic majority announced that they had met in caucus and voted 58–33 to cast out the eighteen, just as they had banished Liebknecht. The eighteen responded immediately that it was they who acted in accordance with Social Democratic principles and the dictates of the party congresses. Moreover, to serve the interests of their electorate, they declared that they were forming their own Social Democratic Collaborative (Sozialdemokratische Arbeitsgemeinschaft, or SAG). The notice was signed by all eighteen, including Bernstein, Wilhelm Dittmann, Geyer, Haase, Georg Ledebour, Arthur Stadthagen, and Emanuel Wurm. The next day Haase resigned as cochair of the Social Democratic Party executive to assume the same position with Ledebour in the new organization.[64] The rampant dissidence was now officially a party split.

CHAPTER NINETEEN

WAR FOR WAR'S SAKE: POLITICAL ALIENATION AND REALIGNMENT (1916–1917)

M AURICE HANKEY, secretary of the War Council in London, advised Prime Minister Asquith in June 1915 that Britain's blockade of Germany would work in time "when the psychological moment arrives and the cumulative effects reach their maximum."[1] Anticipating problems in supply and distribution of foodstuffs, the German government had implemented controls in the first months of the war and sought alternatives to customary staples. In January 1915 potatoes replaced grain as the source of flour in *Kriegsbrot* (war bread), an *Ersatz*, or substitute, for the genuine article. Dearth and greed combined to drive speculation. The cost of a liter of milk in the capital went up by 175 percent in 1915, from 12 to 33 pfennige.[2] During the Berlin "butter riots" in mid-October angry crowds smashed shop windows and fought with police over shortages and exorbitant prices. *Vorwärts* reported unrest in Münster and Aachen as well.[3] With the failed potato crop of 1916 conditions worsened. Germany's increasing reliance on imports of foods such as herring, pork, and cheese prompted the British and French to buy up critical stores from neutral Sweden and Holland.[4] Although the troops and munitions workers were adequately fed, the civilian populace was in dire need. The press was rife with accounts of food-profiteering, which the Far Right in particular attributed to parasitic Jewish middlemen.[5] In an attempt to silence criticism from the Left, the military governors tightened state-of-siege restrictions, banning Social Democratic meetings and harassing members of the opposition with searches of domiciles and seizure of papers.[6]

In April 1916 Kurt Eisner witnessed proof of Hankey's prophesied psychological moment when an emaciated cart-horse collapsed on a Munich street. Despite the best efforts of the driver, a policeman, and well-meaning bystanders, the beast could not be coaxed back up. "It lay there as though dead, only the labored, anxious breathing and sad black eyes betrayed that it still clung to life." A crew of six fireman arrived, assembled a steel tripod, and by means of block and tackle succeeded in lifting the limp horse and lowering it onto a truck. A wag in the crowd shouted that fresh horsemeat would be on sale the next day. "The point is," someone answered, "the creature has no feed in its gut!"[7] Eisner documented the scene for the *Arbeiter-Feuilleton* and in another piece satirized the panoply of substitute products being turned out by chemists at Berlin's Kaiser Wilhelm Institute, from powdered eggs to dehydrated, cubed essence of roast goose.[8] Virtually every form of natural nutrition had a replacement now, he noted, "not to mention intellectual sustenance, where absolutely everything printed, spoken, thought, felt is a substitute for what was formerly truth and reason." To impose more rigorous food controls, the government created the War Food Office (Kriegsernährungsamt) the next month, directed by Adolf von Batocki, an East Prussian Junker.[9]

A presentiment of worse things to come was Karl Liebknecht's arrest for sedition at a May Day peace demonstration in the capital when the government was increasingly beleaguered by critics at home and abroad. Washington now faulted Berlin for instigating a deadly raid by the Mexican guerrilla Pancho Villa on a border town in New Mexico. Pressed by a Spanish journalist on the question of German-American relations, Foreign Minister Gottlieb von Jagow deftly changed the topic by expressing his great admiration for Cervantes, whose literary achievement was being celebrated at the three hundredth anniversary of his death.[10] Deflection and denial were rampant as prospects for victory dimmed.

Eisner took heart though from the continued interest of Munich's proletariat in cultural offerings. Monday evening, 15 May, the federated trade unions' education committee sponsored a dramatic reading of Strindberg's *Dream Play* by Oscar Vogelmann-Vollrath, prefaced by Eisner's remarks on the work's artistry and meaning. Two days earlier the *Post* printed a summary of the play and notes on its genesis so that the audience might better follow the reading. The union hall on Pestalozzistraße was filled to capacity by workers who had paid 30 pfennige per ticket, "despite the privations of war and their overload of work," just to hear the poetry of the spoken word.[11] A few weeks later Eisner celebrated the world premiere of the second and third parts of Strindberg's *To Damascus* trilogy by Falckenberg's Chamber Players, with Friedrich Kayßler and Helene Fehdmer in the leading roles. The critique touted their interpretation as "a model for all future productions" and lauded Falckenberg's spare staging for its "marvels" of ingenuity. Those present at the two performances had "a real idea of what it once meant for the Greeks to free themselves from the weight of human existence through the violent emotional tumult of their tragedies of fate, to be cast down and lifted up at the same time."[12]

In the wake of Social Democracy's split and Liebknecht's arrest the stakes and risks were mounting. Having determined that "the time for daring" had arrived, Eisner launched a sortie against the state and its apostate Social Democratic champions with a commentary on the spurious pretext for Germany's war with France. Printed in the 24 June issue of the *Arbeiter-Feuilleton*, "The Aerial Bombs of Nuremberg" probed the genesis and effect of the 2 August 1914 report by Bavaria's Hoffmann News Agency that "on the Nuremberg-Kissingen line as well as on the Nuremberg-Ansbach line, aircraft were sighted dropping bombs on the tracks." The *Kölnische Zeitung* then printed the claim and speculated that the airplanes in question were French, an allegation that became grounds for Berlin's declaration of war, delivered in Paris the next day. "In France, however," Eisner wrote, "the story was pronounced an absurd fabrication from the start, which we in turn took as proof of the brazen mendacity of the French."

But now that the alleged bombings had been confirmed as pure fiction, the German public was doggedly indifferent to their own government's subterfuge in plunging the nation into disastrous conflict. In light of what could be fully documented to date as to the declarations of war on Russia and France, Eisner demanded that the government ministers and their agents in the press be held accountable for their deceit. "In truth, the matter cannot possibly go unresolved; after the historical significance it has had there must be *complete* clarification."[13] After printing the exposé, the Karlsruhe *Volksfreund* (Karlsruhe People's Friend), threatened with preventive censorship, canceled subscription to the *Arbeiter-Feuilleton*.[14]

Felix Fechenbach, a convalescing veteran radicalized by his experience, recounts that he and his fellows in Munich increasingly looked to Kurt Eisner for direction after the local party leadership moved in June 1916 to divert its youth movement from autonomous activism to willing wardship. "Together with several friends I approached Eisner with the request to hold separate discussion evenings for us." Eisner agreed but insisted that the meetings be open to all drawn to the opposition, regardless of age.[15]

The government's response to its critics could be gauged by Liebknecht's trial, which concluded on 28 June. He initially drew a sentence of thirty months' hard labor, subsequently increased on 23 August to over four years by the Military High Court.[16] The class of offense entailed disbarment from legal practice and forfeiture of civil rights. Majority Social Democrats had voted with the bourgeois parties to deny Liebknecht immunity from prosecution as a member of the Reichstag. Liebknecht could now neither vote nor represent a state or national constituency.[17] In protest Social Democratic workers mounted mass political strikes—the first in a decade—in Berlin, Braunschweig, Bremen, and Stuttgart. That the strikers were mainly metalworkers at munitions plants infuriated the militarist camp. The social chauvinists vociferously repudiated the walkout and moved to quell it, while the government undertook to cow the opposition by imprisonment or conscription.[18] Rosa Luxemburg was arrested on 10 July 1916 and held without trial in "military protective custody" first at the Women's Prison, then at police headquarters on Alexanderplatz, at Wronke Fortress in Posen, and finally in Breslau Prison until the war's end.[19] Franz Mehring, Julian Marchlewski, Ernst Meyer, Käte Duncker were among the detained; Hugo Eberlein was called to the colors.[20]

In the 20 July edition of *Vorwärts* Eisner supported a wartime party congress to mend the rent in German Social Democracy. Here he broke with other opposition leaders, who held that such a congress would only strengthen the Majority Socialists. "Party clarity and unity," Eisner argued, "will recur on their own once we establish and promptly implement a socialist and democratic program for action . . . to address the present world crisis." By so doing, Social Democracy might actively reclaim its moral authority and dispense with merely denying shared responsibility for the war. The effect would transcend the party itself and even national borders. "A French officer's tragically steeling quote, 'Today we are all just dead men on furlough,' must impel the congress delegates to speak the truth without mortal fear and say what they propose to do."[21] His hope was temporarily thwarted, as there would be no party congress that fall.

Although he had been spared the most recent round of arrests and prosecutions, Eisner's material existence was increasingly threatened by the decline of the *Arbeiter-Feuilleton*. The theater reviews for the *Post* were his only source of regular income now, and he took vital solace in this refuge from factional strife. Upon Erich Ziegel's retirement as manager of the Chamber Players at the end of August, Eisner paid special tribute to the conviction, born in the first months of the war, "that only by presenting the highest art could the monstrosity of our present circumstances be surmounted." Despite limitations of space, fittings, and funding, Ziegel's theater won renown as Germany's Strindberg house, embracing the challenge of dramas that other companies deemed incapable of performance. The impresario's infectious sense of mission animated the entire troupe. Although he staged the work of the avant-garde when other managers banked on a more conventional repertoire, the productions enjoyed long runs. "As they schooled themselves, the Chamber Players cultivated their public too." Under Ziegel the ensemble realized Schiller's didactic ideal of the 'theater as a moral institution.' There could be no higher praise.[22] Ten days later Eisner hailed the debut of Ziegel's successor, Hermann Sinsheimer, who chose Sophocles's *Antigone* as his first production. The tale of conflicted loyalty, fratricide, suicide, and dishonor spoke to the moment and signaled a welcome commitment to Ziegel's activist legacy.[23]

The infighting between Social Democratic factions in Berlin had become as acute as in 1905, with improbable realignments occurring with each new series of arrests, denunciations, and recriminations. The attempt by centrists Adolf Braun and Emanuel Wurm to convene a conference in Nuremberg on 23 July in hope of reuniting the SAG and the Majority Socialists had failed.[24] The SAG and the Spartacists seemed for awhile to be on the point of an alliance advocated by Haase, but this compact proved illusory as well.[25] Tensions between the Majority and the SAG erupted at the national conference of Social Democratic officialdom 21–23 September 1916 in Berlin, which Eisner attended as a delegate from Munich's second Reichstag district.[26] Another purge at *Vorwärts* was brewing in the party executive. Apprised of circumstances in Berlin by Haase, Eisner confined himself for the moment to watching and waiting.[27]

In mid-September Eisner had visited his children in Nuremberg on the way to Berlin, where his declining mother suffered from the food shortage. Every compartment on the overnight train to the capital was packed with soldiers on leave. Nuremberg, he wrote to Belli on the nineteenth, was a ghost town, Berlin a virtual matriarchate.[28] The next day he apprised her that if his subscribers did not settle their arrears, an amount totaling nearly 100 marks, he would be stranded at his mother's flat on Geisbergstraße.[29] He was in "strictly confidential" negotiations for a choice assignment of which he had been assured, one that would finally afford him financial security. The formal offer was to be made shortly, he wrote on the twenty-fourth, but if he accepted, the work would entail his relocation to Berlin for the duration of the war. He would continue to publish the *Arbeiter-Feuilleton*, sending her manuscripts to be typed, mimeographed, and posted. At the moment, though, he was still without means for a return ticket to Munich and would have to postpone departure. He closed with the request that she not mention the business to anyone until he could discuss it with her in person.[30]

The enterprise, it appears certain, was a commission from the pacifist organization New Fatherland, which had issued Eisner's anti-Pan-German article "Driving Forces" as a pamphlet in 1915. Wilhelm Herzog writes in his memoirs that New Fatherland was in contact with him as well. "I was secretly commissioned to found a press to prepare publications that were to appear immediately upon the outbreak of the revolution. Among them were works by Gustav Landauer, Kurt Eisner, and an anthology I conceived, *The World Course of Intellect*, which was to incorporate all the revolutionizing works of world literature: fiction, manifestos, pamphlets. Eisner, with whom I had already discussed the plan repeatedly in Munich, took the lead in organizing this collection."[31] The rapidly changing political environment evidently militated against Eisner's indefinite transfer from Großhadern to the capital.

On 11 October 1916 Majority Socialist Eduard David rejected foreign allegations of German war guilt in a speech before the Reichstag. In support of his argument he parroted Berlin's official version of events from July and August 1914—"in the style of a government commissioner," as Eisner later remarked—and, citing an article from *L'Humanité* the day after Jaurès's assassination, asserted that Jaurès himself laid blame on the French government. Hugo Haase immediately challenged David's claims, but further debate was terminated by a procedural vote.[32] Addressing the Foreign Press Association in London on 23 October, Lord Grey reiterated his position that "this war . . . was not forced upon Germany, but forced by Germany upon Europe." No state, he declared, had designed to invade Germany in the summer of 1914.[33] In a statement to members of the Reichstag's central committee Bethmann underscored on 9 November the import of Grey's linking responsibility for the war with terms of peace.[34]

In a four-part article Eisner examined the question of war guilt and expounded his documentation of German culpability. He opened with remarks on the English proposal that a court determine the instigator. "The English statesman demands a tribunal to decide war guilt, and the German chancellor replies that he need not fear a tribunal." Since both sides agreed in principle to a trial, Eisner suggested that the parties present their evidence and let the chips fall where they may. He had already endorsed Grey's initiative in a letter to the *Chemnitzer Volksstimme*, written and posted in October but held back until a month later, when it ran together with Ernst Heilmann's rebuttal on 21 November.[35] Now he chronicled every discrepancy between various official and actual chronologies of the Austrian, Russian, and German mobilizations of 1914. Russia's mobilization, Eisner argued, was prompted by the alarmist extra edition of the *Berliner Lokal-Anzeiger* on 30 July 1914, a paper with close ties to the government. He understood the chronology all too well, for it was he, at Adolf Müller's summons, who had apprised Heilmann by telephone two days earlier that Russia's muster was imminent. Yet mobilizations in and of themselves were defensive measures, "neither threats nor causes of war." Even Berlin's best intelligence sources confirmed that the Russian military was in no position to make war on Germany. It was solely to Germany's strategic advantage to launch a first strike. Thus Baron Beyens, the Belgian ambassador, suspected all along that Vienna's fateful ultimatum to Serbia had originated in Berlin.[36]

Faulted by Heilmann for having misread events in July 1914, Eisner responded that if it were "a lack of judgment to be mistaken about the causes of a war at its onset," then Marx and Engels had been guilty of the same offense in 1870. Just as they had been deluded by long antipathy to Napoleon III, he was swayed by deep distrust of Russian foreign policy. But he, like them, had the capacity to recheck bearings and change course.[37] The Majority Social Democrats in contrast had descended the slippery slope straight into the abyss. Eisner conceded that the approval of war credits on 4 August 1914 was the party's only course of action then, but what followed was unthinkable. Having acquiesced in the war, Social Democracy by and large rushed to embrace German militarism, imperialism, and absolutism, easily rivaling Chauvin in blind patriotism. Rather than remaining reluctant partners in an inescapable enterprise, the party's leaders joyfully took up the cause of their most insidious class enemy: the Junker generals, for whom "war for war's sake" was their raison d'être. It was the worst capitulation since the National Liberals' collapse of 1866. For his part, Eisner publicly declared his allegiance here at the beginning of December to the opposition.[38] The German Foreign Office and the military high command expressly forbade the article's publication in the *Volksstimme*.[39] It would not come to print until after the war.

Felix Fechenbach recalls in his biography of Eisner that after long consultation as to program and participants, invitations to the first of the requested "discussion evenings" went out on 7 December. Two dozen dissidents, mainly the expelled radicals of the Social Democratic Association's Youth Section assembled in the private room of a tavern to hear Eisner trace the fragmentation of Social Democracy effected by the war.[40] In this personal following was the core of Eisner's future revolutionary cadre. At the starting point of his rise to power he was on the brink of penury. Hausenstein often saw him in town, his familiar rucksack filled with books and a few "modest provisions for the household outside the city walls."[41] One evening after speaking at the union hall on Pestalozzistraße, Eisner uncharacteristically declined to join members of his audience for continued discussion at a café. "After much coaxing," Fechenbach recollects, "he finally confessed to us with some embarrassment that he lacked the 25 pfennige for a cup of coffee."[42]

Eleven years after Eisner had been forced out at *Vorwärts* by the party executive, the same body sacked his surviving successors in mid-October 1916 and installed Eisner's former ally Friedrich Stampfer, now firmly in the Majority camp, as head editor.[43] Stampfer in turn undertook to woo Eisner back. Untempted, Eisner remarked the irony to Kautsky in a note of 12 December: "Just think, *V.* has solemnly invited me repeatedly to contribute." Yet the requests caused him to wonder. "What," he posed to Kautsky, "do they hope to gain by it?"[44] At the end of the month the *Münchener Post* apprised Eisner that beginning 1 January 1917 the rate for his theater reviews would be raised to 15 marks regardless of line count.[45] Effectively proscribed from publishing his political commentary and wary of Stampfer's overtures, he no doubt welcomed any increase in income.

On Sunday, 7 January 1917, Haase, Ledebour, and Ewald Vogtherr of the SAG executive succeeded in convening at the Reichstag a national conference of the Left's opposition leadership to discuss joint goals and tactics. It was a remarkable coup. The Reichstag president, Left Liberal Johannes Kaempf, banned the police, press, and public from observing the proceedings, which were to follow the decorum of a regular deputation caucus. Delegates were selected by the same rules as those to the Social Democratic Party congress. The conference was attended by 157 persons representing 72 Social Democratic electoral districts, 35 of whom were Spartacists.[46] Ledebour opened the meeting by stating the ground rules and agenda. Haase, as first scheduled speaker, addressed the state of Social Democracy, attacking the Majority executive for abandoning class struggle, serving as lackey to the German chancellor, and turning *Vorwärts* into a government organ. The opposition, he declared, was committed to reclaim the Social Democratic Party for the masses and restore it to its historical purpose so that it not sink to the trade unionism that now defined English socialism. Former editor of the *Leipziger Volkszeitung* Richard Lipinski, closely aligned with the SAG, spoke to how the opposition might best coordinate its efforts. He rejected the tactic of withholding local monies from the national party as potentially undermining the very structure the opposition hoped to regain from the rogue executive. "Stay in the party, make use of every means within the party to strengthen our line. . . . Our power lies in the masses, but only in the organization we can unite the masses." Since that executive now controlled the party press, Lipinski urged a word-of-mouth campaign of agitation in every electoral district and among troops in the field.[47]

Speaking for the Spartacists, Ernst Meyer claimed that what separated the Spartacists from the SAG was their bearing toward the International. The Spartacists categorically rejected any defense of Germany's imperialist, militarist regime. The class struggle therefore had to be waged against the Majority leadership at all costs, even if it meant the disintegration of the tainted Social Democratic Party. "Taken as a whole," Meyer charged, "the Collaborative still espouses the fiction of party unity."[48] Julian Borchardt, representative of the newly formed International Socialists of Germany, preferred occasional joint action with the SAG to formal political union and advocated withholding dues from the national Social Democratic Party regardless of effect on the national organization.[49] The three opposition factions presented resolutions delineating their respective stances.

When conference chairman Wilhelm Dittmann opened discussion, Kurt Eisner, representing his circle of Munich's dissidents, generally agreed with Meyer's critique of the party, "for even before the war . . . what we perversely, unconsciously imitated in our organization was the Prussian barrack-state's organization." Over time any deviation from the executive line was classed as mutiny. "In particular it is the concept of discipline," he professed, "which has absolutely nothing to do with democracy and socialism, deriving instead from militarism, that has crippled us intellectually and morally." On the other hand he took exception to the Spartacists' quasimystical faith in collective motive will. "This blunting of the personal consciousness of individual party comrades, this skulking behind the masses is what has always inspired the heroes of bureaucracy." If the Spartacists indeed rejected continued socialist support for national defense then they should have the courage to call for comrades to lay down their arms. He personally believed that the opposition deputies could invoke mass actions from the rostrum of the Reichstag, the last free forum, by demanding directly that the government abdicate: "We must tell the government: what you are witnessing today, what you yourselves call the most terrible crime is your fault. Your system has failed. New people, new men must take over. Out with you! Only those not responsible for the war can conclude peace with other nations."[50]

After heated debate the SAG resolution to retake Social Democracy was approved by 111 votes, the Spartacists garnered 34, the International Socialists but 6. Before adjournment Kautsky presented a resolution urging the socialist parties in the warring states to demand that their governments define their war goals; to require a comprehensive peace without humiliating terms, forced annexations, and crippling reparations; to press for courts of arbitration to resolve international conflicts and for universal arms-limitation accords. Eisner followed with a resolution condemning Bethmann's peace proposal of 12 December 1916 as a ploy, for the German government had rejected President Wilson's subsequent offer to broker talks. "For the German people," Eisner clarified, "there are only two paths left: either we support, directly or indirectly, the Pan-German politics of conquest or we call on the proletarian masses to mount against the responsible government an autonomous campaign of propaganda for a *European*, democratic, and socialist peace." Both resolutions were unanimously endorsed.[51]

The Majority Socialists responded with yet more recriminations. At the meeting of the Social Democratic Party advisory board on 18 January 1917 Friedrich Ebert refuted point by point, over objections from Collaborative adherents Lipinski and Hermann Fleißner, the criticisms voiced at the opposition conference. The Collaborative and the Spartacists had already broken with the party, Ebert contended, and now the time had come for the Majority to purge the menace. In a resolution beginning with a pointed rejection of Eisner's remarks on discipline, the advisory board pronounced affiliation with the opposition organizations fundamentally "incompatible with membership in the greater party."[52] Three days later Eisner wrote to the bourgeois pundit Maximilian Harden, who having initially supported the war, now committed his journal, *Die Zukunft*, to the peace initiative: "For two and a half years I have fought against my party, which had the duty and might to be savior to the world yet betrayed its mission for the basest and vilest motives." Having been silenced too long, he was now fully committed "to attack the press pestilence (in its most virulent organ) and to chastise a parliamentary swindler who is the mastermind of a party he ruined." Eisner proposed to Harden that they meet for further discussion when he visited Munich.[53]

Beginning in January the discussion evenings of Eisner's cohort were held each Monday at various pubs on Schillerstraße near Munich's main train station. Attendance grew with each meeting. Their purpose, Fechenbach recounted, was "the education of the participants in independent political thought and judgment, particularly to emancipate ourselves from the crush of lies in the daily press." Eisner briefed the group on developments and publications abroad, news of which was suppressed in Germany. The implications were discussed openly until consensus emerged. For Fechenbach and his comrades the meetings were an extraordinary revelation. "Kurt Eisner taught us to read accurately, showed us what was between the lines and words and what had been left unsaid in newspaper articles, government proclamations, and other documents." The local Majority Party ridiculed the ring as an amateur "debate club" adrift.[54]

On 22 January the *Post* featured Eisner's review of the German premiere of *The Persians* at the Munich Playhouse. Aeschylus's jeremiad on a ruinous war of conquest spanned millennia to grip its modern audience. The choral lament of Xerxes's defeat seemed poignantly topical, as the tyrant's ambition was dashed by the resolve of the Athenian republic. "It is the martial tragedy of hubris, arrogance, immoderation—for the ancient Greeks the worst crime against divine fate." For Eisner himself, no doubt, the 1917 revival of *The Persians* might well have been recast as *The Prussians*. The comparison was all the more apt amid the debate over renewal of unrestricted submarine warfare; the crushing blow to the would-be conquerors was the sea battle at Salamis, joined when the Persian admirals rashly pressed an imagined advantage. At end the chorus's lament turns into a curse on the king: "Woe to Xerxes the fool!"[55]

Marshaled to do Auer's bidding, Franz Schmitt, secretary of Munich's SPD and its Voters' League, informed Eisner by registered letter of 27 January that the consolidated board proposed he be expelled from the party for maliciously dishonoring his contract for the voters' handbook. Eisner responded on the the thirty-first, coolly explaining that at issue here was merely an ordinary case of literary rights to a project. He candidly confessed that he was in default, declared that he had already agreed to dissolution of the contract, and added that he had made arrangements with Auer to repay the advances. He appended a dig of his own: "I take note of this communication as an indication of how far the incitement in the party has progressed at present."[56] The same day he forwarded a postal order for a thousand marks to Auer with notice that the full sum of the received advances would be returned within fourteen days.[57] Else Belli commented in retrospect that her father, reluctant to believe that Social Democratic comrades could be so petty, balked a year earlier at a loan to cover the remaining debt. Eisner and she "were firmly resolved to commit suicide if the expulsion occurred," as his life's work would have been effectively nullified. Joseph Belli begrudgingly lent the money against a promissory note, eventually made good by the posthumous sale of Eisner's library.[58]

The German high command's U-boat campaign against merchant shipping began anew on 1 February.[59] On leave from his posting, Fechenbach wrote to Eisner on the thirteenth to arrange an afternoon meeting at Café Stefanie near the university, *Stammlokal* (regular venue) of Munich's bohemians and Eisner's favored haunt.[60] At the moment Eisner was engaged in a sharp exchange with the high command of the First Bavarian Army Corps over prohibition of his serialized mobilization article "for jeopardizing the interests of national defense." The order banning its dissemination in any form had been relayed to him by the mayor of Großhadern. Eisner responded directly to the military authorities: "I confirm communication of this proscription, however, I reject it objectively in its entirety." In contrast to Prussian code, the legislators drafting the Bavarian state-of-war law of October 1912 expressly guaranteed freedom of political expression and forbade only unauthorized military reports. "No one can forbid me in advance to write and publish political and interpretive historical reflections." If indeed his writings violated civil law, he was fully prepared to answer charges in a civil court.

Continuing, Eisner made clear that his was a sacred obligation. "It is the journalist's office to seek the truth conscientiously and, when he has found it, to profess and publicize it for the benefit of the general public. That is the journalist's civic duty, among the essential trusts and inalienable rights of modern society. It would be contemptible cowardice, especially in the present world catastrophe, to conceal one's meticulously hard-won conviction. Truth is the most precious of all national treasures. A state, a nation, a system in which truth is suppressed or won't be heard needs to fall as swiftly and utterly as possible." If the high command could substantiate that anything he had written in the article was false or misleading, he pledged to gratefully incorporate their corrections. The formal protest closed with notice that he intended to file suit if the censor persisted.[61]

Fechenbach records that both the banned article and the letter on censorship were discussed in detail at the Monday evening gathering. Now a frequent guest in Eisner's home, Fechenbach perceived him as a scholar at heart, a secular rabbi grappling with the ethical problem of the age. "I often found him at work on his war archives, ensconced amid the books, journals, and newspapers stacked up on his desk." The Jewish baker's son from Würzburg was emerging as a virtual aide-de-camp. Calling at the cottage in Großhadern, Fechenbach and his fellows took tea with Eisner beneath the firs, weather permitting, or in the ground-floor parlor. Their conversations turned invariably to the war and what might be done to end it.[62] In March 1917 there was much to mull. The Americans, incensed by revelation of German foreign minister Arthur Zimmermann's secret proposed alliance with Mexico and by renewed submarine attacks on passenger vessels, were finally readying for the fight. In Petrograd munitions workers at the Putilov Iron Works went on strike on 7 March. Their marches were joined by the disaffected bourgeoisie. When Tsar Nicholas ordered the army to quell the unrest, mutiny ensued. He was deposed by his war-weary ministers and generals on the fifteenth. A liberal provisional government was formed the next day, contested by the newly formed Petrograd Soviet.

On Saturday, 24 March, art student Josef Breitenbach put out the invitation to Monday's discussion evening at Wiesmayr's Beer Garden.[63] The Social Democratic opposition was to assemble again the first week in April; arrangements had to be made to send a delegate. Eisner was chosen and a collection taken up to cover his travel expenses.[64] Two days later, in response to Kautsky's request for a book review, Eisner took the opportunity to report on events in Munich. "The official party's cause is hopeless," he assessed, citing a recent meeting scheduled to counter his discussion evenings. "If the opposition had not come, the room would have been nearly empty."[65] At the same time Eisner found himself in the unexpected position of being courted to succeed Ernst Heilmann at the helm of the *Chemnitzer Volksstimme*. Severely wounded at the front, Heilmann resettled to Berlin-Charlottenburg to edit the annexationist *Internationale Korrespondenz*, which counted Eduard David, Konrad Haenisch, Wolfgang Heine, Gustav Noske, and Philipp Scheidemann among its contributors.[66] Although the offer from Chemnitz was like manna from heaven, Eisner unwaveringly imposed a critical condition that could not be met: "Only if the *Volksstimme* might transform into an organ of the opposition—which I of course would ardently welcome—could I personally come into consideration as managing editor. Otherwise it is impossible."[67]

On 6 April, Good Friday, the founding congress of the Independent Social Democratic Party convened in Gotha. Forty-two years earlier the rival Lasalleans and Eisenacher had come together here to form the Social Democratic Party. The compound symbolism was surely not lost on Eisner, who habitually drew inspiration from the Christian calendar: Gotha at Easter signaled the resurrection of German socialism. The military authorities had approved the meeting but decreed that it must be held in camera, without publicity, and that the minutes were to be submitted to the censor. Despite the hindrances 143 representatives were present to consider the three-point agenda: the fracture of the German Left, the opposition's preferred organizational structure, and the new entity's course of action.[68]

In his opening report Haase blamed the moral collapse of the old party on two elements: the trade unions' short-sighted leadership and the ideologically corrupt social imperialists. Dittmann asserted that the opposition had not left the party, but rather the party had forsaken its principles. "In truth *we* are the party." Yet he argued now for the creation of a new organization with a distinct hierarchy, one in which power would be decentralized, concentrated in the electoral districts (Wahlkreise) so as to keep the bureaucracy in check and afford full latitude of opinion. Spartacist Fritz Rück, unconvinced by Dittmann's call for formal unification, countered that the Collaborative was too wedded to parliamentary action. The opposition's appeal, Rück preached, should be made to the workers themselves to rise up, end the war, and topple the state. Utopian notions had to be dispelled. "In the age of capitalism precisely nothing can be expected from courts of arbitration, nothing from international law." Accordingly, the Spartacists preferred a "cartel relationship" that would safeguard their autonomy and freedom of action from yet another tyrannical majority.[69]

Eisner answered that the Spartacists' outmoded rhetoric and outlook condemned them to impotence. To deny the proletariat's power to alter capitalist society seemed to him nonsensical in light of socialist influence on the new provisional government in Russia. Rejection of courts of arbitration, he continued, followed Bethmann's line, supported by the Majority Social Democrats, and wildcat agitation programs by the Spartacists would only further fragment the masses. "I call that actionless." He still believed it possible, as did Adolf Braun in Nuremberg, to achieve rapprochement with the Majority given the current developments in Russia and America. In Munich the Majority at least claimed to want to hear out the dissidents, although individual opposition leaders were being ostracized. "We want to win the Munich organization for ourselves." For that reason he argued that the tactics of the opposition would and should vary from state to state. In this sense he supported a cartel relationship *with the Majority* where personal relationships allowed for it. And wherever opposition members could sway the Majority, there they should retain their party affiliation.[70]

The advocates of a unified, separate party won out. Jakob Rieper of Hamburg-Altona urged the Spartacists to accept the vote and work within the construct to achieve their ends. He was seconded by Georg Ledebour, who defended parliamentary participation as a necessity: "*We are democrats*, not just socialists but democrats as well. We seek to implement democracy in the state and society."[71] By the second day of deliberations the delegates knew that the US Congress had approved President Wilson's request for a declaration of war against Germany. The new party came into being that afternoon. Its stated purpose was to represent the interests of the working class in keeping with Social Democracy's founding principles and the dictates of both party and international congresses. It pledged to oppose the ruling state and the government's war policy, which the nominal Social Democratic Party's leadership had determined to support. By a vote of 77 to 42, the name Independent Social Democratic Party of Germany (Unabhängige Sozialdemokratische Partei Deutschlands, or USPD) was adopted. The choice was opposed by Hugo Haase, Eduard Bernstein, Karl Kautsky, Kurt Eisner, and Luise Zietz, who laid claim to the original name and branded the rival Majority Social Democrats "the Government Socialists."[72]

On Easter Monday, the day after adjournment, Eisner wrote to Else Belli that he was departing Gotha for Berlin that morning and would return to Munich on Thursday evening. "I leave Gotha with mixed emotions. The separation is an accomplished fact. We have no other option than to establish our own organization in Munich too. I fought against it to the end, to no avail. If it will be better for us—who knows?"[73] That same day Vladimir Lenin and his Bolshevik cohort disembarked from exile in Bern for Petrograd. By special arrangement of the German Foreign Office, they boarded a sealed railroad car and were transported to the Swedish border via Karlsruhe, Franfurt am Main, and Berlin. On the platform in Bern a group of Russian expatriates assembled in protest, having heard that Lenin was now in the pay of the German high command.[74]

CHAPTER TWENTY

THE MOST BEAUTIFUL
DAYS OF MY LIFE: LEADING THE
OPPOSITION (1917–1918)

WEDNESDAY MORNING, 18 April 1917, Friedrich Ebert opened a meeting of the Majority expanded advisory council with the announcement that the first item of business would be the split formalized at Gotha, superseding consideration of food shortages, electoral reform, and peace initiatives. In the ensuing discussion Paul Reißhaus of Erfurt reported that most of his Thuringian comrades feared that their organization was rapidly evolving into a national-social party. Other speakers downplayed the threat posed by the Independents. Hermann Beims ventured that in Magdeburg the opposition's numbers were insignificant, perhaps 150 adherents. Erhard Auer too believed the Independents' strength overrated. "Munich was represented at Gotha as well, by Eisner. He was not elected but rather appointed a delegate at a meeting of 22 people—11 masters and 11 misses, almost all of them Jewish elements." The insult induced ripples of laughter.[1] In 1982 historian Freya Eisner remarked that many Munich Jews blamed her grandfather's revolution for a surge of anti-Semitism unknown in Bavaria to his contemporaries. Auer's demeaning characterization of Kurt Eisner's cadre suggests, however, that Jew-baiting was already manifest among his professed comrades in the South.[2]

Upon his return from the founding congress of the USPD Eisner felt reinvigorated, refocused as he resumed his critiques for the *Münchener Post*. In a review of Rudolf Franz's book on contemporary drama he reaffirmed the necessity of social and political engagement of both artist and critic, applauding Franz's attempt to apply Marxist historical materialism to interpretation of theater. Reprising the premise of his 1896 essay "Party Art," Eisner stated: "In the age of the proletarian class struggle the great artist must himself be a socialist. The more profoundly and ardently his entire personality is shaped by this worldview, the clearer and bolder he examines men and matters from this perspective, the greater his artistic stature will become through socialist virtue and insight."[3] The next week a dance performance by Lisa Kresse, Primavera and Beatrice Mariagraete, and Lala Herdmenger evoked the observation that "even today there is still something that one may call feeling for life."[4] And on Monday, 30 April, Eisner hailed as a revelation the Chamber Players' premiere of Georg Kaiser's 1912 expressionist masterpiece on the spiritual poverty of material greed, *Von morgens bis mitternachts* (From Morning to Midnight). "Since Saturday we can be confident of having among us a German dramatist of original vitality, fertile imagination, and intellectual magnitude."[5]

May Day 1917 the Munich branch of the Independent Social Democratic Party issued a card recognizing the charter membership of "author Curt Eisner."[6] On the tenth Eisner informed Haase that the local organization would be legally constituted the next week and that its leaders hoped to schedule a public rally to win a broader following. He asked if Haase might find time to speak in such a forum. Although the trip from Berlin would cost time and effort, Eisner coaxed, "ultimately it is not wholly unimportant what becomes of the opposition in the German Empire's second capital."[7] Registration papers were filed with the police department 16 May 1917; the new party stood "in fundamental opposition to the ruling state system and to the Imperial government's war policy."[8]

In light of Eisner's reluctance at Gotha to break with the Social Democratic Party altogether, it would have been indecorous, at the least, for him to serve as chair of the Munich USPD, yet other factors came into consideration. Eisner himself held that a worker should have the authority if the proletariat was indeed to own the movement. For that reason he preferred to serve in an advisory capacity.[9] Fechenbach notes that the discussion evenings continued, independent of the USPD.[10] Perhaps Eisner hesitated to subordinate his critical judgment to another party line, however greatly he might figure in formulating it. Then too he and his cohort surely understood his value as what Falk Wiesemann terms "chief ideologue" of the Munich Independents. With the rival Majority Socialists abetting the government, with the police monitoring the upstarts at every turn, the chair of the new organization was prominently at risk for arrest and detainment: better that a lieutenant be carted off. Police intelligence believed this to be the case.[11] In any case Eisner declined the titular role in favor of master cabinetmaker Albert Winter, a participant together with his son in the discussion evenings.[12] Although Wiesemann dismisses Winter as "otherwise politically insignificant," he was clearly an engaged and trusted comrade. Some weeks earlier he and Eisner had jointly sought to bring the Collaborative executive member Ewald Vogtherr to Munich to address the Independents.[13] Winter became a key agitator in the January 1918 munitions strike.

Eisner's range of action was altered by the establishment of the USPD. He spoke frequently at the regular meetings of its membership at the Lampl Garden, arguing that "the most practical and natural organization would be by plant, where shop stewards would necessarily constitute the vital link to the Independent Party."[14] The 22 May issue of the *Arbeiter-Feuilleton* went out with the notice that regular circulation had to be suspended temporarily. The entire final issue was banned by the censor.[15] Incredibly, despite Eisner's national prominence in the USPD and Auer's niggling enmity, the *Münchener Post* continued to employ the local opposition leader as its chief theater critic.

Worn down by his travails and domestic tensions, Eisner repaired to the spa at Wörishofen in Swabia for a brief cure. The town had transformed into a military convalescent center, he reported to Belli on Wednesday, 23 May, and "my host is himself an ailing officer." Although there was sufficient food and drink, no one had socks.[16] The next day he instructed her to have his daughter Ilse, now twenty-one and living with them, to fetch his weekend theater tickets from the *Post*, as he planned to return on Saturday morning.[17] His critique of Max Dreyer's comedy *Die reiche Frau* (The Rich Woman) as saccharine fluff appeared early the next week: "Apparently the Munich Court Theater has finally decided to withdraw from all contact with the art of the present. No one active there has literary ambition or would have the pluck and proclivity to realize it."[18] In contrast the review of 8 June heralded the Chamber Players' premiere of René Schickele's *Hans im Schnakenloch* (Hans in the Gnat Hole), dramatizing the dilemma of Alsatians torn between Germany and France, as "an earnest attempt to come to grips with the World War through art."[19]

His divorce having been finalized in April, Kurt Eisner wed Else Belli 31 May 1917 in a civil ceremony at Großhadern's town hall. Her father and Richard Kämpfer, a regular participant in the discussion evenings, served as witnesses. Eisner claimed both daughters, Freia and Ruth, as his. The marriage certificate listed him as Jewish.[20] His house was now officially in order, come what may.

On 5 July the *Post* reported that preparations were underway in the United States to equip a two-million-man army.[21] In May 1916 General Ludendorff, the supreme high command's chief of staff under Hindenburg, had remarked disparagingly to Friedrich von der Ropp that the United States had "no soldiers." In January 1917 Ludendorff convinced Kaiser Wilhelm, over Bethmann's objection, that the return to unrestricted submarine warfare would void Washington's threat, for Britain and France would soon capitulate. Bethmann further alienated the Right when, in an address to the Reichstag on 29 March, he categorically rejected any German initiative to restore the tsar to power. Worse yet, he prompted Wilhelm at Easter to endorse abolition of three-tiered voting in Prussia, in light of the Social Democrats' service in arms. Ludendorff denounced the promised reform as an unforgivable "kowtowing before the Russian Revolution." Then on 23 April at a meeting called by Wilhelm to discuss war aims, Bethmann broached the renunciation of annexations, which both the Majority and Independent Socialists advocated as the way to a negotiated peace. Yet at the same time the Reichstag had come to regard Bethmann as too accommodating to the high command. Exasperated by Wilhelm's vacillations, Ludendorff finally tendered his resignation on 12 July. The chancellor followed suit. It was his offer that the kaiser reluctantly accepted. Georg Michaelis, the Prussian food-rationing commissioner was appointed in his stead. The *Münchener Post* applauded Bethmann's dismissal as "a success for Social Democracy" and a rebuke to the annexationists.[22]

The *Arbeiter-Feuilleton* now shelved, Eisner turned to a series of vast editorial projects with his literary partners. The publishing enterprise mandated by New Fatherland became a top priority. He composed a detailed business plan spelling out the new press's purpose and practice. The preamble proclaims that the founders aspired to promote a modern, humane order by dispelling "the necrotic, the medieval, the contradictory of our public life." Their vehicle of enlightenment would be an encyclopedia like that of Diderot and d'Alembert. Contributors of international reputation were on board, and archives were being compiled. Eisner projected that 150,000 marks were required to launch the enterprise, of which 90,000 had already been borrowed or donated. Full-scale publication could commence once the war ended.[23] Besides Eisner, Herzog cites Heinrich Mann, Raoul Francé, and Friedrich Wilhelm Foerster, professor of ethics at Munich's Ludwig Maximilian University, as chief collaborators.[24]

On 1 August 1917 Eisner completed a prospectus for *Der Weltweg des Geistes*, expanding its purview considerably beyond the revolutionary texts Herzog had envisioned. Eisner had in mind another encyclopedia, a "comprehensive compilation . . . to recapitulate uniformly through documents mankind's *entire* intellectual life across epochs and peoples." Each volume was to include an introduction clarifying the historical context and import of its contents. For the intitial series he proposed sixty-some topics, including antiwar drama by Aristophanes, the heretical astronomical treatises of Giordano Bruno, Abraham Lincoln's speeches, and the Boxer Rebellion from the Chinese perspective. The individual tomes were to cost no more than 2 marks.[25] By the end of the month it had been determined that Eisner and Landauer would serve as coeditors. To Herzog, the business manager, Eisner wrote on 30 August of their progress, outlining the first two series of ten volumes each. He proposed that Heinrich Mann prepare a new translation of Zola's *La fortune des Rougon*, whereas he himself would render Jaurès's history of the Franco-Prussian War.[26] Everything appeared to be on track. A third planned series drew on Eisner's mass-education endeavor in Nuremberg and his special concern for shaping adolescent minds. The Young People's Library was intended to present an overview of socialist life, thought, and culture through illustrated biographies, literary texts, songbooks, histories, and annotated collections of documents pertaining to war and its aftermath. Among the books and chapters slated for inclusion were the causes of poverty, Rousseau's social contract, pacifism, the Russian revolutions of 1905 and 1917, Booker Washington, and letters from fallen soldiers worldwide.[27]

As Herzog, Landauer, and Eisner busied themselves with the print campaign that was to follow Germany's expected defeat, Lenin, threatened with arrest by Kerensky's provisional government, was directing his outlawed Bolshevik Red Guard from hiding in Finland. General Kornilov, whom Kerensky had named the Russian Army's supreme commander, withdrew troops from the front to wrest control of Petrograd and impose a military dictatorship. Kerensky then appealed to the Bolshevik militia he had sought to disarm. On Lenin's orders twenty-five thousand Red Guard recruits amassed to crush the reaction.[28]

As Lenin issued instructions from Helsinki to his vanguard in Russia, Eisner's discussion group in Munich was growing in number and influence, attracting a broad spectrum of leftist dissidents. The German sailors' mutiny of 2 August in Wilhelmshaven and the execution by firing squad of its leaders, seamen Albin Kölbis and Max Reichpietsch, on 5 September fueled the question whether a revolution in Germany could succeed.[29] Oskar Maria Graf, former disciple of the anarchist Erich Mühsam, made his way to the weekly meetings fall 1917. He had been discharged from the military as mentally ill in December 1916 after refusing a menial order at the eastern front and then going on hunger strike while in detention. He found work at a biscuit factory in Munich and chanced upon an acquaintance from Mühsam's circle who invited him to a meeting of antiwar socialists at the Black Eagle Tavern on Schillerstraße. Two days later Graf appeared at the pub expecting a clandestine gathering. He was amazed when the owner openly directed him to a smoky sideroom where between forty and fifty participants, including some of his fellow syndicalists, a large contingent of working women, a few intellectuals, and an army sergeant sat listening to a speaker, "a man of slight build with long gray hair, mustache, and goatee."

The figure in casual dress and pince-nez impressed Graf as a retired academic. "He had a rather toneless, raspy voice but spoke most fluently," punctuating his lines with upheld index finger or a brief arm gesture. Whoever he was, his message was purely incendiary and moved the audience to cries of agreement and calls for action: 'In 1914 German Social Democracy failed. The proletariat was shamefully, pitiably betrayed by its leaders. The bloodbath began. But now the first signs of awakening are evident. . . . It is no longer a matter of mere protest, comrades, we must realize that our purpose is to progress to revolution!' Graf asked the man next to him who the speaker might be. "That's Eisner," came the reply. Thereafter Graf regularly attended the Independent Socialists' discussion evenings, "of which everyone in the city was aware." The sergeant he had seen that first night was Felix Fechenbach, who opened the meetings and always sat next to Eisner. Filled with the holy spirit of his master's humanity, as Graf writes, Fechenbach became known to the discussants as "the apostle." Their gatherings struck Graf as critically momentous; in 1936 he wrote that "the Bavarian Revolution literally started at the Black Eagle."[30]

Part of the appeal of the discussion evenings was the earnest debate that followed the presentation. All views were initially entertained, even those of Eisner's harshest critics, most prominently Erich Mühsam, another transplanted North German litterateur and friend of Gustav Landauer. Founder of the anarchosyndicalist group Act, to which Graf had belonged, Mühsam now aligned himself with the Spartacist camp, although Karl Liebknecht, like Eisner, regarded him as a divisive influence.[31] Mühsam in turn lumped Eisner together with Bernstein. The disagreement escalated over Lenin, whom Eisner profoundly mistrusted after Kerensky's government made public the German funding for Lenin's mission. "The Bolsheviks' passage through Germany," Mühsam wrote, "signaled betrayal to him and he took it as proof that Lenin and Trotsky were tools of Ludendorff." To counter Eisner's "democratic-pacifist stance," Mühsam attacked Kerensky at the Schillerstraße meetings as a stooge of the Entente who undermined the interests of the Russian proletariat so as to curry favor in Paris and London.[32]

Angered by Mühsam's attempt to hijack the discussion evenings, Eisner struck back after Lenin overthrew Kerensky's regime and seized power. Having attended a reading by Mühsam in Munich's Alfred Schmid Hall, Eisner reviewed it for the *Post* on 26 November. Although he professed some discomfort at pronouncing critical judgment on a man to whose public engagement he wished to do justice, a man whose art mirrored gentle humanity, Eisner pulled no punches. Mühsam's verse he deemed hopelessly artificial, conventional, and prosaic. "Nor can the lack of original novelty be replaced by the author's perception—bespeaking the egocentric requirements so technically necessary to inhabitants of the lyrical realm—that his I is the force behind world events. . . . It is not just the thinking of anarchy but much more the anarchy of thinking that pervades these reflections."[33] Mühsam wrote to publisher Carl Georg von Maassen on the day the review appeared that Eisner alone of the critics present had savaged him "such that no intact shred is left hanging on me."[34]

The Bolshevik coup of 6–7 November and Lenin's peace proclamation on the eighth, the first day of Soviet control, redoubled the German militarists' zeal. That day Max Weber's student Ernst Toller, a twenty-three-year-old veteran, posted to Eisner for comment a draft appeal to students nationwide to back the USPD initiative for peace without annexations.[35] Soon the two men would be in constant contact. Convinced that Russia's withdrawal from the war also presented the opposition its best chance to force the government's hand, Eisner sought a ready platform for mass agitation. "Forever and a day we have been cut off from all the world by the bourgeois and 'Social Democratic' press," he complained to Haase on the tenth. Eisner disclosed that the feuilleton editor of Berlin's liberal *Vossische Zeitung* had invited him to become a regular contributor with full license. He asked Haase's advice. Given their isolation at the critical moment, might it not be prudent to have some voice in the capital's media?[36] On Sunday, 25 November, Eisner was able to address a wider audience than his discussion group at a peace rally in Munich's Colosseum Beer Hall, telling two hundred participants that the fastest way to peace was, as the Soviets had shown, the seizure of power by the proletariat of all warring states. "If this comes to pass, there will be peace tomorrow."[37]

The fateful hour was approaching. Eisner spent much of December and January in Berlin pressing for a mass strike to compel the government to relinquish expansionist claims in peace talks with the Soviets, begun on 3 December at Brest-Litovsk. On 11 December he reported in veiled language to Else Eisner that he had arrived in Berlin and circulated among his associates. "They all share my opinion, but it will be difficult to move them to an appropriate action."[38] His suspicion that his mail was being intercepted by the police seemed confirmed when her response arrived unsealed. He bade her reply via simple postcard, sent to his cousin Grete Chain's address in Alt-Moabit. The need to reach a broader public was being met, for he had been asked to reprise his discussion evenings for the capital's intelligentsia in spacious, illuminated halls. "I appear to be almost exotic to the people here," Eisner noted on the fifteenth. "My language of political will is foreign to them. They acknowledge my proposals as fitting and necessary, but they lack any measure of resolve. Perhaps something will come of it though."[39] Three days later he pushed back his departure for Munich, informing his wife that he needed to go first to Leipzig, then back to Berlin. He expressed optimism that he had indeed accomplished something: "They have asked me to direct the activity here." He agreed, but only until someone else stepped forward.[40]

At 14:00 Monday, 17 December, the armistice concluded between the Soviet government and the Central powers came into effect. The USPD leadership in Berlin believed that prospects for a comprehensive peace effectively precluded the projected general strike, especially in light of the 'widespread exhaustion' of the German proletariat. "I myself vehemently challenged this view," Eisner declared to police interrogators three months later, "and told my friends that, from my knowledge of the masses, there was a shared, burning desire for an idealistic action and that it was the fault of their leaders, who themselves lacked the requisite confidence for it, that this action had never yet occurred." As it became clear that the German high command and government intended to exact a dear price for the peace Lenin wanted, sentiment among the opposition shifted to Eisner's favor.[41] Ernst Toller, expelled from Heidelberg for political agitation, arrived in Berlin a few days before Christmas. Along with pacifist poet Armin Wegner he spoke at a meeting called to link the protests of intellectuals and workers.[42]

Food prices in Berlin that week were astronomical: nearly 100 marks for a goose, 20 for a pound of butter.[43] In Leipzig, Eisner noted, the dining room of the elegant Astoria Hotel was desolate. He would be returning to Munich for the holiday with commissions from publisher Paul Cassirer for a book on political theater and a drama. In Eisner's luggage was a trove of precious papers—manuscripts from Georg Herwegh's literary remains—entrusted to him for the *Weltweg des Geistes* project. He asked Else to meet him at the station with a cart.[44] On Christmas day he broke from family festivities to write to Kautsky's wife of plans to launch a USPD newspaper. Titles under consideration included *Befreiung* (Liberation), *Neue Menschheit* (New Humanity), and *Freie Welt* (Free World). He regarded Hermann Weise, arrested in August 1916 for publishing SAG appeals, as point man in the Independents' organizational efforts in Berlin. "I am in agreement with him on all details," Eisner declared. Nonetheless he confided his foreboding on the eve of the great strike action: "I have the darkest anxieties for January. We are nearing a world-historical abyss. Will we once again succeed only in a new demonstration of our impotence?"[45]

Preparing to return to Berlin, Eisner reviewed the Chamber Players' premiere of Reinhard Johannes Sorge's religious mystery cycle *Metanoeite* for the 28 December edition of the *Münchener Post*. The Catholic convert had been killed at the Somme in July 1916 at the age of twenty-four. Germany's young poets, Eisner observed, fell into two categories: devotees to their earthly existence and refugees from it, the politically conscious and the reborn romantics. Sorge he classed as the latter, a mystic sharing "something of the menacing ardor of the later Görres." Despite the enthusiasm Sorge had generated, there was sadly no more promise to realize.[46] It was the last review Eisner would file for the *Post*.

Early in the new year Eisner was summoned back to Berlin.[47] The German delegation to the Brest-Litovsk peace talks had stipulated Polish and Lithuanian autonomy from the Soviet state, a sticking point prompting renewed outcry at home for an immediate peace accord. Strikes erupted in Austria and rapidly gained momentum. On 8 January 1918 Eisner checked into the Excelsior Hotel across from the Anhalter railway station.[48] On the tenth the proclamation of President Wilson's Fourteen Points was reported by *Vorwärts*.[49] After conferring with his contacts on a timetable for the strike action, Eisner wrote the same day to his wife, expressing disappointment that the USPD leaders in the capital had not yet reached a decision but rather were relying on him to help organize the action. Walking back along the Landwehr Canal to the hotel the previous night, he felt oppressed by the presentiment of his own doom. "I know that my path is filled with perils I clearly see and yet to which I prefer to be blind. But I can do no other. I could never again breathe freely if I did not do now what I consider my duty." He had no illusions about the probable sacrifice. "Never have I been more passionately and joyfully bound to life than in these years: I am attached to you, the children, the work still to be done, the thoughts still stirring in my mind, the tranquil cottage, the books. Nevertheless I must risk it all." He hoped she would not be unsettled by these portents, but he deemed it prudent at the moment not to let them go unsaid.[50]

At the urging of rank and file the USPD parliamentarians resolved to call a three-day strike.[51] On 14 January workers at Vienna's sprawling Daimler Motor Works joined the Austrian action, driving a swell of popular support.[52] Two days later Eisner outlined the German Independent Socialists' objectives in a flier and circulated it among friends for review, but the Reichstag deputation settled on another statement for publication.[53] Before he returned to Munich on 19 January, Eisner met with Ernst Toller, who determined to join him there.[54] No decision had yet been reached as to whether the strike was to commence on 21 or 28 January. Eisner asked Albert Winter to convene Munich's USPD executive board and advisory council at the Golden Anchor Tavern before the scheduled Monday discussion evening on 21 January. There he briefed the leadership on the coming strike and agreed to speak at a USPD peace rally slated for Sunday, 27 January, at the Colosseum Beer Hall.[55]

Eisner then presented the strike resolution to the discussion group, underscoring that the end goals were the abolition of monarchy and militarism. "It is regrettable," he remarked to the 150 in attendance, "that now when the movement has begun in Austria we comrades have not responded immediately from Berlin." Among those present were metalworker Hans Unterleitner; USPD chairman Albert Winter; Albert Winter Jr.; Karl Kröpelin and his partner, Emilie Landauer, treasurer of Munich's Independents; her sisters Mathilde and Betty; the young clerk Fritz Schröder; Sonja Lerch; and about thirty soldiers.[56] Toller and Oskar Maria Graf recorded their impressions of the participants. Toller, to whom the politicized working class had previously been suspect, was struck by "worker figures whom I had never before encountered: men of clear mind, social insight, immense practical knowledge, steeled will."[57] Graf recalled in particular the "women with worn, hard faces, hands ragged from work, determined eyes" who had been the first to join the demonstrations against food shortages and now made ready to mount the strike. "They were the most earnest, the most courageous," he wrote. "They worked in the grenade factories, as tram conductors, in war-vital industries."[58]

On Saturday, the twenty-sixth, Toller met with Eisner, who invited him to Sunday's peace rally. There Eisner and Dr. Sarah Sonja Rabinowitz Lerch, a Polish-Russian émigré and member of the discussion group, announced the strike and clarified its goals before a crowd of 250 sympathizers: immediate peace without annexations or reparations, the restoration of freedom of the press and the right to assemble, the lifting of martial law and emergency regulation of labor, and the release of political prisoners.[59] Hindenburg and Ludendorff, Eisner declared, were doing everything in their power to prolong the fighting, convinced that their campaign of conquest would soon succeed. When a police official tried to interrupt, Eisner assured the crowd that what he was telling them was so, however unsettling, for "I have the courage to say what is true!" He received a long ovation before Sonja Lerch then reiterated the need for action.[60] Electrified by their message, Toller came to the Golden Anchor the next evening and in Eisner's absence railed against the war, captivating the assembly with his eloquence.[61] Graf, who was present, recorded Toller's effect. "Ardently, ecstatically, with wild gesticulations and twisted face he shouted his emotions. . . . 'You mothers!' he began repeatedly and portrayed with poetic-rhetorical fervor the horrors of war: 'You brothers and sisters!' He held everyone in thrall. Some women wept or raged."[62]

Earlier that afternoon Munich's Majority Socialists and federated unions (Gewerkschaftsverein) had held a joint meeting at the Schwabinger Brewery with workers from the local Krupp Artillery Works. Eisner reckoned the crowd in the overpacked hall at several thousand; police estimated the turnout at under a thousand. Franz Schmitt's scheduled talk was to address the transition of the German economy from war to peace, but shop stewards from Krupp had invited Eisner after Sunday's rally to speak on the planned strike at Monday's assembly. When union secretary Joseph Kurth called the meeting to order, Krupp workers demanded that the focus be shifted from the future economy to the acute political situation and that Schmitt share the rostrum with Eisner. Kurth and Schmitt reluctantly agreed. To his prepared report on the economy Schmitt appended remarks on the efforts of his colleagues in the Reichstag. Eisner then announced, to a roar of approval, that the strike had already started in Berlin. He outlined its purpose and significance. Schmitt and a representative of the Christian unions emphatically opposed the strike, without evident effect, but the time limit imposed by police allowed Kurth to adjourn the meeting before a vote could be taken. The Krupp stewards asked Eisner to confer with them privately the next afternoon at the Ingolstädter Inn.[63]

Monday's evening edition of the *Münchner Neueste Nachrichten* prematurely reported to its bourgeois readership that the mass strike called by Berlin's USPD and the Spartacists had apparently been averted, opposed as it was by the MSPD and its affiliated trade unions.[64] But Tuesday morning the paper nervously confirmed that a hundred thousand workers had walked off the line at forty plants in Berlin, and that in Nuremberg some younger workers, male and female, were parading through the streets with placards bearing the single word Peace.[65] Eisner, Albert Winter, and Sonja Lerch attended Tuesday's meeting of the Krupp stewards, who determined after earnest deliberation to join the general strike on Thursday morning.[66] Tuesday and Wednesday Eisner, Winter, Lerch, and Toller agitated for the strike at meeting after meeting.[67] The lead article Tuesday evening in the *Münchner Neueste Nachrichten* announced that half of Berlin's industrial workers were on strike, supported now by comrades in Kiel and Hamburg. At a meeting Wednesday evening in the Colosseum attended by workers in Munich's printing industry, Eisner, Sonja Lerch, and Fritz Schröder pressed the assembly to declare sympathy with the strikers, a motion that narrowly passed.[68] That night Eisner took a room at the Reichshof Hotel on Sonnenstraße to be ready for action.[69]

On Thursday, 31 January, eight thousand employees of Munich's weapons plants—including Krupp, Maffei, Rapp, and BMW—joined half a million Berlin workers in the walkout.[70] Fifteen years later Toller recounted in his autobiography: "The Krupp workers, mostly North Germans, were the first to leave the factories. No threat could intimidate them." The decision to strike was based on principle rather than personal gain, on the imperative to liberate their fellows in the trenches.[71] The *Münchner Neueste Nachrichten* reported in its evening edition Thursday that a thousand workers from the Bavarian Artillery Works in Freimann had met that morning at the Schwabinger Brewery, where Eisner led them to adopt a resolution proclaiming solidarity with Belgian, French, English, Italian, Russian, and American comrades demanding an immediate cessation of hostilities.[72] He made clear that this was no demonstration for increased suffrage, for reform, but rather for "the ultimate."[73] The strikers were reclaiming the civil freedoms of which they had been deprived. They needed no permission to assemble, march in the streets, or disseminate truth. He urged them to act on their own authority. "The Bavarian government no longer exists," he proclaimed. "Censorship is abolished!" Eisner warned of military intervention but ventured that the soldiers themselves would likely join them, once they were informed what was at stake. The potential for violence was undeniable, but it would be better to die for peace than to die in the trenches. "I made these remarks because I wanted to impress in all earnestness on those present that political struggles of this nature are no mere child's play, rather the stuff of grave contingencies, and each much decide for himself whether he is up to it."[74]

After the meeting Eisner, Winter, Lerch, and Hans Reck, chair of the Krupp stewards, marched with strikers past Munich's huge factories and main train station to the Mathäser Brewery.[75] There Auer was pleading with workers from Rapp Motor Works for calm. Citing Eisner's solidarity resolution, Auer ridiculed him as an arrogant extremist, a utopist with delusions of grandeur. Eisner answered from the floor that his name commanded more credence abroad than Auer's or any other Majority Socialist's. Urged to the podium, Eisner revealed the MSPD's role in prolonging the war. When Auer's fellow functionary Johannes Timm joined the attempt to discredit their rival, both were shouted down by the crowd, as was the antistrike stewards' committee. A new committee was constituted on the spot to approve the strike. Eisner told the assembly that he had just received word that thousands of strikers in Berlin were refusing the punitive call-up for duty at the front. The news was greeted with tumultuous acclaim.[76]

Following the Rapp meeting Eisner spoke at the same beer hall to the radical element of aircraft workers from the Otto Plant, who unanimously endorsed the solidarity resolution. He returned to his hotel, where he was arrested the same evening.[77] At 03:00 Friday police took Sonja Lerch from her home on Clemenstraße.[78] Emilie and Betty Landauer, Albert Winter, Hans Unterleitner, and Lorenz Winkler were also rounded up. All of the detained strike organizers were charged with treason.[79] On Saturday, 2 February, Eisner wrote to Else from police headquarters that he had missed the last streetcar home Thursday evening by a few minutes. He had engaged Dr. Benedikt Bernheim for his defense and expected to be transferred to Neudeck Prison on Mariahilfplatz east of the Isar. Having been cut off from all news since his arrest, Eisner asked her to fetch his standing order of Swiss and French newspapers from the kiosk at Karlsplatz and to apply to the court for permission to visit him.[80] On Monday he commenced a prison journal with an entry recording the events of the previous week. "Those were the most beautiful days of my life, the days of revolt, of struggle," he began. "I saw human souls again, not just animal maws."[81]

CHAPTER TWENTY-ONE

OUR POWER TO ACT NOW GROWS: FROM PRISONER TO PREMIER (1918)

E RNST TOLLER ELUDED ARREST until Monday, 4 February 1918, when the strike ended after repeated appeals from the Majority Socialist leadership. At noon he was taken from his room at gunpoint and held until trial at a military prison on Leonrodstraße.[1] Upon reporting back to his garrison, Felix Fechenbach was interrogated at length by officers who had been apprised of his involvement with the strike. He was transferred to Passau on the Austrian border, where he was kept under close surveillance.[2] Eisner was already resigned to a lengthy stay behind bars. On Tuesday he wrote to Else from Neudeck with detailed directives. His daughter Ilse was to bring him an array of a dozen prominent German, French, and Swiss newspapers every other day, taking care that no issue was skipped. In addition he asked for a number of books from his desk, including Marx and Engels's political works and correspondence, English and French dictionaries, and the manuscript of the play he had begun while incarcerated at Plötzensee in Berlin. Stationery, pens and ink, marking pencils, a soft shirt, vest, slippers, and teaspoon rounded out the list. He urged that she procure a ticket to the Court Theater's upcoming production of Beethoven's *Fidelio*, "the work for our days now."[3] The last directive signaled undiminished optimism. It must have been of no small consolation that Wilhelm Herzog had authorized payment of 250 marks a few days earlier for Eisner's work on *Weltweg des Geistes*, income that continued for the duration of his incarceration.[4]

In response to Eisner's urgent request Hugo Haase sent word on Wednesday from Berlin that he would join Dr. Bernheim as counsel. Representation was being arranged for Eisner's codefendants as well.[5] A week later the court rejected motions for release on bail.[6] In his cell Eisner immersed himself in writing. Else's appeal to send him the requested items was granted on the twelfth. The next day she wrote that she would bring additional archival materials on her next visit and confessed that she was concerned about his wretched appearance. For solace she intended to read in the New Testament of "the struggle for truth by one who refuses to keep it to himself but rather speaks out against the world's lies. . . . And mankind has risen to the task: then it was a deity who took up this arduous mission, today it is just mortal men."[7] On Friday, 15 February, Eisner reported to her good progress on the play despite the dreariness of his surroundings. He bade her be happy with the children at home. "If I know that, it allows me to bear even my lack of freedom more easily."[8]

A few days later he read in the local papers that Munich's factories had resumed normal operations after the brief disruption fomented by "foreign agitators." Indeed, Bavarian prime minister Otto von Dandl had thanked Auer and Timm for their role in defusing the strike. His gratitude, Eisner remarked bitterly, was well justified: "Had I been given two more days to lead the masses to truth by force of reason, the entire proletariat would have been won over." He concluded that the old union and party structure that accorded disproportionate influence to the most phlegmatic elements subverted revolutionary action. German socialism had to be liberated from its leaders. "The organization must be built up from the natural cells, the plants. The politicization of the plants: that is the determinant of the German proletariat's strength and impotence. Far more important than requisite unity of the workers is their independence. . . . The workers' collective itself in each plant, in its mass and in organized collaboration with other plants, has to retain the leadership. They must not let themselves be 'represented,' not by anyone at all."[9]

With Eisner imprisoned, his cadre continued to meet. At the same time Eisner wholeheartedly embraced decentralization of authority in the workers' movement, anarchist Erich Mühsam told the discussion group that Eisner and his jailed comrades were victims of a "shameful betrayal." The strike should have been extended until they were released from custody. Now it fell to those present to "follow in Eisner's footsteps." Mühsam was seconded by Josef Sontheimer, who derided "the flock of red sheep" that heeded Auer's call to return to work.[10] Of those in custody Sonja Rabinowitz Lerch suffered the worst. Her husband, lecturer in French at Munich University, filed for divorce, fearing that her political activism threatened his career. He posted announcement of the pending divorce in the local press. During an exercise break Eisner saw her wet and shivering in the jailyard at Neudeck, utterly downcast, "a symbolic representation of homelessness." Under constant watch they nodded in passing. Soon she was transferred to Stadelheim Prison in Munich's Giesing quarter on the edge of Perlacher Forest.[11]

Having done time twenty years earlier in Berlin, Eisner knew better what to expect, but conditions varied with time and place. Wartime food shortages were most pressing in the waning winter; prison fare barely sustained subsistence. Similarly, the smallest liberties were curtailed in the interest of the state apparatus. On Sunday, 10 March, Eisner noted in his journal that only inmates who were Catholic and sole defendants in their individual cases were allowed to attend church services. Upon reflection he realized that the stipulations were intended to prevent conspirators from plotting their legal defense. "Thus even in clerical, Catholic Bavaria the magistrate and prosecutor's convenience takes precedence over a sinner's right to spiritual edification!"[12] His hopes for release or timely trial dimmed as Germany's military woes worsened. The admiralty's boast that submarines would prevent US troops from landing in Europe had proven illusory. Well over three hundred thousand were safely in France and preparing for action. Ludendorff's final gambit to break the stalemate before the Americans fully deployed was Operation Michael, a massive artillery and infantry assault launched the morning of 21 March against British positions along the Somme. The time seemed right: a week earlier Lenin had persuaded the Soviet congress to accept the Brest-Litovsk peace treaty. The German divisions outnumbered the British, but despite losing ground, the defenders inflicted far heavier casualties on their attackers. After an initial dramatic advance the assault bogged down. The British regrouped and counterattacked.[13]

The day before Operation Michael began, Hugo Haase made plans to travel to Munich after the end of the Reichstag session on Friday, 22 March, to confer with Eisner and Dr. Bernheim. He arrived Monday morning and following the consultation took part in the regularly scheduled discussion evening, where he had to submit to a police identification check of the fifty persons in attendance.[14] In addition to his literary projects Eisner outlined a four-part study on the theory and practice of democratic socialism and drafted a detailed review of Franz Mehring's biography *Karl Marx: Geschichte seines Lebens* (Karl Marx: His Life Story).[15] Mehring responded to Eisner's request for advance copy on 30 March, adding that Eisner had been much on his mind in recent months: "In what spirit and sense I hope to be able to tell you in person once more."[16]

Among the literary works with which Eisner busied himself was a cycle of one-act plays under the general working title "Behind the Front."[17] Over the course of two days, 21–22 March, he wrought the verse prologue to "The Egyptian Woman," the title of which refers to a princess who loves a foreign-born slave in the distant past. In this piece

Eisner depicts the anguish and absurdity of his prison life, dramatizing the mealtime ritual and exercise regimen, incomprehensible regulations, disquieting dreams through the long nights, the piteous wailing of forlorn detainees, pointless consultation with his attorney, and a visit by his wife and their eight-year-old daughter. "I know that I shall be free as soon as my country suffers a collapse," says the inmate. "Defeat would be victory for me. I know that I shall perish in prison if we win."[18] At the end of the month Eisner clipped an article for his war archives. The *Deutsche Tageszeitung* reported the deployment of German artillery with a range of 120 kilometers against the fortification of Paris. The author gushed with boundless admiration at "this marvel of German ingenuity" and wondered what might yet be achieved. Eisner appended in a grim note that "the Thirty Years' War provided the answer."[19]

Two weeks before her scheduled court appearance in the divorce case, Sonja Lerch hanged herself in her cell at Stadelheim. She was buried Easter Monday, 1 April, at Munich's New Israelite Cemetery. Police strictly prohibited any political demonstration at the grave. The rabbi briefly addressed mourners, remarking that the victim was mentally deranged at the time of her death. Josef Sontheimer retorted that she had fallen in the revolution. After an unseemly chase through the grounds he was collared and arrested at the gates. The next day Eisner wrote an open letter from Neudeck to Sonja Lerch's comrades, including her friend Clara Zetkin, to explain that the suicide stemmed from the humiliation by her husband, who had publicly repudiated her and refused to visit her in jail. "Prison psychosis and the long, lonely, sleepless nights completed the work of emotional ruin."[20] Zetkin, who herself had been jailed repeatedly during the war, thanked Eisner for passing on the sad news, communicated with "profound humanity" despite the circumstances. "The thought of your lot too, of that of your wife and children, depressed me while reading your so sensitive lines. What your detention means for your loved ones, for all of us was clear and present to me."[21] The grave concern for his well-being was only heightened when *Le Temps* reported his death, a notice Eisner read in his cell on Tuesday, 16 April. "I am living now somewhat withdrawn from the world," he wrote wryly to Kautsky the same day. "But only somewhat."[22]

That month Eisner sent to Else detailed instructions for typing his Plötzensee play for submission to Paul Cassirer in Berlin.[23] The working title of the manuscript had changed from "The Prince's Trial" to "The Trial of the Gods." The hero is Guldar, the heroine his lover Warana, female personification of the true, derived from the adjective *wahr*. It is a strangely evocative, mythic work: a Schillerian theme of despotism versus enlightenment, masked as farce, rendered in irregular pentameter, imbued with the surreal, sensual ambience of Strindberg's later dramas. With its righteous, crusading hero and heroine, its rapacious villains, and its just outcome, *Die Götterprüfung* resembles nothing so much as a *Märchen* in five acts. If Maurice Ravel's *La valse* scores Europe's mad reeling into world war, Eisner's stage allegory scripts the instigators' fate.

The play represents more though than a melodramatic protest against Kaiser Wilhelm and the war by a jailed opponent. It serves as an indictment both of the autocratic, feudal state structure as, true to the definition of farce, a grotesque and therefore comic anachronism, and of the incomprehensible willing servility of the oppressed to the Imperial regime. The farce ends to give way to hope. Guldar's illicit union with Warana produces the first child born in the sterile land since the rulers, in accordance with ancient laws they neither understood nor questioned, proscribed procreation. The birth of the child at Guldar's moment of triumph conforms to the expressionist ideal: the rebirth of man in a new age. Undeniably, Guldar must be read as Eisner's literary alter ego, whose triumphant return from exile mirrors the sublimated yet fervent desire of the perpetual outsider for validation, the displaced Prussian Jew in Catholic Bavaria, renegade in the eyes of his former comrades. The hope shines through in the prophetic observation of an old man whom Guldar has won to the cause: "Is it not wondrous how our power to act now grows after all the doubt and despair?"[24] Equally undeniable was the improbability of a German revolution at the moment. Yet Eisner remained indomitable even in custody, buoyed by the knowledge that against all odds he had successfully marshaled a mass action in Bavaria's capital. He directed Else to post the typescript via registered mail to Leo Kestenberg at Cassirer, insuring it for 100 marks. "The manuscript of the comedy, which I kept as neat as possible for you, I present to you as the only thing I have to give now—other than reflections on you in my solitude."[25] In her autobiographical novel Else adopted the name Warana for herself, Guldar for Eisner.[26]

In a postscript to his instructions Eisner added that he would soon forward the one-act tetralogy. Two of the component works, "The Teletype" and "The Afreet," he deemed too revolutionary for performance at present, but "Morning Song" and "The Egyptian Woman" might pass the censor. Once she received the manuscripts, Belli was to prepare copy for Otto Falckenberg, director of the Chamber Players. Should Falckenberg express interest, Eisner proposed that they be submitted to the censor's office under the pseudonym Ernst Bidt.[27] The first component of this dark cycle, "Morning Song," characterizes their bleakness. It plays out in a hotel suite in southwestern Germany at the end of November 1917. There are but two characters: Walter, a disillusioned civil servant who has arranged a tryst with Brigitte, the aristocratic wife of an abusive staff officer. "What dreadful madness of chance," Walter voices their discontent, "to be born in a nation where there is no great and just cause for which one can die and no way of escape, chained immobile to the collective guilt!" In an act of defiance rather than despair, the two lovers deliver themselves from bondage with a poisoned draught of champagne.[28]

On 29 April 1918 Lieutenant Otto Braun, only son of Heinrich and Lily, was killed in action on the Somme. The prodigious poet and devotee of Stefan George was twenty years old. He had enlisted at seventeen in 1914, been wounded on the eastern front in 1916, and been posted to France in February 1918 after a long convalescence in Berlin.[29] In the past Eisner had typically observed Pentecost with a piece commemorating spiritual rebirth and renewed commitment to cause. This year's offering, however, took the form of five mordant vignettes on disfigured heroes, unreported casualties, "light" wounds, infinite buffer zones, and the problematic interment of remains after an artillery attack.[30]

On 31 May, a perfect spring day, Else Eisner reminded her husband of their first anniversary.[31] He had been held without trial now for four months. Toller and the Landauer sisters had been released from remand. Toller was posted to a reserve unit in Neu-Ulm. Mühsam had been arrested the last week of April; he and Sontheimer were in the custody of military authorities in Traunstein.[32] Concerned at how their long separation weighed on his wife, Eisner composed a poem for her the first week of June. Titled "B.I.D.T.," for *bis in den Tod*, it reaffirmed that their lives were ever joined.[33] On the seventeenth he took delight in nesting titmice that used the bleak exercise yard at Neudeck as the "flight school" for their young, watched by 150 men through barred windows.[34]

The four-part review of Franz Mehring's biography of Marx was serialized in the *Leipziger Volkszeitung*, beginning 8 June as the lead article. Eisner's critique served multiple purposes: to present a candid evaluation of the text, to demonstrate the depth of his own knowledge of Marx's writings, to reground German socialism in the international revolutionary construct, and to pay homage to a former adversary, even while acknowledging their differences. He began by recalling how the Social Democratic press had once scoffed at the stunted liberal bourgeoisie's commemoration of Schiller and his like as intellectual leaders of their revolution. Now it was the Majority Social Democrats themselves who rated as the corrupted epigoni at the hundredth anniversary of their professed master's birth, the same lot who currently supported Germany's monarchic-militarist regime in the attempt to cripple the Russian Revolution. The party once hailed as Marxism's standard-bearer had degenerated into a "colossally bloated organization devoid of soul," "a timid, petit-bourgeois, philistine creature," "a comically authentic popular edition of the state, . . . but lacking precisely the force in which the ruling state's power reposed: the military executive." The world war that effected the party's tragic assimilation Marx himself would have greeted as impetus to world revolution.

The delayed publication of Mehring's biography, Eisner declared, was a boon. The distracting din of the Majority Social Democrats' shameful observances on 5 May had subsided, and this earnest endeavor could be accorded due study and reflection. Mehring's achievement was threefold. He had addressed the work to a general rather than scholarly audience without oversimplifying the subject matter; the bibliography provided sources for readers desiring a more thorough explication of complex economic concepts and theories. He framed Marx's life and thought in historical and cultural context of the nineteenth century. And he presented an objective, balanced reckoning of the quarrels between Marx and rival theorists in the workers' movement. Still, Eisner did not shrink from citing what he believed to be weaknesses of the book, most notably inconsistencies and internal contradictions in Mehring's interpretation of Prussian politics of the 1860s and his treatment of Bismarck's war with France. Alluding to the author's fiery temperament and their own former enmity, Eisner remarked that Mehring would not have understood Marx's combative disposition so well "if he himself did not share the strength of rancor, anger, and hatred." Fortunately the text was free of all polemic against contemporary comrades, only a few fleeting asides aroused memories of past unpleasantness.

All told, Eisner judged the tome a sure guide for the young generation who would realize Marx's ideals. "I do not know if there is much that can be achieved with the older generation," Eisner concluded. "The hour will come in the not-too-distant future when the 'proven leaders' will frantically rush to con the forgotten language of 'international, revolutionary, masses-liberating' Social Democracy again. But no one will take that seriously anymore." It would fall to the regenerated, reconsecrated proletariat to deliver Marx from the Marxists.[35]

In failing health Mehring wrote from Berlin-Steglitz on 22 June to express his gratitude for the detailed review. That Eisner's intellectual vigor remained "fresh and whole" despite his sad lot was a great solace, Mehring warranted, "and I must be chief among those to attest how brilliantly you have realized the promise you customarily exhibited in past conflicts." In light of their circumstances he doubted if they would be able to shake hands again, but he assured Eisner that their reestablished friendly relations had greatly brightened the last dark years.[36] That same day Eisner was composing a slow march to the muffled tread of prisoners walking their circle in the yard. The accompanying lyrics mirror the taut anxiety of August Stramm's expressionist combat verse. Still, the march ends defiantly: "We who believe / Shall yet besiege!"[37] Mehring's letter, received on the twenty-seventh, considerably lifted his spirits. He responded immediately to venture that they would see each other again in better circumstances. He cheerfully reported that he was making the most of ample time to write and that he was now permitted three five-minute visits each week with his wife. His youngest daughter, Ruth, thought it amusing that she would be grown to womanhood before he might be released.[38]

At the end of the month Paul Cassirer requested that Eisner forward the work on political theater they had discussed in December. In the same missive the Berlin publisher tactfully expressed concern that *Die Götterprüfung* might be too controversial for publication at the moment but offered to reconsider it at a later date.[39] More and worse aggravation soon followed. Eisner was transferred at the first of July from Neudeck to Stadelheim, where conditions were worse. Visiting her husband there the evening of 9 July, Else found him highly agitated by his inability to work. She pleaded with Bernheim to intervene on his behalf.[40] Eisner reported his change of address to Kautsky on the nineteenth and groused that he had now been held nearly half a year without trial.[41] The next week Else clashed with the prison warden, who forbade her to bring prepared meals to supplement the standard fare of nettle boiled in brine.[42] After detailing conditions to Bernheim, she lodged a formal protest with district attorney Matthias Hahn. Likening Eisner to Socrates, who ate but to preach truth, she argued that "his mind is too precious for his belly to be ruined by the nettle of our glorious age."[43] On the twenty-seventh the Supreme Court (Reichsgericht) at Leipzig rejected the request for release from custody filed on behalf of Eisner, Lorenz Winkler, Albert Winter, and his son.[44]

Ludendorff's final offensive had been launched on the Marne in mid-July. The troops at his disposal were ravaged by the onset of the influenza pandemic that would rage for months. The French, heavily reinforced now by fresh American divisions, repelled the assault and forced the Germans into massive retreat. Senior officers on Ludendorff's staff openly called for peace negotiations with the Entente. British, Canadian, Australian, and French forces under command of Field Marshal Haig and Marshal Foch amassed on the Somme for the crushing blow, which came on 8 August, pushing the weary enemy back toward the Hindenburg

Line, the designated demarcation of last resort. Ludendorff himself pronounced the date "the black day."[45] The general staff now knew beyond all doubt that the war was lost.[46] Within weeks the Entente armies were poised for the final breakthrough. From cell 70 at Stadelheim Eisner satirized the commander who, ensconced in his posh headquarters replete with well-stocked wine cellar, fervently asserted the humble desire to die with honor at the front as a regular soldier.[47]

On 28 August the Supreme Court denied the request for release on bail, filed by Eisner's counsel on the fifteenth.[48] But the situation was changing rapidly. The military collapse on the western front prompted sober political reassessments. At his Berlin-Zehlendorf villa Majority Socialist Albert Südekum drafted a comprehensive review of the current state of affairs on Friday, 6 September. The popular alarm was all the greater, he surmised, because the press had led readers to believe that the British and French were too depleted to hold out long. Moreover, the Entente's recognition of the Czechoslovaks had severely undermined Austrian unity. Südekum was convinced that Wilson aimed "to create a set of European republics that would remain dependent on America financially and for supply of raw materials, and consequently have to dance to its tune politically as well." It was clear now that the Soviets had readily ratified the Brest-Litovsk peace treaty in the belief that the terms would be revised after Germany's defeat. Equally clear was that the Entente had no intention of negotiating with defeated autocrats: "Germany will be democratic or it will cease to be." It was therefore critical that the governing parties act immediately in concert to end the state of siege, introduce equal suffrage in Prussia, and release from service all soldiers other than those required to defend the borders. To prevent American domination of Europe, Germany needed to come to terms with Britain and France quickly, possibly ceding French-speaking Lorraine if necessary. Otherwise he fully expected that the nation would be compelled to surrender unconditionally by spring 1919.[49]

A few days later Eisner wrote that "we are all just on leave from death." After four years of war "the realm of consciousness previously known as life" was merely the vestibule of doom.[50] This was the darkest hour before dawn. On 12 September the American commander in France, General John Pershing, having consolidated his army, launched an overwhelming assault at St. Mihiel, which the Germans had held for four years. The doughboy onslaught, Ludendorff conceded, imbued his rank and file with the languor of "looming defeat." The presentiment became reality when French, British, American, and Belgian forces attacked simultaneously on 26 September. Within two days Ludendorff personally informed Hindenburg that the fight was over. On the twenty-ninth the German high command urged the kaiser to sue for peace on the basis of Wilson's Fourteen Points. The democratization of which Südekum had written was about to begin. Chancellor Hertling, who opposed it, tendered his resignation, and the kaiser asked his kinsman Prince Max von Baden to form a new government. Max immediately named Majority Socialists Philipp Scheidemann and Gustav Bauer to his cabinet and wrote to the American president.[51]

In this new context the disparate elements of the German Left jockeyed for primacy. On 20 September Kautsky posted to Eisner a draft theoretical critique of Bolshevism and urgently requested Eisner's commentary.[52] While the Independent Socialists sought to distinguish themselves in the public eye from Lenin's chief allies, the Spartacists, the MSPD painted both rival factions as dominated by transplanted Russian Jews intent on herding Germany into the Soviet fold. In Bavaria the state of flux had been heightened in August when Georg von Vollmar, ailing and confined to a wheelchair at age sixty-eight, resigned his seats in the Reichstag and Landtag. Erhard Auer, Vollmar's protégé, was the Majority Socialists' candidate in the special Reichstag election for Munich's second district, to be held on 17 November.[53] At a closed meeting on 14 September the Independent Socialists determined to nominate Eisner for the vacated Reichstag seat and Albert Winter Sr. for the Landtag.[54] Eisner wrote to Haase on the twenty-ninth that although his candidacy had been reported by the press, the nomination was not yet formalized. He compared his incarceration, soon to be in the ninth month, to gestation: "Is it only a psychological superstition when I imagine now that I shall soon see the light of day?" The court had rejected his repeated requests for release on the grounds that he might flee Bavaria before trial. Now that he was to be a candidate for the Reichstag that suspicion was "nonsensical." Turning to national politics, Eisner went on to ridicule the demands made by Paul Lensch, Friedrich Ebert, and their MSPD cohorts "to conclude their transformation from government agency to government proper" as short even of the National Liberals' reform agenda.[55]

Dr. Bernheim appealed by telegram to Leipzig on 7 October for Eisner's immediate release, citing both his client's Reichstag candidacy and the "altered political situation."[56] For markedly different reasons Erhard Auer also opposed his rival's prosecution, at least for the moment. A Bavarian Interior Ministry official summarized intelligence Auer had provided the government: "Eisner's nomination is, of course, a sham, as the Independents have at most three hundred actual members here, and even if the Jewish money flows for their brother Eisner, he [Auer] thinks that the Independents and their sympathizers would generate no more than two thousand votes. Nonetheless it would be desirable that the case against Eisner not proceed before the scheduled election, for the trial would certainly be exploited by the Independents and the Jews."[57] On 14 October the release was granted, and that evening Eisner departed Stadelheim for Großhadern.[58] Seven days later the Winters and Hans Unterleitner were cleared for discharge from detention.[59]

As events of the next weeks would prove, Auer had once again colossally miscalculated Eisner's influence and effect, which were bolstered no doubt by President Wilson's hardening line against negotiation with an autocratic regime, as evinced by notes of 8, 14, and 23 October to Max von Baden.[60] The hopes of Germany's revolutionary Left were on the rise. Rosa Luxemburg wrote from her cell at Breslau to Liebknecht's wife on the eighteenth: "If Dittmann and Eisner have been released, they can no longer keep me imprisoned, and soon Karl will be free too."[61] And, indeed, by terms of the general amnesty implemented by Prince Max's government on 12 October, political prisoners who had been formally tried and sentenced were let go. Liebknecht arrived in Berlin on the twenty-third, but Luxemburg, who like Eisner had never been brought to trial, remained in confinement until 9 November.[62] Incredibly, even as the German populace learned for the first time the scope of the military's dire defeat, elements of the collapsing regime, desperate to maintain their privilege, pleaded maniacally for a last stand. The Pan-German press organs urged boys and old men capable of bearing arms to mount the critical "national defense." While jailed opponents of the war were being released, Felix Fechenbach was transferred from Passau to Munich to face a court martial the last week of October on charges of subversive political activity.[63]

In her novel Else recorded Eisner's transformation in captivity. "Something strange had come over her husband since his seclusion. Something otherworldly, as if imprisonment, doom, intellectual demise, physical decline were one with life, with love." At home he stared at his spectral likeness in the mirror, met by a gaze far removed from the mundane.[64] Gaunt and wan, with lined brow, streaming gray hair and beard, he was the very image of Elijah returned from the wilderness to ascend with the whirlwind. For a few brief days he reacclimated to freedom, marshaled his energies, and then launched a frenetic campaign—not for the Reichstag but for the revolution that, he told his constituency, "will void this election."[65] He made the remark at his first public address on Wednesday, 23 October, at the Schwabinger Brewery before a standing-room crowd of two thousand supporters, including, as the police observer noted, many from "the best" bourgeois circles among the munitions workers who formed the backbone of the Munich USPD.[66] Oskar Maria Graf, who was present, records in his memoirs how Eisner flaunted his disheveled appearance, now clearly cultivated as an image. Only the pince-nez distinguished him from some biblical hero. Standing at the podium amid his crouching retinue, he declared hoarsely to thunderous applause: "You behold me thus as Stadelheim consigned me to freedom!" In February he believed he had taken Munich's militant proletariat to within forty-eight hours of revolt. Now he was determined not to fail. Eisner gravely warned the audience against the false prophets who would once again mislead them to the pit. "Whoever casts his vote for those approvers of war credits, those criminals who helped conjure the consummate misery of this bloodiest mass murder, whoever chooses the false flame validates this crime as lawful!" The word he used for "false flame" left no doubt as to the villain's identity: *Auerlicht*.[67]

Those responsible for, or complicit in the Imperial government's war, Eisner made clear, had no place in the coming democratic government that must supplant the crumbling monarchy. Without reservation he endorsed Wilson's peace plan and rejected the national defense initiative, which he denounced as a subterfuge to safeguard the culpable. In place of the Hohenzollern prince who now headed the government Eisner proposed Karl Liebknecht, "the first citizen of New Germany," and called for the unification of Germany and German-speaking Austria as a social republic.[68] In the course of the next ten days Eisner advised Fechenbach on his successful trial defense, reassembled an activist vanguard, and established contact with the brothers Ludwig and Karl Gandorfer, leaders of the radicalized Bavarian Peasants' League (Bayerischer Bauernbund), secular counterpart to the consolidated Christian agrarian associations under Center Party champion Georg Heim. Even as the Bavarian government, backed by the Majority Socialists, established a constitutional monarchy, Eisner flayed the advocates of woefully belated, stopgap political reform. He sought to coax Haase, Dittmann, and Liebknecht to come to Munich to speak at mass rallies. Both Fechenbach and Liebknecht's eldest son, Helmi, took up temporary residence at Eisner's home in Großhadern.[69] At a campaign appearance at the Löwenbräu Cellar on Wednesday, 30 October, Eisner called for the abolition of the Imperial state and its constituent monarchies. If no peace agreement could be concluded in the next days, he urged that workers and peasants seize control of the government so as to prevent an Entente invasion of Bavaria.[70]

Eisner wrote on 1 November to Luise Zietz, member of the USPD central committee (Zentralkomitee) in Berlin, to report the status of the special election. "My opponent is relying on open and secret organizational work; the entire press, the Social Democratic Party and trade-union apparatus, the liberal and black infrastructures are in operation for him." Yet Auer was having difficulty galvanizing his base. The mood of the audience at his sole public meeting was skeptical. For his part Eisner intended to use the next week's campaign rallies to impress "the immediate exigencies of political mass action." In his last speech nothing had evoked greater enthusiasm, he related, than the declaration that "if necessary the Bavarian Republic would be proclaimed of its own accord in the name of Germany."[71] The next evening Eisner led young Krupp workers in the disruption of a meeting of the association Free Munich, where they shouted down the Left Liberal Reichstag deputy Ernst Müller-Meiningen when he parroted Ludendorff's slur of antiwar activists as backstabbers.[72] Then on the night of 2/3 November Fechenbach and his fellows fanned out in the city's proletarian quarters to post mimeographed handbills for a USPD peace demonstration at the towering statue of Bavaria on Theresa's Green (Theresienwiese). Sunday morning, 3 November, a thousand people assembled to hear Eisner speak. The police permit expressly forbade proclamation of a republic and, on the same day the sailors' mutiny at Kiel erupted in violence, any exhortation to soldiers to disobey orders.[73] Eisner hailed the collapse of the Habsburg monarchy in Vienna and urged that the people of Bavaria join Austrian republicans to proclaim the war's end "since neither the will nor the power exists in Berlin to reach an immediate peace."[74]

Confident now that the long-awaited day of reckoning was at hand, Eisner moved to consolidate his forces. That same day Wilhelm Herzog in Berlin received a two-word telegram from Eisner: "visit desired."[75] At the critical moment Ernst Toller and Gustav Landauer were suffering from influenza, Toller at his mother's residence in Landsberg, Landauer in Krumbach. Erich Mühsam had been released from custody four days earlier.[76] Immediately after his address Eisner boarded a train to Pfaffenberg, south of Regensberg, to confer with Ludwig Gandorfer, who days earlier had called for regime change in Bavaria.[77] While Eisner rode north, Fechenbach led two hundred of the rally audience on a march across the Isar to Stadelheim, where they demanded the immediate release of Richard Kämpfer, Fritz Schröder, and Lorenz Winkler, the three remaining detainees from the leadership of the January munitions strike.[78] From noon through early evening the demonstrators faced off with security forces at the gates of Stadelheim while a delegation negotiated first with prison officials, then with Interior Minister Friedrich von Brettreich. The Bavarian Justice Ministry telegraphed the court in Leipzig to report that soldiers had joined the crowd at Stadelheim and there was danger of an assault on the prison. Officially assured that their demands would be met shortly, the victorious throng then paraded into town, swelling in number along the way. Before the Wittelsbach Palace Fechenbach spoke to those now gathered—thousands by his estimate—enjoining them to make ready for the momentous events of the coming days. He closed with the ringing benediction "Long live peace, long live freedom, long live the social republic!" At 19:20 Kämpfer, Schröder, and Winkler were freed.[79] Eisner returned to Munich assured of Gandorfer's critical support for the planned action.[80]

Despite the evident epochal change in progress, fighting on the western front still raged as Entente forces thrust toward the German border. That morning Else Eisner fetched Wilhelm Herzog from the railway station. Upon arrival at Großhadern they waited in the foyer as Eisner conferred individually with Munich University professors Friedrich Wilhelm Foerster and Friedrich Muckle, two of the intellectuals whom he had recruited to the cause. Eisner had also enlisted Edgar Jaffé, coeditor of the *Archiv für Sozialwissenschaft und Sozialpolitik* (Archive for Social Science and Social Policy). For the next days Herzog was at Eisner's side from early until late, closely observing the interaction.[81] Also on Monday, the fourth, the same day that Herzog joined the Bavarian revolutionaries, Max Weber spoke on the topic "Germany's Political New Orientation" at a Left Liberal meeting in Munich's Wagner Hall, denouncing as criminally stupid the delusion "that bourgeois society can be transformed by revolution into a utopia based on socialist ideals." Erich Mühsam and the Spartacist Max Levien, in attendance, roared their derision, and Oskar Maria Graf mounted the stage to herald the imminent uprising. "The revolution will come!" he shouted. "It is coming! I call upon soldiers to disobey orders and leave the barracks!"[82] Indeed, as Herzog recorded forty years on, Eisner was preparing to launch. "With astonishing composure he deliberated with the spokesmen of Munich's working class, to whom he gave minutely precise instructions after their discussions. Everything was accomplished dispassionately, with complete detachment."[83]

The next day news of the revolt in Kiel led by Karl Artelt and Lothar Popp, both Independent Socialists, reached Munich, spurring the restive populace. That evening Eisner was to make a campaign appearance at the Hacker Cellar, but the crowd that gathered, far too large for the space, moved to the Theresienwiese. A legion of nearly twenty thousand awaited his arrival at the colossus of Bavaria. Fritz Schröder and the young poet Bruno Frank, both combat veterans, spoke first, followed by Eisner, who was hard pressed to prevent a premature putsch. The impatience of men long stifled threatened the desired goal. Some called for an immediate march to the barracks where weapons might be seized. "I too was disappointed," confessed Oskar Maria Graf. Eisner's reassurance and resolve held sway. "Just a bit longer," he pleaded and raised his hand in oath, "but I stake my life that before forty-eight hours pass, Munich will rise up!"[84]

Wednesday, 6 November, placards throughout the city announced a peace demonstration Thursday afternoon on the Theresienwiese. The rally's USPD organizers had turned to the trade unions to broker joint sponsorship by the MSPD so as to attract the widest following. On the sixth yet, while the Bavarian interior minister pondered security measures and weighed the advisability of Eisner's immediate arrest, "a small group of not even ten friends" met at Eisner's home to plot their strategy for the next day.[85] In Berlin the Majority Socialist leadership told General Wilhelm Groener, Ludendorff's successor, that they were prepared to accept a constitutional monarchy and a socialist-led parliamentary government, but that Wilhelm must abdicate forthwith. To his later regret Groener refused to negotiate, and Ebert declared a parting of ways. That evening Max von Baden announced to the kaiser that only his abdication could secure the monarchy. The next morning Max informed Ebert of having issued the ultimatum.[86]

In a 1988 interview in the German Democratic Republic Dr. Ruth Strahl, youngest daughter of Kurt Eisner and Else Belli, recounted the events of 7–8 November 1918: "My parents called in my eleven-year-old sister Freia and me and spoke with us as to adults. They planned something great to end the war and to overthrow the monarchy. We shouldn't worry. If anything happened, we should turn to our grandfather in Stuttgart. That night my parents did not come back. Workers did instead, and they told us 'We've chased away the king.' The next day our mother came: 'Bavaria is now a republic.' We had no idea what that meant, but that the king was gone—that we understood."[87]

Thursday noon, 7 November, the USPD leadership met once more for final instructions while Interior Minister Brettreich conferred with Erhard Auer, who reassured him that Eisner had been neutralized and the situation was well in hand.[88] At 13:00 the factories shut down, and streams of factory workers bearing red flags made their way to the Theresienwiese. Uniformed soldiers, many absent without leave from their barracks, artisans, students, townspeople, shopkeepers, women, and children joined the procession. Eisner himself, accompanied by Herzog, led a column of "several hundred workers."[89] Oskar Maria Graf witnessed a female worker ripping down every cautionary placard against unruliness and violence, posted that morning on Brettreich's order. "Not a single policeman was to be seen," he records in reminiscences.[90] At 15:00 the scheduled speakers were to address the multitude briefly and present a resolution for conclusion of an immediate ceasefire, rejection of the *levée en masse*, and sweeping democratic reform of government. Auer was positioned on the steps at the great statue's base, Eisner far below on the lawn, with ten further speakers interspersed between them every 50 meters or so. Fechenbach estimated the crowd at well over a hundred thousand.

At the behest of one of their standard bearers, the soldiers gathered around Eisner. The various speakers simultaneously harangued their listeners. Graf notes that whenever Eisner paused for breath, the other spokesmen could be heard in the distance. Herzog recalls that Auer made a timid speech ending with the announcement that the kaiser had abdicated in favor of the crown prince. "So everything is resolved. And now I advise you, comrades, to maintain peace and order and to proceed home in customary discipline." On this point Herzog's recollection is subject to question. If Auer did indeed announce Wilhelm's decision to abdicate as emperor, the disclosure was slightly premature, based perhaps on intelligence divulged by Ebert and Scheidemann as to their ongoing negotiations with Max von Baden.[91] In any case, upon approval of the resolution Auer strode off down Landwehrstraße with his followers behind a brass band. At the Angel of Peace Monument on the right bank of the Isar, MSPD Reichstag deputy Franz Schmitt once again urged the crowd to disperse peacefully.[92] Even as Auer pleaded with his constituents to return to their homes, Eisner shouted to his retinue: "You have just heard the charge directed to you. No, you will not go home but rather remain here. And afterwards we will march together in closed ranks into the city!" The audience was jubilant as he declared that the people would no longer be stymied. His call to action Herzog paraphrased four decades later: "We want neither a crown prince nor any other. . . . The old system, the German Empire with its megalomaniacal Hohenzollern as chief, laden with the curse of war, is dead. Long live the German Republic of Workers and Soldiers! Long live the free Republic of Bavaria! And now we shall proceed to the Wittelsbach Palace!"[93]

In response the crowd roared "Long live Eisner!"[94] Ludwig Gandorfer, gone blind over years, stepped forward to pledge peasant support for their Munich comrades. Fechenbach then consolidated the revolutionary alliance of urban proletariat, peasantry, and soldiery by exhorting his fellows to liberate the barracks. "Our leader Kurt Eisner has spoken," he cried. "There's no point to more talk. Whoever is for the revolution, follow us! Follow me! March!" Turning to Fechenbach and Herzog, Eisner said they needed to make haste. Eisner linked arms with Gandorfer and moved to the head of the ranks with Fechenbach, Hans Unterleitner, Herzog, Erich Mühsam, and Oskar Maria Graf. Far from grim, the mood of the crowd, by Graf's account, was positively festive, although Eisner's face was drawn and pallid.[95] They led their train to the nearby Guldein School, where army reserve units were garrisoned, a ten-minute walk from the northern edge of the Theresienwiese. The crowd waited on the street as Fechenbach and one other soldier entered the school through a broken window to persuade the reserves to open the entrance. Once five minutes passed, Eisner's forces were to storm the building. Fechenbach negotiated with the unyielding major in command. On signal the vanguard breached the door. The armed reserves came out, red handkerchiefs tied to the barrels of their rifles, to welcoming cheers. Fechenbach ordered the distribution of weapons and ammunition.[96]

Crossing the Donnersberger Bridge over the railroad, the swelling throng swarmed the barracks complex between the king's summer palace and the heart of town. Infantry, artillery, cavalry, air, rail, signal, and cadet units all went over to their besiegers.[97] Fechenbach writes that for the most part officers were peacefully disarmed, "only in isolated cases did it come to a beating." Token resistance was offered by a sergeant at the brig, who was overpowered after firing an aimless pistol shot, and by the King's Own Regiment at the Turkish Barracks near the Wittelsbach Palace, who briefly sought to scatter marchers with tear gas.[98] Eisner's entourage advanced from Odeon Square (Odeonsplatz) past the Royal Residence. The court guards deserted their posts to join the parade. Rather than occupy the king's private quarters, Eisner and his legion continued on their way. Inside, the septuagenarian Ludwig III, the last king of Bavaria, attended his ailing wife. He had been fetched from a stroll in the English Garden by a courtier on bicycle and found all but one entrance to the Residence blocked upon their return.[99]

On Max-Joseph-Platz before the Court Theater the marchers encountered Erhard Auer pleading with a small group to desist and go home. "This is enough now," he implored in desperation. The tens of thousands with Eisner marched on triumphantly to the Isar, stopping at the foot of the Maximilian Bridge. There he had his adjutants disband the procession.[100] In the city's center the Landtag deputies, unaware of the tumult outside, had halted the day's deliberations on potato shortages at 18:00. An hour later General Philipp von Hellingrath, head of the Bavarian War Ministry, apprised Dandl that he had no more troops at his disposal. Brettreich was either in stark denial or stalling for time. Asked by

Fritz Wahl, Munich correspondent for the *Frankfurter Zeitung*, for confirmation of the situation, Brettreich adamantly asserted that by his order Eisner had been jailed earlier that afternoon.[101] Yet by 20:00 Brettreich accompanied Dandl to the Residence to advise Ludwig to flee his capital. The Bavarian king, queen, and crown prince departed at once by car for Wildenwart Castle overlooking the Chiemsee, 35 kilometers from the Austrian border.[102]

At about the same time Dandl and Brettreich were meeting with King Ludwig, Oskar Maria Graf was among an anxious crowd gathered across the Isar at the Franziskaner Cellar, where Eisner was expected to speak. All appeared to be going to plan. Graf and a friend entered the beer hall for a quick repast. The regular clientele seemed utterly unconcerned by the furor at the threshold. Making his way back into town, Graf noted that the trams were not in service and that armed bands stood at the ready. The red flag fluttered over the Residence guardhouse. He heard on the street that an election was being held for the Workers' and Soldiers' Council at the Mathäser Brewery on Karlsplatz.[103] Eisner had in fact gone there. While the soldiers chose their deputation upstairs, between ten and twenty representatives of Munich's workers met with Eisner on the ground floor. The two groups' designated leaders then conferred and jointly issued orders for their militia to patrol the city, secure government buildings, seize communications exchanges, commandeer public transport and press organs.[104]

Trucks with rifles and ammunition pulled up before the beer hall. Soldiers and workers were armed and dispatched. By 22:00, Fechenbach writes, "all government ministries, the army headquarters, main rail terminal, post and telegraph offices were in the hands of the revolutionaries." The duly constituted Workers' and Soldiers' Council, escorted by sixty armed guards, then marched to the Landtag on Prannerstraße.[105] The porter initially refused to surrender the keys. The exchange that followed was at once pathetic and comical. Patting the doorman's shoulders, a worker said simply: "No need for a scene, man! Don't you know yet which hour has struck?" The poor fool looked at his watch. "You've lost your wits," exclaimed the other. "No wonder, among these mummies here!" The porter quietly relinquished the key ring. Striding into the chamber where he had so often observed proceedings, Eisner made straightaway for the podium and claimed the president's chair, with Fechenbach and Herzog at his side in the secretaries' places. The Council filed in and occupied the deputies' benches. Gandorfer and several others from his organization were present. Herzog recalls seeing women with red umbrellas among the workers in the chamber.[106]

Fritz Wahl, with whom Eisner had sat together for years in the journalists' gallery at the Landtag, had been cleared by guards to enter the
chamber. Just a few hours earlier Wahl had been covering the food-short-
age debate. He was surprised by the sight of his former colleague standing on the podium, presidential bell in hand, ready to commence. "But,
Eisner," he queried, "what are you doing here? Brettreich told me you
were under arrest." With understandable pleasure Eisner replied: "Well,
then tell Mr. Ex-Minister that is not quite right. Moreover, you are truly
in luck, dear fellow! I am just about to proclaim the Bavarian Republic,
and besides the two of us there is not a single journalist present who
would be able to file a report on it." Thus it was that the *Frankfurter
Zeitung* broke the story.[107]

Moments later at 22:30 Eisner signaled for order. As the first order
of business he was elected the Council's first chairman, Hans Unterleitner
its second.[108] Staving off evident exhaustion, Eisner then spoke for twenty
minutes "with remarkable assurance, complete clarity, utmost discipline,
and yet with such passion that his words' impact could be read on every
face." A hush fell over the hall as he commenced: "The Bavarian Revolution
has triumphed. It has swept away the rubbish of the Wittelsbach kings. We
have proclaimed the Republic, the Free State of Bavaria. Now we must proceed to the formation of a government. We must mount elections. He who
addresses you now presumes your consent that he shall act as provisional
prime minister." Exultant acclamation confirmed the new head of state. He
went on to underscore that the elections would be conducted on the basis
of proportional representation via direct, universal suffrage and secret ballot. The establishment of the Republic, he reiterated, was the sole means of
concluding a favorable peace with the Entente.

His speech done, Eisner leaned over to Herzog and asked that he
draft a proclamation for immediate release to the public. For over an
hour, while discussion continued on the floor, he worked through the
text. Then they withdrew to a closet where Eisner copied the statement,
making few changes, then summoned a typist to generate multiple copies
for the local press and Wolff News Agency. Dr. Karl Eugen Müller, editor in chief of the bourgeois *Münchner Neueste Nachrichten*, had come
to the Landtag and requested an audience. Eisner designated Herzog the
Republic's press secretary and bade him receive Müller, who complained
indignantly that workers had occupied his offices and were preventing
publication—for the first time in the paper's history—of the morning
edition. It was just after midnight then. Herzog calmly apprised Müller
that his paper would be allowed to continue operations and, handing him
copy from the typist, with the proclamation on its front page.[109]

Just before 01:00 it occurred to the Council leadership that in the absence of police intervention against the Revolution, no one had bothered to secure police headquarters on Ettstraße, just a few hundred meters to the south. Eisner dispatched Fechenbach with a contingent to redress the oversight. Among them was the young physician Erich Katzenstein, a friend of Ernst Toller. There they found Police Chief Rudolf von Beckh in conference with his senior staff. Fechenbach apprised Beckh that the Council authorized him to continue for the moment to discharge his duties under its direction. After five minutes' reflection Beckh signed a pledge placing his force at the new regime's disposal.[110] Within the hour a reserve artillery officer, Lieutenant Kurt Königsberger, reported to Eisner that he had eight hundred men, twenty machine guns, and several howitzers in Schleißheim, north of the city, ready to defend the Revolution. The prime minister asked him to rush his troops to the Landtag. Having returned from police headquarters, Fechenbach located a red plush sofa in a caucus room. He and Herzog coaxed Eisner to lie down and sleep for a bit. Lowering himself onto the couch, Eisner remarked to Herzog: "Isn't it wondrous that we made a revolution without spilling a drop of blood? That's never happened in history."[111]

CHAPTER TWENTY-TWO

THE TERROR OF TRUTH: FORGING THE REPUBLIC, COMBATTING REACTION (1918)

DURING THE NIGHT OF 7/8 November 1918 the Bavarian ancien régime desperately sought to perpetuate itself. Interior Minister Brettreich summoned Erhard Auer for consultation as to how the revolutionary uprising might be quelled. Meeting with Brettreich past midnight, Auer and the trade-union secretary Gustav Schiefer assured him that the workers of Munich would establish order. Although Workers' and Soldiers' Council forces had seized the telephone exchange, General von Hellingrath was able to reach the garrison commander at Landsberg and request reinforcements. Bavarian infantry and Prussian reserve units were dispatched by train to Pasing on Munich's outskirts. At dawn Lieutenant Königsberger, whom Herzog dubbed "the savior from Schleißheim," had his men take up positions in defense of the Landtag, now Eisner's command center. Accompanied by three of his staff officers, Hellingrath personally met his presumed loyalist reinforcements at Pasing, but the reserves were soon persuaded to join the Revolution by a carload of men dispatched by Eisner once he learned of Hellingrath's plan.[1]

After a night of celebration with his friend Anthony van Hoboken, Oskar Maria Graf tottered through Schwabing's empty streets, bawling his approval of the sea change.[2] By midmorning a notice, printed black on a red background, was placarded on walls and advertisement columns across Bavaria: "In order to rebuild after years of destruction, the people have seized the power of the civil and military authorities and taken control of the government. The Bavarian Republic is hereby proclaimed. The supreme authority is the popularly elected Workers', Soldiers', and Peasants' Council (Arbeiter-, Soldaten- und Bauernrat, or ASB), provisionally empowered until a definitive representative body is constituted. It has legislative power. The entire garrison has placed itself at the Republican Government's disposal. Military and police headquarters are under our command. The Wittelsbach dynasty is deposed. Long live the Republic!"[3]

The morning edition of the *Münchner Neueste Nachrichten* led with the revolutionary proclamation addressed to the citizenry by Kurt Eisner as Council chair. "The terrible fate visited upon the German people has led to an elemental movement of Munich's workers and soldiers. A provisional Workers', Soldiers', and Peasants' Council was formed in the Landtag the night of 8 November. Bavaria is henceforth a republic." He went on to clarify events of the previous day, promised prompt, free, and fair election of the constituent national assembly to determine the government of the Republic. "The democratic and social Republic of Bavaria," he asserted, "has the moral authority to effect a peace for Germany . . . before enemy armies surge over the border or demobilized German troops cause chaos after the armistice." He guaranteed the security of person, of property and, for military officers and government officials who wished to serve the new state, of position, although sweeping social and political reforms were forthcoming. He emphatically rejected all bloodshed after so many years of mass murder, for "every human life should be sacred." The townspeople were assured of a steady food supply, which would be rationally apportioned. Both in recognition of the imperative for political solidarity and in a charitable gesture toward his meanest rivals, Eisner declared that "the fratricidal war between socialists is over for Bavaria."[4]

The appeal worked favorably even on as conservative a reader as Karl Alexander von Müller, coeditor with Paul Nikolaus Cossmann of the *Süddeutsche Monatshefte* (South German Monthly) and later champion of the reaction. "Shall I confess it?" he writes in his memoirs. "So deep was the stress of the past weeks, so paralyzing the mindless debility of the old government, that the journalistic verve of these proclamations, the humane idealism that appeared to resonate in them left an impression momentarily on me as well."[5] Others of Müller's stamp were impressed for greater duration. On the Republic's first day members of the old Landtag, oblivious to the new reality, arrived at the building to resume discussion of food shortages, only to be confronted by Königsberger's guns. More sentient stewards of the former regime, among them military officers in mufti, presented themselves to offer their services, including Lieutenant Colonel Falkner von Sonnenburg, censor at the Bavarian War Ministry. Lieutenant Friedrich Burschell of the Bavarian cavalry, having just met with Eisner, encountered his friend the poet Rainer Maria Rilke on Ludwigstraße: "The deep, at times desperate melancholy, readily apparent during my visits to his studio apartment on Ainmillerstraße in the last weeks of the war, appeared to have vanished. I recall how he stretched out his hands while conversing, opened and closed them several times as if grasping something. 'The time is so ripe,' he told me, 'one can shape it now.'"[6]

Having slept briefly, Eisner set about to expand the Provisional National Council and select a cabinet for his coalition government. Four Liberal Union (Liberale Vereinigung) members of the Landtag, Karl Köhl, Karl Hübsch, Friedrich Scheu, and the prominent pacifist Ludwig Quidde, were asked to join the Provisional Council. Erhard Auer was summoned to the Landtag and offered the position of interior minister.[7] While Eisner reconfigured the Bavarian state, the German government's armistice commission, led by the Center Party's Matthias Erzberger, met with Marshal Foch at Compiègne on the Oise to hear the Entente's terms: evacuation of occupied territories east and west, including Alsace-Lorraine, massive reparations, surrender of military hardware, impoundment of the fleet, and continuation of the Entente blockade. No ceasefire would be granted until the terms were accepted, which was required within seventy-two hours. Erzberger's delegation was stunned by the severity of the demands. His request for an additional day to confer with Berlin was categorically rejected.[8]

Late that morning Eisner strode into the elegant Montgelas Palace, around the block from the Landtag, for a two-hour meeting with members of the displaced Dandl cabinet in the Foreign Ministry offices. (Traditionally, the Bavarian prime minister also served as foreign minister.) Still dressed in the clothes he had slept in, he spoke about the task at hand: "I am prepared to work with you, provided that you are openly and honestly at our disposal." But he also stated that he was more disposed to collaborate with capable individuals whose station had previously precluded them from consideration for public service.[9] Auer, with a list of Eisner's proposed cabinet in hand, met at noon with Brettreich at the Interior Ministry to report that a new government was to be formed that afternoon. Unaware yet that Hellingrath's attempted military intervention had failed, Auer pledged loyalty to Dandl's government if the anticipated counterstrike could be launched no later than 15:00.[10] When no assault materialized, Auer determined to commit to Eisner's new government.

In midafternoon the Provisional National Council assembled at the Landtag for its first plenary session. In addition to representatives of the Workers', Soldiers', and Peasants' Council, the membership included the Social Democratic and Peasants' League deputations to the old Landtag as well as the select Liberal Union invitees.[11] Eisner opened the session at 15:38, underscoring its significance in his inaugural address. "Gentlemen, in a few hours over the last days we have shown how history is made, how facts are revolutionarily established for all future time. . . . Bavaria became a republic yesterday and will remain a republic." He repeated the rationale for decisive action to prevent invasion and anarchy. As President Wilson had made clear that the current government in Berlin was suited only to surrender, not to negotiate peace, a revolutionary government, "the driving forces of which, in isolated and dangerous opposition, stood up against the German war policy from the beginning," would surely be a more palatable broker and ensure more favorable terms. The Bavarian people themselves would freely exercise the right of self-determination. "A constituent national assembly will determine Bavaria's final constitution in times of calmer development."

The task at hand was to settle on those who would conduct the Republic's business of state. To that end Eisner put forward his cabinet nominees for approval, with the declaration that the ministers were responsible to the Provisional Council. Four Majority Socialists, three Independents, and one unaligned technocrat would head the nine ministries. Eisner himself was to serve as prime and foreign minister. Fellow Independents Edgar Jaffé and Hans Unterleitner were tabbed to lead Finance and the new Ministry of Social Welfare, respectively. The choice for Interior Minister Brettreich's successor was Erhard Auer, with his MSPD comrades Johannes Timm, Johannes Hoffmann, and Albert Roßhaupter assuming the portfolios for Justice, Education and Culture, and War, the latter rechristened the Ministry of Military Affairs. The politically unaffiliated Heinrich von Frauendorfer, a man with a reputation for impartiality as transportation minister in Podewil's government, was slated to reassume his former office. Eisner also asked the Council to confirm trade-union official and USPD activist Josef Staimer as the capital's police chief. Only the nomination of Erhard Auer elicited jeers, which Eisner defused with a call for socialist unity. "You see that we are not biased, we have neither favored orientations nor excluded bourgeois experts," he remarked before asking for approval.

Eisner then recognized Auer, who nominated Franz Schmitt as president of the Council, Fritz Schröder and Ludwig Quidde as vice presidents, Hans Vogel, Karl Gandorfer, Gustav Schiefer, and Bruno Körner as secretaries. No objection having been raised from the floor, Eisner declared Auer's nominees confirmed, and Schmitt conducted the vote on each of the proposed ministers. All were duly approved, Eisner first and unanimously. Schmitt then read the new government's proclamation to the citizenry, pronouncing the Revolution accomplished, pledging defense of Bavaria's borders and nourishment of the cities, assuring the bureaucracy and military of continued employment, and appealing for the productive collaboration of all. On behalf of the Peasants' League, Karl Gandorfer requested that the agricultural areas in closest proximity to the cities be patrolled to prevent plundering of crops. Schmitt read a telegram from Munich's Christian Trade Unions and the Regional Association of Catholic Workers, offering support in maintaining order and discipline. He then closed the session promptly at 16:30.[12] That night the novelist Thomas Mann, who would later repudiate his staunch support of the monarchy and the war, gave credence in his diary to the unfounded rumor that officers seeking refuge in a Munich hotel had been ferreted out and shot. "Both Munich and Bavaria governed by Jewish scribblers," he rued. "How long will the city put up with that?"[13]

Saturday, 9 November 1918, is a momentous date in German history. The Republic's leadership took up the offices of their predecessors, Eisner at Dandl's desk in the Foreign Ministry at Montgelas Palace. In the anteroom sat Felix Fechenbach, whom Eisner had chosen as his personal secretary.[14] Encouraged by Eisner's success, a workers' and soldiers' council in Berlin mobilized for revolutionary action. The USPD and Spartacists had called a general strike for 09:00 to force the monarchy's dissolution.[15] Deluded to the end, Wilhelm II devised to lead the German Army in person against the rebels and restore domestic order. It fell to Groener to apprise his liege that the military's oath to defend the crown to the death was passé, effectively voided by circumstance. Just before luncheon Wilhelm determined to step down as German emperor but remain king of Prussia. The meal was interrupted by word from Berlin that Max von Baden, in a bid to save the government from complete collapse, had already announced Wilhelm's abdication as emperor and king. Even before his indignation at this "treason" could pass to enervating cognitive dissonance, the high command informed the Hohenzollern stub that the army had lost control of the capital, his own guard battalion could no longer be deemed reliable, his person was in peril.[16] At last comprehending the situation, Wilhelm ordered his train and initiated a request for asylum in Holland. By permission of Queen Wilhelmina he crossed the border the next morning.

By that time Prince Max had already resigned as chancellor in favor of Friedrich Ebert, who insisted that only the Majority Socialists might form a credible provisional government. Max held out hope that the monarchy might yet be saved, and Ebert himself believed the issue would be decided by a constituent assembly yet to be called.[17] At moments of epochal transition, however, history moves in fits and starts. Eating potato soup in the Reichstag dining hall, Philipp Scheidemann was accosted by workers and soldiers from the street who said that Karl Liebknecht was about to proclaim a soviet republic from the balcony of the palace. A crowd had assembled outside the Reichstag. Scheidemann hurried upstairs, stepped to the French windows of the reading room, announced that Ebert was now chancellor, and then hailed the new German Republic. The crowd burst into cheers. Arriving at the Reichstag, Ebert furiously confronted Scheidemann for having overstepped his legal authority and "invalidated the existing constitution" by declaring Germany a republic.[18] After proclaiming his socialist republic that afternoon, Liebknecht led an armed contingent of Soldiers' Council men in the seizure of the *Berliner Lokal-Anzeiger* press offices. Rosa Luxemburg, freed from her cell in Breslau, rushed to the capital to take over launch of the Spartacist central organ, *Die rote Fahne* (The Red Flag).[19] In his first hours as chancellor Ebert had already had his hand forced. Bowing to USPD demands, he reluctantly formed an all-socialist government the next day, with Independents Haase, Dittmann, and Emil Barth joining Scheidemann, Otto Landsberg, and himself as its ministers. The Workers' and Soldiers' Council of Berlin voted that afternoon to approve the new government.[20]

Oskar Maria Graf, having slept off his stupor, wandered through Munich late Saturday afternoon, 9 November, observing reaction to the day's events. Hoarders lined up outside the bakeries. A rumor circulated that Ludwig III had been captured and would be shot like the tsar. Reading a newspaper account of armistice terms, an elderly man reeled and cried out that Germany would be destroyed. "That's the revenge for Brest-Litovsk!" a soldier in a ragged uniform shouted.[21] Fechenbach also recorded his impressions of the day. Citizens gathered on the squares and engaged in lively debate. Crests and inscriptions identifying purveyors to the court were being removed from the show windows of elegant shops. Police, military, and armed workers patrolling the town suddenly sprang into action, placing machine guns around the train station and on the thoroughfares. Rumor was rife that a counterrevolution was afoot: Crown Prince Rupprecht was approaching the capital with an army, or a Prussian division was poised to strike against the Republic. Eisner dispatched spokesmen onto the streets to quell disquiet. Comic relief came a few days later when a maidservant to Ludwig III arrived at the Foreign Ministry to ask permission to fetch the former king's underwear from the palace. Eisner readily approved the request.[22]

Eisner's scholarly biographers have disproportionately emphasized the last hundred days of his life, the brief tenure as head of the Bavarian Republic, as the zenith of a political trajectory. Yet, as his and Else Eisner's instructions to their children on the eve of the Revolution as well as Eisner's instructions to Wilhelm Herzog at the first meeting of the Workers' and Soldiers' Council indicate, the success of their planned enterprise was neither assured nor anticipated. Indeed, his first biographer and indispensable collaborator in the Revolution, Felix Fechenbach, maintained ten years after Eisner's death that his great "historic and national service" was achieved on 7 November 1918, when his proclamation of the Republic thwarted the Bavarian Center Party's scheme to negotiate an autonomous peace accord with the Entente and establish a separatist monarchical state.[23] Far more suspect than inflated treatments of Eisner's brief time in government are those by his monarchist and fascist detractors who belittle him as a literatus out of his depth, an amateur meddling in statecraft. Certainly few of his contemporaries were as qualified by intellect, erudition, experience, motivation, and work ethic to lead the Bavarian state. For years he had minutely observed and reported the sessions of the German, Prussian, and Bavarian parliaments. As one of Social Democracy's most prominent publicists, that is, an expert commentator on public affairs, he had long shaped mass opinion through his writing and speaking. In any case the Eisner government of 9 November 1918 through 21 February 1919 has been thoroughly documented, scrutinized, analyzed, and interpreted by Marxist and non-Marxist historians from various schools of thought in Germany, Europe, and the United States. Complete stenographic records were made of each cabinet meeting and the ten sessions of the Provisional National Council. Meticulously annotated transcripts or minutes of the cabinet meetings, with all pertinent documents appended, can be studied ad litteram in Franz J. Bauer's exhaustive tome. It is therefore not the purpose of this book to present a day-by-day account of the affairs of state but rather to examine in more general terms Kurt Eisner's initiatives as prime minister and the rationale behind them against the backdrop of Europe in upheaval.

The first casualty of the Bavarian Revolution was Ludwig Gandorfer, killed 10 November in an automobile accident near Schleißheim while being driven home to woo the rural populace's support for the Republic.[24] A sea of troubles was rising. The harsh terms of the armistice threatened to undermine the new German governments even as they repudiated the Imperial regime that fomented war. After conferring with his fellow ministers, Eisner composed an appeal to the Entente. It was telegraphed on Sunday, the tenth, to the Swiss cabinet in Bern with the request that the text be forwarded to the American, French, British, and Italian governments and distributed to the Swiss press. "The democratic nations," Eisner wrote incredulously, "cannot desire that the revolutionary creation of German democracy be undone by the victors' mercilessness."

The resultant anarchy would in turn produce "an intellectual and moral degeneration, a sociopolitical madness" that would have devastating consequences for the victors as well.[25] The same night Wilhelm Herzog returned by train to Berlin. He carried with him a missive from Eisner to Haase. Immediately upon his arrival on Monday, the eleventh, Herzog was driven directly to the chancellery. "In his letter," Herzog reveals in his memoirs, "Eisner warned Haase about Ebert and Noske, who were still closely allied with the Wilhelmine generals and who, as he suspected, were planning a counterrevolution in cooperation with those generals."[26] And in truth Ebert had already made his pact with Groener by telephone on the night of the ninth to crush the Spartacists.[27]

On Tuesday, 12 November, Eisner named the pacifist academic Friedrich Wilhelm Foerster as Bavaria's provisional envoy to Bern to emphasize the Republic's orientation, an appointment formalized two days later.[28] In his telegram of 12 November appointing Foerster to the post, Eisner concluded with the dire assessment: "If the armistice conditions are not moderated, all is lost for us."[29] Informed by the Swiss government that it was "not in the position" to forward his appeal, Eisner sought to have Foerster approach the American socialist theologian George D. Herron, a private international-relations analyst with close ties to the US embassy there, about relaying the message to President Wilson.[30] Having collaborated with both Foerster and Edgar Jaffé on peace initiatives during the war, Herron obliged and wrote directly to Wilson, urging him to encourage Eisner's hope.[31] Thursday afternoon, 14 November, Herron optimistically counseled Eisner and Jaffé jointly by telegram not to confuse the harsh armistice terms with the those of the future peace treaty, which would surely guarantee economic assistance rather than hardship. "Especially you, as antimilitarists, should see that the purpose of this armistice is to destroy your own enemies in Germany and clear the way for your program."[32]

But Eisner had already resolved to act independently against the militarists. Convinced that Matthias Erzberger, a fanatical advocate of annexations, unrestricted submarine warfare, and the bombing of London, was a disastrous choice to lead Berlin's armistice commission, Eisner determined to discredit him and his allies in the national Foreign Office by exposing their complicity in Germany's war guilt. On the thirteenth Eisner demanded that Sigmund von Lößl, privy councilor to the Bavarian Foreign Ministry, produce the reports of the Bavarian envoy to Berlin from July and August 1914. Lößl confessed that he had destroyed critical documents a week earlier to protect the culpable. Eisner turned to Dr. Friedrich Muckle, Bavaria's new envoy in Berlin, to obtain copies there.[33]

Muckle and Eisner concurred that the German Republic had to demonstrate its complete break with the Imperial old guard by publishing secret
papers and bringing to trial those responsible for the debacle of August
1914. Perhaps the momentous change would persuade the Entente to
validate and sustain nascent German democracy. If Prussia blocked the
effort, then Bavaria should threaten secession.[34]

The same day that Herron telegraphed Munich, Eisner once again
asked Gustav Landauer to join the effort to shape public opinion. "What
I would like from you is for you to contribute to the remolding of souls
through oratorical engagement."[35] The next day Eisner outlined his government's program in a detailed statement addressing further democratization, political and social reform, economic exigencies, freedom of
expression, the armistice, and the character of a new German state. The
opening sentence set the elevated tone: "The revolutionary government
of the Bavarian Republic is committed to the great attempt to transform
the old misery into the new age in complete, guaranteed freedom and
in moral regard for human sentiments, and by so doing to provide an
example of the possibilities of politics based on confidence in the spirit
of the masses, on full and clear recognition of the necessities and means
of development, on frank honesty and truthfulness." For the sake of
transparency the government eschewed its own press organ. Despite the
notorious particularism of German newspapers, freedom of the press
was assured in the hope that critical judgment would eventually prevail.
Likewise, religious and academic freedom was held inviolable. The government promised equal access to education, sweeping curricular change,
and reform of pedagogical practice. Just as the schools had to be restructured, so too did the justice system, the army, and tax code, all according
to principles of social equality.

With regard to the armistice, his direct appeal to the Entente leaders, Eisner remarked here, had already borne fruit. He foresaw the creation of a United States of Germany, including Austria, "without any
predominance of a single state" such as Prussia had enjoyed to the detriment of the nation. In Bavaria he wanted to achieve greater direct
democracy even before the constituent national assembly was convened.
To that end he proposed a massive expansion of councils representing
every trade, profession, and pursuit. These councils of civil servants,
educators, artists, craftsmen, merchants, and others would constitute an
"associate parliament" complementing the "central parliament" of the
existing Workers', Soldiers', and Peasants' Council. Representatives of
the new body would meet in the National Theater, previously the Court
Theater, in Munich.

Eisner took a consummately pragmatic approach to the question of nationalizing industry. "It is Karl Marx's view that the economy must be transferred to public ownership once productivity has developed to the point of bursting the too narrow confines of capitalist regulation." The war had exhausted Germany's productive capacity; there was nothing left to socialize. Only after the International had reconstituted itself within the democratic League of Nations would prolonged peaceful economic growth fulfill the requisite conditions for collectivization. For the moment Auer's Ministry of the Interior would oversee food rationing, seizing all military stores for immediate distribution to the populace. Unterleitner's Ministry of Social Welfare undertook finding work for demobilized soldiers and displaced munitions workers. The bourgeois *Bayerische Staatszeitung* printed the program in full on Sunday, 17 November.[36]

That morning a postcard portrait of Eisner as prime minister, with the slogan "For Freedom and Justice!" above the image, was being sold throughout town for 20 pfennige. "He has had his hair trimmed, beard too, a cross between Marx and Bethmann," observed Dr. Josef Hofmiller, a teacher at Munich's Ludwigsgymnasium, who purchased one so that acquaintances in the village of Palling might see "how the red regent looks."[37] Later that evening a stately observance of the Bavarian Revolution was held at the National Theater, with benefits assisting wounded and ill soldiers. Eisner's long experience in organizing impressive celebrations and commemorations was evident in the event's resplendent staging. It was his first public appearance as head of state. Tickets were distributed by the Workers', Soldiers', and Peasants' Council, with seating determined by lottery. Government ministers were scattered throughout the audience, a mix of new guard, municipal dignitaries, and theater crowd in appropriately sober attire brightened by the occasional red armband or ribbon.[38] The hall had been decorated by society architect Emanuel von Seidl.[39] Rainer Maria Rilke, theater director Viktor Schwanneke, and German Museum of Science and Technology founder Oskar von Miller were among the attendees.[40] The program featured orchestral perfomances of two Beethoven pieces fraught with symbolism, both for the new Republic and for Eisner personally: the third *Leonore* Overture, adumbrating the political prisoner's deliverance from bondage, and the *Egmont* Overture, memorializing the martyred hero of the Netherlands' revolt against Spanish oppression. After Bruno Walter conducted the music from *Fidelio*, Eisner paid tribute to Ludwig Gandorfer and consecrated the Revolution to democracy and socialism, that everyone might best "cultivate his talents" and lead a fulfilled, productive life in peace. A reading from Goethe was followed by the second overture, a Handel aria sung by Paul Bender accompanied by Walter, a recitation of Conrad Ferdinand Meyer's poem "Peace on Earth," and the audience's singing of the final verse of Eisner's own composition, "The Peoples' Hymn," with conductors Hugo Röhr and Otto Heß sharing the baton for the second Beethoven piece and the finale.[41]

Karl Gandorfer had assumed his brother's mantle as head of the Bavarian Peasants' League, but Georg Heim, whom Erhard Auer had proposed for membership in the Provisional National Council, was now demanding that his Bavarian Christian Peasants' Association (Bayerischer Christlicher Bauernverein) be accorded majority representation proportionate to its numbers on the Peasants' Central Council.[42] Preparing to depart for a conference of government officials in Berlin, Eisner took time out to write to Heim on Friday, 22 November. Although Eisner would welcome Heim's addition to the Provisional National Council as an expert on agricultural economy, his organization's dominance on the Peasants' Council was out of the question, for "it is the basis and precept of the new system that supporters of the old who share responsibility for Germany's collapse remain excluded." Well aware of the renascent fervor of the dispossessed to restore their privilege, he underscored his resolve for lasting change: "Nor is my determination weakened by the observation that across the country all the familiar means of demagoguery are being employed now in an attempt to interrupt or even prevent the new construction of state and society."[43] Defeating reaction was much on his mind. The Workers' Council too was concerned about broader dissemination of the Revolution's ideals and policy. Its members, Gustav Landauer reported to Eisner the same Friday, "all wanted to establish a newspaper." In committee Landauer proposed that Eisner as the government's executive might be moved to create a propaganda arm, an idea enthusiastically endorsed by Richard Scheid, education panel chair of the Munich trade unions.[44]

Saturday, 23 November, Eisner departed Munich for Berlin. There he met with Karl Liebknecht at Bavaria's legation in a personal attempt to bridge divides between the USPD and the Spartacists, but Liebknecht was disinclined to compromise. Eisner then met with Theodor Wolff, editor of the *Berliner Tageblatt*, and passed on the secret exchanges obtained from Muckle: a report of 18 July 1914 from the Bavarian chargé d'affaires in Berlin, Hans von Schoen, to Prime Minister Hertling in Munich; transcripts of two telephone calls of 31 July from the legation in Berlin to the Bavarian Foreign Ministry; and chief envoy Hugo von Lerchenfeld's report of 4 August to Hertling. Eisner himself selected the critical passages. The four communiqués detailed preparations for mobilization, outlined constellations of alliance, disclosed the imminent violation of Belgian neutrality, and demonstrated that, far from moderating Vienna's stance, Berlin contrived to take advantage of Austria's "favorable hour" for intervention in Serbia.[45] On Saturday yet the Hoffmann News Agency of Bavaria circulated the documents, which Wolff's paper published the next day, followed on Monday by the major newspapers of Germany and Europe.[46]

Writing three and a half years later, Bavarian archivist and historian Pius Dirr construed Eisner's intent in releasing the documents as twofold, serving both his domestic and foreign policy. "Above all he wanted to brand the previous Imperial government and former ruling classes as war criminals and thereby 'blow up' all manner of counterrevolution. He hoped thereby to deal a blow to the Majority Socialists as well, whose politics he had already opposed during the war and whose leaders he accepted only with reluctance . . . as executives of the new federal government. . . . The confession of war guilt was to show the ethical force of the Revolution, its character as moral revolt against the old system! Thus Germany's absolution was to be accomplished, the way prepared to a better peace with the nation's enemies, and doors opened to Wilson's League of Nations, the coming age of peaceful international cooperation, the age of humanity, begun."[47]

When Ebert opened the national conference at the Chancellor's Palace that morning, Eisner's action had already effectively preempted the agenda. Of the 110 participants, 9 were members of the Bavarian delegation: Eisner, Muckle, Fechenbach, consular economic attaché Josef Gunz, Finance Ministry adviser Philipp von Kohl, banker Hans Schmelzle, Federal Council representative (Bundesratsbevollmächtigter) Adam von Nüßlein, ministry department heads Ludwig Huber and Gustav Rohmer. Many of Eisner's former allies and adversaries—Eduard Bernstein, Georg Gradnauer, Paul Göhre, Wolfgang Heine, Karl Kautsky, Georg Ledebour, Heinrich Ströbel, Philipp Scheidemann, Albert Südekum, Emanuel Wurm—were present in their new capacities as cabinet secretaries, privy councilors, commissioners, and attachés, yet none was as highly placed now as he.[48] In his introductory remarks Ebert hailed the work of Erzberger's armistice commission and warned that for Germany's preservation "nothing would be more disastrous in this situation than internal divisiveness." He was immediately challenged by Eisner, who declared that an entirely new polity was precisely the imperative.

Reporting on the state of the peace negotiations, German foreign minister Wilhelm Solf, who had held office since 3 October, decried as unconscionable "the publication of misleading statements" lifted from official files and insisted that the federal government alone, not individual states or local workers' and soldiers' committees, was empowered to conduct negotiations with foreign powers. Erzberger echoed Ebert's call for unity and speculated that the Entente would use any pretext to invade. Eisner responded with incendiary ire, remarking the irony that Clemenceau, whom Solf and Erzberger doubtlessly regarded as the ultimate chauvinist, was poised to begin food shipments. To cries of support, the man who had been jailed nine months for treason accused the two of counterrevolution, of attempting to save the very parties guilty of plunging Germany into the abyss by redirecting the fury of the people toward "merciless enemies" who were willing to feed them. The Entente's demand to negotiate with the unsullied he deemed entirely justified. "One could but wish that all compromised representatives of the old system find their way to Holland as quickly as possible so as not to be arrested as traitors."

Whereas Heine protested Eisner's vituperation, Kautsky and Bernstein voiced their agreement that Germany was ill served by negotiators who were clearly suspect to the victors. Spartacist August Merges, president of the Braunschweig Council of People's Deputies, went further than Eisner. The Majority Socialists, he alleged, had compromised themselves for four years. "Herr Solf could easily take refuge under the wings of Ebert and Scheidemann, who have recanted all things socialist." Although Ebert pushed through a unity resolution, roiling discord was manifest, particularly on the issue of monarchists and annexationists continuing to conduct affairs of state.[49] Solf left the conference "entirely broken."[50] In Munich the next day Eisner briefed the cabinet that Erzberger and Solf, closely allied with the army's general staff, personified the Imperial "apparatus of corruption" still functioning unchecked.[51] At midnight he composed a telegram to the Bavarian legation in Berlin, asking that Ebert be informed of his decision to terminate dealings between the Foreign Ministry in Munich and the tainted leadership of the German Foreign Office. The next day the executive committee of the Workers', Soldiers', and Peasants' Council in Munich appealed to its Berlin counterpart to interdict influence of "counterrevolutionary elements" on foreign policy, lumping Majority Socialists Scheidemann and Eduard David with Erzberger and Solf among compromised undesirables.[52] In the cabinet session of Thursday, 28 November, Eisner reported that the American ambassador to Switzerland vigorously denied any intention of the Entente to resume hostilities, an action Erzberger deemed imminent. Nonetheless, the yellow press had seized on the scaremongering and branded Eisner a foreign agent and worse.[53]

Among Eisner's papers in the Bundesarchiv at Berlin-Lichterfelde is a copious file of threatening cards and letters. A postcard dated the twenty-eighth asks: "How many millions in English-French money did you pocket, Jewish swine, for your betrayal of the fatherland?" A lengthy letter written the same day reads: "Bribed by money from Russian Bolshevists, you base your power on the bayonets of adolescent boys. . . . You decline to deal with honorable men because they allegedly come to you with dirty hands, you, who in your life have never had anything else. . . . We shall give you time, until six in the evening on 5 December. If you have not resigned your 'office' by then, we will shoot you down, we swear it." One of the postcard portraits of Eisner was received with eyes gouged out and "your hours will be numbered" typed on the verso.[54] While Eisner's enemies plotted his demise, Gustav Landauer was preparing to move with his daughters from Krumbach to Eisner's home in Großhadern so as to be more engaged with shoring up the Republic.[55]

As purposefully as Eisner championed more direct democracy and proscription of Imperial linchpins from the new government, Erhard Auer was equally committed to channel power away from the councils and back to the MSPD organizations that he controlled. Repeatedly Auer blocked Karl Gandorfer's efforts to win greater influence for his Peasants' League, which enjoyed Eisner's express support.[56] While Eisner was away in Berlin, Auer complained in the cabinet meeting of Monday, 25 November, of the burgeoning costs of maintaining the Soldiers' Council in particular. A week earlier he had presented draft guidelines calling for the consolidation of the Workers' and Peasants' Councils, declaring that the two bodies had no executive power to enforce policy, and enjoining them to desist from meddling with duly installed state and local officials discharging their duties. The guidelines were approved in Eisner's absence.[57] A tempest was brewing.

In Berlin Eisner had addressed the executive body of the Workers' and Soldiers' Council. There he underscored that his Munich Independents, "a tiny minority, perhaps four hundred comrades," had taken the lead in the German Revolution and succeeded despite fierce opposition from the Majority Socialists. The revolutionary impulse was embodied in the Workers', Soldiers', and Peasants' Council, which formed the legitimate government until the constituent assembly could be convened. He was convinced that the greatest threat to democratization was a return to conventional parliamentarism, the fondest desire of the counterrevolution. "Revolution is not democracy," he declared, but rather its precursor. The councils must first "lay the foundation for new development," imbue society with new ideals before there could be any thought of a constituent assembly. Only the consolidation of the Revolution, of more direct democracy would prevent the reemergence of a Berlin dictatorship. Having been urged by Foerster to avoid any appearance of Leninist sympathies, Eisner unequivocally stated his commitment to peaceful transformation. The council system he envisioned, far from being Bolshevist, prevented authoritarian rule. "I have no love for the method of Bolshevism. I believe in the power of the idea."[58]

Thursday evening, 28 November, Eisner reprised and expanded the Berlin talk in a speech for the Workers', Soldiers', and Peasants' Council in Munich, a meeting he called in order to clarify the changing political situation, to take the offensive against a hostile press, and to refute the accusation of despotism. Citing reports that his actual name was Salomon Kuschinski, that he had ridden in King Ludwig's private car to Berlin, that Entente troops were about to march into Munich, Eisner remarked that "the gentlemen of the press who lied to the German people for four and a half years have, after a brief respite, found their way back to their old calling and are lying once more." Why? Because he had exposed how the counterrevolution was already in control in Berlin and thus threatened their parasitic existence. It was they and their financiers who were leading the call for the state and national constituent assemblies so as to "neutralize once again the direct, vital participation of the masses" in government. "The bankrupt politicians who want to sweep aside the new revolutionary organizations are gathering beneath the banner of national assembly, and the criminal politicians who started and prolonged the World War, who plunged us into the abyss, seek anew to stoke the German people's hatred and ire against the Entente so that we forget them and their wretchedness." What must the Entente powers infer from such developments? That the Revolution was nothing more than a puppeteers' farce, that the kaiser would soon return and restore the military dictatorship, that he or his son would plunge Europe back into war. Eisner appealed to two representatives from the Berlin Workers' and Soldiers' Council executive who were present, Gustav Heller and Hermann Bergmann, to support the purge of compromised individuals from the Foreign Office and to help forge a democratic, socialist United States of Germany. His remarks prompted a tumultuous ovation.[59]

Far more contentious was the four-day meeting of the Soldiers' Council, beginning on Saturday, 30 November. As the initial speaker, Eisner resumed his attack on the press, which pandered to every absurd rumor spawned by agents of Berlin's Foreign Office. He, one of the most prominent victims of state censorship during the "slavery of the last years, the dictatorship of the high command," had now to suffer both the scurrilous sensationalism of a venal press to which he accorded complete freedom and the charge that his government, which shared power with its bitter rival, aspired to Bolshevist absolutism. He chronicled how for the duration of the war the Majority Socialists teamed with the high command to suppress any contradiction. Now Ebert, Erzberger, Groener, and their former allies were determined to persist on that course by subverting the revolutionary councils' influence. Even worse, their agents had infiltrated the councils themselves. And here Eisner pointedly cast aspersions on the rival members of his government, whom the press reported were at odds with his leadership. "We have been unified in all things up to now, but it is most clear that those gentlemen in the cabinet who opposed the Revolution, who pursued a policy different from ours during the war, cannot quite bring themselves in line yet now with the new spirit."

Erhard Auer, who had also been invited to address the gathering, immediately confirmed Eisner's surmise by endorsing the national assembly. The entire populace, Auer argued, had to weigh in on Germany's future. It was insufficient that people merely be apprised of decisions, rather all segments of society had to share in making decisions. "A dictatorship cannot and must not be permitted to exist in a free republic." The very man who had done everything in his power to prevent the Bavarian monarchy's fall was now the Republic's staunchest defender. Fritz Schröder jeered from his bench. Eisner had to hear worse yet. Lieutenant Nieberl, representative of Thirty-Ninth Bavarian Reserve Division, warned against placing the same kind of blind faith in Eisner as had been entrusted to General Ludendorff. Citing a report from the MSPD tool *Vorwärts*, Anton Kothieringer of Augsburg pointed out that Eisner himself had initially supported the war and wondered if he could be counted as uncompromised.[60] The coalition Eisner had forged was disintegrating. Encouraged by Auer and Frauendorfer, the transportation workers' union threatened on Sunday, 1 December, to strike if the government failed to schedule prompt elections as promised.[61] The same day, a twenty-year-old student, goaded by the relentless press barrage, was foiled in an attempt to shoot Eisner, whom he held for the scourge of the land. Contrite, the young man confessed his confusion and expressed remorse. Eisner consoled his would-be assassin and pleaded for leniency.[62]

On Monday the *Münchener Post* printed Friedrich Wilhelm Foerster's affirmation of the national assembly as "the symbol for indispensable reconciliation of all classes in the enterprise of saving our fatherland from disintegration and disgraceful foreign domination."[63] In *Vorwärts* Eisner's former protégé Friedrich Stampfer attacked the "quixotic presidency" of the Bavarian Republic.[64] That morning Auer, Timm, and Frauendorfer

396 + THE TERROR OF TRUTH

tendered their resignations from the cabinet. Through the day Eisner was closeted with them in an attempt to reach a viable compromise. Late in the afternoon he read to the Soldiers' Council a statement with the consent of all members of the cabinet. In essence he had bought time to shore up the councils' continuation as an associate representative forum by honoring his original commitment to elections for a Bavarian constituent assembly. The announcement was received with enthusiastic applause.[65] Behind the closed doors of the cabinet chamber the squabbles, invective, and recriminations intensified.

Wednesday morning, 4 December, five hundred armed soldiers of Bavaria's First Engineer Reserve Battalion formed in ranks before the Foreign Ministry to demand announcement of the date for elections. They were confronted by the Republican Guard assembled in Eisner's defense. The tense stand-off ended when Eisner himself came out and disclosed that the cabinet was indeed in the process of scheduling the ballot.[66] Later that day he thwarted a plot hatched by the anti-Semitic free-booter Rudolf Glauer, self-styled Freiherr von Sebottendorff, founder of the protofascist, paramilitary Thule Society and the newspaper *Völkischer Beobachter*, which would become the Nazi Party organ in December 1920. Glauer, who regarded Eisner as the personification of an "international Jewish conspiracy," planned to abduct him from a meeting in Bad Aibling on Wednesday, 4 December, hold him hostage in the mountains, and proclaim Auer head of the government. The coup was abandoned when Eisner and Karl Gandorfer were well received by the audience of workers and peasants.[67]

At the next day's cabinet session Eisner warned while discussing details of the upcoming election that further agitation against Munich's Workers' Council could incite "a second revolution." Timm and Frauendorfer in turn denounced Eisner as an anarchist. Frauendorfer charged that Eisner was "no statesman" and alleged that "all the world says you cannot govern." Eisner answered that Frauendorfer was "no politician" and that "the world also supported the World War." Hoffmann came to Eisner's defense, reproaching both Timm and Frauendorfer for ill-considered allusions to Bolshevism. Eisner conceded that the councils would act merely in an advisory capacity to the constituent assembly. The cabinet approved 12 January 1919 as the date for elections.[68]

The second revolution indeed began Friday night, 6 December, and only Eisner's intervention prevented certain violent reprisals. Mass meetings held in support of direct democracy induced immediate action. After a rally at the Schwabinger Brewery Erich Mühsam's adherents seized and "socialized" the offices of the Catholic, conservative *Bayerischer Kurier*, turning the operation over to the typesetters, who set to work composing a morning edition the likes of which its loyal readers had never beheld. A parade of pro-Eisner demonstrators commandeered other bourgeois papers. At midnight three hundred marchers, among them many former soldiers, made their way through the streets to Erhard Auer's residence on Nußbaumstraße, where a delegation entered the building and roughly demanded that he resign from the government. Among the intruders was Auer's future would-be assassin, Alois Lindner, who that night accused him of treason. Auer apprised the crowd that he had offered to quit earlier in the week but then duly signed a statement that he was stepping down under duress. The parade then proceeded to the Foreign Ministry to report their triumph, but Eisner had rushed to the *Bayerischer Kurier* pressroom. There he persuaded the Spartacists to disperse and required that the compositors reset the edition their employers had presented. When the marchers appeared with Auer's resignation in hand, Eisner gratefully acknowledged their allegiance but confirmed that he had asked Auer to remain in office. He bade them all return home peaceably and then hurried to Auer to repudiate the extorted renunciation of his post. In retrospect Mühsam judged that Eisner had dug his grave that night.[69]

On Saturday, 7 December, 400 members of Munich's workers' councils met to elect 25 representatives to the Bavarian Workers' Council, which was to comprise 210 delegates. The 50 members of the Revolutionary Workers' Council (Revolutionärer Arbeiterrat, or RAR), constituted on 8 November, stridently objected to the attempt by Majority Socialist unions to control the election and banished their leaders from the hall. Continuing on Sunday morning, the body, dominated by MSPD councils, chose the 25 allotted delegates, none of whom was from the Revolutionary Workers' Council. The Bavarian Workers' Council then met on Monday and Tuesday to elect 50 delegates to the constituent national assembly.[70] Hans Reck and Ernst Toller served as first and second chairs.[71] Despite their exclusion from voting, the Revolutionary Workers' Council members, led by Gustav Landauer, attended the meetings on Monday and Tuesday and were permitted to participate in discussion.

In a spirited and compelling address Eisner wryly apologized for having launched the Revolution without prior approval from the provinces, then earnestly deplored the disenfranchisement of the vanguard. At least ten of the revolutionaries, he entreated, should have seats in the constituent national assembly. He reminded all present of how impotent the mighty Social Democratic Party had proven in preventing the war, despite the strength and wealth of its unions and press, the envy of the entire International. Citing historical precedent, he argued that the Revolution of 1848 had been subverted by bourgeois avarice and exploitation. To the accusation that he would institute dictatorship and rule by terror, that he would banish the bourgeoisie from power, he answered that what he aimed to prevent was their cherished goal of repealing the Revolution, a contagion that unfortunately had infected the Soldiers' Council. "If that be terror, then it is the terror of truth, the terror of necessity, the terror of the future that will be."[72]

Auer then spoke briefly, repeating his opposition to any form of dictatorship. Landauer presented a lengthy report of the Revolutionary Workers' Council's activities and proposals for democratizing and socializing Bavaria. He accused Auer of attempting to restore the antediluvian order of the nineteenth century. Erich Mühsam lashed out at the Majority Socialists' attempt at cooption: "I warn you, the Revolution will not be voted down."[73] On the second day of the meeting USPD affiliate August Hagemeister alleged that Auer and two of his fellow cabinet members had hatched a "conspiracy" in the previous week with the stated purpose of toppling Eisner, and that Auer had announced in a secret meeting of his backers that Eisner would fall within days. Before Auer could rush back to the hall to answer the charge, the Council approved fifty nominees to the constituent assembly, ten of whom were from the Revolutionary Council, including Landauer, Karl Kröpelin, Lorenz Winkler, and Hedwig Kämpfer. Having been telephoned by one of his allies, Auer reappeared and adamantly denied Hagemeister's representation of events at Munich's Red Cock Hotel, although he readily admitted that "Eisner and I are political opponents." Nonetheless, he asserted, they were working together for the common good.[74] When Landauer, Mühsam, Breitenbach, and Gandorfer challenged Auer on multiple points, Auer retorted that his patience was wearing exceedingly thin and that soon the choice would have to be made between one line or the other. The meeting ended after sustained uproar from the benches.

The next day Dr. Max Levien, a native Muscovite and associate of Mühsam, organized the Munich branch of the Spartacus Group at a beer-hall meeting of supporters of the Workers', Soldiers', and Peasants' Council as the supreme authority. Like Sonja Lerch, Levien had taken part in the Russian revolution of 1905 and studied in Switzerland before settling in Germany. In Switzerland he met Lenin and joined the Bolsheviks. Having served at the front in the Bavarian infantry, Levien became a member of the fifteen-man Munich Soldiers' Council executive, together with Fechenbach, Richard Kämpfer, and Schröder. Eisner and Jaffé were present at the meeting in hope of moderating its proceedings and averting further direct actions such as had been orchestrated a week earlier. Eisner pleaded with those present not to overestimate their strength. The time to protest the national assembly was past, and conditions in Russia were far different from those in Germany. Divisive demonstrations and meetings against the government were breaking down its ability to preserve order while the reaction was gathering momentum. The very spirit of the new Republic, he averred, hinged at the moment on a united socialist front.[75] Mühsam answered in his journal *Kain* (Cain): "Herr Eisner has declared publicly that the election may now be considered an accomplished fact already. He is wrong. The revolutionaries are resolved, firmly resolved to offer the most extreme, determined resistance to the incalculable misfortune that the convocation of a counterrevolutionary legislative body would mean for the nation."[76]

The message of united front was one Eisner repeated the next evening, Thursday, 12 December, at a rousing USPD election rally in the Mathäser Brewery. "Every Social Democrat stands on the basis of class struggle, but class struggle for us has never been rule by one class, but rather its elimination." Revolution had to fit its national context. What worked in Russia was no formula for Bavaria or Germany. Still, he espoused the council system as indispensable, the schools where the masses learned political and economic engagement. "The councils are the foundation of democracy. The National Assembly, the Landtag crown the structure. But if they do not rest on the strength and will of those workers' councils . . . , this crown will collapse just like the monarchical crowns." For this notion and for his assertion of Germany's war guilt, Eisner told those present, the same press that had blithely printed the high command's lies for four and a half years celebrated its new freedom by casting him as an ideologue, a dreamer, a poet out of place in politics. Spurred on by the press, the same citizenry of Munich that could endure every privation and indignity under Wittelsbach kings and Catholic clerics had become impatient overnight. If the Isar's flow dropped and the hydroelectric plant could not power the streetcars, it was now the fault of his government. Yet he remained optimistic, for just four weeks after he and his party had effected the Revolution and established the Republic, they had already implemented the eight-hour day and women's suffrage, more than the Social Democratic Party had ever achieved, "and those are things that cannot be undone."[77]

CHAPTER TWENTY-THREE

THE FANTASIES OF A VISIONARY: MARTYR OF THE REVOLUTION (1918–1919)

A SSAILED BY LEFT AND RIGHT, Eisner struggled to maintain equilibrium. The Swiss press in particular regarded developments in Bavaria as ominous. "One watches with dismay," the progressive *National-Zeitung* of Basel wrote, "as the hate campaign in the disheveled, so politically imprudent German nation turns on precisely the one man who thus far has demonstrated understanding of reality." In Bern the democratic *Freie Zeitung* warned "if Eisner falls, the immensely polymorphous counter-revolution is victorious."[1] Amid the miasma of division and intrigue the Provisional National Council convened for its second session on Friday, 13 December 1918. Since 8 November the affairs of state had been conducted by Eisner and his cabinet ministers. Now that elections for the Bavarian National Assembly, the new Landtag, were set for 12 January 1919, the Provisional National Council—expanded to include 67 representatives from various professional organizations, 50 delegates from each branch of the Workers', Soldiers', and Peasants' Council, 29 members of the Social Democratic deputation from the old Landtag, 4 of their Liberal Union colleagues, and 6 from the Bavarian Peasants' League—met four times over the course of six days.[2]

Faced with imminent dissolution once the new Landtag was seated, the caretaker lawmakers pursued cross purposes, some pressing for immediate reform while others exhorted conscientious deference to their successors. Wednesday, 18 December, Minister of Education Johannes Hoffmann began the fifth session with the announcement of one of the most significant reforms undertaken by the Eisner government. Two days earlier the cabinet had approved the secularization of public-school administration, curriculum, and instruction by proscribing dominant clerical oversight of local and regional school boards and church funding for school inspectors. The costs previously borne by the parishes would be assumed by the state.[3] "The seventh of November and the sixteenth of December," Hoffmann declared, "mark the end of the Church and Center State of Bavaria. It would be a shame for Bavarian Social Democracy, a shame for the liberal Bavarian middle class, and a shame for Bavarian schoolteachers if it were ever to return." The hall resounded with acclaim.[4] In absence of industry to socialize, society itself might be reshaped.

For the most part, however, genuine debate on most issues gave way to campaign harangue as MSPD loyalists exerted their upper hand and attacked Eisner as an alien interloper unpalatable to true Bavarians. To jeers from the Independent Socialist camp, Konrad Lotter, Workers' Council representative from Neustadt an der Aisch in Central Franconia, asserted that 99 percent of the populace would back a government headed by "a man such as Auer," whereas Eisner's heritage and politics, particularly his suspect foreign policy, "aroused the mistrust of the people."[5] The criticism of the Republic's foreign policy was echoed by Ludwig Quidde of the Liberal Union, who alleged that Eisner had overestimated Clemenceau's goodwill.[6] Speaking repeatedly in his own defense, Eisner maintained that conventional conceptions of leadership, statecraft, and order were no longer applicable in the postwar world. He noted too the personal prejudice against him. Should he enunciate Quidde's cherished pacifist ideals, they would be pronounced "the fantasies of a visionary." Turning the tables on his critics from the old Landtag, Eisner asked what their bourgeois parliamentarism had accomplished in the four and a half years of war. The very nature of politics had changed since the Revolution, and imaginative, creative vision was the essential attribute of leadership. "The function of the truly productive politician is to see already realized in his mind's eye what will be tomorrow or the next day, and therefore only the future, not the present, can ever judge such statesmen." Like poets, politicians had to visualize the shape of things to come, "and it is a delusion of our apolitical German people that something can be achieved in the world without just such poetic vitality."[7]

Demonstrations the press deplored as woeful disorder, Eisner claimed, were actually the first attempts by a liberated society at self-actualization, regardless of how distasteful and irresponsible their vocal excesses. For him to tolerate criticism that no past head of state would have brooked, to decline to impose censorship, to engage in dialogue with his detractors, even to rein in his own overly enthusiastic defenders evinced his ultimate commitment to nonviolence and freedom of expression. "What is expected of a government determined to maintain order without bloodshed and without prisons, prosecutors, and convicts either?

. . . A democratic government is not in the position to suppress theories by force of arms. A fine democracy that would be! . . . But, gentlemen, once blood is shed, we cannot know where the slaughter will end. . . . For my part I have truthfully done as much as I could to keep the peace." For all the talk of his dictatorship and reign of terror, Eisner reminded the body, the first armed military force to threaten to destabilize the Republic was the reserve engineers assembled before the Foreign Ministry two weeks earlier to demand a return to bourgeois parliamentarism.[8]

The first issue of the Independent Socialist paper that Eisner had envisioned a year earlier was published on Friday, 20 December 1918. Its title, derived from the new age begun by the Revolution, was simply *Neue Zeitung*. For the inaugural edition Eisner contributed an article on the nature of the bourgeois press, which he characterized as an inherently venal enterprise. He explained that such concerns came into existence when some entrepreneur secured office space and presses, hired personnel, and directed them to turn out his product: a newspaper. "More and more the press has evolved from a vehicle for dissemination of political and social ideas into a venture to generate profits or into the agent of capitalist interest groups." Thus it was that the German high command, the Foreign Office, and the press could engage in a war-long conspiracy to delude the populace as to the possibility of ultimate victory after the first battle of the Marne. The daily press conferences jointly orchestrated at the Reichstag by Lieutenant Colonel Erhard Deutelmoser and Mumm von Schwarzenstein, conducted solely to sway public opinion rather than to inform, and the willing cooperation of the papers in spreading the distortions were "the main cause of the German nation's frightful catastrophe." Not until the masses mastered independent thought and the servile press turned from commercial enterprise to critical judgment could the new democracy prosper.[9]

Frank Arnau, Bern correspondent for the Associated Press, visited Munich on assignment and went to Fechenbach to request an interview with Eisner. Returning late from a meeting and having to depart for another without lunch, Eisner apologized and asked if Arnau might come to his residence later that evening. Arnau gladly assented. Fechenbach fetched him at his hotel shortly after eight, and the two walked back to the Foreign Ministry, where Eisner and his wife occupied a small loft apartment. (The Eisners' two daughters were residing in Krumbach with Gustav Landauer's daughters, Charlotte, Gudula, and Brigitte. Landauer's wife, Hedwig Lachmann, had died of influenza on 21 February 1918 there.)[10] The chairs, table, and cabinet in the parlor, Arnau surmised, had been moved upstairs from offices below. A grand piano and cello case were in one corner of the room. Dressed in a flannel robe, Eisner rose from his seat to receive the guest and called into the adjacent room. "His young wife came in and greeted me as if I were an old acquaintance," the reporter recalled. She said she thought she had enough tea and coffee for everyone to have some.

In the course of the following conversation Eisner asked Arnau about his having interviewed Lenin, answered questions on the challenges Bavaria now faced, and disclosed that he planned to attend the first post-war congress of the Socialist International in Bern in February. There he hoped to sway those yet hostile by honestly confessing Germany's machinations to induce world war. "If we are able to convince Wilson that there is another Germany, the course of which is being charted by new men committed to peace, then the American president will bring all his influence to bear in Paris to impress on the chauvinistic elements the necessity of a just peace." Nearly two hours had passed. As tired as he was, Eisner seated himself at the piano and asked first if Arnau loved Beethoven, then what he would like to hear. Fechenbach dimmed the lights. Upon request the prime minister, completely absorbed, played the *Moonlight* Sonata from memory. Arnau never forgot the moment.[11]

Whereas the USPD looked to their new newspaper to rally the electorate, the Majority Socialists, acutely conscious of potential radical volatility after Erhard Auer's rude awakening at his residence by Mühsam's cohort, cozied up to the paramilitary groups determined to unseat the revolutionary leaders. The government forces funded by Albert Roßhaupter's defense ministry comprised the amorphous complement of soldiers' councils, the Munich Military Police unit of about 150 men, and the 1,500-strong Republican Guard. As interior minister, Auer had already authorized funding for a handful of rural militias to uphold order in the provinces. Former Bavarian reserve lieutenant Rudolf Buttmann, who would become the fourth official member of the Nazi Party in February 1925, had begun to organize a counterrevolutionary militia to oppose the soldiers' councils. When approached by Buttmann with a request for arms, Military Police Chief Oskar Dürr told him that he and his ilk should be shot.[12] The reactionary militias planned a coup for Christmas Eve on the pretexts that the Spartacists were about to mount a revolt and that Auer's life was in danger. Buttmann was being advised by Captain Hans Karl von Zwehl of the First Bavarian Field Artillery, staff officers Karlfried von Dürckheim and Emmerich von Godin of the Bavarian Infantry King's Own Regiment, under the command of the Freikorps organizer Colonel Franz von Epp. Their first objective was to oust Dürr.[13]

That day Buttmann met with Auer, who inquired as to the militia's readiness to move against the Spartacists and expressed his own willingness to reinstate the monarchy. For his safety Auer was urged to spend the evening at the Turkish Barracks, where he was hosted by Lieutenant Anton von Arco auf Valley, commanding officer of the fifth company of Epp's regiment. Dürkheim was also present. As a veteran of the regiment, Auer seemed at ease as he sat conversing with Count Arco at length, although he later denied their tête-à-tête ever took place. Silken armbands in Bavarian blue and white, to be worn by the militiamen, were festively distributed in Auer's presence.[14] Georg Heim, head of the new Bavarian People's Party (Bayerische Volkspartei, or BVP), was apparently well informed of the scheduled operation; a week earlier in Würzburg he had told soldiers in the conservative camp to arm themselves in preparation for the planned reckoning.[15]

Militia coorganizer Julius Lehmann, Munich publisher of Pan-Germanist tracts, had appealed to Archbishop Michael von Faulhaber to have the church bells rung as the call to action. When the pealing commenced, Lehmann rushed armed to the city's center, where he expected to meet the nationalist element to whom he had distributed army pistols made available by the deputy command of the First Bavarian Army Corps, but evidently too few of his fellows were willing to forsake hearth and home on the holy night to bring off their putsch.[16] Eisner himself, who had already been apprised of rumors of mischief, was spending the holiday with his family at the Landauers' home in Krumbach before a meeting of South German state governments in Stuttgart 27–28 December.[17] On Christmas Day and again two days later Buttmann met with counterrevolutionary groups to stoke zeal against the Independent Socialists, Spartacists, and Bolshevists. Capitalizing on a rumor born of streetfighting in Berlin, Buttmann reported to Auer at his home in the wee hours of Wednesday, 27 December, that Liebknecht and Ledebour had supplanted Ebert and Haase and now controlled the government.[18] Buttmann persuaded Auer to sign a "Call for the Establishment of a Citizens' Militia." A few hours later Timm and Sigmund von Haller, one of Eisner's prominent critics during his time in Nuremberg, added their signatures. Roßhaupter refused to sign.[19]

Shrewdly worded so as to imply the blessing of the entire government, the appeal was publicly posted that same morning throughout Munich and generated both support and suspicion. It announced that security troops had been summoned to reinforce local police in protecting the community from violent unrest. "Nevertheless," the critical sentence read, "in the belief that the citizenry in the broadest sense is not content merely to let others shield it at this perilous time but stands ready to answer Prime Minister Kurt Eisner's call for the voluntary collaboration of all, also in accomplishing this most urgent mission at present, and thus to defend the current form of government from every assault, the undersigned appeal for the creation of a citizens' militia."[20] Meeting in absence of Eisner, Auer, and Unterleitner, the cabinet treated what Roßhaupter now regarded as a crisis. Called to account, Timm lamely asserted that he envisioned the citizens' militia as an organization of trade-union homeguards to check the Bolshevist threat emanating from Berlin. The unions, he claimed, were to meet the next day to discuss the matter. Roßhaupter advised that the "brakes be applied if at all possible" at the union meetings, for the establishment of such a militia had the potential "to arouse the greatest mistrust in the soldiers" whose councils underpinned the revolutionary Republic. Any government distribution of arms to militiamen he now deemed out of the question.[21]

Indeed, the executive committee of the Soldiers' Council immediately condemned the proposed citizens' militia as an incitement to civil war and reaffirmed loyalty to Dürr.[22] That night Buttmann presided over an organizational meeting of his recruits in the Germania Lodge and Thule Society club rooms at the Four Seasons Hotel. One of Roßhaupter's men gained entry and confirmed in a detailed report his chief's assessment of the peril. Buttmann announced that Lieutenant Colonel Friedrich von Haack, chief of staff of the First Bavarian Army Corps, would serve as the Militia's tactical commander, that Auer would provide arms, and that the Militia already enjoyed active support from the King's Own Regiment. Haack then unveiled a plan of attack by which government buildings were to be occupied, critical transit routes blocked, and adversarial demonstrations dispersed by firing into the crowd with machine guns.[23]

Apprised of the crisis, Eisner departed Stuttgart by car Saturday morning, 28 December, to return to Munich. Acting on intelligence from his informant, Dürr ordered a raid on a secret meeting of Militia leadership at the Four Seasons at 11:00. Haack and Lehmann were among forty men taken into custody. Buttmann, who came to the meeting late, avoided arrest. That evening he intercepted Auer's train at Pasing on the outskirts of town and took him by car into the city, for an angry contingent from the workers' councils were waiting at the central terminal to confront Auer. During the drive Auer reiterated his support for the Citizens' Militia, pledged to appeal for release of the detained, and welcomed the opportunity to settle accounts with Eisner.[24] Yet by the next day's full cabinet meeting, attended by Dürr, Police Chief Staimer, and two officers from the Ministry of Military Affairs, Auer's bravado had vanished. Lieutenant

Albert Kranold, Roßhaupter's ordnance officer, present at the organizational meeting of the Citizens' Militia on the twenty-seventh, briefed the cabinet on what he had witnessed. Staimer and Dürr complemented Kranold's disclosures with details from their informants.[25] Dürr remarked the outrage of the soldiers' councils at the complicity of Auer, Timm, and Haller. The putschists, Dürr demanded, had to be dealt with. "We cannot be constrained by earlier laws," he declared ominously. Roßhaupter and Unterleitner reported that fighting had already broken out between soldiers' councils and militiamen in Plattling and Ingolstadt.[26]

A habitual and accomplished liar, Auer claimed he was "the scapegoat," unwitting "victim of a terrible hoax" and offered to resign his ministry. Although Eisner found it suspicious that the call had been published on the day he left for Stuttgart, he sought to defuse the tension by coming to Auer's defense. The man Frauendorfer had derided as no statesman once again showed humility, forbearance, and charity. The critical consideration was to avoid bloody mayhem just two weeks before the Landtag elections. "The masses are seething," Eisner warned. "Either we shall all come to ruin, to Bolshevism, or we have to find ways to political resolution." He proposed that Auer simply withdraw his signature from Buttmann's appeal. Roßhaupter and Jaffé agreed. The latter underscored that Auer and Timm had to refrain from their divisive tactics and "sincerely cooperate." Eisner noted that even if the government held together, the Spartacists might move to establish a council dictatorship. "I do not know if I can prevent that," he added. Hoffmann pleaded for unity lest the antagonism between Auer and Eisner lead to the kind of mass violence Berlin had experienced. Unterleitner, however, lashed out at Auer and Timm, insisting that they both resign. Citing chronic attacks by the *Münchener Post*, he charged that the Majority leaders were engaged in vile campaign of defamation against the USPD and that Auer was behind it. Unterleitner went further yet. Despite his penchant for feigning ignorance when called to account, Auer "somehow though can recall every particular when it matters." Eisner remained unmoved; political considerations had to take precedence over personal differences.[27]

The seventh session of the Provisional National Council, held on Monday, 30 December 1918, was devoted to discussion of the Citizens' Militia debacle. With the demeanor of a state prosecutor Ernst Toller drew on informants' reports to expose the motives and machinations of the Militia organizers and their financiers, implicating Auer, Timm, and Haller as willing pawns at best, at worst trusted coconspirators of Bavaria's fanatic monarchists. "The Citizens' Militia," Toller scoffed, "is to safeguard elections to the National Assembly. From whom then? Are you unaware that even the most radical leftists intend to take part in this election for the National Assembly and do you not believe that the soldiers and police would arrest the few people who might want to sabotage the elections?" Noting that the Left Liberal *Fränkischer Kurier* had endorsed Auer as Bavaria's potential savior, Landauer joined Toller in calling upon the Majority Socialists to turn to new leadership committed to democratic, socialist ideals.[28] Ludwig Kraus of Fürth, himself a first lieutenant, conceded that the threat from the Left was miniscule compared with that posed by the unregenerate officer corps. Opponents of the Revolution, Fritz Schröder recalled, had branded the council government a tyranny of terror. Had they not been derailed, he gibed, precisely "they would have then introduced a real dictatorship of machine guns."[29]

Auer and Timm, who had both formally recanted their support for Buttmann's venture, presented their rationale for signing his announcement four days earlier. As promised, Eisner then whitewashed the vipers' nest with the statement that "the cabinet is united in the resolve to utilize every means against any threat to the Revolution's achievements." There could be no doubt, he emphasized, that the temporarily thwarted champions of capitalist exploitation were behind every secretive, cowardly, and insidious plot to regain their former preserve.[30] Confident that he had averted the collapse of his government, Eisner moved to further institutionalization of the Revolution. That same day he wrote to Kautsky to inquire if he was comfortable working with the Anglophobe Ulrich von Brockdorff-Rantzau at Berlin's Foreign Office or whether he might prefer succeeding the renowned Lujo Brentano as economics chair at Munich University.[31] The next day a sailor guarding Eisner's building affronted Auer and Timm as they entered for the scheduled cabinet meeting. "You're to be shot," Auer was told, "we've already decided that."[32]

Rumors abounded of a putsch by the extreme Left on New Year's Eve. The din of riotous soldiers and sporadic gunfire kept the Bavarian capital on edge through the night.[33] Even as Eisner pressed for Social Democratic unity in the face of counterrevolution, his Prussian USPD comrades Haase, Dittmann, and Barth resigned from the Berlin government on 28 December over Ebert's use of troops to quell demonstrations. The Spartacus Group, the Bremen Left Radicals (Bremer Linksradikale), and affiliated outliers merged as the German Communist Party (Kommunistische Partei Deutschlands, or KPD) on the thirtieth. Their inaugural congress concluded on 1 January 1919 in Berlin.[34] In Munich Levien's Spartacists and Mühsam's United Revolutionary Internationalists (Vereinigung revolutionärer Internationalisten, or VRI) soon joined. Eisner's chief concern before the 12 January polling was to win cabinet approval for his draft constitution to serve as legal basis for the transition to elective, republican government. The document recapitulated the ideals and directives of the revolutionary regime, codified its sweeping democratic and secular reforms, and subjected future controversial legislation to popular referendum. The cabinet considered and amended the draft in its meetings of 3 and 4 January, advised by privy councilors and legal experts Robert Piloty and Josef von Graßmann, the latter of whom had recorded the cabinet minutes since its inception.[35]

Aristocratic title and privilege having been abolished, Eisner's constitution prescribed a unicameral Landtag elected directly by secret ballot of Bavaria's citizens, male and female, who had reached the age of twenty-one. Executive authority reposed in the ministerial cabinet, which was empowered to call for a referendum on any parliamentary law within four weeks of its passage. Were the measure upheld by a simple majority of the popular vote, the cabinet was obligated to step down. If, however, the measure were rejected, the Landtag was to be dissolved. Eisner believed that the option for referendum effectively precluded uprisings against the state, as the people would have immediate recourse. He was well aware too that the new Landtag might attempt to restore an autocratic monarchy and dispense with a constitution altogether. The revolutionary government's provisional constitution for the Republic was therefore to be submitted to the Landtag as the first order of business. Until the Landtag formulated a permanent constitution, the revolutionary government retained all executive and legislative power. By this stipulation Eisner hoped to ensure that reactionaries of Buttmann's ilk could perpetuate no "election swindle" and repeal the Revolution by guile.[36]

By Eisner's draft, Bavaria was to be a democratic, socialist republic abiding by the principles of the League of Nations as a constituent member of the United States of Germany. He argued in discussion that all Germans residing in Bavaria should have the right to vote in Bavaria so as to lift restrictions on workers sent to factories there during the war. Discounting reservations of the legal advisers, the cabinet concurred, requiring only registration by 8 January.[37] After a line-by-line reading of the draft, debate and amendment of some finer points, Eisner was unanimously authorized to publish the constitution. Concerned about potential conflict between the Provisional Council and the Landtag, Timm moved that the Council be disbanded forthwith.[38] Indeed, the Council's final session was held the morning of 4 January.

On Sunday, 5 January, Eisner traveled north to Ingolstadt for a campaign speech in the riding hall of the engineer corps. He told the audience of several thousand that a new epoch was beginning, that on 12 January they would not be casting their ballots for candidates but for themselves, for freedom and self-affirmation. The bankrupt bourgeois parties, having exhausted their credit, had reorganized and changed their names, yet they remained the parties that propelled Germany into war. "You ask if a black Landtag were to assemble, would I then have it dispersed with machine guns. Yes, I have built myself a machine gun with a special feature: it spills no blood and fells only the liars. This machine gun is called popular referendum. If the black deputies wanted to establish monarchy, for example, then the government would call up the people for a vote. If the people decide against the deputies, then the Landtag goes home. That is true rule of the people."[39]

The machine-gun fire in Berlin the next day was anything but proverbial. In mass protest of Ebert's decision to replace the USPD's Emil Eichhorn as Berlin's police chief with Eugen Ernst, the Independent Socialists and Communists turned out in force, occupied police headquarters on Alexanderplatz, distributed arms, and launched a general strike on Monday morning. From the balcony of police headquarters Liebknecht proclaimed to his followers that their moment had arrived. The Spartacus Uprising was begun. Ebert turned to the military and anticommunist Freikorps auxiliaries to crush the revolt. The campaign was coordinated by Gustav Noske, one of the most extreme social chauvinists during the war. He gave his commanders and their men free rein in the operation. The protestors, estimated to number two hundred thousand, had taken control of train stations, newspaper offices, and critical vantage points in the heart of the city.[40] From his room in the Kaiserhof Hotel the diarist Harry von Kessler observed soldiers moving into position on the street. "At half past five violent shooting," he noted, "the rat-tat-tat of machine guns, the pounding of artillery or trench mortars, the blast of grenades, the roar of battle."[41] On Saturday, 11 January, the Freikorps Potsdam Regiment, commanded by Major Franz von Stephani, stormed the *Vorwärts* compound on Lindenstraße, redoubt of about 350 armed Spartacists. Howitzers blasted away at the facade, then a tank breached the entrance. The rebels attempted to negotiate terms. Seven of their messengers were executed by Stephani's men, who after their victorious assault brutalized nearly 300 prisoners.[42] The police headquarters was retaken by Freikorps troops that night with yet more slaughter. In less than a fortnight the failed insurrection claimed over 1,000 dead.[43]

The unrest spread to Munich as well, even though Independent Socialists controlled the government there. Eisner's principled resolve to preserve freedom of expression and to prevent violence was taxed to the limit. What a study in contrast with the imperatives of Ebert and Noske in Berlin. At noon on Tuesday, 7 January, several thousand unemployed demonstrated on the Theresienwiese for an increase of benefits. Participants marched to the Foreign Ministry building, which housed the Social Welfare office of Hans Unterleitner, to present their demands. Unterleitner met at length with a delegation while the crowd on Promenadeplatz became increasingly agitated. The representatives emerged with a compromise agreement in hand, but as the demonstrators paraded away, shots were exchanged with the Republican Guard, leaving three people dead.[44] On the ninth the cabinet met all day to deal with the crisis. The executive committee of the Workers' Council, leaders of soldiers' councils, the Independent Socialists' executive, and other officials were called in to confer. Intelligence indicated that the demonstration had been orchestrated by the extreme Left as a provocation; the ranks of the unemployed with legitimate complaints had been infiltrated by anarchist rabble. Unterleitner reported that on the day of the riot Erich Mühsam had made "the boldest inflammatory speeches" and a general strike was to begin the next day to coincide with the burial of the martyrs. Staimer and Dürr disclosed that armed demonstrations were being planned as well. At a Wednesday rally led by Josef Sontheimer the audience was exhorted to seize the newspaper offices. Dürr warned that his men were stretched thin and demoralized by constant deployment. Both he and Staimer averred that a Communist putsch was imminent and called for an immediate ban on all assemblies and demonstrations. "We must prohibit meetings too," Staimer pleaded, "for the demonstrations arise from them."[45]

Eisner deplored the rashness of Liebknecht and Ledebour. "Luxemburg is perhaps the only rationale one," he remarked. (She had indeed chastised Liebknecht for jumping the gun.)[46] Eisner had no doubt that opportunistic elements were manipulating the protests in Munich to provoke violence. "Demonstrations by revolutionaries against revolutionary government," he fulminated, "make no sense and are merely counterrevolution in disguise." He agreed to a ban on all demonstrations not approved in advance by the Workers' or Soldiers' Council, but he declined to impose a ban on meetings. He was willing to accept full responsibility for the decision. He warned against the government's use of deadly force and reiterated his stance: "I am against any bloodshed."[47] Eisner reluctantly endorsed his security chiefs' plan to arrest the leaders of the next day's slated demonstrations, including Levien, Mühsam, Sontheimer, and Landauer.[48] That night, in response to Hugo Haase's urgent request, he telegraphed Berlin to protest the fratricide that threatened to engulf all of Germany. "Berlin's example is having a ruinous effect everywhere and generating a pandemic of madness. A government borne by popular confidence, uniting all factions of socialism, and determined to erect democracy and socialism on the foundation of revolution seems the only salvation."[49]

The ordered arrests of Bavaria's extreme Left leaders, carried out early Friday, prompted their supporters, many of whom were soldiers, to parade to the Foreign Ministry that afternoon to secure release of the detained. Rudolf Egelhofer, a sailor in the Communist camp who was suspected of fomenting Tuesday's firefight, climbed into Eisner's office through the window in an attempt to arrange a conference with a dozen spokesmen. Eisner refused to meet under duress with the delegation but proposed they return the next day.[50] Fifty "totally dissolute rabble, subproletarians" then breached the building's entrance. Volunteer naval guards stood at the ready with hand grenades and machine guns to repel the rioters. For two hours, Eisner later complained, his staff attempted to telephone Dürr and Roßhaupter for reinforcements, but no one answered. Finally, so as to avoid "a great bloodbath," Eisner ordered the prisoners' release. Unterleitner was dispatched to Stadelheim. There he was shot at by guards embittered by the order. Mühsam was beaten before being freed. That evening he and Levien addressed jubilant partisans at the Mathäser Brewery. After the meeting Communists clashed with police guarding the nearby central railway terminal. The fighting yielded six fatalities.[51]

In the next day's cabinet meeting Eisner angrily confronted Dürr and Roßhaupter with their failure to prevent the siege at the Foreign Ministry: "Why wasn't Promenadeplatz blocked off?" Dürr first claimed that there had been no calls to his office, then confessed that he had been out on the streets with his overwhelmed force. He countered that his hands were tied anyway by the obsessive "fear of bloodshed" on the part of irresponsible parties. Moreover, the Spartacists had infiltrated the barracks. Roßhaupter proposed to bring in reliable reinforcements from Ingolstadt and Freising. Timm expressed alarm at the government's loss of authority. "I would rather be torn to shreds than to bow to political demands under pressure from a demonstration," Eisner said. "I informed the released prisoners that the next time we will shoot, which they readily acknowledged." Anticipating another demonstration that day, he ordered police to seal off Promenadeplatz and be prepared to "work their wonders." Sufficiently chidden, Staimer and Dürr announced they would gladly resign. "We all want to go," Eisner retorted, but that was no option.[52] Thus the state of affairs on the eve of Landtag elections.

On Sunday, 12 January, seven of Bavaria's eight provinces voted in the Republic's first Landtag election; the Rhenish Palatinate's polling took place on 2 February. At stake were 180 seats to be filled by proportional representation of the vying parties. Candidates could stand in multiple districts. Eisner was entered in thirty-nine races. Although he headed the government of the state he had called into being, it nonetheless stood to reason that the Independent Socialists, a splinter party formed in April 1917, were at a distinct disadvantage. Only in Upper Franconia—home to Bamberg, Bayreuth, Coburg, Hof, and Kulmbach—was the USPD in control of the old Social Democratic bureaucracy, organizations, and press. The first issue of Munich's *Neue Zeitung* had been printed hardly three weeks earlier.[53] Many of Bavaria's Independent Socialists had been transplanted there from North Germany during the war and were regarded, like their leader, as alien. Far more established and indigenous was the Bavarian Peasants' League (BBB), with which Eisner had forged a critical alliance on the eve of 7 November. The party of Ludwig and Karl Gandorfer claimed 16 seats. For a Prussian-born, Jewish, naturalized Bavarian who had never held elective office, Eisner scored significant personal totals in the final tally, garnering 17,302 votes, compared with 40,269 won by Auer, native leader of the firmly entrenched Majority Socialists. Only two other Independents won election: Max Blumtritt and Fritz Goßler in Hof's first and second districts, respectively. The largest prize belonged to Georg Heim's Bavarian People's Party, the rechristened Center Party, with 35 percent of the nearly 3.41 million votes cast and 66 seats. At the last moment the Communists had thrown their negligible support to the BVP, both to repudiate Eisner's governing coalition and to sharpen class conflict. The Majority Socialists were in second place at 33 percent and 61 seats.[54] Whatever government emerged would be by necessity another coalition.

Since coming to power Eisner had stressed socialist unity against both reaction and Bolshevism. On 8 November, with the councils in control of the government and the radicalized ranks of soldiers as enforcers, he might well have moved against his rivals at the same time he deposed the monarchy. Acting on principles and ideals, he chose instead to share power, forming a coalition government of Independents Socialists, Majority Socialists, and one unaffiliated bourgeois minister (Frauendorfer). Liberal democrats were accorded representation in the Provisional National Council. Eisner had envisioned the Workers', Soldiers', and Peasants' Council replacing the aristocratic chamber of the bicameral Landtag. To preserve the gains of the Revolution, he had drafted a provisional constitution granting his coalition ministry the power to nullify the Landtag's constitution and dissolve the assembly via popular referendum. Early in December 1918 he had spoken of a "second revolution" if the attempt were made to void the first. After the Landtag balloting he was compelled to take stock of the new reality.

Eisner's first address after the election was on Tuesday, 14 January, to select members of the Workers' and Soldiers' Council in special session at the German Theater on Schwanthalerstraße. A month earlier, in his campaign speech of 12 December 1918 at the Mathäser Brewery, he had pledged to "stand and fall" with the council system.[55] Now he reasserted his abiding commitment to direct democracy, socialist unity, and non-violence. The Communists had embraced Bolshevism and were therefore excluded from the fold; equally abhorrent was the "organizational fanaticism" that begat the Ebert-Noske regime in Berlin. Socialism would be achieved by the people, not by a party. In contrast to the Communists, whose slogan was "all power to the councils," he held to his conception of formalized, grassroots control bodies monitoring all aspects of public policy, a shadow assembly of sorts, or *Nebenparlament*, for informing and articulating mass opinion. At the same time Eisner sought to disabuse his audience of delusions of grandeur propagated by the KPD. "Do you want the executive and legislative? Then we need neither parliament nor government. Then you are everything at once, and I wish you much pleasure in this enterprise." By his design the councils would be part of the state construct, but the Landtag alone would enact legislation. "The parliament, however, is dependent on the constitutionally mandated plebescites." And here the councils held the trump card.[56]

Neue Zeitung printed Eisner's "Guidelines for Future Socialist Policy" on the fifteenth. He still believed that a unified front of the coalition he had created—USPD, MSPD, BBB—could legitimately retain power and continue to govern.[57] Indeed, in light of the present political configuration, he argued that "the restoration of a unified party has become possible and necessary," an appeal that had been published by the USPD organ on the thirteenth.[58] The new government, Eisner maintained, would be either socialist or bourgeois; on that score there could be no doubt or compromise. By his schema, "no socialist may join a bourgeois government," but a socialist government might invite bourgeois experts to serve as cabinet ministers.[59] The sticking point for the Majority Socialists in reunification with the Independents was precisely the councils, which they regarded as too radicalized. As January's violent demonstrations had shown, the soldiers' councils in particular were deeply divided and could scarcely be counted on to back a cabinet determined to marginalize the advocates of the councils' supreme authority: Levien, Mühsam, and Landauer. And now that Auer was in the position to head a new cabinet, he could dictate the terms of merger. The consolidated leadership of Munich's Social Democratic Association (Sozialdemokratischer Verein) expressed willingness to negotiate reunification with the USPD but discounted any role in that discussion for "corporations such as the Workers' Council, in which other political parties are also represented."[60]

Between the Landtag elections and those for the German National Assembly a week later, Noske's operation in Berlin routed the Communist insurgency when Karl Liebknecht and Rosa Luxemburg were captured in hiding on 15 January and brutally murdered by a Freikorps detachment. The effects were lasting and fateful. The murders, historian Eberhard Kolb writes, "aroused indignation and horror among many who in no way shared the victims' political views."[61] In Munich the young dramatist Bertolt Brecht, adamantly apolitical until then, was spurred to a modicum of engagement. He and his friend Hanns Otto Münsterer attended election rallies on the sixteenth and were in the company of Felix Fechenbach until late that night.[62] "After Liebknecht comes Eisner," warned a missive received at the Foreign Ministry; its author, who claimed concern for the prime minister's welfare, urged immediate abdication.[63] The elections for the German National Assembly reflected a decisive shift of opinion in Bavaria. In one week the USPD vote tally rose by 46.6 percent from 78,780 to 115,476 (excluding the Rhenish Palatinate, where the Landtag election was yet to be held), with the greatest increase coming in the capital, more than doubling from 18,331 to 37,121.[64] In Upper Bavaria, that is, Munich and its environs, the gains came primarily at the expense of the BVP and the MSPD.

In Munich the cabinet braced for another putsch attempt by the Communists, whose Berlin organization Eisner was now convinced had been secretly funded by General Ludendorff, rumored to have returned from exile in Scandinavia.[65] A second conference of German heads of state was scheduled for Saturday, 25 January, in Berlin—one week after the Entente's Paris Peace Conference had commenced—to discuss the centralist constitution penned by Hugo Preuß, Ebert's interior minister, for approval by the German National Assembly.[66] In the days before the trip Eisner spoke at the inaugural session of the Bavarian Socialization Commission (Bayerischer Sozialisierungs-Ausschuß) and conferred with Swedish socialist Hjalmar Branting, the neutral states' most influential intermediary at Paris. Opening the forum on collectivization Wednesday, the twenty-second, Eisner counseled transparency and public dialogue in all their dealings. Economic transformation, he held, must follow the political revolution, but it could not occur from one day to the next. A beginning must nonetheless be made. "I would consider our work utterly pointless if, like earlier inquests and commissions, nothing came of it other than impulses and ambitions, no immediately feasible plan of action." He envisioned that the process would start with agriculture and land redistribution.[67] On Thursday he told the cabinet that Branting painted a bleak picture. France's position had hardened. Key figures in the current German government, men such as Erzberger and Brockdorff-Rantzau, were regarded as "the most despised personalities to the Entente." In response to the query as to how some progress might occur, Branting despaired that the upcoming first postwar assembly of the International in Bern could break the impasse, given the bitter divisions. Perhaps a South German initiative would be in order. "Bavaria has good press abroad," Eisner remarked to his fellow ministers. Something positive might yet be achieved.[68]

Friday, 24 January, Eisner was accompanied by Jaffé, Josef von Graßmann, and privy councilor Ernst Müller to Berlin. At Bamberg they were joined by the delegations from Baden and Württemberg. On the train the three groups voiced joint concerns about recurring Prussian preeminence and determined to oppose the Preuß draft. Saturday morning Eisner hosted his counterparts from the two neighboring South German states, Hesse, and Saxony at the Bavarian mission. By agreement Eisner presented to the full conference Graßmann's federalist "Guidelines for the National Constitution," already endorsed by the South German contingent in transit from Bamberg, and a proposal requiring ratification of the constitution by a commission from the individual states. In addition, he moved that the German National Assembly be relocated from Weimar, within 20 kilometers of the Prussian border, to Würzburg in Bavaria. None of the initiatives was destined to succeed. Back in Munich Eisner reported to his cabinet on Tuesday. "I believe," he conceded, "that the unitarian faction is very strong, the great majority in the [German] National Assembly as well."[69] The previous day Auer's acquaintance Count Arco had arranged for publication of a placard charging Eisner with forestalling popular will enunciated in the Landtag balloting. Through "childish political maneuvers," the twenty-two-year-old monarchist alleged, Eisner was making Bavaria an international laughingstock. The police chief refused permission to post the notice.[70] Eisner now made ready for departure to the potentially more welcoming venue of Bern and the congress of the Socialist International.

Fearing another damning exposé of Germany's war guilt, Ebert's government had gone to extraordinary lengths to block Eisner's participation at Bern.[71] Given Noske's methods of dealing with adversaries, Eisner's application for a pistol permit, granted by Staimer's office on the twenty-eighth, seems justifiable prudence.[72] Wednesday, 29 January, Eisner embarked for Switzerland.[73] The next day Gustav Landauer invited Else Eisner to stay with his family in Krumbach in her husband's absence.[74] Eisner's position was increasingly tenuous. Quidde's German Democratic Party (Deutsche Demokratische Partei, or DDP) and Heim's Bavarian People's Party both strenuously opposed further impediments to the duly elected Landtag. On Friday the BVP leadership called for immediate convocation of the new parliament and for consequent disempowerment of the revolutionary councils.[75] Eighty-four delegates of the Bavarian MSPD met in Munich the weekend of 1–2 February to consider their course. Auer told them that the majority of voters had sided with the bourgeois parties. Backed by Hoffmann, he urged that the revolutionary government step aside, but he rejected his party's relegation to the opposition and proposed potential coalition partners. Despite perceptions of "unreliablility of the Democrats and Peasants' Leaguers" by his fellow conferees, Auer revealed that negotiations were already underway with both.[76]

That same Sunday, the day before the week-long congress opened, Fechenbach accompanied Eisner and a French attendee on a brief mountain hike.[77] Conditions in Bern were far more to Eisner's favor than at home, as Germany's Majority Socialists and Independents had equal representation. Further, he was completely in his element, at the center of an open exchange of ideas in cosmopolitan company. He held court in the parlor of the Bellevue Hotel and the smoking room of the Café du Théâtre, delighting friends and strangers alike with his reflections, witticisms, and self-deprecating humor. The Basel sociologist Robert Michels recalls encountering Eisner looking for newspapers in the salon of the sumptuous Bernerhof Hotel. "I need to see," he explained with a smile, "if I have been deposed."[78]

The MSPD sent Hermann Müller, Otto Wels, and old Hermann Molkenbuhr as delegates. The Independents were represented by Haase, Kautsky, and Hermann Jäckel, with Eisner attending by choice in quasiofficial capacity as leader of the Bavarian Independents and on a mission of peace as head of a socialist government.[79] But when Haase left to join the German National Assembly in Weimar after the International preconference deliberations, Eisner, by dint of his prominence as, in Fechenbach's words, "the great man" there, emerged as chief spokesman for the USPD. Boycotted by the communist parties and the Belgian socialists—the latter in protest of the German MSPD's presence—the Bern congress attracted ninety-six delegates from twenty-six nations. Fechenbach noted that the German Majority Socialists were clearly "on the stand" as accomplices of the German Imperial government.[80] And Otto Wels embraced that role, obdurately and absurdly defending his party's wartime policy under a system that was no more. When Eisner rose to speak, he repudiated Wels's assertions so eloquently as to move Germany's harshest critics to reconciliation and to leave an indelible impression on the audience.

With reluctance, for he had no desire "to cast stones at what is already dead," Eisner characterized Wels's reflections as a product of an "outmoded mindset." Most Social Democrats, including himself, were persuaded by government lies in July and August 1914 that Germany was threatened by tsarist imperialism. "We were deluded at the beginning of the war, after fourteen days we could no longer be so. . . . We knew that once war begins, the individual soldier has no choice, but Social Democracy's duty was in the political arena. We had to overthrow the government, seize political power, and make peace." To shouts of protest from Wels and of agreement from others, Eisner stated categorically: "You, Majority Socialist comrades, helped plunge Germany into the abyss." Socialist unity, Eisner's paramount hope, hinged on the Majority's recognition that the old line was as indefensible as it was passé. Perhaps, he speculated, his errant comrade-compatriots had been emboldened by the nearly twelve million votes they won in the National Assembly elections, but experience demonstrated that "truth is no product of multiplication."

"Today there is no question," Eisner declared, "that this war was made by a small band of insanely Prussian officers allied with heavy industrialists, champions of Weltpolitik, capitalists, and princes, all wholly lacking political foresight and military insight." By their inability or unwillingness to acknowledge four years' complicity in the tragic enterprise, the Majority Socialists had "undermined the moral credit of the German people." Yet, even in the fall of 1914, there were those who rose up against the government, and for the duration of the fighting the prisons were full of them. He appealed now, invoking Jaurès's prophecy of humanity's triumph after the bloodbath, to French socialists, to English comrades to forgo thoughts of vengeance and instead to nurture nascent German democracy. "We want to expiate our guilt by moving forward on the way to socialism. And now give us your hand!" Thunderous applause echoed through the People's Hall.[81]

The effect of Eisner's speech was immediate and tangible. The congress passed his resolution for rapid repatriation of German prisoners of war. It was cosponsored by Pierre Renaudel, Jaurès's successor as editor of *L'Humanité*. In presenting it Eisner described his efforts to relieve the suffering of twelve thousand Entente POWs in Munich, whose temporary barracks he inspected together with French officers. There they saw the ravages of influenza: the dead and dying lay among the yet uninfected. His credibility, Michels judged, was epically enhanced by a single remark:

"Those of you, my comrades of conscience, who have been impris-oned, understand how these men feel."[82] Citing statistics indicating his detailed knowledge of the destruction wrought by four years of fighting in France—wrecked railways, bridges, canal locks—Eisner pleaded that the use of forced labor to rebuild the country was morally and economi-cally toxic. German workers, students, and artists were honor-bound to volunteer their services in making whole the land their military had rav-aged, and he pledged to call them to action in this undertaking for rec-onciliation. Once again his message found its resonance, signaled by a prolonged, deafening ovation.[83]

In diametric contrast to Eisner's reception at the Bern congress was the response of the German nationalist and Majority Socialist press. Here Eisner was vilified as an egomaniacal traitor personally bent on destruc-tion of the fatherland, for he himself had quoted Wilhelm Solf's lament that the revelation of Berlin's determination to provoke war "costs Germany 100 billion more" in reparations—and declared that the truth must be told even if it spelled ruin.[84] In the desperate hysteria of humili-ation and denial the culpable and their minions now set upon the scape-goat with savage fury. Every scurrilous lie that might galvanize ire against their nemesis was brought to bear. The man who would soon be eulo-gized as Christlike and the noblest Bavarian of all was scathed by those, in the words of Frank Arnau, "who had learned nothing from the German defeat" as a Polish-born Bolshevik bought by French bribes to advocate enslavement of German prisoners of war.[85] One of the few papers to strive for clarity was the *Frankfurter Zeitung*. "Whoever distorts, impugns, and diminishes Eisner's work in Bern in the exceedingly malicious man-ner as has recently occurred failed to understand what was at stake at the International Socialist congress and what . . . was achieved."[86]

In his January conversation with Eisner, Hjalmar Branting had expressed incredulity at the Germans' persistent inability to appreciate the psyche of other nations.[87] Although the populace had certainly suffered from the British blockade, no fighting had taken place within its borders; the land had been spared the frightful devastation visited upon north-ern France. And yet the very factions that had so frenetically advocated war now somehow believed that Germany's abasement alone squared all accounts. The national conscience had been so warped by blind self-righ-teousness that it could neither abide truth nor accept consequences.

Friday, 7 February, Timm and Jaffé telegraphed Eisner in Bern to request he come back to Munich as soon as possible. Demands for transfer of authority to the Landtag were at a peak, civil servants were poised to go on strike, and Communist agitation was destabilizing the government.[88] His light in Munich nearly eclipsed, Eisner opted to return by way of Basel, where he had been invited by the university's democratically restructured student government to give the inaugural talk in a series on vital political perspectives.[89] He left Bern on Monday, the tenth, before the congress concluded. His work there was already done, and he was depressed by reports of the first sessions of the Weimar National Assembly, which he believed could nurture no international hope for a new Germany. He sensed too that he could no longer rely on French public opinion for critical support.[90] That evening Eisner and Italian socialist Giulio Casalini were slated to speak at the Casino, Basel's opulent concert hall. Every seat was filled. The audience included town and gown.[91] One of the bourgeois ladies present recorded in her journal that the speaker "looked to be sixty-five" and had the bearing of "a sage, a prophet." His vision for the future left her enthralled.[92] Michels observed that despite his jarring, staccato cadence, Eisner's speech had "profound oratorical effect."[93]

The talk was titled "Socialism and Youth." Fichte's emphasis on intellectual cultivation and ideation in his *Reden an die deutsche Nation*, Eisner told the audience, was born of humbling military defeat by Napoleon. Now, once again, the way to national liberation lay in transformative conceptualization about postwar society. He declared all politics to be an effort to educate. Required at present was a thorough schooling in socialism and democracy. The only alternative was more conflict and chaos. The older generation, so inured to political and economic inequity, might well be incapable of helping shape a just world order. It therefore fell to young people to reconfigure the social contract, to redefine the nature of human relations. However daunting the proposition, his own immediate experience proved the feasibility of change against all odds. When, in the darkest days of the war, he and his few confederates set out to oppose the rampant, monolithic Prussian military state, their only succor came from disillusioned youth. The revolution in the Bavarian capital came about because young minds had been won "for the single greatest idea known to man: that there be neither inconsistency nor delay between thought and deed."

One war was over, Eisner reflected, but the war that drove it, class struggle, had to end as well if all war were to be done with. Yet violent seizure of the means of production could change nothing: "It is a delusion that has taken hold of many workers today who believe that it is socialism when they themselves begin to be capitalists." Bolshevism, archbogey of the bourgeoisie, was a predictable consequence of the military anarchy that voided all right to life, liberty, and property. Capitalism would wither and socialism flourish, he ventured, only through thorough democratization, collective consciousness, dynamic work, and the thoughtful application of just, moral principles. For the third time in a week his remarks generated ardent acclaim.[94]

Having invited Eisner to dinner at his home, Professor Michels was beset by mysterious callers telephoning to inquire after the premier's whereabouts and schedule. When Michels voiced concern to his guest, Eisner replied that he was resigned to his fate, come what may. His work nearly accomplished, he was eager to return to his writing and music. Perhaps he might serve as head of a school for farm youth he hoped to establish.[95] After two weeks abroad he returned to Munich on Wednesday, 12 February. Levien's arrest on the seventh had elicited vociferous protests from the Communists, which Roßhaupter used as pretext to resurrect a citizens' militia, a force that was to be independent of what he deplored as the undisciplined and disorderly influence of the soldiers' councils. Despite Levien's release on the eleventh, the Munich Workers' Council, at Landauer's urging, voted to stage on Sunday a mass demonstration for the preservation of the council system. At Wednesday's cabinet session Unterleitner charged that Roßhaupter and Auer had provoked the councils while ignoring the reactionary menace. Staimer worried about the threats from both Left and Right; the latter, he believed, were exacerbated by attacks on Eisner in the press.

Eisner opposed banning Sunday's demonstration, which Roßhaupter feared as potential impulse to the second revolution preached by Levien, Mühsam, and Landauer. Majority Socialist rigidity at Bern had steeled Eisner's resolve. "By second revolution," he said of the councils' champions, "they do not mean a Bolshevist regime but rather a socialist democracy. The old bureaucracy has to go. Up to now there has been no real revolution in Germany." He suggested that the cabinet join the demonstration on the sixteenth. Confounded, Auer asserted that if the tyranny of minority views, Left or Right, could not be quelled, the government had no choice but to step down. "I shall be glad when I can go back to my books again," Eisner said, "therefore I do not want any draconian measures now, no parliamentary chicanery."[96] That same day Roßhaupter issued his call for volunteers to enlist in the People's Homeland Militia (Volksheimatschutz) to combat the threat of Bolshevism in Bavaria, and Auer, by his authority as interior minister, announced that the Landtag would convene on Friday, 21 February.[97]

The next morning Eisner addressed the assembled Bavarian Workers', Soldiers', and Peasants' Council at the German Theater. Reporting on the proceedings of the Bern congress, he lashed out so vehemently against the lies of the press that reporters present walked out and the Council determined to publish his speeches at Bern at government expense so as to counter the orchestrated calumny. He also registered his disgust at the coalition of Majority Socialists, the reconstituted Center Party, and the Left Liberal German Democratic Party that had emerged in Weimar, best suited "to muddle through for all eternity by the cherished methods of parliamentarism." With regard to Bavaria he saw but two viable choices: "that the entire government steps down and consigns policy to the bourgeois parties, or that the socialist government closes ranks."[98] Later that day Eisner objected in the cabinet meeting to Roßhaupter's "white guard," the People's Homeland Militia. Auer in turn questioned Landauer's posture on "second revolution," and Timm voiced his exasperation: "No one is thinking of counterrevolution. We have reached a critical juncture, yet everything is being done to weaken the authority of the government. The prime minister is doing the most to that end. I regard the situation as hopeless, I have to say in all honesty."[99] Speaking to the Council congress again on the fifteenth, Eisner reaffirmed his commitment to the council system but rejected demands for the Majority Socialists to quit the government.[100]

At Sunday's demonstration Eisner, Jaffé, and Unterleitner rode in an open car at the head of some twenty thousand marchers supporting direct democracy, the councils, economic socialization, total separation of church and state, purge of the Imperial bureaucracy, and demolition of the capitalist press monopoly. The crowd cheered Eisner, Liebknecht, Luxemburg, Lenin, and Trotsky and reviled Auer, Timm, Roßhaupter, Scheidemann, and Noske. Eisner had his car divert to the German Theater, where the Workers', Soldiers', and Peasants' Council was meeting. There he parleyed with a delegation headed by Landauer. Eisner said that he would have all charges against Levien and Mühsam dropped, but he stressed that a civil war provoked by escalation of violent confrontation would be ruinous to their cause. The next day Roßhaupter agreed to cede to the Council recruitment for the People's Militia. At the three-day meeting of the Bavarian MSPD convened Tuesday, 18 February, at the Landtag, delegates affirmed the councils' continued function as political-action committees for the working class but made clear that the councils would have no legislative or executive role.[101]

Late Wednesday afternoon a militia funded by Auer and led by Konrad Lotter attempted a putsch to depose Eisner, disband the Council, and install Auer as premier. Reinforced by soldiers from the suspect First Engineer Reserve Battalion and reactionary students, elements of a Bavarian marine unit occupied the rail terminal, telegraph hub, police and Republican Guard headquarters, and government buildings. Dürr, Staimer, and Fechenbach were arrested. About fifty sailors entered the Landtag, to which the Workers', Soldiers', and Peasants' Council congress had relocated from the German Theater. The reserve engineers and their auxiliaries, commanded by Sergeant Kraus, set up a machine gun outside and detonated a hand grenade to signal an assault to clear out Council members. Auer, present at the MSPD deliberations in another part of the building, emerged and spoke with Kraus: "We don't need you right now. Be ready tomorrow." The chidden train forsook its mischief for the moment and slunk away. The prisoners were released unharmed.[102]

The Council congress concluded Thursday, having passed Landauer's resolution to reconvene after pressing the Landtag to legitimize the councils in the constitution. Eisner was the final speaker. He made use of the opportunity to plead for a nonviolent continuation of what the first revolution began: the organization of the urban and rural masses to achieve democratic socialism. Auer's socialist-bourgeois coalition he regarded as untenable and fleeting. He made indirect reference to perverse alliances exemplified by Wednesday's putsch and to the leaders such unions favored. "The Bavarian people have elected the Landtag as it now exists. Imbecilic organizations have certainly played a role in it too. The bourgeois majority will now pursue bourgeois politics. . . . I yearn for socialists of every hue to become the opposition again. . . . Tomorrow the Landtag begins, tomorrow the activity of the councils should begin anew."[103]

The final cabinet meeting of Eisner's government—for which no minutes exist—took place that evening. A charged discussion raged between Eisner and Auer as to the transfer of power to the Landtag. Determined to prevent bloodshed between rival factions, Eisner agreed to amend his provisional constitution's stipulation that the revolutionary government would remain in power until the Landtag's constitution won approval. The entire cabinet would tender its resignation the next morning. He had already had his papers moved from the apartment at the Foreign Ministry back to his home in Großhadern.[104] That night he drafted a resignation speech in which he elucidated the ideological bases and practical achievements of his revolution and regime. He made clear that the new Landtag owed its existence to the determination of the revolutionary provisional government to create a free, democratic republic rather than a repressive, class dictatorship. Indispensable in that enterprise had been the councils of workers, soldiers, and peasants, which Eisner fervently hoped would continue as agents of "active democracy" and "the necessary development toward socialism" in Bavaria. However impatiently and impetuously his government promoted change, it remained acutely conscious of its responsibility to reestablish civil discourse under colossally inauspicious circumstances so as "to safeguard the masses, morbidly agitated after long conflict and severe privation, from the horrors of civil war by means of rational discussion instead of brute force." Thus Bavaria, in stark contrast to Prussia, had avoided grievous intramural bloodletting.

The effort to forge peace with embittered enemies abroad was coupled with insistence on a federal German state with no predominant member. The preservation of Bavarian autonomy and identity within the new configuration he deemed essential to a viable, vibrant union. Turning to the work of his cabinet, Eisner praised the Interior Ministry for equitable distribution of food and coal, the latter procured by special arrangement with the Czechoslovak Republic. Military Affairs, aided by the soldiers' councils, presided over the orderly demobilization of troops and democratization of the army. Justice maintained peace and order by implementing a crucial amnesty for officials and opponents of the defunct Imperial regime. Education introduced overdue reforms prescribing separation of church and state. Despite the coal shortage and Bavaria's forfeiture of half its freight locomotives to the Entente, the Transportation Ministry managed delivery of critical goods to the populace. Faced with massive unemployment and relief expenditures, Finance nonetheless kept the state solvent, while Social Welfare addressed problems of inadequate housing, public health, and working conditions. In tendering the revolutionary government's resignation to the Landtag it had called into being, the prime minister proferred the provisional constitution "as legacy of our democratic and socialist conviction . . . , on which history shall pass the final judgment."[105]

While Eisner composed his text past midnight at the Foreign Ministry, Count Arco sat in his elegant guest-house quarters at Prinzregentenstraße 18, across from the English Garden. After an evening of barhopping, he too was writing his political testament: "I hate Bolshevism! I am and think German! I hate the Jews! I *love* the true Bavarian people! I am a loyal monarchist until death! I am a loyal Catholic! People will say: He's a murderer! There is cause enough for murder!" Earlier in the evening he had confided to the chambermaid that he intended to shoot Eisner the next day. He instructed her to wake him promptly in the morning and to have a bath drawn. She doubted the earnestness of his plan: "He was really still often like a child." At 07:00 Friday, 21 February, she knocked, but the count was already up. Waiting for his bath, Arco perused the *Münchener Zeitung*, *Bayerischer Kurier*, and *Augsburger Abendzeitung*. The young chambermaid, Walburga Kästele, later asserted in a formal statement that she considered the lieutenant a victim of the Catholic press, "for the gentleman count read only the black newspapers, which really wrote nothing good about Eisner." After his bath and breakfast Arco telephoned the Landtag to ask if seats were yet available in the gallery and when the ministers might arrive. He donned a heavy coat over his suit and left shortly after 09:15.[106]

At the Foreign Ministry Eisner was making ready to deliver his final speech as head of state. The Landtag was but a block away. He was determined to walk there, accompanied by Fechenbach and Dr. Benno Merkle, now serving as his office manager. Fechenbach, Unterleitner, and others expressed concern for Eisner's safety, but he dismissed the suggestion that he cut through the Bayerischer Hof, a luxury hotel behind the Palais Montgelas. The attempt to cheat fate was pointless in the end, he said, "and they can only shoot me dead just that once." Besides, the military had blocked access routes to outside traffic. A minute before ten Eisner exited the palace with Fechenbach on his left, Merkle on his right. They were preceded by two escorts, Eisner's personal orderly, Wilhelm Klebsch, and the premier's hulking bodyguard, Sergeant Huber. Turning left onto Promenadestraße, they walked a short way, Merkle recalled, deep in thought.

When his target stepped out of the Foreign Ministry, Arco was skulking in the doorway of the Bavarian Commercial Bank on the opposite corner of Promenadestraße. Beneath his left arm was a smart portfolio. His hands were thrust into his coat pockets, in the right a Walther automatic pistol. When the prime minister's party filed past, Arco slipped across the nearly deserted street, hurried up behind them on the sidewalk, drew his weapon and fired two rounds point-blank into the back of Eisner's head. Fechenbach whirled around and seized Arco's arm. Jolted upright by the bullets' impact, Eisner tottered for an instant before collapsing. The escorts rushed to help Fechenbach subdue the assailant. Arco was flat on his back on the pavement when Huber fired down on him at least four times with a revolver. Dazed and believing that he was the sole survivor of a machine-gun attack, Merkle turned to see Eisner's body twitching in a pool of blood. Everything had occurred in a matter of seconds. Heavily armed soldiers were running to the scene.[107]

CHAPTER TWENTY-FOUR

NOW DEAD, AS IT STANDS:
OUTCOMES AND LEGACY (1919–2017)

RECOVERING FROM INFLUENZA, art historian Julie Vogelstein departed Berlin by rail Friday morning, 21 February, for Munich, where she planned to visit a friend. The only other occupant of her compartment was a Prussian aristocrat, one Von der Schulenburg. They were conversing about forestry when he glanced down at his watch and casually remarked: "Eisner now has twenty minutes to live." He handed her his calling card and suggested that she might show it to the director of the Fürstenhof Hotel in Nuremberg to obtain a room for the night. "The train will run only as far as Nuremberg," he said. When they arrived there the platform was swarming with military guards; newspaper extras reported Eisner's assassination by Graf Arco. The track to the Bavarian capital was indeed closed.[1]

Moments after the gunfire on Promenadestraße ended, three soldiers with rifles and hand grenades rushed to Merkle and shouted: "Now to the Landtag where we'll clean house!" Pulling them over to Eisner's corpse, he pleaded with the infuriated trio to desist. "Could he but speak a few more words, he would tell you: Do not avenge me!" Merkle and Fechenbach had soldiers from the Foreign Ministry guard carry the two limp bodies to the Palais Montgelas. Eisner was laid out on a couch in the porter's room, his assailant dropped at the building's entrance. When Arco showed signs of life, enraged sailors had to be prevented from killing him on the spot. An angry crowd gathered. Merkle insisted that Arco be brought inside. Dr. Steudemann, police physician, officially pronounced Eisner dead.[2]

At the Landtag, where the deputies awaited the prime minister's entrance, word of the shootings arrived within minutes. Fechenbach strode into the hall, approached the ministers' table, and spoke briefly with Auer and Roßhaupter. The two ministers turned deathly pale.[3] A few moments later Sergeant Huber entered the journalists' gallery,

tearfully showed Eisner's bloodstained pince-nez, and brandishing his
service revolver menacingly, declared that he had dispatched the assassin.[4] At 10:10 Dr. Eugen Jäger of the Bavarian People's Party, president
by seniority at age seventy-seven, opened the proceedings with a frightful statement: "Ladies and gentlemen, before we commence I must
report rumor has it that Prime Minister Eisner was shot to death today.
The murderer is also said to have been shot dead." The ensuing tumult
in the gallery necessitated an hour-long recess. Dr. Franz Lochbrunner,
also representing the BVP, testified that soldiers purportedly guarding the Landtag became "extremely hostile toward the deputies" once
announcement was made of Eisner's murder.[5] Behind closed doors
Edgar Jaffé ventured that the assassination was a conspiracy and bitterly
implied Auer's complicity. Dürr arrived to warn Auer and Roßhaupter
that they were marked men.[6]

From the third-floor "Red Room" of the Landtag building, where
the Workers' Council leadership met, Richard Moses went downstairs to
the courtyard. There he saw Else Eisner weeping. She had been waiting
to hear her husband's speech. Moses went back upstairs. He, Mühsam,
Landauer, RAR chair Hans Köberl, Oskar Deubler, Fritz Weigel, Alois
Lindner, and Georg Frisch were among those gathered in the Red Room.
Lindner, a founding member of the RAR, was so incensed that he foamed
at the mouth while waving a pistol and vowing to shoot Auer. "No one
but Auer is to blame for Eisner's death." Lindner raged. "That Judas
is guilty!" Threatening his comrades who attempted to block the door,
Lindner shoved his way past them, joined by Frisch.[7]

Oskar Maria Graf records that word spread quickly through the
streets that Eisner was dead. Every bell tolled, the streetcars ceased running, a red flag trimmed with black crape was displayed from a window.
People with anguished faces streamed toward the city's center. Rifles were
stacked upright on the place Eisner had fallen. His framed portrait, fixed
to the rifles, was encircled by a wreath and draped in black. Men hardened
by war wept openly, the disconsolate dipped handkerchiefs in the martyr's blood for relics. Guards with fixed bayonets stood ready to knock
hats from the heads of gawkers failing to register respect.[8] Elsewhere
news of Eisner's murder evoked a far different response. "The idiocy of
Arco's deed at this moment," Thomas Mann wrote in his journal, "must
be immediately obvious, but many people are delighted by it. Our boys'
schoolmates applauded and danced when the news came."[9] Ernst Toller,
who had visited friends after the Bern congress, was en route to the
Bavarian capital on the twenty-first. At one of the stops a Swiss conductor
shouted from the platform that Eisner had been slain. Inside the train a

German bourgeois greeted the announcement with a hearty bravo.[10] The gloating soon turned into stark terror.

Following the recess the Landtag session resumed at 11:14. Auer rose to confirm that Eisner had been murdered on the way to tender the government's resignation. "The political conflict in Bavaria," Auer lamented, "was on the verge of peaceful resolution." The infamy of the cowardly crime was compounded by its senselessness. He paid tribute to "the leader of the Revolution and at the same time a man imbued with purest idealism and genuine concern for the proletariat."[11] Just after Auer was seated, a man in a gray overcoat and hat pushed through the velvet curtains of the same entrance Fechenbach had taken. Ranting unintelligibly, the stocky figure with black mustache walked straight to the ministers, stopped directly in front of Auer, took aim with a large Browning automatic pistol, and fired twice. Auer clutched his chest and slumped down over the table.

Several witnesses recognized the shooter as Alois Lindner. Still spitting epithets, Lindner turned to flee. Major Paul von Jahreis, adviser to the Ministry of Military Affairs, blocked the aisle to prevent his escape. Lindner felled him with a single shot to the throat and strode out. Through the parted curtains of the entry someone fired into the hall. Legislators and attendants reported that shots rained down from the public gallery as well. BVP deputy Heinrich Osel was mortally wounded. Panic-stricken members of the Landtag rushed for the exits, only to be halted by guards who vowed that no one would leave the hall alive. In the chamber a soldier fidgeting with a hand grenade demanded that Majority Socialist deputy Johann Gentner point out Timm and Roßhaupter. Gentner claimed neither was there.[12] Still conscious, Auer was bandaged and rushed to the university's surgery clinic, where Professor Ferdinand Sauerbruch had just performed a life-saving operation on Arco.[13] After the flurry of gunfire in the Landtag chamber Commandant Dürr confronted Lindner in the hallway outside the press gallery. Lindner admitted that he had just shot Auer. Drawing his pistol, Dürr attempted to arrest his quarry, but the soldiers present refused the order. Instead, they surrounded Lindner and escorted him from the building to freedom. That evening Lindner appeared in an infantry uniform, sans mustache, at a session of the Munich workers' council in the German Theater.[14]

Oskar Maria Graf notes that even while the crowd wept at the makeshift shrine on Promenadestraße, a red-flagged truck bristling with machine guns roared past. Its passengers exhorted "revenge for Eisner!" The call was taken up by hundreds. A USPD handbill bearing the names of Eisner's trusted lieutenants from 7 November—Fechenbach, Fritz

Schröder, and Richard Kämpfer—called for a general strike to combat the counterrevolution.[15] Soon another notice rained down from aircraft. Signed by Dürr, Staimer, and Bavarian Soldiers' Council chair Josef Simon, this one announced that Eisner had been killed, Auer critically wounded, and that a 19:00 curfew was being imposed on the city.[16] Columns of marchers assembled on the Theresienwiese. By then Toller had reached the city and was one of the many speakers. Soldiers and sailors led a parade to the German Theater and forced the locked doors. "From today on," a sailor cried, "the Workers' and Soldiers' Council is in permanent session!"[17]

Elements of the Munich and Bavarian councils, complemented by representatives of the MSPD, USPD, and KPD, met in special session that afternoon and formed an action committee that in turn created a Central Council (Zentralrat der Republik Bayern). The eleven members were drawn from the councils' executive bodies and included Karl Kröpelin, Ernst Niekisch, Josef Simon, Karl Gandorfer, August Hagemeister, and Max Levien.[18] Its chair was Niekisch, a Majority Socialist from Augsburg who had supported Eisner's call for a united front in the January elections. By order of the Central Council the presses of the bourgeois newspapers and the *Münchener Post* were commandeered for the printing of handbills and placards. Only the USPD *Neue Zeitung* continued publication.[19] Eisner's body was transported Friday evening to the mortuary of the city's East Cemetery where it was to lie in state before a state funeral the following Wednesday.[20] In Berlin, Harry Kessler noted in his diary entry for 21 February that in retaliation for Eisner's assassination Communists had killed Roßhaupter and wounded Auer. In fact Roßhaupter had been taken into protective custody and remained unharmed.[21]

On Saturday a new gazette appeared in lieu of the bourgeois and Catholic newspapers, the *Nachrichtenblatt des Zentralrats* (Bulletin of the Central Council). The lead article memorialized Eisner as "the mind of the Revolution" who at the darkest hour unified the proletariat for decisive, concerted action against their enemies. "The preponderance of his personality was strong enough, despite every attack from Left and Right, to prevent chaos, the struggle of all against all."[22] Already hundreds of citizens were queuing to view Eisner's corpse.[23] The Landtag having been chased, remaining members of Eisner's cabinet, still technically the government of Bavaria, were in limbo. The Central Council announced that it would consult with the "rump cabinet" before naming new ministers.[24] In an ominous development the Central Council ordered the taking of fifty hostages as surety against reprisals, among them Julius Lehmann and Kreß von Kressenstein. The hostages were housed at the Bayerischer

Hof. A notice signed on Sunday by Niekisch, Fritz Sauber, and Gandorfer guaranteed the hostages' safety "so long as no assassination attempts arise from counterrevolutionary efforts." Two days later Karl Kröpelin publicly declared that ten hostages would be shot for every comrade who fell victim to counterrevolutionary attack.[25] Aided by his comrades, Alois Lindner was provided with false papers and money and driven across the border to Salzburg.[26]

Saturday afternoon the Central Council undertook the reunification of socialist parties that Eisner sought in his declaration of 8 November. A six-man panel of Central Council members and party and trade-union representatives approved an accord deploring political fratricide in the face of reaction and supporting constitutional recognition of the councils, expansion of the existing cabinet to include an agriculture minister from the BBB, resumption of the Landtag, replacement of the army by republican and trade-union forces, limited restoration of press freedoms.[27] The Communists were understandably less than enthused. On Tuesday, 25 February, the Bavarian council congress was reconvened by Ernst Niekisch. The first speaker he recognized after honoring Eisner's legacy was Gustav Landauer, who promptly challenged the formulation of the second order of business, "Council Republic or Democracy," as pejorative. Mühsam asserted that at the moment the very existence of the councils' congress was at stake. Levien characterized the combination of Landtag and councils as "a mating of fish and fowl" and upheld the "absolute sovereignty of the ASB." Rudolf Egelhofer announced that five thousand soldiers and workers assembled at the Wagner Hall had just demanded that the Landtag be abolished, Commandant Dürr dismissed, the bourgeoisie disarmed, a Red Guard formed, alliance with Soviet Russia concluded, and the Workers', Soldiers', and Peasants' Council purged of suspect elements.[28] That same day Hoffmann, Jaffé, Unterleitner, Frauendorfer, and Fechenbach conferred on behalf of the Central Council with Dr. Wilhelm Muehlon, an expatriate technocrat from Foerster's circle in Bern, about assuming the office of foreign minister. Auer was clinging to life; Timm and Roßhaupter had quit their posts. Discouraged by the precariousness of the government, Muehlon declined the offer.[29]

On Wednesday, 26 February, Eisner's state funeral was held, as elaborate a spectacle as the citizenry of Munich had ever witnessed. The unbroken train of mourners joining the cortege stretched 5 kilometers from the Theresienwiese to the Ostfriedhof. Among them were a score of brass bands playing dirges, wreath-bearing deputations, luminaries from the arts community, Russian POWs, and Lance Corporal Adolf Hitler with a red armband. "From every province of Bavaria the people had converged," Oskar Maria Graf recalled. "In front marched the Penzberg and Hausham miners in their black costume, then followed thousands upon thousands." The bourgeoisie gaped in amazement at the sheer numbers on parade, nearly a hundred thousand by conservative estimate. Priests were made to toll the church bells. Unterleitner, Haase, Levien, and Landauer spoke eulogies. Karl Kautsky was present.[30]

In his panegyric Landauer likened his fallen friend and comrade to Christ and Hus, avatars of enlightenment silenced by self-serving fools. "Kurt Eisner, the Jew, was a prophet who fought mercilessly against faint-hearted, contemptible men because he loved humanity and believed in it and wanted it. He was a prophet because he empathized with the poor and downtrodden and perceived the possibility and necessity to end want and servitude. He was a prophet because he was a seer, this poet who dreamed of beauty to come and at the same time looked hard, ugly facts in the face undaunted."[31] Toller's verse graced the monument holding the urn with Eisner's ashes: "He who prepares the paths succumbs on the threshold, yet death bows before him in reverence."[32] But decades earlier Eisner had penned his own epitaph in his student journal:

Kurt Eisner lies below,
the one with big plans:
genius once, or no,
now dead, as it stands.[33]

Far more tributes came in the next weeks and months at solemn public ceremonies and in print. Two days after the funeral Heinrich Ströbel, Eisner's relentless critic at *Vorwärts* in 1905, redressed the old feud: "Yes, we have to confess that Eisner . . . demonstrated greater insight into the fatal flaws of our age than we ourselves who fancied we saw the particulars more clearly and perhaps actually did so." The man who then was branded an opportunist chose internal exile in 1914 at Social Democracy's perfect capitulation to opportunism, then reemerged as voice of the wayward party's abandoned ideals and as redeemer of national honor. "For Kurt Eisner was not just the most highminded patriot but also a genuine disciple of democracy, a sworn opponent of every violent minority regime, even a proletarian one."[34] At a memorial service on 16 March in the Odeon, the stately concert hall on Ludwigstraße, Heinrich Mann told the audience that Eisner was "the first true intellectual at the head of a German state," whose brief government "brought more ideas, more of reason's delights, more mental stimulation than the previous fifty years."[35]

For the April issue of *Der Neue Merkur* Wilhelm Hausenstein provided the most subtle and penetrating biography of Eisner by any contemporary, a shrewd psychological portrait of "a complex, modern personality" born of "intellectual and ethical ideality" coupled with the "asceticism of a medieval monk." In a balanced critique of his friend's conceptual strengths and weaknesses, Hausenstein paid homage to Eisner's apically astute historical and philosophical writings, his discerning theater reviews, and the classically enlightened draft constitution for the Bavarian Republic, while dismissing the literary and poetic work as undistinguished. That the attempt to realize politically Kant's and Fichte's "formulations of the moral applications of society" foundered in Catholic, clerical Bavaria could hardly be reckoned solely to Eisner's account, for the reconciliation of obdurate bias to progressive idealism was destined to fail, even under the best of circumstances. Still, the categorical imperative dictated that he try. History, Hausenstein opined, would be Eisner's judge, and its verdict would be more lenient than that passed on his rivals and epigoni.[36] Robert Michels in Basel ventured that worse was in store with Eisner's demise. "His death will embitter the civil war in Germany and reinforce the conviction among non-German peoples that the new Germany cannot abide new individuals and there the forces of darkness continue to dominate political life. There can be no doubt that Germany will have to pay for Eisner's murder in the conditions for peace."[37] Ruth Eisner, who at age nine lost her father, recalled eighty-seven years later that she, her sister, and mother had "missed Patro terribly."[38]

In the eleven weeks following the assassination Bavaria suffered five governments. Eisner's "terror of truth" was supplanted first by the red terror, then by the white as the South spiraled down into butchery more cruel and ruthless than that of the trenches. Hostages and prisoners were executed by both sides. Even Georg Heim yearned for the relative reasonability of Eisner's leadership.[39] Michels's predictions proved accurate on all points. When the Treaty of Versailles was approved on 28 June, the harshness of its terms prompted English economist John Maynard Keynes to prophesy that the "Carthaginian peace" would provoke within Germany frightful political violence, "which will destroy, whoever is victor, the civilization and the progress of our generation."[40] The groundwork had been laid for the Nazis' rise to power.

As to outcomes and fates of Kurt Eisner's friends and enemies, few died peacefully at home in their beds. Of his eulogists, Gustav Landauer was kicked to death in the yard at Stadelheim on 2 May 1919, as emigré Oskar Maria Graf told the German-Jewish Club of New York in 1940, "by the subhumans who today are Hitler's SS men."[41] Toller and two other Workers' Council leaders were led past Landauer's crumpled body. "There he lies now, your chum," one of their guards remarked.[42] On 8 October Hugo Haase was shot on the steps of the Reichstag by a disgruntled worker and died a month later of blood poisoning. Max Levien managed to escape to Soviet Russia, where he was arrested during the Great Purge by the NKVD in 1936 and executed the next year. After going over to the Majority Socialists, Hans Unterleitner served in the Reichstag for twelve years before he was arrested and sent to the concentration camp at Dachau. Released through the intercession of friends in Switzerland and Britain, he fled to Switzerland in 1936, then to the United States in 1939. In New York he chaired the German-American Council for the Liberation of Germany from Nazism. After the war Bavarian prime minister Wilhelm Hoegner offered Eisner's son-in-law a cabinet post, which he declined. Unterleitner died in New York in August 1971.[43]

Ernst Toller served as field commander of Red Army forces of the Bavarian Soviet Republic headed by Eugen Leviné. Toller led the assault that wrested Dachau from White irregulars. He defied orders to execute prisoners, released them, and a week later resigned his command. As Freikorps troops surrounded Munich in the last days of April, Red Guards shot eight hostages, seven of whom were members of the Thule Society, at the Luitpoldgymnasium. (Two Communist doctors saved Count Arco from facing the firing squad.) Toller publicly decried the killings. By 3 May Munich had fallen to the Freikorps, who executed the Soviet's leaders and massacred a thousand of its supporters and sympathizers. Tried for treason by the military government's provisional court, Toller drew a lenient sentence of five years' imprisonment after Max Weber and Thomas Mann testified on his behalf.[44]

In 1933 Toller was forced into exile. Moving from Zurich to London to New York, to Los Angeles, and back to New York, he spoke out against the Nazis, championed initiatives of the League for Human Rights, and organized relief operations during the Spanish Civil War. In his autobiography, published 1933 in Amsterdam, Toller recalled a beloved mentor. "Eisner was a man of another intellectual cast than Ebert, Scheidemann, Noske, Auer. German classicism and Romantic rationalism shaped and molded him. His political ideal was complete democracy. . . . One thing distinguished him from all other republican ministers: his will to act, his courage in the face of death."[45] On 22 May 1939 Toller's secretary found him dead in his suite at the Mayflower Hotel in New York. The authorities ruled that he hanged himself on the hook of the bathroom door, yet he had recently booked a berth on a liner to England, and in conversation the previous night at the home of friends he had adamantly countered his host's defense of suicide. "If ever you read that I committed suicide," Toller told the English author Robert Payne, "I beg you not to believe it."[46]

Eisner's essential famulus and factotum, Felix Fechenbach, the man Graf dubbed "the apostle," served but two years of an eleven-year sentence for treason. His show trial later became known as Germany's Dreyfus affair. Released from prison on 20 December 1924 in response to public outrage, Fechenbach worked as an editor for J. H. W. Dietz in Berlin. In 1929 he published his biography of Eisner and became editor of the Majority Socialist *Volksblatt* in Detmold. There he wrote and spoke against the fascists. He was arrested by the Nazis in March 1933 and killed in August while being transported to Dachau, "shot while escaping." He had already told comrades that the formulaic justification would be code for his murder.[47] Although Fechenbach was dismissed by some more cultivated minds in Eisner's orbit as a valiant plodder, his synopsis and analysis of Eisner's policy are consistently cogent and illuminating.[48] Certainly no one else serving in an official capacity had more immediate, daily insight into its formulation than did he.

Erich Mühsam was sentenced to fifteen years for treason. Released from Niederschönenfeld Prison in December 1924, he relocated to Berlin, published his memoirs, and resumed his political activism. Arrested the night of the Nazis' Reichstag arson, he was tortured for months before his murder by a Bavarian SS contingent at Oranienburg in July 1934. While being forced to dig his own grave, he defiantly sang the "Internationale." His killers then strung up the body in a lavatory and claimed that Mühsam had hanged himself.[49] Distraught at the tragic turn of events, the economist Edgar Jaffé suffered a complete breakdown and died in a Munich sanatorium in April 1921, two weeks shy of his fifty-fifth birthday.[50]

The irrational fervor and sere conscience of nationalist fanatics claimed unlikely victims from the ranks of chief bourgeois supporters of Germany's war effort as well. For sparing Hindenburg the indignity of inking the armistice at Compiègne, Matthias Erzberger was ambushed by two Freikorps officers while strolling at a Black Forest spa on 26 August 1921. Critically wounded and prostrate, he was finished off by multiple shots to the head.[51] Foreign Minister Walther Rathenau, founding director of the War Ministry's raw materials department, proponent of conscripting Belgian civilians to work in Germany, and foremost advocate of a *levée en masse* for last-ditch national defense in 1918, fell prey to a machine gun and hand-grenade attack while being driven to the Berlin Foreign Office the morning of 24 June 1922. His crime was being Jewish.[52]

Thanks to the skill of Dr. Sauerbruch, Erhard Auer survived the attempt on his life. By June 1919 he could be transferred from the surgical clinic to an Alpine sanatorium in Oberstdorf. After two months Sauerbruch was confident that Auer would fully recover. Indeed, he resumed his position as party chair, filled a seat on the Munich city council, and took up his mandates in both the Reichstag and Landtag, serving in the latter as vice president until 1933. A year after Eisner's assassination, while Count Arco was being treated at a Munich clinic, Auer had flowers delivered together "with the wish for a speedy recovery." For many to whom Eisner's memory was sacred the gesture confirmed Auer's complicity in the murder and aroused suspicions even among Majority Socialists. None of the coziness with Arco's ilk proved beneficial once Hitler came to power. In March 1933 Brown Shirts raided Auer's residence. Two months later he was assaulted by Nazis on the city council and jailed at Stadelheim. By year's end he was banished from Munich. Resettling in Baden, Auer was hounded by the Gestapo until his death in March 1945.[53]

Of the other members of Eisner's cabinet, Johannes Hoffmann headed two governments from 17 March 1919 to 14 March 1920, acting largely as a puppet of the reactionaries and militarists who crushed the Bavarian Soviet Republic and extirpated the revolutionary councils' leaders. He sat in the Reichstag until his death in December 1930.[54] Johannes Timm was a member of the Landtag and chair of the SPD caucus until 1933. From 1920 to 1931 he directed the Bavarian branch of the Weimar Republic's national Office of Information (Reichszentrale für Heimatdienst). He survived the Third Reich and died in Munich in 1945.[55] Albert Roßhaupter was also a member of the Bavarian Landtag until the Nazi seizure of power. He was arrested repeatedly and twice interned at Dachau but returned to politics as Labor and Social Welfare secretary in the Schäffer and Hoegner governments during the postwar American occupation.[56] Heinrich von Frauendorfer retained his post through both Hoffmann governments. Chair of the Bavarian Numismatic Society, Frauendorfer was scandalized by his implication in a counterfeiting scheme and committed suicide in July 1921.[57]

Of Eisner's closest colleagues in Berlin, Nuremberg, and Munich, Georg Gradnauer cast his lot with the Majority Socialists when the party split. From March 1919 until April 1920 he served as prime minister of Saxony, as member of the Reichstag from 1920 to 1924, and as head of the Saxon mission in Berlin from 1921 until 1931. At the time of Hitler's suicide Gradnauer was an inmate at Theresienstadt. He expired the next year at age eighty in Berlin.[58] Julius Kaliski was a member of Berlin's Workers' and Soldiers' Council 1918–1919 and worked as an editor for *Sozialistische Monatshefte* until the Nazis forced him into Danish exile in 1934. He died in 1956.[59] Friedrich Stampfer, once Eisner's protégé and later his stark critic, had enlisted in the Austrian Army during the war, was chief editor of *Vorwärts* and member of the Reichstag through the years of the Weimar Republic. In exile he moved from Prague to Paris to New York, where he became editor of the German-language *Neue Volkszeitung*. Stampfer returned to Germany in 1948. In his 1957 autobiography he recalls his former mentor as "one of the best activists and most courageous men" and provides rich detail of Eisner's professional and personal life when they were neighbors in Berlin.[60]

Joseph Bloch, founder of *Sozialistische Monatshefte* who long sought to win Eisner over to social imperialism, died in exile in Prague in 1936.[61] Georges Weill, Eisner's closest ally at the *Fränkische Tagespost* in Nuremberg, who had abandoned his Reichstag seat in August 1914 to enlist in the French Army, never returned to Germany. He served in the French Chamber of Deputies between the world wars and as vice president of Alexandre Millerand's National Republican League. Withdrawing from public life in 1936, he lived in Algiers during the Second World War, then returned to Paris where he died in 1970.[62] The enigmatic Adolf Müller, chief editor of the *Münchener Post*, became such a trusted emissary of the Imperial government during the war that, as biographer Karl Heinrich Pohl writes, "eventually neither Eisner and his friends, who condemned him more or less as a 'collaborator,' nor his party colleagues in Munich, who despite highest personal regard categorized him as too skeptical, acknowledged him as a loyal comrade." The judgments were confirmed by Müller's refusal, when approached by Wilhelm Hoegner in Swiss exile, to write for anti-Nazi journals. Müller preferred a life of political anonymity at his villa on Lake Thun, where he remained until his death in September 1943.[63]

Of Eisner's most prominent rivals in the infamous *Vorwärts* clash and the debate over the elite Party School in Berlin, both Mehring and Kautsky had reconciled with him, if not with each other. Mehring died in Berlin a few weeks before Eisner's assassination. Kautsky rejoined the Social Democratic Party in 1922, but his influence was now minimal, and in 1924 he returned to Vienna, where he had lived as a boy and studied at university, "retiring forever from active political life."[64] After Nazi Germany's annexation of Austria in March 1938 Kautsky fled to Amsterdam where he died in October at the age of eighty-four. Rosa

Luxemburg, murdered two weeks before Mehring's death, became inextricably linked with her old nemesis in the popular, proletarian mentality, as Karl Liebknecht, she, and Kurt Eisner formed the first triumvirate of revolutionary martyrs in 1919. Even more ironic is that her star pupil from the Party School, Wilhelm Pieck, founding president of the German Democratic Republic, evidently betrayed Luxemburg and Liebknecht to the Freikorps.[65]

The gadflies Paul Lensch and Heinrich Cunow were together with Konrad Haenisch the leading social chauvinists—that monstrous contradiction in terms—who championed rapacious annexations from Soviet Russia. Fittingly, Cunow was appointed professor of ethnography at Berlin University in 1919 by the thoroughly pedestrian Haenisch, Prussian minister of education. Their great service to the high command proved of little benefit to Cunow when the Nazis seized power. He was denied his pension and died destitute in 1936 in Hitler's capital.[66] Lensch, likewise named to Berlin's faculty by Haenisch, left the SPD altogether in 1922 to spend the remaining four years of his life writing in support of the German People's Party (Deutsche Volkspartei, or DVP).[67]

Count Arco, under the care and protection of Dr. Sauerbruch, was finally deemed fit for trial after protests from the *Münchener Post* over the long delay. The proceedings opened on 15 January 1920 and were completed the next day. The character witnesses for the defense, fellow comrades in arms, hailed Eisner's murder as an act of profound patriotism by an exemplary, ingenuous, and personable young officer. At end, state prosecutor Matthias Hahn, while paying homage to Arco's motivation, dutifully requested the death penalty for his brutal and senseless act. The court concurred. The record of the trial remained sealed until 1941. The same government that had upheld Eugen Leviné's egregious death sentence in June 1919 despite massive international protest commuted Arco's judgment to life imprisonment. Held at Landsberg, Arco enjoyed every privilege that Ernst Toller and his comrades were denied at Niederschönenfeld: "He was permitted unsupervised visits," Toller recalled, "allowed to burn lights without restriction, to write, to publish monarchist articles in monarchist papers, to go for walks into town, to learn agriculture on an estate near Landsberg, to chance upon BVP deputy Georg Heim there, to have conversations with him, etc., etc."[68]

After four years Arco was released, returned home to a hero's welcome, and was soon named vice president of South German Lufthansa.[69] He wed his cousin Marie Gabrielle von Arco-Zinneberg and had five children by her. Seven weeks after Germany's surrender in 1945 Arco died near Salzburg in a head-on collision with an American Army transport while passing a horsecart.[70] In 1933 Rudolf von Sebottendorff, founder of the Thule Society, from which Arco had been excluded because of his mother's Jewish heritage, advanced a psychological rationale for Eisner's murder: Arco was out to prove that even a "half-Jew" was capable of bold action for the cause.[71]

After his escape from Bavaria, Alois Lindner, under pseudonym and in disguise, took up residence in Budapest as propaganda officer for the Hungarian Soviet Republic, called into being by Béla Kun on 21 March 1919. When Kun's regime was overthrown by reactionary forces, Lindner fled to Austria, where he was arrested on 2 August. He was extradited to Bavaria on 17 September only after the Viennese authorities, repelled by Leviné's show trial and execution, received assurance that Lindner would be spared the death penalty. At his week-long trial Lindner provided detailed testimony and expressed remorse for the rampage in the Landtag. On Monday, 15 December, he was convicted of attempted murder and aggravated homicide. Lindner served eight and a half years of his fourteen-year sentence. He emigrated to the Soviet Union, worked once again as a propagandist, and served in the Red Army during the Nazi invasion. He vanishes from record in 1943, having moved from Moscow to Kalinin.[72]

After Eisner's death his family took refuge in Krumbach. Else Eisner wrote from there, "in my quiet convalescent nest at Gustav Landauer's home," on 25 March 1919 to Siegfried Jacobsohn to thank him for his tribute to her husband in the pages of *Die Weltbühne* and offered a private eulogy of her own. Jacobsohn asked if he might publish it in his journal. Else Eisner's two-page homage was printed in the 10 April issue. "In time, when I feel whole enough for work, I will write my husband's story," she divulged. "It is a singular, thorny passage of the clairvoyant, dogged warrior against the fears of the fainthearted, the shortsightedness of dilettantes, the inability of bunglers whose hatred this hardened and yet benevolent warrior took upon himself."[73] In her journal entry of 4 May she lamented the mindless radicalism of Levien and Leviné, against which her husband had warned incessantly. The shooting of the Thule Society hostages on 30 April had the predictable result, she wrote, of horrific reprisals "applauded by the bourgeoisie as revenge." Returning to her home on Lindenallee in Großhadern, she learned from Eisner's distraught daughter Ilse that Gustav Landauer had been forcibly seized there by White Guards while neighbors cheered.[74]

For months Else Eisner moved with her children from village to village. They were in Reutin on Lake Constance long enough that Freia could attend school for a few weeks in November and December 1919.[75]

Else settled in Gengenbach in Baden the next year, where her father once again bought a house for her. Financially strapped and overburdened by parental responsibilities, Else Eisner gave up her youngest daughter, Ruth, at age fourteen to a foster family for nearly two years. When Else formed a dependent emotional attachment in 1925 to Friedrich Leiser, a chronically unemployed rotary-press operator, both daughters were left to their own devices. While Ruth completed her preparation for university in neighboring Offenburg and began studying medicine in Berlin in 1929, Freia drifted through apprenticeships and odd jobs in Stuttgart, Berlin, Vienna, Paris, struggling with bouts of anxiety and depression.[76] Ruth was briefly jailed as a Communist in 1933 after her eighth semester. Upon release she wed Hermann Strahl, a toolmaker who proposed marriage to provide her a new identity. From 1935 until 1946 they joined the *innere Emigration*, withdrawing to his hometown of Mosigkau on the outskirts of Dessau.[77] Freia's stations in exile were Stockholm, Paris, London, and finally Cambridge, where she assisted refugees and worked as a language tutor, translator, and interpreter.[78]

Her citizenship revoked by the Nazis, Else Eisner fled first to Switzerland, then to France. On 23 September 1938 she wrote to Gerhart Seger, editor of the *Neue Volkszeitung* in New York, to report that she had posted two parcels the previous day to his business address on East 84th Street. In addition to two copies of her manuscript biography of Kurt Eisner, the packages contained a trove of his publications and manuscripts as well as works by other authors about him. Citing the uncertainty of her situation, she entrusted the collection to Seger for safekeeping and declared Friedrich Leiser the executor of Eisner's literary remains and her biography.[79] Three days later she apprised Freia of the letter to Seger and castigated German intellectuals by name for their "blindness" to German evil that Eisner recognized some thirty years earlier: Thomas and Heinrich Mann, Feuchtwanger, Rilke.[80]

Amid the German invasion of France Else Eisner sought refuge at a convent in Dole. On the evening of 16 June 1940 the convent came under deadly artillery fire, and the next day the Wehrmacht occupied the town. The body of Eisner's widow was found hanged in a lavatory and transported at night to the cemetery. Her grave was marked with a cross bearing the name Elise Beli. Freia learned of her mother's death only after the war. She traveled to Dole and spoke with a nun who had pushed the handcart bearing the coffin. Initially Freia Eisner termed her mother's death suicide but in 1972 claimed that "she met her untimely death by the Nazis on 17 June 1940."[81] Like Walter Benjamin's demise some three months later in Spain, where he evidently despaired of escaping the Gestapo and Stalinist agents, Else Eisner's end remains shrouded in mystery.[82]

Eisner's youngest son, Hans Kurt, became a photographer and Social Democratic propagandist after the dissolution of the USPD. He was arrested by the Nazis on 19 April 1933, interned for years, and finally murdered by lethal injection at Buchenwald on 26 August 1942, having taken blame for a theft so as to protect his male lover, a young fellow inmate.[83] In 1946 Ruth Strahl resumed her medical studies at Halle, specialized in internal medicine, and practiced in East Berlin until her retirement in 1973.[84] Freia returned to Germany in 1948 and challenged Friedrich Leiser in court for possession of Kurt Eisner's papers. Her mother had sold some correspondence and manuscripts to archives and private collectors. The remnants of Eisner's vast library—part of which had been sold or given away, part of which was burned by the Nazis—were confiscated and sent to the municipal library. Eventually Eisner's adoptive daughter was materially aided by officials of the German Democratic Republic in acquiring the papers, which she consigned in 1958 to the Socialist Unity Party (Sozialistische Einheitspartei Deutschlands, or SED) archive at Berlin's Institute for Marxism-Leninism. Reinhard Eisner's daughter, the historian and journalist Freya Eisner, protested from Munich to her aunt Freia on 29 December 1958 that "Kurt Eisner was handed over to the Communists, whose terrorist methods he abhorred."[85]

It was just one more perverse indignity. In 1933 the Nazis removed the urns of Kurt Eisner and Gustav Landauer from their places of honor in the Ostfriedhof and Waldfriedhof. The two urns were buried in the same grave at the Jewish cemetery and marked with a single stone fragment from Landauer's destroyed monument.[86] The street on which Eisner was shot, Promenadestraße, was renamed in 1952 to commemorate Cardinal Michael von Faulhaber, his malign critic, a man who ordered a Te Deum mass celebrated at the Frauenkirche when an attempt on Hitler's life failed.[87] After long debate in Munich's city council, a new, "worthy" memorial to Eisner was finally commissioned in 1986. Sculpted by Erika Maria Lankes, it took the form of a cast-steel plate embedded in the sidewalk where Eisner fell. On the plate is the disturbing image of a corpse sprawled out face-down, like the chalk outline drawn by police at a crime scene.[88] What was meant as a celebration of Eisner's humanity and idealism functionally memorializes Count Arco's atrocity. Not until 30 May 2011 was a fitting monument dedicated in Kurt Eisner's capital. Commissioned by the city council, Rotraut Fischer's glass sculpture features a monolithic transparent plate bearing the inscription of Eisner's credo from the revolutionary proclamation of 7/8 November: "Every human life should be sacred." It stands at Oberanger 34/36 near the old town's Sendlinger Gate, a stone's throw from the headquarters of the Bavarian SPD. At the sesquicentennial of Eisner's birth the first exhibition on his life and work, "Revolutionary and Prime Minister," curated by Ingrid Scherf and Günther Gerstenberg, opened 12 May 2017 for a five-month run at Munich's City Museum.

Kurt Eisner's brief achievement of the Bavarian Republic became known to friend and foe alike as the Poets' Revolution and Regime. To his admirers Eisner was at once aesthete and Realpolitiker; to his revilers from the Right a dreamer and iconoclast, to those from the Left a reformist and opportunist—charged terms all. The discrepancy of opinion on Eisner's legacy hinges, no doubt, on fundamentally incompatible views of man's nature and history's mechanics. Is man by nature evil, good, or indeterminate? Is history's dynamic cyclical, linear, or dialectical? And surely the paradigm shift from monarchy to modernity, in which Eisner played so pivotal a role, was as disconcerting as it was disorienting to otherwise astute minds. Thus it was that patrician Thomas Mann, who died a reluctant democrat in Swiss exile, having fled Hitler and Joe McCarthy, could regard Erhard Auer during the Weimar years as the tragically thwarted voice of moderation and reason despite Auer's ominous collusion with unrepentant monarchists and militarists. Still, a new precedent had been set for what sort might conduct affairs of state and formulate foreign policy in postwar central Europe. Two months after Eisner emerged as premier and foreign minister of the Bavarian Republic, the pianist and composer Paderewski became his counterpart in the newly forged Second Republic of Poland.

Writing a decade after the November Revolution, historian Arthur Rosenberg, himself an Independent Socialist before joining the KPD, apprehended well what Eisner sought to accomplish, knowing that nationalization of a ruined economy would but impede his political agenda: "He saw as the mission of German workers and socialists the execution of a radical bourgeois revolution . . . to bring down the military power and dynasties, to secure immediate peace, and to enable an effective democracy under the leadership of peasants and workers."[89] Socialization was to come though, by Eisner's plan, beginning in Bavaria with agriculture. Vain hope. Friedrich Ebert's pact with the Prussian generals proved fateful, restoring the military command after ignominious defeat and so dividing the Left as to cripple effective opposition to the Nazis. If the tumult of 1918 is, as historians assert, "the failed revolution," then the Weimar Republic must be regarded as the stillborn democracy, for neither it nor the Bavarian Republic was much favored by fate. Germany's ethnic, sectarian, and class divides, coupled with privation and the punitive peace, virtually doomed productive development. Whatever criticism of Eisner's brief government may be justified, certainly no one can credibly assert that the regimes of Wilhelm II or Adolf Hitler were in any way preferable. Nor can Eisner be assigned blame for what followed. As Allan Mitchell concludes, the failure of the Weimar Republic, the Prussian-centralist constitution of which Eisner opposed, cannot be ascribed to one who freed Bavaria from Wittelsbach rule, reached out to Germany's bitterest enemies, and willingly relinquished power to the democratic assembly he himself had mandated.[90]

Undeniably, Eisner's revolution struck at both the absolute Prussian-German state and the authoritarian Social Democratic Party. His opponents and their extended brood, Right and Left, for the rest of the blighted twentieth century demonstrated the depravity of their disparate ideologies through *KZ-Lager* (concentration camp) and Gulag, show trials and red scares, My Lai and the Killing Fields, the *Stasi* and Iran-Contra, the arms race and ethnic cleansing. So much so that Genocide Studies is today a discipline at prominent universities. As to the legacy of the Bavarian Republic, fascism could not efface the International ideal or the dream of a cosmopolitan Europe. And neither did Eisner's vision of "libertarian socialism," as Freya Eisner termed it, expire with him. In defiance of the Kremlin's hegemony it flickered up June 1953 in East Berlin and October 1956 in Budapest, then ignited during Alexander Dubček's Prague Spring of 1968, aimed at realizing "socialism with a human face." After the Berlin Wall fell in 1989, the West German author Günter Grass, whose drama *Die Plebejer proben den Aufstand* (*The Plebeians Rehearse the Uprising*) attacked Brecht's perceived reticence during the 1953 uprising, favored the maintenance of separate German states so that democratic socialism might finally find a home. That the Peaceful Revolution's dissidents had ushered in a new epoch without firing a shot was fitting homage to Kurt Eisner's moral courage and ethical resolve.

ABBREVIATIONS

A-F	*Arbeiter-Feuilleton*
BArch-Koblenz	Bundesarchiv Koblenz
CJA	Stiftung Neue Synagoge Berlin–Centrum Judaicum Archiv (Berlin-Mitte)
FT	*Fränkische Tagespost*
IISG	Internationaal Instituut voor Sociale Geschiedenis (Amsterdam)
K	*Die Kritik: Wochenschau des öffentlichen Lebens*
LBI-NY	Leo Baeck Institute of New York
M	*Die Menschheit*
MfL	*Das Magazin für Litteratur*
MNN	*Münchner Neueste Nachrichten*
MP	*Münchener Post*
NG	*Die Neue Gesellschaft: Sozialistische Wochenschrift*
NZ	*Die Neue Zeit*
SAPMO-BArch	Stiftung Archiv der Parteien und Massenorganisationen der DDR im Bundesarchiv (Berlin-Lichterfelde)
SM	*Sozialistische Monatshefte*
UdV	*Unterhaltungsblatt des Vorwärts*
V	*Vorwärts*

NOTES

Because of diverse styles employed by archivists for numeration of recto and verso leaves of correspondence, only the first leaf's number shall be cited.

Introduction

[1] Allan Mitchell, *Revolution in Bavaria, 1918–1919: The Eisner Regime and the Soviet Republic* (Princeton, NJ: Princeton University Press, 1965), 32.

[2] Stefan Großmann, "Kurt Eisner," *Das Tagebuch* 10.14 (April 1929): 558–559; Wilhelm Hausenstein, "Erinnerung an Eisner," *Der Neue Merkur* 3.1 (April 1919): 56.

[3] Hausenstein, "Erinnerung an Eisner," 58, 60–64.

[4] Louis L. Snyder, *The Weimar Republic: A History of Germany from Ebert to Hitler* (Princeton, NJ: D. Van Nostrand, 1966), 32–33.

[5] Michael Doeberl, *Sozialismus, soziale Revolution, sozialer Volksstaat* (Munich: Verlag der Allgemeinen Zeitung, 1920), 42–43; Hans Beyer, *Die Revolution in Bayern 1918/1919*, 2nd ed. (Berlin: VEB Deutscher Verlag der Wissenschaften, 1988), 16.

[6] Ossip K. Flechtheim, "Der einsame Sozialist. Verachtet, verkannt: Kurt Eisner," *Die Zeit*, 2 November 1979.

Chapter One

[1] SAPMO-BArch, NY 4060 (Nachlaß Kurt Eisner)/3/12; Renate Schmolze and Gerhard Schmolze, introduction to Kurt Eisner, *Die halbe Macht den Räten: Ausgewählte Aufsätze und Reden* (Cologne: Jakob Hegner, 1969), 14.

[2] Franz Schade, *Kurt Eisner und die bayerische Sozialdemokratie* (Hanover: Verlag für Literatur und Zeitgeschehen, 1961), 176.

[3] Hausenstein, "Erinnerung an Eisner," 59.

[4] SAPMO-BArch, NY 4060/3/53; Freya Eisner, introduction to Kurt Eisner, *Zwischen Kapitalismus und Kommunismus* (Frankfurt am Main: Suhrkamp, 1996), 22.

5 SAPMO-BArch, BildY 10/202/91 N.

6 SAPMO-BArch, BildY 10/201/91 N.

7 Kurt Eisner, *Taggeist: Culturglossen* (Berlin: John Edelheim, 1901), 5.

8 Peter Gay, *The Dilemma of Democratic Socialism: Eduard Bernstein's Challenge to Marx* (New York: Collier, 1962), 28.

9 SAPMO-BArch, NY 4060/3/49.

10 Schmolze and Schmolze, introduction to Kurt Eisner, *Die halbe Macht*, 15. See also Gordon A. Craig, *Germany, 1866–1945* (New York: Oxford University Press, 1978), 191.

11 Kurt Eisner, *Wilhelm Liebknecht: Sein Leben und Wirken*, 2nd ed. (Berlin: Buchhandlung Vorwärts, 1906), 80.

12 SAPMO-BArch, BildY 10/199/91 N. Published in Kurt Eisner, *Wachsen und Werden: Aphorismen, Gedichte, Tagebuchblätter, dramatische Bruchstücke, Prosa usw* (Leipzig: Roter Türmer Verlag, 1926), 15.

13 SAPMO-BArch, NY 4060/1/66–67.

14 SAPMO-BArch, NY 4060/1/3.

15 Quoted in Schmolze and Schmolze, introduction to Kurt Eisner, *Die halbe Macht*, 15–16.

16 Felix Fechenbach, *Der Revolutionär Kurt Eisner* (Berlin: J. H. W. Dietz, 1929), 4.

17 Kurt Eisner, "Herbst," in Kurt Eisner, *Feste der Festlosen: Hausbuch weltlicher Predigtschwänke* (Dresden: Kaden, [1906]), 132.

18 Kurt Eisner, "Volkstheater—eine sociale Ehrenpflicht Berlins," in Kurt Eisner, *Taggeist*, 250.

19 SAPMO-BArch, NY 4060/2/310–334.

20 ke [Kurt Eisner], "Der Born der Liebe," "König Humbert in Neapel," "Idyllen und Scherze," *Deutsche Roman-Zeitung* 22.46 (1885): 499–502; SAPMO-BArch, NY 4060/38.1/140.

21 SAPMO-BArch, NY 4060/13/223. The German text:

> Religion ist ein sanfter Gaul,
> Geht stets seinen frommen Trab;
> Reit' ihn, wer im Denken faul,
> Er wirft ihn nicht ab.
>
> Ein feuriger Hengst ist die Philosophie,
> Stürmt außer Rand und Band;
> Wer nicht besitzt viel Reitgenie,
> Sitzt balde auf dem Sand.

22 SAPMO-BArch, NY 4060/12/5–6.

23 SAPMO-BArch, NY 4060/1/69–74.

24 SAPMO-BArch, NY 4060/15.2/178–180.

25 SAPMO-BArch, NY 4060/15.2/182.

26 SAPMO-BArch, NY 4060/16.

27 SAPMO-BArch, NY 4060/15.2/184–185.

28 Kurt Eisner, *Psychopathia spiritualis: Friedrich Nietzsche und die Apostel der Zukunft* (Leipzig: Wilhelm Friedrich, [1892]), 32, 71n.

29 [Kurt Eisner], "Friedrich Wilhelm IV. 50 Jahre nach seinem Tod," *A-F*, Sonder-Nummer (January 1911); SAPMO-BArch, NY 4060/52/5–6; *MP*, 1 January 1911.

30 SAPMO-BArch, NY 4060/9/286.

31 SAPMO-BArch, NY 4060/2/5–6.

32 SAPMO-BArch, NY 4060/16.

33 Schmolze and Schmolze, introduction to Kurt Eisner, *Die halbe Macht*, 15.

34 Tat-Twam [Kurt Eisner], "Sehr geehrter Herr Wrede!" *K* 3.92 (4 July 1896): 1241–1242.

35 SAPMO-BArch, NY 4060/12/17–25.

36 Kurt Eisner, "Volkstheater," 243–258.

37 SAPMO-BArch, NY 4060/15.2/146.

38 Kurt Eisner, "Errichtung eines Volkstheaters eine soziale Ehrenpflicht Berlins," *Die Gesellschaft*, September 1889, 1278–1290. Reprinted as "Volkstheater," in Kurt Eisner, *Taggeist*, 243–258.

39 SAPMO-BArch, NY 4060/1/165.

40 Lee Baxandall, "The Naturalist Innovation on the German Stage: The Freie Bühne and Its Influence," *Modern Drama* 5.4 (February 1963): 473.

41 Bruno Wille, *Aus Traum und Kampf: Mein 60jähriges Leben*, 2nd ed. (Berlin: Kultur-Verlag, 1920), 29.

42 The verdict on Friedrich Wilhelm IV appears in a leatherbound journal that Eisner kept from 1886 to 1890. It was presented as a gift to his betrothed, Lisbeth Hendrich. Excerpts were published in *Wachsen und Werden*. The university journal was made available to the author in 1981 by Eisner's granddaughter, Dr. Freya Eisner of Munich.

43 SAPMO-BArch, NY 4060/13/309.

44 SAPMO-BArch, NY 4060/13/319.

45 SAPMO-BArch, NY 4060/13/328.

⁴⁶ SAPMO-BArch, NY 4060/69/1, 6.

⁴⁷ SAPMO-BArch, NY 4060/69/8.

⁴⁸ SAPMO-BArch, NY 4060/70/3.

⁴⁹ SAPMO-BArch, NY 4060/1/113.

⁵⁰ SAPMO-BArch, NY 4060/71/3; 4060/15.2/135–138.

⁵¹ Kurt Eisner, "Sieben Briefe: An eine Freundin," in Kurt Eisner, *Gesammelte Schriften*, 2 vols. (Berlin: Paul Cassirer, 1919), 2:65–68.

⁵² SAPMO-BArch, NY 4060/15.2/135–138.

⁵³ Kurt Eisner, "Quittung," in Kurt Eisner, *Wachsen und Werden*, 10.

⁵⁴ Kurt Eisner, "Herbst," 130.

⁵⁵ SAPMO-BArch, NY 4060/15.2/133. The German:

> Ich weihe dir dies Buch, daß all mein Sinnen
> In deine Seele dring' wie in sein Heim,
> Daß bildend liebumhegt es wohne drinnen,
> Daß es beglückt werd' deines Glückes Keim.

⁵⁶ SAPMO-BArch, NY 4060/15.2/169.

⁵⁷ SAPMO-BArch, NY 4060/2/328. The German:

> Und thätest du als heller Stern
> Den Abendhimmel schmücken,
> Dann möcht' ich wohl ein Blümchen sein,
> Um ungestört im Wald allein
> Zum Aether aufzublicken. . . .

⁵⁸ SAPMO-BArch, NY 4060/65/98.

⁵⁹ Schade, *Kurt Eisner*, 27, 104–105.

⁶⁰ SAPMO-BArch, NY 4060/31/14.

Chapter Two

¹ Quoted in Koppel S. Pinson, *Modern Germany: Its History and Civilization*, 2nd ed. (New York: Macmillan, 1966), 277.

² Ibid., 297.

³ Kurt Eisner, "Rein Menschlich!" in Kurt Eisner, *Taggeist*, 34–35.

⁴ Kurt Eisner, "Bilder in Max Klingers Weise," *Die Gesellschaft*, April 1891, 504–505.

⁵ Kurt Eisner, "Mainacht: Ein Lebensblatt," *Die Gesellschaft*, June 1891, 787–790. The German text:

> Wir lauschen Leib an Leib geschmiegt der Nacht.
> Auf traulichem Balkon, den wilder Wein

Umrankt, blicken hinaus wir in das Dunkel
Und in den Atem heilger Stille quillt
Der heiße Liebeshauch aus unsren Seelen.

[6] SAPMO-BArch, NY 4060 (Nachlaß Kurt Eisner)/1/85.

[7] SAPMO-BArch, NY 4060/1/80.

[8] SAPMO-BArch, NY 4060/1/85.

[9] Kurt Eisner, "Das Stehaufmännchen: Eine Erscheinung aus der Studentenzeit," *SM* 5.2 (July 1901): 519–524.

[10] SAPMO-BArch, NY 4060/71/3.

[11] Pinson, *Modern Germany*, 153, 172, 197, 253.

[12] Freya Eisner, "Kurt Eisners Ort in der sozialistischen Bewegung," *Vierteljahrshefte für Zeitgeschichte* 43.3 (1995): 413.

[13] SAPMO-BArch, NY 4060/74/174.

[14] Freya Eisner, "Kurt Eisners Ort in der sozialistischen Bewegung," 413.

[15] Bernhard Grau, *Kurt Eisner 1867–1919: Eine Biographie* (Munich: C. H. Beck, 2001), 80–81.

[16] Kurt Eisner, "Psychopathia spiritualis: Friedrich Nietzsche und die Apostel der Zukunft," *Die Gesellschaft*, November 1892, 1505–1536; December 1892, 1600–1664. Parenthetical page citations within the text are to Kurt Eisner, *Psychopathia spiritualis*.

[17] The German novelist Martin Walser, speaking on the topic "What Makes an Author" at Duke University on 3 April 1985, ventured that the writer writes to redress a deficiency he perceives in himself.

[18] SAPMO-BArch, NY 4060/68/131.

[19] SAPMO-BArch, NY 4060/71/23.

[20] *Die Gesellschaft*, March 1892, endpages.

[21] Franz Mehring, "Kurt Eisner, *Psychopathia spiritualis: Friedrich Nietzsche und die Apostel der Zukunft*," *NZ* 10.2 (1891–1892): 667–669.

[22] SAPMO-BArch, NY 4060/66/108.

[23] George Brandes [Georg Morris Cohen], *Friedrich Nietzsche*, trans. A. G. Chater (London: William Heinemann, 1914), 62–63, 87.

[24] SAPMO-BArch, NY 4060/65/79.

[25] C. Vedente, "Psychopathia spiritualis," *Die Gesellschaft*, May 1892, 629–633.

[26] Kurt Eisner, "Nochmals Psychopathia spiritualis: Ein Scheidewort," *Die Gesellschaft*, August 1892, 1053–1059.

[27] Reprinted in Kurt Eisner, *Taggeist*, 259–279.

28 SAPMO-BArch, NY 4060/65/102.

29 SAPMO-BArch, NY 4060/32/12.

30 Kurt Eisner, "Neue deutsche Belletristik: Kritische Lese," *Frankfurter Zeitung*, 30 September–1 October 1892.

31 SAPMO-BArch, NY 4060/70/9.

32 SAPMO-BArch, NY 4060/71/68.

33 SAPMO-BArch, NY 4060/74/93.

34 SAPMO-BArch, NY 4060/3/9.

35 SAPMO-BArch, NY 4060/74/93; 4060/67/79.

36 SAPMO-BArch, NY 4060/67/12.

37 Schmolze and Schmolze, introduction to Kurt Eisner, *Die halbe Macht*, 21.

38 SAPMO-BArch, NY 4060/1/96.

39 SAPMO-BArch, NY 4060/67/79.

40 SAPMO-BArch, NY 4060/1/96.

41 SAPMO-BArch, NY 4060/65/114.

42 Sperans [Kurt Eisner], "Militarismus," *MfL* 62.20 (20 May 1893): 313–316. Reprinted in Kurt Eisner, *Taggeist*, 13–21.

43 Matthäus Becker, "Kurt Eisner und der 'Bauernkönig,'" *Die Weltbühne: Wochenschrift für Politik, Kunst, Wirtschaft* 3.7/8 (1948): 187; Philipp Scheidemann, *Memoiren eines Sozialdemokraten*, 2 vols. (Dresden: Carl Reissner, 1928), 1:58.

44 Becker, "Kurt Eisner und der 'Bauernkönig,'" 187; Sperans [Kurt Eisner], "Sporen," *MfL* 62.23 (10 June 1893): 363–365 (reprinted in Kurt Eisner, *Taggeist*, 22–29); Uriel Tal, *Christians and Jews in Germany: Religion, Politics, and Ideology in the Second Reich, 1870–1914*, trans. Noah Jonathan Jacobs (Ithaca, NY: Cornell University Press, 1975), 233, 240, 299; Scheidemann, *Memoiren eines Sozialdemokraten*, 1:57.

45 Becker, "Kurt Eisner und der 'Bauernkönig,'" 187.

46 Sperans [Kurt Eisner], "Sporen."

47 Pinson, *Modern Germany*, 602.

48 Sperans [Kurt Eisner], "Talarsozialismus," *MfL* 62.24 (17 June 1893): 381–383. Reprinted in Kurt Eisner, *Taggeist*, 171–177.

49 See Pinson, *Modern Germany*, 167.

50 Sperans [Kurt Eisner], "Eine Reise um die Welt in drei Tagen: Romfahrt via Eisenach, Frankfurt, Zürich," *MfL* 62.34 (26 August 1893): 542–546. Reprinted in Kurt Eisner, *Taggeist*, 56–68.

51 Mitchell, *Revolution in Bavaria*, 42n.

52 SAPMO-BArch, NY 4060/74/109.

53 SAPMO-BArch, NY 4060/74/112.

54 SAPMO-BArch, NY 4060/75/6.

Chapter Three

1 Quoted in Schmolze and Schmolze, introduction to Kurt Eisner, *Die halbe Macht*, 24.

2 Ibid., 23.

3 Mitchell, *Revolution in Bavaria*, 46.

4 Harry van der Linden, *Kantian Ethics and Socialism* (Indianapolis, IN: Hackett, 1988), 303.

5 Ibid., 222. The summary of Cohen's thought here derives primarily from Van der Linden's study.

6 Ibid., 266, 272.

7 Adolf Koester, "Hermann Cohen," *März: Eine Wochenschrift* 6.3 (1912): 157–158.

8 Kurt Eisner, "Hermann Cohen: Zum 70. Geburtstag des Philosophen," *MP*, 5–6 July 1912; "Parteikunst," in Kurt Eisner, *Taggeist*, 280–282.

9 SAPMO-BArch, NY 4060 (Nachlaß Kurt Eisner)/66/72.

10 Kurt Eisner, "Hermann Cohen."

11 Becker, "Kurt Eisner und der 'Bauernkönig,'" 187.

12 Sperans [Kurt Eisner], "Ein Fäulnisprozeß," *MfL* 62.45 (11 November 1893): 720–723. Reprinted in Kurt Eisner, *Taggeist*, 44–55.

13 Sperans [Kurt Eisner], "Boykottierte Wahlen!" *MfL* 62.46 (18 November 1893): 736–738. Reprinted in Kurt Eisner, *Taggeist*, 36–43.

14 Diether Raff, *A History of Germany from the Medieval Empire to the Present*, trans. Bruce Little (Oxford: Berg, 1988), 113; J. Alden Nichols, *Germany after Bismarck: The Caprivi Era, 1890–1894* (Cambridge: Harvard University Press, 1958), 36–37.

15 SAPMO-BArch, NY 4060/65/152.

16 SAPMO-BArch, NY 4060/1/113.

17 Sperans [Kurt Eisner], "Der grüne Hannes," *MfL* 62.49 (9 December 1893): 781–783. Reprinted in Kurt Eisner, *Taggeist*, 341–348.

18 Quoted in Nichols, *Germany after Bismarck*, 87.

19 Quoted in Freya Eisner, "Kurt Eisners Ort in der sozialistischen Bewegung," 414.

20 Sperans [Kurt Eisner], "Der Zweite," *MfL* 63.1 (6 January 1894): 11–15. Reprinted in Kurt Eisner, *Taggeist*, 69–76.

21 Nichols, *Germany after Bismarck*, 32–33.

22 Sperans [Kurt Eisner], "Politisches Temperenzlertum," *MfL* 63.4 (27 January 1894): 103–107. Reprinted in Kurt Eisner, *Taggeist*, 178–184.

23 Sperans [Kurt Eisner], "Das Glück der Esel," *MfL* 63.10 (10 March 1894): 294–297. Reprinted in Kurt Eisner, *Taggeist*, 77–82.

24 Sperans [Kurt Eisner], "Die Tragödie des Mittelstandes," *MfL* 63.24 (16 June 1894): 744–748. Reprinted in Kurt Eisner, *Taggeist*, 83–89.

25 Scheidemann, *Memoiren eines Sozialdemokraten*, 1:55–58.

26 Rudolf Schmidt, *Geschichte der Stadt Eberswalde*, 3 vols. (Eberswalde: Rudolf Müller, 1941), 2:395.

27 SAPMO-BArch, NY 4060/1/166, 167.

28 Sperans [Kurt Eisner], "Die Allmacht der Korpsstudenten," *MfL* 64.9 (2 March 1895): 270–274. Reprinted in Kurt Eisner, *Taggeist*, 90–97.

29 *** [Kurt Eisner], "Muster für Umsturzgesetze: Eine historische Studie," *Hessische Landeszeitung*, 7 April 1895.

30 E. [Kurt Eisner], "Ein Volksfest auf der Schwalm," *Frankfurter Zeitung*, 14 August 1895.

31 Reinhard Fern [Kurt Eisner], "Shakespeares Verfasser: Das Ende des Bacon-Streites," *Hessische Landeszeitung*, 29 September 1895.

32 SAPMO-BArch, NY 4060/74/129; 4060/1/113.

33 SAPMO-BArch, NY 4060/75/15; Kurt Eisner, "Herrn Schönes Triumph," in Kurt Eisner, *Taggeist*, 225.

34 Becker, "Kurt Eisner und der 'Bauernkönig,'" 188; *Die Hilfe: Gotteshilfe, Selbsthilfe, Staatshilfe, Bruderhilfe* 2.26 (1896): 7. The deadline for entries was 15 September 1896, the award was announced 27 December 1896, and the story ran in weekly installments from 17 January to 27 June 1897.

35 Becker, "Kurt Eisner und der 'Bauernkönig,'" 188.

36 In his reply to C. Vedente ("Nochmals Psychopathia spiritualis," 1056), Eisner sarcastically summarized his critic's interpretation of Nietzsche: "He ripped the mask from people's faces and thundered at them—fluent as we are now in Sanskrit!—Tat twam asi—you are thus—and added (presumably in translation): And well you should be."

37 Tat-Twam [Kurt Eisner], "Sehr geehrter Herr Wrede!" 1241–1242.

38 Tat-Twam [Kurt Eisner], "Advokatenpolitik," *K* 92 (4 July 1896): 1242–1246.

[39] Tat-Twam [Kurt Eisner], "Raus!" *K* 93 (11 July 1896): 1285–1292. Reprinted in Kurt Eisner, *Taggeist*, 98–105.

[40] Tat-Twam [Kurt Eisner], "Der Einbund," *K* 97 (8 August 1896): 1472–1478. Reprinted in Kurt Eisner, *Taggeist*, 106–114.

[41] Tat-Twam [Kurt Eisner], "Um Manchester," *K* 98 (15 August 1896): 1519–1529. Reprinted in Kurt Eisner, *Sozialismus als Aktion: Ausgewählte Aufsätze und Reden*, ed. Freya Eisner (Frankfurt am Main: Suhrkamp, 1975), 9–15.

[42] Sperans [Kurt Eisner], "Parteikunst," *MfL* 65.44 (31 October 1896): 1348–1353. Reprinted in Kurt Eisner, *Taggeist*, 280–288.

[43] Eisner's didactic fiction is treated in Albert E. Gurganus, *The Art of Revolution: Kurt Eisner's Agitprop*, Studies in German Literature, Linguistics, and Culture 15 (Columbia, SC: Camden House, 1986).

[44] Tat-Twam [Kurt Eisner], "Allerlei Kulturkämpfer," *K* 109 (31 October 1896): 2047–2058. Reprinted in Kurt Eisner, *Taggeist*, 115–127.

[45] Tat-Twam [Kurt Eisner], "Almela," *K* 114 (5 December 1896): 2287–2296. Reprinted in Kurt Eisner, *Taggeist*, 184–193.

[46] Horace B. Davis, *Nationalism and Socialism: Marxist and Labor Theories of Nationalism to 1917* (New York: Monthly Review Press, 1967), 100.

[47] Carl E. Schorske, *German Social Democracy, 1905–1917: The Development of the Great Schism* (New York: Wiley, 1955), 12–13.

[48] Tat-Twam [Kurt Eisner], "Die Limonadenseele," *K* 99 (22 August 1896): 1567–1576. Reprinted in Kurt Eisner, *Taggeist*, 349–359.

[49] Tat-Twam [Kurt Eisner], "Die Philosophie der Untat," *K* 104 (26 September 1896): 1807–1815.

Chapter Four

[1] Roger Chickering, *Imperial Germany and a World without War: The Peace Movement and German Society, 1892–1914* (Princeton, NJ: Princeton University Press, 1975), 85–86.

[2] Mephisto [Kurt Eisner?], "Hieb und Stich," *K* 70 (1 February 1896): 235–236. In that Mephisto vanishes when Tat-Twam appears and that their subjects, style, and diction are so similar, it is a reasonable assumption that Mephisto was Kurt Eisner.

[3] Max Falkenfeld, "Majestätsbeleidigung," *K* 103 (19 September 1896): 1770–1774.

[4] Tat-Twam [Kurt Eisner], "Morituri," *K* 100 (29 August 1896): 1615–1623.

5 Tat-Twam [Kurt Eisner], "Fürsten-Visiten," *K* 101 (5 September 1896): 1663–1671.

6 Tat-Twam [Kurt Eisner], "Die heilige Güter-Alliance," *K* 103 (19 September 1896): 1759–1769.

7 Tat-Twam [Kurt Eisner], "Das Ende der Monarchie," *K* 111 (14 November 1896): 2143–2150.

8 Tat-Twam [Kurt Eisner], "X," *K* 115 (12 December 1896): 2336–2343. Reprinted in Kurt Eisner, *Taggeist*, 128–137.

9 Tat-Twam [Kurt Eisner], "Fernwerthungen," *K* 113 (28 November 1896): 2239–2247.

10 Tat-Twam [Kurt Eisner], "Ein undiplomatischer Neujahrs-Empfang," *K* 118 (2 January 1897): 1–9.

11 Richard Wrede, "Haussuchung," *K* 121 (23 January 1897): 145–146.

12 SAPMO-BArch, NY 4060 (Nachlaß Kurt Eisner)/4/144.

13 Tat-Twam [Kurt Eisner], "Herrn Schönes Triumph," *K* 126 (27 February 1897): 430–432. Reprinted in Kurt Eisner, *Taggeist*, 222–225.

14 Tat-Twam [Kurt Eisner], "Kriminelle Majestätsverherrlichung," *K* 122 (30 January 1897): 193–203. Reprinted in Kurt Eisner, *Taggeist*, 212–222.

15 "Herrn Schönes Triumph," 223–224.

16 Ibid.; SAPMO-BArch, NY 4060/4/165.

17 SAPMO-BArch, NY 4060/4/168; Fechenbach, *Der Revolutionär Kurt Eisner*, 5.

18 Sperans [Kurt Eisner], "Banquier-Symbolismus," *SM* 1.1 (February 1897): 87–97. Reprinted in Kurt Eisner, *Taggeist*, 289–305.

19 Kurt Eisner, "Nationalsoziale Grundirrtümer," *Hessische Landeszeitung*, 17, 20, 23 January; 7, 12 February 1897. Reprinted in Kurt Eisner, *Taggeist*, 194–210.

20 Tat-Twam [Kurt Eisner], "Weltpolitik," *K* 131 (3 April 1897): 625–634. Reprinted in Kurt Eisner, *Taggeist*, 149–158.

21 SAPMO-BArch, NY 4060/4/15.

22 SAPMO-BArch, NY 4060/4/147.

23 Tat-Twam [Kurt Eisner], "Dolus eventualissimus," *K* 136 (8 May 1897): 865–876. Reprinted in Kurt Eisner, *Taggeist*, 225–240.

24 SAPMO-BArch, NY 4060/1/113.

25 Tat-Twam [Kurt Eisner], "Dolus eventualissimus."

26 *Verhandlungen des Reichstags: 9. Legislaturperiode, 4. Session 1895/97*, vol. 8 (3 May–25 June 1897), 5864–5865.

27 Tat-Twam [Kurt Eisner], "Heinrich Stephan," *K* 133 (17 April 1897): 721–729.

28 Tat-Twam [Kurt Eisner], "Männer der Praxis," *K* 137 (15 May 1897): 913–920.

29 Tat-Twam [Kurt Eisner], "Konflikt!" *K* 138 (22 May 1897): 961–970.

30 Tat-Twam [Kurt Eisner], "Die Mitregierung," *K* 141 (12 June 1897): 1105–1114.

31 Richard Wrede, "Mixed Pickles," *K* 143 (26 June 1897): 1246–1248.

32 SAPMO-BArch, NY 4060/4/68; "Majestätsbeleidigungsprozeß," *LV*, 25 September 1897.

33 SAPMO-BArch, NY 4060/4/150; 4060/4/89.

34 SAPMO-BArch, NY 4060/4/91.

35 Roger Fletcher, *Revisionism and Empire: Socialist Imperialism in Germany, 1897–1914* (London: Allen & Unwin, 1984), 113.

36 SAPMO-BArch, NY 4060/4/91; 4060/67/118.

37 SAPMO-BArch, NY 4060/14/1.

38 Kurt Eisner, "Wie ich in Plötzensee verdurstete: Erinnerungen aus meiner Strafvollzugszeit," typescript, SAPMO-BArch, NY 4060/14/11–15. Published in *NG* 1.27 (1905): 326–328.

39 Ein schwerer Junge [Kurt Eisner], "Plötzenseer Bilderbuch mit Original-Illustrationen," *Der wahre Jacob: Illustrierte Zeitung für Satire, Humor und Unterhaltung* 396.20 (24 September 1901): 3598–3599; 398.22 (22 October 1901): 3618–3619; 400.24 (19 November 1901): 3638–3639; 402.26 (17 December 1901): 3658–3659.

40 Kurt Eisner, "Wie ich in Plötzensee verdurstete."

41 K. E., "Der konfiszierte Weihnachtsbaum: Eine Erinnerung," *Die Furche*, 24 December 1908.

42 SAPMO-BArch, NY 4060/67/118; 4060/67/97; Kurt Eisner, "Briefe aus Plötzensee," *Die Weltbühne: Wochenschrift für Politik, Literatur, Wirtschaft* 21.7 (1925): 233–235.

43 SAPMO-BArch, NY 4060/14.

44 SAPMO-BArch, NY 4060/14/185–186.

45 Ein schwerer Junge [Kurt Eisner], "Plötzenseer Bilderbuch mit Original-Illustrationen," 3617. The German text:

> Hier sperrt ein man auch "Polit'sche,"
> Deren Ansichten "verwerflich,"
> Anarchisten und die Rothen,
> Daß sie nicht durch Agitiren
> Kränken unschuldsvolle Seelen.

46 The plot of "Rauschglück" is summarized in SAPMO-BArch, NY 4060/67/106.

47 SAPMO-BArch, NY 4060/6/263; Kurt Eisner, *Die Götterprüfung: Eine weltpolitische Posse in fünf Akten und einer Zwischenaktspantomime* (Berlin: Paul Cassirer, 1920), titlepage.

48 SAPMO-BArch, NY 4060/14/107. Eisner executed the illustrations for *Der wahre Jacob*, originals of which are preserved in SAPMO-BArch, NY 4060/14/91–106. Item 4060/14/93 shows his face as that of the convict guilty of Majestätsbeleidigung.

49 SAPMO-BArch, NY 4060/67/118; Ein schwerer Junge [Kurt Eisner], "Plötzenseer Bilderbuch mit Original-Illustrationen," 3619.

50 IISG, Kleine Korrespondenz; SAPMO-BArch, NY 4060/67/118.

51 Kurt Eisner, "Der Zuhälter: Eine Erinnerung," in Kurt Eisner, *Gesammelte Schriften*, 2:110–115.

52 SAPMO-BArch, NY 4060/71/88.

53 Kurt Eisner, "Briefe aus Plötzensee," 235.

54 SAPMO-BArch, NY 4060/75/15.

55 SAPMO-BArch, NY 4060/67/2.

56 SAPMO-BArch, NY 4060/75/11.

57 SAPMO-BArch, NY 4060/67/165. Reprinted in part in Kurt Eisner, "Briefe aus Plötzensee," 234–235.

58 SAPMO-BArch, NY 4060/75/11.

Chapter Five

1 SAPMO-BArch, NY 4060 (Nachlaß Kurt Eisner)/1/97.

2 Kurt Eisner, "Die zweite Zukunft: Ein grammatikalischer Reformvorschlag," *Neue Deutsche Rundschau* 10 (1899): 766–772; "Das Testament des Jahrhunderts," 10 (1899): 1328–1333. Reprinted as "Die Meinungen des Dritten," in Kurt Eisner, *Taggeist*, 316–337.

3 Freya Eisner, introduction to Kurt Eisner, *Zwischen Kapitalismus und Kommunismus*, 64.

4 Scheidemann, *Memoiren eines Sozialdemokraten*, 1:58.

5 Walther G. Oschilewski, *Zeitungen in Berlin: Im Spiegel der Jahrhunderte* (Berlin: Haude & Spenersche Verlagsbuchhandlung, 1975), 128. Braun resettled in Bavaria and went to work for the party press in Nuremberg.

6 SAPMO-BArch, NY 4034/147/91.

[7] Quoted in Helmut Holzhey, *Cohen und Natorp*, 2 vols. (Basel: Schwabe, 1986), 1:248.

[8] SAPMO-BArch, NY 4060/1/132.

[9] Freya Eisner, introduction to Kurt Eisner, *Zwischen Kapitalismus und Kommunismus*, 64–65.

[10] Friedrich Stampfer, *Erfahrungen und Erkenntnisse: Aufzeichnungen aus meinem Leben* (Cologne: Verlag für Politik und Wirtschaft, 1957), 75; Joc [Kurt Eisner], "Sonntagsplauderei," *UdV*, 18 November 1900.

[11] Oschilewski, *Zeitungen in Berlin*, 118–120; Gary P. Steenson, *"Not One Man! Not One Penny!" German Social Democracy*, 1863–1914 (Pittsburgh, PA: University of Pittsburgh Press, 1981), 21–23.

[12] Oschilewski, *Zeitungen in Berlin*, 120–121; Steenson, *"Not One Man!"* 28–29.

[13] Quoted in Steenson, *"Not One Man!"* 29.

[14] Kurt Eisner, *Wilhelm Liebknecht* (1906), 79.

[15] Gay, *The Dilemma of Democratic Socialism*, 45–47; Steenson, *"Not One Man!"* 34–39. See also Ernst Engelberg, *Revolutionäre Politik und Rote Feldpost 1878–1890* (Berlin: Akademie, 1959).

[16] Oschilewski, *Zeitungen in Berlin*, 126–127; Steenson, *"Not One Man!"* 133; Dieter Fricke, *Handbuch zur Geschichte der deutschen Arbeiterbewegung 1869 bis 1917*, 2 vols. (Berlin: Dietz, 1987), 1:553.

[17] Steenson, *"Not One Man!"* 133.

[18] Eduard Bernstein, *Die Voraussetzungen des Sozialismus und die Aufgaben der Sozialdemokratie*, Internationale Bibliothek 61 (1921; reprint of 2nd ed., Berlin: J. H. W. Dietz, 1977), 5–13, 229–230. See also Harry J. Marks, "The Sources of Reformism in the Social Democratic Party of Germany, 1890–1914," *Journal of Modern History* 11 (March–December 1939): 334–356; Georg Sinowjew, *Der Krieg und die Krise des Sozialismus* (Vienna: Verlag für Literatur und Politik, 1924), 549.

[19] Craig, *Germany, 1866–1945*, 267–268.

[20] Quoted in Fricke, *Handbuch zur Geschichte der deutschen Arbeiterbewegung*, 1:555.

[21] Victor Adler, *Briefwechsel mit August Bebel und Karl Kautsky*, ed. Friedrich Adler (Vienna: Wiener Volksbuchhandlung, 1954), 283.

[22] Großmann, "Kurt Eisner," 558.

[23] Oschilewski, *Zeitungen in Berlin*, 121.

[24] Fricke, *Handbuch zur Geschichte der deutschen Arbeiterbewegung*, 1:556.

[25] Stampfer, *Erfahrungen und Erkenntnisse*, 73.

26 SAPMO-BArch, NY 4060/1/180, 181.

27 Kurt Eisner, *Eine Junkerrevolte: Drei Wochen preußischer Politik* (Berlin: Buchhandlung Vorwärts, 1899).

28 Freya Eisner, introduction to Kurt Eisner, *Zwischen Kapitalismus und Kommunismus*, 76–77.

29 This letter, contained in SAPMO-BArch, NY 4023 (Nachlaß Eduard Bernstein)/6, was called to the author's attention by Dr. Veli-Matti Rautio, author of *Die Bernstein-Debatte: Die politisch-ideologischen Strömungen und die Parteiideologie in der Sozialdemokratischen Partei Deutschlands 1898–1903* Studia Historica 47 (Helsinki: Suomen Historiallinen Seura, 1994).

30 Joc [Kurt Eisner], "Sonntagsplauderei," *UdV*, 25 June 1899.

31 See Craig, *Germany, 1866–1945*, 265.

32 Kurt Eisner, "Die falsche Krise," *Die Wage: Wiener Wochenschrift* 2.36 (3 September 1899): 613–614; "Weltmanchester," 3.2 (7 January 1900): 26–28; "Von der Weltpolitik und den Sauen," 3.12 (18 March 1900): 186–189.

33 Bernstein, *Die Voraussetzungen des Sozialismus*, 13, 256.

34 Gay, *The Dilemma of Democratic Socialism*, 79–81.

35 Kurt Eisner, "Unser Tag," *V*, 10–12 October 1899; "Nach Hannover," 15 October 1899. Reprinted in Kurt Eisner, *Zwischen Kapitalismus und Kommunismus*, 136–156.

36 Bebel's opinion was shared by the bourgeois novelist Theodor Fontane, who wrote in 1896: "The new, the better world begins with the fourth estate. . . . What the workers think, speak, and write has in fact overtaken the thinking, speaking, and writing of the old ruling classes; it is all more genuine, more truthful, more full of life. The workers have attacked everything in a new way; they not only have new goals but new methods of attaining them." Quoted in Craig, *Germany, 1866–1945*, 269–270.

37 Luxemburg's animosity against Eisner, arising from profound conflicts of philosophy and personality, was later vitriolic. See J. P. Nettl, *Rosa Luxemburg*, 2 vols. (London: Oxford, 1966), 1:21.

38 Victor Adler, *Briefwechsel mit August Bebel und Karl Kautsky*, 329.

39 Ibid., 330.

40 Nettl, *Rosa Luxemburg*, 1:171–172; Rosa Luxemburg, *Gesammelte Briefe*, ed. Annelies Laschitza and Günter Radczun, 5 vols. (Berlin: Dietz, 1982–1984), 1:501.

41 SAPMO-BArch, NY 4060/65/3.

42 SAPMO-BArch, NY 4060/3/52.

[43] Kurt Eisner, "Der Probetod: Eine Geschichte," *Deutsche Dichtung* 27.4 (15 November 1899): 81–88. Reprinted in Kurt Eisner, *Feste der Festlosen*, 169–183.

[44] Joc [Kurt Eisner], "Sonntagsplauderei," *UdV*, 14 January 1900.

[45] Michael Meyer, *Ibsen: A Biography* (Harmondsworth, England: Penguin, 1985), 830.

[46] Kurt Eisner, "Professor Rubeks Puppenheim," in Kurt Eisner, *Taggeist*, 306–315.

[47] SAPMO-BArch, NY 4060/15.1/130.

[48] Joc [Kurt Eisner], "Sonntagsplauderei," *UdV*, 4 February 1900.

[49] Kurt Eisner, *Wilhelm Liebknecht* (1900), 58.

[50] Quoted in Freya Eisner, *Kurt Eisner: Die Politik des libertären Sozialismus* (Frankfurt am Main: Suhrkamp, 1979), 22.

[51] SAPMO-BArch, NY 4060/66/60.

[52] Joc [Kurt Eisner], "Sonntagsplauderei," *UdV*, 25 February 1900.

[53] Joc [Kurt Eisner], "Sonntagsplauderei," *UdV*, 4 March 1900.

[54] Joc [Kurt Eisner], "Sonntagsplauderei," *UdV*, 1 April 1900.

[55] SAPMO-BArch, NY 4060/66/123.

[56] Joc [Kurt Eisner], "Sonntagsplauderei," *UdV*, 15 April 1900. Reprinted as "Beim Wissenden," in Kurt Eisner, *Feste der Festlosen*, 67–71.

[57] Joc [Kurt Eisner], "Sonntagsplauderei," *UdV*, 8 April 1900.

[58] Kurt Eisner, "Der alte Abgott," *SM* 4.1 (May 1900): 251–255.

[59] Joc [Kurt Eisner], "Sonntagsplauderei," *UdV*, 20 May 1900.

[60] Joc [Kurt Eisner], "Sonntagsplauderei," *UdV*, 27 May 1900.

[61] Joc [Kurt Eisner], "Sonntagsplauderei," *UdV*, 10 June 1900.

[62] Joc [Kurt Eisner], "Sonntagsplauderei," *UdV*, 1 July 1900.

[63] Davis, *Nationalism and Socialism*, 100.

[64] Bernstein, *Die Voraussetzungen des Sozialismus*, 207–211.

[65] Ibid., 211.

[66] Joc [Kurt Eisner], "Sonntagsplauderei," *UdV*, 8, 29 July 1900.

[67] SAPMO-BArch, NY 4060/65/15.

[68] Joc [Kurt Eisner], "Sonntagsplauderei," *UdV*, 12 August 1900. Reprinted as "Der Alte," in Kurt Eisner, *Feste der Festlosen*, 257–260.

[69] Kurt Eisner, "Liebknechts Erbe," *SM* 4.2 (September 1900): 519–521.

[70] IISG, Kleine Korrespondenz.

[71] Kurt Eisner, *Wilhelm Liebknecht* (1900), 2.

[72] Ibid., 56.

[73] Kurt Eisner, *Wilhelm Liebknecht* (1906), 4; advertisement, *V*, 27 September 1900.

[74] Fricke, *Handbuch zur Geschichte der deutschen Arbeiterbewegung*, 1:553–556.

Chapter Six

[1] [Kurt Eisner], "Mainz," *V*, 16 September 1900; "Kulturdienst," 22 September 1900. Reprinted in part in Kurt Eisner, *Zwischen Kapitalismus und Kommunismus*, 156–159.

[2] Gay, *The Dilemma of Democratic Socialism*, 239.

[3] Ibid., 237.

[4] Steenson, *"Not One Man!"* 70–72.

[5] Luxemburg, *Gesammelte Briefe*, 1:504–505.

[6] Joc [Kurt Eisner], "Sonntagsplauderei," *UdV*, 30 September 1900. Reprinted as "Bienchen," in Kurt Eisner, *Feste der Festlosen*, 111–115.

[7] Kurt Eisner, "Kulturdienst," *V*, 22 September 1900.

[8] Kurt Eisner, "Der goldene Magnetberg," *SM* 4.2 (October 1900): 653–664. Reprinted in Kurt Eisner, *Gesammelte Schriften*, 1:264–284.

[9] Addressing troops about to depart Bremerhaven for China in July 1900, Wilhelm remarked: "When you encounter the enemy, he is to be routed. There will be no quarter shown, no prisoners taken! Whoever falls into your hands is a casualty. Just as the Huns made a name for themselves a thousand years ago under their King Attila . . . so too may you impress the name 'German' in China for a thousand years in such a way that no Chinese will ever again dare look askance at a German!" This excerpt from the infamous "Hun Speech," as reported by Bremerhaven's *Nordwestdeutsche Zeitung*, appeared as the underscored headline to the Sunday edition of *Vorwärts* on 29 July, followed by a comparison of versions of the speech printed in the right-wing press. Looking back half a century later on the kaiser's gaffe, Friedrich Stampfer recorded in his memoirs: "Whenever the Germans were called Huns by their adversaries, they owe it to the man whom they let rule them for thirty years" (*Erfahrungen und Erkenntnisse*, 63).

[10] Joc [Kurt Eisner], "Sonntagsplauderei," 30 September 1900.

[11] Oschilewski, *Zeitungen in Berlin*, 125.

[12] Gradnauer, Robert Schmidt, and Ströbel were destined to serve as government cabinet ministers following the First World War. Cunow later taught at the Party School in Berlin, became a university professor, directed the

Museum of Ethnology, and published monographs on the Germanic tribes and the Incas. John served as a district mayor in Berlin.

13 Joc [Kurt Eisner], "Sonntagsplauderei," *UdV*, 21 October 1900.

14 Joc [Kurt Eisner], "Sonntagsplauderei," *UdV*, 28 October 1900.

15 Stampfer, *Erfahrungen und Erkenntnisse*, 75.

16 Joc [Kurt Eisner], "Sonntagsplauderei," *UdV*, 4 November 1900.

17 Joc [Kurt Eisner], "Sonntagsplauderei," *UdV*, 4 November 1900; "Sonntagsplauderei," 18 November 1900. The latter reprinted as "Nebelwahn," in Kurt Eisner, *Feste der Festlosen*, 157–160.

18 Joc [Kurt Eisner], "Sonntagsplauderei," *UdV*, 25 November 1900.

19 Joc [Kurt Eisner], "Sonntagsplauderei," *UdV*, 2 December 1900.

20 Kurt Eisner, "Raskolnikow: Zu Dostojewskijs Bild," *SM* 5.1 (January 1901): 48–52.

21 Joc [Kurt Eisner], "Sonntagsplauderei," *UdV*, 27 January 1901. Reprinted as "Der unsittliche Frack," in Kurt Eisner, *Feste der Festlosen*, 117–122.

22 SAPMO-BArch, NY 4060 (Nachlaß Kurt Eisner)/67/81.

23 SAPMO-BArch, NY 4060/66/61.

24 Pinson, *Modern Germany*, 248; "Stumm," *V*, 10 March 1901.

25 [Kurt Eisner], "Auferstehung," *V*, 7 April 1901; "Pfingstgeist," 26 May 1901.

26 Joc [Kurt Eisner], "Sonntagsplauderei," *UdV*, 30 June 1901. Reprinted as "Die Bank," in Kurt Eisner, *Feste der Festlosen*, 123–127.

27 Kurt Eisner, "Parlamentarismus und Ministerialismus," *NZ* 19.2 (1900–1901): 484–491.

28 Ladislaus Gumplowicz, "Revuen," *SM* 5.2 (September 1901): 757–758.

29 Victor Adler, "Unmaßgebliche Betrachtungen," *NZ* 19.2 (1900–1901): 775–780.

30 SAPMO-BArch, NY 4060/1/111.

31 Ernst Gystrow, "Rundschau: Bücher," *SM* 5.2 (September 1901): 756–57. Goethe's verse:

Wer in der Weltgeschichte lebt,
Dem Augenblick sollt' er sich richten?
Wer in die Zeiten schaut und strebt,
Nur der ist wert, zu sprechen und zu dichten.

32 [Kurt Eisner], "Lübeck," *V*, 22 September 1901. Reprinted in part in Kurt Eisner, *Zwischen Kapitalismus und Kommunismus*, 159–162.

33 [Kurt Eisner], "Der Ertrag," *V*, 29 September 1901. Reprinted in part in Kurt Eisner, *Zwischen Kapitalismus und Kommunismus*, 162–164.

[34] Gay, *The Dilemma of Democratic Socialism*, 156–158; Lily Braun, *Memoiren einer Sozialistin: Kampfjahre*, vol. 3 of *Gesammelte Werke* (Berlin-Grunewald: Hermann Klemm, n.d.), 317–318; Heinrich Ströbel, "Erklärung," *V*, 27 September 1901.

[35] Lily Braun, *Memoiren einer Sozialistin: Kampfjahre*, 318.

[36] Heinrich Ströbel, "Erklärung."

[37] Joc [Kurt Eisner], "Sonntagsplauderei," *UdV*, 20 October 1901. Reprinted as "Herbst," in Kurt Eisner, *Feste der Festlosen*, 129–132.

[38] Victor Adler, *Briefwechsel mit August Bebel und Karl Kautsky*, 374.

[39] SAPMO-BArch, NY 4060/65/17, 19.

[40] Joc [Kurt Eisner], "Sonntagsplauderei," *UdV*, 24 November 1901. Reprinted as "Die Verleumdung des Sterbens," in Kurt Eisner, *Feste der Festlosen*, 161–164.

[41] Joc [Kurt Eisner], "Prager Brief," *UdV*, 3 November 1901. Reprinted as "Prag," in Kurt Eisner, *Feste der Festlosen*, 133–137.

[42] Karl Kautsky Jr., ed., *August Bebels Briefwechsel mit Karl Kautsky* (Assen: Van Gorcum, 1971), 122n4.

[43] [Kurt Eisner], "Die Unmöglichkeit der Wahrheit: Der Chinaprozeß des *Vorwärts*," *V*, 3 December 1901.

[44] [Kurt Eisner], "Entweihte Nacht," *V*, 25 December 1901.

[45] Luxemburg, *Gesammelte Briefe*, 1:548.

[46] SAPMO-BArch, NY 4060/66/72.

[47] [Kurt Eisner], "Jahreswende," *V*, 1 January 1901; "Das Ausland im Jahre 1901," 3 January 1901.

[48] [Kurt Eisner], "Die Kinderausbeutung," *V*, 2 February 1902.

[49] Luxemburg, *Gesammelte Briefe*, 1:576–577.

[50] Ibid., 585–587.

[51] Ibid., 594.

[52] SAPMO-BArch, NY 4060/65/21.

[53] Hans Wandrer [Kurt Eisner], "Das Bettelgewerbe," *V*, 9 February 1902.

[54] [Kurt Eisner], "Bürgertum und Revolution," *V*, 18 March 1902.

[55] [Kurt Eisner], "Im Friedrichshain," *V*, 19 March 1902; Joc [Kurt Eisner], "Sonntagsplauderei," *UdV*, 23 March 1902. The latter reprinted as "Die Schere," in Kurt Eisner, *Feste der Festlosen*, 231–234.

[56] SAPMO-BArch, NY 4060/66/49. Luxemburg, *Gesammelte Briefe*, 1:632. Luxemburg's review of volumes 2 and 3 appeared under the title "Aus dem Nachlaß unserer Meister," *V*, 9 November 1902.

57 [Kurt Eisner], "Neue Ostern," *V*, 30 March 1902.

58 See Vernon L. Lidtke, *The Alternative Culture: Socialist Labor in Imperial Germany* (New York: Oxford University Press, 1985), 77–84.

59 [Kurt Eisner], "Rüstet das Maifest!" *V*, 20 April 1902.

60 [Kurt Eisner], "Zum 1. Mai," *V*, 1 May 1902.

61 Stampfer, *Erfahrungen und Erkenntnisse*, 68–75.

62 Joc [Kurt Eisner], "Sonntagsplauderei: Episoden der Vorortbahn," *UdV*, 29 June 1902. Reprinted as "Episoden von der Vorortbahn," in Kurt Eisner, *Feste der Festlosen*, 139–143.

Chapter Seven

1 See Nettl, *Rosa Luxemburg*, 1:186–189.

2 SAPMO-BArch, NY 4060 (Nachlaß Kurt Eisner)/67/83.

3 [Kurt Eisner], "Die Tagesordnung des Parteitags," *V*, 31 July 1902.

4 SAPMO-BArch, NY 4060/65/86.

5 Eduard Bernstein, "Zur Frage der preußischen Landtagswahlen," *V*, 9 September 1902.

6 [Kurt Eisner], "Kriegsrat," *V*, 14 September 1902.

7 [Kurt Eisner], "Unser Parteitag," *V*, 21 September 1902.

8 Luxemburg, *Gesammelte Briefe*, 1:646n328.

9 [Kurt Eisner], "Emile Zola—tot!" *V*, 30 September 1902.

10 Kurt Eisner, "Zolas Werk," *NZ* 21.1 (1902–1903): 133–141. Reprinted in Kurt Eisner, *Gesammelte Schriften*, 2:310–326.

11 E__r [Kurt Eisner], "Zola," *Neue Deutsche Rundschau* 13 (1902): 1221–1223.

12 [Kurt Eisner], "Ins neue Heim," *V*, 30 September 1902; "Unser neues Heim," 14 October 1902. See also Oschilewski, *Zeitungen in Berlin*, 130.

13 SAPMO-BArch, NY 4060/67/85.

14 Quoted in William Manchester, *The Arms of Krupp, 1587–1968* (Boston: Little, Brown, 1968), 225.

15 Ibid., 221–225.

16 Stampfer, *Erfahrungen und Erkenntnisse*, 98–99.

17 Ibid., 99.

18 Manchester, *The Arms of Krupp*, 226–227.

19 Ibid., 228–230.

20 "Die Krupp-Presse," *V*, 25 November 1902.

21 Stampfer, *Erfahrungen und Erkenntnisse*, 99.

22 SAPMO-BArch, NY 4060/65/127.

23 Stampfer, *Erfahrungen und Erkenntnisse*, 99.

24 Manchester, *The Arms of Krupp*, 230.

25 Quoted in [Kurt Eisner], "Wilhelm II. gegen den *Vorwärts*," *V*, 28 November 1902.

26 Ibid.

27 [Franz Mehring], "Der Fall Krupp," *NZ* 21.1 (1902–1903): 257–260.

28 Paul Göhre, "Die Sozialdemokratie und die Monarchie," *SM* 7.1 (February 1903): 169–179.

29 Manchester, *The Arms of Krupp*, 231–232.

30 Freya Eisner, introduction to Kurt Eisner, *Zwischen Kapitalismus und Kommunismus*, 84.

31 Kurt Eisner, "Rantum," *Die Neue Welt: Illustrierte Beilage für Wissenschaft, Belehrung und Unterhaltung* (1903): 1:3–6, 2:11–12.

32 Kurt Eisner, "Der junge Ibsen," *SM* 7.1 (January 1903): 47–53.

33 [Kurt Eisner], "Aus dem Sumpfe der Berliner politischen Polizei," *V*, 15 January 1903.

34 [Kurt Eisner], "Karl Marx," *V*, 14 March 1903.

35 [Kurt Eisner], "Jahreswende," *V*, 1 January 1903.

36 Steenson, *"Not One Man!"* 42–46.

37 See Stampfer, *Erfahrungen und Erkenntnisse*, 77–79.

38 [Kurt Eisner], "Koloniale Sklaverei," *V*, 6 March 1903.

39 [Kurt Eisner], "Fünf Jahre," *V*, 17 March 1903.

40 [Kurt Eisner], "Die Auslandsflotte," *V*, 4 April 1903.

41 [Kurt Eisner], "Alte und neue Pfingsten," *V*, 31 May 1903.

42 [Kurt Eisner], "Der Wahltag ein Feiertag," *V*, 9 June 1903.

43 [Kurt Eisner], "Wahlschluß um 7 Uhr!" and "Volkstag!" *V*, 16 June 1903.

44 Stampfer, *Erfahrungen und Erkenntnisse*, 81–82.

45 "Ergebnisse der Berliner Reichstagswahlen," *V*, 17 June 1903; Steenson, *"Not One Man!"* 50.

46 Steenson, *"Not One Man!"* 45–46.

47 [Kurt Eisner], "Berlin die Hauptstadt der Sozialdemokratie! Deutschland das Reich der Sozialdemokratie!" *V*, 17 June 1903.

48 Stampfer, *Erfahrungen und Erkenntnisse*, 82; Kurt Eisner, "Die Wahlnacht," in *Feste der Festlosen*, 244.

49 Joc [Kurt Eisner], "Sonntagsplauderei," *UdV*, 21 June 1903. Reprinted as "Die Wahlnacht," in Kurt Eisner, *Feste der Festlosen*, 241–244.

50 Stampfer, *Erfahrungen und Erkenntnisse*, 80.

51 Ibid., 79; BArch-Koblenz, R 117 (*Sozialistische Monatshefte* 1894–1911)/4/231.

52 [Kurt Eisner], "Sozialpolitische Aufgaben des neuen Reichstages," *V*, 4 July 1903.

53 Kurt Eisner to Victor Adler on 2 September 1903, quoted in Fletcher, *Revisionism and Empire*, 113–114.

54 "Parteinachrichten: Zur Tagesordnung des Parteitags," *V*, 18 August 1903; "Die Fürstenwalder Resolution," 23 August 1903; "Parteinachrichten: Erklärung," 26 August 1903; "Versammlungen: Zuschrift von Wolfgang Heine," 28 August 1903.

55 "Die Berliner Parteiversammlungen: Dritter Wahlkreis," *V*, 27 August 1903.

56 [Kurt Eisner], "'Neue Taktik,'" *V*, 30 August 1903.

57 SAPMO-BArch, NY 4060/59/9.

58 Karl Kautsky Jr., *August Bebels Briefwechsel mit Karl Kautsky*, 157–59. Bebel's allegation of Eisner's "historical gaffes" is particularly ironic here, as his own correspondence constantly confounded its compiler because of the author's confusion over dates. In this letter too Bebel errs as to the year of the party congress at Frankfurt, writing 1895 rather than 1894.

59 SAPMO-BArch, NY 4060/59/13.

60 August Bebel, "Die Meinungsfreiheit in der Partei," *LV*, 5 September 1903.

61 August Bebel, "Ein Nachwort zur Vizepräsidentenfrage und Verwandtem," *NZ* 21.2 (1902–1903): 718.

62 Karl Kautsky Jr., *August Bebels Briefwechsel mit Karl Kautsky*, 159–160.

63 SAPMO-BArch, NY 4060/59/19.

64 August Bebel, "Parteinachrichten: Erklärung," *V*, 9 September 1903.

65 Karl Kautsky Jr., *August Bebels Briefwechsel mit Karl Kautsky*, 160–162.

66 [Kurt Eisner], "Die Einheit der Aktion," *V*, 11 September 1903.

67 Karl Kautsky Jr., *August Bebels Briefwechsel mit Karl Kautsky*, 161n4; Stampfer, *Erfahrungen und Erkenntnisse*, 88.

68 Stampfer, *Erfahrungen und Erkenntnisse*, 88.

[69] Ibid., 87.

[70] Luxemburg, *Gesammelte Briefe*, 2:238nn116–117, 239n127; Stampfer, *Erfahrungen und Erkenntnisse*, 88–89.

[71] SAPMO-BArch, NY 4060/59/19. For Kraus's thoughts on the controversy and details of Wilhelm Liebknecht's articles for the journal, see "Schimpfen," *Die Fackel* 143 (6 October 1903): 1–15.

[72] Freya Eisner, *Kurt Eisner: Die Politik des libertären Sozialismus*, 25.

[73] [Kurt Eisner], "Dresden," *V*, 13 September 1903.

[74] *Protokoll über die Verhandlungen des Parteitages der Sozialdemokratischen Partei Deutschlands 1903* (Berlin: Buchhandlung Vorwärts, 1903), 158–264.

[75] Luxemburg, *Gesammelte Briefe*, 2:39–40.

[76] *Protokoll über die Verhandlungen des Parteitages der Sozialdemokratischen Partei Deutschlands 1903*, 315.

[77] [Kurt Eisner], "Der Parteitag," *V*, 22 September 1903.

[78] Stampfer, *Erfahrungen und Erkenntnisse*, 92.

Chapter Eight

[1] "An die Wähler zum preußischen Landtag!" *V*, 18 October 1903.

[2] [Kurt Eisner], "Der preußische Wahlkampf," *V*, 4 October 1903.

[3] Stampfer, *Erfahrungen und Erkenntnisse*, 102–103.

[4] Ibid., 100.

[5] Ibid.

[6] [Kurt Eisner], "Deutsches Reich: Die Kaiserinsel," *V*, 18, 19 August 1903.

[7] [Kurt Eisner], "Deutsches Reich: Die Kaiserinsel," *V*, 21 August 1903.

[8] Stampfer, *Erfahrungen und Erkenntnisse*, 102.

[9] [Kurt Eisner], "Der Majestätsbeleidigungs-Prozeß des *Vorwärts*," *V*, 17 October 1903.

[10] Stampfer, *Erfahrungen und Erkenntnisse*, 101–102.

[11] Barbara W. Tuchman, *The Proud Tower: A Portrait of the World before the War, 1880–1914* (New York: Macmillan, 1966), 330–331.

[12] Stampfer, *Erfahrungen und Erkenntnisse*, 102.

[13] "Der Majestätsbeleidigungs-Prozeß des *Vorwärts*," *V*, 17 October 1903.

[14] Luxemburg, *Gesammelte Briefe*, 2:43–44. See also Oschilewski, *Zeitungen in Berlin*, 86–89.

15 [Kurt Eisner], "Preußische Justiz," *V*, 22 October 1903; Grau, *Kurt Eisner 1867–1919*, 150.

16 "Berliner Partei-Angelegenheiten," *V*, 5 November 1903.

17 "Wahl-Berichterstattung!"; [Kurt Eisner], "Zum Kampf um Preußen!" *V*, 10 November 1903.

18 "Wahl-Ergebnisse," *V*, 13 November 1903.

19 [Kurt Eisner], "Die Wahl der Entrechteten," *V*, 14 November 1903.

20 [Kurt Eisner], "Der alte neue Reichstag," *V*, 29 November 1903.

21 SAPMO-BArch, NY 4060 (Nachlaß Kurt Eisner)/1/113.

22 [Kurt Eisner], "Johann Gottfried Herder," *UdV*, 17 December 1903.

23 [Kurt Eisner], "Revolutionäre Humanität! Zum Gedächtnis Herders (gestorben am 18. Dezember 1803)," *V*, 18 December 1903. Reprinted in Kurt Eisner, *Gesammelte Schriften*, 2:153–164.

24 "Preußen—Eine russische Spitzelprovinz," *V*, 3 January 1904.

25 Kurt Eisner, *Der Geheimbund des Zaren: Der Königsberger Prozeß wegen Geheimbündelei, Hochverrat gegen Rußland und Zarenbeleidigung vom 12. bis 25. Juli 1904* (Berlin: Buchhandlung Vorwärts, 1904), 51.

26 "Rußland und Japan," *V*, 14, 23 January 1904.

27 K. E., "Kant (Gestorben am 12. Februar 1804)," *V*, 12–14 February 1904. Reprinted as "Kant," in Kurt Eisner, *Gesammelte Schriften*, 2:165–186.

28 Kurt Eisner, "Kant," 2:165.

29 Luxemburg, *Gesammelte Briefe*, 2:56–57.

30 [Kurt Eisner], "Revolution," *V*, 18 March 1904.

31 Joc [Kurt Eisner], "Die Kinderuhr," *UdV*, 13 March 1904. Reprinted in Kurt Eisner, *Feste der Festlosen*, 151–154.

32 [Kurt Eisner], "Das feiernde Berlin," *V*, 3 May 1904; "Die Maifeier der Partei," 3 May 1904.

33 "Zum russisch-japanischen Krieg," *V*, 18 June 1904.

34 [Kurt Eisner], "Der Prozeß des Zaren," *V*, 12 July 1904; "Königsberg," 24 July 1904.

35 Kurt Eisner, *Der Geheimbund des Zaren*, 380.

36 Joc [Kurt Eisner], "Prophetenkraft," *UdV*, 3 July 1904. Reprinted in Kurt Eisner, *Feste der Festlosen*, 275–279.

37 [Kurt Eisner], "Das Urteil," *V*, 26 July 1904.

38 Kurt Eisner, *Der Geheimbund des Zaren*, 501–506.

39 Ibid., 509.

40 Ibid., 500.

41 Kurt Eisner, "Krottingen: Eine Erinnerung," *A-F* 6.10 (March 1915); SAPMO-BArch, NY 4060/56. Reprinted in Kurt Eisner, *Gesammelte Schriften*, 1:75–87. See also Kurt Eisner, *Der Geheimbund des Zaren*, 215.

42 Kurt Eisner, *Der Geheimbund des Zaren*, 48, 54, 213.

43 Karl Liebknecht, "Ein Dokument zur Zeitgeschichte: Der Königsberger Prozeß," *NZ* 23.1 (1904–1905): 756–759.

44 [Kurt Eisner], "Die Internationale," *V*, 7, 9 August 1904.

45 [Kurt Eisner], "Amsterdam," *V*, 14 August 1904.

46 [Kurt Eisner], "Einheit!" *V*, 21 August 1904.

47 Kurt Eisner, "Sozialdemokratie und Staatsform: Eine öffentliche Diskussion zwischen Kurt Eisner und Karl Kautsky 1904," in *Gesammelte Schriften*, 1:285.

48 Karl Kautsky, "Der Kongreß zu Amsterdam," *NZ* 22.2 (1903–1904): 673–682.

49 K. E., "Sozialdemokratie und Staatsform," *V*, 30 August 1904.

50 IISG, Karl Kautsky, DX/148.

51 H. S. [Heinrich Ströbel], "Sozialdemokratie und Staatsform," *V*, 31 August 1904.

52 Karl Kautsky, "Sozialdemokratie und Staatsform," *V*, 2 September 1904.

53 Karl Kautsky Jr., *August Bebels Briefwechsel mit Karl Kautsky*, 196.

54 Ibid., 165–166.

55 "Nochmals Sozialdemokratie und Staatsform," *V*, 7 September 1904. The debate is reprinted as "Sozialdemokratie und Staatsform: Eine öffentliche Diskussion zwischen Kurt Eisner und Karl Kautsky 1904," in Kurt Eisner, *Gesammelte Schriften*, 1:285–325.

56 Karl Kautsky Jr., *August Bebels Briefwechsel mit Karl Kautsky*, 167.

57 Luxemburg, *Gesammelte Briefe*, 2:65–67.

58 [Kurt Eisner], "Die rote Hansa," *V*, 18 September 1904.

59 "Parteitag der sozialdemokratischen Partei Deutschlands," *V*, 20 September 1904.

60 See Joc [Kurt Eisner], "Der Parteitag auf See," *V*, 27 September 1904. Eisner's account of the day voyage on the steamer *Glückauf* rates as one of his more humorous pieces, circumlocuting "vomit" with half a dozen euphemisms.

61 See Schorske, *German Social Democracy, 1905–1917*, 69.

62 [Kurt Eisner], "Neue Kraft," *V*, 25 September 1904.

[63] *SM* 8.1 (January 1904): 93; 8.2 (December 1904): 1011.

[64] Stampfer, *Erfahrungen und Erkenntnisse*, 97.

[65] IISG, Kautsky, DX/150. See Z. A. B. Zeman and W. B. Scharlau, *The Merchant of Revolution: The Life of Alexander Israel Helphand (Parvus), 1867–1924* (London: Oxford University Press, 1965), 175–176.

[66] "Parteinachrichten," *V*, 19 October 1904.

[67] [Kurt Eisner], "Militarismus und Demokratie," *V*, 6 November 1904.

[68] Karl Kautsky, "Militarismus und Demokratie: Die Demokratisierung der Spitzelei," *V*, 9 November 1904.

[69] [Kurt Eisner], "Militarismus und Demokratie," *V*, 10 November 1904.

[70] Karl Kautsky, "Militarismus und Demokratie: Demokratie und Spitzelei," *V*, 13 November 1904.

[71] [Kurt Eisner], "Militarismus und Demokratie: Demokratie und Spitzelei," *V*, 13 November 1904.

[72] Ke [Kurt Eisner], "Der Veitstanz des Todes," *UdV*, 20 November 1904. Reprinted in Kurt Eisner, *Feste der Festlosen*, 165–168.

[73] SAPMO-BArch, NY 4060/3/9.

[74] Kesr [Kurt Eisner], "Magdeburger Sauerkraut," *A-F* 1.24/25 (September 1910); SAPMO-BArch, NY 4060/51; *MP*, 18–19 September 1910.

[75] Freya Eisner, *Kurt Eisner: Die Politik des libertären Sozialismus*, 27–28.

[76] Ibid., 27.

[77] Victor Adler, *Briefwechsel mit August Bebel und Karl Kautsky*, 444–445.

[78] Ibid.; Freya Eisner, *Kurt Eisner: Die Politik des libertären Sozialismus*, 24–25.

[79] IISG, Kautsky, DX/152.

Chapter Nine

[1] [Kurt Eisner], "Die Streik-Revolution in Rußland," *V*, 22 January 1905.

[2] "Der Blutsonntag," *V*, 24 January 1905.

[3] [Kurt Eisner], "Die Streik-Revolution in Rußland."

[4] "Der Blutsonntag."

[5] J. P. Nettl, *The Soviet Achievement* (Norwich, England: Harcourt, Brace & World, 1971), 27.

[6] "Der Blutsonntag."

[7] [Kurt Eisner], "Die Schlacht des Zaren!" *V*, 24 January 1905.

8 Rosa Luxemburg, "Die Revolution in Rußland," *V*, 9–10 February 1905.

9 Nettl, *The Soviet Achievement*, 27.

10 See Joc [Kurt Eisner], "Tapferkeiten," *UdV*, 8 January 1905. Reprinted in Kurt Eisner, *Feste der Festlosen*, 281–284. Here Eisner treated the European press's lamentations at the impending capitulation of the "heroic" Russian general Stössel, who commanded 50,000 besieged troops at Port Arthur. The bourgeois papers reported that over the course of eleven months 42,000 Russian troops had fallen to the cruel, fanatical enemy. Despite his vow to fight to the death for the tsar, Stössel and his subordinate generals, beaten to the pit, preferred surrender. "With the sobriety of a laundry ticket tallying in figures the returned socks, shirts, and underwear," Eisner wrote, "the Japanese general counted up the captured human booty: 48,000 men, among them 16,000 sick and wounded!" The jingoist press was incontrovertibly exposed, and its favorite revealed as "a farce's buffoon, perhaps a coward."

11 Kurt Eisner, "Die Heimat der Neunten," in *Feste der Festlosen*, 293.

12 Stampfer, *Erfahrungen und Erkenntnisse*, 97–98.

13 "Freie Volksbühne in Berlin," *SM* 9.2 (November 1905): 991–992.

14 Kurt Eisner, "Die Heimat der Neunten," *NG* 1.1 (1905): 9–10. Reprinted in Kurt Eisner, *Feste der Festlosen*, 291–294.

15 Stampfer, *Erfahrungen und Erkenntnisse*, 98.

16 See J. Hampden Jackson, *Clemenceau and the Third Republic* (New York: Collier, 1962), 95–97.

17 Quoted in Kurt Eisner, *Der Sultan des Weltkrieges: Ein marokkanisches Sittenbild deutscher Diplomaten-Politik* (Dresden: Kaden, 1906), 68. Reprinted in part in Kurt Eisner, *Gesammelte Schriften*, 1:326–341.

18 Craig, *Germany, 1866–1945*, 318–319.

19 Ibid., 318.

20 [Kurt Eisner], "Marokko-Lärm," *V*, 25 March 1905.

21 [Kurt Eisner], "Marokko-Konflikt?" *V*, 31 March 1905.

22 [Kurt Eisner], "Das marokkanische 'Mißverständnis,'" *V*, 8 April 1905.

23 Kurt Eisner, "Über Schillers Idealismus," in *Gesammelte Schriften* 2:217–234. The article appeared in March 1905 in a sixteen-page commemorative pamphlet printed in house by the Vorwärts Bookstore Press. Featuring essays by Eisner, Friedrich Stampfer, Lily Braun, John Schikowski, Eduard David, and Hermann Molkenbuhr, the pamphlet sold out two printings, a total of 96,000 copies, within a month ("Parteinachrichten: Die Schiller-Märznummer," *V*, 19 March 1905; "Aus der Partei," 12 April 1905).

24 Quoted in Fricke, *Handbuch zur Geschichte der deutschen Arbeiterbewegung*, 2:930.

25 Luxemburg, *Gesammelte Briefe*, 2:121–123.

26 [Kurt Eisner], "Gewerkschaft und Partei," *V*, 8 June 1905.

27 [Kurt Eisner], "Über politischen Streik," *V*, 25 June 1905.

28 Schorske, *German Social Democracy, 1905–1917*, 85.

29 Quoted in Ibid., 41.

30 Victor Adler, *Briefwechsel mit August Bebel und Karl Kautsky*, 461–462.

31 Fricke, *Handbuch zur Geschichte der deutschen Arbeiterbewegung*, 1:559.

32 Kurt Eisner, "Der Sultan des Weltkrieges," in *Gesammelte Schriften*, 1:326–327.

33 Paul Büttner et al., eds., *Der Vorwärts-Konflikt: Gesammelte Aktenstücke* (Munich: G. Birk, [1905]), 115–116; [Kurt Eisner], "Eine Kundgebung des Weltfriedens!" *V*, 1 July 1905.

34 SAPMO-BArch, NY 4060 (Nachlaß Kurt Eisner)/65/135.

35 Luxemburg, *Gesammelte Briefe*, 2:145–146.

36 [Kurt Eisner], "Eine Kundgebung des Weltfriedens!"

37 [Kurt Eisner], "Weltblamage," *V*, 7 July 1905.

38 [Kurt Eisner], "Parteigenossen und Genossinen Berlins."

39 [Kurt Eisner], "Die Furcht vor dem Sozialismus: Jaurès' Antwort," *V*, 8 July 1905.

40 "Bülow im Urteil Englands," *V*, 8 July 1905.

41 Jean Jaurès, "Die Friedensidee und die Solidarität des internationalen Proletariats," *V*, 9 July 1905.

42 [Kurt Eisner], "Für den Weltfrieden des Proletariats! Gegen die Weltstörung durch Polizei und Diplomatie!" *V*, 11 July 1905.

43 Büttner et al., *Der Vorwärts-Konflikt*, 79.

44 Kurt Eisner, "Der Sultan des Weltkrieges," 1:327.

45 [Kurt Eisner], "Die Tagesordnung des Parteitages," *V*, 6 July 1905.

46 "Zur Tagesordnung des Parteitages," *V*, 7 July 1905.

47 Karl Kautsky, "Die Folgen des japanischen Sieges und die Sozialdemokratie," *NZ* 23.2 (1904–1905): 461n.

48 Ibid., 492–499.

49 [Franz Mehring], "In eigener Sache II," *LV*, 11 July 1905.

50 Victor Adler, *Briefwechsel mit August Bebel und Karl Kautsky*, 459.

51 Ibid., 463–464.

[52] Arthur Stadthagen, "Der Parteitag zu Jena," *NZ* 23.2 (1904–1905): 521–528.

[53] Luxemburg, *Gesammelte Briefe*, 2:153.

[54] Ibid., 2:155. The important letter to which she refers is lost. Annelies Laschitza and Günter Radczun, editors of Luxemburg's correspondence, attribute it to either Kurt Eisner or Luxemburg's attorney, Kurt Rosenfeld, but nowhere in Luxemburg's extant correspondence from 1905 is Rosenfeld mentioned.

[55] [Franz Mehring], "Die Vorwärts-Frage IV," *LV*, 30 August 1905.

[56] [Franz Mehring], "Über 'guten Ton,'" *LV*, 5 August 1905.

[57] Kurt Eisner, "Von schlechtem Ton und guter Logik I–II," *V*, 11–12 August 1905.

[58] [Franz Mehring], "Aus der Partei," *LV*, 16 August 1905.

[59] [Kurt Eisner], "Aus der Partei: Gezänke," *V*, 22 August 1905.

[60] Freya Eisner, *Kurt Eisner: Die Politik des libertären Sozialismus*, 30; quoted in [Franz Mehring], "Die Vorwärts-Frage VII," *LV*, 6 September 1905.

[61] See Luxemburg, *Gesammelte Briefe*, 2:164; Karl Kautsky, "Die Fortsetzung einer unmöglichen Diskussion," *NZ* 23.2 (1904–1905): 681–692.

[62] "Aus der Partei: Zum Parteitage," *V*, 26 August 1905.

[63] [Franz Mehring], "Die Vorwärts-Frage I–IX," *LV*, 26, 28–30 August, 4–8 September 1905.

[64] [Franz Mehring], "Die Vorwärts-Frage IV."

[65] [Franz Mehring], "Die Vorwärts-Frage VI," *LV*, 5 September 1905.

[66] [Franz Mehring], "Die Vorwärts-Frage VIII," *LV*, 7 September 1905.

[67] Ibid.

[68] [Franz Mehring], "Die Vorwärts-Frage I," *LV*, 26 August 1905.

[69] [Franz Mehring], "Die Vorwärts-Frage IX," *LV*, 8 September 1905.

[70] Karl Kautsky, "Die Fortsetzung einer unmöglichen Diskussion," *NZ* 23.2 (1904–1905): 717–727.

[71] [Kurt Eisner], "Debatten über Wenn und Aber I–VII," *V*, 2, 5–6, 8–10, 13 September 1905.

[72] [Kurt Eisner], "Debatten über Wenn und Aber III," *V*, 6 September 1905.

[73] [Kurt Eisner], "Debatten über Wenn und Aber V," *V*, 9 September 1905.

[74] Fricke, *Handbuch zur Geschichte der deutschen Arbeiterbewegung*, 1:557.

[75] Ibid., 1:348–349.

[76] Victor Adler, *Briefwechsel mit August Bebel und Karl Kautsky*, 466–467.

[77] See Büttner et al., *Der Vorwärts-Konflikt*, 88; Fricke, *Handbuch zur Geschichte der deutschen Arbeiterbewegung*, 1:352, 557.

[78] Büttner et al., *Der Vorwärts-Konflikt*, 5.

[79] Ibid., 13.

[80] Fricke, *Handbuch zur Geschichte der deutschen Arbeiterbewegung*, 1:557.

[81] Büttner et al., *Der Vorwärts-Konflikt*, 79.

[82] Luxemburg, *Gesammelte Briefe*, 2:184–185.

[83] Gary P. Steenson, *Karl Kautsky, 1854–1938: Marxism in the Classical Years* (Pittsburgh, PA: Univeristy of Pittsburgh Press, 1978), 147–148.

[84] Fricke, *Handbuch zur Geschichte der deutschen Arbeiterbewegung*, 1:353; Steenson, *"Not One Man!"* 104–106.

[85] *Protokoll über die Verhandlungen des Parteitages der Sozialdemokratischen Partei Deutschlands 1905* (Berlin: Buchhandlung Vorwärts, 1905), 104–105, 115–116, 130–131, 175–176, 185.

[86] Ibid., 43.

[87] Ibid., 144. The other members of Dietz's commission were Ottilie Baader, Friedrich Ebert, Eugen Ernst, Ludwig Frank, Hugo Haase, Klemens Hengsbach, Paul Kleemann, Joseph Rother, Franz Schmitt, Theodor Schwartz, Fritz Seger, Karl Sperka, Otto Stolten, and Hugo Woldersky.

[88] Stampfer, *Erfahrungen und Erkenntnisse*, 109; *Protokoll über die Verhandlungen des Parteitages 1905*, 128.

[89] Ibid., 179–180. Wels's second solution, in the case that *Vorwärts* was to continue as central organ, parroted Kautsky's opinion in a letter of 2 August 1905 to Victor Adler.

[90] Ibid., 187–188, 347.

[91] Büttner et al., *Der Vorwärts-Konflikt*, 6, 15.

[92] *Protokoll über die Verhandlungen des Parteitages 1905*, 350.

[93] Büttner et al., *Der Vorwärts-Konflikt*, 16–17.

[94] Ibid., 17.

[95] *Protokoll über die Verhandlungen des Parteitages 1905*, 144.

[96] Büttner et al., *Der Vorwärts-Konflikt*, 15.

[97] *Protokoll über die Verhandlungen des Parteitages 1905*, 285–313.

[98] Ibid., 320–321.

[99] Ibid., 142–143.

[100] Ibid., 342–343.

[101] [Kurt Eisner], "Jena," *V*, 24 September 1905.

[102] Karl Kautsky, "Der Parteitag von Jena," *NZ* 24.1 (1905–1906): 5–10.

[103] Luxemburg, *Gesammelte Briefe*, 2:174, 178, 180–181.

[104] Ibid., 2:175–177.

[105] Büttner et al., *Der Vorwärts-Konflikt*, 94–95.

[106] Luxemburg, *Gesammelte Briefe*, 2:180.

[107] Büttner et al., *Der Vorwärts-Konflikt*, 95.

[108] Luxemburg, *Gesammelte Briefe*, 2:183–185.

[109] Büttner et al., *Der Vorwärts-Konflikt*, 5, 94–95.

[110] Ibid., 95–96.

[111] Ibid., 5–9.

[112] Ibid., 9–11.

[113] Ibid., 12.

[114] Luxemburg, *Gesammelte Briefe*, 2:211, 215.

[115] Büttner et al., *Der Vorwärts-Konflikt*, 20.

[116] Ibid., 20–21.

[117] Luxemburg, *Gesammelte Briefe*, 2:215.

[118] Büttner et al., *Der Vorwärts-Konflikt*, 21.

[119] Luxemburg, *Gesammelte Briefe*, 2:221–222.

[120] Büttner et al., *Der Vorwärts-Konflikt*, 29–30.

[121] Luxemburg, *Gesammelte Briefe*, 2:226.

Chapter Ten

[1] Großmann, "Kurt Eisner," 558–559.

[2] Fricke, *Handbuch zur Geschichte der deutschen Arbeiterbewegung*, 1:557.

[3] Büttner et al., *Der Vorwärts-Konflikt*, 97; Fricke, *Handbuch zur Geschichte der deutschen Arbeiterbewegung*, 1:558.

[4] Karl Kautsky, "Die Freiheit der Meinungsäußerung," *NZ* 24.1 (1905–1906): 152–155.

[5] Georg Ledebour, "Eine Literatenrevolte," *NZ* 24.1 (1905–1906): 189–194.

[6] Kurt Eisner, "Zur Literaten-Psychologie," *NG* 1.34 (22 November 1905): 404–408.

[7] IISG, Karl Kautsky, DX/155.

[8] IISG, Kleine Korrespondenz.

9 A. Bebel, "Meine Antwort," *V*, 7 November 1905.

10 BArch-Koblenz, R 117 (*Sozialistische Monatshefte* 1894–1911)/3/39.

11 Büttner et al., *Der Vorwärts-Konflikt*, 77–83.

12 IISG, Karl Kautsky, DX/156.

13 IISG, Karl Kautsky, DX/157.

14 Fricke, *Handbuch zur Geschichte der deutschen Arbeiterbewegung*, 1:558.

15 Büttner et al., *Der Vorwärts-Konflikt*, 18.

16 Ibid., 64–65, 70.

17 Steenson, *"Not One Man!"* 104–105; Fricke, *Handbuch zur Geschichte der deutschen Arbeiterbewegung*, 1:353.

18 Luxemburg, *Gesammelte Briefe*, 2:230. See also Stampfer, *Erfahrungen und Erkenntnisse*, 112.

19 Nettl, *Rosa Luxemburg*, 1:312n1.

20 Victor Adler, *Briefwechsel mit August Bebel und Karl Kautsky*, 663n4.

21 "Briefe von Kurt Eisner und Gustav Landauer," *Die Fackel* 601–607 (November 1922): 66.

22 SAPMO-BArch, NY 4060 (Nachlaß Kurt Eisner)/65/132.

23 SAPMO-BArch, NY 4060/65/88, 89, 91.

24 Kurt Eisner, "Die Expropriation der Eltern," *NG* 1.36 (6 December 1905): 427–428; Paul Göhre, "Volksschule und Religionsunterricht," 428–430.

25 See for example "Eine ostelbische Schul'reform,'" *V*, 11 April 1901; "Die Regierung und die Volksschule," 30 October 1903; "Volksschule und Landtag in Preußen," 4 November 1903; "Wem gehört die Volksschule?" 6 November 1903; "Trinkgeld-Pädagogik," 31 March 1904; "Sozialdemokratie und Volksschule," 18 December 1904; "Preußische Volksschule," 26 February 1905.

26 Thomas Alexander, *The Prussian Elementary Schools* (New York: Macmillan, 1919), v.

27 Leo Berg, "Die Feste des Proletariats," *NG* 2.1 (3 January 1906): 8–10.

28 Karl Liebknecht to Kurt Eisner, 16 February 1906, IISG, Kleine Korrespondenz.

29 Kurt Eisner, *Wilhelm Liebknecht* (1906), 100–101.

30 LBI-NY, Julie Braun-Vogelstein Collection.

31 Kurt Eisner, "Der Sultan des Weltkrieges," 1:328.

32 Kurt Eisner, *Der Sultan des Weltkrieges*, 6.

33 Ibid., 3.

34 SAPMO-BArch, NY 4060/67/61.

35 Kurt Eisner, "Der Sultan des Weltkrieges," 1:329.

36 BArch-Koblenz, R 117/4/206.

37 Kurt Eisner, "Der Sultan des Weltkrieges," 1:328–329.

38 Kurt Eisner, "Diplomaten," NG 2.6 (7 February 1906): 63–65.

39 Kurt Eisner, "Der Sultan des Weltkrieges," 1:327, 328–329.

40 Kurt Eisner, "Englische Grotesken," NG 2.8 (21 February 1906): 89–91; "Nationale Verantwortlichkeit," 2.15 (11 April 1906): 171–173; "Bundestreue," 2.17 (26 April 1906): 195–196.

41 LBI-NY, Julie Braun-Vogelstein Collection.

42 Ibid.

43 BArch-Koblenz, R 117/4/205.

44 Kurt Eisner, "Heine, ein Wintermärchen," NG 2.7 (14 February 1906): 82–84.

45 Kurt Eisner, "Preußische Völkerrechts-Verbrechen," NG 2.19 (9 May 1906): 219–221; "Preußen-Pranger," 2.21 (23 May 1906): 243–244.

46 Kurt Eisner, "Petition Nr. 70," NG 2.23 (6 June 1906): 267–269.

47 Kurt Eisner, Das Ende des Reichs: Deutschland und Preußen im Zeitalter der großen Revolution, 2nd ed. (Berlin: Buchhandlung Vorwärts, 1907), vi.

48 Ibid., iii.

49 SAPMO-BArch, NY 4060/66/134–135.

50 Kurt Eisner to Joseph Bloch, 6 February 1907, BArch-Koblenz, R 117/4/209.

51 See Fricke, Handbuch zur Geschichte der deutschen Arbeiterbewegung, 1:669–670.

52 Kurt Eisner, Das Ende des Reichs, vi–vii.

53 Kurt Eisner, "Jena," NG 2.26 (27 June 1906): 303–305.

54 Kurt Eisner, Das Ende des Reichs, iv.

55 Ibid., iii.

56 Pinson, Modern Germany, ix, 622.

57 BArch-Koblenz, R 117/4/208.

58 "Die Philosophie Friedrich Nietzsches," Volksblatt: Organ für die werktätige Bevölkerung in Hessen und Waldeck, 24 November 1906.

59 Ibid., 27, 28, 29 November, 1, 4 December 1906; SAPMO-BArch, NY 4060/28/13–20.

60 SAPMO-BArch, NY 4060/60/3.

[61] IISG, Kleine Korrespondenz. From 1 January 1904 Stampfer's *Berliner Korrespondenz für die sozialdemokratische Presse* appeared six days a week and exerted immense influence on the party press.

[62] Gert Rückel, *Die Fränkische Tagespost: Geschichte einer Parteizeitung*, Veröffentlichungen der Stadtbibliothek Nürnberg 8 (Nuremberg: Fränkische Verlagsanstalt und Buchdruckerei, 1964), 40–44, 139; Grau, *Kurt Eisner 1867–1919*, 226; Fricke, *Handbuch zur Geschichte der deutschen Arbeiterbewegung*, 1:559.

[63] George Dunlap Crothers, *The German Elections of 1907* (New York: Columbia University Press, 1941), 34, 74–75, 90–96.

[64] Quoted in Ibid., 105.

[65] Eduard von Liebert, *Aus einem bewegten Leben* (Munich: J. F. Lehmann, 1925), 181.

[66] Kurt Eisner, "Die Blockade des Reichstags," *NG* 3.13 (26 December 1906): 147–148.

[67] Max Schippel, "Rundschau: Literatur," *SM* 11.2 (February 1907): 152–153.

[68] BArch-Koblenz, R 117/4/209.

[69] BArch-Koblenz, R 117/4/207, 211, 214.

[70] BArch-Koblenz, R 117/4/213. Rose's two-volume *Napoleon I* was reviewed by Kautsky two weeks earlier in *NZ* 25.1 (1906–1907): 610–612.

[71] SAPMO-BArch, NY 4060/12/111.

[72] Crothers, *German Elections of 1907*, 166–184; Erika Rikli, *Der Revisionismus: Ein Revisionsversuch der deutschen marxistischen Theorie 1890–1914* (Zurich: H. Girsberger, 1936), 3; Pinson, *Modern Germany*, 602; Stampfer, *Erfahrungen und Erkenntnisse*, 115–116.

[73] Eduard Bernstein, "Was folgt aus dem Ergebnis der Reichstagswahlen?" *SM* 11.2 (February 1907): 108–114.

[74] Richard Calwer, "Der 25. Januar," *SM* 11.2 (February 1907): 101–107.

[75] Karl Kautsky, "Der 25. Januar," *NZ* 25.1 (1906–1907): 588–596.

[76] Karl Kautsky, "Die Situation des Reiches," *NZ* 25.1 (1906–1907): 484–500.

[77] Crothers, *German Elections of 1907*, 58n97.

[78] Stampfer, *Erfahrungen und Erkenntnisse*, 116–117.

[79] Kurt Eisner, "Der Fall Molkenbuhr," *NG* 3.21 (20 February 1907): 247–249.

[80] SAPMO-BArch, NY 4060/76/13.

[81] SAPMO-BArch, NY 4060/76/18.

Chapter Eleven

[1] SAPMO-BArch, NY 4060 (Nachlaß Kurt Eisner)/3/48.

[2] SAPMO-BArch, NY 4060/74/8.

[3] BArch-Koblenz, R 117 (*Sozialistische Monatshefte* 1894–1911)/4/217.

[4] "Aus der Redaktion der *Fränkischen Tagespost*," *FT*, 22 February 1907; H, "Das Ende des Reichs," 9 March 1907.

[5] [Kurt Eisner], "Die Gefahr der Presse," *FT*, 28 March 1907.

[6] [Kurt Eisner], "Der verbotene Witz," *FT*, 8 April 1907.

[7] [Kurt Eisner], "Das Recht der Kritik," *FT*, 8 April 1907.

[8] [Else Belli], "Die Kulturarbeit der Frau," *FT*, 9 April 1907.

[9] [Kurt Eisner], "Ignaz Auer," *FT*, 10 April 1907.

[10] "Ignaz Auer," *NZ* 25.2 (1906–1907): 41–43.

[11] SAPMO-BArch, NY 4060/76/36.

[12] Kurt Eisner, "Ein Führer," *FT*, 11 April 1907.

[13] "Zum Gedächtnis Ignaz Auers," *FT*, 25 April 1907.

[14] BArch-Koblenz, R 117/4/218.

[15] "Eingelaufene Schriften: *Das Ende des Reichs*," *FT*, 24 April 1907.

[16] Kurt Eisner, *Das Ende des Reichs*, viii.

[17] Schorske, *German Social Democracy, 1905–1917*, 72–79; *Verhandlungen des Reichstags: 12. Legislaturperiode, 1. Session 1907/09*, vol. 228 (17 April–14 May 1907), 1089.

[18] [Kurt Eisner], "Hervé and Bebel," *FT*, 4 May 1907.

[19] BArch-Koblenz, R 117/4/227.1.

[20] SAPMO-BArch, NY 4060/76/62.

[21] SAPMO-BArch, NY 4060/76/67.

[22] SAPMO-BArch, NY 4060/76/79.

[23] BArch-Koblenz, R 117/4/224.

[24] BArch-Koblenz, R 117/4/225.

[25] BArch-Koblenz, R 117/4/226.

[26] Kesr [Kurt Eisner], "Im Wahlauto," *FT*, 1 June 1907.

[27] "Der Mai des Sieges," *FT*, 1 June 1907.

[28] "Afrikanische Bestien," *FT*, 27 June 1907.

29 Kesr [Kurt Eisner], "Unsere Afrikaner: Persönliche Eindrücke vom Peters-Prozeß," *FT*, 6 July 1907.

30 "Ein neuer Prozeß Peters: Peters verklagt die *Fränkische Tagespost*," *FT*, 25 July 1907.

31 [Kurt Eisner,] "Ein Schritt zum sozialistischen Bildungsideal," *FT*, 16 July 1907.

32 See Max Maurenbrecher, "Parteischule," *NG* 2.30 (25 July 1906): 353–354; and Fricke, *Handbuch zur Geschichte der deutschen Arbeiterbewegung*, 1:691–696.

33 "Aus der Partei," *FT*, 25, 29 July, 2 August 1907; Fricke, *Handbuch zur Geschichte der deutschen Arbeiterbewegung*, 1:611–612.

34 "Generalversammlung des Sozialdemokr. Vereins Nürnberg," *FT*, 10 August 1907.

35 BArch-Koblenz, R 117/4/230.

36 BArch-Koblenz, R 117/8/21.

37 BArch-Koblenz, R 117/8/26.

38 BArch-Koblenz, R 117/8/27.

39 Quoted in Schorske, *German Social Democracy, 1905–1917*, 81.

40 Quoted in Ibid., 83.

41 Ibid., 82.

42 [Kurt Eisner], "Die Internationale," *FT*, 26 August 1907.

43 Kurt Eisner, "Kopenhagen: Nachschrift," in *Gesammelte Schriften*, 2:148–149.

44 BArch-Koblenz, R 117/4/231.

45 [Kurt Eisner], "Der Parteitag in Essen," *FT*, 14 September 1907.

46 "Bericht über die Generalversammlung vom 14. u. 15. September 1907 zu Essen," *Mitteilungen des Vereins Arbeiterpresse* 8.69 (31 October 1907).

47 *Protokoll über die Verhandlungen des Parteitages der Sozialdemokratischen Partei Deutschlands 1907* (Berlin: Buchhandlung Vorwärts, 1907), 257–258.

48 Ibid., 164–165.

49 Ibid., 341, 344–345.

50 Kesr [Kurt Eisner], "Ein Friedhof der Lebenden," *FT*, 28 September 1907. Reprinted in Kurt Eisner, *Gesammelte Schriften*, 2:10–14.

51 BArch-Koblenz, R 117/4/228.

52 SAPMO-BArch, NY 4060/76/157.

53 SAPMO-BArch, NY 4060/76/163.

54 [Kurt Eisner], "Der Parteitag," *FT*, 23 September 1907.

55 "Berichterstattung vom Parteitag," *FT*, 28 September 1907.

56 Kesr [Kurt Eisner], "Der Kreis um Ihn," *FT*, 26 October 1907.

57 Kesr [Kurt Eisner], "Winterangst," *FT*, 16 November 1907.

58 SAPMO-BArch, NY 4060/12/138–144.

59 [Kurt Eisner], "Die Ethik des Sozialismus," *FT*, 22–23, 25 November 1907.

60 Kesr [Kurt Eisner], "Fünfhunderttausend Teufel," *FT*, 30 November 1907.

61 "Karl Peters contra Tagespost," *FT*, 2 December 1907.

62 [Kurt Eisner], "Das teuerste Land der Welt," *FT*, 19 December 1907.

63 [Kurt Eisner], "Licht in der Not," *FT*, 28 December 1907.

64 "Journalist oder Schmock?" *FT*, 10 January 1908.

65 "Das Urteil im Mohr-Prozeß," *FT*, 14 January 1908.

66 [Kurt Eisner], "Das Jubiläum der Junkerbefreiung: Zum 9. Oktober 1907," *FT*, 8–9 October 1907.

67 [Kurt Eisner], "Der preußische Weg," *FT*, 13 January 1908.

68 Kesr [Kurt Eisner], "Ein preußischer Junker," *FT*, 18 January 1908.

69 [Kurt Eisner], "Biegen oder Brechen," *FT*, 25 January 1908.

70 BArch-Koblenz, R 117/4/237.

Chapter Twelve

1 Kesr [Kurt Eisner], "Massenlust: Ein unparlamentarischer Abend," *FT*, 3 March 1908.

2 "Parteitag in Nürnberg 1908," *FT*, 16 March 1908.

3 "Preisausschreiben," *FT*, 31 March 1908.

4 BArch-Koblenz, R 117 (*Sozialistische Monatshefte* 1894–1911)/4/256.

5 [Kurt Eisner], "Zum Würzburger Gautag," *FT*, 25 April 1908.

6 "Der Gautag der Sozialdemokratie Nordbayerns," *FT*, 27 April 1908.

7 Kurt Eisner, "Kommunismus des Geistes," *Dokumente des Fortschritts: Internationale Revue* 1.6 (May 1908): 586–591. Reprinted in Kurt Eisner, *Gesammelte Schriften*, 2:15–26.

8 [Kurt Eisner], "Das neue Haus," *FT*, 30 May 1908.

9 "Die Auflage der *Tagespost*," *FT*, 23 June 1908.

10 Kurt Eisner, "Preußische Erinnerungen," *FT*, 27 June 1908.

[11] Kurt Eisner, "Organisation der Bildung," *FT*, 19 August 1908.

[12] Quoted in Karl Heinrich Pohl, *Die Münchener Arbeiterbewegung: Sozialdemokratische Partei, Freie Gewerkschaften, Staat und Gesellschaft in München 1890–1914*, Schriftenreihe der Georg-von-Vollmar-Akademie 4 (Munich: K. G. Sauer, 1992), 497.

[13] Kurt Eisner, "Vier Fragen," *FT*, 28–29 August 1908. Reprinted in Kurt Eisner, *Sozialismus als Aktion*, 26–39.

[14] BArch-Koblenz, R 117/4/249.

[15] Victor Adler, *Briefwechsel mit August Bebel und Karl Kautsky*, 488–489.

[16] Quoted in Grau, *Kurt Eisner 1867–1919*, 543–544n24.

[17] Pohl, *Die Münchener Arbeiterbewegung*, 497–498.

[18] Karl Kautsky, "Budgetbewilligung," *NZ* 26.2 (1907–1908): 809–826.

[19] Kurt Eisner, "Das vorgeschrittene Hinterpommern," *FT*, 8–11 September 1908. Reprinted in Kurt Eisner, *Sozialismus als Aktion*, 40–57.

[20] "Bildungsarbeit: Das Nürnberger Programm," *FT*, 12 September 1908.

[21] Max Maurenbrecher, "Arbeiterbildung," *FT*, 12 September 1908.

[22] *Protokoll über die Verhandlungen des Parteitages der Sozialdemokratischen Partei Deutschlands 1908* (Berlin: Buchhandlung Vorwärts, 1908), 217–221.

[23] Ibid., 227–229.

[24] Ibid., 230–235.

[25] Ibid., 235–237.

[26] Ibid., 190, 423–424.

[27] [Kurt Eisner], "Die Klärung: Nach dem Nürnberger Parteitag," *FT*, 21 September 1908.

[28] [Kurt Eisner], "Neue Saat," *FT*, 25 September 1908.

[29] "An die gesamte Arbeiterschaft Nürnbergs!" *FT*, 29 September 1908.

[30] BArch-Koblenz, R 117/4/250.

[31] Quoted in "Die *Tagespost* im Munde der Gegner," *FT*, 7 October 1908.

[32] Kurt Eisner, "Religion des Sozialismus," in *Gesammelte Schriften*, 2:27–38.

[33] "Die Nürnberger Parteigenossen über den Nürnberger Parteitag," *FT*, 12 October 1908. In his history of the Nuremberg workers' movement Georg Gärtner, a staff member at the *Tagespost*, documents the increase in subscriptions during Eisner's time at the helm from 19,920 in 1907 to 22,800 on 1 July 1908. See Georg Gärtner, *Die Nürnberger Arbeiterbewegung 1868–1908* ([1908]; reprint, Berlin: J. H. W. Dietz, 1977), 214.

[34] Grau, *Kurt Eisner 1867–1919*, 229.

35 "Die Nürnberger Parteigenossen über den Nürnberger Parteitag," *FT*, 13 October 1908.

36 [Kurt Eisner], "Sozialistische Briefe an eine Freundin: Natur und Kultur," *Der Volksbildner* 1.3 (October 1908).

37 H. M., "Entfremdung," *Die Furche*, 26 October 1908.

38 SAPMO-BArch, NY 4060/110/82; 4060/77/1, 71, 87.

39 SAPMO-BArch, NY 4060/60/11.

40 SAPMO-BArch, NY 4060/60/12.

41 SAPMO-BArch, NY 4060/110/27.

42 "Sozialistische Briefe an eine Freundin: Die große Unruhe," "Der verlorene Einzelne," "Solidarität," "Eine Weltfahrt in 50 Kilometern," "Wagenklassen," "Fremde Seelen," *Der Volksbildner* 1.5, 7, 8, 9, 13, 2.4 (November 1908–January 1909). Reprinted as "Sieben Briefe," 2:39–69. Lisbeth Eisner's response to the *Sozialistische Briefe* was a children's book, *Hamelébuku und Allerhand: Ein lustiges Büchlein vom Kinderland* (Nuremberg: Fränkische Verlagsanstalt und Buchdruckeri, n.d.). In the preface she writes that her inspiration was the happy family life in her seventeen-year marriage with Kurt Eisner. SAPMO-BArch, NY 4060/93/1.

43 SAPMO-BArch, NY 4060/1/121; Fricke, *Handbuch zur Geschichte der deutschen Arbeiterbewegung*, 1:529; Luxemburg, *Gesammelte Briefe*, 2:403.

44 CJA, 6.4 (Nachlaß Freia Eisner)/13/2; Wilhelm Seytter, *Unser Stuttgart: Geschichte, Sage und Kultur unserer Stadt und Umgebung* (Stuttgart: Max Kielmann, 1903).

45 CJA 6.4/13/2.

46 Else Belli, "Der Flüchtling," *Die Gleichheit: Zeitschrift für die Interessen der Arbeiterinnen*, 31 October 1906; SAPMO-BArch, NY 4060/96/1.

47 Peter Mugay, "'Patro hat uns sehr gefehlt,'" *Abendzeitung*, 21 August 2006.

48 CJA Findbuch Nachlässe 6.4 (Nachlaß Freia Eisner 1907–1989) D/31; CJA 6.4/31/2, 3; SAPMO-BArch, NY 4060/1/121; Freya Eisner, introduction to Kurt Eisner, *Zwischen Kapitalismus und Kommunismus*, 105.

49 [Else Belli], "Die Kulturarbeit der Frau," *FT*, 9 April 1907.

50 Karl Kautsky Jr., *August Bebels Briefwechsel mit Karl Kautsky*, 200n1; Luxemburg, *Gesammelte Briefe*, 2:382.

51 E. B., "Das Schreibmaschinenfräulein," *Die Gleichheit*, 6 January 1908.

52 SAPMO-BArch, NY 4060/77/30; Karl Kautsky Jr., *August Bebels Briefwechsel mit Karl Kautsky*, 199–200; Luxemburg, *Gesammelte Briefe*, 2:382.

53 SAPMO-BArch, NY 4060/77/117–118.

[54] "Leitungen und Aufgaben der Kommunalpolitik: Vorbemerkung," *FT*, 14 November 1908.

[55] "An die Gemeindewähler Nürnbergs," *FT*, 21 November 1908.

[56] SAPMO-BArch, NY 4060/60/16.

[57] SAPMO-BArch, NY 4060/60/17.

[58] "Ein sozialdemokratischer Vizepräsident," *FT*, 11 December 1908.

[59] Kesr [Kurt Eisner], "Weihnachtsausverkauf," *FT*, 18 December 1908.

[60] See the first and last paragraphs of "Sozialistische Briefe an eine Freundin: Wagenklassen," *Der Volksbildner* 1.13 (December 1908); SAPMO-BArch, NY 4060/77/6.

[61] Grau, *Kurt Eisner 1867–1919*, 242–243.

[62] Fricke, *Handbuch zur Geschichte der deutschen Arbeiterbewegung*, 1:658.

Chapter Thirteen

[1] [Georges Weill], "Deutsche 'Weltpolitik' 1908," *FT*, 31 December 1908, 2 January 1909.

[2] IISG, Kleine Korrespondenz.

[3] SAPMO-BArch, NY 4060 (Nachlaß Kurt Eisner)/77/1.

[4] SAPMO-BArch, NY 4060/72/1.

[5] SAPMO-BArch, NY 4060/77/4.

[6] "Die Zentralbibliothek," *FT*, 19 January 1909.

[7] SAPMO-BArch, NY 4060/77/14.

[8] SAPMO-BArch, NY 4060/77/17.

[9] "Sozialistische Briefe an eine Freundin: Fremde Seelen," *Der Volksbildner* 2.4 (January 1909). Reprinted in Kurt Eisner, *Gesammelte Schriften*, 2:64–69; SAPMO-BArch, NY 4060/77/26.

[10] SAPMO-BArch, NY 4060/77/26.

[11] SAPMO-BArch, NY 4060/77/28.

[12] SAPMO-BArch, NY 4060/77/30.

[13] "Kurt Eisner gegen v. Dallwitz," *Volksblatt für Anhalt*, 30 January 1909; SAPMO-BArch, NY 4060/35/54.

[14] SAPMO-BArch, NY 4060/77/35.

[15] SAPMO-BArch, NY 4060/77/40.

[16] SAPMO-BArch, NY 4060/77/42.

[17] SAPMO-BArch, NY 4060/77/44.

[18] Kesr [Kurt Eisner], "Theater-Elend," *FT*, 4 February 1909.

[19] SAPMO-BArch, NY 4060/77/51.

[20] SAPMO-BArch, NY 4060/72/5.

[21] Kesr [Kurt Eisner], "Darwinismus und Sozialismus," *FT*, 11–12 February 1909; SAPMO-BArch, NY 4060/77/55.

[22] SAPMO-BArch, NY 4060/77/57.

[23] SAPMO-BArch, NY 4060/77/59.

[24] Grau, *Kurt Eisner 1867–1919*, 243; SAPMO-BArch, NY 4060/66/78.

[25] "Reichstags-Kandidatur," *FT*, 15 February 1909.

[26] SAPMO-BArch, NY 4060/77/78.

[27] SAPMO-BArch, NY 4060/77/84.

[28] SAPMO-BArch, NY 4060/77/71, 97, 100, 104.

[29] "Bildungs-Ausschuß," *FT*, 13 March 1909.

[30] Kesr [Kurt Eisner], "Nacktheit mit Badehosen," *FT*, 18 March 1909.

[31] SAPMO-BArch, NY 4060/77/134.

[32] "Bildungs-Ausschuß," *FT*, 24 March 1909.

[33] Kurt Eisner, "Mairuf," *FT*, 30 April 1909.

[34] BArch-Koblenz, R 117 (*Sozialistische Monatshefte* 1894–1911)/8/187.

[35] BArch-Koblenz, R 117/8/214.

[36] BArch-Koblenz, R 117/8/265; Karl Leuthner, "Herrenvolk und Sklaven-volk," *SM* 13.8 (April 1909): 475–481.

[37] BArch-Koblenz, R 117/8/270. In 1895 Berthold Heymann was cofounder with Bloch of *Der sozialistische Akademiker*, forerunner to *Sozialistische Monatshefte*.

[38] [Georges Weill], "Hurrah!" *FT*, 5 May 1909. See BArch-Koblenz, R 117/8/158.

[39] Karl Leuthner, "Umlernen," *SM* 13.9 (May 1909): 558–559; Fricke, *Handbuch zur Geschichte der deutschen Arbeiterbewegung*, 1:605.

[40] Kurt Eisner, "Ungelernter Sozialismus," *FT*, 10 May 1909.

[41] BArch-Koblenz, R 117/8/295. Moritz Gottlieb Saphir (1795–1858) was a controversial theater critic and satirist active in Vienna, Berlin, Munich, and Paris.

[42] BArch-Koblenz, R 117/8/302.

[43] SAPMO-BArch, NY 4060/67/162.

[44] SAPMO-BArch, NY 4060/77/216.

[45] BArch-Koblenz, R 117/8/302.

46 [Kurt Eisner], "Die *Sozialistische Monatshefte*," *FT*, 10 June 1909.

47 BArch-Koblenz, R 117/4/253; SAPMO-BArch, NY 4060/65/35.

48 BArch-Koblenz, R 117/4/256.

49 M. Beer, "*Sozialistische Monatshefte* und *Vorwärts* kontra *Fränkische Tagespost*: Fragen der äußeren Politik," *FT*, 21 June 1909.

50 SAPMO-BArch, NY 4060/77/207.

51 SAPMO-BArch, NY 4060/77/247, 250, 254.

52 SAPMO-BArch, NY 4060/72/26.

53 "Gegen den Steuerraub der schwarz-blauen Reaktion," *FT*, 4 August 1909.

54 SAPMO-BArch, NY 4060/77/254.

55 "Die Sozialdemokratie in Nordbayern," *FT*, 9 August 1909.

56 SAPMO-BArch, NY 4060/77/254.

57 E. W. [Kurt Eisner], "Fettchen," *Die Furche*, 6, 9–13, 16–17 August 1909.

58 SAPMO-BArch, NY 4060/77/254.

59 SAPMO-BArch, NY 4060/70/57.

60 SAPMO-BArch, NY 4060/77/275; Speranza [Else Belli], "Der große Angler," *Die Furche*, 31 August 1909.

61 BArch-Koblenz, R 117/4/258.

62 Kurt Eisner, "Zum 'Fall Bernstein,'" *FT*, 26 August 1909.

63 Kesr [Kurt Eisner], "Künstlertheater," *FT*, 26 August 1909.

64 Kesr [Kurt Eisner], "Der weiße Vogel," *FT*, 28 August 1909; SAPMO-BArch, NY 4060/77/277.

65 SAPMO-BArch, NY 4060/77/283.

66 [Kurt Eisner], "Leipzig," *FT*, 11 September 1909. Reprinted in part in Kurt Eisner, *Zwischen Kapitalismus und Kommunismus*, 221–222.

67 *Protokoll über die Verhandlungen des Parteitages der Sozialdemokratischen Partei Deutschlands 1909* (Berlin: Buchhandlung Vorwärts, 1909), 221.

68 Ibid., 322–324.

69 Ibid., 326.

70 Ibid., 332–333.

71 Ibid., 352.

72 Ibid., 363–364.

73 SAPMO-BArch, NY 4060/77/295.

[74] Kurt Eisner, "Der Sultan des Weltkrieges," 1:330. See John Keegan, *The First World War* (New York: Vintage, 1998), 42–43.

[75] [Kurt Eisner], "Kraft," *FT*, 20 September 1909.

[76] "Sozialdemokratischer Verein," *FT*, 25 September 1909.

Chapter Fourteen

[1] Freya Eisner, introduction to Kurt Eisner, *Zwischen Kapitalismus und Kommunismus*, 105.

[2] SAPMO-BArch, NY 4060 (Nachlaß Kurt Eisner)/77/316.

[3] See Murray Bookchin, *The Spanish Anarchists: The Heroic Years, 1868–1936* (New York: Free Life Editions, 1977), 129–132, 153–154.

[4] "Arbeiter, Volk Nürnbergs!" *FT*, 16 October 1909.

[5] SAPMO-BArch, NY 4060/77/330.

[6] SAPMO-BArch, NY 4060/77/332, 336.

[7] SAPMO-BArch, NY 4060/72/38.

[8] SAPMO-BArch, NY 4060/72/39.

[9] SAPMO-BArch, NY 4060/77/342.

[10] SAPMO-BArch, NY 4060/77/354.

[11] "Eine Anti-Ferrer-Versammlung," *FT*, 12 November 1909.

[12] "Redaktionswechsel," *FT*, 15 November 1909.

[13] SAPMO-BArch, NY 4060/51/1.

[14] Kurt Eisner, "Die ewigen Arbeiter (aus einem Reich 24stündiger Arbeitszeit): Eine soziale Wanderung," *Die Furche*, 20–22 December 1909. Reprinted in Kurt Eisner, *Gesammelte Schriften*, 2:70–85.

[15] SAPMO-BArch, NY 4060/77/402.

[16] *A-F* 1.1a (January 1910); SAPMO-BArch, NY 4060/51.

[17] SAPMO-BArch, NY 4060/78/1.

[18] SAPMO-BArch, NY 4060/78/3.

[19] [Kurt Eisner], "Bennigsen: Die Tragikomödie des deutschen Liberalismus," *A-F* 1.2 (January 1910); SAPMO-BArch NY 4060/51. The ten-part article, which appeared in *Die Furche* 18–19 January; 14, 21–22 April; 3, 6, 25 May; 6–7 June 1910, is reprinted in its entirety in Kurt Eisner, *Gesammelte Schriften*, 1:342–405.

[20] Kurt Eisner, "Die Tragikomödie des deutschen Liberalismus," in *Gesammelte Schriften*, 1:342–343.

[21] Ibid., 345–346.

[22] See Pinson, *Modern Germany*, 104.

[23] Kurt Eisner, "Die Tragikomödie des deutschen Liberalismus," 1:362.

[24] Ibid., 364.

[25] Ibid., 374.

[26] Ibid., 380–381.

[27] Pinson, *Modern Germany*, 207; Craig, *Germany, 1866–1945*, 95.

[28] Kurt Eisner, "Die Tragikomödie des deutschen Liberalismus," 1:395–396.

[29] Ibid., 387.

[30] See Ernst Feise and Harry Steinhauer, eds., *German Literature since Goethe* (Boston: Houghton Mifflin, 1958), 9.

[31] Kurt Eisner, "Die Tragikomödie des deutschen Liberalismus," 1:389.

[32] SAPMO-BArch, NY 4060/78/24.

[33] SAPMO-BArch, NY 4060/78/17.

[34] SAPMO-BArch, NY 4060/78/24.

[35] SAPMO-BArch, NY 4060/72/41.

[36] SAPMO-BArch, NY 4060/78/29.

[37] SAPMO-BArch, NY 4060/78/36.

[38] SAPMO-BArch, NY 4060/78/41.

[39] SAPMO-BArch, NY 4060/60/46.

[40] SAPMO-BArch, NY 4060/78/41.

[41] "Bebels Geburtstag: Bebel-Feier in der Parteischule," *FT*, 24 February 1910.

[42] Kesr [Kurt Eisner], "Kleine Märchen vom Tage," *A-F* 1.3 (February 1910); SAPMO-BArch, NY 4060/51. Reprinted in part as "Anekdoten vom Tage," in Kurt Eisner, *Gesammelte Schriften*, 1:406–410.

[43] SAPMO-BArch, NY 4060/78/43.

[44] SAPMO-BArch, NY 4060/15.2/15.

[45] SAPMO-BArch, NY 4060/78/58.

[46] "August Bebel," *FT*, 21 February 1910.

[47] SAPMO-BArch, NY 4060/78/58.

[48] SAPMO-BArch, NY 4060/78/65.

[49] SAPMO-BArch, NY 4060/60/59.

[50] SAPMO-BArch, NY 4060/60/60.

[51] BArch-Koblenz, N 1190 (Nachlaß Südekum)/8/1.

[52] SAPMO-BArch, NY 4060/78/83, 89.

53 Quoted in Grau, *Kurt Eisner 1867–1919*, 231, 243.

54 "Die Märzfeier der Nürnberger Arbeiterschaft," *FT*, 17 March 1910.

55 SAPMO-BArch, NY 4060/60/142.

56 SAPMO-BArch, NY 4060/78/89.

57 BArch-Koblenz, N 1190/8/1.

58 Zero [Kurt Eisner], "Auferstehung," *A-F* 1.4 (March 1910); SAPMO-BArch, NY 4060/51. The German:

> Ein Falter flattert hell auf gelben Schwingen,
> In allen Höhen tönt ein suchend Singen.
> Die Ferne quillt in meine durstge Seele.

59 SAPMO-BArch, NY 4060/78/94.

60 SAPMO-BArch, NY 4060/66/81.

61 SAPMO-BArch, NY 4060/78/89, 94.

62 SAPMO-BArch, NY 4060/78/97. For an appreciation of Wilhelm Herzberg see Rückel, *Die Fränkische Tagespost*, 46.

63 SAPMO-BArch, NY 4060/78/119.

64 SAPMO-BArch, NY 4060/78/89, 127.

65 "Die Kultur der Arbeiterbewegung," *FT*, 30 April, 4 May 1910.

66 BArch-Koblenz, N 1190/8/1.

67 SAPMO-BArch, NY 4060/78/156.

68 SAPMO-BArch, NY 4060/72/42.

69 SAPMO-BArch, NY 4060/78/162.

70 SAPMO-BArch, NY 4060/78/164.

71 SAPMO-BArch, NY 4060/60/111.

Chapter Fifteen

1 SAPMO-BArch, NY 4060 (Nachlaß Kurt Eisner)/78/172.

2 BArch-Koblenz, N 1190 (Nachlaß Südekum)/8/1.

3 "Rücktritt von den Reichstagskandidaturen," *FT*, 8 August 1910.

4 Grau, *Kurt Eisner 1867–1919*, 236.

5 SAPMO-BArch, NY 4060/51/38.

6 Quoted in Freya Eisner, introduction to Kurt Eisner, *Zwischen Kapitalismus und Kommunismus*, 106.

7 BArch-Koblenz, R 117 (*Sozialistische Monatshefte* 1894–1911)/4/271.

8 SAPMO-BArch, NY 4060/78/166.

9 Kurt Eisner to Heinrich Braun, 17 July 1910, and Heinrich Braun to Kurt Eisner, 22 October 1911, LBI-NY, Julie Braun-Vogelstein Collection. See also Kurt Eisner to Joseph Bloch, 22 November 1910, BArch-Koblenz R 117/4/267. Braun's wife, Lily von Kretschmann Gizycki Braun, had a geneaological link to Napoleon. Her grandmother Jenny von Gustedt was the extramarital child of Napoleon's brother Jérôme Bonaparte and Diana von Pappenheim.

10 SAPMO-BArch, NY 4060/78/166.

11 [Kurt Eisner], "Die preußische Heilige: Zum hundertjährigen Todestag der Königin Luise," *A-F* 1.17/18 (July 1910); SAPMO-BArch NY 4060/51. Reprinted as "Luise: Eine Heiligengeschichte aus dem 19. Jahrhundert," in Kurt Eisner, *Gesammelte Schriften*, 1:411–420.

12 E. B., "Die unanständige Welt"; —t —r, "Das Besitzrecht am Menschen: Zur Stuttgarter Künstlertragödie," *A-F* 1.17/18 (July 1910); SAPMO-BArch, NY 4060/51.

13 K. E., "Ernst Màtrays Tanzpantomimen," *MP*, 10 August 1910.

14 "Der Zölibat," *A-F* 1.21 (August 1910); SAPMO-BArch, NY 4060/51.

15 "Kleines Feuilleton," *A-F* 1.23 (August 1910); SAPMO-BArch, NY 4060/51.

16 E. B., "Das Reich der Stummen," *A-F* 1.21 (August 1910); SAPMO-BArch, NY 4060/51.

17 Kurt Eisner, "Kopenhagen," in *Gesammelte Schriften*, 2:141–149. See also e. [Kurt Eisner], "Kopenhagener Stimmungen," *MP*, 3–4, 7–8 September 1910.

18 SAPMO-BArch, NY 4060/78/174.

19 SAPMO-BArch, NY 4060/78/179.

20 Kesr [Kurt Eisner], "Madgeburger Sauerkraut," *A-F* 1.24/25 (September 1910); SAPMO-Barch, NY 4060/51. Printed in the *MP*, 18/19 September 1910.

21 Karl Heinrich Pohl, *Adolf Müller: Geheimagent und Gesandter in Kaiserreich und Weimarer Republik* (Cologne: Bund-Verlag, 1995), 86.

22 Pohl, *Die Münchener Arbeiterbewegung*, 404–407.

23 Freya Eisner, *Kurt Eisner: Die Politik des libertären Sozialismus*, 56–57.

24 Pohl, *Adolf Müller*, 103.

25 Ibid., 121.

26 Pohl, *Münchener Arbeiterbewegung*, 370–371.

27 Ibid., 405.

28 Pohl, *Adolf Müller*, 85.

29 LBI-NY, Julie Braun-Vogelstein Collection.

30 Kurt Eisner to Heinrich Braun, 17 October 1910, LBI-NY, Julie Braun-Vogelstein Collection. The planned volume appears never to have come to print.

31 [Kurt Eisner], "Die Gründung der Universität Berlin: Zur Jahrhundertfeier (9. Oktober)," *A-F* 1.28 (October 1910); SAPMO-BArch, NY 4060/51.

32 [Kurt Eisner], "Arbeit und Tuberkulose," *A-F* 1.29 (October 1910); K. E., "Evangelium Tolstoi," 1.35 (November 1910); SAPMO-BArch, NY 4060/51.

33 "Die Ausdehnung amerikanischer Städte," *A-F* 1.35 (November 1910); SAPMO-BArch, NY 4060/51.

34 [Kurt Eisner], "Zentrumstaktik," *MP*, 4 November 1910.

35 K. E., "Schule Gladbach," *MP*, 4/5 December 1910.

36 BArch-Koblenz, R 117/4/259.

37 BArch-Koblenz, R 117/4/260.2.

38 BArch-Koblenz, R 117/4/261.

39 BArch-Koblenz, R 117/4/263.

40 Kurt Eisner, "Der Dramatiker der Revolution," *SM* 15.4 (February 1911): 246–253. "Marie-Joseph Chénier: Zum 100. Todestag des Dichters der Revolution," *A-F* 2.1 (January 1911); SAPMO-BArch, NY 4060/52. Reprinted in part in Kurt Eisner, *Gesammelte Schriften* 2:304–309.

41 Ke. [Else Belli], "Der Kinematograph in der Schule," *Die Furche*, 31 December 1910.

42 Kurt Eisner [Else Belli], "Die rosarothe Watte," *New Yorker Volkszeitung*, 16 January 1911; SAPMO-BArch, NY 4060/96/18.

43 SAPMO-BArch, NY 4060/1/119.

44 SAPMO-BArch, NY 4060/78/89.

45 SAPMO-BArch, NY 4060/78/183, 191.

46 SAPMO-BArch, NY 4060/78/191.

47 K. E., "Ehe: Zum 'Grenzfall' Herberich," *A-F* 2.4 (January 1911); SAPMO-BArch, NY 4060/52.

48 Hugo Friedländer, *Interessante Kriminal-Prozesse von kulturhistorischer Bedeutung: Darstellung merkwürdiger Strafrechtsfälle aus Gegenwart und Jüngstvergangenheit*, vol. 5 (Berlin: Hermann Barsdorf, 1912), 164–166.

49 Venturus [Kurt Eisner], "Die Meineidslinde von Essen," *Pan* 1.8 (February 1911): 258–260. Reprinted in Kurt Eisner, *Gesammelte Schriften*, 1:421–424.

[50] See the unsigned two-part review "Aus den jungen Tagen der Sozialdemokratie," *MP*, 2–3 July 1912.

[51] K. E., "Die Politik des Unmöglichen," *MP*, 24 March 1911.

[52] LBI-NY, Julie Braun-Vogelstein Collection.

[53] K. E., "Lily Brauns *Kampfjahre*," *MP*, 19 May 1911.

[54] Heinrich Braun to Kurt Eisner, 30 August 1911, LBI-NY, Julie Braun-Vogelstein Collection.

[55] ke., "Nach 25 Jahren," *MP*, 20, 22, 27, 29 June, 6, 11 July 1911.

[56] Kurt Eisner, "Die hohen Stühle," in *Gesammelte Schriften*, 1:481–493.

[57] Craig, *Germany, 1866–1945*, 328–329.

[58] "Eine deutsche Marokko-Aktion," *MP*, 4 July 1911.

[59] "Die Besetzung von Agadir: Warum wurde der Landtag heimgeschickt?" *MP*, 5 July 1911.

[60] "Die deutsche Marokko-Aktion: Jaurès zur Marokkofrage," *MP*, 8 July 1911.

[61] ke., "Marokko-Blödsinn," *MP*, 30/31 July 1911. Reprinted as "Aus der Panther-Zeit: Sus—die deutsche Existenzfrage," in Kurt Eisner, *Gesammelte Schriften*, 1:467–468.

[62] Kesr [Kurt Eisner], "Diplomatische Verständigungen," *MP*, 8 August 1911.

[63] "Gegen das Marokko-Abenteuer!" *MP*, 10 August 1911.

[64] "Der Friede in Gefahr!" *MP*, 12 August 1911.

[65] Kurt Eisner, "Meinungsbetrieb," *Pan* 1.20 (August 1911): 647–652. Reprinted in Kurt Eisner, *Gesammelte Schriften*, 1:437–443.

[66] SAPMO-BArch, NY 4060/21/82.

[67] Kurt Eisner, "Jonathan Swift," *SM* 15.18–20 (September 1911): 1234–1242. Reprinted in Kurt Eisner, *Gesammelte Schriften*, 2:288–303.

[68] Kurt Eisner, "Aus der Panther-Zeit: Innere und äußere Kolonisation," in *Gesammelte Schriften* 1:468–474. See also "Marokko als Wahlparole," *MP*, 26 August 1911; "Das Märchen von Sus," 27/28 August 1911; "Konfusion," 3/4 September 1911; "Innere und äußere Kolonisation," 24 October 1911.

[69] SAPMO-BArch, NY 4060/78/186.

[70] SAPMO-BArch, NY 4060/78/188.

[71] Kurt Eisner to Heinrich Braun, 30 September 1911, LBI-NY, Julie Braun-Vogelstein Collection.

[72] Ke., "Bebels Erinnerungen: Der zweite Band," *MP*, 3–4 October 1911.

73 [Kurt Eisner,] "Tam Tam," *MP*, 5 October 1911. Reprinted as "Aus der Panther-Zeit: Frankreichs Friedensbürgschaft," in Kurt Eisner, *Gesammelte Schriften*, 1:474–476.

74 Kurt Eisner, "Was nun?" in *Gesammelte Schriften*, 1:476–480. See also "Das Märchen ist aus!" *MP*, 1 December 1911; "Weltkrieg oder Abrüstung," 5 December 1911.

75 Kurt Eisner, "Meinungsbetrieb," 1:443.

76 Kurt Eisner, "Das Preußentum Heinrich Kleists: Zum Gedächtnistage seines Untergangs," *MP*, 22–23 November 1911. Reprinted in Kurt Eisner, *Gesammelte Schriften*, 2:259–271.

Chapter Sixteen

1 "Gau Südbayern: Öffentliche Wählerversammlungen finden statt," *MP*, 5 January 1912.

2 "Die letzten Reichstagswählerversammlungen," *MP*, 12 January 1912.

3 [Kurt Eisner], "Das Volksgericht," *MP*, 14/15 January 1912.

4 K. E., "Patrioten," *MP*, 17 January 1912.

5 [Kurt Eisner], "Die Sozialdemokratie und die auswärtige Politik," *MP*, 23 January 1912.

6 Pohl, *Die Münchener Arbeiterbewegung*, 488; Fricke, *Handbuch zur Geschichte der deutschen Arbeiterbewegung*, 2:722–735, 758–760. See also Wilhelm Heinz Schröder, *Sozialdemokratische Parlamentarier in den deutschen Reichs- und Landtagen 1867–1933: Biographien—Chronik—Wahldokumentation*, Handbücher zur Geschichte des Parlamentarismus und der politischen Parteien 7 (Düsseldorf: Droste, 1995), 496, 794–795.

7 Pohl, *Adolf Müller*, 103–105.

8 K. E., "Charles Dickens: Geboren am 7. Februar 1812," *MP*, 8–9 February 1912.

9 SAPMO-BArch, NY 4060 (Nachlaß Kurt Eisner)/78/202.

10 SAPMO-BArch, NY 4060/65/50.

11 [Kurt Eisner], "Das rote Blatt," *A-F* 3.9/10 (April 1912); SAPMO-BArch, NY 4060/53.

12 Kurt Eisner, "Der Philosoph des sozialen Enthusiasmus: Zu Fichtes 150. Geburtstag," *SM* 16.10 (May 1912): 611–621.

13 K. E., "Rousseau," *MP*, 29 June 1912.

14 Eisner, "Hermann Cohen."

15 Kurt Eisner, "Der Zufall des Dramas," *MP*, 14 July 1912. Reprinted in *Freie Volksbühne: Zum neuen Spieljahr 1912/13*, 27–29.

16 Ke., "*Oaha*: Eine Schriftstellerkatastrophe," *MP*, 9 August 1912.

17 SAPMO-BArch, NY 4060/78/206.

18 SAPMO-BArch, NY 4060/78/210.

19 Kurt Eisner, "Der Untergang der großen Armee: Der Krieg von 1812," *A-F* 3.21 (July 1912); SAPMO-BArch, NY 4060/53.

20 SAPMO-BArch, NY 4060/78/210.

21 SAPMO-BArch, NY 4060/78/208.

22 K. E., "Wilhelm Grimm: *Märchen*," *A-F* 3.29/30 (October 1912); SAPMO-BArch, NY 4060/53.

23 SAPMO-BArch, NY 4060/78/220.

24 SAPMO-BArch, NY 4060/78/225; 4060/15.1/133.

25 SAPMO-BArch, NY 4060/78/225.

26 *A-F* 3.33/34 (December 1912); SAPMO-BArch, NY 4060/53.

27 "Parteitag der preußischen Sozialdemokratie," *MP*, 8–9 January 1913; *Protokoll über die Verhandlungen des Parteitages der Sozialdemokratischen Partei Preußens 1913* (Berlin: Buchhandlung Vorwärts, 1913), 246–266.

28 Houyhnhnm [Kurt Eisner], "Professor Hertling," *März: Eine Wochenschrift* 7.1 (January–March 1913): 58–62. Reprinted as "Hertling," in Kurt Eisner, *Gesammelte Schriften*, 1:494–502.

29 K. E., "Die Verstaatlichung der Köpfe," *März* 7.1 (January–March 1913): 82–83. For Frick's curriculum vitae see Matthias Lau, *Pressepolitik als Chance: Staatliche Öffentlichkeitsarbeit in den Ländern der Weimarer Republik*, Beiträge zur Kommunikationsgeschichte 14 (Stuttgart: Franz Steiner, 2003), 65n174.

30 * * * [Kurt Eisner], "Ein Militärprogramm der Linken," *März* 7.1 (January–March 1913): 235–240.

31 Kurt Eisner, "Mein Gefängnistagebuch: Neudeck, 5. 2. 1918," *M* 4 (27 January 1928): 27; *M* 5 (3 February 1928): 38. Reprinted in "Januarstreik 1918," in Kurt Eisner, *Sozialismus als Aktion*, 63–72.

32 SAPMO-BArch, NY 4060/66/141.

33 Wilhelm Herzog, *Menschen, denen ich begegnete* (Bern: Francke, 1959), 55–56.

34 Hausenstein, "Erinnerung an Eisner," 63.

35 Kurt Eisner, "Die neue Lehre von Bethlehem," *Die Neue Rundschau* 24.1 (1913): 593–602; "Taylorismus," 24.2 (1913): 1448–1453.

[36] Kurt Eisner, "Karl Marx' Kunstauffassung," *A-F* 4.8 (March 1913); SAPMO-BArch, NY 4060/54. Reprinted in Kurt Eisner, *Gesammelte Schriften*, 2:272–278.

[37] SAPMO-BArch, NY 4060/65/59.

[38] K. E., "*Leonce und Lena*: Von Georg Büchner," *MP*, 5 June 1913.

[39] ke., "Gastspiel der Düsseldorfer," *MP*, 8 June 1913.

[40] K. E., "Tschechows *Onkel Wanja*," *MP*, 17 June 1913.

[41] SAPMO-BArch, NY 4060/70/62.

[42] CJA 6.4 (Nachlaß Freia Eisner)/9/31.

[43] Quoted in Freya Eisner, introduction to Kurt Eisner, *Zwischen Kapitalismus und Kommunismus*, 107.

[44] SAPMO-BArch, NY 4060/62/1.

[45] Kurt Eisner, "Marx und Bakunin," *A-F* 4.26–27 (August 1913); SAPMO-BArch, NY 4060/54.

[46] Quoted in Nettl, *Rosa Luxemburg*, 2:468.

[47] SAPMO-BArch, NY 4060/67/87.

[48] "Zur Nachricht!" *A-F* 4.28 (August 1913); SAPMO-BArch, NY 4060/54.

[49] Kurt Eisner, "Shelley," *SM* 17.18–20 (September 1913): 1173–1180.

[50] Kurt Eisner, "Arno Holz: *Ignorabimus*, ein Weckruf," *A-F* 4.29 (September 1913); SAPMO-BArch, NY 4060/54. Printed in the *MP*, 21, 23 September 1913. Reprinted in Kurt Eisner, *Gesammelte Schriften*, 2:279–287.

[51] SAPMO-BArch, NY 4060/78/235, 273.

[52] SAPMO-BArch, NY 4060/65/70.

[53] "Militarismus und Armee," *MP*, 1 July 1913.

[54] Pinson, *Modern Germany*, 288–289; David Schoenbaum, *Zabern 1913: Consensus Politics in Imperial Germany* (London: Allen & Unwin, 1982), 95–114.

Chapter Seventeen

[1] Kurt Eisner, "Die Kabinettsorder von 1820: Ein deutsches Sittenbild aus dem 20. Jahrhundert," *MP*, 15–16 January 1914. Reprinted in Kurt Eisner, *Gesammelte Schriften*, 1:509–520.

[2] Hausenstein, "Erinnerung an Eisner," 63.

[3] K. E., "*Rösselsprung* von Karl Rößler: Uraufführung im Schauspielhaus," *MP*, 20 January 1914.

[4] K. E., "*Das vierte Gebot*: Erstaufführung im Residenztheater," *MP*, 21 January 1914.

[5] K. E., "*Die Wölfe* von Romain Rolland: Deutsche Uraufführung in den Kammerspielen," *MP*, 6–7 March 1914.

[6] SAPMO-BArch, NY 4060 (Nachlaß Kurt Eisner)/66/109.

[7] Quoted in Keegan, *The First World War*, 17.

[8] "Öffentliche Volksversammlung," *MP*, 22 March 1914.

[9] Kurt Eisner, "Preßprobleme," in *Gesammelte Schriften*, 1:444–462.

[10] BArch-Koblenz, N 1190 (Nachlaß Südekum)/101.1/76–77; 1190/103/3.

[11] K. E., "*Herodes und Mariamne*: Osterfestspiele in den Kammerspielen," *MP*, 19 April 1914.

[12] SAPMO-BArch, NY 4060/15.2/55. The German:

> . . . im Dunst
> Düstrer Sorgen
> Singend ist heut
> Der Freiheit Morgen.

[13] Keegan, *The First World War*, 48.

[14] "Untergang des Thronfolgers," *MP*, 30 June 1914.

[15] "Die Katastrophe des Hauses Habsburg," *MP*, 1 July 1914.

[16] David Fromkin, *Europe's Last Summer: Who Started the Great War in 1914?* (New York: Knopf, 2004), 156; Keegan, *The First World War*, 53–54.

[17] "Ein Ultimatum an Serbien?" *MP*, 23 July 1914.

[18] "Will Österreich Serbien zum Kriege zwingen?" *MP*, 25 July 1914.

[19] "Vor der Kriegserklärung: Ein Aufruf des Berliner Parteivorstandes," *MP*, 26/27 July 1914.

[20] "Der Krieg in München," *MP*, 28 July 1914.

[21] Keegan, *The First World War*, 57–58.

[22] "Friedenskundgebung!" *MP*, 28 July 1914.

[23] Fechenbach, *Der Revolutionär Kurt Eisner*, 10–11; "Für Freiheit und Völkerfrieden," *MP*, 29 July 1914; "An die Bevölkerung Münchens!" 26/27 July 1914.

[24] Kurt Eisner, "Mein Gefängnistagebuch: Am Neudeck, 1. 3. 18," *M* 7 (17 February 1928): 57; *M* 9 (2 March 1928): 76. SAPMO-BArch, NY 4060/23.2/17. "Für Kultur und Völkerfrieden," "Für Freiheit und Völkerfrieden," *MP*, 29 July 1914.

25 Kurt Eisner, "Die Mobilmachung als Kriegsursache und Anderes," in *Unterdrücktes aus dem Weltkrieg* (Munich: Georg Müller Verlag, 1919), 19.

26 "Für Kultur und Völkerfrieden."

27 "Für Freiheit und Völkerfrieden."

28 Kurt Eisner, "Krieg! Drei Szenen," *A-F* 5.26 (July 1914); SAPMO-BArch, NY 4060/55. Reprinted in Kurt Eisner, *Gesammelte Schriften*, 1:9–14. See Fechenbach, *Der Revolutionär Kurt Eisner*, 10.

29 Fromkin, *Europe's Last Summer*, 217–220; Fritz Fischer, *Germany's Aims in the First World War* (New York: Norton, 1967), 71–74, 85–86; Michael Duffy, "Primary Documents: Austria-Hungary's Declaration of War with Serbia, 28 July 1914," firstworldwar.com, 22 August 2009, www.firstworldwar.com/source/autrohungariandeclarationofwar_serbia.htm.

30 Kurt Eisner, "Mein Gefängnistagebuch: Am Neudeck, 1. 3. 18," 76; SAPMO-BArch, NY 4060/23.2/6.

31 Keegan, *The First World War*, 62; Schorske, *German Social Democracy, 1905–1917*, 288–289.

32 See Scheidemann, *Memoiren eines Sozialdemokraten*, 1:238–242.

33 Schorske, *German Social Democracy, 1905–1917*, 287.

34 "Jaurès assassiné," *L'Humanité*, 1 August 1914. See Scheidemann, *Memoiren eines Sozialdemokraten*, 1:247–248; Susanne Miller, *Burgfrieden und Klassenkampf: Die deutsche Sozialdemokratie im Ersten Weltkrieg*, Beiträge zur Geschichte des Parlamentarismus und der politischen Parteien 53 (Düsseldorf: Droste, 1974), 52–53.

35 Kurt Eisner, "Kopenhagen: Nachschrift," 2:148.

36 *Von den Ursachen des Krieges bis etwa zum Schluß des Jahres 1914*, vol. 1 of *Kriegs-Rundschau: Zeitgenössische Zusammenstellung der für den Weltkrieg wichtigen Ereignisse, Urkunden, Kundgebungen, Schlacht- und Zeitberichte* (Berlin: Verlag der Täglichen Rundschau: 1915), 43.

37 Schorske, *German Social Democracy, 1905–1917*, 289.

38 Scheidemann, *Memoiren eines Sozialdemokraten*, 1:248–249; Miller, *Burgfrieden und Klassenkampf*, 55–56.

39 Miller, *Burgfrieden und Klassenkampf*, 59.

40 Fechenbach, *Der Revolutionär Kurt Eisner*, 14. In the 24 June 1916 edition of the *Arbeiter-Feuilleton* Eisner exposed the alleged bombing as a calculated lie of the Imperial German government to cloak its indubitable war guilt. Hitler would stage an attack by Poland to justify the Nazi invasion on 1 September 1939. See William L. Shirer, *The Rise and Fall of the Third Reich: A History of Nazi Germany* (New York: Simon and Schuster, 1960), 518–520, 594–595.

[41] Scheidemann, *Memoiren eines Sozialdemokraten*, 1:258; Keegan, *The First World War*, 69, 81.

[42] "Ein Opfer des Chauvinismus: Jaurès ermordet!" *MP*, 2/3 August 1914.

[43] [Kurt Eisner], "Jean Jaurès †," *MP*, 4 August 1914. Reprinted in part as "Jaurès," in Kurt Eisner, *Gesammelte Schriften*, 1:15–20.

[44] Kurt Eisner, "Jaurès: Nachtrag, Stadelheim 1918," in *Gesammelte Schriften*, 1:19–20; Kurt Eisner, "Mein Gefängnistagebuch: Neudeck, 5. 2. 1918," *M 4* (27 January 1928): 38.

[45] Nettl, *Rosa Luxemburg*, 2:610.

[46] Freya Eisner, introduction to Kurt Eisner, *Zwischen Kapitalismus und Kommunismus*, 109.

[47] Kurt Eisner, "Mein Gefängnistagebuch: Neudeck, 5. 2. 1918," 38.

[48] Fricke, *Handbuch zur Geschichte der deutschen Arbeiterbewegung*, 1:644; Luxemburg, in Kurt Eisner, *Gesammelte Briefe*, 5:467, 471, 472, 477.

[49] Quoted in Eugen Prager, *Das Gebot der Stunde: Geschichte der USPD*, 4th ed. (Berlin: J. H. W. Dietz, 1980), 31.

[50] Kurt Eisner, "Das Verhängnis Europas," "Weltgeschichte von Jean Jaurès," *A-F* 5.27/28 (August 1914); SAPMO-BArch, NY 4060/55.

[51] SAPMO-BArch, NY 4060/66/69.

[52] SAPMO-BArch, NY 4060/102/525.

[53] K. E., "*Zopf und Schwert*," *MP*, 26 August 1914.

[54] Kurt Eisner, "Mein Gefängnistagebuch: Neudeck, 5. 2. 1918," 38; Hermann Müller, *Die November-Revolution: Erinnerungen* (Berlin: Der Bücherkreis, 1928), 156.

[55] Kurt Eisner, "Mein Gefängnistagebuch: Neudeck, 5. 2. 1918," 38.

[56] Kurt Eisner, "Presse," *Neue Zeitung: Unabhängiges sozialistisches Organ*, 20 December 1918. Reprinted in Kurt Eisner, *Sozialismus als Aktion*, 97–101.

[57] Keegan, *The First World War*, 150.

[58] SAPMO-BArch, NY 4060/78/247.

[59] Ibid.; *Protokolle der Sitzungen des Parteiausschusses der SPD 1912 bis 1921*, Reprints zur Sozialgeschichte, ed. Dieter Dowe, 2 vols. (Berlin: J. H. W. Dietz, 1980), 1:83–84.

[60] SAPMO-BArch, NY 4060/78/247.

[61] Pohl, *Adolf Müller*, 133–134.

[62] See Herzog, *Menschen, denen ich begegnete*, 56.

[63] K. E., "*Grüne Ostern* von Heinrich Lee: Kammerspiele," *MP*, 8 October 1914.

64 SAPMO-BArch, NY 4060/65/74.

65 Kurt Eisner, "Völkerrecht," *Der Neue Merkur* 1.2 (October 1914–March 1915): 225–236; "Volkswehr im Völkerrecht," 479–489. Reprinted as "Völkerrecht: Einige Anmerkungen," in Kurt Eisner, *Gesammelte Schriften*, 1:21–51.

66 "Herr Georg Weill," *MP*, 24 December 1914.

67 SAPMO-BArch, NY 4060/67/163.

68 K. E., "Weihnachtsfeier der Kammerpiele," *MP*, 25 December 1914.

Chapter Eighteen

1 K. E., "*Viel Lärmen* [*sic*] *um Nichts*: Residenztheater," *MP*, 1 January 1915.

2 "Zeitungsverbot," *MP*, 15 January 1915.

3 K. E., "*Der letzte Kuß*: Uraufführung im Schauspielhaus," *MP*, 16 January 1915; Karl Kraus, "In dieser großen Zeit," in *1914–1925: In dieser großen Zeit*, vol. 2 of *Ausgewählte Werke*, ed. Dietrich Simon (Berlin: [Verlag Volk und Welt], [1971]), 9–22.

4 "Gegen Täuschungsversuche der ausländischen Genossen," *MP*, 21 January 1915.

5 Grau, *Kurt Eisner 1867–1919*, 311–312.

6 Kurt Eisner, "Die Zensur," *Chemnitzer Volksstimme*, 29 January 1915.

7 Quoted in Grau, *Kurt Eisner 1867–1919*, 561n39.

8 Wolfgang Heine, *Gegen die Quertreiber!* (Dessau: Verlag Volksblatt für Anhalt, [1915]).

9 Kurt Eisner, "Brief an Wolfgang Heine (11. Februar 1915)," in *Die halbe Macht*, 253–259.

10 Luxemburg, *Gesammelte Briefe*, 5:19n.

11 Kurt Eisner, "Zur Psychologie des Weltkriegs," *A-F* 6.5/6 (February 1915); SAPMO-BArch, NY 4060 (Nachlaß Kurt Eisner)/56.

12 [Kurt Eisner], "Karl Marx' nationale Auffassungen: Eine geschichtliche Betrachtung zum 18. März," *A-F* 6.9 (March 1915); SAPMO-BArch, NY 4060/56.

13 Kurt Eisner, "Die Neunte: Das Werk der Zeit," *A-F* 6.10 (March 1915); SAPMO-BArch, NY 4060/56. Reprinted in Kurt Eisner, *Gesammelte Schriften*, 1:69–74.

14 K. E., "Kleist 1914," *MP*, 2 February 1915.

15 K. E., "Schildkraut als Lear: Volkstheater," *MP*, 14 March 1915.

16 *Protokolle der Sitzungen des Parteiausschusses der SPD 1912 bis 1921*, 1:68–72.

17 Kurt Eisner, "Treibende Kräfte," *NZ* 33.2 (1914–1915): 97–106.

18 Kurt Eisner, *Treibende Kräfte*, Flugschriften des Bundes Neues Vaterland 4, 2nd ed. (Berlin: Verlag Neues Vaterland, 1915).

19 Karl Bücher, *Unsere Sache und die Tagespresse* (Tübingen: J. C. B. Mohr, 1915).

20 Kurt Eisner, "Die Presse im Krieg," in *Gesammelte Schriften*, 1:106–115.

21 SAPMO-BArch, NY 4060/21/24.

22 Kurt Eisner, "Aus Tagheften 1914–1918: Humor und Idylle," in *Gesammelte Schriften*, 1:182–184.

23 [Kurt Eisner], "Die Schwierigkeiten des Komparativs," *A-F* 5.37 (October 1914); SAPMO-BArch, NY 4060/55. Reprinted in "Aus Tagheften 1914–1918," in Kurt Eisner, *Gesammelte Schriften*, 1:190–192.

24 SAPMO-BArch, NY 4060/78/254.

25 SAPMO-BArch, NY 4060/78/258.

26 SAPMO-BArch, NY 4060/78/261.

27 SAPMO-BArch, NY 4060/78/258, 268.

28 SAPMO-BArch, NY 4060/78/268.

29 Fechenbach, *Der Revolutionär Kurt Eisner*, 13.

30 IISG, Karl Kautsky, DX/160.

31 Kurt Eisner, "Hus: Ein halbes Jahrtausend nach seinem Feuertod," *A-F* 6.24 (July 1915); SAPMO-BArch, NY 4060/56. Reprinted in Kurt Eisner, *Gesammelte Schriften*, 1:123–130.

32 K. E., "Strindberg-Abend der Kammerspiele: *Gläubiger*, *Mit dem Feuer spielen*," *MP*, 8 December 1914.

33 K. E., "Strindbergs *Scheiterhaufen*: Erstaufführung der Kammerspiele," *MP*, 12 February 1915. Reprinted as "Strindberg nach der Höllenfahrt I," in Kurt Eisner, *Gesammelte Schriften*, 2:327–330.

34 K. E., "*Gespenstersonate*: Uraufführung im Strindberg-Zyklus der Kammerspiele," *MP*, 4 May 1915. Reprinted as "Strindberg nach der Höllenfahrt III," in Kurt Eisner, *Gesammelte Schriften*, 2:334–339.

35 IISG, Karl Kautsky, DX/161.

36 SAPMO-BArch, NY 4060/65/147.

37 "Aus dem Gefängnis zum Militär," *MP*, 3 September 1915.

38 Fricke, *Handbuch zur Geschichte der deutschen Arbeiterbewegung*, 1:634.

[39] "Aus der Haft entlassen," *MP*, 14 October 1915; Luxemburg, *Gesammelte Briefe*, 5:67n82.

[40] SAPMO-BArch, NY 4060/79/1.

[41] IISG, Karl Kautsky, DX/162.

[42] [Kurt Eisner], "Die diplomatischen Kriegsurkunden I–II," *A-F* 6.37 (December 1915); SAPMO-BArch, NY 4060/56.

[43] [Kurt Eisner], "Die diplomatischen Kriegsurkunden III," *A-F* 6.38 (December 1915); SAPMO-BArch, NY 4060/56.

[44] Fricke, *Handbuch zur Geschichte der deutschen Arbeiterbewegung*, 2:785–788; Prager, *Das Gebot der Stunde*, 77.

[45] *Verhandlungen des Reichstags: 13. Legislaturperiode, 2. Session*, vol. 306 (4 August 1914–16 March 1916), 506–508.

[46] K. E., "Strindbergs *Advent*: Uraufführung in den Münchener Kammerspielen," *MP*, 1 January 1916. Reprinted as "Strindberg nach der Höllenfahrt VI," in Kurt Eisner, *Gesammelte Schriften*, 2:343–350.

[47] Kurt Eisner, "Zusammenbruch! Ein Jahrwendgespräch," *A-F* 6.39 (December 1915); SAPMO-BArch, NY 4060/56. Reprinted in Kurt Eisner, *Gesammelte Schriften*, 1:145–154.

[48] Fricke, *Handbuch zur Geschichte der deutschen Arbeiterbewegung*, 1:615, 641; Freya Eisner, introduction to Kurt Eisner, *Zwischen Kapitalismus und Kommunismus*, 115.

[49] Fricke, *Handbuch zur Geschichte der deutschen Arbeiterbewegung*, 1:385; Nettl, *Rosa Luxemburg*, 2:639.

[50] Quoted in Fricke, *Handbuch zur Geschichte der deutschen Arbeiterbewegung*, 1:386–389.

[51] Ibid., 1:385–386, 625–627.

[52] IISG, Karl Kautsky, DX/163.

[53] Quoted in Fechenbach, *Der Revolutionär Kurt Eisner*, 14.

[54] Fricke, *Handbuch zur Geschichte der deutschen Arbeiterbewegung*, 2:788; Prager, *Das Gebot der Stunde*, 86.

[55] SAPMO-BArch, NY 4060/62/1.

[56] IISG, Karl Kautsky, DX/164.

[57] Peter-Christian Witt, *Friedrich Ebert: Parteiführer, Reichskanzler, Volksbeauftragter, Reichspräsident*, 4th ed. (Bonn: J. H. W. Dietz, 2008), 77–78.

[58] Fechenbach, *Der Revolutionär Kurt Eisner*, 15–16.

[59] SAPMO-BArch, NY 4060/79/10.

[60] SAPMO-BArch, NY 4060/67/75.

61 Quoted in Fricke, *Handbuch zur Geschichte der deutschen Arbeiterbewegung*, 1:389.

62 Ibid., 2:789.

63 *Verhandlungen des Reichstags: 13. Legislaturperiode, 2. Session*, vol. 307 (22 March–6 June 1916), 843–844.

64 Prager, *Das Gebot der Stunde*, 91–92; Fricke, *Handbuch zur Geschichte der deutschen Arbeiterbewegung*, 1:348–349.

Chapter Nineteen

1 Quoted in Hew Strachan, *The First World War* (New York: Viking, 2004), 215.

2 Ibid., 218–221.

3 Belinda J. Davis, *Home Fires Burning: Food, Politics, and Everyday Life in World War I Berlin* (Chapel Hill, NC: University of North Carolina Press, 2000), 80–88, 100.

4 Strachan, *The First World War*, 217, 218.

5 Davis, *Home Fires Burning*, 107–110, 132–133, 159–160.

6 Schorske, *German Social Democracy, 1905–1917*, 308–309.

7 K. E., "Die Lebenswinde," *A-F* 7.[1] (April 1916); SAPMO-BArch, NY 4060 (Nachlaß Kurt Eisner)/57. Reprinted in Kurt Eisner, *Gesammelte Schriften*, 1:155–158.

8 K. E., "Mensch-Ersatz-Würfel: Ein Triumph deutscher Wissenschaft," *A-F* 7.[2] (April 1916); SAPMO-BArch, NY 4060/57. Reprinted in Kurt Eisner, *Gesammelte Schriften*, 1:159–163.

9 Bert Becker, "Germany, Home Front," in *World War I Encyclopedia: A Political, Social, and Military History*, ed. Spencer C. Tucker and Priscilla Roberts, 5 vols. (Santa Barbara, CA: ABC CLIO, 2005), 2:478.

10 K. E., "Cervantes-Feier in München," *MP*, 2 May 1916.

11 "Bildungsausschuß des Gewerkschaftsvereins München," *MP*, 14 May 1916; "Strindbergs *Traumspiel*: Zur Vorlesung im Gewerkschaftshaus (15. Mai)," 13 May 1916; "Bildungsausschuß," 21 May 1916.

12 k. e., "Die Uraufführung von Strindbergs *Damaskus*-Trilogie," *MP*, 11 June 1916; Kurt Eisner, "Strindbergs *Damaskus*-Trilogie: Zur Münchener Uraufführung," *A-F* 7.[6] (June 1916); SAPMO-BArch, NY 4060/57.

13 [Kurt Eisner], "Kleines Feuilleton: Die Fliegerbomben von Nürnberg," *A-F* 7.[7] (June 1916); SAPMO-BArch, NY 4060/57.

14 Fechenbach, *Der Revolutionär Kurt Eisner*, 14.

[15] Ibid., 16.

[16] Luxemburg, *Gesammelte Briefe*, 5:126n95, 133n132.

[17] Nettl, *Rosa Luxemburg*, 2:649nn1–2.

[18] Prager, *Das Gebot der Stunde*, 103.

[19] Luxemburg, *Gesammelte Briefe*, 5:130n116; Nettl, *Rosa Luxemburg*, 2:651–652.

[20] Fricke, *Handbuch zur Geschichte der deutschen Arbeiterbewegung*, 1:393; Schorske, *German Social Democracy, 1905–1917*, 309–310.

[21] Kurt Eisner, "Für einen Kriegsparteitag," *V*, 20 July 1916.

[22] K. E., "Direktion Ziegel," *MP*, 3 September 1916.

[23] K. E., "*Antigone* in den Kammerspielen," *MP*, 13 September 1916.

[24] Fricke, *Handbuch zur Geschichte der deutschen Arbeiterbewegung*, 2:790.

[25] Schorske, *German Social Democracy, 1905–1917*, 309.

[26] Fricke, *Handbuch zur Geschichte der deutschen Arbeiterbewegung*, 2:790; Vorstand der Sozialdemokratischen Partei Deutschlands, *Protokoll der Reichskonferenz der Sozialdemokratie Deutschlands vom 21., 22. und 23. September 1916* (1916; reprint, Glashütten im Taunus: Detlev Auvermann, 1974), 12, 181.

[27] Freya Eisner, *Kurt Eisner: Die Politik des libertären Sozialismus*, 66.

[28] SAPMO-BArch, NY 4060/78/275.

[29] SAPMO-BArch, NY 4060/78/277.

[30] SAPMO-BArch, NY 4060/78/279.

[31] Herzog, *Menschen, denen ich begegnete*, 59.

[32] *Verhandlungen des Reichstags: 13. Legislaturperiode, 2. Session*, vol. 307 (22 March–6 June 1916), 1735–1741; Kurt Eisner, "Die Historien des Reichstagsabgeordneten David," in *Unterdrücktes aus dem Weltkrieg*, 63.

[33] Edward Grey, *Why Britain Is in the War and What She Hopes from the Future* (London: Unwin, [1916]), 5.

[34] Ralph Haswell Lutz, *Fall of the German Empire, 1914–1918*, trans. David G. Rempel and Gertrude Rendtorff, Hoover War Library Publications 1, 2 vols. (New York: Octagon Books, 1969), 1:35.

[35] Kurt Eisner, "Die Mobilmachung als Kriegsursache und Anderes," 7, 9, 39.

[36] Ibid., 10–11, 21–23.

[37] Ibid., 19.

[38] Ibid., 34–37, 50.

[39] Grau, *Kurt Eisner 1867–1919*, 317; Kurt Eisner, "Die Mobilmachung als Kriegsursache und Anderes," 52–53.

[40] Fechenbach, *Der Revolutionär Kurt Eisner*, 16–17; Schmolze and Schmolze, introduction to Kurt Eisner, *Die halbe Macht*, 33.

[41] Hausenstein, "Erinnerung an Eisner," 63.

[42] Fechenbach, *Der Revolutionär Kurt Eisner*, 14.

[43] Nettl, *Rosa Luxemburg*, 2:655; Freya Eisner, *Kurt Eisner: Die Politik des libertären Sozialismus*, 66.

[44] IISG, Karl Kautsky, DX/165.

[45] SAPMO-BArch, NY 4060/66/40.

[46] Emil Eichhorn, ed., *Protokoll über die Verhandlungen des Gründungs-Parteitages der USPD vom 6. bis 8. April 1917 in Gotha. Mit Anhang: Bericht über die Gemeinsame Konferenz der Arbeitsgemeinschaft und der Spartakusgruppe vom 7. Januar 1917 in Berlin* (Berlin: A. Seehof, 1921), in facsimile reprint *Protokolle der Parteitage der Unabhängigen Sozialdemokratischen Partei Deutschlands*, vol. 1, *1917–1919* (Glashütten im Taunus: Detlev Auvermann, 1975), 84. See Freya Eisner, *Kurt Eisner, Die Politik des libertären Sozialismus*, 224n1 for a caveat on Emil Eichhorn's selective stenography.

[47] *Protokolle der Parteitage der Unabhängigen Sozialdemokratischen Partei Deutschlands*, 1:85–92.

[48] Ibid., 92–94.

[49] Prager, *Das Gebot der Stunde*, 120–121.

[50] *Protokolle der Parteitage der Unabhängigen Sozialdemokratischen Partei Deutschlands*, 1:100–101.

[51] Ibid., 1:118–119; Prager, *Das Gebot der Stunde*, 122–124.

[52] *Protokolle der Sitzungen des Parteiausschusses der SPD 1912 bis 1921*, 1:389–429.

[53] SAPMO-BArch, NY 4060/67/44.

[54] Fechenbach, *Der Revolutionär Kurt Eisner*, 16–17, 19.

[55] K. E., "*Die Perser* des Aischylos: Uraufführung im Schauspielhaus," *MP*, 22 January 1917.

[56] SAPMO-BArch, NY 4060/62/4.

[57] SAPMO-BArch, NY 4060/62/3.

[58] SAPMO-BArch, NY 4060/79/13.

[59] Keegan, *The First World War*, 352.

[60] SAPMO-BArch, NY 4060/65/93.

[61] SAPMO-BArch, NY 4060/61/27, 34. Eisner's response is printed in "Die Mobilmachung als Kriegsursache und Anderes," 53–59.

[62] Fechenbach, *Der Revolutionär Kurt Eisner*, 20.

[63] SAPMO-BArch, NY 4060/65/84.

[64] Fechenbach, *Der Revolutionär Kurt Eisner*, 18.

[65] IISG, Karl Kautsky, DX/166.

[66] Fricke, *Handbuch zur Geschichte der deutschen Arbeiterbewegung*, 1:645.

[67] SAPMO-BArch, NY 4060/63/9.

[68] Prager, *Das Gebot der Stunde*, 137.

[69] *Protokolle der Parteitage der Unabhängigen Sozialdemokratischen Partei Deutschlands*, 1:12, 16–18, 20–22; Prager, *Das Gebot der Stunde*, 139.

[70] *Protokolle der Parteitage der Unabhängigen Sozialdemokratischen Partei Deutschlands*, 1:25–26.

[71] Ibid., 1:35–36, 52.

[72] Ibid., 1:47–50.

[73] SAPMO-BArch, NY 4060/78/289.

[74] Robert Payne, *The Life and Death of Lenin* (New York: Simon and Schuster, 1964), 290–300.

Chapter Twenty

[1] *Protokolle der Sitzungen des Parteiausschusses der SPD 1912 bis 1921*, 1:431, 440, 451, 457.

[2] In an interview with the author in Munich, 12 March 1982. Kurt Eisner's adoptive daughter, Freia, made the same claim when annotating his and Else Belli Eisner's papers: "Anti-Semitism in Bavaria began under Eisner. . . . For that reason Eisner was unpopular and remains so among Jews who recall that time" (SAPMO-BArch, NY 4060 (Nachlaß Kurt Eisner)/101/9).

[3] K. E., "Eine sozialistische Dramaturgie," *MP*, 13 April 1917.

[4] K. E., "Tanzabend in den Kammerspielen," *MP*, 19 April 1917.

[5] K. E., "*Von morgens bis mitternachts* von Georg Kaiser: Uraufführung in den Kammerspielen," *MP*, 30 April 1917.

[6] SAPMO-BArch, NY 4060/1/142.

[7] SAPMO-BArch, NY 4060/67/27.

[8] Quoted in Grau, *Kurt Eisner 1867–1919*, 328.

[9] Kurt Eisner, "Mein Gefängnistagebuch: Neudeck, 19. 2. 1918," *M 7* (17 February 1928): 57. Reprinted in "Januarstreik 1918," in Kurt Eisner,

Sozialismus als Aktion, 73–74. The complete manuscript and typed copy of the prison journal are preserved in SAPMO-BArch, NY 4060/23.1 (ms) and 23.2 (copy). Excerpts appeared in *Die Menschheit*, a Berlin weekly, at the tenth anniversary of the strike. The prison journal is reprinted in part as "Januarstreik 1918" in *Sozialismus als Aktion*, 58–74.

[10] Fechenbach, *Der Revolutionär Kurt Eisner*, 18.

[11] Falk Wiesemann, "Kurt Eisner: Studie zu seiner politischen Biographie," in *Bayern im Umbruch: Die Revolution von 1918, ihre Voraussetzungen, ihr Verlauf und ihre Folgen*, ed. Karl Bosl (Munich: R. Oldenbourg, 1969), 400, 422n84; Freya Eisner, *Kurt Eisner: Die Politik des libertären Sozialismus*, 72.

[12] Freya Eisner, *Kurt Eisner: Die Politik des libertären Sozialismus*, 74.

[13] *Protokolle der Sitzungen des Parteiausschusses der SPD 1912 bis 1921*, 1:457.

[14] SAPMO-BArch, NY 4060/4/227.

[15] Kurt Eisner, "Werte Kollegen!" *A-F* 8.[no issue number] (May 1917); SAPMO-BArch, NY 4060/57.

[16] SAPMO-BArch, NY 4060/78/291.

[17] SAPMO-BArch, NY 4060/78/293.

[18] K. E., "Residenztheater: Max Dreyer, *Die reiche Frau*," *MP*, 29 May 1917.

[19] K. E., "*Hans im Schnakenloch* von René Schickele: Erstaufführung in den Kammerspielen—Gastspiel Ziegel-Horwitz," *MP*, 8 June 1917.

[20] SAPMO-BArch, NY 4060/1/116–118, 121; Freya Eisner, *Kurt Eisner: Die Politik des libertären Sozialismus*, 74.

[21] "Die Kriegslage: Amerika," *MP*, 5 July 1917.

[22] Friedrich von der Ropp, *Zwischen Gestern und Morgen: Erfahrungen und Erkenntnisse*, 2nd ed. (Stuttgart: J. F. Steinkopf, 1963), 101; Karl Georg von Treutler, *Die graue Exzellenz: Zwischen Staatsräson und Vasallentreue*, ed. Karl-Heinz Janßen (Frankfurt am Main: Propyläen, 1971), 210–211; Georg Alexander von Müller, *Regierte der Kaiser? Kriegstagebücher, Aufzeichnungen und Briefe des Chefs des Marine-Kabinetts 1914–1918*, ed. Walter Görlitz (Göttingen: Musterschmidt, 1959), 246–249; Michael B. Barrett, "Erich Ludendorff," in Tucker and Roberts, *World War I Encyclopedia*, 2:715–716; Gerhard Ritter, *The Sword and the Scepter: The Problem of Militarism in Germany*, trans. Heinz Norden, 4 vols. (Coral Gables, FL: University of Miami Press, 1969–72), 3:314, 405, 418–419, 451–454, 4:258–259; Manfred Nebelin, *Ludendorff: Diktator im Ersten Weltkrieg* (Munich: Siedler, 2010), 311–315; Craig, *Germany, 1866–1945*, 385; "Ein Erfolg der Sozialdemokratie," *MP*, 16 July 1917.

[23] SAPMO-BArch, NY 4060/22/33–34.

[24] Herzog, *Menschen, denen ich begegnete*, 58.

[25] SAPMO-BArch, NY 4060/22/6–7.

[26] SAPMO-BArch, NY 4060/22/22; IISG, Gustav Landauer Archive, 118.

[27] SAPMO-BArch, NY 4060/22/31–32.

[28] W. H. Chamberlin, "The Kornilov Mutiny," in *The Russian Revolution: An Anthology*, ed. M. K. Dziewanowski (New York: Thomas Y. Crowell, 1970), 101–137.

[29] Fechenbach, *Der Revolutionär Kurt Eisner*, 21; SAPMO-BArch, NY 4060/4/224–225.

[30] Oskar Maria Graf, *Wir sind Gefangene: Ein Bekenntnis* (Munich: Süddeutscher Verlag, 1978), 312, 316–318; Oskar Maria Graf, "In Memoriam Felix Fechenbach," in *Reden und Aufsätze aus dem Exil*, ed. Helmut F. Pfanner (Munich: Süddeutscher Verlag, 1989), 66–71. The Black Eagle's address was Schillerstraße 32, whereas the Golden Anchor, the regular meeting place, was number 34. It is possible that the two establishments shared the room where the discussion evenings were held.

[31] Erich Mühsam, *Tagebücher 1910–1924*, ed. Chris Hirte (Munich: Deutscher Taschenbuch Verlag, 1994), 171.

[32] Erich Mühsam, *Von Eisner bis Leviné: Die Entstehung der bayerischen Räterepublik* (Berlin-Britz: FANAL-Verlag Erich Mühsam, 1929), 11.

[33] K. E., "Erich Mühsam," *MP*, 26 November 1917.

[34] Erich Mühsam, *In meiner Posaune muß ein Sandkorn sein: Briefe 1900–1934*, ed. Gerd W. Jungblut, 2 vols. (Vaduz: Topos, 1984), 1:246–247.

[35] Richard Dove, *He Was a German: A Biography of Ernst Toller* (London: Libris, 1990), 35; SAPMO-BArch, NY 4060/66/112.

[36] SAPMO-BArch, NY 4060/67/31.

[37] Quoted in Grau, *Kurt Eisner 1867–1919*, 329.

[38] SAPMO-BArch, NY 4060/78/296.

[39] SAPMO-BArch, NY 4060/78/298.

[40] SAPMO-BArch, NY 4060/78/300.

[41] SAPMO-BArch, NY 4060/4/228–229.

[42] Dove, *He Was a German*, 36, 40–41; Wolfgang Frühwald and John M. Spalek, eds., *Der Fall Toller: Kommentar und Materialien* (Munich: Carl Hanser, 1979), 13.

[43] SAPMO-BArch, NY 4060/78/300.

[44] SAPMO-BArch, NY 4060/78/302.

[45] IISG, Karl Kautsky, DX/167. For reference to Hermann Weise see Ottokar Luban, "Die Rolle der Spartakusgruppe bei der Entstehung und Entwicklung

der USPD Januar 1916 bis März 1919," *JahrBuch für Forschungen zur Geschichte der Arbeiterbewegung* 7.2 (2008): 69–76.

46 K. E., "Reinhard Johannes Sorge, *Metanoeite*: Uraufführung in den Kammerspielen," *MP*, 28 December 1917.

47 SAPMO-BArch, NY 4060/4/229.

48 SAPMO-BArch, NY 4060/1/207.

49 "Wilsons Weltfriedensprogramm," *V*, 10 January 1918.

50 SAPMO-BArch, NY 4060/78/304.

51 SAPMO-BArch, NY 4060/4/229–230.

52 "Jännerstreik 1918," *Weblexikon der Wiener Sozialdemokratie*, http://www.dasrotewien.at/jaennerstreik-1918.html. See also Hans Mommsen, "Victor Adler und die Politik der österreichischen Sozialdemokratie im Ersten Weltkrieg," in *Politik und Gesellschaft im alten und neuen Österreich: Festschrift für Rudolf Neck zum 60. Geburtstag*, ed. Isabella Ackerl et al., 2 vols. (Vienna: Verlag für Geschichte und Politik, 1981), 1:403–405.

53 SAPMO-BArch, NY 4060/4/230.

54 Dove, *He Was a German*, 43.

55 SAPMO-BArch, NY 4060/4/230–231.

56 Freya Eisner, introduction to Kurt Eisner, *Zwischen Kapitalismus und Kommunismus*, 117n289; Paul Nikolaus Cossmann, ed., "Vorbereitung des Münchner Munitionsarbeiterstreiks vom Januar 1918: Nach unveröffentlichten Geheimakten," *Süddeutsche Monatshefte* 21 (1923/24): 27–28. There is some discrepancy in the record of what information Eisner then shared with his discussion group. Although a detailed police report of the meeting documents discussion of the strike, Eisner himself denied to police interrogators that he had divulged any information about the strike, knowing that outside observers were among the audience. He maintained that his report on preparations for the strike was confined to the executive meeting prior to the regular gathering. In any case some participants were present at both forums. See SAPMO-BArch, NY 4060/4/231.

57 Ernst Toller, *Eine Jugend in Deutschland*, in *Gesammelte Werke*, ed. Wolfgang Frühwald and John M. Spalek, 2nd ed., 5 vols. (Munich: Carl Hanser, 1996), 4:88.

58 Graf, "In Memoriam Felix Fechenbach," 68–69.

59 Dove, *He Was a German*, 43; Fechenbach, *Der Revolutionär Kurt Eisner*, 22–23; Kurt Eisner, "Mein Gefängnistagebuch: Untersuchungsgefängnis München am Neudeck, 4. 2. 1918," *M* 3 (20 January 1928): 19; *M* 4 (27 January 1928): 27. Reprinted in "Januarstreik 1918," 58–62.

60 Cossmann, "Vorbereitung des Münchner Munitionsarbeiterstreiks," 28–29.

61 Dove, *He Was a German*, 44; SAPMO-BArch, NY 4060/4/246.

62 Graf, *Wir sind Gefangene*, 342.

63 Cossmann, "Vorbereitung des Münchner Munitionsarbeiterstreiks," 29; SAPMO-BArch, NY 4060/4/234–235; Kurt Eisner, "Mein Gefängnistagebuch: . . . Neudeck, 4. 2. 1918," 19, 27.

64 "Streikpläne in Groß-Berlin," "Der Umfang der Ausstände am Montag," *MNN*, 28 January 1918.

65 "Der Demonstrationsstreik in Berlin," *MNN*, 29 January 1918.

66 SAPMO-BArch, NY 4060/4/235–236.

67 Dove, *He Was a German*, 44; Toller, *Eine Jugend in Deutschland*, 4:88; Fechenbach, *Der Revolutionär Kurt Eisner*, 23; Kurt Eisner, "Mein Gefängnistagebuch: . . . Neudeck, 4. 2. 1918," 19, 27.

68 "Die Ausstandsbewegung in München," *MNN*, 31 January 1918, evening ed.

69 SAPMO-BArch, NY 4060/4/242.

70 Mitchell, *Revolution in Bavaria*, 67–68; Dove, *He Was a German*, 45; "Die Ausstandsbewegung in München," *MNN*, 31 January 1918, evening ed.

71 Toller, *Eine Jugend in Deutschland*, 4:88.

72 "Die Ausstandsbewegung in München," *MNN*, 31 January 1918.

73 Cossmann, "Vorbereitung des Münchner Munitionsarbeiterstreiks," 28–29.

74 SAPMO-BArch, NY 4060/4/237–239.

75 SAPMO-BArch, NY 4060/4/237, 240.

76 SAPMO-BArch, NY 4060/4/240–241; Kurt Eisner, "Mein Gefängnistagebuch: Neudeck, 5. 2. 1918," 27, 38. Cossmann, "Vorbereitung des Münchner Munitionsarbeiterstreiks," 30–31.

77 SAPMO-BArch, NY 4060/4/241–242.

78 Toller, *Eine Jugend in Deutschland*, 4:89.

79 SAPMO-BArch, NY 4060/4/220.

80 SAPMO-BArch, NY 4060/78/306.

81 Kurt Eisner, "Mein Gefängnistagebuch: . . . Neudeck, 4. 2. 1918," 19.

Chapter Twenty-One

[1] Toller, *Eine Jugend in Deutschland*, 4:92–94; "Das Ende der Streikbewegung in München," *MNN*, 4 February 1918.

[2] Fechenbach, *Der Revolutionär Kurt Eisner*, 28–29.

[3] SAPMO-BArch, NY 4060 (Nachlaß Kurt Eisner)/78/308. The requested newspapers were the *Berliner Tageblatt, Frankfurter Zeitung, National-Zeitung Basel, Vorwärts, Leipziger Volkszeitung, Wiener Arbeiterzeitung, Neue Zürcher Zeitung, Le Temps, L'Humanité, Deutsche Zeitung,* and *Deutsche Tageszeitung*. See Eisner's anonymous essay on *Fidelio* in *Freie Volksbühne* 17.6–7 (December 1912–January 1913): 53–60.

[4] SAPMO-BArch, NY 4060/22/36–47.

[5] SAPMO-BArch, NY 4060/4/219.

[6] SAPMO-BArch, NY 4060/4/220.

[7] SAPMO-BArch, NY 4060/73/86.

[8] SAPMO-BArch, NY 4060/78/314.

[9] Kurt Eisner, "Mein Gefängnistagebuch: Neudeck, 19. 2. 1918," 57.

[10] Freya Eisner, *Kurt Eisner: Die Politik des libertären Sozialismus*, 76.

[11] Albert E. Gurganus, "Sarah Sonja Lerch, née Rabinowitz: The Sonja Irene L. of Toller's *Masse-Mensch*," *German Studies Review* 28.3 (2005): 611–614.

[12] SAPMO-BArch, NY 4060/23.1/39.

[13] Keegan, *The First World War*, 372–373, 387, 393–394, 400–405.

[14] SAPMO-BArch, NY 4060/4/247; Freya Eisner, *Kurt Eisner, Die Politik des libertären Sozialismus*, 77.

[15] Freya Eisner, introduction to Kurt Eisner, *Zwischen Kapitalismus und Kommunismus*, 119–120.

[16] SAPMO-BArch, NY 4060/66/63.

[17] SAPMO-BArch, NY 4060/78/317.

[18] SAPMO-BArch, NY 4060/12/319–337.

[19] SAPMO-BArch, NY 4060/23.1/40–41. Printed as "Aus Tageheften 1914–1918: Märzstürme 1918," in Kurt Eisner, *Gesammelte Schriften*, 1:199–200.

[20] Gurganus, "Sarah Sonja Lerch," 614; SAPMO-BArch, NY 4060/23.2/44.

[21] SAPMO-BArch, NY 4060/23.2/47.

[22] IISG, Karl Kautsky, DX/168.

[23] SAPMO-BArch, NY 4060/78/317.

[24] Kurt Eisner, *Die Götterprüfung*. The play was performed May Day 1921 in Berlin. The critic Julius Bab panned it as thoroughly conventional, a hackneyed tirade against absolute monarchy, saying nothing that could not have been said by Voltaire or Diderot. See Gurganus, *The Art of Revolution*, 98–99.

[25] SAPMO-BArch, NY 4060/78/317.

[26] SAPMO-BArch, NY 4060/102/496–497.

[27] SAPMO-BArch, NY 4060/78/317.

[28] SAPMO-BArch, NY 4060/12/162–177.

[29] Julie Braun-Vogelstein, *Was niemals stirbt: Gestalten und Erinnerungen* (Stuttgart: Deutsche Verlagsanstalt, 1966), 279–302.

[30] Kurt Eisner, "Kleine Kriegsmärchen," in *Gesammelte Schriften*, 1:204–208.

[31] SAPMO-BArch, NY 4060/72/96.

[32] Dove, *He Was a German*, 47; Freya Eisner, *Kurt Eisner: Die Politik des libertären Sozialismus*, 76–77.

[33] SAPMO-BArch, NY 4060/23.1/47.

[34] Kurt Eisner, "Kleine Kriegsmärchen: Die Schule des Fliegens," in *Gesammelte Schriften*, 1:213–216.

[35] K. E., "Unveränderte Lage: Franz Mehrings Marx," *LV*, 8 June 1918. Reprinted as "Marx-Feier," in Kurt Eisner, *Gesammelte Schriften*, 1:221–239.

[36] SAPMO-BArch, NY 4060/66/65.

[37] Kurt Eisner, "Letzter Marsch," in *Gesammelte Schriften*, 1:7–8; SAPMO-BArch, NY 4060/15.2/1.

[38] SAPMO-BArch, NY 4060/67/91.

[39] SAPMO-BArch, NY 4060/65/85.

[40] SAPMO-BArch, NY 4060/4/272.

[41] IISG, Karl Kautsky, DX/170.

[42] SAPMO-BArch, NY 4060/4/273.

[43] SAPMO-BArch, NY 4060/4/249.

[44] SAPMO-BArch, NY 4060/4/251.

[45] Keegan, *The First World War*, 408–412.

[46] Fechenbach, *Der Revolutionär Kurt Eisner*, 30.

[47] Kurt Eisner, "Kleine Kriegsmärchen: Der Lebenshaß," in *Gesammelte Schriften*, 1:218–220.

[48] SAPMO-BArch, NY 4060/4/255.

[49] BArch-Koblenz, N 1190 (Nachlaß Südekum)/20/37–48.

[50] Kurt Eisner, "Wir Toten auf Urlaub," in *Gesammelte Schriften*, 1:5–6.

[51] Keegan, *The First World War*, 411–413; Snyder, *The Weimar Republic*, 12–13; Erich Eyck, *A History of the Weimar Republic*, trans. Harlan P. Hanson and Robert G. L. Waite, 2 vols. (New York: Atheneum, 1970), 1:35, 102.

[52] SAPMO-BArch, NY 4060/65/148.

[53] Mitchell, *Revolution in Bavaria*, 77.

[54] Paul Nikolaus Cossmann, ed., "In der Heimat: Vom Munitionsarbeiterstreik zur Revolution," *Süddeutsche Monatshefte* 21 (1923/24): 92.

[55] SAPMO-BArch, NY 4060/67/36.

[56] SAPMO-BArch, NY 4060/4/257.

[57] Cossmann, "In der Heimat," 92.

[58] SAPMO-BArch, NY 4060/4/258; Cossmann, "In der Heimat," 93.

[59] SAPMO-BArch, NY 4060/4/260.

[60] Snyder, *The Weimar Republic*, 13; Eyck, *A History of the Weimar Republic*, 1:35, 37.

[61] Luxemburg, *Gesammelte Briefe*, 5:412–413.

[62] Nettl, *Rosa Luxemburg*, 2:709, 713; Cossmann, "In der Heimat," 92.

[63] Fechenbach, *Der Revolutionär Kurt Eisner*, 31–33.

[64] SAPMO-BArch, NY 4060/102/498–499.

[65] Graf, *Wir sind Gefangene*, 385.

[66] Freya Eisner, introduction to Kurt Eisner, *Zwischen Kapitalismus und Kommunismus*, 120.

[67] Graf, *Wir sind Gefangene*, 384–385.

[68] Grau, *Kurt Eisner 1867–1919*, 346–347.

[69] Fechenbach, *Der Revolutionär Kurt Eisner*, 32–34; SAPMO-BArch, NY 4060/67/171.

[70] Grau, *Kurt Eisner 1867–1919*, 347; Fechenbach, *Der Revolutionär Kurt Eisner*, 34.

[71] SAPMO-BArch, NY 4060/67/171.

[72] Cossmann, "In der Heimat," 93.

[73] Fechenbach, *Der Revolutionär Kurt Eisner*, 35.

[74] Quoted in Mitchell, *Revolution in Bavaria*, 87.

[75] Herzog, *Menschen, denen ich begegnete*, 60.

[76] Toller, *Eine Jugend in Deutschland*, 4:112; Dove, *He Was a German*, 61; IISG, Gustav Laundauer Archive, 120; Jürgen Schiewe and Hanne Maußner,

eds., *Trotz allem Mensch sein: Gedichte und Aufsätze*, by Erich Mühsam (Stuttgart: Reclam, 1984), 169.

[77] Fechenbach, *Der Revolutionär Kurt Eisner*, 35–36; Mitchell, *Revolution in Bavaria*, 89.

[78] Fechenbach, *Der Revolutionär Kurt Eisner*, 36; Hermann Schueler, *Auf der Flucht erschossen: Felix Fechenbach 1894–1933* (Cologne: Kiepenheuer & Witsch, 1981), 51; Hermann Kurt Schueler, "Felix Fechenbach 1894–1933: Die Entwicklung eines republikanischen Journalisten" (PhD diss., Rheinische Friedrich-Wilhelms-Universität, 1980), 56n1.

[79] Fechenbach, *Der Revolutionär Kurt Eisner*, 36–37; Cossmann, "In der Heimat," 93.

[80] Fechenbach, *Der Revolutionär Kurt Eisner*, 35–36.

[81] Mitchell, *Revolution in Bavaria*, 90; Herzog, *Menschen, denen ich begegnete*, 60–61.

[82] M. Rainer Lepsius, "Max Weber in München: Rede anläßlich der Enthüllung einer Gedenktafel," *Zeitschrift für Soziologie* 6.1 (January 1977): 106; Graf, *Wir sind Gefangene*, 385–386.

[83] Herzog, *Menschen, denen ich begegnete*, 61.

[84] Fechenbach, *Der Revolutionär Kurt Eisner*, 37; Graf, *Wir sind Gefangene*, 387–388.

[85] Fechenbach, *Der Revolutionär Kurt Eisner*, 38–39.

[86] Eyck, *A History of the Weimar Republic*, 1:42–44.

[87] Bernhard Meyer, "Sanitätsrat Ruth Strahl—ein ungewöhnlicher Lebensweg," *Humanitas, Zeitschrift für Medizin und Gesellschaft* 21 (1988): 9; CJA 6.4 (Nachlaß Freia Eisner)/31/17–18. See also Hans-Dieter Schütt, "Hoffnung ist nicht aus der Welt zu schaffen: Interview mit Ruth Strahl, der Tochter Kurt Eisners," *Neues Deutschland*, 17/18 August 1996.

[88] Fechenbach, *Der Revolutionär Kurt Eisner*, 39; Mitchell, *Revolution in Bavaria*, 91–92.

[89] Fechenbach, *Der Revolutionär Kurt Eisner*, 39; Herzog, *Menschen, denen ich begegnete*, 61.

[90] Graf, *Wir sind Gefangene*, 393; Mitchell, *Revolution in Bavaria*, 92.

[91] Fechenbach, *Der Revolutionär Kurt Eisner*, 39–40; Graf, *Wir sind Gefangene*, 393; Herzog, *Menschen, denen ich begegnete*, 61. Writing forty years after the events, Herzog mistakenly cites the date of the Bavarian Revolution as 6 November.

[92] Fechenbach, *Der Revolutionär Kurt Eisner*, 40; Mitchell, *Revolution in Bavaria*, 95.

[93] Herzog, *Menschen, denen ich begegnete*, 61–62.

[94] Graf, *Wir sind Gefangene*, 393.

[95] Fechenbach, *Der Revolutionär Kurt Eisner*, 40; Herzog, *Menschen, denen ich begegnete*, 62; Graf, *Wir sind Gefangene*, 393–394.

[96] Fechenbach, *Der Revolutionär Kurt Eisner*, 40–41; Graf, "In Memoriam Felix Fechenbach," 70–71; *Wir sind Gefangene*, 395.

[97] Mitchell, *Revolution in Bavaria*, 93, 96; Graf, *Wir sind Gefangene*, 395–396; "In Memoriam Felix Fechenbach," 71.

[98] Fechenbach, *Der Revolutionär Kurt Eisner*, 41.

[99] Herzog, *Menschen, denen ich begegnete*, 62–63, Fechenbach, *Der Revolutionär Kurt Eisner*, 42.

[100] Herzog, *Menschen, denen ich begegnete*, 63.

[101] Fechenbach, *Der Revolutionär Kurt Eisner*, 42; Fritz Wahl, "Rätezeit in München," in *Gegenwart, Sonderheft zum 29. Oktober 1956: Ein Jahrhundert* Frankfurter Zeitung *1856–1956*, ed. Max von Brück et al. (Frankfurt am Main: Societäts-Druckerei, 1956), 15–16.

[102] Fechenbach, *Der Revolutionär Kurt Eisner*, 42.

[103] Graf, *Wir sind Gefangene*, 398–399.

[104] Mitchell, *Revolution in Bavaria*, 98–99; Herzog, *Menschen, denen ich begegnete*, 63.

[105] Fechenbach, *Der Revolutionär Kurt Eisner*, 42–43.

[106] Herzog, *Menschen, denen ich begegnete*, 63–64; Fechenbach, *Der Revolutionär Kurt Eisner*, 43.

[107] Wahl, "Rätezeit in München," 15.

[108] Fechenbach, *Der Revolutionär Kurt Eisner*, 43.

[109] Ibid.; Herzog, *Menschen, denen ich begegnete*, 64–66. Eisner's own handwritten copy, replete with strikethroughs, cigarette burns, and ink smears, is preserved by the Bavarian State Archive in Munich (Bayerisches Hauptstaatsarchiv-München, MA 1027/100–102).

[110] Fechenbach, *Der Revolutionär Kurt Eisner*, 44; Lepsius, "Max Weber in München," 106–107.

[111] Herzog, *Menschen, denen ich begegnete*, 67–68.

Chapter Twenty-Two

[1] Fechenbach, *Der Revolutionär Kurt Eisner*, 46; Herzog, *Menschen, denen ich begegnete*, 67; Cossmann, "In der Heimat," 93–94; Franz J. Bauer, ed., *Die Regierung Eisner 1918/19: Ministerratsprotokolle und Dokumente*,

Quellen zur Geschichte des Parlamentarismus und der politischen Parteien, 1st ser., 10 (Düsseldorf: Droste, 1987), xvi.

[2] Graf, *Wir sind Gefangene*, 399.

[3] Mitchell, *Revolution in Bavaria*, 100–101.

[4] "An die Bevölkerung Münchens!" *MNN*, 8 November 1918; Bauer, *Die Regierung Eisner*, 409–411.

[5] Karl Alexander von Müller, *Mars und Venus: Erinnerungen 1914–1919* (Stuttgart: Gustav Kilpper, 1954), 269.

[6] Herzog, *Menschen, denen ich begegnete*, 68; Friedrich Burschell, "*Revolution und Neue Erde*: München 1918/19 aus meinen Erinnerungen," in *Imprimatur: Ein Jahrbuch für Bücherfreunde*, n.s., 3, ed. Siegfried Buchenau (Frankfurt am Main: Gesellschaft der Bibliophilen, 1961/62), 244.

[7] Schade, *Kurt Eisner*, 135n144; Bauer, *Die Regierung Eisner*, xxv.

[8] Keegan, *The First World War*, 418; Snyder, *The Weimar Republic*, 13–14.

[9] Mitchell, *Revolution in Bavaria*, 105; Kurt Eisner, "Wahlrede vor den Unabhängigen," in *Die neue Zeit: Zweite Folge* (Munich: Georg Müller, 1919), 27–28. The speech is reprinted in Tankred Dorst, ed., *Die Münchner Räterepublik: Zeugnisse und Kommentar* (Frankfurt am Main: Suhrkamp, 1980), 23–44.

[10] Bauer, *Die Regierung Eisner*, xxv.

[11] Fechenbach, *Der Revolutionär Kurt Eisner*, 46.

[12] *Verhandlungen des provisorischen Nationalrates des Volksstaates Bayern im Jahre 1918/1919: Stenographische Berichte Nr. 1 bis 10* (8 November 1918–4 January 1919), 1–5. For biographies of the new goverment ministers see Bauer, *Die Regierung Eisner*, xxx–xlvii.

[13] Thomas Mann, *Diaries, 1918–1939*, trans. Richard and Clara Winston (New York: Harry N. Abrams, 1982), 19.

[14] Fechenbach, *Der Revolutionär Kurt Eisner*, 47.

[15] Richard M. Watt, *The Kings Depart: The Tragedy of Germany; Versailles and the German Revolution* (New York: Simon and Schuster, 1968), 192.

[16] Ibid., 191–192.

[17] Snyder, *The Weimar Republic*, 22, 24; Watt, *The Kings Depart*, 195.

[18] Scheidemann, *Memoiren eines Sozialdemokraten*, 2:309–314; Watt, *The Kings Depart*, 196–197.

[19] Watt, *The Kings Depart*, 198.

[20] Snyder, *The Weimar Republic*, 25–26.

[21] Graf, *Wir sind Gefangene*, 399–400.

22 Fechenbach, *Der Revolutionär Kurt Eisner*, 47–48.

23 Ibid., 38–39.

24 Ibid., 47.

25 Bauer, *Die Regierung Eisner*, 11n3, 414–415.

26 Herzog, *Menschen, denen ich begegnete*, 68.

27 Watt, *The Kings Depart*, 199–200.

28 Fechenbach, *Der Revolutionär Kurt Eisner*, 48–49; Pius Dirr, ed., *Bayerische Dokumente zum Kriegsausbruch und zum Versailler Schuldspruch* (Munich: R. Oldenbourg, 1922), 28–30.

29 Dirr, *Bayerische Dokumente*, 28–29.

30 Bauer, *Die Regierung Eisner*, 11n5.

31 Ibid., xliv; Mitchell, *Revolution in Bavaria*, 130–131n26.

32 Dirr, *Bayerische Dokumente*, 30–31.

33 Fechenbach, *Der Revolutionär Kurt Eisner*, 49–50.

34 Mitchell, *Revolution in Bavaria*, 132.

35 IISG, Gustav Landauer Archive, 124.

36 Kurt Eisner, "Das Regierungsprogramm: An das bayerische Volk," in *Die neue Zeit*, ed. Benno Merkle (Munich: Georg Müller, 1919), 20–29. Reprinted in Bauer, *Die Regierung Eisner*, 420–423.

37 Josef Hofmiller, *Revolutionstagebuch 1918/19: Aus den Tagen der Münchner Revolution* (Leipzig: Karl Rauch, [1938]), 65.

38 Benno Merkle, introduction to "Ansprache anläßlich der Revolutionsfeier im Nationaltheater am 17. November 1918," in Kurt Eisner, *Die neue Zeit*, 30–31.

39 Karl Alexander von Müller, *Mars und Venus*, 285.

40 Rilke's letter of 16 November 1918 to Elya Maria Nevar, in Rainer Maria Rilke, *Briefe zur Politik*, ed. Joachim W. Storck (Frankfurt am Main: Insel, 1992), 234; Hofmiller, *Revolutionstagebuch*, 71–72; Wilhelm Füßl, *Oskar von Miller 1855–1934: Eine Biographie* (Munich: C. H. Beck, 2005), 182.

41 Hofmiller, *Revolutionstagebuch*, 59–60, 67; Münchener Stadtbibliothek, Monacensia-Abteilung, Flugblätter: F Mon 2564, "Revolutions-Feier für verwundete und kranke Soldaten."

42 *Verhandlungen des provisorischen Nationalrates des Volksstaates Bayern*, 4–5; Grau, *Kurt Eisner 1867–1919*, 372.

43 Kurt Eisner, "Brief an Georg Heim," in Kurt Eisner, *Sozialismus als Aktion*, 81–82.

44 SAPMO-BArch, NY 4060 (Nachlaß Kurt Eisner)/66/4.

[45] Fechenbach, *Der Revolutionär Kurt Eisner*, 50–51; Dirr, *Bayerische Dokumente*, 3–16.

[46] Fechenbach, *Der Revolutionär Kurt Eisner*, 51; Mitchell, *Revolution in Bavaria*, 133.

[47] Dirr, *Bayerische Dokumente*, vii–viii.

[48] Erich Matthias, Susanne Miller, and Heinrich Potthoff, eds., *Die Regierung der Volksbeauftragten 1918/19: Erster Teil*, Quellen zur Geschichte des Parlamentarismus und der politischen Parteien, 1st ser., 6.1 (Düsseldorf: Droste, 1969), 149–152.

[49] Ibid., 152–175.

[50] Mitchell, *Revolution in Bavaria*, 135n36.

[51] Bauer, *Die Regierung Eisner*, 83.

[52] Dirr, *Bayerische Dokumente*, 72.

[53] Bauer, *Die Regierung Eisner*, 99.

[54] SAPMO-BArch, NY 4060/64/38, 88, 95.

[55] IISG, Gustav Landauer Archive, 122.

[56] Bauer, *Die Regierung Eisner*, 107, 109–113; Mitchell, *Revolution in Bavaria*, 156–160.

[57] Bauer, *Die Regierung Eisner*, 74, 424–425.

[58] Kurt Eisner, "Rede im Berliner Vollzugsrat der Arbeiter- und Soldatenräte," in Kurt Eisner, *Sozialismus als Aktion*, 75–77; Dirr, *Bayerische Dokumente*, 33–39.

[59] *Verhandlungen des provisorischen Nationalrates des Volksstaates Bayern im Jahre 1918/1919: Beilagen-Band*, 1–11. Reprinted in Kurt Eisner, *Die neue Zeit*, 38–60.

[60] *Verhandlungen des provisorischen Nationalrates des Volksstaates Bayern: Beilagen-Band*, 13–56. Reprinted in Kurt Eisner, *Die neue Zeit*, 61–124.

[61] Mitchell, *Revolution in Bavaria*, 166–167.

[62] Freya Eisner, *Kurt Eisner: Die Politik des libertären Sozialismus*, 122.

[63] F. W. Foerster, "Die Unhaltbarkeit der gegenwärtigen politischen Lage in Bayern," *MP*, 2 December 1918.

[64] [Friedrich Stampfer], "Der Fall Kurt Eisner: Eine Münchener Revolutions-Episode," *V*, 2 December 1918.

[65] Bauer, *Die Regierung Eisner*, 105–106nn1–3, 109; Mitchell, *Revolution in Bavaria*, 167–169.

[66] Bauer, *Die Regierung Eisner*, 118–119n4.

[67] Ibid., 128n4.

[68] Ibid., 123–129.

[69] Ibid., 133–134n1; Schade, *Kurt Eisner*, 76–77; Fechenbach, *Der Revolutionär Kurt Eisner*, 53; Friedrich Hitzer, *Anton Graf Arco: Das Attentat auf Kurt Eisner und die Schüsse im Landtag* (Munich: Knesebeck & Schuler, 1988), 268; Mühsam, *Von Eisner bis Leviné*, 15.

[70] Schade, *Kurt Eisner*, 77–78.

[71] *Verhandlungen des provisorischen Nationalrates des Volksstaates Bayern: Beilagen-Band*, 127–128.

[72] Ibid., 129–133.

[73] Ibid., 133, 135, 149.

[74] Ibid., 153, 184–185, 193–194, 195.

[75] Schade, *Kurt Eisner*, 78, 155n124; Freya Eisner, *Kurt Eisner: Die Politik des libertären Sozialismus*, 142; Georg Köglmeier, "Münchner Soldatenrat 1918/19," *Historisches Lexikon Bayerns*, 23 November 2012, http://www.historisches-lexikon-bayerns.de/artikel/artikel_44340.

[76] Quoted in Freya Eisner, *Kurt Eisner: Die Politik des libertären Sozialismus*, 143.

[77] Kurt Eisner, "Wahlrede vor den Unabhängigen," 12–46.

Chapter Twenty-Three

[1] Quoted in Freya Eisner, *Kurt Eisner: Die Politik des libertären Sozialismus*, 125–126.

[2] Ibid., 140.

[3] Bauer, *Die Regierung Eisner*, 176–178.

[4] *Verhandlungen des provisorischen Nationalrates des Volksstaates Bayern im Jahre 1918/1919: Stenographische Berichte Nr. 1 bis 10* (8 November 1918–4 Januar 1919), 102.

[5] Ibid., 42.

[6] Ibid., 58.

[7] Ibid., 62, 63, 70.

[8] Ibid., 119–120.

[9] Kurt Eisner, "Presse," *Neue Zeitung: Unabhängiges sozialistisches Organ*, 20 December 1918. Reprinted in Kurt Eisner, *Sozialismus als Aktion*, 97–101.

[10] SAPMO-BArch, NY 4060 (Nachlaß Kurt Eisner)/101/5.

[11] Frank Arnau [Heinrich Karl Schmitt], *Gelebt, geliebt, gehaßt: Ein Leben im 20. Jahrhundert* (Munich: Kurt Desch, 1972), 94–105.

[12] Mitchell, *Revolution in Bavaria*, 198–201.

[13] Karl Alexander von Müller, *Mars und Venus*, 293–294; Freya Eisner, *Kurt Eisner: Die Politik des libertären Sozialismus*, 146–147.

[14] Bauer, *Die Regierung Eisner*, 212n; Freya Eisner, *Kurt Eisner: Die Politik des libertären Sozialismus*, 147.

[15] *Verhandlungen des provisorischen Nationalrates des Volksstaates Bayern*, 225.

[16] Ibid., 188; Bauer, *Die Regierung Eisner*, 222–223; Freya Eisner, *Kurt Eisner: Die Politik des libertären Sozialismus*, 147–148.

[17] Bauer, *Die Regierung Eisner*, 188; Mitchell, *Revolution in Bavaria*, 194n32; Fechenbach, *Der Revolutionär Kurt Eisner*, 54.

[18] Bauer, *Die Regierung Eisner*, 211–213n1; *Verhandlungen des provisorischen Nationalrates des Volksstaates Bayern*, 187.

[19] Bauer, *Die Regierung Eisner*, 217, 226, 228, 439.

[20] Fechenbach, *Der Revolutionär Kurt Eisner*, 54; *Verhandlungen des provisorischen Nationalrates des Volksstaates Bayern*, 186.

[21] Bauer, *Die Regierung Eisner*, 211–214.

[22] Mitchell, *Revolution in Bavaria*, 202.

[23] *Verhandlungen des provisorischen Nationalrates des Volksstaates Bayern*, 188–189; Bauer, *Die Regierung Eisner*, 212–213n1.

[24] Bauer, *Die Regierung Eisner*, 213n1.

[25] Ibid., 214–215, 220–222.

[26] Ibid., 224, 228, 230.

[27] Ibid., 226–231.

[28] *Verhandlungen des provisorischen Nationalrates des Volksstaates Bayern*, 186, 197–198.

[29] Ibid., 211, 214.

[30] Ibid., 224.

[31] IISG, Karl Kautsky, DX/172.

[32] Bauer, *Die Regierung Eisner*, 234–235.

[33] Ibid., 226–227; Mitchell, *Revolution in Bavaria*, 207–208.

[34] Eberhard Kolb, *The Weimar Republic*, trans. P. S. Falla (London: Unwin Hyman, 1990), 15–16.

[35] Bauer, *Die Regierung Eisner*, 245–257.

[36] Ibid., 250.

[37] Joseph Würsdörfer, "Die Wahlen zum Bayer. Landtag am 12. Januar 1919," *Politische Zeitfragen: Lose Mitteilungen über alle Gebiete des öffentlichen Lebens* 1.3/4 (15 March 1919): 47–49.

[38] Bauer, *Die Regierung Eisner*, 245–257; text of approved draft in ibid., 440–442.

[39] "Kurt Eisner in Ingolstadt," *Neue Zeitung: Unabhängiges sozialistisches Organ*, 7 January 1919; SAPMO-BArch, NY 4060/29/3–4; Bauer, *Die Regierung Eisner*, 256n.

[40] Otto Friedrich, *Before the Deluge: A Portrait of Berlin in the 1920s* (New York: Harper & Row, 1972), 39–40.

[41] Harry Kessler, *In the Twenties: The Diaries of Harry Kessler*, trans. Charles Kessler (New York: Holt, Rinehart and Winston, [1971]), 53.

[42] Watt, *The Kings Depart*, 261–262; http://www.gedenktafeln-in-berlin. de/nc/gedenktafeln/gedenktafel-anzeige/tid/spartakusaufstand-1/.

[43] Friedrich, *Before the Deluge*, 44.

[44] Bauer, *Die Regierung Eisner*, 258n3, 267.

[45] Ibid., 257–280.

[46] Ibid., 261; Friedrich, *Before the Deluge*, 43.

[47] Bauer, *Die Regierung Eisner*, 262, 265–270.

[48] Ibid., 274, 286.

[49] Ibid., 258n1; quoted in Schade, *Kurt Eisner*, 82.

[50] Bauer, *Die Regierung Eisner*, 258n3, 281n1, 286; Schade, *Kurt Eisner*, 81–82; Freya Eisner, *Kurt Eisner: Die Politik des libertären Sozialismus*, 159.

[51] Bauer, *Die Regierung Eisner*, 281n1, 282, 285–287.

[52] Ibid., 282–283, 289–290.

[53] Würsdörfer, "Die Wahlen zum Bayer. Landtag," 42–49; Fechenbach, *Der Revolutionär Kurt Eisner*, 54–55.

[54] Mitchell, *Revolution in Bavaria*, 213–219; Würsdorfer, "Die Wahlen zum Bayer. Landtag," 58; *Verhandlungen des Bayerischen Landtages 1919: Stenographische Berichte Nr. 1 bis 27* (21 February–24 October 1919), xxxii, xxxiv; Schade, *Kurt Eisner*, 82. For statistics on the female vote see *Statistisches Jahrbuch für den Freistaat Bayern 1919* (Munich: J. Lindauersche Universitäts-Buchhandlung, [1920]), 584–589.

[55] Kurt Eisner, "Wahlrede vor den Unabhängigen," 29.

[56] Schade, *Kurt Eisner*, 83–84; Freya Eisner, *Kurt Eisner: Die Politik des libertären Sozialismus*, 163–165; Kurt Eisner, "Die Stellung der Arbeiter-, Soldaten- und Bauernräte," in Kurt Eisner, *Zwischen Kapitalismus und Kommunismus*, 273.

[57] Kurt Eisner, "Richtlinien für die künftige sozialistische Politik," *Neue Zeitung: Unabhängiges sozialistisches Organ*, 15 January 1919. Reprinted in Kurt Eisner, *Zwischen Kapitalismus und Kommunismus*, 274–276. Mitchell, *Revolution in Bavaria*, 219–220.

[58] Quoted in Mitchell, *Revolution in Bavaria*, 219.

[59] Kurt Eisner, "Richtlinien für die künftige sozialistische Politik," 274.

[60] Quoted in Schade, *Kurt Eisner*, 84.

[61] Kolb, *The Weimar Republic*, 16.

[62] Klaus Völker, *Brecht-Chronik: Daten zu Leben und Werk* (Munich: Carl Hanser, 1971), 13.

[63] SAPMO-BArch, NY 4060/64/326.

[64] Mitchell, *Revolution in Bavaria*, 218. Schade, *Kurt Eisner*, 161n195.

[65] Bauer, *Die Regierung Eisner*, 306.

[66] Ibid., 340n4.

[67] Kurt Eisner, "Die Aufgabe des bayerischen Sozialisierungs-Ausschusses," in Kurt Eisner, *Sozialismus als Aktion*, 124–132.

[68] Bauer, *Die Regierung Eisner*, 330–337.

[69] Ibid., 339–348; Mitchell, *Revolution in Bavaria*, 254.

[70] Freya Eisner, *Kurt Eisner: Die Politik des libertären Sozialismus*, 167–168.

[71] Bauer, *Die Regierung Eisner*, 361–362n2.

[72] SAPMO-BArch, NY 4060/1/203.

[73] Bauer, *Die Regierung Eisner*, 361–362n2.

[74] IISG, Gustav Landauer Archive, 121.

[75] Mitchell, *Revolution in Bavaria*, 207, 230.

[76] Schade, *Kurt Eisner*, 84, 162nn211–212, 163nn213–215.

[77] Freya Eisner, *Kurt Eisner: Die Politik des libertären Sozialismus*, 169.

[78] Robert Michels, "Kurt Eisner: Unter Benützung von persönlichen Erinnerungen," *Archiv für die Geschichte des Sozialismus und der Arbeiterbewegung* 14 (1929): 379, 383, 385.

[79] See Bauer, *Die Regierung Eisner*, 375–376.

[80] Freya Eisner, *Kurt Eisner: Die Politik des libertären Sozialismus*, 168–169; Bauer, *Die Regierung Eisner*, 361–362n2.

[81] The entire speech, with an introduction by Heinrich Ströbel, is printed in Kurt Eisner, *Schuld und Sühne*, Flugschriften des Bundes Neues Vaterland 12 (Berlin: Verlag Neues Vaterland, 1919). Reprinted in part in Kurt Eisner, *Sozialismus als Aktion*, 133–138.

[82] Michels, "Kurt Eisner," 375.

[83] Fechenbach, *Der Revolutionär Kurt Eisner*, 57–60.

[84] Kurt Eisner, *Schuld und Sühne*, 25.

[85] Freya Eisner, *Kurt Eisner: Die Politik des libertären Sozialismus*, 175–176; Mitchell, *Revolution in Bavaria*, 275–276; Arnau, *Gelebt, geliebt, gehaßt*, 95.

[86] Quoted in Fechenbach, *Der Revolutionär Kurt Eisner*, 60.

[87] Bauer, *Die Regierung Eisner*, 337.

[88] Ibid., 362n2; Schade, *Kurt Eisner*, 85.

[89] Kurt Eisner, *Der Sozialismus und die Jugend: Vortrag gehalten zu Basel auf Einladung der Basler Studentenschaft im Großen Musiksaal am 10. Februar 1919* (Basel: Druck und Verlag der National-Zeitung), 3.

[90] Michels, "Kurt Eisner," 376.

[91] Ibid., 377–378.

[92] LBI-NY, Transcript of Diary Written by the Grandmother of Mr. Cyril Jalon.

[93] Michels, "Kurt Eisner," 378.

[94] Kurt Eisner, *Der Sozialismus und die Jugend*.

[95] Michels, "Kurt Eisner," 380–381.

[96] Bauer, *Die Regierung Eisner*, 358n2, 361n1, 366–371.

[97] Ibid., 362n4; Schade, *Kurt Eisner*, 85.

[98] Freya Eisner, *Kurt Eisner: Die Politik des libertären Sozialismus*, 178–179; Schade, *Kurt Eisner*, 85.

[99] Bauer, *Die Regierung Eisner*, 374–379.

[100] Schade, *Kurt Eisner*, 85–86.

[101] Ibid., 86; Freya Eisner, *Kurt Eisner: Die Politik des libertären Sozialismus*, 180–182; Bauer, *Die Regierung Eisner*, 393–394.

[102] Freya Eisner, *Kurt Eisner: Die Politik des libertären Sozialismus*, 182–184.

[103] Mitchell, *Revolution in Bavaria*, 268–270. The most complete text of Eisner's address, drawn from the *Bayerische Staatszeitung*, is printed in Bauer, *Die Regierung Eisner*, 444–446.

[104] Bauer, *Die Regierung Eisner*, 401–402; Freya Eisner, *Kurt Eisner: Die Politik des libertären Sozialismus*, 184.

[105] Bauer, *Die Regierung Eisner*, 446–452.

[106] Hitzer, *Anton Graf Arco*, 384–389, 391–392.

[107] Fechenbach, *Der Revolutionär Kurt Eisner*, 62; Hitzer, *Anton Graf Arco*, 53, 58–67, 395–397; Wahl, "Rätezeit in München," 16. Fechenbach believed

that it was Klebsch who shot Arco (Hitzer, *Anton Graf Arco*, 59), but Wahl reports that Huber claimed to have fired the shots.

Chapter Twenty-Four

[1] Braun-Vogelstein, *Was niemals stirbt*, 308–309.

[2] Hitzer, *Anton Graf Arco*, 65–67; Fechenbach, *Der Revolutionär Kurt Eisner*, 62; "Die neuen Umsturztage in München," *MNN*, 25 February 1919.

[3] Hitzer, *Anton Graf Arco*, 145, 187.

[4] Wahl, "Rätezeit in München," 16.

[5] *Verhandlungen des Bayerischen Landtags 1919: Stenographische Berichte Nr. 1 bis 27* (21 February–24 October 1919), 1:1; Hitzer, *Anton Graf Arco*, 176.

[6] Schade, *Kurt Eisner*, 88; Hitzer, *Anton Graf Arco*, 189, 279.

[7] Hitzer, *Anton Graf Arco*, 179, 183–185, 226.

[8] Graf, *Wir sind Gefangene*, 444–445; Michels, "Kurt Eisner," 390; Ricarda Huch, "Kurt Eisners Todestag: Eine Münchner Erinnerung," in *Gesammelte Schriften: Essays, Reden, autobiographische Aufzeichnungen* (Freiburg im Breisgau: Atlantis, 1964), 134.

[9] Thomas Mann, *Diaries, 1918–1939*, 34.

[10] Toller, *Eine Jugend in Deutschland*, 4:116.

[11] *Verhandlungen des Bayerischen Landtags 1919*, 1:1–2.

[12] Hitzer, *Anton Graf Arco*, 145–155, 158.

[13] Ibid., 54–58, 160.

[14] Ibid., 227.

[15] Graf, *Wir sind Gefangene*, 444–445.

[16] "Eisner, Kurt: Kurt Eisner zum Gedächtnis!" [Kleine Drucksachen], München 1919–1921, *Münchener DigitalisierungsZentrum*, http://daten. digitalesammlungen.de/0001/bsb00013318/images/index.html?fip=193.1. 74.98.30&id=00013318&seite=19.

[17] Graf, *Wir sind Gefangene*, 446.

[18] Freya Eisner, *Kurt Eisner: Die Politik des libertären Sozialismus*, 187.

[19] Mitchell, *Revolution in Bavaria*, 278–279; Graf, *Wir sind Gefangene*, 446–448.

[20] "Die neuen Umsturztage."

[21] "Ein Aufruf der USP," *Nachrichtenblatt des Zentralrats*, 22 February 1919.

[22] "Ein Märtyrer der Revolution," *Nachrichtenblatt des Zentralrats*, 22 February 1919.

23 "Die neuen Umsturztage."

24 "Nachmittagssitzung des Münchner Arbeiterrats," *Nachrichtenblatt des Zentralrats*, 22 February 1919.

25 "Dokument: Bekanntmachung," *Historisches Lexikon Bayerns*, 17 October 2012, http://www.historisches-lexikon-bayerns.de/document/artikel_44593_bilder_value_1_roter-terror1.jpg; *Verhandlungen des Kongresses der Arbeiter-, Bauern- und Soldatenräte vom 25. Februar bis 8. März 1919*, 3.

26 Hitzer, *Anton Graf Arco*, 228–229.

27 Mitchell, *Revolution in Bavaria*, 279–280.

28 *Verhandlungen des Kongresses der Arbeiter-, Bauern- und Soldatenräte*, 1–2, 10, 14, 17.

29 Bauer, *Die Regierung Eisner*, 402–406.

30 Freya Eisner, *Kurt Eisner: Die Politik des libertären Sozialismus*, 189–190; Graf, *Wir sind Gefangene*, 455–456; Jeffrey S. Gaab, *Munich Hofbräuhaus: Beer, Culture, and Politics* (New York: Peter Lang, 2006), 61; Mitchell, *Revolution in Bavaria*, 275–276; Bernhard Grau, "Beisetzung Kurt Eisners, München, 26. Februar 1919," *Historisches Lexikon Bayerns*, 20 May 2015, http://www.historisches-lexikon-bayerns.de/artikel/artikel_44676.

31 Gustav Landauer, *Gustav Landauer und die Revolutionszeit 1918/19: Die politischen Reden, Schriften, Erlasse und Briefe Landauers aus der November-Revolution 1918/1919*, ed. Ulrich Linse (Berlin: Karin Kramer, 1974), 153–158.

32 Gavriel D. Rosenfeld, "Monuments and the Politics of Memory: Commemorating Kurt Eisner and the Bavarian Revolutions of 1918–1919 in Postwar Munich," *Central European History* 30.2 (1997): 230–231.

33 Kurt Eisner, *Welt werde froh! Ein Kurt-Eisner-Buch*, ed. Erich Knauf (Berlin: Büchergilde Gutenberg, 1929), 7. The German:

> Kurt Eisner lieget hie,
> Der Plänereiche:
> Einst zweifelhaft Genie,
> Jetzt sicher Leiche.

34 Heinrich Ströbel, introduction to Kurt Eisner, *Schuld und Sühne*, 4, 7–8.

35 Heinrich Mann, "Kurt Eisner: Gedenkrede, gehalten am 16. März 1919," in *Macht und Mensch* (Munich: Kurt Wolff, 1919), 170–175.

36 Hausenstein, "Erinnerung an Eisner," 56–68.

37 Michels, "Kurt Eisner," 390.

38 Mugay, "'Patro hat uns sehr gefehlt.'"

39 Mitchell, *Revolution in Bavaria*, 297.

[40] John Maynard Keynes, *The Economic Consequences of the Peace* (New York: Harcourt, Brace, and Howe, 1920), 36, 268.

[41] Oskar Maria Graf, "Die Juden stehen nicht allein," in Graf, *Reden und Aufsätze aus dem Exil,* 160–161, 445.

[42] Ernst Toller, "Justiz: Erlebnisse," in Toller, *Gesammelte Werke,* 1:98–101.

[43] Bauer, *Die Regierung Eisner,* xlvii; Stampfer, *Erfahrungen und Erkenntnisse,* 74.

[44] Dove, *He Was a German,* 76–80, 82–84, 88–93; Hermann Gilbhard, "Thule-Gesellschaft, 1918–1933," *Historisches Lexikon Bayerns,* 28 May 2015, http://www.historisches-lexikon-bayerns.de/artikel/artikel_44318; Hitzer, *Anton Graf Arco,* 367–370.

[45] Frühwald and Spalek, *Der Fall Toller,* 21–24; Dove, *He Was a German,* 199–249; Toller, *Eine Jugend in Deutschland,* 4:116–118.

[46] Dove, *He Was a German,* 262; Robert Payne, *Forever China* (New York: Dodd, 1945), 221–225.

[47] Schueler, *Auf der Flucht erschossen,* 187–192, 203–208, 211, 219–225, 240–248.

[48] Stefan Großmann, for example, characterizes Fechenbach as a "naive soul" in "Kurt Eisner," 558.

[49] Schiewe and Maußner, *Trotz allem Mensch sein,* 167–171; Graf, "Die Juden stehen nicht allein," 160–161; Christian Linder, "'Sich fügen heißt lügen': Vor 80 Jahren ermordeten die Nazis den Schriftsteller Erich Mühsam," *Deutschland Radiokultur,* 10 July 2014, http://www.deutschlandradiokultur.de/erich-muehsam-sich-fuegen-heisst-luegen.932.de.html?dram%3Aarticle_id=291354.

[50] Bauer, *Die Regierung Eisner,* xlv.

[51] Eyck, *A History of the Weimar Republic,* 1:188; Watt, *The Kings Depart,* 522.

[52] Snyder, *The Weimar Republic,* 49–50, 153–154. See also Friedrich, *Before the Deluge,* 118–119.

[53] Hitzer, *Anton Graf Arco,* 160–162; Bauer, *Die Regierung Eisner,* xxxvi–xxxviii, lvi n2; Joachim Lilla, "Auer, Erhard," *Bayerische Landesbibliothek Online,* 12 November 2014, http://verwaltungshandbuch.bayerische-landesbibliothek-online.de/auer-erhard; Herzog, *Menschen, denen ich begegnete,* 69.

[54] Bauer, *Die Regierung Eisner,* xli–xliii.

[55] Ibid., xxxviii–xxxvix; Joachim Lilla, "Timm, Johannes," *Bayerische Landesbibliothek Online,* 8 Oktober 2012, http://verwaltungshandbuch.bayerische-landesbibliothek-online.de/timm-johannes.

56 Bauer, *Die Regierung Eisner*, xl; Joachim Lilla, "Roßhaupter, Albert," *Bayerische Landesbibliothek Online*, 27 June 2014, http://verwaltungshand buch.bayerische-landesbibliothek-online.de/rosshaupter-albert. See also http://www.hdbg.de/parlament/content/persDetail.php?id=1825.

57 Bauer, *Die Regierung Eisner*, xlv–xlvi; Joachim Lilla, "Frauendorfer, Heinrich Ritter von," *Bayerische Landesbibliothek Online*, 19 Februar 2015, http://verwaltungshandbuch.bayerische-landesbibliothek-online.de/frauendorfer-heinrich.

58 Wilhelm Heinz Schröder, "Gradnauer, Georg," in *Sozialdemokratische Parlamentarier*, 69.

59 "Kaliski, Julius," *Katalog der deutschen Nationalbibliothek*, https://portal.dnb.de/opac.htm?method=showFullRecord&currentResultId=%221335139 47%22%26any&currentPosition=3.

60 Franz Osterroth, "Friedrich Stampfer," in *Biographisches Lexikon des Sozialismus* (Hanover: J. H. W. Dietz, 1960), 297–299; Stampfer, *Erfahrungen und Erkenntnisse*, 123.

61 Franz Osterroth, "Joseph Bloch," in *Biographisches Lexikon des Sozialismus*, 25–26.

62 Wilhelm Heinz Schröder, "Weill, Georges," in *Sozialdemokratische Parlamentarier*, 794–795.

63 Pohl, *Adolf Müller*, 259–260, 361, 371.

64 Steenson, *Karl Kautsky, 1854–1938*, 228.

65 Friedrich, *Before the Deluge*, 45–46. See also Hans Schmelz and Martin Virchow, "'Ich liess Rosa Luxemburg richten': SPIEGEL-Gespräch mit dem Putsch-Hauptmann Waldemar Pabst," *Der Spiegel* 16.16 (18 April 1962): 38–44.

66 Helga Grebing, "Cunow, Heinrich Wilhelm Carl," in *Neue Deutsche Biographie*, vol. 3 (1957), 439–440.

67 Gisela M. Krause, "Lensch, Paul," in *Neue Deutsche Biographie*, vol. 14 (1985), 215–217.

68 Hitzer, *Anton Graf Arco*, 250–255, 257, 308–314; Toller, "Justiz: Erlebnisse," 1:101–102.

69 Schueler, *Auf der Flucht erschossen*, 126; Toller, "Justiz: Erlebnisse," 1:102n.

70 Hitzer, *Anton Graf Arco*, 379–380.

71 Rudolf von Sebottendorff [Rudolf Glauer], *Bevor Hitler kam: Urkundliches aus der Frühzeit der nationalsozialistischen Bewegung* (Munich: Deukala, 1933), 82.

[72] Hitzer, *Anton Graf Arco*, 258–272, 306–307; Norman Dankerl, *Alois Lindner: Das Leben eines bayerischen Abenteurers und Revolutionärs* (Viechtach: Lichtung, 2007), 134–139.

[73] Siegried Jacobsohn, "Antworten: Wilhelm A.," *Die Weltbühne: Wochenschrift für Politik, Kunst, Wirtschaft* 15.10 (27 February 1919): 238–239; Else Eisner, "Brief über Kurt Eisner," *Die Weltbühne* 15.16 (10 April 1919): 403–404.

[74] SAPMO-BArch, NY 4060 (Nachlaß Kurt Eisner)/103/18.

[75] Freia Eisner, "Ansätze zu einem Lebenslauf," *Sinn und Form* 38.4 (July/August 1986): 696.

[76] Frank Flechtmann, "Das 'Haus an der Stirn': Familie Eisner in Gengenbach," in *Die Ortenau*, ed. Karl Maier, Veröffentlichungen des Historischen Vereins für Mittelbaden 72 (Offenburg: Verlag des Historischen Vereins für Mittelbaden, 1992), 305, 307–309, 333n25a; Freia Eisner, "Ansätze zu einem Lebenslauf," 696–701. See also Claudia Schoppmann, *Zeit der Maskierung: Lebensgeschichten lesbischer Frauen im "Dritten Reich"* (Berlin: Orlanda Frauenverlag, 1993), 144–160.

[77] Meyer, "Sanitätsrat Ruth Strahl," 9; Schütt, "Hoffnung ist nicht aus der Welt zu schaffen."

[78] Freia Eisner, "Ansätze zu einem Lebenslauf," 705–712.

[79] CJA 6.4 (Nachlaß Freia Eisner)/30/5–6.

[80] CJA 6.4/13/1.

[81] Flechtmann, "Familie Eisner in Gengenbach," 318–319; SAPMO-BArch, NY 4060/101/9; Freia Eisner, "Ansätze zu einem Lebenslauf," 703.

[82] See Stephen Schwartz, "The Mysterious Death of Walter Benjamin," *The Weekly Standard* 6.37 (11 June 2001).

[83] CFA 6.4/31/15; Ernst Federn, "Eros hinter Stacheldraht," in *Stimmen aus Buchenwald: Ein Lesebuch*, ed. Holm Kirsten and Wulf Kirsten (Göttingen: Wallstein, 2002), 71–72; Wolfgang Röll, *Sozialdemokraten im Konzentrationslager Buchenwald 1937–1945: Unter Einbeziehung biographischer Skizzen* (Göttingen: Wallstein, 2000), 85–87.

[84] Meyer, "Sanitätsrat Ruth Strahl," 9.

[85] Flechtmann, "Familie Eisner in Gengenbach," 306–307, 317, 323–325, 328–331.

[86] Rosenfeld, "Monuments and the Politics of Memory," 232.

[87] Guenter Lewy, "Mit festem Schritt ins Neue Reich: Die katholische Kirche zwischen Kreuz und Hakenkreuz," *Der Spiegel* 19.15 (7 April 1965): 85–86.

88 Erika Maria Lankes, "Das Denkmal heute: Funktion und Umsetzung," in *Geschichte zwischen Kunst und Politik*, ed. Ulrich Baumgärtner and Monika Fenn, Münchner geschichtsdidaktisches Kolloquium 4 (Munich: Herbert Utz, 2002), 83–94.

89 Quoted in Schmolze and Schmolze, introduction to Kurt Eisner, *Die halbe Macht*, 36–37.

90 Mitchell, *Revolution in Bavaria*, 336.

SOURCES AND REFERENCES

As a professional writer for the serial press, Kurt Eisner brought work to print nearly every day for a quarter century. Individual articles, essays, editorials, reviews, and columns cited in this study are fully documented in the endnotes; the newspapers and journals that circulated his cited writings and those of his allies and adversaries are listed below in sections IV and V. Eisner's book-length writings and separately published tracts are listed in section I. With regard to secondary sources, only those works that were consulted or might be of special interest to the researcher appear here.

I. Primary Literature

Adler, Victor. *Briefwechsel mit August Bebel und Karl Kautsky*. Edited by Friedrich Adler. Vienna: Wiener Volksbuchhandlung, 1954.

Alexander, Thomas. *The Prussian Elementary Schools*. New York: Macmillan, 1919.

Arnau, Frank [Heinrich Karl Schmitt]. *Gelebt, geliebt, gehaßt: Ein Leben im 20. Jahrhundert*. Munich: Kurt Desch, 1972.

Becker, Matthäus. "Kurt Eisner und der 'Bauernkönig.'" *Die Weltbühne: Wochenschrift für Politik, Kunst, Wirtschaft* 3.7/8 (1948): 187–188.

Bernstein, Eduard. *Die Voraussetzungen des Sozialismus und die Aufgaben der Sozialdemokratie*. Internationale Bibliothek 61. 1921. Reprint of 2nd ed., Berlin: J. H. W. Dietz, 1977.

Braun, Lily. *Memoiren einer Sozialistin: Kampfjahre*, Vol. 3 of *Gesammelte Werke*. Berlin-Grunewald: Hermann Klemm, n.d.

Braun-Vogelstein, Julie. *Was niemals stirbt: Gestalten und Erinnerungen*. Stuttgart: Deutsche Verlagsanstalt, 1966.

Bücher, Karl. *Unsere Sache und die Tagespresse*. Tübingen: J. C. B. Mohr, 1915.

Büttner, Paul, Georg Gradnauer, Kurt Eisner, Julius Kaliski, Wilhelm Schröder, and Heinrich Wetzker, eds. *Der Vorwärts-Konflikt: Gesammelte Aktenstücke*. Munich: G. Birk, [1905].

Burschell, Friedrich. "*Revolution* und *Neue Erde*: München 1918/19 aus meinen Erinnerungen." In *Imprimatur: Ein Jahrbuch für Bücherfreunde*, edited by Siegfried Buchenau, n.s., 3:244–248. Frankfurt am Main: Gesellschaft der Bibliophilen, 1961/62.

Cossmann, Paul Nikolaus. "In der Heimat: Vom Munitionsarbeiterstreik zur Revolution." *Süddeutsche Monatshefte* 21 (1923/24): 92–94.

———, ed. "Vorbereitung des Münchner Munitionsarbeiterstreiks vom Januar 1918: Nach unveröffentlichten Geheimakten." *Süddeutsche Monatshefte* 21 (1923/24): 26–32.

Doeberl, Michael. *Sozialismus, soziale Revolution, sozialer Volksstaat.* Munich: Verlag der Allgemeinen Zeitung, 1920.

Dorst, Tankred, ed. *Die Münchner Räterepublik: Zeugnisse und Kommentar.* Frankfurt am Main: Suhrkamp, 1980.

Eisner, Freia. "Ansätze zu einem Lebenslauf." *Sinn und Form* 38.4 (July/August 1986): 696–710.

Eisner, Kurt. *Psychopathia spiritualis: Friedrich Nietzsche und die Apostel der Zukunft.* Leipzig: Wilhelm Friedrich, [1892].

———. *Eine Junkerrevolte: Drei Wochen preußischer Politik.* Berlin: Buchhandlung Vorwärts, 1899.

———. *Wilhelm Liebknecht: Sein Leben und Wirken.* Berlin: Buchhandlung Vorwärts, 1900, 2nd ed., 1906.

———. *Taggeist: Culturglossen.* Berlin: John Edelheim, 1901.

———. *Der Geheimbund des Zaren: Der Königsberger Prozeß wegen Geheimbündelei, Hochverrat gegen Rußland und Zarenbeleidigung vom 12. bis 25. Juli 1904.* Berlin: Buchhandlung Vorwärts, 1904.

———. *Feste der Festlosen: Hausbuch weltlicher Predigtschwänke.* Dresden: Kaden, [1906].

———. *Der Sultan des Weltkrieges: Ein marokkanisches Sittenbild deutscher Diplomaten-Politik.* Dresden: Kaden, 1906.

———. *Das Ende des Reichs: Deutschland und Preußen im Zeitalter der großen Revolution.* 2nd ed. Berlin: Buchhandlung Vorwärts, 1907.

———. *Treibende Kräfte.* Flugschriften des Bundes Neues Vaterland 4. 2nd ed. Berlin: Verlag Neues Vaterland, 1915.

———. *Gesammelte Schriften.* 2 vols. Berlin: Paul Cassirer, 1919.

———. *Die neue Zeit.* Edited by Benno Merkle. Munich: Georg Müller, 1919.

———. *Die neue Zeit: Zweite Folge.* Munich: Georg Müller, 1919.

———. *Schuld und Sühne.* Introduced by Heinrich Ströbel. Flugschriften des Bundes Neues Vaterland 12. Berlin: Verlag Neues Vaterland, 1919.

———. *Der Sozialismus und die Jugend: Vortrag gehalten zu Basel auf Einladung der Basler Studentenschaft im Großen Musiksaal am 10. February 1919.* Basel: Druck und Verlag der National-Zeitung, 1919.

———. *Unterdrücktes aus dem Weltkrieg.* Munich: Georg Müller Verlag, 1919.

———. *Die Götterprüfung: Eine weltpolitische Posse in fünf Akten und einer Zwischenaktspantomime.* Berlin: Paul Cassirer, 1920.

———. *Wachsen und Werden: Aphorismen, Gedichte, Tagebuchblätter, dramatische Bruchstücke, Prosa usw.* Leipzig: Roter Türmer, 1926.

———. *Mein Gefängnistagebuch: Untersuchungsgefängnis München am Neudeck.* In *Die Menschheit* 3–7, 9 (20, 27 January, 3, 10, 17 February, 2 March 1928): 19, 27, 38, 48, 57, 76.

———. *Welt werde froh! Ein Kurt-Eisner-Buch.* Edited by Erich Knauf. Berlin: Büchergilde Gutenberg, 1929.

———. *Die halbe Macht den Räten: Ausgewählte Aufsätze und Reden.* Edited and introduced by Renate and Gerhard Schmolze. Cologne: Jakob Hegner, 1969.

———. *Sozialismus als Aktion: Ausgewählte Aufsätze und Reden.* Edited by Freya Eisner. Frankfurt am Main: Suhrkamp, 1975.

———. *Zwischen Kapitalismus und Kommunismus.* Edited and introduced by Freya Eisner. Frankfurt am Main: Suhrkamp, 1996.

Fechenbach, Felix. *Der Revolutionär Kurt Eisner.* Berlin: J. H. W. Dietz, 1929.

Federn, Ernst. "Eros hinter Stacheldraht." In *Stimmen aus Buchenwald: Ein Lesebuch,* edited by Holm Kirsten and Wulf Kirsten, 69–72. Göttingen: Wallstein, 2002.

Friedländer, Hugo. *Interessante Kriminal-Prozesse von kulturhistorischer Bedeutung: Darstellung merkwürdiger Strafrechtsfälle aus Gegenwart und Jüngstvergangenheit.* Vol. 5. Berlin: Hermann Barsdorf, 1912.

Gärtner, Georg. *Die Nürnberger Arbeiterbewegung 1868–1908.* [1908]. Reprint, Berlin: J. H. W. Dietz, 1977.

Graf, Oskar Maria. *Wir sind Gefangene: Ein Bekenntnis.* Munich: Süddeutscher Verlag, 1978.

———. *Reden und Aufsätze aus dem Exil.* Edited by Helmut F. Pfanner. Munich: Süddeutscher Verlag, 1989.

Grey, Edward. *Why Britain Is in the War and What She Hopes from the Future.* London: Unwin, [1916].

Großmann, Stefan. "Kurt Eisner." *Das Tagebuch* 10.14 (6 April 1929): 558–562.

Hausenstein, Wilhelm. "Erinnerung an Eisner." *Der neue Merkur* 3.1 (April 1929): 56–68.

Heine, Wolfgang. *Gegen die Quertreiber!* Dessau: Verlag Volksblatt für Anhalt, [1915].

Herzog, Wilhelm. *Menschen, denen ich begegnete.* Bern: Francke, 1959.

Hofmiller, Josef. *Revolutionstagebuch 1918/19: Aus den Tagen der Münchner Revolution.* Leipzig: Karl Rauch, [1938].

Huch, Ricarda. *Gesammelte Schriften: Essays, Reden, autobiographische Aufzeichnungen.* Freiburg im Breisgau: Atlantis, 1964.

Kautsky, Karl Jr., ed. *August Bebels Briefwechsel mit Karl Kautsky.* Assen: Van Gorcum, 1971.

Kessler, Harry. *In the Twenties: The Diaries of Harry Kessler.* Translated by Charles Kessler. New York: Holt, Rinehart and Winston, [1971].

———. *Journey to the Abyss: The Diaries of Count Harry Kessler, 1880–1918.* Translated and edited by Laird M. Easton. New York: Knopf, 2011.

Keynes, John Maynard. *The Economic Consequences of the Peace.* New York: Harcourt, Brace, and Howe, 1920.

Koester, Adolf. "Hermann Cohen." *März: Eine Wochenschrift* 6.3 (1912): 157–158.

Kraus, Karl. *1914–1925: In dieser großen Zeit.* Vol. 2 of *Ausgewählte Werke.* Edited by Dietrich Simon. Berlin: [Verlag Volk und Welt], [1971].

Landauer, Gustav. *Gustav Landauer und die Revolutionszeit 1918/19: Die politischen Reden, Schriften, Erlasse und Briefe Landauers aus der November-Revolution 1918/1919.* Edited by Ulrich Linse. Berlin: Karin Kramer, 1974.

Liebert, Eduard von. *Aus einem bewegten Leben.* Munich: J. F. Lehmann, 1925.

Luxemburg, Rosa. *Gesammelte Briefe.* Edited by Annelies Laschitza and Günter Radczun. 5 vols. Berlin: Dietz, 1982–1984.

Mann, Heinrich. *Macht und Mensch.* Munich: Kurt Wolff, 1919.

Mann, Thomas. *Diaries, 1918–1939.* Translated by Richard and Clara Winston. New York: Harry N. Abrams, 1982.

Meyer, Bernhard. "Sanitätsrat Ruth Strahl—ein ungewöhnlicher Lebensweg." *Humanitas: Zeitschrift für Medizin und Gesellschaft* 21 (1988): 9.

Michels, Robert. "Kurt Eisner: Unter Benützung von persönlichen Erinnerungen." *Archiv für die Geschichte des Sozialismus und der Arbeiterbewegung* 14 (1929): 364–391.

Mühsam, Erich. *Von Eisner bis Leviné: Die Entstehung der bayerischen Räterepublik.* Berlin-Britz: FANAL-Verlag Erich Mühsam, 1929.

———. *In meiner Posaune muß ein Sandkorn sein: Briefe 1900–1934.* Edited by Gerd W. Jungblut. 2 vols. Vaduz: Topos, 1984.

———. *Trotz allem Mensch sein: Gedichte und Aufsätze.* Edited by Jürgen Schiewe and Hanne Maußner. Stuttgart: Reclam, 1984.

———. *Tagebücher 1910–1924.* Edited by Chris Hirte. Munich: Deutscher Taschenbuch Verlag, 1994.

Müller, Georg Alexander von. *Regierte der Kaiser? Kriegstagebücher, Aufzeichnungen und Briefe des Chefs des Marine-Kabinetts 1914–1918.* Edited by Walter Görlitz. Göttingen: Musterschmidt, 1959.

Müller, Hermann. *Die November-Revolution: Erinnerungen.* Berlin: Der Bücherkreis, 1928.

Müller, Karl Alexander von. *Mars und Venus: Erinnerungen 1914–1919.* Stuttgart: Gustav Kilpper, 1954.

Mugay, Peter. "'Patro hat uns sehr gefehlt.'" *Abendzeitung,* 21 August 2006.

Payne, Robert. *Forever China.* New York: Dodd, Mead and Co., 1945.

Prager, Eugen. *Das Gebot der Stunde: Geschichte der USPD.* 4th ed. Berlin: J. H. W. Dietz, 1980.

Rikli, Erika. *Der Revisionismus: Ein Revisionsversuch der deutschen marxistischen Theorie 1890–1914.* Zurich: H. Girsberger, 1936.

Rilke, Rainer Maria. *Briefe zur Politik.* Edited by Joachim W. Storck. Frankfurt am Main: Insel, 1992.

Ropp, Friedrich von der. *Zwischen Gestern und Morgen: Erfahrungen und Erkenntnisse.* 2nd ed. Stuttgart: J. F. Steinkopf, 1963.

Rückel, Gert. *Die Fränkische Tagespost: Geschichte einer Parteizeitung.* Veröffentlichungen der Stadtbibliothek Nürnberg 8. Nuremberg: Fränkische Verlagsanstalt und Buchdruckerei, 1964.

Scheidemann, Philipp. *Memoiren eines Sozialdemokraten.* 2 vols. Dresden: Carl Reissner, 1928.

Schmelz, Hans, and Martin Virchow. "'Ich liess Rosa Luxemburg richten': SPIEGEL-Gespräch mit dem Putsch-Hauptmann Waldemar Pabst." *Der Spiegel* 16.16 (18 April 1962): 38–44.

Schoppmann, Claudia. *Zeit der Maskierung: Lebensgeschichten lesbischer Frauen im "Dritten Reich."* Berlin: Orlanda Frauenverlag, 1993.

Schütt, Hans-Dieter. "Hoffnung ist nicht aus der Welt zu schaffen: Interview mit Ruth Strahl, der Tochter Kurt Eisners." *Neues Deutschland,* 17/18 August 1996.

Sebottendorff, Rudolf von [Rudolf Glauer]. *Bevor Hitler kam: Urkundliches aus der Frühzeit der nationalsozialistischen Bewegung.* Munich: Deukala, 1933.

Stampfer, Friedrich. *Erfahrungen und Erkenntnisse: Aufzeichnungen aus meinem Leben.* Cologne: Verlag für Politik und Wirtschaft, 1957.

Toller, Ernst. *Gesammelte Werke.* Edited by Wolfgang Frühwald and John M. Spalek, 2nd ed. 5 vols. Munich, Carl Hanser, 1996.

Von den Ursachen des Krieges bis etwa zum Schluß des Jahres 1914. Vol. 1 of *Kriegs-Rundschau: Zeitgenössische Zusammenstellung der für den Weltkrieg wichtigen Ereignisse, Urkunden, Kundgebungen, Schlacht- und Zeitberichte.* Berlin: Verlag der Täglichen Rundschau, 1915.

Wahl, Fritz. "Rätezeit in München." In *Gegenwart, Sonderheft zum 29. Oktober 1956: Ein Jahrhundert* Frankfurter Zeitung *1856–1956,* edited by Max von Brück et al., 15–16. Frankfurt am Main: Societäts-Druckerei, 1956.

Wille, Bruno. *Aus Traum und Kampf: Mein 60jähriges Leben.* 2nd ed. Berlin: Kultur-Verlag, 1920.

Würsdörfer, Joseph. "Die Wahlen zum Bayer. Landtag am 12. Januar 1919." *Politische Zeitfragen: Lose Mitteilungen über alle Gebiete des öffentlichen Lebens* 1.3/4 (15 March 1919): 41–76.

II. Secondary Literature

Altieri, Riccardo. *Der Pazifist Kurt Eisner.* Hamburg: Verlag Dr. Kovač, 2015.

Barrett, Michael B. "Erich Ludendorff." In Tucker et al., *World War I Encyclopedia*, 2:715–16.

Bauer, Gerhard. *Gefangenschaft und Lebenslust: Oskar Maria Graf in seiner Zeit.* Munich: Süddeutscher Verlag, 1987.

Baxandall, Lee. "The Naturalist Innovation on the German Stage: The Freie Bühne and Its Influence." *Modern Drama* 5.4 (February 1963): 454–476.

Becker, Bert. "Germany, Home Front." In Tucker et al., *World War I Encyclopedia*, 2:478–479.

Beyer, Hans. *Die Revolution in Bayern 1918/1919.* 2nd ed. Berlin: VEB Deutscher Verlag der Wissenschaften, 1988.

Bookchin, Murray. *The Spanish Anarchists: The Heroic Years, 1868–1936.* New York: Free Life Editions, 1977.

Brandes, Georg [Georg Morris Cohen]. *Friedrich Nietzsche.* Translated by A. G. Chater. London: William Heinemann, 1914.

Chamberlin, W. H. "The Kornilov Mutiny." In *The Russian Revolution: An Anthology*, edited by M. K. Dziewanowski, 101–137. New York: Thomas Y. Crowell, 1970.

Chickering, Roger. *Imperial Germany and a World without War: The Peace Movement and German Society, 1892–1914.* Princeton, NJ: Princeton University Press, 1975.

Craig, Gordon A. *Germany, 1866–1945.* New York: Oxford University Press, 1978.

Crothers, George Dunlap. *The German Elections of 1907.* New York: Columbia University Press, 1941.

Dankerl, Norman. *Alois Lindner: Das Leben eines bayerischen Abenteurers und Revolutionärs.* Viechtach: Lichtung, 2007.

Davis, Belinda J. *Home Fires Burning: Food, Politics, and Everyday Life in World War I Berlin.* Chapel Hill, NC: University of North Carolina Press, 2000.

Davis, Horace B. *Nationalism and Socialism: Marxist and Labor Theories of Nationalism to 1917.* New York: Monthly Review Press, 1967.

Dove, Richard. *He Was a German: A Biography of Ernst Toller*. London: Libris, 1990.

Easton, Laird M. *The Red Count: The Life and Times of Harry Kessler*. Berkeley: University of California Press, 2002.

Eisner, Freya. *Kurt Eisner: Die Politik des libertären Sozialismus*. Frankfurt am Main: Suhrkamp, 1979.

———. "Kurt Eisners Ort in der sozialistischen Bewegung." *Vierteljahrshefte für Zeitgeschichte* 45.3 (July 1995): 407–435.

Engelberg, Ernst. *Revolutionäre Politik und Rote Feldpost 1878–1890*. Berlin: Akademie, 1959.

Eyck, Erich. *A History of the Weimar Republic*. Translated by Harlan P. Hanson and Robert G. L. Waite. 2 vols. New York: Atheneum, 1970.

Feise, Ernst, and Harry Steinhauer, eds. *German Literature since Goethe*. Boston: Houghton Mifflin, 1958.

Fischer, Fritz. *Germany's Aims in the First World War*. New York: Norton, 1967.

Flechtheim, Ossip K. "Der einsame Sozialist. Verachtet, verkannt: Kurt Eisner." *Die Zeit*, 2 November 1979.

Flechtmann, Frank. "Das 'Haus an der Stirn': Familie Eisner in Gengenbach." In *Die Ortenau*, edited by Karl Maier, 303–339. Veröffentlichungen des Historischen Vereins für Mittelbaden 72. Offenburg: Verlag des Historischen Vereins für Mittelbaden, 1992.

Fletcher, Roger. *Revisionism and Empire: Socialist Imperialism in Germany, 1897–1914*. London: Allen and Unwin, 1984.

Fricke, Dieter. *Handbuch zur Geschichte der deutschen Arbeiterbewegung 1869 bis 1917*. 2 vols. Berlin: Dietz, 1987.

Friedrich, Otto. *Before the Deluge: A Portrait of Berlin in the 1920s*. New York: Harper & Row, 1972.

Fromkin, David. *Europe's Last Summer: Who Started the Great War in 1914?* New York: Knopf, 2004.

Frühwald, Wolfgang, and John M. Spalek, eds. *Der Fall Toller: Kommentar und Materialien*. Munich: Carl Hanser, 1979.

Füßl, Wilhelm. *Oskar von Miller 1855–1934: Eine Biographie*. Munich: C. H. Beck, 2005.

Gaab, Jeffrey S. *Munich Hofbräuhaus: Beer, Culture, and Politics*. New York: Peter Lang, 2006.

Gay, Peter. *The Dilemma of Democratic Socialism: Eduard Bernstein's Challenge to Marx*. New York: Collier, 1962.

Grau, Bernhard. *Kurt Eisner 1867–1919: Eine Biographie*. Munich: C. H. Beck, 2001.

Gurganus, Albert E. *The Art of Revolution: Kurt Eisner's Agitprop.* Studies in German Literature, Linguistics, and Culture 15. Columbia, SC: Camden House, 1986.

———. "Sarah Sonja Lerch, née Rabinowitz: The Sonja Irene L. of Toller's *Masse-Mensch.*" *German Studies Review* 28.3 (2005): 607–620.

Historische Kommission bei der Bayerischen Akademie der Wissenschaften, ed. *Neue Deutsche Biographie.* 25 vols. Berlin: Duncker & Humblot, 1953–.

Hitzer, Friedrich. *Anton Graf Arco: Das Attentat auf Kurt Eisner und die Schüsse im Landtag.* Munich: Knesebeck & Schuler, 1988.

Holzhey, Helmut. *Cohen und Natorp.* 2 vols. Basel: Schwabe, 1986.

Jackson, J. Hampden. *Clemenceau and the Third Republic.* New York: Collier, 1962.

Keegan, John. *The First World War.* New York: Vintage, 1998.

Kolb, Eberhard. *The Weimar Republic.* Translated by P. S. Falla. London: Unwin Hyman, 1990.

Lankes, Erika Maria. "Das Denkmal Heute: Funktion und Umsetzung." In *Geschichte zwischen Kunst und Politik,* edited by Ulrich Baumgärtner and Monika Fenn, 83–89. Münchner geschichtsdidaktisches Kolloquium 4. Munich: Herbert Utz, 2002.

Lau, Matthias. *Pressepolitik als Chance: Staatliche Öffentlichkeitsarbeit in den Ländern der Weimarer Republik.* Beiträge zur Kommunikationsgeschichte 14. Stuttgart: Franz Steiner, 2003.

Lepsius, M. Rainer. "Max Weber in München: Rede anläßlich der Enthüllung einer Gedenktafel." *Zeitschrift für Soziologie* 6.1 (January 1977): 103–118.

Lewy, Guenter. "Mit festem Schritt ins Neue Reich: Die katholische Kirche zwischen Kreuz und Hakenkreuz." *Der Spiegel* 19.15 (7 April 1965): 85–105.

Lidtke, Vernon L. *The Alternative Culture: Socialist Labor in Imperial Germany.* New York: Oxford University Press, 1985.

Linden, Harry van der. *Kantian Ethics and Socialism.* Indianapolis: Hackett, 1988.

Linder, Christian. "'Sich fügen heißt lügen': Vor 80 Jahren ermordeten die Nazis den Schriftsteller Erich Mühsam." *Deutschland Radiokultur,* 10 July 2014, http://www.deutschlandradiokultur.de/erich-muehsam-sich-fuegen-heisst-luegen.932.de.html?dram%3Aarticle_id=291354.

Luban, Ottokar. "Die Rolle der Spartakusgruppe bei der Entstehung und Entwicklung der USPD Januar 1916 bis März 1919." *JahrBuch für Forschungen zur Geschichte der Arbeiterbewegung* 7.2 (2008): 69–76.

Lutz, Ralph Haswell. *Fall of the German Empire, 1914–1918.* Translated by David G. Rempel and Gertrude Rendtorff. Hoover War Library Publications, no. 1. 2 vols. New York: Octagon Books, 1969.

Mackey, Richard William. *The Zabern Affair, 1913–1914.* Lanham, MD: University Press of America, 1991.

Manchester, William. *The Arms of Krupp, 1587–1968.* Boston: Little, Brown, 1968.

Marks, Harry J. "The Sources of Reformism in the Social Democratic Party of Germany, 1890–1914." *Journal of Modern History* 10 (March–December 1939): 334–356.

Matthias, Erich, Susanne Miller, and Heinrich Potthoff, eds. *Die Regierung der Volksbeauftragten 1918/19: Erster Teil.* Quellen zur Geschichte des Parlamentarismus und der politischen Parteien, 1st ser., 6.1. Düsseldorf: Droste, 1969.

Meyer, Michael. *Ibsen: A Biography.* Harmondsworth, England: Penguin, 1985.

Miller, Susanne. *Burgfrieden und Klassenkampf: Die deutsche Sozialdemokratie im Ersten Weltkrieg.* Beiträge zur Geschichte des Parlamentarismus und der politischen Parteien 53. Düsseldorf: Droste, 1974.

Miller, Susanne, and Heinrich Potthoff. *Kleine Geschichte der SPD, Darstellung und Dokumentation 1848–1980.* 4th ed. Bonn: Verlag Neue Gesellschaft, 1981.

Mitchell, Allan. *Revolution in Bavaria, 1918–1919: The Eisner Regime and the Soviet Republic.* Princeton, NJ: Princeton University Press, 1965.

Mommsen, Hans. "Victor Adler und die Politik der österreichischen Sozialdemokratie im Ersten Weltkrieg." In *Politik und Gesellschaft im alten und neuen Österreich: Festschrift für Rudolf Neck zum 60. Geburtstag,* edited by Isabella Ackerl, Walter Hummelberger, and Hans Mommsen, 1:378–408. 2 vols. Vienna: Verlag für Geschichte und Politik, 1981.

Nebelin, Manfred. *Ludendorff: Diktator im Ersten Weltkrieg.* Munich: Siedler, 2010.

Nettl, J. P. *Rosa Luxemburg.* 2 vols. London: Oxford University Press, 1966.

———. *The Soviet Achievement.* Norwich, England: Harcourt, Brace & World, 1971.

Nichols, J. Alden. *Germany after Bismarck: The Caprivi Era, 1890–1894.* Cambridge: Harvard University Press, 1958.

Oschilewski, Walther G. *Zeitungen in Berlin: Im Spiegel der Jahrhunderte.* Berlin: Haude und Spenersche Verlagsbuchhandlung, 1975.

Osterroth, Franz. *Biographisches Lexikon des Sozialismus.* Hanover: J. H. W. Dietz, 1960.

Payne, Robert. *The Life and Death of Lenin.* New York: Simon and Schuster, 1964.

Pinson, Koppel S. *Modern Germany: Its History and Civilization.* 2nd ed. New York: Macmillan, 1966.

Pohl, Karl Heinrich. *Die Münchener Arbeiterbewegung: Sozialdemokratische Partei, Freie Gewerkschaften, Staat und Gesellschaft in München 1890–1914.* Schriftenreihe der Georg-von-Vollmar-Akademie 4. Munich: K. G. Sauer, 1992.

———. *Adolf Müller: Geheimagent und Gesandter in Kaiserreich und Weimarer Republik.* Cologne: Bund-Verlag, 1995.

Raff, Diether. *A History of Germany from the Medieval Empire to the Present.* Translated by Bruce Little. Oxford: Berg, 1988.

Rautio, Veli-Matti. *Die Bernstein-Debatte: Die politisch-ideologischen Strömungen und die Parteiideologie in der Sozialdemokratischen Partei Deutschlands 1898–1903.* Studia Historica 47. Helsinki: Suomen Historiallinen Seura, 1994.

Ritter, Gerhard. *The Sword and the Scepter: The Problem of Militarism in Germany.* Translated by Heinz Norden. 4 vols. Coral Gables, FL: University of Miami Press, 1969–1972.

Röll, Wolfgang. *Sozialdemokraten im Konzentrationslager Buchenwald 1937–1945: Unter Einbeziehung biographischer Skizzen.* Göttingen: Wallstein, 2000.

Rosenfeld, Gavriel D. "Monuments and the Politics of Memory: Commemorating Kurt Eisner and the Bavarian Revolutions of 1918–1919 in Postwar Munich." *Central European History* 30.2 (1997): 221–251.

Rumold, Rainer. *Archaeologies of Modernity: Avant-Garde "Bildung."* Evanston, IL: Northwestern University Press, 2015.

Sackett, Robert Eben. *Popular Entertainment, Class, and Politics in Munich, 1900–1923.* Cambridge: Harvard University Press, 1982.

Schade, Franz. *Kurt Eisner und die bayerische Sozialdemokratie.* Hanover: Verlag für Literatur und Zeitgeschehen, 1961.

Schmidt, Rudolf. *Geschichte der Stadt Eberswalde.* 3 vols. Eberswalde: Rudolf Müller, 1941.

Schoenbaum, David. *Zabern 1913: Consensus Politics in Imperial Germany.* London: Allen & Unwin, 1982.

Schorske, Carl E. *German Social Democracy, 1905–1917: The Development of the Great Schism.* New York: Wiley, 1955.

Schröder, Wilhelm Heinz. *Sozialdemokratische Reichstagsabgeordnete und Reichstagskandidaten 1898–1918: Biographisch-statistisches Handbuch.* Düsseldorf: Droste, 1986.

———. *Sozialdemokratische Parlamentarier in den deutschen Reichs- und Landtagen 1867–1933: Biographien—Chronik—Wahldokumentation.* Handbücher zur Geschichte des Parlamentarismus und der politischen Parteien 7. Düsseldorf: Droste, 1995.

Schueler, Hermann Kurt. "Felix Fechenbach 1894–1933: Die Entwicklung eines republikanischen Journalisten." PhD diss., Rheinische Friedrich-Wilhelms-Universität, Bonn, 1980.

———. *Auf der Flucht erschossen: Felix Fechenbach 1894–1933.* Cologne: Kiepenheuer & Witsch, 1981.

Schwartz, Stephen. "The Mysterious Death of Walter Benjamin." *The Weekly Standard* 6.37 (11 June 2001): http://www.weeklystandard.com/the-mysterious-death-of-walter-benjamin/article/1487.

Seytter, Wilhelm. *Unser Stuttgart: Geschichte, Sage und Kultur unserer Stadt und Umgebung.* Stuttgart: Max Kielmann, 1903.

Shirer, William L. *The Rise and Fall of the Third Reich: A History of Nazi Germany.* New York: Simon and Schuster, 1960.

Sinowjew, Georg. *Der Krieg und die Krise des Sozialismus.* Vienna: Verlag für Literatur und Politik, 1924.

Snyder, Louis L. *The Weimar Republic: A History of Germany from Ebert to Hitler.* Princeton, NJ: D. Van Nostrand, 1966.

Steenson, Gary P. *Karl Kautsky, 1854–1938: Marxism in the Classical Years.* Pittsburgh, PA: Univeristy of Pittsburgh Press, 1978.

———. *"Not One Man! Not One Penny!" German Social Democracy, 1863–1914.* Pittsburgh, PA: University of Pittsburgh Press, 1981.

Strachan, Hew. *The First World War.* New York: Viking, 2004.

Tal, Uriel. *Christians and Jews in Germany: Religion, Politics, and Ideology in the Second Reich, 1870–1914.* Translated by Noah Jonathan Jacobs. Ithaca, NY: Cornell University Press, 1975.

Treutler, Karl Georg von. *Die graue Exzellenz: Zwischen Staatsräson und Vasallentreue.* Edited by Karl-Heinz Janßen. Frankfurt am Main: Propyläen, 1971.

Tuchman, Barbara W. *The Proud Tower: A Portrait of the World before the War, 1880–1914.* New York: Macmillan, 1966.

Tucker, Spencer, Priscilla Roberts, Cole C. Kingseed, Malcolm Muir Jr., and David Zabecki, eds. *World War I Encyclopedia.* 5 vols. Santa Barbara, CA: ABC CLIO, 2005.

Völker, Klaus. *Brecht-Chronik: Daten zu Leben und Werk.* Munich: Carl Hanser, 1971.

Watt, Richard M. *The Kings Depart: The Tragedy of Germany; Versailles and the German Revolution.* New York: Simon and Schuster, 1968.

Wiesemann, Falk. "Kurt Eisner: Studie zu seiner politischen Biographie." In *Bayern im Umbruch: Die Revolution von 1918, ihre Voraussetzungen, ihr Verlauf und ihre Folgen,* edited by Karl Bosl, 387–426. Munich: R. Oldenbourg, 1969.

Witt, Peter-Christian. *Friedrich Ebert: Parteiführer, Reichskanzler, Volksbeauftragter, Reichspräsident.* 4th ed. Bonn: J. H. W. Dietz, 2008.

Zeman, Z. A. B., and W. B. Scharlau. *The Merchant of Revolution: The Life of Alexander Israel Helphand (Parvus), 1867–1924*. London: Oxford University Press, 1965.

III. Government Publications, Proceedings, Protocols

Bauer, Franz J., ed. *Die Regierung Eisner 1918/19: Ministerratsprotokolle und Dokumente*. Quellen zur Geschichte des Parlamentarismus und der politischen Parteien, 1st ser., 10. Düsseldorf: Droste, 1987.

Dirr, Pius, ed. *Bayerische Dokumente zum Kriegsausbruch und zum Versailler Schuldspruch*. Munich: R. Oldenbourg, 1922.

Hahlweg, Werner, ed. *Lenins Rückkehr nach Rußland 1917: Die deutschen Akten*. Studien zur Geschichte Osteuropas 4. Leiden: E. J. Brill, 1957.

Protokoll der Reichskonferenz der Sozialdemokratie Deutschlands vom 21., 22. und 23. September 1916. 1916. Reprint, Glashütten im Taunus: Detlev Auvermann, 1974.

Protokoll über die Verhandlungen des Gründungs-Parteitages der USPD vom 6. bis 8. April 1917 in Gotha. Mit Anhang: Bericht über die Gemeinsame Konferenz der Arbeitsgemeinschaft und der Spartakusgruppe vom 7. Januar 1917 in Berlin. Edited by Emil Eichhorn. Berlin: A. Seehof, 1921. Facsimile reprint in *Protokolle der Parteitage der Unabhängigen Sozialdemokratischen Partei Deutschlands*. Vol. 1, *1917–1919*. Glashütten im Taunus: Detlev Auvermann, 1975.

Protokoll über die Verhandlungen des Parteitages der Sozialdemokratischen Partei Deutschlands. Berlin: Buchhandlung Vorwärts, 1903, 1905, 1907, 1908, 1909.

Protokoll über die Verhandlungen des Parteitages der Sozialdemokratischen Partei Preußens: Abgehalten in Berlin vom 6. bis 8. Januar 1913. Berlin: Buchhandlung Vorwärts, 1913.

Protokolle der Sitzungen des Parteiauschusses der SPD 1912 bis 1921. Reprints zur Sozialgeschichte, edited by Dieter Dowe. 2 vols. Berlin: J. H. W. Dietz, 1980.

Statistisches Jahrbuch für den Freistaat Bayern 1919. Munich: J. Lindauersche Universitäts-Buchhandlung, [1920].

Verhandlungen des Bayerischen Landtags 1919: Stenographische Berichte Nr. 1 bis 27 (21 February–24 October 1919).

Verhandlungen des Kongresses der Arbeiter-, Bauern- und Soldatenräte vom 25. Februar bis 8. März 1919.

Verhandlungen des provisorischen Nationalrates des Volksstaates Bayern im Jahre 1918/1919: Beilagen-Band.

Verhandlungen des provisorischen Nationalrates des Volksstaates Bayern im Jahre 1918/1919: Stenographische Berichte Nr. 1 bis 10 (8 November 1918–4 January 1919).

Verhandlungen des Reichstags: 9. Legislaturperiode, 4. Session 1895/97. Vol. 8. (3 May–25 June 1897). Berlin: Verlag der Norddeutschen Buchdruckerei, 1897.

Verhandlungen des Reichstags: 12. Legislaturperiode, 1. Session 1907/09. Vol. 228 (17 April–14 May 1907). Berlin: Verlag der Norddeutschen Buchdruckerei, 1907.

Verhandlungen des Reichstags: 13. Legislaturperiode, 2. Session 1914/16. Vol. 306 (4 August 1914–16 March 1916), Vol. 307 (22 March 1916–6 June 1916). Berlin: Verlag der Norddeutschen Buchdruckerei, 1916.

IV. Cited Period Journals

Deutsche Dichtung
Deutsche Roman-Zeitung
Dokumente des Fortschritts: Internationale Revue
Die Fackel
Freie Volksbühne: Zum neuen Spieljahr 1912/13
Die Gesellschaft: Monatsschrift für Litteratur, Kunst und Sozialpolitik
Die Gleichheit: Zeitschrift für die Interessen der Arbeiterinnen
Die Hilfe: Gotteshilfe, Selbsthilfe, Staatshilfe, Bruderhilfe
Die Kritik: Wochenschau des öffentlichen Lebens
März: Eine Wochenschrift
Das Magazin für Litteratur
Die Menschheit
Mitteilungen des Vereins Arbeiterpresse
Neue Deutsche Rundschau
Die Neue Gesellschaft: Sozialistische Wochenschrift
Der Neue Merkur
Die Neue Rundschau
Die Neue Welt: Illustrierte Beilage für Wissenschaft, Belehrung und Unterhaltung
Die Neue Zeit
Pan
Politische Zeitfragen: Lose Mitteilungen über alle Gebiete des öffentlichen Lebens
Sozialistische Monatshefte
Süddeutsche Monatshefte
Das Tagebuch
Die Wage: Wiener Wochenschrift
Der wahre Jacob: Illustrierte Zeitung für Satire, Humor und Unterhaltung

Die Weltbühne: Wochenschrift für Politik, Kunst, Wirtschaft

V. Cited Period Newpapers, Supplements

Chemnitzer Volksstimme
Fränkische Tagespost
Frankfurter Zeitung
Die Furche (supplement to the *Fränkische Tagespost*)
Hessische Landeszeitung
L'Humanité
Leipziger Volkszeitung
Münchener Post
Münchner Neueste Nachrichten
Nachrichtenblatt des Zentralrats
Neue Zeitung: Unabhängiges sozialistisches Organ
New Yorker Volkszeitung
Unterhaltungsblatt des Vorwärts
Der Volksbildner (supplement to the *Fränkische Tagespost*)
Volksblatt: Organ für die werktätige Bevölkerung in Hessen und Waldeck
Volksblatt für Anhalt
Vorwärts

VI. Archives, Library Special Collections

Bayerisches Geheimes Staatsarchiv (now Abteilung III, Geheimes Hausarchiv, Bayerisches Hauptstaatsarchiv München)
Bayerisches Hauptstaatsarchiv München
Bundesarchiv Koblenz
Internationaal Instituut voor Sociale Geschiedenis (Amsterdam)
Leo Baeck Institute (New York)
Münchener Stadtbibliothek, Monacensia-Abteilung
Stadtbibliothek Nürnberg
Stiftung Archiv der Parteien und Massenorganisationen der DDR im Bundesarchiv (Berlin-Lichterfelde)
Stiftung Neue Synagoge Berlin—Centrum Judaicum Archiv (Berlin-Mitte)

INDEX